The Critical Pedagogy Reader

Second Edition

Since its publication, *The Critical Pedagogy Reader* has firmly established itself as the leading collection of classic and contemporary essays by the major thinkers in the field of critical pedagogy. While retaining its comprehensive introduction, this thoroughly revised second edition includes more fully developed section introductions, updated and expanded bibliographies, and up-to-date classroom questions. For ease of use and navigation, the book is arranged topically around such issues as class, racism, gender/sexuality, language and literacy, and classroom issues. In addition, two entirely new sections focused on teacher education and critical issues beyond the classroom provide readers with the all-important tools needed to put critical pedagogical theory into practice in their own classrooms. Carefully attentive to both theory and practice, this new edition remains the definitive source for teaching and learning about critical pedagogy.

Antonia Darder is Professor of Educational Policy Studies and Latina and Latino Studies at the University of Illinois, Urbana-Champaign.

Marta P. Baltodano is Associate Professor of Education at Loyola Marymount University.

Rodolfo D. Torres is Professor of Urban Planning at the University of California, Irvine.

The Critical Pedagogy Reader

Second Edition

Edited by
Antonia Darder, Marta P. Baltodano,
and Rodolfo D. Torres

Routledge
Taylor & Francis Group

NEW YORK AND LONDON

First published 2009
by Routledge
711 Third Avenue, New York, NY 10017

Simultaneously published in the UK
by Routledge
2 Park Square, Milton Park, Abingdon, Oxon OX14 4RN

Routledge is an imprint of the Taylor & Francis Group, an informa business

© 2009 Taylor & Francis

Typeset in Minion
by RefineCatch Limited, Bungay, Suffolk

Library of Congress Cataloging in Publication Data
The critical pedagogy reader / Antonia Darder, Marta Baltodano, and Rodolfo D. Torres. — 2nd ed.
  p. cm.
  Includes bibliographical references and index.
  ISBN 978–0–415–96121–9 (hb : alk. paper) — ISBN 978–0–415–96120–2 (pb : alk. paper)
1. Critical pedagogy. I. Darder, Antonia, II. Baltodano, Marta. III. Torres, Rodolfo D., 1949– .
  LC196.C758 2008
  370.11′5—dc22   2008004095

ISBN10: 0–415–96121–1 (hbk)
ISBN10: 0–415–96120–3 (pbk)

ISBN13: 978–0–415–96121–9 (hbk)
ISBN13: 978–0–415–96120–2 (hbk)

Dedicated to the lasting memory of
Paulo Freire and Myles Horton

Contents

Acknowledgments

On a Public Note

We wish to acknowledge Catherine Bernard, our editor at Routledge, for having the foresight to invite us to complete this second edition of the Reader. Her consistent support and editorial assistance was invaluable. We would also like to acknowledge Routledge for their continuing commitment to publishing risky books on the edge and remaining committed to democratizing education.

On a Scholarly Note

We thank our colleagues and comrades, too numerous to mention, for their sustaining and continuing support. We could not move forward with our projects, teaching, advising, committee meetings, conferences, reviews, more meetings, and, of course, our writing, were we not committed to a larger political vision of emancipation and solidarity.

On a Pedagogical Note

We wish to acknowledge and express our most sincere appreciation to our students, who struggle with us each day to learn what it truly means to live a critical pedagogy.

On a Personal Note

A.D: Thank you Christy & Michael, Kelly & Lawrence, Gabriel & Vicky, and especially my beautiful granddaughters, Jessica, Naomi, Sophia, & Azul, who keep my spirit fluid and supple with their love.

M.B: Thank you Alberto and Emanuel for your love and patience.

RDT: Thank you Patricia and Jacob for making my life complete.

Critical Pedagogy: An Introduction

Antonia Darder, Marta P. Baltodano, and Rodolfo D. Torres

A society which makes provision for participation in its good of all members on equal terms and which secures flexible readjustment of its institutions through interaction of the different forms of associated life is in so far democratic. Such a society must have a type of education which gives individuals a personal interest in social relationships and control, and the habits of mind which secure social changes.

> John Dewey
> *Democracy and Education*, 1916

The education of any people should begin with the people themselves.

> Carter G. Woodson
> *The Mis-education of the Negro*, 1933

We believe that Education leads to action.

> Myles Horton
> Founder of the Highlander Folk School, 1932

Students live in a historical situation, in a social, political and economic moment. Those things have to be part of what we teach.

> Herbert Kohl
> Founder of the Open School Movement, 1964

The dual society, at least in public education, seems in general to be unquestioned.

> Jonathan Kozol
> *Death at an Early Age*, 1967

If situations cannot be created that enable the young to deal with feelings of being manipulated by outside forces, there will be far too little sense of agency among them. Without a sense of agency, young people are unlikely to pose significant questions, the existentially rooted questions in which learning begins.

> Maxine Greene
> *The Dialectics of Freedom*, 1988

Many students, especially those who are poor, intuitively know what the schools do for them. They school them to confuse process and substance. Once these become blurred, a new logic is assumed: the more treatment there is, the better are the results; or escalation leads to success. The pupil is thereby "schooled" to confuse teaching with learning, grade advancement with education, a diploma with competence and fluency with the ability to say something new.

> Ivan Illich
> *Deschooling Society*, 1971

Knowledge emerges only through invention and re-invention, through the restless, impatient continuing, hopeful inquiry [we] pursue in the world, with the world, and with each other.

Paulo Freire
Pedagogy of the Oppressed, 1971

Our analysis of the repressiveness, inequality, and contradictory objectives of contemporary education in America is not only a critique of schools and educators, but also of the social order of which they are a part.

Samuel Bowles and Herbert Gintis
Schooling in Capitalist America, 1976

These words and concerns illustrate that the struggles for public democratic schooling in America have been a multidimensional enterprise, which for over a century occupied the dreams, hearts, and minds of many educators. These educators were not only firmly committed to the ideal and practice of social justice within schools, but to the transformation of structures and conditions within society that functioned to thwart the democratic participation of all people.

Hence, critical pedagogy loosely evolved out of a yearning to give some shape and coherence to the theoretical landscape of radical principles, beliefs and practices that contributed to an emancipatory ideal of democratic schooling in the United States during the twentieth century. The development of this school of thought reflected a significant attempt to bring an array of divergent views and perspectives to the table, in order to invigorate the capacity of radical educators to engage critically with the impact of capitalism and gendered, racialized, and homophobic relations on students from historically disenfranchised populations.

The first textbook use of the term *critical pedagogy* is found in Henry Giroux's *Theory and Resistance in Education*, published in 1983. During the 1980s and 1990s, Giroux's work, along with that of Paulo Freire, Stanley Aronowitz, Michael Apple, Maxine Greene, Peter McLaren, bell hooks, Donaldo Macedo, Michelle Fine, Jean Anyon, and many others was, inarguably, one of the most central and potent forces in the revitalization of emancipatory educational debates in this country. However, Giroux would be the first to adamantly insist that critical pedagogy emerged from a long historical legacy of radical social thought and progressive educational movements, which aspired to link practices of schooling to democratic principles of society and transformative social action in the interest of oppressed communities.

There is no doubt that in the last decade, monumental historical events tied to 9/11, the politics of indigeneity, global warming, the incalcitrant nature of the Iraq war, and the expanding economic divisions between the rich and the poor have all challenged critical educators to rethink the meaning of schooling. This process has required the cultivation of greater suppleness and fluidity in defining and expanding the limits of rationality. For only through such awareness could critical theories of education remain inextricably rooted to the actual conditions of everyday life, and conscious of the political and economic landscapes that give rise to their formation. In keeping with the spirit of such a commitment, critical pedagogical scholarship has also undertaken rigorous examination into societal concerns that intersect with the process of schooling. Included here are aspects of popular culture, media literacy, indigenous struggles, ecological conditions, and the liberatory possibilities of public pedagogy.

Major Influences on the Formation of Critical Pedagogy

Twentieth Century Educators and Activists

The views of American philosopher and educator, John Dewey, often referred to as the *father of the progressive education movement*, had a significant influence on progressive educators concerned with advancing democratic ideals. During the early 1900s, Dewey sought to articulate his pragmatic philosophy and expand on the idea of community to explain the purpose of education in a democratic society. His beliefs centered on a variety of basic principles, including the notion that education must engage with an enlarged experience; that thinking and reflection are central to the act of teaching; and that students must freely interact with their environments in the practice of constructing knowledge. Although there are those who have sharply criticized Dewey's faith in creative intelligence as eminently naïve and accused him of underestimating the sociopolitical and economic forces that shape inequality and injustice, Dewey's work is consistent in "his attempt to link the notion of individual and social (cooperative) intelligence with the discourse of democracy and freedom" (McLaren, 1989, p.199). By so doing, John Dewey provided "a language of possibility"—a philosophical construct of foremost significance to the evolution of critical pedagogy.

The works of W.E.B. DuBois and Carter G. Woodson, often referred to as the *father of Black History*, rightly merit recognition for their important contributions to the evolution of critical pedagogical thought, particularly with respect to the education of African American students and other racialized inequalities (Graves, 1998). Published in 1902, DuBois' *The Souls of Black Folk* still stands as a poignant treatise on the impact of racism on racialized populations. Woodson's volume, *The Mis-education of the Negro* published in 1933, boldly speaks to the destructive nature of mainstream education. Ardently convinced that education was essential to liberation, the two men shared a deep desire to transform the social inequalities and educational injustices suffered by African Americans. Moreover, DuBois and Woodson clearly foresaw the importance of an oppressed people regaining access to their own history. They tirelessly championed the right of African American students to a process of schooling that would prepare them to critically challenge socially prevailing notions of the time—notions which denied them their humanity and trampled their self-respect. Most importantly, the historical influence of DuBois and Woodson set the stage for many of the contemporary educational struggles associated with anti-racism, multiculturalism, and social justice today.

Myles Horton, considered by some to be one of the sparks that ignited the civil rights movement in the United States, channeled his belief in the political potential of schooling into the founding of the Highlander Folk School (known today as the Highlander Research and Education Center) in Monteagle, Tennessee. His wife, Zilphia Johnson Horton, brought an important cultural dimension to the work through her integration of singing into the school curriculum and labor organizing activities. The purpose of the school was to provide a place for the education of blacks and whites in defiance of segregation laws. Over the years, Horton and Zilphia's work resulted in the participation of thousands of people, challenging entrenched social, economic and political structures of a deeply segregated society. One of the most noted among them was the civil rights activist Rosa Parks, who had attended Highlander just a few months prior to her refusal to move to the back of the bus. Key to Horton's political practice was the notion that in order for education or institutional change to be effective, it had to begin with the people themselves—a particularly significant tenet of critical pedagogical thought.

In the early 1960s, the views of Herbert Kohl provided the impetus for the development of the Open School Movement in the United States. His efforts to challenge and address issues of democratic schooling were fundamentally rooted upon a tradition of radical politics and radical history that could counter the structures of oppression at work in public schools. Kohl's deep commitment to community interaction and his tremendous faith in students, set a significant example for the practice of teaching diverse students from working class populations. And although he has been known to take issue with the academic writings of critical educators today, Kohl's uncompromising political views on schooling and activism were significant in helping to lay the groundwork for the development of critical pedagogical practices in the years to come.

Beginning with his first book *Death at an Early Age*, the work of long-time author and social activist, Jonathan Kozol, has consistently examined issues of racism, class and schooling inequalities, grounding his conclusions upon the actual stories and experiences of dispossessed populations in this country. More importantly, he has sought to address the material conditions and expose the social consequences of poverty and racism to those children and their families who have been relegated to an existence at the margins of American life. For Kozol, questions of education could not only be engaged in terms of the theoretical, programmatic, or technical; they also had to be reconceptualized along human, spiritual, as well as political grounds. In *The Shame of the Nation: The Restoration of Apartheid Schooling in America*, Kozol again exposed the immorality of human oppression, documenting the worsening conditions of schools in poor and racialized communities. During the summer of 2007, both stunned by the U.S. Supreme Court decision that reversed Brown v. Board of Education by prohibiting state-ordered integration programs and in protest of *No Child Left Behind*, Kozol began a partial fast to call attention to the issue.

The internationally recognized philosopher and educator, Maxine Greene, has played a pivotal role in her work with critical educators in the United States. Often referred to as the *mother of aesthetic education*, Greene was the first woman to be hired at Teachers College as a philosopher. In the midst of the hostility she faced as a woman and a Jew within the academy in the early 1960s, Greene persevered to become a formidable force in the theoretical arena of aesthetics and its relationship to education and society. Many of her views on education and democracy today still echo thoughts and concerns raised by Dewey, almost a century ago. For Greene, democracy constitutes a way of life that must be practiced within both social and political arenas, made living through our relationships, our educational experiences, as well as our moments of beauty and enjoyment out in the world. Greene's contribution to critical pedagogy is most evident by the manner in which her reflective theories of knowledge, human nature, learning, curriculum, schooling and society have influenced the practice of progressive educators for over 30 years.

In the arena of schooling and the political economy, the work of such noted theorists as Samuel Bowles and Herbert Gintis, Martin Carnoy, and Michael Apple all contributed significantly to the forging of a critical pedagogical perspective. The work of these scholars consistently upheld the centrality of the economy in the configuration of power relations within schools and society. Through their persistent critique of capitalism, these theorists argued, in a variety of ways, that the problems associated with schooling are deeply tied to the reproduction of a system of social relations that perpetuates the existing structures of domination and exploitation. Michael Apple, in particular, linked notions of cultural capital with the school's reproduction of official knowledge—knowledge that primarily functioned to sustain the inequality of class relations within schools and society.

Ivan Illich, who in the 1950s worked as a parish priest among the poor Irish and Puerto Rican communities of New York City, has been considered by many to be one of the most radically political social thinkers in the second half of the twentieth century. His critical writings on schooling and society, including *Deschooling Society* published in 1971, sought to analyze the institutional structures of industrialization and to provide both rigorous criticism and an alternative to what he perceived as the crisis of a society that endorses growth economy, political centralization, and unlimited technology. In very important ways, Illich's views on education and the institutionalization of everyday life inspired critical education theorists and activists during the latter half of the twentieth century to rethink their practice in schools and communities. The most notable among these was the Brazilian educator, Paulo Freire.

The Brazilian Influence

While progressive educators and social activists such as Myles Horton, Martin Luther King, Herbert Kohl, Angela Davis, Cesar Chavez, Malcom X, and many others challenged the disgraceful conditions of oppressed people in the United States, Brazilian educator Paulo Freire and his contemporary Augusto Boal were also involved in challenging the horrendous conditions they found in the cities and countryside of Brazil—a struggle that was historically linked to the emancipatory efforts of many educators and political activists across Latin America.

Paulo Freire would be forced to live in exile for over 15 years for his writings on education and the dispossessed members of Brazilian society. In the early 1970s, Paulo Freire was extended an invitation to come to Harvard University as a visiting professor. It was his presence in the United States during that precise historical moment, along with the translation of *Pedagogy of the Oppressed* into English, that became a watershed for radical educators in schools, communities, and labor organizations, struggling to bring about social change to public health, welfare, and educational institutions across the country.

As a consequence, Paulo Freire is considered by many to be the most influential educational philosopher in the development of critical pedagogical thought and practice. From the 1970s until his death in 1997, Freire continued to publish and speak extensively to educators throughout the United States. Although Freire's writings focused on questions of pedagogy, his thought widely influenced post-colonial theory, ethnic studies, cultural studies, adult education, media studies, and theories of literacy, language and social development. Most importantly, Freire labored consistently to ground the politics of education within the existing framework of the larger society.

As with so many of the influential educators previously mentioned, Freire's efforts were never simply confined to discussions of methodology or applications of teaching practice. Instead, Freire forthrightly inserted questions of power, culture and oppression within the context of schooling. In so doing, he reinforced the Frankfurt School's focus on theory and practice as imperative to the political struggles against exploitation and domination. Through his views on emancipatory education, Freire made central pedagogical questions related to social agency, voice and democratic participation—questions that strongly inform the recurrent philosophical expressions of critical pedagogical writings even today.

Augusto Boal's book *Theatre of the Oppressed* was released in 1971, the same year as Freire's seminal text, *Pedagogy of the Oppressed.* In the 1960s Boal developed an experimental theater approach whereby the cast would stop a performance and invite members of the audience to provide or demonstrate new suggestions on stage. By so doing, he unexpectedly discovered an effective pedagogical form of praxis that evolved directly from the audience's participation, collective reflection, and the action generated by participants. Excited and inspired by the process of empowerment he witnessed among participants, Boal began to develop what was to be known as the "spec-actor" (in contrast to spectator) theater approach.

Seeing the possibilities of his approach as a vehicle for grassroots activism, Boal's work in communities began to give shape to his *Theatre of the Oppressed.* Similar to Freire, Boal's work as a cultural activist was repressed by the military junta that came to power during the 1960s. Also like Freire, Boal was arrested, tortured, and eventually exiled for his activities, but he continued to develop his work in Argentina and later in Paris. He returned to Brazil in 1986, when the military junta was removed from power. Boal's work was first linked to Freire's work in the U.S. at the Pedagogy and Theatre of the Oppressed Conference in 1994. Boal's contribution was to mark a significant turning point for those critical educators and artists who had become frustrated with what they perceived as, on one hand, the deeply theoretical nature of critical pedagogy and, on the other, the absence of more practical and affective strategies to enliven their work. For these critical educators, Boal's *Theatre of the Oppressed* provided a new avenue upon which to build and rethink their educational practice in schools and communities.

Gramsci and Foucault

Although it is impossible to discuss here all the "classical" theorists who influenced the intellectual development of critical pedagogy, the contributions of Antonio Gramsci and Michel Foucault to a critical understanding of education merit some discussion. These philosophers extended existing notions of power and its impact on the construction of knowledge. Their writings also strengthen the theoretical foundation upon which to conduct critical readings of culture, consciousness, history, domination, and resistance.

Antonio Gramsci, imprisoned by Mussolini during World War II for his active membership in the Communist party and public rejection of fascism, was deeply concerned with the manner in which domination was undergoing major shifts and changes within advanced industrial Western societies. In *Prison Notebooks* (1992), Gramsci carefully articulated a theory of hegemony, as he sought to explain how the historical changes of the time were being exercised less and less through brutal physical force. Instead, he argued that the mechanism for social control was exercised through the moral leaders of society (including teachers), who participated and reinforced universal "common sense" assumptions of "truth."

This phenomenon can be understood within the context of schooling in the following way. Through the daily implementation of specific norms, expectations, and behaviors, that incidentally conserve the interests of those in power, students are ushered into consensus. Gramsci argued that by cultivating such consensus through personal and institutional rewards, students could be socialized to support the interest of the ruling elite, even when such actions were clearly in contradiction with the students' own class interests. As such, this reproduction of ideological hegemony within schools functioned to sustain the hegemonic processes that reproduced cultural and economic domination within the society. This process of reproduction was then perpetuated through what Gramsci termed "contradictory consciousness." However, for Gramsci this was not a clean and neat act of one-dimensional reproduction. Instead, domination existed here as a complex combination of thought and practices, in which could also be found the seeds for resistance.

The French philosopher, Michel Foucault, deeply questioned what he termed "regimes of truth" that were upheld and perpetuated through the manner in which particular knowledge was legitimated within a variety of power relationships within society. However, for Foucault, power did not represent a static entity, but rather an active process constantly at work on our bodies, our relationships, our sexuality, as well as on the ways we construct knowledge and meaning in the world. Power, in Foucault's conceptualization, is not solely at play in the context of domination, but also in the context of creative acts of resistance—creative acts that are produced as human beings interact across the dynamic of relationships, shaped by moments of dominance and autonomy. Such a view of power challenged the tendency of radical education theorists to think of power solely from the dichotomized standpoint of either domination or powerlessness. As such, Foucault's writings on knowledge and power shed light on the phenomenon of student resistance within the classroom and opened the door to a more complex understanding of power relationships within our teaching practice.

The Frankfurt School

Critical educational thought is fundamentally linked to those critical theories of society that emerged from the members of the Frankfurt School and their contemporaries. These theorists sought to challenge the narrowness of traditional forms of rationality that defined the concept of meaning and knowledge in the Western world, during a very critical moment in the history of the twentieth century. As such, their work was driven by an underlying commitment to the notion that theory, as well as practice, must inform the work of those who seek to transform the oppressive conditions that exist in the world.

The Institute for Social Research (*Das Institut für Sozialforschung*) was officially established in Frankfurt in 1923 and was the home of the Frankfurt School. The institute came under the direction of Max Horkheimer in 1930. Although there were a number of other prominent thinkers who worked under the direction of Horkheimer, those most prominent in the development of critical social theory included Theodor Adorno, Walter Benjamin, Leo Lowenthal, Erich Fromm, and Herbert Marcuse. Herbert Marcuse, in particular, is considered by some as the most prominent scholar of the Frankfurt School to influence critical pedagogical thought. As others in his tradition, Marcuse incorporated the thought of Hegel, Marx, and Heidegger, in his efforts to imagine a society in which all aspects of our humanity—our work, play, love, and sexuality—functioned in sustaining a free society. More recently, the work of Jürgen Habermas has also received much attention within the arena of critical theory.

In the early years, the Frankfurt theorists were primarily concerned with an analysis of bourgeois society's substructure, but with time their interest focused upon the cultural superstructures. This overarching emphasis was, undoubtedly, a result of the disruptions and certain fragmentation experienced in the process of emigration and repeated relocation in the 1930s and 1940s—a process that was precipitated by the threat of Nazism, the members' avowedly Marxist orientation, and the fact that most of them were Jews.

One cannot attempt to understand the foundations of critical theory without considering the historical context that influenced its development and shaped the minds of its foremost thinkers. The Frankfurt School came into being as a response to the important political and historical transformations taking place in the early part of the twentieth century. The political shifts in Germany's governing structure had a significant impact upon its founders. During the early part of the century, Germany had managed to temporarily contain class conflict. But within two years following World War I, the foundations of the German imperial system were undermined and a republic was declared in Berlin (Held, 1980). What followed were thirteen years of chaotic political struggles between the German Communist Party (KPD) and the more conservative forces of the Social Democratic Party (SPD).

As the KPD became increasingly ineffective in its efforts to organize a majority of the working class, the Social Democratic Leadership of the Weimar Republic supervised the destruction of the competing radical and revolutionary movements. In the process, the SDP did not only fail to implement the promised democratization and socialization of production in Germany, but it failed to stop the monopolistic trends of German industrialists and the reactionary elements which eventually paved the way for the emergence of Nazism. As the forces of the Nazis, under Hitler's control, seized power in Germany, Italy and Spain came under the fascist leaderships of Mussolini and Franco. A similar fate befell the workers' struggle in these countries, where all independent socialist and liberal organizations were suppressed.

In light of the Marxist orientation shared by the members of the Frankfurt School, "the emergence of an antidemocratic political system in the country of the first socialist revolution" (Warren, 1984: 145), consequently had a profound impact upon the development of critical theory. Moreover, the Russian revolution had been systematically weakened by foreign interventions, blockades, and civil war; and Lenin's revolutionary vision was rapidly losing ground. After Lenin's death in 1924, Stalin advanced in Russia with the expansion of centralized control and censorship, a process created to maintain European Communist parties under Moscow's leadership. In 1939, the Hitler–Stalin pact was enacted representing an ironic historical moment for those committed to the struggle of the working class and the socialist principles espoused by Marx.

A final event that strongly influenced the thinking of the Frankfurt School theorists was the nature and impact of unconfined forces of advanced capitalism in the West. The rapid development of science and technology and their persuasive penetration into the political and social systems summoned a new and major transformation in the structure of capitalism. This accelerated development of an advanced industrial-technological society represented a serious area of concern.

The major historical and political developments of capitalist society, as well as the rise of bureaucratic communist orthodoxy, affirmed for the founders of critical theory the necessity to address two basic needs: (1) the need to develop a new critical social theory within a Marxist framework that could deal with the complex changes arising in industrial-technological, postliberal, capitalist society; and (2) the need to recover the philosophical dimensions of Marxism which had undergone a major economic and materialistic reduction by a new Marxist orthodoxy (Warren, 1984).

The Frankfurt School intended their findings to become a material force in the struggle against domination of all forms. Based upon the conditions they observed, the following questions were central to the work of the Institute (Held, 1980: 35):

The European labor movements did not develop in a unified struggle of workers. What blocked these developments?

Capitalism was a series of acute crises. How could these better be understood? What was the relation between the political and the economic? Was the relation between the political and the economic? Was the relation changing?

Authoritarianism and the development of the bureaucracy seemed increasingly the order of the day. How could the phenomena be comprehended? Nazism and fascism rose to dominate central and southern Europe. How was this possible? How did these movements attain large-scale support?

Social relationships, for example those created by the family, appeared to be undergoing radical social change. In what directions? How were these affecting individual development?

The arena of culture appeared open to direct manipulation. Was a new type of ideology being formed? If so, how was this affecting everyday life?

Given the fate of Marxism in Russia and Western Europe, was Marxism itself nothing other than a state orthodoxy? Was there a social agent capable of progressive change? What possibilities were there for effective socialist practices?

Philosophical Principles of Critical Pedagogy

In response to many of these questions, Horkheimer, Adorno, Marcuse, Fromm and others wrote seminal essays that were to serve as the building blocks for a critical theory of society. It was this critical perspective that ultimately provided the foundation for the philosophical principles that were to determine the set of *heterogeneous* ideas that were later to be known as critical pedagogy. We highlight the use of heterogeneous here because it is important to emphasize that there does not exist a formula or homogeneous representation for the universal implementation of any form of critical pedagogy. In fact, it is precisely this distinguishing factor that constitutes its critical nature, and therefore its most emancipatory and democratic function.

The philosophical heterogeneity of its array of radical expressions is then only consolidated through an underlying and explicit intent and commitment to the unwavering liberation of oppressed populations. Toward this end, a set of principles tied to the radical belief in the historical possibility of transformation can be tentatively fleshed out for the purpose of teaching and to better understand what is implied by a critical perspective of education, society, and the world. The following provides a very brief and general introduction to the principles that inform critical pedagogy. However, it is imperative that readers bear in mind that a multitude of both specific and complex expressions of these philosophical ideas has emerged within a variety of intellectual traditions—traditions that have sought to explore the relationship between human beings, schooling, and society, via a myriad of epistemological, political, economic, cultural, ideological, ethical, historical, aesthetic, as well as methodological points of reference.

Cultural Politics

Critical pedagogy is fundamentally committed to the development and enactment of a culture of schooling that supports the empowerment of culturally marginalized and economically disenfranchised students. By so doing, this pedagogical perspective seeks to help transform those classroom structures and practices that perpetuate undemocratic life. Of particular importance then is a critical analysis and investigation into the manner in which traditional theories and practices of public schooling thwart or influence the development of a politically emancipatory and humanizing culture of participation, voice, and social action within the classroom. The purpose for this is intricately linked to the fulfillment of what Paulo Freire defined as our "vocation"—to be truly humanized social (cultural) agents in the world.

In an effort to strive for an emancipatory culture of schooling, critical pedagogy calls upon teachers to recognize how schools have historically embraced theories and practices that serve to unite knowledge and power in ways that sustain asymmetrical relations of power. Under the guise of neutral and apolitical views of education, practices of meritocracy, for example, rooted in ideologies of privilege, shaped by power, politics, history, culture and economics have prevailed. Schools, thus, function as a terrain of on-going cultural struggle over what is accepted as legitimate knowledge. In response, critical pedagogy seeks to address the concept of cultural politics by both legitimizing, as well as challenging, experiences and perceptions shaped by the histories and socioeconomic realities that give meaning to the everyday lives of students and their constructions of what is perceived as truth.

Political Economy

Critical education contends that, contrary to the traditional view, schools actually work against the class interests of those students who are most politically and economically vulnerable within society. The role of competing economic interests of the marketplace in the production of knowledge and in the structural relationships and policies that shape public schools are recognized as significant factors, particularly in the schooling of disenfranchised students. From the standpoint of the political economy, public schools serve to position select groups within asymmetrical power relations that replicate the existing cultural values and privileges of the dominant class. It is this uncontested relationship between schools and society that critical pedagogy seeks to challenge, unmasking traditional claims that education provides equal opportunity and access for all.

Hence, what is at issue here is the question of class reproduction and how schooling practices are deceptively organized to perpetuate racialized inequalities. This is to say that within the context of critical pedagogy, the relationship between culture and class is intricately linked and cannot be separated within the context of daily life in schools. The concept of class here refers to the economic, social, ethical, and political relationships that govern particular sectors of the social order. More importantly, critical pedagogy acknowledges the myriad of ways in which social class, within the lives of students and teachers, contributes to their understanding of who they are and how they are perceived within schools and society.

Historicity of Knowledge

Critical pedagogy supports the notion that all knowledge is created within a historical context and it is this historical context which gives life and meaning to human experience. True to this principle, schools must be understood not only within the boundaries of their social practice but within the boundaries of the historical events that inform educational practice. Along these lines, students and the knowledge they bring into the classroom must be understood as historical—that is, being constructed and produced within a particular historical moment and under particular historical conditions.

As such, critical pedagogy urges teachers to create opportunities in which students can come to discover that "there is no historical reality which is not human" (Freire, 1971, p.125). By so doing, students come to understand themselves as subjects of history and to recognize that conditions of injustice, although historically produced by human beings, can also be transformed by human beings. This concept of student social agency is then tied to a process of collective and self-determined activity. This historical view of knowledge also challenges the traditional emphasis on historical continuities and historical development. Instead, it offers a mode of analysis that stresses the breaks, discontinuities, conflicts, differences, and tensions in history, all which serve in bringing to light the centrality of human agency as it presently exists, as well as within its possibilities for change (Giroux, 1983).

Dialectical Theory

In opposition to traditional theories of education that serve to reinforce certainty, conformity, and technical control of knowledge and power, critical pedagogy embraces a dialectical view of knowledge that functions to unmask the connections between objective knowledge and the cultural norms, values and standards of the society at large. Within this dialectical perspective, all analysis begins first and foremost with human existence and the contradictions and disjunctions that both shape and make problematic its meaning. Hence, the problems of society are not seen as merely random or isolated events, but rather as moments that arise out of the interaction between the individual and society (McLaren, 1989).

An important emphasis here is that students are encouraged to engage the world within its complexity and fullness, in order to reveal the possibilities of new ways of constructing thought and action beyond how it currently exists. Rooted in a dialectical view of knowledge, critical pedagogy seeks to support dynamic interactive elements, rather than participate in the formation of absolute dichotomies or rigid polarizations of thought or practice. By so doing, it supports a supple and fluid view of humans and nature that is relational; an objectivity and subjectivity that is interconnected; and a coexistent understanding of theory and practice. Most importantly, this perspective resurfaces the power of human activity and human knowledge as both a product and a force in the shaping of the world, whether it is in the interest of domination or the struggle for liberation.

Ideology and Critique

Ideology can best be understood as a societal lens or framework of thought, used in society to create order and give meaning to the social and political world in which we live. Also important here is the notion that ideology be understood as existing at the deep, embedded psychological structures of the personality. Ideology then, more often than not, manifests itself in the inner histories and experiences that give rise to questions of subjectivity as they are constructed by individual needs, drives, and passions, as well as the changing material conditions and class formations within society. As such, a critical notion of ideology provides the means for not only a critique of educational curricula, texts and practices, but the fundamental ethics that inform their production.

As a pedagogical tool, ideology can be used to interrogate and unmask the contradictions that exist between the mainstream culture of the school and the lived experiences and knowledge that students use to mediate the reality of school life. Ideology in this instance provides teachers with the necessary insight and language to examine how their own views about knowledge, human nature, values, and society are mediated through the commonsense assumptions they employ to structure classroom experiences. In this way, the principle of ideology in critical pedagogy serves as a useful starting point for asking questions that will help teachers to evaluate critically their practice and to better recognize how the culture of the dominant class becomes embedded in the hidden curriculum—a curriculum informed by ideological views that structurally reproduce dominant cultural assumptions and practices that silence and thwart democratic participation.

Hegemony

Hegemony refers to a process of social control that is carried out through the moral and intellectual leadership of a dominant sociocultural class over subordinate groups (Gramsci, 1971). Critical pedagogy incorporates this notion of hegemony in order to demystify the asymmetrical power relations and social arrangements that sustain the interests of the ruling class. This critical principle acknowledges the powerful connection that exists between politics, economics, culture, and pedagogy. By making explicit hegemonic processes in the context of schooling, teachers are challenged to recognize their responsibility to critique and transform those classroom relationships that perpetuate the economic and cultural maginalization of subordinate groups.

What is important to recognize here is that the process of critique must be understood as an on-going phenomenon, for hegemony is never static or absolute. On the contrary, hegemony must be fought for constantly in order to retain its privileged position as the status quo. As a consequence, each time a radical form threatens the integrity of the status quo, generally this element is appropriated, stripped of its transformative intent, and reified into a palatable form. This process serves to preserve intact the existing power relations. Hence, understanding how hegemony functions in society provides critical educators with the basis for understanding not only how the seeds of domination are produced, but also how they can be challenged and overcome through resistance, critique and social action.

Resistance and Counter-Hegemony

Critical pedagogy incorporates a theory of resistance in an effort to better explain the complex reasons why many students from subordinate groups consistently fail within the educational system. It begins with the assumption that all people have the capacity and ability to produce knowledge and to resist domination. However, how they choose to resist is clearly influenced and limited by the social and material conditions in which they have been forced to survive and the ideological formations that have been internalized in the process.

The principle of resistance seeks to uncover the degree to which student oppositional behavior is associated with their need to struggle against elements of dehumanization or are simply tied to the perpetuation of their own oppression. As in other aspects of critical pedagogy, the notion of emancipatory interests serves here as a central point of reference in determining when oppositional behavior reflects a moment of resistance that can support counter-hegemonic purposes.

The term counter-hegemony is used within critical pedagogy to refer to those intellectual and social spaces where power relationships are reconstructed to make central the voices and experiences of those who have historically existed at the margins of public institutions. This is achieved whenever a new social context is forged out of moments of resistance, through establishing alternative structures and practices that democratize relations of power, in the interest of liberatory possibilities. It is significant to note here that given the powerful and overarching hegemonic political apparatus of advanced capitalist society, there is often great pressure placed upon individuals and groups, who rather than simply conform to the status quo, seek to enact counter-hegemonic alternatives of teaching and learning.

In response to the stress of this political pressure faced by many critical educators, Freire consistently stressed that it is a political imperative to develop a strong command of one's particular academic discipline. He believed that a solid knowledge of the authorized curriculum was essential, whether one taught in pre-school or primary education, the middle or high school grades, or higher education, or the university, if radical educators were to create effective counterhegemonic alternatives for their students. By so doing, they could competently teach the "official transcript" of their field or discipline, while simultaneously creating the opportunities for students to engage critically classroom content, from their existing knowledge and the events and experiences that comprise their living history.

Praxis: The Alliance of Theory and Practice
A dialectical view of knowledge supports the notion that theory and practice are inextricably linked to our understanding of the world and the actions we take in our daily lives. In keeping with this view, all theory is considered with respect to the practical intent of transforming asymmetrical relations of power. Unlike deterministic notions of schooling practice that focus primarily on an instrumental/technical application of theory, praxis is conceived as self-creating and self-generating free human activity. All human activity is understood as emerging from an on-going interaction of reflection, dialogue, and action—namely praxis—and as praxis, all human activity requires theory to illuminate it and provide a better understanding of the world as we find it and as it might be.

Hence, within critical pedagogy, all theorizing and truth claims are subject to critique, a process that constitutes analysis and questions that are best mediated through human interaction within democratic relations of power. Critical pedagogy places a strong emphasis on this relationship of *question-posing* within the educational process. Freire argued that a true praxis is impossible in the undialectical vacuum driven by a separation of the individual from the object of their study. For within the context of such a dichotomy, both theory and practice lose their power to transform reality. Cut off from practice, theory becomes abstraction or "simple verbalism." Separated from theory, practice becomes ungrounded activity or "blind activism."

Dialogue and Conscientization

The principle of dialogue as best defined by Freire is one of the most significant aspects of critical pedagogy. It speaks to an emancipatory educational process that is above all committed to the empowerment of students through challenging the dominant educational discourse and illuminating the right and freedom of students to become subjects of their world. Dialogue constitutes an educational strategy that centers upon the development of critical social consciousness or what Freire termed "conscientizaçao."

In the practice of critical pedagogy, dialogue and analysis serve as the foundation for reflection and action. It is this educational strategy that supports a problem-posing approach to education—an approach in which the relationship of students to teacher is, without question, dialogical, each having something to contribute and receive. Students learn from the teacher; teachers learn from the students. Hence, the actual lived experiences cannot be ignored nor relegated to the periphery in the process of coming to know. Instead, they must be actively incorporated as part of the exploration of existing conditions and knowledge, in order to understand how these came to be and to consider how they might be different.

Conscientizaçao or conscientization is defined as the process by which students, as empowered subjects, achieve a deepening awareness of the social realities which shape their lives and discover their own capacities to recreate them. This constitutes a recurrent, regenerating process of human interaction that is utilized for constant clarification of reflections and actions that arise in the classroom, as students and teachers move freely through the world of their experiences and enter into dialogue anew.

Critiques of Critical Pedagogy

The fundamental purpose of this volume is to provide a starting place for the study of critical pedagogy, through providing a short historical overview of those theoretical perspectives and philosophical principles that inform a critical theory of pedagogy. However, it would be contrary to its philosophical origins and intent not to mention, albeit briefly, some of the fundamental critiques that over the last two decades have fueled major debates within the context of critical pedagogical circles. Many of the critiques raised have effectively served to prompt a deepening consciousness as to our interpretations of critical pedagogical theories and practices within school and society.

Feminist Critiques

Numerous criticisms of critical pedagogy have been rooted in feminist views and articulations of identity, politics, and pedagogy. Some of the most significant critiques have been issued by such notable feminist scholars as Elizabeth Ellsworth, Carmen Luke, Jennifer Gore, Patti Lather, and Magda Lewis. As one might instantly recognize in the preceding discussion, the leading recognized scholars considered to have most influenced the development of critical theory and critical pedagogy have all been men, with the exception of Maxine Greene. From this standpoint alone, there has been much suspicion and concern about the failure of critical pedagogy to engage forthrightly questions of women, anchored within the context of female experience and knowledge construction. As such, critical pedagogy has often been accused of challenging the structures and practices of patriarchy in society, solely from a myopic and superficial lens.

Within the context of these critiques, questions have been launched against the underlying carte blanche acceptance of the Enlightenment's emphasis on the emancipatory function of cognitive learning that informs the Marxian perspective of reason—a view that underpins critical philosophical views of human beings, knowledge and the world. Along the same lines, there has been concern with the integration of Freudian analytical views within the work of the Frankfurt School—theories that clearly have served as a guiding light for the evolvement of critical pedagogical thought. Hence, in an effort to challenge the privileging of reason as the ultimate sphere upon which knowledge is constructed, feminists have passionately argued for the inclusion of personal biography, narratives, a rethinking of authority, and an explicit engagement with the historical and political location of the knowing subject—all aspects essential to questioning patriarchy and reconstructing the sexual politics that obstruct the participation of women as full and equal contributing members of society.

The Language of Critical Pedagogy

In very practical ways, the language of critical pedagogy has often been a serious point of contention not only among feminist scholars but also working-class educators, who argue that the theoretical language ultimately functions to create a new form of oppression. Hence, rather than liberating those who historically have found themselves at the margins of classical intellectual discourse, the language reinscribes power and privilege. Accordingly, the language was not only critiqued in the early days for its incessant use of the masculine pronoun in reference to both male and female subjects, but also for its elitism and consequent inaccessibility to those most affected by social inequalities. On one hand, these critiques challenged critical theorists to rethink the direction of their work and reconsider alternative strategies and approaches to the articulation of theoretical concerns. On another, they encouraged critical theorists to engage forthrightly with deeper questions being stirred by the debates, in terms of literacy, class, gender, culture, power and the emancipatory potential of diverse political projects within different traditions of struggle and pedagogy.

Critiques from the Borderlands

As might be expected, similar concerns have been raised among those scholars intimately involved in the struggle against racialized inequalities within schools and society. Although it cannot be denied that the writings of feminist scholars of color, such as Audre Lorde, Toni Morrison, Gloria Anzaldua, Trinh Minh-Ha, and bell hooks have had a tremendous impact on contemporary perspectives of gender, sexuality, and race in critical pedagogy, much of the work of these scholars remains primarily associated with ethnic, cultural, or feminist studies, with the exception of bell hooks.

Hence, another "obvious" characteristic of the leading critical scholars provoked some controversy—the fact that most of them are "white." At moments in the history of critical pedagogy, this factor became a major source of contention, as concerns were raised about the failure of critical pedagogy to explicitly treat questions of race, culture, or indigeneity as central concerns or from the specific location of racialized and colonized populations, themselves. When such concerns were raised, they were often silenced by accusations of "essentialism." Hence, questions of voice, agency and identity politics have fueled massive debates that have often created great suspicion and strife in efforts to work across diverse cultural perspectives.

From such debates sprung the intersectionality argument, grounded in the notion that critical theorists with their link to Marxist analysis and classical European philosophical roots were not only ethnocentric but also reductionist. Feminists and critics of color insisted that questions of race/gender/sexuality be given equal weight in any critical analysis of schooling in the United States. Such efforts were not only focused on the production of different readings of history and society, but on the empowerment of those groups who had existed historically at the margins of mainstream life.

Toward this end, a variety of culturally and racially defined strands of critical pedagogy emerged. Prominent discourses emerged in the field that included, for example, a critical race theory (CRT) of education that made central the issue of race in pedagogical discussions, as well as indigenous and ecological reinterpretations of emancipatory schooling and society. These contributions were significant to the field in that they concretely signaled an organic resistance to reification, inherent in critical pedagogical principles. Hence, critical scholars from a variety of cultural contexts challenged the Western predisposition toward orthodoxy in the field, reinforcing Freire's persistent assertion that critical pedagogical principles exist and remain open to reinvention.

The Postmodern Twist

In many ways, the impact of such postmodernist notions as intersectionality upon the direction of critical pedagogy has been considered by some as truly a double-edged sword. As postmodern theories brought into question many of the philosophical "sacred cows" of Western Enlightenment, they were also thought to stoke the coals of identity politics. Postmodern theories sought to move away from all-consuming meta-narratives, rejecting traditional notions of totality, reason and universality of absolute knowledge. As a consequence, the boundaries of traditional configurations of power and their impact on what constitutes legitimate knowledge were suddenly pushed wide open by new methods of deconstruction and reconstruction in the intellectual act of *border crossing.*

Although such a view appeared to hold real promise for a more serious theoretical engagement with developing notions of cultural hybridity, racialized subjects, sexualities, and the politics of difference, its intense fragmenting influence on formally effective organizing strategies across communities of difference led to the dismantling of former political visions. Those political visions that once offered some unifying direction to diverse political projects, were now called into question or simply met wholesale abandonment. As a consequence, the educational left found itself in a disheartening state of disarray, tension, and befuddlement. What is most unfortunate is that this philosophical shift in our understanding of diversity and the multicultural body politic often failed to acknowledge the similar oppressive conditions and human suffering experienced across cultural communities of the same socioeconomic class. An important recognition that had once functioned historically as a significant common ground for social justice struggles in the US and around the world.

The Retreat from Class

For almost two decades, a class-blind perspective seemed to dominate much of the debates, as post-civil-rights education activists attempted to stave off the impact of the rapidly growing conservative trend of the latter decades of the twentieth century. Critical theorists, who were particularly concerned with the totalizing impact of capitalism, its growing internationalization of capital, and its deleterious impact on working class people in the United States and abroad, lamented the retreat from class in postmodern writings about issues of culture, race, gender, and sexuality. The "postmodern" trend to see "power everywhere and nowhere" (Naiman, 1996) signaled for many a dangerous form of political abstraction, which failed to acknowledge forthrightly the manner in which advanced capitalism whipped wildly around the globe, well-consolidated in neoliberal efforts to perpetuate structures of economic domination and exploitation.

Without question, there were critical pedagogical theorists who were also tremendously concerned about the destructive impact that this intensified globalization of the economy was having upon the commercialization of public schooling. In light of these growing concerns, critical theorists such as Michael Apple, Stanley Aronowitz, Jean Anyon, Peter McLaren, Joel Spring, Alex Molnar, and others urged educators to remain ever cognizant of the centrality of social class in shaping the conditions students experienced within schools and communities. As a consequence, they worked rigorously to draw attention to the continuing significance of class analysis, by challenging the changing nature of the "post-industrial" economy and its consequences on knowledge production and schooling.

However, in the foreground of this concern remained questions of how to engage class as both an analytical and political category, without falling prey to "red-herring" accusations of economic determinism and reductionism. In response, a number of critical educators began to rethink post-civil-rights notions of class, race, and gender, in an effort to begin formulating new language for our understanding of gendered and racialized class relations and its impact on education. Hence, at a time in our history when critical educators most needed an economic understanding of schooling, a revived historical materialist approach began to reinvigorate critical pedagogical debates in the age of "globalization." This perspective challenged the destruction of the "safety-net" once afforded disenfranchised populations, the politics of privatization, the corporate bureaucratization of society, and the growing impoverishment and pollution of the planet.

The Ecological Critique

Ecological scholars, who question the Western modernizing legacy of progress that anchors much of the theoretical underpinnings of critical pedagogy, have also heavily criticized the field. Here, many of the concerns are linked to the manner in which the ideas of critical theory structure assumptions and meanings associated with notions of humanity, freedom, and empowerment. As such, critical educators are accused of intensifying or reinscribing dominant values, particularly within contexts where non-Western traditions or indigenous knowledge challenges critical pedagogical definitions of the world. As such, critical pedagogical principles tied to knowledge production and dialogical relations are questioned for their potentiality to essentialize and absolutize knowledge, despite its dialogical intents.

C. A. Bowers (1987; Bowers & Apffel-Marglin, 2004), one of the most strident critics, claims, for example, that the drawback with Freire's perspective of dialogue is not its emphasis on critical reflection, but the manner in which individual reflection is privileged —in the name of empowerment. At issue here are concerns related to the tensions that exist between the privileging of traditional forms of community knowledge and individual knowledge enacted within the praxis of dialogue. Hence, from an ecological standpoint, there has been concern that critical pedagogy, albeit unintentionally, fractures knowledge and supports the further alienation of human beings from nature. Moreover, the lethargic pace at which critical pedagogical scholars have addressed questions of the planet's ecological deterioration has been seen as cause for alarm.

However, in light of such critiques, it is significant to note that, more recently, critical education scholars have begun to seriously engage these critiques, in an effort to explore the manner in which critical pedagogy might become more proactive in the face of the ecological crisis at hand. The Paulo Freire Institute for Ecopedagogy, for example, is expressly committed to "the construction of a planetary citizenship, so that all, with no exception or exclusion, may have healthy conditions, in a planet able to offer life because its own life is being preserved." Rooted in a deep sense of ecological awareness, an eco-pedagogy cultivates critical approaches of learning that go beyond mastery and manipulation, encouraging students to develop a sense of kinship with all life, through an integrated commitment to the ecological welfare of the world.

Silencing of Dissent

Despite the efforts of critical education theorists to counter the oppressive forces at work in society today, conservative and liberal educators, including public school officials and educational policy makers, adamantly claim that "critical pedagogy is only about politics," dismissing the constitutive role of politics and dissent to democratic life. Hence, it is not uncommon to hear bitter attacks against the political nature of critical pedagogy, as opponents smugly assert the futility and lack of practical value of radical approaches in the classroom. Yet, such expressions of opposition, more often than not, are sly and unjustified proclamations to obstruct the establishment of democratic approaches to teaching and learning within schools—approaches that seek to alter asymmetrical power relations of schooling practices and reconstruct relationships that deceptively function to retain control over the majority.

More importantly, such critiques are often generated by the fear, confusion and hysteria generated among school officials, mainstream educators, and scholars within schools, communities and universities, whenever teachers, students or parents voice oppositional views that challenge the undemocratic contradictions at work in public schools. Tensions often become heightened at moments when those in power attempt to obstruct efforts by teachers, students and parents to integrate their voices and participation in the governance of public schools—an act that if successful might signal substantive changes to business as usual. Here we must note that what is brought into question, by those who hold power, is the legitimacy of critical social action among poor, working class and racialized populations. Hence, overtures for people to conduct themselves in "reasonable" or "civilized ways," are too often a means to silence and derail the expression of legitimate anger, frustration, and concerns. By so doing, opponents of critical pedagogical efforts deflect the possibility of any substantive public dialogue that might potentially lead to the development of new ideas, new language, new practices, and perhaps even new relationships of power within schools.

In efforts to survive conservative assaults, the ideas of critical pedagogy have been, at times, reified into simplistic fetishized methods that are converted into mere instrumentalized formulas for intervention, discouraging dissent and leaving untouched the ideologies that sustain inequities in schools today. To counter this trend, critical educators attempt to reach beyond the boundaries of the classroom, into communities, workplaces, and public arenas where people congregate, reflect, and negotiate daily survival. Furthermore, it is within this context, of what Giroux terms a *public pedagogy*, that critical educators can develop their capacity to read power effectively and thus enact political and pedagogical interventions, in the interest of social justice and critical democratic life.

The Future of Critical Pedagogy

Understanding critical pedagogy within a long tradition of progressive educational movements and on-going struggles of reinvention offers a possible safeguard against the temptation to inadvertently reify and reduce critical pedagogy to a teaching "method." This has been particularly at issue in the last decade, where conservative policies have retained a stronghold on the rigid standardization of the curriculum, championed high-stakes testing, dismantled anti-bilingual education efforts, and upheld a conservative national agenda for public schooling practice and educational research. Accordingly, the responses of many, even progressive, educators to the reactionary policies of *No Child Left Behind*, for example, has been to abandon overt emancipatory approaches in the classroom or, at best, enact palatable versions of critical pedagogy. This strategy, unfortunately, has functioned to thwart the forthright advancement of an emancipatory educational agenda.

We should, however, not be too surprised, concerned, or discouraged when we find an acceleration of such efforts. Rather, in keeping with the tradition of critical pedagogy, such efforts generally signal, for progressive educators, the importance of learning to read the formal and informal power relationships within schools. But even more importantly, conservative strategies serve as a clear reminder that no political struggle in a school or society can be waged by one lone voice in the wilderness, nor are democratic principles of education ever guaranteed. It is precisely for this reason that on-going emancipatory efforts within schools must be linked to collective emancipatory efforts within and across communities.

Although we have included a variety of works by prominent thinkers in the tradition of critical educational theory, critical pedagogy as a school of thought has often been associated with the work of Paulo Freire. Yet, as we have attempted to illustrate here, critical pedagogy does not begin and end with Freire. Nevertheless, it cannot be denied that Freire's influence as a Brazilian or Latin-American (that is to say not "white" or European) played a significant role in the inspiration his writings brought to many radical educators of color in this country and other parts of the world. His presence, consciously or unconsciously, legitimated our right to express and define, on our own terms, the educational needs of working class and racialized students in the US. But, simultaneously, we also found in Freire a living politics that defied the iconography of his own contribution to the political project of critical pedagogy. As such, his loving ethics of education sought to reinforce the necessity for greater solidarity among critical theorists and critical educators during these perilous times. In this spirit, Freire's understanding of solidarity challenges critical educators to break with alienating practices of competition, internalized notions of superiority, tendencies to demonize difference, and our "colonized" dependence and yearning to be recognized or legitimated by those who hold official power. For it is only through such a politics of solidarity that the principles of critical pedagogy can be enacted, in order to affirm and solidly nourish an on-going emancipatory educational movement.

In light of the long-standing historical tradition of progressive educational efforts in the United States and around the world, we can safely guarantee that the underlying commitment and intent of critical pedagogy will persist, as long as there are those who are forced to exist under conditions of suffering and alienation—and there are those who refuse to accept such conditions as a "natural" evolution of humankind.

References

Boal, A. (1982). *Theatre of the Oppressed*. New York: Routledge.

Bowers, C.A. (1987). *Elements of a Post-liberal Theory of Education*. New York: Teachers College Press.

Bowers, C.A. and F. Apffel-Marglin (2004). *Re-Thinking Freire: Globalization and the Environmental Crisis*. New York: Lawrence Erlbaum.

Bowles, S. and Gintis, H. (1976). *Schooling in Capitalist America*. New York: Basic Books.

Dewey, J. (1916). *Democracy and Education*. New York: The Free Press.

DuBois, W.E.B. (1902). *The Souls of Black Folk*. Chicago: A.C. McClurg & Co.

Freire, P. (1971). *Pedagogy of the Oppressed*. New York: Seabury.

Giroux, H. (1983). *Theory and Resistance in Education*. South Hadley, MA: Bergin & Garvey.

Gramsci, A. (1971/1992). *Prison Notebooks*. New York: Columbia University Press.

Graves, K. (1998). "Outflanking Oppression: African American Contributions to Critical Pedagogy as Developed in the Scholarship of W. E. B. DuBois and Carter G. Woodson." Paper presented at the *Annual Meeting of the American Educational Research Association*.

Greene, M. (1988). *The Dialectics of Freedom*. New York: Teachers College Press.

Held, D. (1980). *Introduction to Critical Theory: Horkheimer to Habermas*. Berkeley and Los Angeles: University of California Press.

Illich, I. (1971). *Deschooling Society*. New York: Harper & Row.

Kozol, J. (1967). *Death at an Early Age*. Boston: Houghton Mifflin.

Kozol, J. (2006). *Shame of the Nation: The Restoration of Apartheid Schooling in America*. New York: Three Rivers Press.

McLaren, P. (1989). *Life in Schools: An introduction to critical pedagogy and the foundations of education*. New York: Longman.

Naiman, J. (1996). "Left feminism and the return to class," in *Monthly Review* vol. 48, no. 2, June.

Warren, S. (1984). *The Emergence of Dialectical Theory*. Chicago: University of Chicago Press.

Woodson, C.G. (1933). *The Mis-education of the Negro*. Washington: Associated Publishers.

Part One

Foundations of Critical Pedagogy

Introduction to Part One

As illustrated in the introduction to this volume, the foundations of critical pedagogy have truly emerged from a variety of intellectual traditions. Yet, what has loosely united these traditions has been their uncompromising allegiance to the liberation of oppressed populations. In keeping with this underlying commitment, critical pedagogy was founded upon philosophical traditions that critically interrogate the pedagogical interrelationships between culture, economics, ideology, and power. In so doing, critical educational approaches cultivate a process of teaching and learning that deeply nurtures the development of critical consciousness among teachers and their students.

Vital to this critical understanding of the world is the intentional and deliberate development of both theoretical faculties and practical capacities that challenge educators to define and critique power relations, in ways that promote the transformation of existing educational inequalities. This entails the ability to read both overt, as well as hidden, relations of power tied to mainstream norms and standards of knowledge, upheld by positivist contentions and conservative social arrangements embedded in the nature and structures of schools and society. Toward this end, a critical theoretical perspective seeks to contest mainstream practices of schooling and explore democratic strategies and interventions that can shift relations of power and alter meaning. This is particularly true when working with students from working class, poor, and racialized communities, whose cultural perspectives and histories fundamentally challenge many of the philosophical assumptions of the standardized curriculum. Hence, it is not unusual for critical education theorists to refer to schools as a "terrain of struggle."

The purpose of critique then, within critical pedagogy, is to serve as a powerful lens of analysis from which social inequalities and oppressive institutional structures can be unveiled, critiqued, and, most importantly, transformed through the process of political engagement and social action. A capacity for critique arms educators and students with the language and theoretical organizing principles to disrupt and transgress the hegemonic expectations of the official curriculum. In this way, teachers learn to assess inequalities in their lives and to question commonsensical notions of the world that perpetuate our cultural, linguistic, economic, gendered, and sexual subordination.

But true to the principle of hegemony, critical pedagogy also assists educators to understand why students who have been oppressed do not necessarily embrace readily the possibility of transformation in the classroom. In an educational context where students from subordinated groups are taught early to believe in their own inherent deficit and to accept the uncompromising authority of standardized knowledge, the possibility of transgression can often signal a moment of crisis, anxiety, and intense fear. Hence, an understanding of resistance, within critical pedagogy, encompasses a realization that expressions of resistance are expected, multidimensional, and significant pedagogical moments from which a democratic process of education is forged.

It is precisely for this reason that a critical pedagogy is also founded on the principle of dialogue, which can only be enacted through on-going, interactive classroom spaces, where teachers and students together can reflect, critique, and act upon their world. This critical dialogical approach seeks to counter the traditional "banking concept" of education, where the teacher functions as all-knowing subject and students are rendered passive objects in the dynamics of their own learning. As such, critical educators are engaged in an on-going reconfiguration of oppressive classroom relationships tied to power and authority, knowledge construction, and democratic participation, while simultaneously making central the lived histories of their students.

Integrating principles of a critical pedagogy in one's teaching practice requires the willingness to seriously interrogate one's ideological understanding of the world. This process also necessitates an examination of the underlying consequences of, and alternatives to, traditional curriculum, teaching methods, classroom relationships, and educational policies. However, for teachers to undertake this enormous task effectively necessitates the development of a clear understanding of the theoretical foundations which inform both an emancipatory vision and practice of critical pedagogy. The articles featured in this section are meant to assist teachers in beginning this journey.

Summary of Articles

This first section of the volume synthesizes further many of the foundational ideas of Critical Pedagogy discussed earlier. "Critical Theory and Educational Practice" by Henry Giroux begins the journey through this evolution of progressive education ideas coalescing into what is today known in the field as critical pedagogy. Without question, Giroux's work is credited with repositioning the education debates of the "New Left" beyond the boundaries of reproduction theories and the hidden curriculum. He presents an analysis that clearly initiates an important turning point in the development of the progressive educational agenda of the 1980s. In this article, Giroux traces the history and development of critical theory back to the members of the Frankfurt School, examining the major themes that informed their work. Namely, rejection of orthodox Marxism, critique of late capitalism, analysis of instrumental reason, deep concerns about the culture industry, and their psychoanalytical view of domination. Giroux's exploration into the historical development of the Frankfurt School provided a strong analytical basis upon which to develop one of the most distinctive features of critical pedagogy—the principle of resistance.

The second contribution to this section is a chapter from the internationally acclaimed book, *Pedagogy of the Oppressed*, by the Brazilian educator Paulo Freire. Freire's work provided a solid foundation and impetus for the development of a critical pedagogical philosophy of education. The essay included here truly captures the essence of Freire's contribution to the field. Freire's critique of the traditional banking concept of education along with a discussion of authoritarian teacher–student interaction represents one of the most powerful critiques of schooling. His discussion of the historical nature of knowledge— including the false duality between theory and practice—and the need to transcend the "problem-solving" approach in order to engage students in a "problem-posing" pedagogy, became an important point of departure in the articulation of a critical pedagogical practice.

"Critical Pedagogy: A Look at the Major Concepts," by Peter McLaren, a former Canadian schoolteacher and a recognized leader in the critical educational movement, articulates for the reader the theoretical principles that underscore a critical pedagogical perspective. McLaren's analysis focuses on the significance of dialectical theory, the nature of knowledge, the concepts of hegemony and ideology, and the effects of the hidden curriculum on public schooling. McLaren's discussion of these concepts is intended to assist teachers in considering more closely what ideas inform their teaching practice. Through this interrogation of their daily practice, teachers are encouraged to seek ways in which they might disrupt oppressive tendencies in the process of teaching and learning.

Maxine Greene, a noted philosopher and remarkable educator, has often been referred to as the *mother of aesthetic education*. In her essay, "In Search of a Critical Pedagogy," she reflects on the historical traditions of the progressive education movement in the United States. Her purpose here is to link the development of critical pedagogy, both historically and philosophically, to the foundations of American social activism. Since many of the philosophical roots of critical theory are linked to the European experience, Greene felt it important to find an analogous experience from which to relate the project of critical pedagogy to the American struggle for "life, liberty and the pursuit of happiness." She discusses the impact of compulsory public education and "the appearance of utopian communities and socialist societies" in the nineteenth century in the United States. More importantly, Greene takes the reader through a journey of re-discovery to highlight American "rebellious figures," where innumerable names emerge that speak to the struggles for the abolition of slavery, women's rights, anti-racism, freedom schools, and the civil rights movement. She argues passionately for reclaiming these struggles—erased from the American psyche—in an effort to invigorate the contribution of critical pedagogy to the struggles in education today.

Questions for Reflection and Dialogue

1. Describe the school of thought known as Critical Theory. What was the role of the Frankfurt School in the development of critical theory?
2. Identify the major themes addressed by the Frankfurt School and why these were important to the development of critical theory.
3. In what ways does Paulo Freire's vision of education differ from traditional approaches to schooling?
4. What are the fundamental changes that Freire proposes to help teachers counteract the banking approach to education?
5. Explain how Freire defines knowledge and the implications of his view to democratic schooling.
6. What are the major distinctions between a "problem-solving" and a "problem-posing" pedagogy? What are the political implications of these approaches for classroom instruction?
7. How does Freire define "praxis" and how does this concept relate to teaching and learning?
8. How does McLaren define dialectical thinking and its importance to critical pedagogy?

9. Define hegemony. What role do class, culture, and ideology play in the process of hegemony?

10. How do notions of the "hidden curriculum" and "cultural capital" relate to the standardization of knowledge in schools today?

11. What is Greene's interpretation of U.S. history? What account of American radical thinkers is found in the K-12 curriculum? Reflect on your own school experience and describe the major historical events and how these influenced your views of yourself, education, and the world.

12. According to Greene, what are the challenges faced by the present generation of Americans? Elaborate in what ways critical pedagogy can help in addressing these challenges.

1

Critical Theory and Educational Practice

Henry A. Giroux

Introduction

This chapter attempts to contribute to the search for a theoretical foundation upon which to develop a critical theory of education. Within the parameters of this task, the notion of critical theory has a two-fold meaning. First, critical theory refers to the legacy of theoretical work developed by certain members of what can be loosely described as "the Frankfurt School." What this suggests is that critical theory was never a fully articulated philosophy shared unproblematically by all members of the Frankfurt School. But it must be stressed that while one cannot point to a single universally shared critical theory, one can point to the common attempt to assess the newly emerging forms of capitalism along with the changing forms of domination that accompanied them. Similarly, there was an attempt on the part of all the members of the Frankfurt School to rethink and radically reconstruct the meaning of human emancipation, a project that differed considerably from the theoretical baggage of orthodox Marxism. Specifically, I argue in this chapter for the importance of original critical theory and the insights it provides for developing a critical foundation for a theory of radical pedagogy. In doing so, I focus on the work of Adorno, Horkheimer, and Marcuse. This seems to be an important concern, especially since so much of the work on the Frankfurt School being used by educators focuses almost exclusively on the work of Jürgen Habermas.

Second, the concept of critical theory refers to the nature of SELF-CONSCIOUS CRITIQUE and to the need to develop a discourse of social transformation and emancipation that does not cling dogmatically to its own doctrinal assumptions. (In other words, critical theory refers to both a "school of thought" and a process of critique.) It points to a body of thought that is, in my view, invaluable for educational theorists; it also exemplifies a body of work that both demonstrates and simultaneously calls for the necessity of ongoing critique, one in which the claims of any theory must be confronted with the distinction between the world it examines and portrays, and the world as it actually exists.

The Frankfurt School took as one of its central values a commitment to penetrate the world of objective appearances to expose the underlying social relationships they often conceal. In other words, penetrating such appearances meant exposing through critical analysis social relationships that took on the status of things or objects. For instance, by examining notions such as money, consumption, distribution, and production, it becomes clear that none of these represents an objective thing or fact, but rather all are historically contingent contexts mediated by relationships of domination and subordination. In adopting such a perspective, the Frankfurt School not only broke with forms of rationality that wedded science and technology into new forms of domination, it also rejected all forms of rationality that subordinated human consciousness and action to the imperatives of universal laws. Whether it be the legacy of Victorian European positivist intellectual thought or the theoretical edifice developed by Engels, Kautsky, Stalin, and other heirs of Marxism, the Frankfurt School argued against the suppression of "subjectivity, consciousness, and culture in history" (Breines 1979–80). In so doing it articulated a notion of negativity or critique that opposed all theories that celebrated social harmony while leaving unproblematic the basic assumptions of the wider society. In more specific terms, the Frankfurt School stressed the importance of critical thinking by arguing that it is a constitutive feature of the struggle for self-emancipation and social change. Moreover, its members argued that it was in the contradictions of society that one could begin to develop forms of social inquiry that analyzed the distinction between *what is* and *what should be*. Finally, it strongly supported the assumption that the basis for thought and action should be grounded, as Marcuse argued just before his death, "in compassion, [and] in our sense of the sufferings of others" (Habermas 1980).

In general terms, the Frankfurt School provided a number of valuable insights for studying the relationship between theory and society. In so doing, its members developed a dialectical framework by which to understand the mediations that link the institutions and activities of everyday life with the logic and commanding forces that shape the larger social totality. The characteristic nature of the form of social inquiry that emerged from such a framework was articulated by Horkheimer when he suggested that members of the Institute for Social Research explore the question of "the interconnection between the economic life of society, the psychic development of the individual, and transformations in the realm of culture . . . including not only the so-called spiritual contents of science, art, and religion, but also law, ethics, fashion, public opinion, sport, amusement, life style, etc." (Horkheimer 1972).

The issues raised here by Horkheimer have not lost their importance with time; they still represent both a critique and a challenge to many of the theoretical currents that presently characterize theories of social education. The necessity for theoretical renewal in the education field, coupled with the massive number of primary and secondary sources that have been translated or published recently in English, provide the opportunity for American- and English-speaking pedagogues to begin to appropriate the discourse and ideas of the Frankfurt School. Needless to say, such a task will not be easily accomplished, since both the complexity of the language used by members of the School and the diversity of the positions and themes they pursued demand a selective and critical reading of their works. Yet their critique of culture, instrumental rationality, authoritarianism, and ideology, pursued in an interdisciplinary context, generated categories, relationships, and forms of social inquiry that constitute a vital resource for developing a critical theory of social education. Since it will be impossible in the scope of this chapter to analyze the diversity of themes examined by the Frankfurt School, I will limit my analysis to the treatment of *rationality, theory, culture,* and *depth psychology*. Finally, I will discuss the implications of these for educational theory and practice.

History and Background of the Frankfurt School

The Institute for Social Research (*Das Institut für Sozialforschung*), officially created in Frankfurt, Germany, in February, 1923, was the original home of the Frankfurt School.

Established by a wealthy grain merchant named Felix Weil, the Institute came under the directorship of Max Horkheimer in 1930. Under Horkheimer's directorship, most of the members who later became famous joined the Institute. These included Erich Fromm, Herbert Marcuse, and Theodor Adorno. As Martin Jay points out in his now-famous history of the Frankfurt School: "If it can be said that in the early years of its history the Institute concerned itself primarily with an analysis of bourgeois society's socio-economic substructure, in the years after 1930 its prime interests lay in its cultural superstructure" (Jay 1973).

The change in the Institute's theoretical focus was soon followed by a shift in its location. Threatened by the Nazis because of the avowedly Marxist orientation of its work and the fact that most of its members were Jews, the Institute was forced to move for a short time in 1933 to Geneva, and then in 1934 to New York City, where it was housed in one of Columbia University's buildings. Emigration to New York was followed by a stay in Los Angeles in 1941, and by 1953 the Institute was re-established in Frankfurt, Germany.

The strengths and weaknesses of the Frankfurt School project become intelligible only if seen as part of the social and historical context in which it developed. In essence, the questions it pursued and the forms of social inquiry it supported represent both a particular moment in the development of Western Marxism and a critique of it. Reacting to the rise of Fascism and Nazism, on the one hand, and to the failure of orthodox Marxism, on the other, the Frankfurt School had to refashion and rethink the meaning of domination and emancipation. The rise of Stalinism, the failure of the European or Western working class to contest capitalist hegemony in a revolutionary manner, and the power of capitalism to reconstitute and reinforce its economic and ideological control forced the Frankfurt School to reject the orthodox reading of Marx and Engels, particularly as developed through the conventional wisdom of the Second and Third Internationals. It is particularly in the rejection of certain doctrinal Marxist assumptions, developed under the historical shadow of totalitarianism and through the rise of the consumer society in the West, that Horkheimer, Adorno, and Marcuse attempted to construct a more sufficient basis for social theory and political action. Certainly, such a basis was not to be found in standard Marxist assumptions such as (a) the notion of historical inevitability, (b) the primacy of the mode of production in shaping history, and (c) the notion that class struggle as well as the mechanisms of domination take place primarily within the confines of the labor process. For the Frankfurt School, orthodox Marxism assumed too much while simultaneously ignoring the benefits of self-criticism. It had failed to develop a theory of consciousness and thus had expelled the human subject from its own theoretical calculus. It is not surprising, then, that the focus of the Frankfurt School's research de-emphasized the area of political economy to focus instead on the issues of how subjectivity was constituted and how the spheres of culture and everyday life represented a new terrain of domination. It is against this historical and theoretical landscape that we can begin to abstract categories and modes of analysis that speak to the nature of schooling as it presently exists, and to its inherent potential for developing into a force for social change.

Rationality and the Critique of Instrumental Reason

Fundamental to an understanding of the Frankfurt School's view of theory and of its critique of instrumental reason is its analysis of the heritage of Enlightenment rationality. Echoing Nietzsche's earlier warning about humanity's unbounded faith in reason, Adorno

and Horkheimer voiced a trenchant critique of modernity's unswerving faith in the promise of Enlightenment rationality to rescue the world from the chains of superstition,
ignorance, and suffering. The problematic nature of such a promise marks the opening
lines of *Dialectic of Enlightenment*: "In the most general sense of progressive thought
the Enlightenment has always aimed at liberating men from fear and establishing their
sovereignty. Yet the fully enlightened earth radiates disaster triumphant" (Adorno &
Horkheimer 1972).

Faith in scientific rationality and the principles of practical judgement did not constitute a legacy that developed exclusively in the seventeenth and eighteenth centuries, when
people of reason united on a vast intellectual front in order to master the world through an
appeal to the claims of reasoned thought. According to the Frankfurt School, the legacy of
scientific rationality represented one of the central themes of Western thought and
extended as far back as Plato (Horkheimer 1974). Habermas, a later member of the
Frankfurt School, argues that the progressive notion of reason reaches its highest point
and most complex expression in the work of Karl Marx, after which it is reduced from
an all-encompassing concept of rationality to a particular instrument in the service of
industrialized society. According to Habermas:

> On the level of the historical self-reflection of a science with critical intent, Marx for the last
> time identifies reason with a commitment to rationality in its thrust against dogmatism. In the
> second half of the nineteenth century, during the course of the reduction of science to a
> productive force in industrial society, positivism, historicism, and pragmatism, each in turn,
> isolate one part of this all-encompassing concept of rationality. The hitherto undisputed
> attempt of the great theories to reflect on the complex of life as a whole is henceforth itself
> discredited as dogma . . . The spontaneity of hope, the art of taking a position, the experience
> of relevance or indifference, and above all, the response to suffering and oppression, the
> desire for adult autonomy, the will to emancipation, and the happiness of discovering one's
> identity—all these are dismissed for all time from the obligating interest of reason.
>
> (Habermas 1973)

Marx may have employed reason in the name of critique and emancipation, but it was
still a notion of reason limited to an overemphasis on the labor process and on the
exchange rationality that was both its driving force and ultimate mystification. Adorno,
Horkheimer, and Marcuse, in contrast to Marx, believed that "the fateful process of rationalization" (Wellmer 1974) had penetrated all aspects of everyday life, whether it be the
mass media, the school, or the workplace. The crucial point here is that no social sphere
was free from the encroachments of a form of reason in which "all theoretical means of
transcending reality became metaphysical nonsense" (Horkheimer 1974).

In the Frankfurt School's view, reason has not been permanently stripped of its positive
dimensions. Marcuse, for instance, believed that reason contained a critical element and
was still capable of reconstituting history. As he put it, "Reason represents the highest
potentiality of man and existence; the two belong together" (Marcuse 1968a). But if reason
was to preserve its promise of creating a more just society, it would have to demonstrate
powers of critique and negativity. According to Adorno (1973), the crisis of reason takes
place as society becomes more rationalized; under such historical circumstances, in the
quest for social harmony, it loses its critical faculty and becomes an instrument of the
existing society. As a result, reason as insight and critique turns into its opposite—
irrationality.

For the Frankfurt School, the crisis in reason is linked to the more general crises in
science and in society as a whole. Horkheimer argued in 1972 that the starting point for

understanding "the crisis of science depends on a correct theory of the present social situation." In essence, this speaks to two crucial aspects of Frankfurt School thought. First, it argues that the only solution to the present crisis lies in developing a more fully self-conscious notion of reason, one that embraces elements of critique as well as of human will and transformative action. Second, it means entrusting to theory the task of rescuing reason from the logic of technocratic rationality or positivism. It was the Frankfurt School's view that positivism had emerged as the final ideological expression of the Enlightenment. The victory of positivism represented not the high point but the low point of Enlightenment thought. Positivism became the enemy of reason rather than its agent, and emerged in the twentieth century as a new form of social administration and domination. Friedman sums up the essence of this position:

> To the Frankfurt School, philosophical and practical positivism constituted the end point of the Enlightenment. The social function of the ideology of positivism was to deny the critical faculty of reason by allowing it only the ground of utter facticity to operate upon. By so doing, they denied reason a critical moment. Reason, under the rule of positivism, stands in awe of the fact. Its function is simply to characterize the fact. Its task ends when it has affirmed and explicated the fact. . . . Under the rule of positivism, reason inevitably stops short of critique.
>
> (Friedman 1981)

It is in its critique of positivistic thought that the Frankfurt School makes clear the specific mechanisms of ideological control that permeate the consciousness and practices of advanced capitalist societies. It is also in its critique of positivism that it develops a notion of theory that has major implications for educational critics. But the route to understanding this concept necessitates that one first analyze the Frankfurt School's critique of positivism, particularly since the logic of positivist thought (though in varied forms) represents the major theoretical impetus currently shaping educational theory and practice.

The Frankfurt School defined positivism, in the broad sense, as an amalgam of diverse traditions that included the work of Saint-Simon and Comte, the logical positivism of the Vienna Circle, the early work of Wittgenstein, and the more recent forms of logical empiricism and pragmatism that dominate the social sciences in the West. While the history of these traditions is complex and cluttered with detours and qualifications, each of them has supported the goal of developing forms of social inquiry patterned after the natural sciences and based on the methodological tenets of sense observation and quantification. Marcuse provides both a general definition of positivism as well as a basis for some of the reservations of the Frankfurt School regarding its most basic assumptions:

> Since its first usage, probably in the school of Saint-Simon, the term "positivism" has encompassed (1) the validation of cognitive thought by experience of facts; (2) the orientation of cognitive thought to the physical science as a model of certainty and exactness; (3) the belief that progress in knowledge depends on this orientation. Consequently, positivism is a struggle against all metaphysics, transcendentalisms, and idealisms as obscurantist and regressive modes of thought. To the degree to which the given reality is scientifically comprehended and transformed, to the degree to which society becomes industrial and technological, positivism finds in the society the medium for the realization (and validation) of its concepts—harmony between theory and practice, truth and facts. Philosophic thought turns into affirmative thought; the philosophic critique criticizes within the societal framework and stigmatizes non-positive notions as mere speculation, dreams or fantasies.
>
> (Marcuse 1964)

Positivism, according to Horkheimer, presented a view of knowledge and science that stripped both of their critical possibilities. Knowledge was reduced to the exclusive province of science, and science itself was subsumed within a methodology that limited "scientific activity to the description, classification, and generalization of phenomena, with no care to distinguish the unimportant from the essential" (Horkheimer 1972). Accompanying this view are the ideas that knowledge derives from sense experience and that the ideal it pursues takes place "in the form of a mathematically formulated universe deducible from the smallest possible number of axioms, a system which assures the calculation of the probable occurrence of all events" (ibid).

For the Frankfurt School, positivism did not represent an indictment of science; instead it echoed Nietzsche's insight that "It is not the victory of science that is the distinguishing mark of our nineteenth century, but the victory of the scientific method over science" (Nietzsche 1966). Science, in this perspective, was separated from the question of ends and ethics, which were rendered insignificant because they defied "explication in terms of mathematical structures" (Marcuse 1964). According to the Frankfurt School, the suppression of ethics in positivist rationality precludes the possibility for self-criticism, or, more specifically, for questioning its own normative structure. Facts become separated from values, objectivity undermines critique, and the notion that essence and appearance may not coincide is lost in the positivist view of the world. The latter point becomes particularly clear in the Vienna Circle pronouncement: "The view that thought is a means of knowing more about the world than may be directly observed . . . seems to us entirely mysterious" (Hahn 1933). For Adorno, the idea of value freedom was perfectly suited to a perspective that was to insist on a universal form of knowledge while simultaneously refusing to inquire into its own socio-ideological development and function in society.

According to the Frankfurt School, the *outcome of positivist rationality and its technocratic view of science represented a threat to the notion of subjectivity and critical thinking.* By functioning within an operational context free from ethical commitments, positivism wedded itself to the immediate and "celebrated" the world of "facts." The question of essence—the difference between the world as it is and as it could be—is reduced to the merely methodological task of collecting and classifying facts. In this schema, "Knowledge relates solely to what is, and to its recurrence" (Horkheimer 1972). Questions concerning the genesis, development, and normative nature of the conceptual systems that select, organize, and define the facts appear to be outside the concern of positivist rationality.

Since it recognizes no factors behind the "fact," positivism freezes both human beings and history. In the case of these, the issue of historical development is ignored since the historical dimension contains truths that cannot be assigned "to a special fact-gathering branch of science" (Adorno, quoted in Gross 1979). Of course, positivism is not impervious to history, or to the relationship between history and understanding, at any rate. On the contrary, its key notions of objectivity, theory, and values, as well as its modes of inquiry, are paradoxically a consequence of and a force in the shaping of history. In other words, positivism may ignore history but it cannot escape it. What is important to stress is that fundamental categories of socio-historical development are at odds with the positivist emphasis on the immediate, or more specifically with that which can be expressed, measured, and calculated in precise mathematical formulas. Russell Jacoby (1980) points concisely to this issue in his claim that "the natural reality and natural sciences do not know the fundamental historical categories: consciousness and self-consciousness, subjectivity and objectivity, appearance and essence."

By not reflecting on its paradigmatic premises, positivist thought ignores the value of historical consciousness and consequently endangers the nature of critical thinking itself. That is, inherent in the very structure of positivist thought, with its emphasis on objectivity and its lack of theoretical grounding with regard to the setting of tasks (Horkheimer 1972), are a number of assumptions that appear to preclude its ability to judge the complicated interaction of power, knowledge, and values and to reflect critically on the genesis and nature of its own ideological presuppositions. Moreover, by situating itself within a number of false dualisms (facts *vs.* values, scientific knowledge *vs.* norms, and description *vs.* prescription) positivism dissolves the tension between potentiality and actuality in all spheres of social existence. Thus, under the guise of neutrality, scientific knowledge and all theory become rational on the grounds of whether or not they are efficient, economic, or correct. In this case, a notion of methodological correctness subsumes and devalues the complex philosophical concept of truth. As Marcuse points out, "The fact that a judgement can be correct and nevertheless without truth, has been the crux of formal logic from time immemorial" (quoted in Arato & Gebhardt 1978).

For instance, an empirical study that concludes that native workers in a colonized country work at a slower rate than imported workers who perform the same job may provide an answer that is correct, but such an answer tells us little about the notion of domination or the resistance of workers under its sway. That the native workers may slow down their rate as an act of resistance is not considered here. Thus, the notions of intentionality and historical context are dissolved within the confines of a limiting quantifying methodology.

For Adorno, Marcuse, and Horkheimer, the fetishism of facts and the belief in value neutrality represented more than an epistemological error; more importantly, such a stance served as a form of ideological hegemony that infused positivist rationality with a political conservatism that made it an ideological prop of the status quo. This is not to suggest, however, an intentional support for the status quo on the part of all individuals who work within a positivist rationality. Instead, it implies a particular relationship to the status quo; in some situations this relationship is consciously political, in others it is not. In other words, in the latter instance the relationship to the status quo is a conservative one, but it is not self-consciously recognized by those who help to reproduce it.

The Frankfurt School's Notion of Theory

According to the Frankfurt School, any understanding of the nature of theory has to begin with a grasp of the relationships that exist in society between the particular and the whole, the specific and the universal. This position appears in direct contradiction to the empiricist claim that theory is primarily a matter of classifying and arranging facts. In rejecting the absolutizing of facts, the Frankfurt School argued that in the relation between theory and the wider society mediations exist that give meaning not only to the constitutive nature of a fact but also to the very nature and substance of theoretical discourse. As Horkheimer writes, "The facts of science and science itself are but segments of the life process of society, and in order to understand the significance of facts or of science, generally one must possess the key to the historical situation, the right social theory" (Horkheimer 1972).

This speaks to a second constitutive element of critical theory. If theory is to move beyond the positivist legacy of neutrality, it must develop the capacity of meta-theory. That is, it must acknowledge the value-laden interests it represents and be able to reflect critically on both the historical development or genesis of such interests and the limitations they may present within certain historical and social contexts. In other words, "methodological correctness" does not provide a guarantee of truth, nor does it raise the fundamental question of why a theory functions in a given way under specific historical conditions to serve some interests and not others. Thus, a notion of self-criticism is essential to a critical theory.

A third constitutive element for a critical theory takes its cue from Nietzsche's dictum that "A great truth wants to be criticized, not idolized" (quoted in Arato & Gebhardt 1978). The Frankfurt School believed that the critical spirit of theory should be represented in its unmasking function. The driving force of such a function was to be found in the Frankfurt School's notions of immanent criticism and dialectical thought. Immanent critique is the assertion of difference, the refusal to collapse appearance and essence, the willingness to analyze the reality of the social object against its possibilities. As Adorno wrote:

> Theory . . . must transform the concepts which it brings, as it were, from outside into those which the object has of itself, into what the object, left to itself, seeks to be, and confront it with what it is. It must dissolve the rigidity of the temporally and spatially fixed object into a field of tension of the possible and the real: each one in order to exist, is dependent upon the other. In other words, theory is indisputably critical.
>
> (Adorno et al. 1976)

Dialectical thought, on the other hand, speaks to both critique and theoretical reconstruction (Giroux 1981). As a mode of critique, it uncovers values that are often negated by the social object under analysis. The notion of dialectics is crucial because it reveals "the insufficiencies and imperfections of 'finished' systems of thought. . . . It reveals incompleteness where completeness is claimed. It embraces that which is in terms of that which is not, and that which is real in terms of potentialities not yet realized" (Held 1980). As a mode of theoretical reconstruction, dialectical thought points to historical analysis in the critique of conformist logic, and traces out the "inner history" of the latter's categories and the way in which these are mediated within a specific historical context. By looking at the social and political constellations stored in the categories of any theory, Adorno (1973) believed their history could be traced and their existing limitations revealed. As such, dialectical thought reveals the power of human activity and human knowledge as both a product of and force in the shaping of social reality. But it does not do so to proclaim simply that humans give meaning to the world. Instead, as a form of critique, dialectical thought argues that there is a link between knowledge, power, and domination. Thus it is acknowledged that some knowledge is false, and that the ultimate purpose of critique should be critical thinking in the interest of social change. For instance, as I mentioned earlier, one can exercise critical thought and not fall into the ideological trap of relativism, in which the notion of critique is negated by the assumption that all ideas should be given equal weight. Marcuse points to the connection between thought and action in dialectical thought:

> Dialectical thought starts with the experience that the world is unfree; that is to say, man and nature exist in conditions of alienation, exist as "other than they are." Any mode of thought which excludes this contradiction from its logic is faulty logic. Thought "corresponds" to reality only as it transforms reality by comprehending its contradictory structure. Here the principle of dialectic drives thought beyond the limits of philosophy. For to comprehend reality means to comprehend what things really are, and this in turn means rejecting their mere

factuality. Rejection is the process of thought as well as of action ... Dialectical thought thus becomes negative in itself. Its function is to break down the self-assurance and self-contentment of common sense, to undermine the sinister confidence in the power and language of facts, to demonstrate that unfreedom is so much at the core of things that the development of their internal contradictions leads necessarily to qualitative change: the explosion and catastrophe of the established state of affairs.

(Marcuse 1960)

According to the Frankfurt School, all thought and theory are tied to a specific interest in the development of a society without injustice. Theory, in this case, becomes a transformative activity that views itself as explicitly political and commits itself to the projection of a future that is as yet unfulfilled. Thus, critical theory contains a transcendent element in which critical thought becomes the precondition for human freedom. Rather than proclaiming a positivist notion of neutrality, critical theory openly takes sides in the interest of struggling for a better world. In one of his most famous early essays comparing traditional and critical theory, Horkheimer spelled out the essential value of theory as a political endeavour:

It is not just a research hypothesis which shows its value in the ongoing business of men; it is an essential element in the historical effort to create a world which satisfies the needs and powers of men. However extensive the interaction between the critical theory and the special sciences whose progress the theory must respect and on which it has for decades exercized a liberating and stimulating influence, the theory never aims simply at an increase of knowledge as such. Its goal is man's emancipation from slavery.

(Horkheimer 1972)

Finally, there is the question of the relationship between critical theory and empirical studies. In the ongoing debate over theory and empirical work, we recognize recycled versions of the same old dualisms in which one presupposes the exclusion of the other. One manifestation of this debate is the criticism that the Frankfurt School rejected the value of empirical work, a criticism that is also being lodged currently against many educational critics who have drawn upon the work of the Frankfurt School. Both sets of criticisms appear to have missed the point. It is certainly true that for the Frankfurt School the issue of empirical work was a problematic one, but what was called into question was its universalization at the expense of a more comprehensive notion of rationality. In writing about his experiences as an American scholar, Adorno spelled out a view of empirical studies that was representative of the Frankfurt School in general:

My own position in the controversy between empirical and theoretical sociology . . . I may sum up by saying that empirical investigations are not only legitimate but essential, even in the realm of cultural phenomena. But one must not confer autonomy upon them or regard them as a universal key. Above all they must terminate the theoretical knowledge. Theory is no mere vehicle that becomes superfluous as soon as data are in hand.

(Adorno 1969)

By insisting on the primacy of theoretical knowledge in the realm of empirical investigations, the Frankfurt School also wanted to highlight the limits of the positivist notion of experience, where research had to confine itself to controlled physical experiences that could be conducted by any researcher. Under such conditions, the research experience is limited to simple observation. As such, abstract methodology follows rules that preclude any understanding of the forces that shape both the object of analysis as well as the subject conducting the research. By contrast, a dialectical notion of society and theory would argue that observation cannot take the place of critical reflection and understanding. That is, one begins not with an observation but with a theoretical framework that situates the observation in rules and conventions that give it meaning while simultaneously acknowledging the limitations of such a perspective or framework. The Frankfurt School's position on the relation between theory and empirical studies thus helps to illuminate its view of theory and practice.

But a further qualification must be made here. While critical theory insists that theory and practice are interrelated, it nonetheless cautions against calling for a specious unity, for as Adorno points out:

> The call for the unity of theory and practice has irresistably degraded theory to the servant's role, removing the very traits it should have brought to that unity. The visa stamp of practice which we demand of all theory became a censor's place. Yet whereas theory succumbed in the vaunted mixture, practice became nonconceptual, a piece of the politics it was supposed to lead out of; it became the prey of power.
>
> (Adorno 1973)

Theory, in this case, should have as its goal emancipatory practice, but at the same time it requires a certain distance from such practice. Theory and practice represent a particular alliance, not a unity in which one dissolves into the other. The nature of such an alliance might be better understood by illuminating the drawbacks inherent in the traditional anti-theoretical stance in American education, in which it is argued that concrete experience is the great "teacher."

Experience, whether on the part of the researcher or others, contains no inherent guarantees to generate the insights necessary to make it transparent to the self. In other words, while it is indisputable that experience may provide us with knowledge, it is also indisputable that knowledge may distort rather than illuminate the nature of social reality. The point here is that the value of any experience "will depend not on the experience of the subject but on the struggles around the way that experience is interpreted and defined" (Bennett 1980). Moreover, theory cannot be reduced to being perceived as the mistress of experience, empowered to provide recipes for pedagogical practice. Its real value lies in its ability to establish possibilities for reflexive thought and practice on the part of those who use it; in the case of teachers, it becomes invaluable as an instrument of critique and understanding. As a mode of critique and analysis, theory functions as a set of tools inextricably affected by the context in which it is brought to bear, but it is never reducible to that context. It has its own distance and purpose, its own element of practice. The crucial element in both its production and use is not the structure at which it is aimed, but the human agents who use it to give meaning to their lives.

In short, Adorno, Horkheimer, and Marcuse provided forms of historical and sociological analysis that pointed to the promise as well as to the limitations of the existing dominant rationality as it developed in the twentieth century. Such an analysis took as a starting-point the conviction that for self-conscious human beings to act collectively against the modes of technocratic rationality that permeated the workplace and other sociocultural spheres, their behaviour would have to be preceded and mediated by a mode of critical analysis. In other words, the pre-condition for such action was a form of critical theory. But it is important to stress that in linking critical theory to the goals of social and political emancipation, the Frankfurt School redefined the very notion of rationality. Rationality was no longer merely the exercise of critical thought, as had been its earlier

Enlightenment counterpart. Instead, rationality now became the nexus of thought and action in the interest of liberating the community or society as a whole. As a higher rationality, it contained a transcendent project in which individual freedom merged with social freedom.

The Frankfurt School's Analysis of Culture

Central to the Frankfurt School's critique of positivist rationality was its analysis of culture. Rejecting the definition and role of culture found in both traditional sociological accounts and orthodox Marxist theory, Adorno and Horkheimer (1972) were noteworthy in developing a view of culture that assigned it a key place in the development of historical experience and everyday life. On the other hand, the Frankfurt School rejected the mainstream sociological notion that culture existed in an autonomous fashion, unrelated to the political and economic life-processes of society. In their view, such a perspective neutralized culture and in so doing abstracted it from the historical and societal context that gave it meaning. For Adorno the conventional view was shot through with a contradiction that reduced culture to nothing more than a piece of ideological shorthand:

> [The conventional view of culture] overlooks what is decisive: the role of ideology in social conflicts. To suppose, if only methodologically, anything like an independent logic of culture is to collaborate in the hypostasis of culture, the ideological *proton pseudos*. The substance of culture . . . resides not in culture alone but in relation to something external, to the material life-process. Culture, as Marx observed of juridical and political systems, cannot be fully "understood either in terms of itself . . . or in terms of the so-called universal development of the mind." To ignore this . . . is to make ideology the basic matter and to establish it firmly.
>
> (Adorno 1967a)

On the other hand, while orthodox Marxist theory established a relationship between culture and the material forces of society, it did so by reducing culture to a mere reflex of the economic realm. In this view, the primacy of economic forces and the logic of scientific laws took precedence over issues concerning the terrain of everyday life, consciousness, or sexuality (Aronowitz 1981a). For the Frankfurt School, changing socioeconomic conditions had made traditional Marxist categories of the 1930s and 1940s untenable. They were no longer adequate for understanding the integration of the working class in the West or the political effects of technocratic rationality in the cultural realm.

Within the Frankfurt School perspective the role of culture in Western society had been modified with the transformation of critical *Enlightenment rationality into repressive forms of positivist rationality*. As a result of the development of new technical capabilities, greater concentrations of economic power, and more sophisticated modes of administration, the rationality of domination increasingly expanded its influence to spheres outside of the locus of economic production. Under the sign of Taylorism and scientific management, instrumental rationality extended its influence from the domination of nature to the domination of human beings. As such, mass-cultural institutions such as schools took on a new role in the first half of the twentieth century as "both a determinant and fundamental component of social consciousness" (Aronowitz 1976). According to the Frankfurt School, this meant that the cultural realm now constitutes a central place in the production and transformation of historical experience. Like Gramsci (1971), Adorno and Horkheimer

(1972) argued that domination has assumed a new form. Instead of being exercised primarily through the use of physical force (the army and police), the power of the ruling classes was now reproduced through a form of ideological hegemony; that is, it was established primarily through the rule of consent, and mediated via cultural institutions such as schools, family, mass media, churches, etc. Briefly put, the colonization of the workplace was now supplemented by the colonization of all other cultural spheres (Aronowitz 1973; Enzenberger 1974; Ewen 1976).

According to the Frankfurt School, culture, like everything else in capitalist society, had been turned into an object. Under the dual rationalities of administration and exchange the elements of critique and opposition, which the Frankfurt School believed inherent in traditional culture, had been lost. Moreover, the objectification of culture did not simply result in the repression of the critical elements in its form and content; such objectification also represented the negation of critical thought itself. In Adorno's words: ". . . Culture in the true sense did not simply accommodate itself to human beings; . . . it always simultaneously raised a protest against the petrified relations under which they lived, thereby honoring them. Insofar as culture becomes wholly assimilated to and integrated into those petrified relations, human beings are once more debased" (Adorno 1975).

As far as the Frankfurt School was concerned, the cultural realm had become a new locus of control for that aspect of Enlightenment rationality in which the domination of nature and society proceeded under the guise of technical progress and economic growth. For Adorno and Horkheimer (1972) culture had become another industry, one which not only produced goods but also legitimated the logic of capital and its institutions. The *term "culture industry" was coined by Adorno as a response to the reification of culture, and it had two immediate purposes.* First, it was coined in order to expose the notion that "culture arises spontaneously from the masses themselves" (Lowenthal 1979). Second, it pointed to the concentration of economic and political determinants that control the cultural sphere in the interest of social and political domination. The term "industry" in the metaphor provided a point of critical analysis. That is, it pointed not only to a concentration of political and economic groups who reproduced and legitimated the dominant belief and value system, it also referred to the mechanisms of rationalization and standardization as they permeated everyday life. In other words, "the expression 'industry' is not to be taken literally. It refers to the standardization of the thing itself—such as the Western, familiar to every movie-goer—and to the rationalization of distribution techniques . . . [and] not strictly to the production process" (Adorno 1975).

At the core of the theory of culture advanced by Horkheimer, Adorno, and Marcuse was an attempt to expose, through both a call for and demonstration of critique, how positivist rationality manifested itself in the cultural realm. For instance, they criticised certain cultural products such as art for excluding the principles of resistance and opposition that once informed their relationship with the world while simultaneously helping to expose it (Horkheimer 1972). Likewise, for Marcuse (1978), "the truth of art lies in its power to break the monopoly of established reality (i.e., of those who established it) to define what is real. In this rupture . . . the fictitious world of art appears as true reality." The Frankfurt School argued that in a one-dimensional society art collapses, rather than highlights, the distinction between reality and the possibility of a higher truth or better world. In other words, in the true spirit of positivist harmony, art becomes simply a mirror of the existing reality and an affirmation of it. Thus, both the memory of a historical truth or the image of a better way of life are rendered impotent in the ultra-realism of Warhol's Campbell-soup painting or the Stakhanovite paintings of socialist realism.

Dictates of positivist rationality and the attendant mutilation of the power of imagination are also embodied in the techniques and forms that shape the messages and discourse of the culture industry. Whether it be in the glut of interchangeable plots, gags, or stories, or in the rapid pace of the film's development, the logic of standardization reigns supreme. The message is conformity, and the medium for its attainment is amusement, which proudly packages itself as an escape from the necessity of critical thought. Under the sway of the culture industry, style subsumes substance and thought is banished from the temple of official culture. Marcuse states this argument superbly:

> By becoming components of the aesthetic form, words, sounds, shapes, and colors are insulated against their familiar, ordinary use and function; . . . This is the achievement of style, which *is* the poem, the novel, the painting, the composition. The style, embodiment of the aesthetic form, in subjecting reality to another order, subjects it to the laws of beauty. True and false, right and wrong, pain and pleasure, calm and violence become aesthetic categories within the framework of the oeuvre. Thus deprived of their [immediate] reality, they enter a different context in which even the ugly, cruel, sick become parts of the aesthetic harmony governing the whole.
>
> (Marcuse 1972)

Inherent in the reduction of culture to amusement is a significant message which points to the root of the ethos of positivist rationality—the structural division between work and play. Within that division, work is confined to the imperatives of drudgery, boredom, and powerlessness for the vast majority; culture becomes the vehicle by which to escape from work. The power of the Frankfurt School's analysis lies in its exposure of the ideological fraud that constitutes this division of labor. Rather than being an escape from the mechanized work process, the cultural realm becomes an extension of it. Adorno and Horkheimer write:

> Amusement under late capitalism is the prolongation of work. It is sought-after as an escape from the mechanized work process, and to recruit strength in order to be able to cope with it again. But at the same time mechanization has such power over a man's leisure and happiness and so profoundly determines the manufacture of amusement goods, that his experiences are after-images of the work process itself. The ostensible content is merely a faded background; what sinks in is an automatic succession of standardized operations.
>
> (Adorno & Horkheimer 1972)

The most *radical critique of the division of labour* among the three theorists under study finds its expression in the work of *Herbert Marcuse* (1955, 1968b). Marcuse (1968b) claims that Marxism has not been radical enough in its attempt to develop a new sensibility that would develop as "an instinctual barrier against cruelty, brutality, ugliness." Marcuse's (1955) point is that a new rationality taking as its goal the erotization of labour and "the development and fulfillment of human needs" would necessitate new relations of production and organizational structures under which work could take place. This should not suggest that Marcuse abandons all forms of authority or that he equates hierarchical relationships with the realm of domination. On the contrary, he argues that work and play can interpenetrate each other without the loss of either's primary character. As Agger points out:

> Marcuse is . . . saying that . . . work and play converge without abandoning the "work" character of work itself. He retains the rational organization of work without abandoning the Marxian goal of creative praxis. As he notes . . . "hierarchical relationships are not unfree

per se." That is, it depends upon the kind of hierarchy which informs relationships. . . . Marcuse . . . suggests two things: in the first place, he hints at a theory of work which rests upon the merger of work and play components. His views in this regard are captured in his vision of the "erotization of labor." In the second place, Marcuse hints at a form of organizational rationality which is nondominating.

(Agger 1978)

According to Marcuse (1964) science and technology have been integrated under the imprint of a dominating rationality that has penetrated the world of communicative interaction (the public sphere) as well as the world of work. It is worth mentioning, by contrast, Habermas's (1973) argument that science and technology in the sphere of work are necessarily limited to technical considerations, and that the latter organization of work represents the price an advanced industrial order must pay for its material comfort. This position has been challenged by a number of theorists, including Aronowitz (1981a), who astutely argues that Habermas separates "communications and normative judgments from the labor process" and thus "cede[s] to technological consciousness the entire sphere of rational purposive action (work)." In further opposition to Habermas, Marcuse (1964) argues that radical change means more than simply the creation of conditions that foster critical thinking and communicative competence. Such change also entails the transformation of the labor process itself and the fusion of science and technology under the guise of a rationality stressing cooperation and self-management in the interest of democratic community and social freedom.

While there are significant differences among Adorno, Horkheimer, and Marcuse in their indictment of positivist rationality and in their respective notions about what constitutes an aesthetic or radical sensibility, their views converge on the existing repressiveness underlying positivist rationality and on the need for the development of a collective critical consciousness and sensibility that would embrace a discourse of opposition and non-identity as a precondition of human freedom. Thus, for them, criticism represents an indispensable element in the struggle for emancipation, and it is precisely in their call for criticism and a new sensibility that one finds an analysis of the nature of domination that contains invaluable insights for a theory of education. The analysis, in this case, includes the Frankfurt School's theory of depth psychology, to which I will now briefly turn.

The Frankfurt School's Analysis of Depth Psychology

As I have pointed out previously, the Frankfurt School faced a major contradiction in attempting to develop a critical tradition within Marxist theory. On the one hand, the historical legacy since Marx had witnessed increased material production and the continued conquest of nature in both the advanced industrial countries of the West and the countries of the socialist bloc as well. In both camps, it appeared that despite economic growth the objective conditions that promoted alienation had deepened. For example, in the West the production of goods and the ensuing commodity fetishism made a mockery of the concept of the Good Life, reducing it to the issue of purchasing power. In the socialist bloc, the centralization of political power led to political repression instead of political and economic freedom as had been promised. Yet in both cases the consciousness of the masses failed to keep pace with such conditions.

For the Frankfurt School it became clear that a theory of consciousness and depth psychology was needed to explain the subjective dimension of liberation and domination.

Marx had provided the political and economic grammar of domination, but he relegated the psychic dimension to a secondary status, believing that it would follow any significant changes in the economic realm. Thus it was left to the Frankfurt School, especially Marcuse (1955, 1964, 1968b, 1970), to analyze the formal structure of consciousness in order to discover how a dehumanized society could continue to maintain its control over its inhabitants, and how it was possible that human beings could participate willingly at the level of everyday life in the reproduction of their own dehumanization and exploitation. For answers, the Frankfurt School turned to a critical study of Freud.

For the Frankfurt School, Freud's metapsychology provided an important theoretical foundation for revealing the interplay between the individual and society. More specifically, the value of Freudian psychology in this case rested with its illumination of the antagonistic character of social reality. As a theoretician of contradictions, Freud provided a radical insight into the way in which society reproduced its powers both in and over the individual. As Jacoby puts it:

> Psychoanalysis shows its strength; it demystifies the claims to liberated values, sensitivities, emotions, by tracing them to a repressed psychic, social, and biological dimension. . . . It keeps to the pulse of the psychic underground. As such it is more capable of grasping the intensifying social unreason that the conformist psychologies repress and forget: the barbarism of civilization itself, the barely suppressed misery of the living, the madness that haunts society.
> (Jacoby 1975)

The Frankfurt School theorists believed that it was only in an understanding of the dialectic between the individual and society that the depth and extent of domination as it existed both within and outside of the individual could be open to modification and transformation. Thus, for Adorno, Horkheimer, and Marcuse, Freud's emphasis on the constant struggle between the individual desire for instinctual gratification and the dynamics of social repression provided an indispensable clue to understanding the nature of society and the dynamics of psychic domination and liberation. Adorno points to this in the following comments:

> The only totality the student of society can presume to know is the antagonistic whole, and if he is to attain to totality at all, then only in contradiction. . . . The jarring elements that make up the individual, his "properties," are invariable moments of the social totality. He is, in the strict sense, a monad, representing the whole and its contradictions, without however being at any time conscious of the whole.
> (Adorno 1967b)

To explore the depth of the conflict between the individual and society, the Frankfurt School accepted with some major modifications most of Freud's most radical assumptions. More specifically, Freud's theoretical schema contained three important elements for developing a depth psychology. First, Freud provided a formal psychological structure for the Frankfurt School theorists to work with. That is, the Freudian outline of the structure of the psyche with its underlying struggle between Eros (the life instinct), Thanatos (the death instinct), and the outside world represented a key conception in the depth psychology developed by the Frankfurt School.

Secondly, Freud's studies on psychopathology, particularly his sensitivity to humanity's capacity for self-destructiveness and his focus on the loss of ego stability and the decline of the influence of the family in contemporary society added significantly to the Frankfurt School analyses of mass society and the rise of the authoritarian personality. For the

Frankfurt School, the growing concentration of power in capitalist society, along with the pervasive intervention of the state in the affairs of everyday life, had altered the dialectical role of the traditional family as both a positive and negative site for identity formation. That is, the family had traditionally provided, on the one hand, a sphere of warmth and protection for its members, while, on the other hand, it also functioned as a repository for social and sexual repression. But under the development of advanced industrial capitalism, the dual function of the family was gradually giving way, and it began to function exclusively as a site for social and cultural reproduction.

Finally, by focusing on Freud's theory of instincts and metapsychology, the Frankfurt School devised a theoretical framework for unraveling and exposing the objective and psychological obstacles to social change. This issue is important because it provides significant insights into how depth psychology might be useful for developing a more comprehensive theory of education. Since Adorno shared some major differences with both Horkheimer and Marcuse regarding Freud's theory of instincts and his view of the relationship between the individual and society, I will treat their respective contributions separately.

Adorno (1968) was quick to point out that while Freud's denunciation of "man's unfreedom" over-identified with a particular historical period and thus "petrified into an anthropological constant," it did not seriously detract from his greatness as a theoretician of contradictions. That is, in spite of the limitations in Freudian theory, Adorno—and Horkheimer as well—firmly believed that psychoanalysis provided a strong theoretical bulwark against psychological and social theories that exalted the idea of the "integrated personality" and the "wonders" of social harmony. True to Adorno's (1968) view that "Every image of man is ideology except the negative one," Freud's work appeared to transcend its own shortcomings because at one level it personified the spirit of negation. Adorno (1967b, 1968) clearly exalted the negative and critical features of psychoanalysis and saw them as major theoretical weapons to be used against every form of identity theory. The goals of identity theory and revisionist psychology were both political and ideological in nature, and it was precisely through the use of Freud's metapsychology that they could be exposed as such. As Adorno put it:

> The goal of the well-integrated personality is objectionable because it expects the individual to establish an equilibrium between conflicting forces, which does not obtain in existing society. Nor should it, because these forces are not of equal moral merit. People are taught to forget the objective conflicts which necessarily repeat themselves in every individual instead of helped to grapple with them.
>
> (Adorno 1968)

While it was clear to the Frankfurt School that psychoanalysis could not solve the problems of repression and authoritarianism, they believed that it did provide important insights into how "people become accomplices to their own subjugation" (Benjamin, J. 1977). Yet beneath the analyses put forth on psychoanalysis by Adorno (1967b, 1968, 1972, 1973) and Horkheimer (1972) there lurked a disturbing paradox: while both theorists went to great lengths to explain the dynamics of authoritarianism and psychological domination, they said very little about those formal aspects of consciousness that might provide a basis for resistance and rebellion. In other words, Horkheimer and Adorno, while recognizing that Freudian psychology registered a powerful criticism of existing society in exposing its antagonistic character, failed to extend this insight by locating in either individuals or social classes the psychological or political grounds for a self-conscious recognition of such contradictions and the ability of human agents to transform them. Consequently, they provided a view of Freudian psychology that consigned Freud to the ambiguous status of radical as well as prophet of gloom.

If Adorno and Horkheimer viewed Freud as a revolutionary pessimist, Marcuse (1955) read him as a revolutionary utopian. That is, though he accepts most of Freud's most controversial assumptions, his interpretation of them is both unique and provocative. In one sense, Marcuse's (1955, 1968a&b, 1970) analysis contained an original dialectical twist in that it pointed to a utopian integration of Marx and Freud. Marcuse (1955) accepted Freud's view of the antagonistic relations between the individual and society as a fundamental insight, but he nevertheless altered some of Freud's basic categories, and in doing so situated Freud's pessimism within a historical context that revealed its strengths as well as limitations. In doing so, Marcuse was able to illuminate the importance of Freud's metapsychology as a basis for social change. This becomes particularly clear if we examine how Marcuse (1955, 1968a&b, 1970) reworked Freud's basic claims regarding the life and death instincts, the struggle between the individual and society, the relationship between scarcity and social repression, and, finally, the issues of freedom and human emancipation.

Marcuse (1955, 1964) begins with the basic assumption that inherent in Freud's theory of the unconscious and his theory of the instincts could be found the theoretical elements for a more comprehensive view of the nature of individual and social domination. Marcuse points to this possibility when he writes:

> The struggle against freedom reproduces itself in the psyche of man as the self-repression of the repressed individual, and his self-repression in turn sustains his masters and their institutions. It is this mental dynamic which Freud unfolds as the dynamic of civilization. . . . Freud's metapsychology is an ever-renewed attempt to uncover, and to question, the terrible necessity of the inner connection between civilization and barbarism, progress and suffering, freedom and unhappiness—a connection which reveals itself ultimately as that between Eros and Thanatos.
>
> (Marcuse 1955)

For Marcuse (1955, 1970) Freudian psychology, as a result of its analysis of the relationship between civilization and instinctual repression, posited the theoretical basis for understanding the distinction between socially necessary authority and authoritarianism. That is, in the interplay between the need for social labor and the equally important need for the sublimation of sexual energy, the dynamic connection between domination and freedom, on the one hand, and authority and authoritarianism, on the other, starts to become discernible. Freud presented the conflict between the individual's instinctual need for pleasure and the society's demand for repression as an insoluble problem rooted in a trans-historical struggle; as a result, he pointed to the continuing repressive transformation of Eros in society, along with the growing propensity for self destruction. Marcuse (1970) believed that the "Freudian conception of the relationship between civilization and the dynamics of the instincts [was] in need of a decisive correction." That is, whereas Freud (1949) saw the increased necessity for social and instinctual repression, Marcuse (1955, 1970) argued that any understanding of social repression had to be situated within a specific historical context and judged as to whether such systems of domination exceeded their bounds. To ignore such a distinction was to forfeit the possibility of analyzing the difference between the exercise of legitimate authority and illegitimate forms of domination. Marcuse (1955) deemed that Freud had failed to capture in his analyses the historical dynamic of organized domination, and thus had given to it the status and dignity of a biological development that was universal rather than merely historically contingent.

While Marcuse (1955) accepts the Freudian notion that the central conflict in society is between the reality principle and the pleasure principle, he rejects the position that the latter had to adjust to the former. In other words, Freud believed that "the price of civilization is paid for in forfeiting happiness through heightening of the sense of guilt" (Freud 1949). This is important because at the core of Freud's notion that humanity was forever condemned to diverting pleasure and sexual energy into alienating labor was an appeal to a trans-historical "truth": that scarcity was inevitable in society, and that labor was inherently alienating. In opposition to Freud, Marcuse argued that the reality principle referred to a particular form of historical existence when scarcity legitimately dictated instinctual repression. But in the contemporary period such conditions had been super-seded, and as such abundance, not scarcity, characterized or informed the reality principle governing the advanced industrial countries of the West.

In order to add a more fully historical dimension to Freud's analysis, Marcuse (1955) introduced the concepts of the performance principle and of surplus-repression. By argu-ing that scarcity was not a universal aspect of the human condition, Marcuse (1955, 1970) claimed that the moment had arrived in the industrial West when it was no longer neces-sary to submit men and women to the demands of alienating labor. The existing reality principle, which Marcuse (1955) labeled the performance principle, had outstripped its historical function, i.e., the sublimation of Eros in the interest of socially necessary labor. The performance principle, with its emphasis on technocratic reason and exchange ration-ality, was, in Marcuse's (1955) terms, both historically contingent and socially repressive. As a relatively new mode of domination, it tied people to values, ideas, and social practices that blocked their possibilities for gratification and happiness as ends in themselves.

In short, Marcuse (1955) believed that inherent in Marx's view of societal abundance and in Freud's theory of instincts was the basis for a new performance principle, one that was governed by principles of socially necessary labor and by those aspects of the pleasure principle that integrated work, play, and sexuality. This leads us to Marcuse's second important idea, the concept of surplus-repression. The excessiveness of the existing nature of domination could be measured through what Marcuse labeled as surplus-repression. Distinguishing this from socially useful repression, Marcuse claims that:

> Within the total structure of the repressed personality, surplus-repression is that portion which is the result of specific societal conditions sustained in the specific act of domination. The extent of this surplus-repression provides the standard of measurement: the smaller it is, the less repressive is the stage of civilization. The distinction is equivalent to that between the biological and the historical sources of human suffering.
>
> (Marcuse 1955)

According to Marcuse (1955, 1970), it is within this dialectical interplay of the personal-ity structure and historically conditioned repression that the nexus exists for uncovering the historical and contemporary nature of domination. Domination in this sense is doubly historical: first, it is rooted in the historically developed socio-economic conditions of a given society; further, it is rooted in the sedimented history or personality structure of individuals. In speaking of domination as a psychological as well as a political phenom-enon, Marcuse did not give a *carte blanche* to wholesale gratification. On the contrary, he agreed with Freud that some forms of repression were generally necessary. What he objected to was the unnecessary repression that was embodied in the ethos and social practices that characterized social institutions like school, the workplace, and the family.

For Marcuse (1964), the most penetrating marks of social repression are generated in the inner history of individuals, in the "needs, satisfactions, and values which reproduce the servitude of human existence." Such needs are mediated and reinforced through the patterns and social routines of everyday life, and the "false" needs that perpetuate toil, misery, and aggressiveness become anchored in the personality structure as second nature; that is, their historical character is forgotten, and they become reduced to patterns of habit.

In the end, Marcuse (1955) grounds even Freud's important notion of the death instinct (the autonomous drive that increasingly leads to self-destruction) in a radical problematic. That is, by claiming that the primary drive of humanity is pleasure, Marcuse redefines the death instinct by arguing that it is mediated not by the need for self-destruction— although this is a form it may take—but by the need to resolve tension. Rooted in such a perspective, the death instinct is not only redefined, it is also politicized as Marcuse argues that in a non-repressive society it would be subordinated to the demands of Eros. Thus, Marcuse (1955, 1964) ends up supporting the Frankfurt School's notion of negative thinking, but with an important qualification. He insists on its value as a mode of critique, but maintains equally that it is grounded in socio-economic conditions that can be transformed. It is the promise of a better future, rather than despair over the existing nature of society, that informs both Marcuse's work and its possibilities as a mode of critique for educators.

Towards a Critical Theory of Education

While it is impossible to elaborate in any detail on the implications of the work of the Frankfurt School for a theory of radical pedagogy, I can point briefly to some general considerations. I believe that it is clear that the thought of the Frankfurt School provides a major challenge and a stimulus to educational theorists who are critical of theories of education tied to functionalist paradigms based on assumptions drawn from a positivist rationality. For instance, against the positivist spirit that infuses existing educational theory and practice, whether it takes the form of the Tyler model or various systems approaches, the Frankfurt School offers an historical analysis and a penetrating philosophical framework that indict the wider culture of positivism, while at the same time providing insight into how the latter becomes incorporated within the ethos and practices of schools. Though there is a growing body of educational literature that is critical of positivist rationality in schools, it lacks the theoretical sophistication characteristic of the work of Horkheimer, Adorno, and Marcuse. Similarly, the importance of historical consciousness as a fundamental dimension of critical thinking in the Frankfurt School perspective creates a valuable epistemological terrain upon which to develop modes of critique that illuminate the interaction of the social and the personal as well as of history and private experience. Through this form of analysis, dialectical thought replaces positivist forms of social inquiry. That is, the logic of predictability, verifiability, transferability, and operationalism is replaced by a dialectical mode of thinking that stresses the historical, relational, and normative dimensions of social inquiry and knowledge. The notion of dialectical thinking as critical thinking, and its implications for pedagogy, become somewhat clear in Jameson's comment that "[D]ialectical thinking is . . . thought about thinking itself, in which the mind must deal with its own thought process just as much as with the material it works on, in which both the particular content involved and the style of thinking suited to it must be held together in the mind at the same time" (Jameson 1971).

What we get here are hints of what a radical view of knowledge might look like. In this case, it would be knowledge that would instruct the oppressed about their situation as a group situated within specific relations of domination and subordination. It would be knowledge that would illuminate how the oppressed could develop a discourse free from the distortions of their own partly mangled cultural inheritance. On the other hand, it would be a form of knowledge that instructed the oppressed in how to appropriate the most progressive dimensions of their own cultural histories, as well as how to restructure and appropriate the most radical aspects of bourgeois culture. Finally, such knowledge would have to provide a motivational connection to action itself; it would have to link a radical decoding of history to a vision of the future that not only exploded the reifications of the existing society, but also reached into those pockets of desires and needs that harbored a longing for a new society and new forms of social relations. It is at this point that the link between history, culture, and psychology becomes important.

It is with regard to the above that the notion of historical understanding in the work of the Frankfurt School makes some important contributions to the notion of radical pedagogy. History, for Adorno and others connected with critical theory, had a two-fold meaning and could not be interpreted as a continuous pattern unfolding under the imperatives of "natural" laws. On the contrary, it had to be viewed as an emerging open-ended phenomenon, the significance of which was to be gleaned in the cracks and tensions that separated individuals and social classes from the imperatives of the dominant society. In other words, there were no laws of history that prefigured human progress, that functioned independently of human action. Moreover, history became meaningful not because it provided the present with the fruits of "interesting" or "stimulating" culture, but because it became the present object of analyses aimed at illuminating the revolutionary possibilities that existed in the given society. For the radical educator, this suggests using history in order "to fight against the spirit of the times rather than join it, to look backward at history rather than 'forward' " (Buck-Morss 1977). To put it another way, it meant, as Benjamin claimed "to brush history against the grain" (Benjamin 1974).

Not only does such a position link historical analysis to the notions of critique and emancipation, it also politicizes the notion of knowledge. That is, it argues for looking at knowledge critically, within constellations of suppressed insights (dialectical images) that point to the ways in which historically repressed cultures and struggles could be used to illuminate radical potentialities in the present. Knowledge in this instance becomes an object of analysis in a two-fold sense. On the one hand, it is examined for its social function, the way in which it legitimates the existing society. At the same time it could also be examined to reveal in its arrangement, words, structure, and style those unintentional truths that might contain "fleeting images" of a different society, more radical practices, and new forms of understanding. For instance, almost every cultural text contains a combination of ideological and utopian moments. Inherent in the most overt messages that characterize mass culture are elements of its antithesis. All cultural artifacts have a hidden referent that speaks to the initial basis for repression. Against the image of the barely clad female model selling the new automobile is the latent tension of misplaced and misappropriated sexual desire. Within the most authoritative modes of classroom discipline and control are fleeting images of freedom that speak to very different relationships. It is this dialectical aspect of knowledge that needs to be developed as part of a radical pedagogy.

Unlike traditional and liberal accounts of schooling, with their emphasis on historical continuities and historical development, critical theory points educators toward a mode of analysis that stresses the breaks, discontinuities, and tensions in history, all of which become valuable in that they highlight the centrality of human agency and struggle while simultaneously revealing the gap between society as it presently exists and society as it might be.

The Frankfurt School's theory of culture also offers new concepts and categories for analysing the role that schools play as agents of social and cultural reproduction. By illuminating the relationship between power and culture, the Frankfurt School provides a perspective on the way in which dominant ideologies are constituted and mediated via specific cultural formations. The concept of culture in this view exists in a particular relationship to the material base of society. The explanatory value of such a relationship is to be found in making problematic the specific content of a culture, its relationship to dominant and subordinate groups, as well as the socio-historical genesis of the ethos and practices of legitimating cultures and their role in constituting relations of domination and resistance. For example, by pointing to schools as cultural sites that embody conflicting political values, histories, and practices, it becomes possible to investigate how schools can be analyzed as an expression of the wider organization of society. Marcuse's (1964) study of the ideological nature of language, Adorno's (1975) analysis of the sociology of music, Horkheimer's (1972) method of dialectical critique and W. Benjamin's (1969, 1977) theory of cognition, all provide a number of valuable theoretical constructs through which to investigate the socially produced nature of knowledge and school experience.

The centrality of culture in the work of the Frankfurt School theorists (despite the differing opinions among its members) points to a number of important insights that illuminate how subjectivities get constituted both within and outside of schools. Though their analysis of culture is somewhat undialectical and clearly underdeveloped, it does provide a foundation for a greater elaboration and understanding of the relationship between culture and power, while simultaneously recognizing the latter as important terrain upon which to analyze the nature of domination and of resistance. By urging an attentiveness to the suppressed moments of history, critical theory points to the need to develop an equal sensitivity to certain aspects of culture. For example, working-class students, women, Blacks, and others need to affirm their own histories through the use of a language, a set of social relations, and body of knowledge that critically reconstructs and dignifies the cultural experiences that make up the tissue, texture, and history of their daily lives. This is no small matter, since once the affirmative nature of such a pedagogy is established, it becomes possible for students who have been traditionally voiceless in schools to learn the skills, knowledge, and modes of inquiry that will allow them to critically examine the role society has played in their own self-formation. More specifically, they will have the tools to examine how this society has functioned to shape and thwart their aspirations and goals, or prevented them from even imagining a life outside the one they presently lead. Thus it is important that students come to grips with what a given society has made of them, how it has incorporated them ideologically and materially into its rules and logic, and what it is that they need to affirm and reject in their own histories in order to begin the process of struggling for the conditions that will give them opportunities to lead a self-managed existence.

While it is true that Adorno, Marcuse, and Horkheimer placed heavy emphasis on the notion of domination in their analyses of culture, and in fact appeared to equate mass culture with mass manipulation, the value of their analyses rests with the mode of critique they developed in their attempt to reconstruct the notion of culture as a political force, as a powerful political moment in the process of domination. There is a paradox in their analyses of culture and human agency—that is, a paradox emerged in their emphasis on the overwhelming and one-sided nature of mass culture as a dominating force, on the one hand, and their relentless insistence on the need for critique, negativity, and critical mediation on the other. It is within this seeming contradiction that more dialectical notions of power and resistance have to be developed, positions that recognize wider structural and ideological determinations while recognizing that human beings never represent simply a reflex of such constraints. Human beings not only make history, they also make the constraints; and needless to say, they also unmake them. It needs to be remembered that power is both an enabling as well as a constraining force, as Foucault (1980) is quick to point out.

It must be stressed that the ideological justification of the given social order is not to be found simply in modes of interpretation that view history as a "natural" evolving process, or in the ideologies distributed through the culture industry. It is also found in the material reality of those needs and wants that bear the inscription of history. That is, history is to be found as "second nature" in those concepts and views of the world that make the most dominating aspects of the social order appear to be immune from historical socio-political development. Those aspects of reality that rest on an appeal to the universal and invariant often slip from historical consciousness and become embedded within those historically specific needs and desires that link individuals to the logics of conformity and domination. There is a certain irony in the fact that the personal and political join in the structure of domination precisely at those moments where history functions to tie individuals to a set of assumptions and practices that deny the historical nature of the political. "Second nature" represents history that has hardened into a form of social amnesia (Jacoby 1975), a mode of consciousness that "forgets" its own development. The significance of this perspective for radical pedagogy is that it points to the value of a *depth psychology* that can unravel how the mechanisms of domination and the possible seeds of liberation reach into the very structure of the human psyche. Radical pedagogy is much too cognitive in its orientation, and it needs to develop a theory of domination that incorporates needs and wants. Radical pedagogy lacks a depth psychology as well as appreciation for a sensibility that points to the importance of the sensual and imaginative as central dimensions of the schooling experience. The Frankfurt School's notion of depth psychology, especially Marcuse's work, opens up new terrain for developing a critical pedagogy. It speaks to the need to fashion new categories of analysis that will enable educators to become more knowledgeable about how teachers, students, and other educational workers become part of the system of social and cultural reproduction, particularly as it works through the messages and values that are constituted via the social practices of the hidden curriculum (Giroux 1981). By acknowledging the need for a critical social psychology, educators can begin to identify how ideologies get constituted, and they can then identify and reconstruct social practices and processes that break rather than continue existing forms of social and psychological domination.

The relevance of Marcuse's analysis of depth psychology for educational theory becomes obvious in the more recent work of Pierre Bourdieu (1977a, 1977b). Bourdieu argues that the school and other social institutions legitimate and reinforce through specific sets of practices and discourses class-based systems of behavior and dispositions that reproduce the existing dominant society. Bourdieu extends Marcuse's insights by pointing to a notion of learning in which a child internalizes the cultural messages of the school not only via the latter's official discourse (symbolic mastery), but also through the messages embodied in the "insignificant" practices of daily classroom life. Bourdieu (1977b) is worth quoting at length on this issue:

> [Schools] . . . set such a store on the seemingly most insignificant details of dress, bearing, physical and verbal manners. . . . The principles embodied in this way are placed beyond the grasp of consciousness, and hence cannot be touched by voluntary, deliberate transformation, cannot even be made explicit. . . . The whole trick of pedagogic reason lies precisely in the way it extorts the essential while seeming to demand the insignificant: in obtaining respect for forms and forms of respect which constitute the most visible and at the same time the best hidden manifestations to the established order.
>
> (Bourdieu 1977b)

Unlike Bourdieu, Marcuse believes that historically conditioned needs that function in the interest of domination can be changed. That is, in Marcuse's view (1955) any viable form of political action must begin with a notion of political education in which a new language, qualitatively different social relations, and a new set of values would have to operate with the purpose of creating a new environment "in which the nonaggressive, erotic, receptive faculties of man, in harmony with the consciousness of freedom, strive for the pacification of man and nature" (Marcuse 1969). Thus the notion of depth psychology developed by the Frankfurt School not only provides new insights into how subjectivities are formed or how ideology functions as lived experience, it also provides theoretical tools to establish the conditions for new needs, new systems of values, and new social practices that take seriously the imperatives of a critical pedagogy.

Conclusion

In conclusion, I have attempted to present selected aspects of the work of critical theorists such as Adorno, Horkheimer, and Marcuse that provide theoretical insights for developing a critical theory of education. Specifically, I have focused on their critique of positivist rationality, their view of theory, their critical reconstruction of a theory of culture, and, finally, on their analysis of depth psychology. It is within the context of these four areas that radical educators can begin the task of reconstructing and applying the insights of critical theory to schooling. Of course, the task of translating the work of the Frankfurt School into terms that inform and enrich radical educational theory and practice will be difficult. This is especially true since any attempt to use such work will have to begin with the understanding that it contains a number of shortcomings and moreover cannot be imposed in grid-like fashion onto a theory of radical pedagogy. For example, the critical theorists I have discussed did not develop a comprehensive theoretical approach for dealing with the patterns of conflict and contradictions that existed in various cultural spheres. To the contrary, they developed an unsatisfactory notion of domination and an exaggerated view of the integrated nature of the American public; they constantly underestimated the radical potential inherent in working-class culture; and they never developed an adequate theory of social consciousness. That is, in spite of their insistence on the importance of the notion of mediation, they never explored the contradictory modes of thinking that characterize the way most people view the world. Of course, the latter selection does not exhaust the list of criticisms that could be made against the work of the critical theorists under analysis here. The point is that critical theory needs to be reformulated to provide the opportunity to both critique and elaborate its insights beyond the constraints and historical conditions under which they were first generated. It must be stressed that the insights critical theory has provided have not been exhausted. In fact, one may argue that we are just beginning to work out the implications of their analyses. The real issue is to reformulate the central contributions of critical theory in terms of new historical conditions, without sacrificing the emancipatory spirit that generated them.

References

Adorno, T. W. 1967a. *Prisms*, trans. Samuel and Shierry Weber. London: Neville Spearman.

———. 1967b. "Sociology and psychology: Part I." *New Left Review*, 46.

———. 1968. "Sociology and psychology: Part II." *New Left Review*, 47.

———. 1969. "Scientific Experiences of a European Scholar in America." In *The Intellectual Migration*, ed. Donald Fleming and Bernard Bailyn. Cambridge, Mass.: Harvard University Press.

Adorno, T. W., and M. Horkheimer, 1972. *Dialectic of Enlightenment*, trans. John Cumming. New York: Seabury Press.

———. 1973. *Negative Dialectics*. New York: Seabury Press.

———. 1975. "The Culture Industry Reconsidered." *New German Critique*, 6 (Fall).

——— 1976. "On the Logic of the Social Sciences." In *The Positivist Dispute in German Sociology*, T. W. Adorno et al. London: Heinemann.

Agger, B. 1978. "Work and Authority in Marcuse and Habermas." *Human Studies*, 2(3) (July).

Aronowitz, S. 1973. *False Promises*. New York: McGraw-Hill.

———. 1976. "Enzenberger on Mass Culture: A Review Essay." *Minnesota Review*, 7 (Fall).

———. 1981a. *The Crisis in Historical Materialism: Class, Politics, and Culture in Marxist Theory*. New York: Bergin.

———. 1981b. "Redefining Literacy." *Social Policy* (Sept.-Oct.).

Benjamin, J. 1977. "The End of Internationalization: Adorno's Social Psychology." *Telos*, 32 (Summer).

Benjamin, W. 1974. In *Über den Begriff der Geschichte: Gesammelte Schriften*, 1(2), ed. Rolf Tiedemann and Hermann Schweppenhauser, Abhandlungen, Suhrkamp Verlag, Frankfurt am Main.

———. 1969. In *Illuminations*, ed. Hannah Arendt. New York: Schocken.

———. 1977. *The Origin of German Tragic Drama*, trans. John Osborne. London: New Left Books.

Bennett, T. 1980. "The Not-So-Good, the Bad, and the Ugly." *Screen Education*, 36 (Autumn).

Bourdieu, P., and J. C. Passeron. 1977a. *Reproduction in Education, Society, and Culture*. Beverly Hills, Cal.: Sage.

———. 1977b. *Outline of Theory and Practice*. Cambridge: Cambridge University Press.

Breines, P. 1979/80. "Toward an Uncertain Marxism." *Radical History Review*, 22 (Winter).

Buck-Morss, S. 1977. *The Origins of Negative Dialectics*. New York: Free Press.

Enzenberger, H. M. 1974. *The Consciousness Industry*. New York: Seabury Press.

Ewen, S. 1976. *Captains of Consciousness: Advertising and the Social Roots of the Consumer Culture*. New York: McGraw-Hill.

Foucault, M. 1980. *Power and Knowledge: Selected Interviews and Other Writings*, ed. C. Gordon. New York: Pantheon.

Freud, S. 1949. *Civilization and Its Discontents*. London: Hogarth Press.

Friedman, G. 1981. *The Political Philosophy of the Frankfurt School*. Ithaca, N.Y.: Cornell University Press.

Giroux, H. A. 1981. *Ideology, Culture, and the Process of Schooling*. Philadelphia: Temple University Press.

Gramsci, A. 1971. *Selections from Prison Notebooks*, ed. and trans. Quinten Hoare and Geoffrey Smith. New York: International Publishers.

Gross, H. 1979. "Adorno in Los Angeles: The Intellectual Emigration." *Humanities in Society*, 2(4) (Fall).

Habermas, J. 1973. *Theory and Practice*. Boston: Beacon Press.

——— 1980. "Psychic Thermidor and the Rebirth of Rebellious Subjectivity." *Berkeley Journal of Sociology*, 25.

Hahn, H. 1933. "Logik Mathematik und Naturerkennen." *In Einheitswissenschaft* ed. Otto Neurath et al. Vienna: n.p.

Held, D. 1980. *Introduction to Critical Theory: Horkheimer to Habermas*. Berkeley: University of California Press.

Horkheimer, M. 1972. *Critical Theory*. New York: Seabury Press.

———. 1974. *Eclipse of Reason*. New York: Seabury Press.

Jacoby, R. 1975. *Social Amnesia*. Boston: Beacon Press.

——— 1980. "What Is Conformist Marxism?" *Telos*, 45 (Fall).

Jameson, F. 1971. *Marxism and Form*. Princeton, N.J.: Princeton University Press.

Jay, M. 1973. *The Dialectical Imagination: A History of the Frankfurt School and the Institute of Social Research 1923–1950*. Boston: Little, Brown.

Lowenthal, L. 1979. "Theodor W. Adorno: An Intellectual Memoir." *Humanities in Society*, 2(4) (Fall).

Marcuse, H. 1955. *Eros and Civilization*. Boston: Beacon Press.

———— . 1960. *Reason and Revolution*, Boston: Beacon Press.

———— . 1964. *One Dimensional Man*. Boston: Beacon Press.

———— . 1968a. *Negations: Essays in Critical Theory*. Boston: Beacon Press.

———— . 1968b. *An Essay on Liberation*. Boston: Beacon Press.

———— . 1970. *Five Lectures*, trans. Jeremy Shapiro and Sheirry Weber. Boston: Beacon Press.

———— . 1969. "Repressive Tolerance." In *A Critique of Pure Tolerance*, ed. Robert Paul Wolff, Benjamin Moor, Jr., and Herbert Marcuse. Boston: Beacon Press.

———— 1972. *Counter-Revolution and Revolt*. Boston: Beacon Press.

———— . 1978. "On Science and Phenomenology." In *The Essential Frankfurt School Reader*, ed. Andrew Arato and Eike Gebhardt. New York: Urizen Books.

Nietzsche, F. 1966. "Aus dem Nachlass der Achtzigerjahre." In *Werke*, vol. 3, ed. Karle Schleckta. Munich: Hanser.

Wellmer, A. 1974. *Critical Theory of Society*, trans. John Cumming. New York: Seabury Press.

2

From *Pedagogy of the Oppressed*

Paulo Freire

A careful analysis of the teacher–student relationship at any level, inside or outside the school, reveals its fundamentally *narrative* character. This relationship involves a narrating Subject (the teacher) and patient, listening objects (the students). The contents, whether values or empirical dimensions of reality, tend in the process of being narrated to become lifeless and petrified. Education is suffering from narration sickness.

The teacher talks about reality as if it were motionless, static, compartmentalized, and predictable. Or else he expounds on a topic completely alien to the existential experience of the students. His task is to "fill" the students with the contents of his narration—contents which are detached from reality, disconnected from the totality that engendered them and could give them significance. Words are emptied of their concreteness and become a hollow, alienated, and alienating verbosity.

The outstanding characteristic of this narrative education, then, is the sonority of words, not their transforming power. "Four times four is sixteen; the capital of Pará is Belém." The student records, memorizes, and repeats these phrases without perceiving what four times four really means, or realizing the true significance of "capital" in the affirmation "the capital of Pará is Belém," that is, what Belém means for Pará and what Pará means for Brazil.

Narration (with the teacher as narrator) leads the students to memorize mechanically the narrated content. Worse yet, it turns them into "containers," into "receptacles" to be "filled" by the teacher. The more completely he fills the receptacles, the better a teacher he is. The more meekly the receptacles permit themselves to be filled, the better students they are.

Education thus becomes an act of depositing, in which the students are the depositories and the teacher is the depositor. Instead of communicating, the teacher issues communiqués and makes deposits which the students patiently receive, memorize, and repeat. This is the "banking" concept of education, in which the scope of action allowed to the students extends only as far as receiving, filing, and storing the deposits. They do, it is true, have the opportunity to become collectors or cataloguers of the things they store. But in the last analysis, it is men themselves who are filed away through the lack of creativity, transformation, and knowledge in this (at best) misguided system. For apart from inquiry, apart from the praxis, men cannot be truly human. Knowledge emerges only through invention and re-invention, through the restless, impatient, continuing, hopeful inquiry men pursue in the world, with the world, and with each other.

In the banking concept of education, knowledge is a gift bestowed by those who consider themselves knowledgeable upon those whom they consider to know nothing. Projecting an absolute ignorance onto others, a characteristic of the ideology of oppression, negates education and knowledge as processes of inquiry. The teacher presents himself to his students as their necessary opposite; by considering their ignorance absolute, he justifies his own existence. The students, alienated like the slave in the Hegelian dialectic, accept their ignorance as justifying the teacher's existence—but, unlike the slave, they never discover that they educate the teacher.

The *raison d'être* of libertarian education, on the other hand, lies in its drive towards reconciliation. Education must begin with the solution of the teacher–student contradiction, by reconciling the poles of the contradiction so that both are simultaneously teachers *and* students.

This solution is not (nor can it be) found in the banking concept. On the contrary, banking education maintains and even stimulates the contradiction through the following attitudes and practices, which mirror oppressive society as a whole:

(a) the teacher teaches and the students are taught;
(b) the teacher knows everything and the students know nothing;
(c) the teacher thinks and the students are thought about;
(d) the teacher talks and the students listen—meekly;
(e) the teacher disciplines and the students are disciplined;
(f) the teacher chooses and enforces his choice, and the students comply;
(g) the teacher acts and the students have the illusion of acting through the action of the teacher;
(h) the teacher chooses the program content, and the students (who were not consulted) adapt to it;
(i) the teacher confuses the authority of knowledge with his own professional authority, which he sets in opposition to the freedom of the students;
(j) the teacher is the Subject of the learning process, while the pupils are mere objects.

It is not surprising that the banking concept of education regards men as adaptable, manageable beings. The more students work at storing the deposits entrusted to them, the less they develop the critical consciousness which would result from their intervention in the world as transformers of that world. The more completely they accept the passive role imposed on them, the more they tend simply to adapt to the world as it is and to the fragmented view of reality deposited in them.

The capability of banking education to minimize or annul the students' creative power and to stimulate their credulity serves the interests of the oppressors, who care neither to have the world revealed nor to see it transformed. The oppressors use their "humanitarianism" to preserve a profitable situation. Thus they react almost instinctively against any experiment in education which stimulates the critical faculties and is not content with a partial view of reality but always seeks out the ties which link one point to another and one problem to another.

Indeed, the interests of the oppressors lie in "changing the consciousness of the oppressed, not the situation which oppresses them";[1] for the more the oppressed can be led to adapt to that situation, the more easily they can be dominated. To achieve this end, the oppressors use the banking concept of education in conjunction with a paternalistic social action apparatus, within which the oppressed receive the euphemistic title of "welfare recipients." They are treated as individual cases, as marginal men who deviate from the general configuration of a "good, organized, and just" society. The oppressed are regarded as the pathology of the healthy society, which must therefore adjust these "incompetent and lazy" folk to its own patterns by changing their mentality. These marginals need to be "integrated," "incorporated" into the healthy society that they have "forsaken."

The truth is, however, that the oppressed are not "marginals," are not men living "outside" society. They have always been "inside"—inside the structure which made them "beings for others." The solution is not to "integrate" them into the structure of oppression, but to transform that structure so that they can become "beings for themselves." Such transformation, of course, would undermine the oppressors' purposes; hence their utilization of the banking concept of education to avoid the threat of student *conscientização*.

The banking approach to adult education, for example, will never propose to students that they critically consider reality. It will deal instead with such vital questions as whether Roger gave green grass to the goat, and insist upon the importance of learning that, on the contrary, *Roger gave green grass to the rabbit*. The "humanism" of the banking approach masks the effort to turn men into automatons—the very negation of their ontological vocation to be more fully human.

Those who use the banking approach, knowingly or unknowingly (for there are innumerable well-intentioned bank-clerk teachers who do not realize that they are serving only to dehumanize), fail to perceive that the deposits themselves contain contradictions about reality. But, sooner or later, these contradictions may lead formerly passive students to turn against their domestication and the attempt to domesticate reality. They may discover through existential experience that their present way of life is irreconcilable with their vocation to become fully human. They may perceive through their relations with reality that reality is really a *process*, undergoing constant transformation. If men are searchers and their ontological vocation is humanization, sooner or later they may perceive the contradiction in which banking education seeks to maintain them, and then engage themselves in the struggle for their liberation.

But the humanist, revolutionary educator cannot wait for this possibility to materialize. From the outset, his efforts must coincide with those of the students to engage in critical thinking and the quest for mutual humanization. His efforts must be imbued with a profound trust in men and their creative power. To achieve this, he must be a partner of the students in his relations with them.

The banking concept does not admit to such partnership—and necessarily so. To resolve the teacher–student contradiction, to exchange the role of depositor, prescriber, domesticator, for the role of student among students would be to undermine the power of oppression and serve the cause of liberation.

Implicit in the banking concept is the assumption of a dichotomy between man and the world: man is merely *in* the world, not *with* the world or with others; man is spectator, not re-creator. In this view, man is not a conscious being (*corpo consciente*); he is rather the possessor of *a* consciousness: an empty "mind" passively open to the reception of deposits of reality from the world outside. For example, my desk, my books, my coffee cup, all the objects before me—as bits of the world which surrounds me—would be "inside" me, exactly as I am inside my study right now. This view makes no distinction between being accessible to consciousness and entering consciousness. The distinction, however, is essential: the objects which surround me are simply accessible to my consciousness, not located within it. I am aware of them, but they are not inside me.

It follows logically from the banking notion of consciousness that the educator's role is to regulate the way the world "enters into" the students. His task is to organize a process which already occurs spontaneously, to "fill" the students by making deposits of information which he considers to constitute true knowledge.[2] And since men "receive" the world as passive entities, education should make them more passive still, and adapt them to the world. The educated man is the adapted man, because he is better "fit" for the world. Translated into practice, this concept is well suited to the purposes of the oppressors, whose tranquility rests on how well men fit the world the oppressors have created, and how little they question it.

The more completely the majority adapt to the purposes which the dominant minority prescribe for them (thereby depriving them of the right to their own purposes), the more easily the minority can continue to prescribe. The theory and practice of banking education serve this end quite efficiently. Verbalistic lessons, reading requirements,[3] the methods for evaluating "knowledge," the distance between the teacher and the taught, the criteria for promotion: everything in this ready-to-wear approach serves to obviate thinking.

The bank-clerk educator does not realize that there is no true security in his hypertrophied role, that one must seek to live *with* others in solidarity. One cannot impose oneself, nor even merely co-exist with one's students. Solidarity requires true communication, and the concept by which such an educator is guided fears and proscribes communication.

Yet only through communication can human life hold meaning. The teacher's thinking is authenticated only by the authenticity of the students' thinking. The teacher cannot think for his students, nor can he impose his thought on them. Authentic thinking, thinking that is concerned about *reality*, does not take place in ivory tower isolation, but only in communication. If it is true that thought has meaning only when generated by action upon the world, the subordination of students to teachers becomes impossible.

Because banking education begins with a false understanding of men as objects, it cannot promote the development of what Fromm calls "biophily," but instead produces its opposite: "necrophily."

> While life is characterized by growth in a structured, functional manner, the necrophilous person loves all that does not grow, all that is mechanical. The necrophilous person is driven by the desire to transform the organic into the inorganic, to approach life mechanically, as if all living persons were things. . . . Memory, rather than experience; having, rather than being, is what counts. The necrophilous person can relate to an object—a flower or a person—only if he possesses it; hence a threat to his possession is a threat to himself; if he loses possession he loses contact with the world. . . . He loves control, and in the act of controlling he kills life.[4]

Oppression—overwhelming control—is necrophilic; it is nourished by love of death, not life. The banking concept of education, which serves the interests of oppression, is also necrophilic. Based on a mechanistic, static, naturalistic, spatialized view of consciousness, it transforms students into receiving objects. It attempts to control thinking and action, leads men to adjust to the world, and inhibits their creative power.

When their efforts to act responsibly are frustrated, when they find themselves unable to use their faculties, men suffer. "This suffering due to impotence is rooted in the very fact that the human equilibrium has been disturbed."[5] But the inability to act which causes men's anguish also causes them to reject their impotence, by attempting

> . . . to restore [their] capacity to act. But can [they], and how? One way is to submit to and identify with a person or group having power. By this symbolic participation in another person's life, [men have] the illusion of acting, when in reality [they] only submit to and become a part of those who act.[6]

Populist manifestations perhaps best exemplify this type of behavior by the oppressed, who, by identifying with charismatic leaders, come to feel that they themselves are active and effective. The rebellion they express as they emerge in the historical process is motivated by that desire to act effectively. The dominant elites consider the remedy to be more domination and repression, carried out in the name of freedom, order, and social peace (that is, the peace of the elites). Thus they can condemn—logically, from their point of view—"the violence of a strike by workers and [can] call upon the state in the same breath to use violence in putting down the strike."[7]

Education as the exercise of domination stimulates the credulity of students, with the ideological intent (often not perceived by educators) of indoctrinating them to adapt to the world of oppression. This accusation is not made in the naïve hope that the dominant elites will thereby simply abandon the practice. Its objective is to call the attention of true humanists to the fact that they cannot use banking educational methods in the pursuit of liberation, for they would only negate that very pursuit. Nor may a revolutionary society inherit these methods from an oppressor society. The revolutionary society which practices banking education is either misguided or mistrusting of men. In either event, it is threatened by the specter of reaction.

Unfortunately, those who espouse the cause of liberation are themselves surrounded and influenced by the climate which generates the banking concept, and often do not perceive its true significance or its dehumanizing power. Paradoxically, then, they utilize this same instrument of alienation in what they consider an effort to liberate. Indeed, some "revolutionaries" brand as "innocents," "dreamers," or even "reactionaries" those who would challenge this educational practice. But one does not liberate men by alienating them. Authentic liberation—the process of humanization—is not another deposit to be made in men. Liberation is a praxis: the action and reflection of men upon their world in order to transform it. Those truly committed to the cause of liberation can accept neither the mechanistic concept of consciousness as an empty vessel to be filled, nor the use of banking methods of domination (propaganda, slogans—deposits) in the name of liberation.

Those truly committed to liberation must reject the banking concept in its entirety, adopting instead a concept of men as conscious beings, and consciousness as consciousness intent upon the world. They must abandon the educational goal of deposit-making and replace it with the posing of the problems of men in their relations with the world. "Problem-posing" education, responding to the essence of consciousness—*intentionality*—rejects communiqués and embodies communication. It epitomizes the special characteristic of consciousness: being *conscious of*, not only as intent on objects but as turned in upon itself in a Jasperian "split"—consciousness as consciousness *of* consciousness.

Liberating education consists in acts of cognition, not transferrals of information. It is a learning situation in which the cognizable object (far from being the end of the cognitive act) intermediates the cognitive actors—teacher on the one hand and students on the other. Accordingly, the practice of problem-posing education entails at the outset that the teacher–student contradiction be resolved. Dialogical relations—indispensable to the capacity of cognitive actors to cooperate in perceiving the same cognizable object—are otherwise impossible.

Indeed, problem-posing education, which breaks with the vertical patterns characteristic of banking education, can fulfill its function as the practice of freedom only if it can overcome the above contradiction. Through dialogue, the teacher-of-the-students and the students-of-the-teacher cease to exist and a new term emerges: teacher-student with students-teachers. The teacher is no longer merely the-one-who-teaches, but one who is himself taught in dialogue with the students, who in turn while being taught also teach. They become jointly responsible for a process in which all grow. In this process, arguments based on "authority" are no longer valid; in order to function, authority must be *on the side of* freedom, not *against* it. Here, no one teaches another, nor is anyone self-taught. Men teach each other, mediated by the world, by the cognizable objects which in banking education are "owned" by the teacher.

The banking concept (with its tendency to dichotomize everything) distinguishes two stages in the action of the educator. During the first, he cognizes a cognizable object while he prepares his lessons in his study or his laboratory; during the second, he expounds to his students about that object. The students are not called upon to know, but to memorize the contents narrated by the teacher. Nor do the students practice any act of cognition, since the object towards which that act should be directed is the property of the teacher rather than a medium evoking the critical reflection of both teacher and students. Hence in the name of the "preservation of culture and knowledge" we have a system which achieves neither true knowledge nor true culture.

The problem-posing method does not dichotomize the activity of the teacher-student: he is not "cognitive" at one point and "narrative" at another. He is always "cognitive," whether preparing a project or engaging in dialogue with the students. He does not regard cognizable objects as his private property, but as the object of reflection by himself and the students. In this way, the problem-posing educator constantly re-forms his reflections in the reflection of the students. The students—no longer docile listeners—are now critical co-investigators in dialogue with the teacher. The teacher presents the material to the students for their consideration, and re-considers his earlier considerations as the students express their own. The role of the problem-posing educator is to create, together with the students, the conditions under which knowledge at the level of the *doxa* is superseded by true knowledge, at the level of the *logos*.

Whereas banking education anesthetizes and inhibits creative power, problem-posing education involves a constant unveiling of reality. The former attempts to maintain the *submersion* of consciousness; the latter strives for the *emergence* of consciousness and *critical intervention* in reality.

Students, as they are increasingly posed with problems relating to themselves in the world and with the world, will feel increasingly challenged and obliged to respond to that challenge. Because they apprehend the challenge as interrelated to other problems within a total context, not as a theoretical question, the resulting comprehension tends to be increasingly critical and thus constantly less alienated. Their response to the challenge evokes new challenges, followed by new understandings; and gradually the students come to regard themselves as committed.

Education as the practice of freedom—as opposed to education as the practice of domination—denies that man is abstract, isolated, independent, and unattached to the world; it also denies that the world exists as a reality apart from men. Authentic reflection considers neither abstract man nor the world without men, but men in their relations with the world. In these relations consciousness and world are simultaneous: consciousness neither precedes the world nor follows it.

> La conscience et le monde sont dormés d'un même coup: extérieur par essence à la conscience, le monde est, par essence relatif à elle.[8]

In one of our culture circles in Chile, the group was discussing (based on a codification[9]) the anthropological concept of culture. In the midst of the discussion, a peasant who by banking standards was completely ignorant said: "Now I see that without man there is no world." When the educator responded: "Let's say, for the sake of argument, that all the men on earth were to die, but that the earth itself remained, together with trees, birds, animals, rivers, seas, the stars ... wouldn't all this be a world?" "Oh no," the peasant replied emphatically. "There would be no one to say: 'This is a world'."

The peasant wished to express the idea that there would be lacking the consciousness of the world which necessarily implies the world of consciousness. *I* cannot exist without a *not-I*. In turn, the *not-I* depends on that existence. The world which brings consciousness into existence becomes the world *of* that consciousness. Hence, the previously cited affirmation of Sartre: "*La conscience et le monde sont dormés d'un même coup.*"

As men, simultaneously reflecting on themselves and on the world, increase the scope of their perception, they begin to direct their observations towards previously inconspicuous phenomena:

> In perception properly so-called, as an explicit awareness [*Gewahren*], I am turned towards the object, to the paper, for instance. I apprehend it as being this here and now. The apprehension is a singling out, every object having a background in experience. Around and about the paper lie books, pencils, ink-well, and so forth, and these in a certain sense are also "perceived", perceptually there, in the "field of intuition"; but whilst I was turned towards the paper there was no turning in their direction, nor any apprehending of them, not even in a secondary sense. They appeared and yet were not singled out, were not posited on their own account. Every perception of a thing has such a zone of background intuitions or background awareness, if "intuiting" already includes the state of being turned towards, and this also is a "conscious experience", or more briefly a "consciousness of" all indeed that in point of fact lies in the co-perceived objective background.[10]

That which had existed objectively but had not been perceived in its deeper implications (if indeed it was perceived at all) begins to "stand out," assuming the character of a problem and therefore of challenge. Thus, men begin to single out elements from their "background awarenesses" and to reflect upon them. These elements are now objects of men's consideration, and, as such, objects of their action and cognition.

In problem-posing education, men develop their power to perceive critically *the way they exist* in the world *with which* and *in which* they find themselves; they come to see the world not as a static reality, but as a reality in process, in transformation. Although the dialectical relations of men with the world exist independently of how these relations are perceived (or whether or not they are perceived at all), it is also true that the form of action men adopt is to a large extent a function of how they perceive themselves in the world. Hence, the teacher-student and the students-teachers reflect simultaneously on themselves and the world without dichotomizing this reflection from action, and thus establish an authentic form of thought and action.

Once again, the two educational concepts and practices under analysis come into conflict. Banking education (for obvious reasons) attempts, by mythicizing reality, to conceal certain facts which explain the way men exist in the world; problem-posing education sets itself the task of demythologizing. Banking education resists dialogue; problem-posing education regards dialogue as indispensable to the act of cognition which unveils reality. Banking education treats students as objects of assistance; problem-posing education makes them critical thinkers. Banking education inhibits creativity and domesticates (although it cannot completely destroy) the *intentionality* of consciousness by isolating consciousness from the world, thereby denying men their ontological and historical vocation of becoming more fully human. Problem-posing education bases itself on creativity and stimulates true reflection and action upon reality, thereby responding to the vocation of men as beings who are authentic only when engaged in inquiry and creative transformation. In sum: banking theory and practice, as immobilizing and fixating forces, fail to acknowledge men as historical beings; problem-posing theory and practice take man's historicity as their starting point.

Problem-posing education affirms men as beings in the process of *becoming*—as unfinished, uncompleted beings in and with a likewise unfinished reality. Indeed, in contrast to other animals who are unfinished, but not historical, men know themselves to be unfinished; they are aware of their incompletion. In this incompletion and this awareness lie the very roots of education as an exclusively human manifestation. The unfinished character of men and the transformational character of reality necessitate that education be an ongoing activity.

Education is thus constantly remade in the praxis. In order to *be*, it must *become*. Its "duration" (in the Bergsonian meaning of the word) is found in the interplay of the opposites *permanence* and *change*. The banking method emphasizes permanence and becomes reactionary; problem-posing education—which accepts neither a "well-behaved" present nor a predetermined future—roots itself in the dynamic present and becomes revolutionary.

Problem-posing education is revolutionary futurity. Hence it is prophetic (and, as such, hopeful). Hence, it corresponds to the historical nature of man. Hence, it affirms men as beings who transcend themselves, who move forward and look ahead, for whom immobility represents a fatal threat, for whom looking at the past must only be a means of understanding more clearly what and who they are so that they can more wisely build the future. Hence, it identifies with the movement which engages men as beings aware of their incompletion—an historical movement which has its point of departure, its Subjects and its objective.

The point of departure of the movement lies in men themselves. But since men do not exist apart from the world, apart from reality, the movement must begin with the men-world relationship. Accordingly, the point of departure must always be with men in the "here and now," which constitutes the situation within which they are submerged, from which they emerge, and in which they intervene. Only by starting from this situation—which determines their perception of it—can they begin to move. To do this authentically they must perceive their state not as fated and unalterable, but merely as limiting—and therefore challenging.

Whereas the banking method directly or indirectly reinforces men's fatalistic perception of their situation, the problem-posing method presents this very situation to them as a problem. As the situation becomes the object of their cognition, the naïve or magical perception which produced their fatalism gives way to perception which is able to perceive itself even as it perceives reality, and can thus be critically objective about that reality.

A deepened consciousness of their situation leads men to apprehend that situation as an historical reality susceptible of transformation. Resignation gives way to the drive for transformation and inquiry, over which men feel themselves to be in control. If men, as historical beings necessarily engaged with other men in a movement of inquiry, did not control that movement, it would be (and is) a violation of men's humanity. Any situation in which some men prevent others from engaging in the process of inquiry is one of violence. The means used are not important; to alienate men from their own decision-making is to change them into objects.

This movement of inquiry must be directed towards humanization—man's historical vocation. The pursuit of full humanity, however, cannot be carried out in isolation or individualism, but only in fellowship and solidarity; therefore it cannot unfold in the antagonistic relations between oppressors and oppressed. No one can be authentically human while he prevents others from being so. Attempting *to be more* human, individualistically, leads to *having more*, egotistically: a form of dehumanization. Not that it is not fundamental *to have* in order *to be* human. Precisely because it *is* necessary, some men's *having* must not be allowed to constitute an obstacle to others' *having*, must not consolidate the power of the former to crush the latter.

Problem-posing education, as a humanist and liberating praxis, posits as fundamental that men subjected to domination must fight for their emancipation. To that end, it enables teachers and students to become Subjects of the educational process by overcoming authoritarianism and an alienating intellectualism; it also enables men to overcome their false perception of reality. The world—no longer something to be described with deceptive words—becomes the object of that transforming action by men which results in their humanization.

Problem-posing education does not and cannot serve the interests of the oppressor. No oppressive order could permit the oppressed to begin to question: Why? While only a revolutionary society can carry out this education in systematic terms, the revolutionary leaders need not take full power before they can employ the method. In the revolutionary process, the leaders cannot utilize the banking method as an interim measure, justified on grounds of expediency, with the intention of *later* behaving in a genuinely revolutionary fashion. They must be revolutionary—that is to say, dialogical—from the outset.

Notes

1. Simone de Beauvoir, *La Pensée de Droite, Aujourd'hui* (Paris); ST, *El Pensamiento político de la Derecha* (Buenos Aires, 1963), p. 34.
2. This concept corresponds to what Sartre calls the "digestive" or "nutritive" concept of education, in which knowledge is "fed" by the teacher to the students to "fill them out." See Jean-Paul Sartre, "Une idée fundamentale de la phénoménologie de Husserl: L'intentionalité," *Situations I* (Paris, 1947).
3. For example, some professors specify in their reading lists that a book should be read from pages 10 to 15—and do this to "help" their students!
4. Fromm, *Escape from Freedom* (New York, 1941), p. 41.
5. *Ibid.*, p. 31.
6. *Ibid.*
7. Reinhold Niebuhr, *Moral Man and Immoral Society* (New York, 1960), p. 130.
8. Sartre, *op. cit.*, p. 32.
9. See Chapter 3.—Translator's note.
10. Edmund Husserl, *Ideas—General Introduction to Pure Phenomenology* (London, 1969), pp. 105–106.

3

Critical Pedagogy: A Look at the Major Concepts

Peter McLaren

In practice, critical pedagogy is as diverse as its many adherents, yet common themes and constructs run through many of their writings. In what follows, I will outline in more detail the major categories within this tradition. A category is simply a concept, question, issue, hypothesis, or idea that is central to critical theory. These categories are intended to provide a theoretical framework within which you may reread my journal entries and perhaps better understand the theories generated by critical educational research. The categories are useful for the purposes of clarification and illustration, although some critical theorists will undoubtedly argue that additional concepts should have been included, or that some concepts have not been given the emphasis they deserve.

The Importance of Theory

Before we discuss individual categories, we need to examine how those categories are explored. Critical theorists begin with the premise that *men and women are essentially unfree and inhabit a world rife with contradictions and asymmetries of power and privilege.* The critical educator endorses theories that are, first and foremost, *dialectical;* that is, theories which recognize the problems of society as more than simply isolated events of individuals or deficiencies in the social structure. Rather, these problems form part of the *interactive context* between individual and society. The individual, a social actor, both creates and is created by the social universe of which he/she is a part. Neither the individual nor society is given priority in analysis; the two are inextricably interwoven, so that reference to one must by implication mean reference to the other. Dialectical theory attempts to tease out the histories and relations of accepted meanings and appearances, tracing interactions from the context to the part, from the system inward to the event. In this way, critical theory helps us focus *simultaneously on both sides of a social contradiction.*[1]

Wilfred Carr and Stephen Kemmis describe dialectical thinking as follows:

> Dialectical thinking involves searching out . . . contradictions (like the contradiction of the inadvertent oppression of less able students by a system which aspires to help all students to attain their "full potential"), but it is not really as wooden or mechanical as the formula of thesis-antithesis-synthesis. On the contrary, it is an open and questioning form of thinking which demands reflection back and forth between elements like *part* and *whole, knowledge* and *action, process* and *product, subject* and *object, being* and *becoming, rhetoric* and *reality,* or *structure* and *function.* In the process, *contradictions* may be discovered (as, for example, in a

political *structure* which aspires to give decision-making power to all, but actually *functions* to deprive some of access to the information with which they could influence crucial decisions about their lives). As contradictions are revealed, new constructive thinking and new construct-ive action are required to transcend the contradictory state of affairs. The complementarity of the elements is dynamic: it is a kind of a tension, not a static confrontation between the two poles. In the dialectical approach, the elements are regarded as mutually constitutive, not separate and distinct. Contradiction can thus be distinguished from paradox: to speak of a contradiction is to imply that a new resolution can be achieved, while to speak of a paradox is to suggest that two incompatible ideas remain inertly opposed to one another. (italics original)[2]

The dialectical nature of critical theory enables the educational researcher to see the school not simply as an arena of indoctrination or socialization or a site of instruction, but also as a cultural terrain that promotes student empowerment and self-transformation. My own research into parochial education for instance, showed that the school functions *simultaneously* as a means of empowering students around issues of social justice and as a means of sustaining, legitimizing, and reproducing dominant class interests directed at creating obedient, docile, and low-paid future workers.[3]

A dialectical understanding of schooling permits us to see schools as sites of *both* domination and liberation; this runs counter to the overdeterministic orthodox Marxist view of schooling, which claims that schools simply reproduce class relations and passively indoctrinate students into becoming greedy young capitalists. This dialectical understand-ing of schooling also brushes against the grain of mainstream educational theory, which conceives of schools as mainly providing students with the skills and attitudes necessary for becoming patriotic, industrious, and responsible citizens.

Critical educators argue that any worthwhile theory of schooling *must be partisan*. That is, it must be fundamentally tied to a struggle for a qualitatively better life for all through the construction of a society based on nonexploitative relations and social justice. The critical educator doesn't believe that there are two sides to every question, with both sides needing equal attention. For the critical educator, there are *many* sides to a problem, and often these sides are linked to certain class, race, and gender interests.

Let's turn for a moment to an example of critical theorizing as it is brought to bear on a fundamental teaching practice: writing classroom objectives. In this example, I will draw on Henry Giroux's important distinction between *micro* and *macro* objectives.[4]

The common use of behavioral objectives by teachers reflects a search for certainty and technical control of knowledge and behavior. Teachers often emphasize classroom man-agement procedures, efficiency, and "how-to-do" techniques that ultimately ignore an important question: "Why is this knowledge being taught in the first place?" Giroux recasts classroom objectives into the categories of macro and micro.

Macro objectives are designed to enable students to make connections between the methods, content, and structure of a course and its significance within the larger social reality. This dialectical approach to classroom objectives allows students to acquire a broad frame of reference or world view; in other words, it helps them acquire a political perspec-tive. Students can then make the hidden curriculum explicit and develop a critical political consciousness.

Micro objectives represent the course content and are characterized by their narrowness of purpose and their content-bound path of inquiry. Giroux tells us that the importance of the relationship between macro and micro objectives arises out of *having students uncover the connections between course objectives and the norms, values, and structural relationships of the wider society.* For instance, the micro objectives of teaching about the Vietnam war might be to learn the dates of specific battles, the details of specific Congressional debates surrounding the war, and the reasons given by the White House for fighting the war. The micro objectives are concerned with the organization, classification, mastery, and manipulation of data. This is what Giroux calls *productive knowledge*. Macro objectives, on the other hand, center on the relationship between means and ends, between specific events and their wider social and political implications. A lesson on the Vietnam war or the more recent invasion of Grenada, for instance, might raise the following macro questions: What is the relationship between the invasion of Grenada as a rescue mission in the interests of U.S. citizens and the larger logic of imperialism? During the Vietnam era, what was the relationship between the American economy and the arms industry? Whose interests did the war serve best? Who benefited most from the war? What were the class relationships between those who fought and those who stayed home in the university?

Developing macro objectives fosters a dialectical mode of inquiry; the process constitutes a socio-political application of knowledge, what Giroux calls *directive knowledge*. Critical theorists seek a kind of knowledge that will help students recognize the *social function of particular forms of knowledge*. The purpose of dialectical educational theory, then, is to provide students with a model that permits them to examine the underlying political, social, and economic foundations of the larger society.

Critical Pedagogy and the Social Construction of Knowledge

Critical educational theorists view school knowledge as historically and socially rooted and interest bound. Knowledge acquired in school—or anywhere, for that matter—is never neutral or objective but is ordered and structured in particular ways; its emphases and exclusions partake of a silent logic. Knowledge is a *social construction* deeply rooted in a nexus of power relations. When critical theorists claim that knowledge is socially constructed, they mean that it is the product of agreement or consent between individuals who live out particular social relations (e.g., of class, race, and gender) and who live in particular junctures in time. To claim that knowledge is socially constructed usually means that the world we live in is constructed symbolically by the mind through social interaction with others and is heavily dependent on culture, context, custom, and historical specificity. There is no ideal, autonomous, pristine, or aboriginal world to which our social constructions necessarily correspond; there is always a referential field in which symbols are situated. And this particular referential field (e.g., language, culture, place, time) will influence how symbols generate meaning. There is no pure subjective insight. We do not stand *before* the social world; we live *in the midst* of it. As we seek the meaning of events we seek the meaning of the social. We can now raise certain questions with respect to the social construction of knowledge, such as: why do women and minorities often view social issues differently than white males? Why are teachers more likely to value the opinions of a middle-class white male student, for instance, than those of a black female?

Critical pedagogy asks how and why knowledge gets constructed the way it does, and how and why some constructions of reality are legitimated and celebrated by the dominant culture while others clearly are not. Critical pedagogy asks how our everyday commonsense understandings—our social constructions or "subjectivities"—get produced and lived out. In other words, what are the *social functions* of knowledge? The crucial factor here is that some forms of knowledge have more power and legitimacy than others. For instance, in many schools in the United States, science and math curricula are favored over the liberal arts. This can be explained by the link between the needs of big business to compete in world markets and the imperatives of the new reform movement to bring "excellence" back to the schools. Certain types of knowledge legitimate certain gender, class, and racial interests. Whose interests does this knowledge serve? Who gets excluded as a result? Who is marginalized?

Let's put this in the form of further questions: What is the relationship between social class and knowledge taught in school? Why do we value scientific knowledge over informal knowledge? Why do we have teachers using "standard English"? Why is the public still unlikely to vote for a woman or a black for president? How does school knowledge reinforce stereotypes about women, minorities, and disadvantaged peoples? What accounts for some knowledge having high status (as in the great works of philosophers or scientists) while the practical knowledge of ordinary people or marginalized or subjugated groups is often discredited and devalued? Why do we learn about the great "men" in history and spend less time learning about the contributions of women and minorities and the struggles of people in lower economic classes? Why don't we learn more about the American labor movement? How and why are certain types of knowledge used to reinforce dominant ideologies, which in turn serve to mask unjust power relations among certain groups in society?

Forms of Knowledge

Critical pedagogy follows a distinction regarding forms of knowledge posited by the German social theorist Jürgen Habermas.[5] Let's examine this concept in the context of class-room teaching. Mainstream educators who work primarily within liberal and conservative educational ideologies emphasize *technical knowledge* (similar to Giroux's *productive knowledge*): Knowledge is that which can be measured and quantified. Technical knowledge is based on the natural sciences, uses hypothetico-deductive or empirical analytical methods, and is evaluated by, among other things, intelligence quotients, reading scores, and SAT results, all of which are used by educators to sort, regulate, and control students.

A second type, *practical knowledge*, aims to enlighten individuals so they can shape their daily actions in the world. Practical knowledge is generally acquired through *describing and analyzing social situations historically or developmentally*, and is geared toward helping individuals understand social events that are ongoing and situational. The liberal educational researcher who undertakes fieldwork in a school in order to evaluate student behavior and interaction acquires practical knowledge, for instance. This type of knowledge is not usually generated numerically or by submitting data to some kind of statistical instrument.

The critical educator, however, is most interested in what Habermas calls *emancipatory knowledge* (similar to Giroux's *directive knowledge*), which attempts to reconcile and transcend the opposition between technical and practical knowledge. Emancipatory knowledge helps us understand how social relationships are distorted and manipulated by relations of power and privilege. It also aims at creating the conditions under which irrationality, domination, and oppression can be overcome and transformed through deliberative, collective action. In short, it creates the foundation for social justice, equality, and empowerment.

Class

Class refers to the *economic, social, and political relationships that govern life in a given social order.* Class relationships reflect the constraints and limitations individuals and groups experience in the areas of income level, occupation, place of residence, and other indicators of status and social rank. Relations of class are those associated with surplus labor, who produces it, and who is a recipient of it. Surplus labor is that labor undertaken by workers beyond that which is necessary. Class relations also deal with the social distribution of power and its structural allocation. Today there are greater distinctions within the working classes and it is now possible to talk about the new *underclasses* within the American social structure consisting of black, Hispanic, and Asian class fractions, together with the white aged, the unemployed and underemployed, large sections of women, the handicapped, and other marginalized economic groups.

Culture

The concept of *culture*, varied though it may be, is essential to any understanding of critical pedagogy. I use the term "culture" here to signify *the particular ways in which a social group lives out and makes sense of its "given" circumstances and conditions of life.* In addition to defining culture as *a set of practices, ideologies, and values from which different groups draw to make sense of the world*, we need to recognize how cultural questions help us understand who has power and how it is reproduced and manifested in the social relations that link schooling to the wider social order. The ability of individuals to express their culture is related to the power which certain groups are able to wield in the social order. The expression of values and beliefs by individuals who share certain historical experiences is determined by their collective power in society.[6]

The link between culture and power has been extensively analyzed in critical social theory over the past ten years. It is therefore possible to offer three insights from that literature that particularly illuminate the political logic that underlies various cultural/power relations. First, culture is intimately connected with the structure of social relations within class, gender, and age formations that produce forms of oppression and dependency. Second, culture is analyzed not simply as a way of life, but as a form of production through which different groups in either their dominant or subordinate social relations define and realize their aspirations through unequal relations of power. Third, culture is viewed as a field of struggle in which the production, legitimation, and circulation of particular forms of knowledge and experience are central areas of conflict. What is important here is that each of these insights raises fundamental questions about the ways in which inequalities are maintained and challenged in the spheres of school culture and the wider society.[7]

Dominant Culture, Subordinate Culture, and Subculture

Three central categories related to the concept of culture—dominant culture, subordinate culture, subculture—have been much discussed in recent critical scholarship. Culture can be readily broken down into "dominant" and "subordinate" parent cultures. *Dominant culture* refers to social practices and representations that *affirm the central values, interests, and concerns of the social class in control of the material and symbolic wealth of society.*

Groups who live out social relations in subordination to the dominant culture are part of the *subordinate culture.* Group *subcultures* may be described as subsets of the two parent cultures (dominant and subordinate). Individuals who form subcultures often use distinct symbols and social practices to help foster an identity outside that of the dominant culture. As an example, we need only refer to punk subculture, with its distinct musical tastes, fetishistic costumery, spiked hair, and its attempt to disconfirm the dominant rules of propriety fostered by the mainstream media, schools, religions, and culture industry. For the most part, working-class subcultures exist in a subordinate structural position in society, and many of their members engage in oppositional acts against the dominant middle-class culture. It is important to remember, however, that people don't inhabit cultures or social classes but *live out class or cultural relations,* some of which may be dominant and some of which may be subordinate.[8]

Subcultures are involved in contesting the cultural "space" or openings in the dominant culture. The dominant culture is never able to secure total control over subordinate cultural groups. Whether we choose to examine British subcultural groups (i.e., working-class youth, teddy-boys, skinheads, punks, rude boys, rastafarians) or American groups (i.e., motorcycle clubs such as Hell's Angels, ethnic street gangs, or middle class suburban gangs), subcultures are more often *negotiated* than truly *oppositional.* As John Muncie points out, this is because they operate primarily in the arena of leisure that is exceedingly vulnerable to commercial and ideological incorporation.[9] Subcultures do offer a symbolic critique of the social order and are frequently organized around relations of class, gender, style, and race. Despite the often ferocious exploitation of the subcultural resistance of various youth subcultures by bourgeois institutions (school, workplace, justice system, consumer industries), subcultures are usually able to keep alive the struggle over how meanings are produced, defined, and legitimated; consequently, they do represent various degrees of struggle against lived subjugation. Many subcultural movements reflect a crisis within dominant society, rather than a unified mobilization against it. For instance, the hippie movement in the 1960s represented, in part, an exercise of petite-bourgeoisie socialism by middle-class radicals who were nurtured both by idealist principles and by a search for spiritual and life-style comfort. This often served to draw critical attention away from the structural inequalities of capitalist society. As Muncie argues, subcultures constitute "a crisis within dominant culture rather than a conspiracy against dominant culture."[10] The youth counterculture of the sixties served as the ideological loam that fertilized my pedagogy. I had learned the rudiments of a middle-class radicalism that was preoccupied with the politics of expressive life and avoided examining in a minded and a critical manner the structural inequalities within the social order.

Cultural Forms

Cultural forms are those symbols and social practices that express culture, such as those found in music, dress, food, religion, dance, and education, which have developed from the efforts of groups to shape their lives out of their surrounding material and political environment. Television, video, and films are regarded as cultural forms. Schooling is also a cultural form. Baseball is a cultural form. Cultural forms don't exist apart from sets of structural underpinnings which are related to the means of economic production, the mobilization of desire, the construction of social values, asymmetries of power/knowledge, configurations of ideologies, and relations of class, race, and gender.

Hegemony

The dominant culture is able to exercise domination over subordinate classes or groups through a process known as *hegemony*.[11] Hegemony refers to the maintenance of domination not by the sheer exercise of force *but primarily through consensual social practices, social forms, and social structures produced in specific sites such as the church, the state, the school, the mass media, the political system, and the family.* By *social practices*, I refer to what people say and do. Of course, social practices may be accomplished through words, gestures, personally appropriated signs and rituals, or a combination of these. *Social forms* refer to the principles that provide and give legitimacy to specific social practices. For example, the state legislature is one social form that gives legitimacy to the social practice of teaching. The term *social structures* can be defined as those constraints that limit individual life and appear to be beyond the individual's control, having their sources in the power relations that govern society. We can, therefore, talk about the "class structure" or the "economic structure" of our society.

Hegemony is a struggle in which the powerful win the consent of those who are oppressed, with the oppressed unknowingly participating in their own oppression. Hegemony was at work in my own practices as an elementary school teacher. Because I did not teach my students to question the prevailing values, attitudes, and social practices of the dominant society in a sustained critical manner, my classroom preserved the hegemony of the dominant culture. Such hegemony was contested when the students began to question my authority by resisting and disrupting my lessons. The dominant class secures hegemony—the consent of the dominated—by supplying the symbols, representations, and practices of social life in such a way that the basis of social authority and the unequal relations of power and privilege remain hidden. By perpetrating the myth of individual achievement and entrepreneurship in the media, the schools, the church, and the family, for instance, dominant culture ensures that subordinated groups who fail at school or who don't make it into the world of the "rich and famous" will view such failure in terms of personal inadequacy or the "luck of the draw." The oppressed blame themselves for school failure—a failure that can certainly be additionally attributed to the structuring effects of the economy and the class-based division of labor.[12]

Hegemony is a cultural encasement of meanings, a prison-house of language and ideas, that is "freely" entered into by both dominators and dominated. As Todd Gitlin puts it,

> both rulers and ruled derive psychological and material rewards in the course of confirming and reconfirming their inequality. The hegemonic sense of the world seeps into popular "common sense" and gets reproduced there; it may even appear to be generated *by* that common sense.[13]

Hegemony refers to the moral and intellectual leadership of a dominant class over a subordinate class achieved not through coercion (i.e., threat of imprisonment or torture) or the willful construction of rules and regulations (as in a dictatorship or fascist regime), but rather through the general winning of consent of the subordinate class to the authority of the dominant class. The dominant class need not impose force for the manufacture of hegemony since the subordinate class actively subscribes to many of the values and objectives of the dominant class without being aware of the source of those values or the interests which inform them.

Hegemony is not a process of active domination as much as an active structuring of the culture and experiences of the subordinate class by the dominant class. The dominant culture is able to "frame" the ways in which subordinate groups live and respond to their own cultural system and lived experiences; in other words, the dominant culture is able to manufacture dreams and desires for both dominant and subordinate groups by supplying "terms of reference" (i.e., images, visions, stories, ideals) against which all individuals are expected to live their lives. The dominant culture tries to "fix" the meaning of signs, symbols, and representations to provide a "common" worldview, disguising relations of power and privilege through the organs of mass media, state apparatus such as schools, government institutions, and state bureaucracies. Individuals are provided with "subject positions," which condition them to react to ideas and opinions in prescribed ways. For instance, most individuals in the United States, when addressed as "Americans," are generally positioned as subjects by the dominant discourse. To be an "American" carries a certain set of ideological baggage. Americans generally think of themselves as lovers of freedom, defenders of individual rights, guardians of world peace, etc.; rarely do Americans see themselves as contradictory social agents. They rarely view their country as lagging behind other industrial economies in the world in providing security for its citizens in such areas as health care, family allowance, and housing subsidy programs. As citizens of the wealthiest country in the world, Americans generally do not question why their government cannot afford to be more generous to its citizens. Most Americans would be aghast at hearing a description of their country as a "terrorist regime" exercising covert acts of war against Latin American countries such as Nicaragua. The prevailing image of America that the schools, the entertainment industry, and government agencies have promulgated is a benevolent one in which the interests of the dominant classes supposedly represent the interests of all groups. It is an image in which the values and beliefs of the dominant class appear so correct that to reject them would be unnatural, a violation of common sense.

Within the hegemonic process, established meanings are often laundered of contradiction, contestation, and ambiguity. Resistance does occur, however, most often in the domain of popular culture. In this case, popular culture becomes an arena of negotiation in which dominant, subordinate, and oppositional groups affirm and struggle over cultural representations and meanings. The dominant culture is rarely successful on all counts. People *do* resist. Alternative groups do manage to find different values and meanings to regulate their lives. Oppositional groups do attempt to challenge the prevailing culture's mode of structuring and codifying representations and meanings. Prevailing social practices are, in fact, resisted. Schools and other social and cultural sites are rarely in the thrall of the hegemonic process since there we will also find struggle and confrontation. This is why schools can be characterized as terrains of transactions, exchange, and struggle between subordinate groups and the dominant ideology. There is a relative autonomy within school sites that allows for forms of resistance to emerge and to break the cohesiveness of hegemony. Teachers battle over what books to use, over what disciplinary practices to use, and over the aims and objectives of particular courses and programs.

One current example of the battle for hegemony can be seen in the challenge by Christian fundamentalists to public schooling. Fundamentalist critics have instigated a debate over dominant pedagogical practices that ranges all the way from textbooks to how, in science classes, teachers may account for the origins of humankind. The important point to remember, however, is that hegemony is always in operation; certain ideas, values, and social practices generally prevail over others.

Not all prevailing values are oppressive. Critical educators, too, would like to secure hegemony for their own ideas. The challenge for teachers is to recognize and attempt to transform those undemocratic and oppressive features of hegemonic control that often structure everyday classroom existence in ways not readily apparent. These oppressive features are rarely challenged since the dominant ideology is so all inclusive that individuals are taught to view it as natural, commonsensical, and inviolable. For instance, subordinate groups who subscribe to an ideology that could be described as right wing are often the very groups hurt most by the Republican government they elect in terms of cutbacks in social services, agricultural aid, etc. Yet the Republican Party has been able to market itself as no-nonsense, get-tought, anti-Communist, and hyper-patriotic—features that appeal to subordinate groups whose cultural practices may include listening to country and western music, following the televangelist programs and crusades, or cheering the pugilistic exploits of Rambo. Those who seek to chart out the ways in which the affluent are favored over subordinate groups are dismissed as wimpish liberals who don't support the "freedom fighters" in Nicaragua. Who needs to use force when ideational hegemony works this well? As Gore Vidal has observed about the United States: "The genius of our system is that ordinary people go out and vote against their interests. The way our ruling class keeps out of sight is one of the greatest stunts in the political history of any country."[14]

Ideology

Hegemony could not do its work without the support of ideology. Ideology permeates all of social life and does not simply refer to the political ideologies of communism, socialism, anarchism, rationalism, or existentialism. Ideology refers to *the production and representation of ideas, values, and beliefs and the manner in which they are expressed and lived out by both individuals and groups.*[15] Simply put, ideology refers to the production of sense and meaning. It can be described as a way of viewing the world, a complex of ideas, various types of social practices, rituals, and representations *that we tend to accept as natural and as common sense.* It is the result of the intersection of meaning and power in the social world. Customs, rituals, beliefs, and values often produce within individuals distorted conceptions of their place in the sociocultural order and thereby serve to reconcile them to that place and to disguise the inequitable relations of power and privilege; this is sometimes referred to as "ideological hegemony."

Stuart Hall and James Donald define ideology as "the frameworks of thought which are used in society to explain, figure out, make sense of or give meaning to the social and political world . . . Without these frameworks, we could not make sense of the world at all. But with them, our perceptions are inevitably structured in a particular direction by the very concepts we are using."[16] Ideology includes both positive and negative functions at any given moment: The *positive function* of ideology is to "provide the concepts, categories, images, and ideas by means of which people make sense of their social and political world, form projects, come to a certain consciousness of their place in the world and act in it;" the *negative function* of ideology "refers to the fact that all such perspectives are inevitably selective. Thus a perspective positively organizes the 'facts of the case' in *this* and makes sense because it inevitably excludes *that* way of putting things."[17]

In order to fully understand the negative function of ideology, the concept must be linked to a theory of domination. *Domination* occurs when relations of power established at the institutional level are systematically asymmetrical; that is, when they are unequal, therefore privileging some groups over others. According to John Thompson, ideology as a

negative function works through four different modes: legitimation, dissimulation, fragmentation, and reification. *Legitimation* occurs when a system of domination is sustained
by being represented as legitimate or as eminently just and worthy of respect. For instance,
by legitimizing the school system as just and meritocratic, as giving everyone the same
opportunity for success, the dominant culture hides the truth of the hidden curriculum—
the fact that those whom schooling helps most are those who come from the most affluent
families. *Dissimulation* results when relations of domination are concealed, denied, or
obscured in various ways. For instance, the practice of institutionalized tracking in schools
purports to help better meet the needs of groups of students with varying academic ability.
However, describing tracking in this way helps to cloak its socially reproductive function:
that of sorting students according to their social class location. *Fragmentation* occurs when
relations of domination are sustained by the production of meanings in a way which
fragments groups so that they are placed in opposition to one another. For instance, when
conservative educational critics explain the declining standards in American education as a
result of trying to accomodate low income minority students, this sometimes results in a
backlash against immigrant students by other subordinate groups. This "divide and rule"
tactic prevents oppressed groups from working together to secure collectively their rights.
Reification occurs when transitory historical states of affairs are presented as permanent,
natural and commonsensical—as if they exist outside of time.[18] This has occurred to a
certain extent with the current call for a national curriculum based on acquiring information about the "great books" so as to have a greater access to the dominant culture. These
works are revered as high status knowledge since purportedly the force of history has
heralded them as such and placed them on book lists in respected cultural institutions
such as universities. Here literacy becomes a weapon that can be used against those groups
who are "culturally illiterate," whose social class, race, or gender renders their own experiences and stories as too unimportant to be worthy of investigation. That is, as a pedagogical tool, a stress on the great books often deflects attention away from the personal
experiences of students and the political nature of everyday life. Teaching the great books is
also a way of inculcating certain values and sets of behaviors in social groups, thereby
solidifying the existing social hierarchy. The most difficult task in analyzing these negative
functions of ideology is to unmask those ideological properties which insinuate themselves
within reality as their fundamental components. Ideological functions which barricade
themselves within the realm of commonsense often manage to disguise the grounds of
their operations.

At this point it should be clear that ideology represents a vocabulary of standardization
and a grammar of design sanctioned and sustained by particular social practices. All ideas
and systems of thought organize a rendition of reality according to their own metaphors,
narratives, and rhetoric. There is no "deep structure," totalizing logic, or grand theory
pristine in form and innocent in effects which is altogether uncontaminated by interest,
value, or judgement—in short, by *ideology*. There is no privileged sanctuary separate from
culture and politics where we can be free to distinguish truth from opinion, fact from
value, or image from interpretation. There is no "objective" environment that is not
stamped with social presence.

If we all can agree that as individuals, we inherit a preexisting sign community, and
acknowledge that all ideas, values, and meanings have social roots and perform social
functions, then understanding ideology becomes a matter of investigating *which* concepts,
values, and meanings *obscure* our understanding of the social world and our place within
the networks of power/knowledge relations, and which concepts, values, and meanings

clarify such an understanding. In other words, why do certain ideological formations cause us to misrecognize our complicity in establishing or maintaining asymmetrical relations of power and privilege within the sociocultural order?

The *dominant ideology* refers to patterns of beliefs and values shared by the majority of individuals. The majority of Americans—rich and poor alike—share the belief that capitalism is a better system than democratic socialism, for instance, or that men are generally more capable of holding positions of authority than women, or that women should be more passive and housebound. Here, we must recognize that the economic system requires the ideology of consumer capitalism to naturalize it, rendering it common-sensical. The ideology of patriarchy also is necessary to keep the nature of the economy safe and secured within the prevailing hegemony. We have been "fed" these dominant ideologies for decades through the mass media, the schools, and through family socialization.

Oppositional ideologies do exist, however, which attempt to challenge the dominant ideologies and shatter existing stereotypes. On some occasions, the dominant culture is able to manipulate alternative and oppositional ideologies in such a way that hegemony can be more effectively secured. For instance, *The Cosby Show* on commercial television carries a message that a social avenue now exists in America for blacks to be successful doctors and lawyers. This positive view of blacks, however, masks the fact that most blacks in the United States exist in a subordinate position to the dominant white culture with respect to power and privilege. The dominant culture secures hegemony by transmitting and legitimating ideologies like that in *The Cosby Show*, which reflect and shape popular resistance to stereotypes, but which in reality do little to challenge the real basis of power of the ruling dominant groups.

The dominant ideology often encourages oppositional ideologies and tolerates those that challenge their own rationale, since by absorbing these contradictory values, they are more often than not able to domesticate the conflicting and contradictory values. This is because the hegemonic hold of the social system is so strong, it can generally withstand dissension and actually come to neutralize it by permitting token opposition. During my teaching days in the suburban ghetto, school dances in the gym often celebrated the values, meanings, and pleasure of life on the street—some of which could be considered oppositional—but were tolerated by the administration because they helped diffuse tension in the school. They afforded the students some symbolic space for a limited amount of time; yet they redressed nothing concrete in terms of the lived subordination of the students and their families on a day-to-day basis.

The main question for teachers attempting to become aware of the ideologies that inform their own teaching is: How have certain pedagogical practices become so habitual or natural in school settings that teachers accept them as normal, unproblematic, and expected? How often, for instance, do teachers question school practices such as tracking, ability grouping, competitive grading, teacher-centered pedagogical approaches, and the use of rewards and punishments as control devices? The point here is to understand that these practices are not carved in stone; but are, in reality, socially constructed. How, then, is the distilled wisdom of traditional educational theorizing ideologically structured? What constitutes the origins and legitimacy of the pedagogical practices within this tradition? To what extent do such pedagogical practices serve to empower the student, and to what extent do they work as forms of social control that support, stabilize, and legitimate the role of the teacher as a moral gatekeeper of the state? What are the functions and effects of the systematic imposition of ideological perspectives on classroom teaching practices?

In my classroom journal, what characterized the ideological basis of my own teaching practices? How did "being schooled" both enable and contain the subjectivities of the students? I am using the word "subjectivity" here to mean forms of knowledge that are both conscious and unconscious and which express our identity as human agents. Subjectivity relates to everyday knowledge in its socially constructed and historically produced forms. Following this, we can ask: How do the dominant ideological practices of teachers help to structure the subjectivities of students? What are the possible consequences of this, for good and for ill?

Prejudice

Prejudice is the negative prejudgment of individuals and groups on the basis of unrecognized, unsound, and inadequate evidence. Because these negative attitudes occur so frequently, they take on a commonsense or ideological character that is often used to justify acts of discrimination.

Critical Pedagogy and the Power/Knowledge Relation

Critical pedagogy is fundamentally concerned with understanding the relationship between power and knowledge. The dominant curriculum separates knowledge from the issue of power and treats it in an unabashedly technical manner; knowledge is seen in overwhelmingly instrumental terms as something to be mastered. That knowledge is always an ideological construction linked to particular interests and social relations generally receives little consideration in education programs.

The work of the French philosopher Michel Foucault is crucial in understanding the socially constructed nature of truth and its inscription in knowledge/power relations. Foucault's concept of "power/knowledge" extends the notion of power beyond its conventional use by philosophers and social theorists who, like American John Dewey, have understood power as "the sum of conditions available for bringing the desirable end into existence."[19] For Foucault, power comes from everywhere, from above and from below; it is "always already there" and is inextricably implicated in the micro-relations of domination and resistance.

Discourse

Power relations are inscribed in what Foucault refers to as *discourse* or a family of concepts. Discourses are made up of discursive practices that he describes as

> a body of anonymous, historical rules, always determined in the time and space that have defined a given period, and for a given social, economic, geographical, or linguistic area, the conditions of operation of the enunciative function.[20]

Discursive practices, then, *refer to the rules by which discourses are formed, rules that govern what can be said and what must remain unsaid, who can speak with authority and who must listen.* Social and political institutions, such as schools and penal institutions, are governed by discursive practices.

> Discursive practices are not purely and simply ways of producing discourse. They are embodied in technical processes, in institutions, in patterns for general behavior, in forms of transmission and diffusion, and pedagogical forms which, at once, impose and maintain them.[21]

For education, discourse can be defined as a "regulated system of statements" that establish differences between fields and theories of teacher education; it is "not simply words but is embodied in the practice of institutions, patterns of behavior, and in forms of pedagogy."[22]

From this perspective, we can consider *dominant* discourses (those produced by the dominant culture) as "regimes of truth," as general economies of power/knowledge, or as multiple forms of constraint. In a classroom setting, dominant educational discourses determine what books we may use, what classroom approaches we should employ (mastery learning, Socratic method, etc.), and what values and beliefs we should transmit to our students.

For instance, neo-conservative discourses on language in the classroom would view working-class speech as undersocialized or deprived. Liberal discourse would view such speech as merely different. Similarly, to be culturally literate within a conservative discourse is to acquire basic information on American culture (dates of battles, passages of the Constitution, etc.). Conservative discourse focuses mostly on the works of "great men." A liberal discourse on cultural literacy includes knowledge generated from the perspective of women and minorities. A *critical* discourse focuses on the interests and assumptions that inform the generation of knowledge itself. A critical discourse is also self-critical and deconstructs dominant discourses the moment they are ready to achieve hegemony. A critical discourse can, for instance, explain how high status knowledge (the great works of the Western world) can be used to teach concepts that reinforce the status quo. Discourses and discursive practices influence how we live our lives as conscious thinking subjects. They shape our subjectivities (our ways of understanding in relation to the world) because it is only in language and through discourse that social reality can be given meaning. Not all discourses are given the same weight, as some will account for and justify the appropriateness of the status quo and others will provide a context for resisting social and institutional practices.[23]

This follows our earlier discussion that knowledge (truth) is socially constructed, culturally mediated, and historically situated. Cleo Cherryholmes suggests that "dominant discourses determine what counts as true, important, relevant, and what gets spoken. Discourses are generated and governed by rules and power."[24] Truth cannot be spoken in the absence of power relations, and each relation necessarily speaks its own truth. Foucault removes truth from the realm of the absolute; truth is understood only as changes in the determination of what can count as true.

> Truth is a thing of this world: it is produced only by virtue of multiple forms of constraint. And it induces regular effects of power. Each society has its regime of truth, its "general politics" of truth: that is, the types of discourse which it accepts and makes function as true; the mechanisms and instances which enable one to distinguish true and false statements, the means by which each is sanctioned; the techniques and procedures accorded value in the acquisition of truth; the status of those who are charged with saying what counts as true.[25]

In Foucault's view, truth (educational truth, scientific truth, religious truth, legal truth, or whatever) must not be understood as a set of "discovered laws" that exist outside power/knowledge relations and which somehow correspond with the "real." We cannot "know" truth except through its "effects." Truth is not *relative* (in the sense of "truths" proclaimed by various individuals and societies are all equal in their effects) but is *relational* (statements considered "true" are dependent upon history, cultural context, and relations of power operative in a given society, discipline, institution, etc.). The crucial question here is that if truth is *relational* and not *absolute*, what criteria can we use to guide our actions in the world? Critical educators argue that *praxis* (informed actions) must be guided by *phronesis* (the disposition to act truly and rightly). This means, in critical terms, that actions and knowledge must be directed at eliminating pain, oppression, and inequality, and at promoting justice and freedom.

Lawrence Grossberg speaks to the critical perspective on truth and theory when he argues

> the truth of a theory can only be defined by its ability to intervene into, to give us a different and perhaps better ability to come to grips with, the relations that constitute its context. If neither history nor texts speak its own truth, truth has to be won; and it is, consequently, inseparable from relations of power.[26]

An understanding of the power/knowledge relationship raises important issues regarding what kinds of theories educators should work with and what knowledge they can provide in order to empower students. *Empowerment* means not only helping students to understand and engage the world around them, but also enabling them to exercise the kind of courage needed to change the social order where necessary. Teachers need to recognize that *power relations correspond to forms of school knowledge that distort understanding and produce what is commonly accepted as "truth"*. Critical educators argue that knowledge should be analyzed on the basis of whether it is oppressive and exploitative, and not on the basis of whether it is "true." For example, what kind of knowledge do we construct about women and minority groups in school texts? Do the texts we use in class promote stereotypical views that reinforce racist, sexist, and patriarchal attitudes? How do we treat the knowledge that working-class students bring to class discussions and schoolwork? Do we unwittingly devalue such knowledge and thereby disconfirm the voices of these students?

Knowledge should be examined not only for the ways in which it might misrepresent or mediate social reality, but also for the ways in which it actually reflects the daily struggle of people's lives. We must understand that knowledge not only distorts reality, but also provides grounds for understanding the actual conditions that inform everyday life. Teachers, then, should examine knowledge both for the way it misrepresents or marginalizes particular views of the world and for the way it provides a deeper understanding of how the student's world is actually constructed. Knowledge acquired in classrooms should help students participate in vital issues that affect their experience on a daily level rather than simply enshrine the values of business pragmatism. School knowledge should have a more emancipatory goal than churning out workers (human capital) and helping schools become the citadel of corporate ideology.[27] School knowledge should help create the conditions productive for student self-determination in the larger society.

Critical Pedagogy and the Curriculum

From the perspective of critical educational theorists, the curriculum represents much more than a program of study, a classroom text, or a course syllabus. Rather, it represents the *introduction to a particular form of life; it serves in part to prepare students for dominant or subordinate positions in the existing society*.[28] The curriculum favors certain forms of knowledge over others and affirms the dreams, desires, and values of select groups of students over other groups, often discriminatorily on the basis of race, class, and gender. In general, critical educational theorists are concerned with how descriptions, discussions, and representations in textbooks, curriculum materials, course content, and social relations embodied in classroom practices benefit dominant groups and exclude subordinate ones. In this regard, they often refer to the *hidden curriculum.*

The Hidden Curriculum

The *hidden curriculum* refers to *the unintended outcomes of the schooling process.* Critical educators recognize that schools shape students both through standardized learning situations, and through other agendas including rules of conduct, classroom organization, and the informal pedagogical procedures used by teachers with specific groups of students.[29] The hidden curriculum also includes teaching and learning styles that are emphasized in the classroom, the messages that get transmitted to the student by the total physical and instructional environment, governance structures, teacher expectations, and grading procedures.

The hidden curriculum deals with the tacit ways in which knowledge and behavior get constructed, outside the usual course materials and formally scheduled lessons. It is a part of the bureaucratic and managerial "press" of the school—the combined forces by which students are induced to comply with dominant ideologies and social practices related to authority, behavior, and morality. Does the principal expel school offenders or just verbally upbraid them? Is the ethos of the office inviting or hostile? Do the administration and teachers show respect for each other and for the students on a regular basis? Answers to these questions help define the hidden curriculum, which refers then, to the *non-subject-related* sets of behaviors produced in students.

Often, the hidden curriculum displaces the professed educational ideals and goals of the classroom teacher or school. We know, for example, that teachers unconsciously give more intellectual attention, praise, and academic help to boys than to girls. A study reported in *Psychology Today* suggests that stereotypes of garrulous and gossipy women are so strong that when groups of administrators and teachers are shown films of classroom discussion and asked who is talking more, the teachers overwhelmingly choose the girls. In reality, however, the boys in the film "out talk" the girls at a ratio of three to one. The same study also suggests that teachers behave differently depending on whether boys or girls respond during classroom discussions. When boys call out comments without raising their hands, for instance, teachers generally accept their answers; girls, however, are reprimanded for the same behavior. The hidden message is "Boys should be academically aggressive while girls should remain composed and passive." In addition, teachers are twice as likely to give male students detailed instructions on how to do things for themselves; with female students, however, teachers are more likely to do the task for them instead. Not surprisingly, the boys are being taught independence and the girls dependency.[30]

Classroom sexism as a function of the hidden curriculum results in the unwitting and unintended granting of power and privilege to men over women and accounts for many of the following outcomes:

- Although girls start school ahead of boys in reading and basic computation, by the time they graduate from high school, boys have higher SAT scores in both areas.

- By high school, some girls are less committed to careers, although their grades and achievement-test scores may be as good as boys. Many girls' interests turn to marriage or stereotypically female jobs. Some women may feel that men disapprove of women using their intelligence.
- Girls are less likely to take math and science courses and to participate in special or gifted programs in these subjects, even if they have a talent for them. They are also more likely to believe that they are incapable of pursuing math and science in college and to avoid the subjects.
- Girls are more likely to attribute failure to internal factors, such as ability, rather than to external factors, such as luck.

The sexist communication game is played at work, as well as at school. As reported in numerous studies it goes like this:

- Men speak more often and frequently interrupt women.
- Listeners recall more from male speakers than from female speakers, even when both use a similar speaking style and cover identical content.
- Women participate less actively in conversation. They do more smiling and gazing; they're more often the passive bystanders in professional and social conversations among peers.
- Women often transform declarative statements into tentative comments. This is accomplished by using qualifiers ("kind of" or "I guess") and by adding tag questions ("This is a good movie, isn't it?"). These tentative patterns weaken impact and signal a lack of power and influence.[31]

Of course, most teachers try hard not to be sexist. The hidden curriculum continues to operate, however, despite what the overt curriculum prescribes. The hidden curriculum can be effectively compared to what Australian educator Doug White calls the *multinational curriculum*. For White,

> [T]he multinational curriculum is the curriculum of disembodied universals, of the mind as an information-processing machine, of concepts and skills without moral and social judgment but with enormous manipulative power. That curriculum proposed the elevation of abstract skills over particular content, of universal cognitive principles over the actual conditions of life.[32]

White reminds us that no curriculum, policy, or program is ideologically or politically innocent, and that the concept of the curriculum is inextricably related to issues of social class, culture, gender, and power. This is, of course, not the way curriculum is traditionally understood and discussed in teacher education. The hidden curriculum, then, refers to learning outcomes not openly acknowledged to learners. But we must remember that not all values, attitudes, or patterns of behavior that are by-products of the hidden curriculum in educational settings are necessarily bad. The point is to identify the structural and political assumptions upon which the hidden curriculum rests and to attempt to change the institutional arrangements of the classroom so as to offset the most undemocratic and oppressive outcomes.

Curriculum as a Form of Cultural Politics

Critical educational theorists view curriculum as a form of *cultural politics*, that is, as a part of the sociocultural dimension of the schooling process. The term cultural politics permits the educational theorist to highlight the political consequences of interaction between teachers and students who come from dominant and subordinate cultures. To view the curriculum as a form of cultural politics *assumes that the social, cultural, political and economic dimensions are the primary categories for understanding contemporary schooling.*[33]

School life is understood not as a unitary, monolithic, and ironclad system of rules and regulations, but as a cultural terrain characterized by varying degrees of accommodation, contestation, and resistance. Furthermore, school life is understood as a plurality of conflicting languages and struggles, a place where classroom and street-corner cultures collide and where teachers, students, and school administrators often differ as to how school experiences and practices are to be defined and understood.

This curriculum perspective creates conditions for the student's self-empowerment as an active political and moral subject. I am using the term *empowerment* to refer to the process through which students learn to critically appropriate knowledge existing outside their immediate experience in order to broaden their understanding of themselves, the world, and the possibilities for transforming the taken-for-granted assumptions about the way we live. Stanley Aronowitz has described one aspect of empowerment as "the process of appreciating and loving oneself;"[34] empowerment is gained from knowledge and social relations that dignify one's own history, language, and cultural traditions. But empowerment means more than self-confirmation. It also refers to the process by which students learn to question and selectively appropriate those aspects of the dominant culture that will provide them with the basis for defining and transforming, rather than merely serving, the wider social order.

Basing a curriculum on cultural politics consists of linking critical social theory to a set of stipulated practices through which teachers can dismantle and critically examine dominant educational and cultural traditions. Many of these traditions have fallen prey to an *instrumental rationality* (a way of looking at the world in which "ends" are subordinated to questions of "means" and in which "facts" are separated from questions of "value") that either limits or ignores democratic ideals and principles. Critical theorists want particularly to develop a language of critique and demystification that can be used to analyze those latent interests and ideologies that work to socialize students in a manner compatible with the dominant culture. Of equal concern, however, is the creation of alternative teaching practices capable of empowering students both inside and outside of schools.

Critical Pedagogy and Social Reproduction

Over the decades, critical educational theorists have tried to fathom how schools are implicated in the process of *social reproduction*. In other words, they have attempted to explore how schools *perpetuate or reproduce the social relationships and attitudes needed to sustain the existing dominant economic and class relations of the larger society.*[35] Social reproduction refers to the intergenerational reproduction of social class (i.e., working-class students become working-class adults; middle-class students become middle-class adults). Schools reproduce the structures of social life through the colonization (socialization) of student subjectivities and by establishing social practices characteristic of the wider society.

Critical educators ask: How do schools help transmit the status and class positions of the wider society? The answers, of course, vary enormously. Some of the major mechanisms of social reproduction include the allocation of students into private versus public schools, the socioeconomic composition of school communities, and the placement of students into curriculum tracks within schools.[36] A group of social reproduction theorists, known as *correspondence theorists*, have attempted to show how schools reflect wider social inequalities.[37] In a famous study by Bowles and Gintis (1976), the authors argue in deterministic terms that there is a *relatively simple correspondence between schooling, class, family, and social inequalities*. Bowles and Gintis maintain that children of parents with upper socioeconomic standing most often achieve upper socioeconomic status while children of lower socioeconomic parents acquire a correspondingly low socioeconomic standing. However, schooling structures are not always successful in ensuring privilege for the students' advantaged class positions. The correspondence theorists *could not explain why some children cross over from the status of their parents*. Social reproduction, as it turns out, is more than simply a case of economic and class position; it also involves social, cultural, and linguistic factors.

This brings into the debate the *conflict* or *resistance theorists*, such as Henry Giroux and Paul Willis, who pay significantly more attention to the *partial autonomy* of the school culture and to the role of conflict and contradiction within the reproductive process itself.[38] *Theories of resistance* generally draw upon an understanding of the complexities of culture to define the relationship between schools and the dominant society. Resistance theorists challenge the school's ostensible role as a democratic institution that functions to improve the social position of all students—including, if not especially, those groups that are subordinated to the system. Resistance theorists question the processes by which the school system reflects and sustains the logic of capital as well as dominant social practices and structures that are found in a class, race, and gender divided society.

One of the major contributions to resistance theory has been the discovery by British researcher Paul Willis that working-class students who engage in classroom episodes of resistance often implicate themselves even further in their own domination.[39] Willis's group of working-class schoolboys, known as "the lads," resisted the class-based oppression of the school by rejecting mental labor in favor of more "masculine" manual labor (which reflected the shop floor culture of their family members). In so doing, they ironically displaced the school's potential to help them escape the shop floor once they graduated. Willis's work presents a considerable advance in understanding social and cultural reproduction in the context of student resistance. Social reproduction certainly exceeds mobility for each class, and we know that a substantial amount of class mobility is unlikely in most school settings. The work of the resistance theorists has helped us understand how domination works, even though students continually reject the ideology that is helping to oppress them. Sometimes this resistance only helps secure to an even greater degree the eventual fate of these students.

How, then, can we characterize student resistance? Students resist instruction for many reasons. As Giroux reminds us, not all acts of student misbehavior are acts of resistance. In fact, such "resistance" may simply be repressive moments (sexist, racist) inscribed by the dominant culture.[40] I have argued that the major drama of resistance in schools is an effort on the part of students to bring their street-corner culture into the classroom. Students reject the culture of classroom learning because, for the most part, it is delibidinalized (eros-denying) and is infused with a cultural capital to which subordinate groups have little legitimate access. Resistance to school instruction represents a resolve on the part of students not to be dissimulated in the face of oppression; it is a fight against the erasure of their street-corner identities. To resist means to fight against the monitoring of passion and desire. It is, furthermore, a struggle against the capitalist symbolization of the flesh. By this I mean that students resist turning themselves into worker commodities in which their potential is evaluated only as future members of the labor force. At the same time, however, the images of success manufactured by the dominant culture seem out of reach for most of them.

Students resist the "dead time" of school, where interpersonal relationships are reduced to the imperatives of market ideology. Resistance, in other words, is a rejection of their reformulation as docile objects where spontaneity is replaced by efficiency and productivity, in compliance with the needs of the corporate marketplace. Accordingly, students' very bodies become sites of struggle, and resistance a way of gaining power, celebrating pleasure, and fighting oppression in the lived historicity of the moment.

What, then, are the "regimes of truth" that organize school time, subject matter, pedagogical practice, school values, and personal truth? How does the culture of the school organize the body and monitor passion through its elaborate system of surveillance? How are forms of social control inscripted into the flesh? How are students' subjectivities and social identities produced discursively by institutionalized power, and how is this institutional power at the same time produced by the legitimization of discourses that treat students as if they were merely repositories of lust and passion (the degenerative animal instincts)? How is reason privileged over passion so that it can be used to quell the "crude mob mentality" of students? What is the range of identities available within a system of education designed to produce, regulate, and distribute character, govern gesture, dictate values, and police desire? To what extent does an adherence to the norms of the school mean that students will have to give up the dignity and status maintained through psychosocial adaptations to life on the street? To what extent does compliance with the rituals and norms of school mean that students have to forfeit their identity as members of an ethnic group? These are all questions that theorists within the critical tradition have attempted to answer. And the answers are as various as they are important.

Some versions of student resistance are undoubtedly romantic: The teachers are villains, and the students are anti-heroes. I am not interested in teacher-bashing, nor in resurrecting the resistant student as the new James Dean or Marlon Brando. I much prefer the image of Giroux's resisting intellectual, someone who questions prevailing norms and established regimes of truth in the manner of a Rosa Luxemburg or a Jean-Paul Sartre.[41]

I would like to stress an important point. Our culture in general (and that includes schools, the media, and our social institutions) has helped educate students to acquire a veritable passion for ignorance. The French psycho-analyst Jacques Lacan suggests that ignorance is not a passive state but rather an active excluding from consciousness. The passion for ignorance that has infected our culture demands a complex explanation, but part of it can be attributed, as Lacan suggests, to *a refusal to acknowledge that our subjectivities have been constructed out of the information and social practices that surround us.*[42] Ignorance, as part of the very structure of knowledge, can teach us something. But we lack the critical constructs with which to recover that knowledge *which we choose not to know.* Unable to find meaningful knowledge "out there" in the world of prepackaged commodities, students resort to random violence or an intellectual purple haze where anything more challenging than the late night news is met with retreat, or despair; and of course, it is the dominant culture that benefits most from this epidemic of conceptual anesthesia. The fewer critical intellectuals around to challenge its ideals, the better.

What do all these theories of resistance mean for the classroom teacher? Do we disregard resistance? Do we try to ignore it? Do we always take the student's side?

The answers to these questions are not easy. But let me sketch out the bare bones of a possible answer. First of all, schooling should be a process of understanding how subjectivities are produced. It should be a process of examining how we have been constructed out of the prevailing ideas, values, and worldviews of the dominant culture. The point to remember is that if we have been made, then we can be "unmade" and "made over". What are some alternative models with which we can begin to repattern ourselves and our social order? Teachers need to encourage students to be self-reflexive about these questions and to provide students with a conceptual framework to begin to answer them. Teaching and learning should be a process of *inquiry*, of critique; it should also be a process of *constructing*, of building a social imagination that works within a language of hope. If teaching is cast in the form of what Henry Giroux refers to as a "language of possibility," then a greater potential exists for making learning relevant, critical, and transformative. Knowledge is relevant only when it begins with the experiences students bring with them from the surrounding culture; it is critical only when these experiences are shown to sometimes be problematic (i.e., racist, sexist); and it is transformative only when students begin to use the knowledge to help empower others, including individuals in the surrounding community. Knowledge then becomes linked to social reform. An understanding of the language of the self can help us better negotiate with the world. It can also help us begin to forge the basis of *social transformation:* the building of a better world, the altering of the very ground upon which we live and work.

Teachers can do no better than to create agendas of possibility in their classrooms. Not every student will want to take part, but many will. Teachers may have personal problems—and so may students—that will limit the range of classroom discourses. Some teachers may simply be unwilling to function as critical educators. Critical pedagogy does not guarantee that resistance will not take place. But it does provide teachers with the foundations for understanding resistance, so that whatever pedagogy is developed can be sensitive to sociocultural conditions that construct resistance, lessening the chance that students will be blamed as the sole, originating source of resistance. No emancipatory pedagogy will ever be built out of theories of behavior which view students as lazy, defiant, lacking in ambition, or genetically inferior. A much more penetrating solution is to try to understand the structures of mediation in the sociocultural world that form student resistance. In other words, what is the larger picture? We must remove the concept of student resistance from the preserve of the behaviorist or the depth psychologist and insert it instead into the terrain of social theory.

Cultural Capital

Resistance theorists such as Henry Giroux focus on *cultural reproduction* as a function of class based differences in *cultural capital.* The concept of *cultural capital,* made popular by French sociologist Pierre Bourdieu, refers to the general cultural background, knowledge, disposition, and skills that are passed on from one generation to another. Cultural capital represents *ways of talking, acting, modes of style, moving, socializing, forms of knowledge, language practices, and values.* Cultural capital can exist in the embodied state, as long-lasting dispositions of the mind and body; in the objectified state, as cultural artifacts such as pictures, books, diplomas, and other material objects; and in the institutionalized state, which confers original properties on the cultural capital which it guarantees. For instance, to many teachers, the cultural traits exhibited by students—e.g., tardiness, sincerity, honesty, thrift, industriousness, politeness, a certain way of dressing, speaking, and gesturing—appear as natural qualities emerging from an individual's "inner essence". However, such traits are to a great extent culturally inscribed and are often linked to the social class standing of individuals who exhibit them. Social capital refers to the collectively owned economic and cultural capital of a group.[43] Taking linguistic competency as just one example of cultural capital, theorists such as Basil Bernstein contend that class membership and family socialization generate distinctive speech patterns. Working-class students learn "restricted" linguistic codes while middle-class children use "elaborated" codes. This means that the speech of working-class and middle-class children is generated by underlying regulative principles that govern their choice and combination of words and sentence structures. These, according to Bernstein, have been learned primarily in the course of family socialization.[44] Critical theorists argue that schools generally affirm and reward students who exhibit the elaborately coded "middle-class" speech while disconfirming and devaluing students who use restricted "working-class" coded speech.

Students from the dominant culture inherit substantially different cultural capital than do economically disadvantaged students, and schools generally value and reward those who exhibit that dominant cultural capital (which is also usually exhibited by the teacher). Schools systematically *devalue* the cultural capital of students who occupy subordinate class positions. Cultural capital is reflective of material capital and replaces it as a form of symbolic currency that enters into the exchange system of the school. Cultural capital is therefore symbolic of the social structure's economic force and becomes in itself a productive force in the reproduction of social relations under capitalism. Academic performance represents, therefore, not individual competence or the lack of ability on the part of disadvantaged students but *the school's depreciation of their cultural capital*. The end result is that the school's academic credentials remain indissolubly linked to an unjust system of trading in cultural capital which is eventually transformed into *economic* capital, as working-class students become less likely to get high-paying jobs.

When I worked with students in my suburban ghetto classroom, those whose cultural capital most closely resembled my own were the students with whom I initially felt most comfortable, spent the most instructional time, and most often encouraged to work in an independent manner. I could relate more readily and positively—at least at the beginning—to those students whose manners, values, and competencies resembled my own. Teachers—including myself—easily spotted Buddy, T. J., and Duke as members of the economically disadvantaged underclass, and this often worked against them, especially with teachers who registered such students as intellectually or socially deficient. Intellectual and social deficiencies had little, if anything, to do with their behavior. Class-specific character traits and social practices did.

Notes

1. The sources for this section are as follows: Bertell Oilman, "The Meaning of Dialectics," *Monthly Review* (1986, November): 42–55; Wilfrid Carr and Stephen Kemmis, *Becoming Critical: Knowing Through Action Research* (Victoria: Deakin University, 1983); Stephen Kemmis and Lindsay Fitzclarence, *Curriculum Theorizing: Beyond Reproduction Theory* (Victoria: Deakin University, 1986); Henry A. Giroux, *Ideology, Culture and the Process of Schooling* (Philadelphia: Temple University Press and London: Falmer Press, Ltd., 1981); Ernst Bloch, "The Dialectical Method," *Man and World* 16 (1983): 281–313.

2. Kemmis and Fitzclarence, *Curriculum Theorizing* 36–37.

3. McLaren, *Schooling as a Ritual Performance.* London: Routledge, 1986.

4. This discussion of micro and macro objectives is taken from Henry A. Giroux, "Overcoming Behavioral and Humanistic Objectives," *The Education Forum* (1979, May): 409–419. Also, Henry A. Giroux, *Teachers as Intellectuals: Towards a Critical Pedagogy of Practical Learning* (South Hadley, MA: Bergin and Garvey Publishers, 1988).

5. See Jürgen Habermas, *Knowledge and Human Interests*, trans. J. J. Shapiro (London: Heinemann, 1972); see also Jürgen Habermas, *Theory and Practice*, trans. J. Viertel (London: Heinemann, 1974). As cited in Kemmis and Fitzclarence, *Curriculum Theorizing*, 70–72.

6. For a fuller discussion of culture, see Enid Lee, *Letters to Marcia: A Teacher's Guide to Anti-Racist Teaching* (Toronto: Cross Cultural Communication Centre, 1985).

7. Henry A. Giroux and Peter McLaren, "Teacher Education and the Politics of Engagement: The Case for Democratic Schooling," *Harvard Educational Review* 56 (1986): 3,232–233. Developed from Giroux's previous work.

8. For this discussion of culture, I am indebted to Raymond A. Calluori, "The Kids are Alright: New Wave Subcultural Theory," *Social Text* 4, 3 (1985): 43–53; Mike Brake, *The Sociology of Youth Culture and Youth Subculture* (London: Routledge and Kegan Paul, 1980); Graham Murdock, "Mass Communication and the Construction of Meaning," in N. Armstead (Ed.) *Reconstructing Social Psychology* (Harmondsworth: Penguin, 1974); Dick Hebidge, *Subculture: The Meaning of Style* (London and New York: Methuen, 1979); Ian Connell, D. J. Ashenden, S. Kessler and G. W. Dowsett, *Making the Difference: Schooling, Families and Social Division* (Sydney, Australia: George Allen and Unwin, 1982). Also: Stuart Hall and Tony Jefferson, *Resistance Through Rituals: Youth Subcultures in Post War Britain* (London: Hutchinson and the Centre for Contemporary Cultural Studies, University of Birmingham, 1980).

9. John Muncie, "Pop Culture, Pop Music and Post-War Youth Subcultures," *Popular Culture*. Block 5 Units 18 and 19/20, The Open University Press (1981): 31–62.

10. Muncie, "Pop Culture," 76.

11. The section on hegemony draws on the following sources: Giroux, *Ideology, Culture and the Process of Schooling*, 22–26; *Popular Culture* (1981), a second level course at The Open University, Milton Keynes, England, published by The Open University Press and distributed in the United States by Taylor and Francis (Philadelphia, PA). Several booklets in this series were instrumental in developing the sections on ideology and hegemony: Geoffrey Bourne, "Meaning, Image and Ideology," *Form and Meaning I*, Open University Press, Block 4, Units 13, 15, and 15, 37–65; see also Tony Bennett, "Popular Culture: Defining Our Terms," *Popular Culture. Themes and Issues I*, Block 1, Units 1 and 2, 77–87; Tony Bennett, "Popular Culture: History and Theory," *Popular Culture: Themes and Issues II*, Block 1, Unit 3, 29–32. Another important source is a booklet for a third level course at The Open University: *The Politics of Cultural Production*, The Open University Press, 1981. Relevant sections include: Geoff Whiny, "Ideology, Politics and Curriculum," 7–52; David Davies, "Popular Culture, Class and Schooling," 53–108. See also P. J. Hills, *A Dictionary of Education* (London: Routledge and Kegan Paul, 1982), 166–167; and Raymond Williams, *Keywords: A Vocabulary of Culture and Society* (London: Fontana, 1983), 144–146.

12. William Ryan, *Blaming the Victim* (New York: Vintage Books, 1976).

13. Todd Gitlin, *The Whole World is Watching: Mass Media in the Making and Unmaking of the New Left* (Berkeley and London: University of California Press, 1980), 253–254.

14. Gore Vidal, *Monthly Review* 19 (1986, October), as cited in Allen Fenichel "Alternative Economic Policies," *The Ecumenist* 25, 4 (1987, May–June): 49.

15. For this section on ideology, I am indebted to Henry A. Giroux, *Theory and Resistance in Education: Pedagogy for the Opposition* (South Hadley, MA: Bergin and Garvey, 1983), 143. See also Stanley Aronowitz and Henry A. Giroux, *Education Under Siege* (South Hadley, MA: Bergin and Garvey, 1985); Douglas Kellner, "Ideology, Marxism, and Advanced Capitalism," *Socialist Review* 8, 6 (1978): 38; Gibson Winter, *Liberating Creation: Foundations of Religious Social Ethics* (New York: Crossroad, 1981), 97. See also: Geoff Whiny, "Ideology, Politics and Curriculum," 7–52 and David Davies, "Popular Culture, Class and Schooling," 53–108; Williams, *Keywords*, 153–157; Tony Bennett, "Popular Culture: Defining our Terms," 77–87; and Geoffrey Bourne, "Meaning, Image and Ideology," 37–53.

16. James Donald and Stuart Hall, "Introduction," in S. Donald and S. Hall (Eds.), *Politics and Ideology* (Milton Keynes: Philadelphia, Open University Press, 1986), ix–x.

17. Donald and Hall, *Politics and Ideology*, x.

18. John Thompson, "Language and Ideology," *The Sociological Review* 35, 3 (1987, Aug.): 516–536.

19. John Dewey, in J. Ratner (Ed.), *Intelligence in the Modern World: John Dewey's Philosophy* (New York: The Modern Library, 1939), 784. See also Michael Foucault *Power/Knowledge*, in C. Gordon (Ed.), (L. Marshall, J. Mepham, and K. Spoer, Trans.), *Selected Interviews and Other Writings 1972–77* (New York: Pantheon, 1980), 187.

20. Michael Foucault, *The Archaeology of Knowledge* (New York: Harper Colophon Books, 1972), 117.

21. Foucault, *Power/Knowledge*, 200.

22. Richard Smith and Anna Zantiotis, "Teacher Education, Cultural Politics, and the Avant-Garde," in H. Giroux and P. McLaren (Eds.), *Schooling and the Politics of Culture* (Albany, NY: SUNY Press, in press), 123.

23. See Chris Weedon, *Feminist Practice and Post-Structuralist Theory* (Oxford: Basil Blackwell, 1987).

24. Cleo Cherryholmes, "The Social Project of Curriculum: A Poststructural Analysis," *American Journal of Education* (in press): 21.

25. Foucault, *Power/Knowledge*, 131.

26. Lawrence Grossberg, "History, Politics and Postmodernism: Stuart Hall and Cultural Studies," *Journal of Communication Inquiry* 10, 2 (1987): 73.

27. For more about the relationship of power and knowledge, see Kathy Borman and Joel Spring, *Schools in Central Cities* (New York: Longman, 1984); Henry Giroux, "Public Education and the Discourse of Possibility: Rethinking the New Conservative and Left Educational Theory," *News for Teachers of Political Science* 44 (1985, Winter): 13–15.

28. See Doug White, "After the Divided Curriculum," *The Victorian Teacher* 7 (1983, March); Giroux and McLaren, "Teacher Education and the Politics of Engagement," 228.

29. See the wide range of articles in H. Giroux and D. Purple (Eds.), *The Hidden Curriculum and Moral Education: Deception or Discovery?* (Berkeley, CA: McCutchen Publishing Corp., 1983).

30. Myra Sadkev and David Sadkev, "Sexism in the Schoolroom of the '80's," *Psychology Today* (1985, March): 55–57.

31. Sadkev and Sadkev, "Sexism in the Schoolroom," 56–57. Also, the 1980 *Nova* television program, *The Pinks and the Blues* (WGBH, Boston), summarized by Anthony Wilden. "In the Penal Colony: The Body as the Discourse of the Other," *Semiotica*, 54, 1/2(1985): 73–76.

32. White, "After the Divided Curriculum," 6–9.

33. Giroux and McLaren, "Teacher Education and the Politics of Engagement," 228–229.

34. Stanley Aronowitz, "Schooling, Popular Culture, and Post-Industrial Society: Peter McLaren Interviews Stanley Aronowitz," *Orbit* (1986): 17, 18.

35. See Kemmis and Fitzclarence, *Curriculum Theorizing*, 88–89. Also, H. A. Giroux, *Ideology, Culture, and the Process of Schooling*.

36. Glenna Colclough and E. M. Beck, "The American Educational Structure and the Reproduction of Social Class," *Social Inquiry* 56, 4 (1986, Fall): 456–476.

37. Samuel Bowles and Herbert Gintis, *Schooling in Capitalist America* (New York: Basic Books, 1976); see also Kemmis and Fitzclarence, *Curriculum Theorizing*, 90; and Colclough and Beck, "The American Educational Structure," 456–476.

38. See, for instance, Peter McLaren, "The Ritual Dimensions of Resistance: Clowning and Symbolic Inversion," *Boston University Journal of Education* 167, 2 (1985): 84–97, and Giroux, *Theory and Resistance*.

39. Paul Willis, *Learning to Labour: How Working Class Kids Get Working Class Jobs* (Westmead, England: Gower, 1977).

40. Giroux, *Theory and Resistance*, 103.

41. Aronowitz and Giroux, *Education under Siege*.

42. Jacques Lacan, "Seminar XX," *Encore* (Paris: Editions du Seuil, 1975): 100. As cited in Constance Penley, "Teaching in Your Sleep: Feminism and Psychoanalysis," in C. Nelson (Ed.), *Theory in the Classroom* (Chicago: University of Chicago Press), 135.

43. Pierre Bourdieu, "Forms of Capital," in John G. Richardson (Ed.), *Handbook of Theory and Research for the Sociology of Education* (New York: Greenwood Press, 1986), 241–258. See also Henry A. Giroux, "Rethinking the Language of Schooling," *Language Arts* 61, 1 (1984, January): 36; and Henry A. Giroux, *Ideology, Culture and the Process of Schooling*, 77.

44. Paul Atkinson, *Language, Structure and Reproduction: An Introduction to the Sociology of Basil Bernstein* (London: Methuen, 1986).

4

In Search of a Critical Pedagogy

Maxine Greene

In what Jean Baudrillard describes as "the shadow of silent majorities"[1] in an administered and media-mystified world, we try to reconceive what a critical pedagogy relevant to this time and place ought to mean. This is a moment when great numbers of Americans find their expectations and hopes for their children being fed by talk of "educational reform." Yet the reform reports speak of those very children as "human resources" for the expansion of productivity, as means to the end of maintaining our nation's economic competitiveness and military primacy in the world. Of course we want to empower the young for meaningful work, we want to nurture the achievement of diverse literacies. But the world we inhabit is palpably deficient: there are unwarranted inequities, shattered communities, unfulfilled lives. We cannot help but hunger for traces of utopian visions, of critical or dialectical engagements with social and economic realities. And yet, when we reach out, we experience a kind of blankness: We sense people living under a weight, a nameless inertial mass. How are we to justify our concern for their awakening? Where are the sources of questioning, of restlessness? How are we to move the young to break with the given, the taken-for-granted—to move towards what might be, what is not yet?

Confronting all of this, I am moved to make some poets' voices audible at the start. Poets are exceptional, of course; they are not considered educators in the ordinary sense. But they remind us of absence, ambiguity, embodiments of existential possibility. More often than not they do so with passion; and passion has been called the power of possibility. This is because it is the source of our interests and our purposes. Passion signifies mood, emotion, desire: modes of grasping the appearances of things. It is one of the important ways of recognizing possibility, "the presence of the future as *that which is lacking* and that which, by its very absence, reveals reality."[2] Poets move us to give play to our imaginations, to enlarge the scope of lived experience and reach beyond from our own grounds. Poets do not give us answers; they do not solve the problems of critical pedagogy. They can, however, if we will them to do so, awaken us to reflectiveness, to a recovery of lost landscapes and lost spontaneities. Against such a background, educators might now and then be moved to go in search of a critical pedagogy of significance for themselves.

Let us hear Walt Whitman, for one:

> I am the poet of the Body and I am the poet of the Soul,
> The pleasures of heaven are with me and the pains of
> hell are with me.

The first I graft and increase upon myself, the latter
  I translate into a new tongue.
I am the poet of the woman the same as the man,
And I say it is as great to be a woman as to be a man,

I chant the chant of dilation or pride.
We have had ducking and deprecating about enough,
I show that size is only development.
Have you outstript the rest? are you the President?,
It is a trifle, they will more than arrive there every one,
   and still pass on.[3]

Whitman calls himself the poet of the "barbaric yawp"; he is also the poet of the child going forth, of the grass, of comradeship and communion and the "en masse." And of noticing, naming, caring, feeling. In a systematized, technicized moment, a moment of violations and of shrinking "minimal" selves, we ought to be able to drink from the fountain of his work.

There is Wallace Stevens, explorer of multiple perspectives and imagination, challenger of objectified, quantified realities—what he calls the "ABC of being . . . the vital, arrogant, fatal, dominant X," questioner as well of the conventional "lights and definitions" presented as "the plain sense of things." We ought to think of states of things, he says, phases of movements, polarities.

But in the centre of our lives, this time, this day,
It is a state, this spring among the politicians
Playing cards. In a village of the indigenes,
One would still have to discover. Among the dogs
  and dung,
One would continue to contend with one's ideas.[4]

One's ideas, yes, and blue guitars as well, and—always and always—"the never-resting mind," the "flawed words and stubborn sounds."

And there is Marianne Moore, reminding us that every poem represents what Robert Frost described as "the triumph of the spirit over the materialism by which we are being smothered," enunciating four precepts:

Feed imagination food that invigorates.
Whatever it is, do with all your might.
Never do to another what you would not wish done to yourself.
Say to yourself, "I will be responsible."

Put these principles to the test, and you will be inconvenienced by being overtrusted, overbefriended, overconsulted, half adopted, and have no leisure. Face that when you come to it.[5]

Another woman's voice arises: Muriel Rukeyser's, in the poem "Käthe Kollwitz."

What would happen if one woman told the truth about her life?
The world would split open[6]

The idea of an officially defined "world" splitting open when a repressed truth is revealed holds all sorts of implications for those who see reality as opaque, bland and burnished, resistant both to protest and to change.

Last, and in a different mood, let us listen to these lines by Adrienne Rich:

> A clear night in which two planets
> seem to clasp each other in which the earthly grasses
> shift like silk in starlight
>   If the mind were clear
> and if the mind were simple you could take this mind
> this particular state and say
> *This is how I would live if I could choose:*
> *this is what is possible*[7]

The poem is called "What Is Possible," but the speaker knows well that no mind can be "simple," or "abstract and pure." She realizes that the mind has "a different mission in the universe," that there are sounds and configurations still needing to be deciphered; she knows that the mind must be "wrapped in battle" in what can only be a resistant world. She voices her sense of the contrast between the mind as contemplative and the mind in a dialectical relation with what surrounds.

They create spaces, these poets, between themselves and what envelops and surrounds. Where there are spaces like that, desire arises, along with hope and expectation. We may sense that something is lacking that must be surpassed or repaired. Often, therefore, poems address our freedom; they call on us to move beyond where we are, to break with sub-mergence, to transform. To transform what—and how? To move beyond ourselves—and where? Reading such works within the contexts of schools and education, those of us still preoccupied with human freedom and human growth may well find our questions more perplexing. We may become more passionate about the possibility of a critical pedagogy in these uncritical times. How can we (decently, morally, intelligently) address ourselves both to desire and to purpose and obligation? How can we awaken others to possibility and the need for action in the name of possibility? How can we communicate the importance of opening spaces in the imagination where persons can reach beyond where they are?

Poets, of course, are not alone in the effort to make us see and to defamiliarize our commonsense worlds. The critical impulse is an ancient one in the Western tradition: we have only to recall the prisoners released from the cave in *The Republic*, Socrates trying to arouse the "sleeping ox" that was the Athenian public, Francis Bacon goading his readers to break with the "idols" that obscured their vision and distorted their rational capacities, David Hume calling for the exposure of the "sophistries and illusions" by which so many have habitually lived. In philosophy, in the arts, in the sciences, men and women repeatedly have come forward to urge their audiences to break with what William Blake called "mind-forg'd manacles." Not only did such manacles shackle consciousness; their effectiveness assured the continuing existence of systems of domination—monarchies, churches, land-holding arrangements, and armed forces of whatever kind.

The American tradition originated in such an insight and in the critical atmosphere specific to the European Enlightenment. It was an atmosphere created in large measure by rational, autonomous voices engaging in dialogue for the sake of bringing into being a public sphere. These were, most often, the voices of an emerging middle class concerned for their own independence from anachronistic and unjust restraints. Their "rights" were being trampled, they asserted, rights sanctioned by natural and moral laws. Among these rights were "life, liberty, and the pursuit of happiness," which (especially when joined to justice or equity) remain normative for this nation: they are goods *to be* secured. Liberty, at the time of the founding of our nation, meant liberation from interference by the state, church, or army in the lives of individuals. For some, sharing such beliefs as those articulated by the British philosopher John Stuart Mill, liberty also meant each person's right to think for himself or herself, "to follow his intellect to whatever conclusions it may lead" in an atmosphere that forbade "mental slavery."[8]

The founders were calling, through a distinctive critical challenge, for opportunities to give their energies free play. That meant the unhindered exercise of their particular talents: inventing, exploring, building, pursuing material and social success. To be able to do so, they had to secure power, which they confirmed through the establishment of a constitutional republic. For Hannah Arendt, this sort of power is kept in existence through an ongoing process of "binding and promising, combining and covenanting." As she saw it, power springs up between human beings when they act to constitute "a worldly structure to house, as it were, their combined power of action."[9] When we consider the numbers of people excluded from this process over the generations, we have to regard this view of power as normative as well. It is usual to affirm that power belongs to "the people" at large; but, knowing that this has not been the case, we are obligated to expand the "wordly structure" until it contains the "combined power" of increasing numbers of articulate persons. A critical pedagogy for Americans, it would seem, must take this into account.

For the school reformers of the early nineteenth century, the apparent mass power accompanying the expansion of manhood suffrage created a need for "self-control" and a "voluntary compliance" with the laws of righteousness.[10] Without a common school to promote such control and compliance, the social order might be threatened. Moreover, the other obligation of the school—to prepare the young to "create wealth"—could not be adequately met. Even while recognizing the importance of providing public education for the masses of children, we have to acknowledge that great numbers of them were being socialized into factory life and wage labor in an expanding capitalist society. Like working classes everywhere, they could not but find themselves alienated from their own productive energies. The persisting dream of opportunity, however, kept most of them from confronting their literal powerlessness. The consciousness of objectively real "open" spaces (whether on the frontier, "downtown," or out at sea) prevented them from thinking seriously about changing the order of things; theoretically, there was always an alternative, a "territory ahead."[11] It followed that few were likely to conceive of themselves in a dialectical relation with what surrounded them, no matter how exploitative or cruel. As the laggard and uneven development of trade unions indicates, few were given to viewing themselves as members of a "class" with a project to pull them forward, a role to play in history.

The appearance of utopian communities and socialist societies throughout the early nineteenth century did call repeatedly into question some of the assumptions of the American ideology, especially those having to do with individualism. The founders of the experimental colonies (Robert Owen, Frances Wright, Albert Brisbane, and others) spoke of communalism, mental freedom, the integration of physical and intellectual work, and the discovery of a common good. Socialists called for a more humane and rational social arrangement and for critical insight into what Orestes Brownson described as the "crisis as to the relation of wealth and labor." He said, "It is useless to shut our eyes to the fact and, like the ostrich, fancy ourselves secure because we have so concealed our heads that we see not the danger."[12] Important as their insights were, such people were addressing themselves to educated humanitarians whose good offices might be enlisted in improving and perfecting mankind. Critical though they were of exploitation, greed, and the division of labor, they did not speak of engaging the exploited ones in their own quests for emancipation. No particular pedagogy seemed required, and none was proposed, except within the specific contexts of utopian communities. Once a decent community or society was created, it was believed, the members would be educated in accord with its ideals.

There were, it is true, efforts to invent liberating ways of teaching for children in the larger society, although most were undertaken outside the confines of the common schools. Elizabeth Peabody and Bronson Alcott, among others, through "conversations" with actual persons in classrooms, toiled to inspire self-knowledge, creativity, and communion. Like Ralph Waldo Emerson, they were all hostile to the "joint-stock company" that society seemed to have become, a company "in which the members agree, for the better securing of his bread to each shareholder, to surrender the liberty and culture of the eater."[13] Like Emerson as well, they were all hostile to blind conformity, to the ethos of "Trade" that created false relations among human beings, to the chilling routines of institutional life. It is the case that they were largely apolitical; but their restiveness in the face of an imperfect society led them to find various modes of defiance. Those at Brook Farm tried to find a communal way of challenging the social order: Fuller found feminism; Emerson, ways of speaking intended to rouse his listeners to create their own meanings, to think for themselves.

The most potent exemplar of all this was Henry David Thoreau, deliberately addressing readers "in the first person," provoking them to use their intellects to "burrow" through the taken-for-granted, the conventional, the genteel. He wanted them to reject their own self-exploitation, to refuse what we would now call false consciousness and artificial needs. He connected the "wide-awakeness" to actual work in the world, to projects. He knew that people needed to be released from internal and external constraints if they were to shape and make and articulate, to leave their own thumbprints on the world. He understood about economic tyranny on the railroads and in the factories, and he knew that it could make political freedom meaningless. His writing and his abolitionism constituted his protests; both *Walden* and *On Civil Disobedience* function as pedagogies in the sense that they seemed aimed at raising the consciousness of those willing to pay heed. His concern, unquestionably, was with his "private state" rather than with a public space; but he helped create the alternative tradition in the United States at a moment of expansion and materialism. And there are strands of his thinking, even today, that can be woven into a critical pedagogy. Whether building his house, hoeing his beans, hunting woodchucks, or finding patterns in the ice melting on the wall, he was intent on *naming* his lived world.

There were more overtly rebellious figures among escaped slaves, abolitionists, and campaigners for women's rights; but the language of people like Frederick Douglass, Harriet Tubman, Sarah Grimke, Susan B. Anthony, and Elizabeth Cady Stanton was very much the language of those who carried on the original demand for independence. The power they sought, however, was not the power to expand and control. For them—slaves, oppressed women, freedmen and freedwomen—the idea of freedom as endowment solved little; they had to take action to *achieve* their freedom, which they saw as the power to act and to choose. Thomas Jefferson, years before, had provided the metaphor of *polis* for Americans, signifying a space where persons could come together to bring into being the "worldly structure" spoken of above. Great romantics like Emerson and Thoreau gave voice to the passion for autonomy and authenticity. Black leaders, including Douglass, W. E. B. Du Bois, the Reverend Martin Luther King, and Malcolm X, not only engaged dialectically with the resistant environment in their pursuit of freedom; they invented languages and pedagogies to enable people to overcome internalized oppression. Struggling for their rights in widening public spheres, they struggled also against what the Reverend King called "nobodiness" as they marched and engaged in a civil disobedience grounded in experiences of the past. Du Bois was in many ways exemplary when he spoke of the "vocation" of twentieth-century youth. Attacking the industrial system "which creates poverty and the children of poverty . . . ignorance and disease and crime," he called for "young women and young men of devotion to lift again the banner of humanity and to walk toward a civilization which will be free and intelligent, which will be healthy and unafraid."[14] The words hold intimations of what Paulo Freire was to say years later when he, too, spoke of the "vocation" of oppressed people, one he identified with "humanization."[15] And the very notion of walking "toward a civilization" suggests the sense of future possibility without which a pedagogy must fail.

Public school teachers, subordinated as they were in the solidifying educational bureaucracies, seldom spoke the language of resistance or transcendence. It is well to remember, however, the courageous ones who dared to go south after the Civil War in the freedmen's schools. Not only did they suffer persecution in their efforts to invent their own "pedagogy of the oppressed"—or of the newly liberated; they often fought for their own human rights against male missionary administrators and even against the missionary concept itself.[16] It is well to remember, too, the transformation of the missionary impulse into settlement house and social work by women like Jane Addams and Lillian Wald. Committing themselves to support systems and adult education for newcomers to the country and for the neighborhood poor, they supported union organization with an explicitly political awareness of what they were about in a class-ridden society. They were able, more often than not, to avoid what Freire calls "malefic generosity" and develop the critical empathy needed for enabling the "other" to find his or her own way.

For all the preoccupations with control, for all the schooling "to order," as David Nasaw puts it,[17] there were always people hostile to regimentation and manipulation, critical of constraints of consciousness. Viewed from a contemporary perspective, for example, Colonel Francis Parker's work with teachers at the Cook County Normal School at the end of the nineteenth century placed a dramatic emphasis on freeing children from competitive environments and compulsions. He encouraged the arts and spontaneous activities; he encouraged shared work. He believed that, if democratized, the school could become "the one central means by which the great problem of human liberty is to be worked out."[18] Trying to help teachers understand the natural learning processes of the young, he was specifically concerned with resisting the corruptions and distortions of an increasingly corporate America. In the Emersonian tradition, he envisioned a sound community life emerging from the liberation and regeneration of individuals. And indeed, there were many libertarians and romantic progressives following him in the presumption that a society of truly free individuals would be a humane and sustaining one.

This confidence may account for the contradictions in the American critical heritage, especially as it informed education within and outside the schools. Structural changes, if mentioned at all, were expected to follow the emancipation of persons (or the appropriate molding of persons); and the schools, apparently depoliticized, were relied upon to effect the required reform and bring about a better world. If individual children were properly equipped for the work they had to do, it was believed, and trained to resist the excesses of competition, there would be no necessity for political action to transform economic relations. The street children, the tenement children, those afflicted and crippled by poverty and social neglect, were often thrust into invisibility because their very existence denied that claim.

John Dewey was aware of such young people, certainly in Chicago, where he saw them against his own memories of face-to-face community life in Burlington, Vermont. Convinced of the necessity for cooperation and community support if individual powers were to be released, he tried in some sense to recreate the Burlington of his youth in the "miniature community" he hoped to see in each classroom.[19] In those classrooms as well, there would be continuing and open communication, the kind of learning that would feed into practice, and inquiries arising out of questioning in the midst of life. Critical thinking modeled on the scientific method, active and probing intelligence: these, for Dewey, were the stuff of a pedagogy that would equip the young to resist fixities and stock responses, repressive and deceiving authorities. Unlike the libertarians and romantics, he directed attention to the "social medium" in which individual growth occurred and to the mutuality of significant concerns.

Even as we question the small-town paradigm in Dewey's treatment of community, even as we wonder about his use of the scientific model for social inquiry, we still ought to be aware of Dewey's sensitivity to what would later be called the "hegemony," or the ideological control, implicit in the dominant point of view of a given society. He understood, for instance, the "religious aureole" protecting institutions like the Supreme Court, the Constitution, and private property. He was aware that the principles and assumptions that gave rise even to public school curricula were so taken for granted that they were considered wholly natural, fundamentally unquestionable. In *The Public and Its Problems*, he called what we think of as ideological control a "social pathology," which "works powerfully against effective inquiry into social institutions and conditions." He went on, "It manifests itself in a thousand ways: in querulousness, in impotent drifting, in uneasy snatching at distractions, in idealization of the long established, in a facile optimism assumed as a cloak, in riotous glorification of things 'as they are,' in intimidation of all dissenters—ways which depress and dissipate thought all the more effectually because they operate with subtle and unconscious pervasiveness."[20] A method of social inquiry had to be developed, he said, to reduce the "pathology" that led to denial and to acquiescence in the status quo. For all his commitment to scientific method, however, he stressed the "human function" of the physical sciences and the importance of seeing them in human terms. Inquiry, communication, "contemporary and quotidian" knowledge of consequence for shared social life: these fed into his conceptions of pedagogy.

His core concern for individual fulfillment was rooted in a recognition that fullfillment could only be attained in the midst of "associated" or intersubjective life. Troubled as we must be fifty years later by the "eclipse of the public," he saw as one of the prime pedagogical tasks the education of an "articulate public." For him, the public sphere came into being when the consequences of certain private transactions created a common interest among people, one that demanded deliberate and cooperative action. Using somewhat different language, we might say that a public emerges when people come freely together in speech and action to take *care* of something that needs caring for, to repair some evident deficiency in their common world. We might think of homelessness as a consequence of the private dealings of landlords, an arms build-up as a consequence of corporate decisions, racial exclusion as a consequence of a private property-holder's choice. And then we might think of what it would mean to educate to the end of caring for something and taking action to repair. That would be *public* education informed by a critical pedagogy; and it would weave together a number of American themes.

Certain of these themes found a new articulation in the 1930s, during the publication of *The Social Frontier* at Teachers College. An educational journal, it was addressed "to the task of considering the broad role of education in advancing the welfare and interests of the great masses of the people who do the work of society—those who labor on farms and ships and in the mines, shops, and factories of the world."[21] Dewey was among the contributors; and, although it had little impact on New Deal policy or even on specific educational practices, the magazine did open out to a future when more and more "liberals" would take a critical view of monopoly capitalism and industrial culture with all their implications for a supposedly "common" school.

In some respect, this represented a resurgence of the Enlightenment faith. Rational insight and dialogue, linked to scientific intelligence, were expected to reduce inequities and exploitation. A reconceived educational effort would advance the welfare and interests of the masses. Ironically, it was mainly in the private schools that educational progressivism had an influence. Critical discussions took place there; attention was paid to the posing of worthwhile problems arising out of the tensions and uncertainties of everyday life; social intelligence was nurtured; social commitments affirmed. In the larger domains of public education, where school people were struggling to meet the challenges of mass education, the emphasis tended to be on "life-adjustment," preparation for future life and work, and "physical, mental, and emotional health."

There is irony in the fact that the progressive social vision, with its integrating of moral with epistemic concerns, its hopes for a social order transformed by the schools, was shattered by the Second World War. The terrible revelations at Auschwitz and Hiroshima demonstrated what could happen when the old dream of knowledge as power was finally fulfilled. Science was viewed as losing its innocence in its wedding to advanced technology. Bureaucracy, with all its impersonality and literal irresponsibility, brought with it almost unrecognizable political and social realities. It took time, as is well known, for anything resembling a progressive vision to reconstitute itself; there was almost no recognition of the role now being played by "instrumental rationality,"[22] or what it would come to signify. On the educational side, after the war, there were efforts to remake curriculum in the light of new inquiries into knowledge structures in the disciplinary fields. On the side of the general public, there were tax revolts and rejections of the critical and the controversial, even as the McCarthyite subversion was occurring in the larger world. Only a few years after the Sputnik panic, with the talent searches it occasioned, and the frantic encouragement of scientific training, the long-invisible poor of America suddenly took center stage. The Civil Rights Movement, taking form since the Supreme Court decision on integration in 1954, relit flames of critical pedagogy, as it set people marching to achieve their freedom and their human rights.

Viewed from the perspective of a critical tradition in this country, the 1960s appear to have brought all the latent tendencies to the surface. The Civil Rights Movement, alive with its particular traditions of liberation, provided the spark; the war in Vietnam gave a lurid illumination to the system's deficiencies: its incipient violence; its injustices; its racism; its indifference to public opinion and demand. The short-lived effort to reform education and provide compensation for damage done by poverty and discrimination could not halt the radical critique of America's schools. And that many-faceted critique—libertarian, Marxist, romantic, democratic—variously realized the critical potentialities of American pedagogies. Without an Emerson or a Thoreau or a Parker, there would not have been a

Free School movement or a "deschooling" movement. Without a Du Bois, there would not have been liberation or storefront schools. Without a social reformist tradition, there would have been no Marxist voices asking (as, for instance, Samuel Bowles and Herbert Gintis did) for a "mass-based organization of working people powerfully articulating a clear alternative to corporate capitalism as the basis for a progressive educational system."[23] Without a Dewey, there would have been little concern for "participatory democracy," for "consensus," for the reconstitution of a public sphere.

Yet, the silence fell at the end of the following decade; privatization increased, along with consumerism and cynicism and the attrition of the public space. We became aware of living in what Europeans called an "administered society";[24] we became conscious of technicism and positivism and of the one-dimensionality Herbert Marcuse described.[25] Popular culture, most particularly as embodied in the media, was recognized (with the help of the critical theorist Theodor Adorno) as a major source of mystification.[26] The schools were recognized as agents of "cultural reproduction," oriented to a differential distribution of knowledge.[27] Numerous restive educational thinkers, seeking new modes of articulating the impacts of ideological control and manipulation, turned towards European neo-Marxist scholarship for clues to a critical pedagogy. In an American tradition, they were concerned for the individual, for the subject, which late Marxism appeared to have ignored; and the humanist dimension of Frankfurt School philosophies held an unexpected appeal. Moreover, what with its concern for critical consciousness and communicative competence, Frankfurt School thinking held echoes of the Enlightenment faith; and, in some profound way, it was recognized.

There is, of course, an important sense in which the Frankfurt School has reappropriated philosophical traditions (Kantian, Hegelian, phenomenological, psychological, psycho-analytical) which are ours as well or which, at least, have fed our intellectual past. But it also seems necessary to hold in mind the fact that European memories are not our memories. The sources of European critical theory are to be found in responses to the destruction of the Workers' Councils after the First World War, the decline of the Weimar Republic, the rise of Stalinism, the spread of fascism, the Holocaust, the corruptions of social democracy. As climactic as any contemporary insight was the realization that reason (viewed as universal in an Enlightenment sense) could be used to justify the application of technical expertise in torture and extermination. Europeans saw a connection between this and the rationalization of society by means of bureaucracy, and in the separating off of moral considerations long viewed as intrinsic to civilized life. The intimations of all this could be seen in European literature for many years: in Dostoevsky's and Kafka's renderings of human beings as insects; in Musil's anticipations of the collapse of European orders; in Camus's pestilence, in Sartre's nausea, in the Dionysian and bestial shapes haunting the structures of the arts. We have had a tragic literature, a critical literature, in the United States. We need only recall Twain, Melville, Crane, Wharton, Hemingway, Fitzgerald. But it has been a literature rendered tragic by a consciousness of a dream betrayed, of a New World corrupted by exploitation and materialism and greed. In background memory, there are images of Jeffersonian agrarianism, of public spheres, of democratic and free-swinging communities. We do not find these in European literature, *nor* in the writings of the critical theorists.

One of the few explicit attempts to articulate aspects of the Western tradition for educators has been the courageous work of Freire, who stands astride both hemispheres. He has been the pioneer of a pedagogy informed by both Marxist and existential-phenomenological thought; his conception of critical reflectiveness has reawakened the themes of a tradition dating back to Plato and forward to the theologies of liberation that have taken hold in oppressed areas of the Western world. His background awareness, however, and that of the largely Catholic peasants with whom he has worked, are not that of most North Americans. It must be granted that his own culture and education transcend his Brazilian origins and make him something of a world citizen when it comes to the life of ideas. Like his European colleagues, however, he reaches back to predecessors other than Jefferson and Emerson and Thoreau and William James and Dewey; his social vision is not that of our particular democracy. This is not intended as criticism, but as a reminder that a critical pedagogy relevant to the United States today must go beyond— calling on different memories, repossessing another history.

We live, after all, in dark times, times with little historical memory of any kind. There are vast dislocations in industrial towns, erosions of trade unions; there is little sign of class consciousness today. Our great cities are burnished on the surfaces, building high technologies, displaying astonishing consumer goods. And on the side streets, in the crevices, in the burnt-out neighborhoods, there are the rootless, the dependent, the sick, the permanently unemployed. There is little sense of agency, even among the brightly successful; there is little capacity to look at things as if they could be otherwise.

Where education is concerned, the discourse widens, and the promises multiply. The official reform reports, ranging from *A Nation at Risk* to the Carnegie Forum's *A Nation Prepared*, call for a restructuring of schools and of teacher education to the end of raising the levels of literacy in accord with the requirements of an economy based on high technology.[28] The mass of students in the schools, including the one third who will be "minorities," are to be enabled to develop "higher order skills" in preparation for "the unexpected, the nonroutine world they will face in the future."[29] The implicit promise is that, if the quality of teachers is improved (and "excellent" teachers rewarded and recognized), the majority of young people will be equipped for meaningful participation in an advanced knowledge-based economy wholly different from the mass-production economy familiar in the past.

On the other hand, there are predictions that we will never enjoy full employment in this country, that few people stand any real chance of securing meaningful work. If the military juggernaut keeps rolling on, draining funds and support from social utilities, daycare centers, arts institutions, schools and universities, we will find ourselves devoid of all those things that might make life healthier, gentler, more inviting and more challenging. At once we are reminded (although not by the authors of the educational reports) of the dread of nuclear destruction (or of Chernobyl, or of Bhopal) that lies below the surface of apparent hope for the future. This dread, whether repressed or confronted, leads numbers of people to a sense of fatalism and futility with respect to interventions in the social world. For others, it leads to a sad and often narcissistic focus on the "now." For still others, it evokes denial and accompanying extravagances: consumerism increases; a desire for heightened sensation, for vicarious violence, grows. And for many millions, it makes peculiarly appealing the talk of salvation broadcast by evangelists and television preachers; it makes seductive the promise of Armageddon.

As young people find it increasingly difficult to project a long-range future, intergenerational continuity becomes problematic. So does the confidence in education as a way of keeping the culture alive, or of initiating newcomers into learning communities, or of providing the means for pursuing a satisfying life. Uncertain whether we can share or constitute a common world, except in its most fabricated and trivialized form, we wonder what the great conversation can now include and whether it is worth keeping alive.

Michael Oakeshott spoke eloquently of that conversation, "begun in the primeval forests and extended and made more articulate in the course of centuries." He said it involves passages of argument and inquiry, going on in public and in private, that it is an "unrehearsed intellectual adventure . . ." Education, for him, "is an initiation into the skill and partnership of this conversation," which gives character in the end "to every human activity and utterance."[30] We know now how many thousands of voices have been excluded from that conversation over the years. We know how, with its oppositions and hierarchies, it demeaned. As we listen to the prescriptions raining down for "common learnings" (which may or may not include the traditions of people of color, feminist criticism and literature, Eastern philosophies) and "cultural literacy," we cannot but wonder how those of us in education can renew and expand the conversation, reconstitute what we can call a common world.

Yes, there are insights into humane teaching in the latest reports; but, taking the wide view, we find mystification increasing, along with the speechlessness. We have learned about the diverse ways we Americans interpret our traditions: about those who identify with the old individualism, those who yearn for old communities, those who seek new modes of justice, those who want to lose themselves in a cause.[31] We know something about the persistence of a commitment to freedom, variously defined, and to the idea of equity. At once, we are bound to confront such extremes as a moral majority usurping talk of intimacy and family values, while neoliberals seek out technocratic, depersonalized solutions to quantified problems and speak a cost-benefit language beyond the reach of those still striving for public dialogue.

People have never, despite all that, had such vast amounts of information transmitted to them—not merely about murders and accidents and scandals, but about crucial matters on which public decisions may some day have to be made: nuclear energy, space vehicles, racism, homelessness, life-support systems, chemotherapies, joblessness, terrorism, abused children, fanatics, saints. There are whole domains of information that arouse frustration or pointless outrage. All we need to do is think of the persecution of the sanctuary-movement leaders, of children living in shelters, of the *contras* in Honduras, of adolescent suicides, of overcrowded jails. At the same time, no population has ever been so deliberately entertained, amused, and soothed into avoidance, denial, and neglect. We hear the cacophonous voices of special interest groups; we hear of discrete acts of sacrifice and martyrdom; we seldom hear of intentionally organized collaborative action to repair what is felt to be missing, or known to be wrong.

Complacency and malaise; upward mobility and despair. Sometimes we detect feelings of shame and helplessness perceived as personal failure. To be dependent, to be on welfare, is to be certified as in some manner deviant or irresponsible since good Americans are expected to fend for themselves. Even as oppressed peasants internalize their oppressors' images of them as helpless creatures, so unsuccessful Americans (young or old) internalize the system's description of them as ineffectual. They are unable to live up to the culture's mandate to control their own lives and contribute to the productivity of the whole. Our institutional responses are ordinarily technical (and we are drawn to technical solutions out of benevolence, as well as out of helplessnesss). Yet we know that to think mainly in terms of techniques or cures or remedies is often to render others and the earth itself as objects to be acted upon, treated, controlled, or used. It is to distance what we believe has to be done (efficiently, effectively) from our own existential projects, from our own becoming among other incomplete and questing human beings. It is to repress or deny the prereflective, tacit understandings that bind us together in a culture and connect us to our history.

Having said all this, I must ask again what a critical pedagogy might mean for those of us who teach the young at this peculiar and menacing time. Perhaps we might begin by releasing our imaginations and summoning up the traditions of freedom in which most of us were reared. We might try to make audible again the recurrent calls for justice and equality. We might reactivate the resistance to materialism and conformity. We might even try to inform with meaning the desire to educate "all the children" in a legitimately "common" school. Considering the technicism and the illusions of the time, we need to recognize that what we single out as most deficient and oppressive is in part a function of perspectives created by our past. It is a past in which our subjectivities are embedded, whether we are conscious of it or not. We have reached a point when that past must be reinterpreted and reincarnated in the light of what we have learned.

We understand that a mere removal of constraints or a mere relaxation of controls will not ensure the emergence of free and creative human beings. We understand that the freedom we cherish is not an endowment, that it must be achieved through dialectical engagements with the social and economic obstacles we find standing in our way, those we have to learn to name. We understand that a plurality of American voices must be attended to, that a plurality of life-stories must be heeded if a meaningful power is to spring up through a new "binding and promising, combining and covenanting." We understand that the Enlightenment heritage must be repossessed and reinterpreted, so that we can over-come the positivism that awaits on one side, the empty universalism on the other. But we cannot and ought not escape our own history and memories, not if we are to keep alive the awarenesses that ground our identities and connect us to the persons turning for fulfillment to our schools.

We cannot negate the fact of power. But we can undertake a resistance, a reaching out towards becoming *persons* among other persons, for all the talk of human resources, for all the orienting of education to the economy. To engage with our students as persons is to affirm our own incompleteness, our consciousness of spaces still to be explored, desires still to be tapped, possibilities still to be opened and pursued. At once, it is to rediscover the value of care, to reach back to experiences of caring and being cared for (as Nel Noddings writes) as sources of an ethical ideal. It is, Noddings says, an ideal to be nurtured through "dialogue, practice, and confirmation,"[32] processes much akin to those involved in opening a public sphere. We have to find out how to open such spheres, such spaces, where a better state of things can be imagined; because it is only through the projection of a better social order that we can perceive the gaps in what exists and try to transform and repair. I would like to think that this can happen in classrooms, in corridors, in schoolyards, in the streets around.

I would like to think of teachers moving the young into their own interpretations of their lives and their lived worlds, opening wider and wider perspectives as they do so. I would like to see teachers ardent in their efforts to make the range of symbol systems available to the young for the ordering of experience, even as they maintain regard for their vernaculars. I would like to see teachers tapping the spectrum of intelligences, encouraging multiple readings of written texts and readings of the world.

In "the shadow of silent majorities," then, as teachers learning along with those we try to provoke to learn, we may be able to inspire hitherto unheard voices. We may be able to empower people to rediscover their own memories and articulate them in the presence of others, whose space they can share. Such a project demands the capacity to unveil and disclose. It demands the exercise of imagination, enlivened by works of art, by situations of speaking and making. Perhaps we can at last devise reflective communities in the interstices of colleges and schools. Perhaps we can invent ways of freeing people to feel and express indignation, to break through the opaqueness, to refuse the silences. We need to teach in such a way as to arouse passion now and then; we need a new camaraderie, a new en masse. These are dark and shadowed times, and we need to live them, standing before one another, open to the world.

Notes

1. Baudrillard, *In the Shadow of Silent Majorities* (New York: Semiotexte, 1983).
2. Jean-Paul Sartre, *Search for a Method* (New York: Knopf, 1968), p. 94.
3. Whitman, *Leaves of Grass* (New York: Aventine Press, 1931), pp. 49–50.
4. Stevens, *Collected Poems* (New York: Knopf, 1963), p. 198.
5. Moore, *Tell Me, Tell Me* (New York: Viking Press, 1966), p. 24.
6. Rukeyser, "Käthe Kollwitz," in *By a Woman Writt*, ed. Joan Goulianos (New York: Bobbs Merrill, 1973), p. 374.
7. Rich, *A Wild Patience Has Taken Me This Far* (New York: Norton, 1981), p. 23.
8. Mill, "On Liberty," in *The Six Great Humanistic Essays* (New York: Washington Square Press, 1963), p. 158.
9. Arendt, *On Revolution* (New York: Viking Press, 1963), pp. 174–175.
10. Horace Mann, "Ninth Annual Report," in *The Republic and the School: Horace Mann on the Education of Free Men*, ed. Lawrence A. Cremin (New York: Teachers College Press, 1957), p. 57.
11. Mark Twain, *The Adventures of Huckleberry Finn* (New York: New American Library, 1959), p. 283.
12. Brownson, "The Laboring Classes," in *Ideology and Power in the Age of Jackson*, ed. Edwin C. Rozwenc (Garden City, NY: Anchor Books, 1964), p. 321.
13. Emerson, "Self-Reliance," in *Emerson on Education*, ed. Howard Mumford Jones (New York: Teachers College Press, 1966), p. 105.
14. Du Bois, *W. E. B. Du Bois: A Reader*, ed. Meyer Weinberg (New York: Harper Torchbooks, 1970), pp. 153–154.
15. Freire, *Pedagogy of the Oppressed* (New York: Continuum, 1970), pp. 27 ff.
16. Jacqueline Jones, "Women Who Were More Than Men: Sex and Status in Freedmen's Teaching," *History of Education Quarterly*, 19 (1979), 47–59.
17. Nasaw, *Schooled to Order* (New York: Oxford University Press, 1981).
18. Parker, *Talks on Pedagogics* (New York: Harper, 1894).
19. Dewey, "The School and Society," in *Dewey on Education*, ed. Martin Dworkin (New York: Teachers College Press, 1959), p. 41.
20. Dewey, *The Public and Its Problems* (Athens, OH: Swallow Press, 1954).
21. Lawrence A. Cremin, *The Transformation of the School* (New York: Knopf, 1961), pp. 231–232.
22. Jürgen Habermas, *Knowledge and Human Interests* (Boston: Beacon Press, 1972).
23. Bowles and Gintis, *Schooling in Capitalist America* (New York: Basic Books, 1976), p. 266.
24. Marcuse, "Some Social Implications of Modern Technology," in *The Essential Frankfurt School Reader*, ed. Andrew Arato and Eike Gebhardt (New York: Urizen Books, 1978), pp. 138–162.
25. Marcuse, *One-Dimensional Man* (Boston: Beacon Press, 1966).
26. Adorno, "Cultural Criticism and Society," in *Prisms* (London: Neville Spearman, 1961), pp. 31–32 ff.
27. See Pierre Bourdieu and Jean-Claude Passeron, *Reproduction* (Beverly Hills: Sage, 1977).
28. The National Commission on Excellence in Education, *A Nation at Risk: The Imperative for Educational Reform* (Washington: U.S. Department of Education, 1983); and Carnegie Forum on Education and the Economy, *A Nation Prepared: Teachers for the 21st Century* (New York: Carnegie Forum, 1986).
29. Carnegie Forum, *A Nation Prepared*, p. 25.
30. Oakeshott, *Rationalism in Politics and Other Essays* (London: Methuen, 1962), pp. 198–199.
31. Robert N. Bellah, Richard Madsen, William M. Sullivan, Ann Swidler, and Steve M. Tipton, *Habits of the Heart: Individualism and Commitment in American Life* (Berkeley: University of California Press, 1985).
32. Noddings, *Caring: A Feminine Approach to Ethics and Moral Education* (Berkeley: University of California Press, 1984).

Suggested Readings for Future Study

Critical Theories

Adorno, T. (1987). *Negative Dialectic*. New York: Continuum.

Adorno, T. W., Benjamin, W., Bloch, E., Brecht, B., and Lukacs, G. (1997). *Aesthetics and Politics*. London: Verso Press.

Althusser, L. (1969). *For Marx*. New York: Vintage Books.

Ashcroft, B., Griffiths, G., and Tiffin, H. (1995). *Postcolonial Studies Reader*. New York: Routledge.

Ball, S., ed. (1990). *Foucault and Education: Disciplines and Knowledge*. New York: Routledge.

Bates, T. R., "Gramsci and the Theory of Hegemony", in *Journal of the History of Ideas* XXXVI, April–June 1975.

Benhabib, S. (1986). *Critique, Norm and Utopia: A Study of the Foundations of Critical Theory*. Columbia University Press.

Benhabib, S. (1992). *Situating the Self*. New York: Routledge.

Bennett, T. et al. (1987). *Culture, Ideology and Social Process*. London: Open University Press.

Best, S. and Kellner, D. (1991). *Postmodern Theory: Critical Interrogations*. New York: Guilford Press.

Bhabha, H. (1994). *The Location of Culture*. New York: Routledge.

Bocock, R. (1986). *Hegemony*. London: Tavistock.

Bourdieu, P. (1977). *Outline of a Theory of Practice*. Cambridge University Press.

Bourdieu, P. (1977). "Cultural Reproduction and Social Reproduction," in Karabel, J. and Halsey, H. A. (eds), *Power and Ideology in Education*. New York: Oxford University Press.

Bourdieu, P. and Passeron, J. (1992). *Reproduction in Education, Society and Culture*. London: Sage.

Buck-Morss, S. (1977). *The Origin of Negative Dialectics: Theodore W. Adorno, Walter Benjamin, and the Frankfurt School*. New York: Free Press.

Cherryholmes, C. (1988). *Power and Criticism: Poststructuralist Investigations in Education*. New York: Teachers College Press.

Cole, M. (2008) *Marxism and Educational Theory*. London and New York: Routledge.

Dubiel, H. (1985). *Theory and Politics: Studies in the Development of Critical Theory*. Cambridge, MA: MIT Press.

Eagleton, T. (1991). *Ideology: An Introduction*. New York: Verso.

Fay, B. (1997). *Critical Social Science*. New York: Cornell University Press.

Fischman, G. and McLaren, P. "Rethinking Critical Pedagogy and the Gramscian and Freirian Legacies," *Cultural Studies/Critical Methodologies*, vol. 5, no. 4, 2005, pp. 1–22.

Foucault, M. (1980). *Power/knowledge: Selected Interviews and Other Writings*. New York: Pantheon Books.

Foucault, M. (1979). *Discipline and Punish—the Birth of the Prison*. New York: Vintage Books.

Foucault, M. (1972). *The Archaeology of Knowledge and the Discourse on Language*. New York: Pantheon Books.

Fromm, E. (1941). *Escape from Freedom*. New York: Avon Books.

Held, D. (1980). *Introduction to Critical Theory: Horkheimer to Habermas*. Berkeley and Los Angeles: University of California Press.

Gramsci, A., Forgacs, D., and Hobsbawm, E. J. (2000). *The Antonio Gramsci Reader: Selected Writings 1916–1935*. New York: NYU Press.

Gramsci, A. (1971). *Selections from the Prison Notebooks*. New York: International Publishers.

Gray, A. and McGuigan, J. (1993). *Studying Culture: An Introductory Reader*. London: Edward Arnold.

Greene, M. (1988). *The Dialectics of Freedom*. New York: Teachers College Press.

Horkheimer, M. (1974). *Critique of instrumental reason; lectures and essays since the end of World War II*. New York: Seabury Press.

Horkheimer, M. (1972). *Critical theory: Selected essays*. New York: Herder & Herder.

Horkheimer, M. and Adorno, T. W. (1944). *Dialectic of Enlightenment.* New York: The Continuum Publishing Company.

Hoy, D. C. (1986). *Foucault—a Critical Reader.* Oxford: Blackwell.

Jardine, G. M. (2005). *Foucault & Education.* New York: Peter Lang.

Jay, M. (1973) *The Dialectical imagination: A history of the Frankfurt School and the Institute of Social Research, 1923–1959.* Boston: Little Brown.

Jay, M. (1984). *Adorno.* Cambridge, MA: Harvard University Press.

Karabel, J. and Halsey, A. H., eds. (1977). *Power and Ideology in Education.* New York: Oxford University Press.

Kellner, D. (1989). *Critical theory, Marxism and modernity.* Cambridge: Polity.

Kellner, D. (1989). *Critical theory and society: a reader.* New York: Routledge.

Kellner, D. (1997). *Herbert Marcuse and the Crisis of Marxism.* Berkeley: University of California Press.

Marcus, J. (1984). *Foundations of the Frankfurt School of Social Research.* New Brunswick: Transaction Books.

Marcuse, H. (1966). *Eros and civilization: A philosophical inquiry into Freud.* Boston: Beacon Press.

Marcuse, H. (1966) *One dimensional man.* Boston: Beacon Press.

Marcuse, H. (1972). *Counter-Revolution and Revolt.* Boston: Beacon Press.

Marcuse, H. (1972). *Studies in critical philosophy.* London: NLB.

Marcuse, H. (1969). *An Essay on Liberation.* Boston: Beacon Press.

Marcuse, H. (1968). *Negations—essays in critical theory.* Boston: Beacon Press.

Marcuse, H. (1941). *Reason and revolution; Hegel and the rise of social theory.* London and New York: Oxford University Press.

Marcuse, H. (1987). *Hegel's ontology and the theory of historicity.* Cambridge, MA: MIT Press.

Marx, K. (1969). *Early writings.* New York: McGraw Hill.

Noble, T. (2000). *Social Theory and Social Change.* New York: St. Martin's Press.

Peters, M. and Besley, C. (2006). *Why Foucault?: New Directions in Educational Research.* New York: Peter Lang.

Popkewitz, T. (1999). *Critical Theories in Education.* New York: Routledge.

Rasmussen, D., ed. (1996). *The handbook of critical theory.* Oxford: Blackwell.

Rosado, R. (1993). *Culture and truth: the remaking of social analysis.* Boston: Beacon Press.

Schindler, R. J. (1998). *The Frankfurt School critique of capitalist culture: a critical theory for post-democratic society and its re-education.* Aldershot, Hants, England and Brookfield, VT: Ashgate.

Stirk, P. M. R. (2005). *Critical theory, politics, and society: an introduction.* New York: Continuum International Publishing.

Trifonas, P. P. (2000). *Revolutionary Pedagogies: Cultural Politics, Instituting Education, and the Discourse of Theory.* New York and London: RoutledgeFalmer.

Tripp, D. "Critical Theory and Educational Research," *Issues In Educational Research*, 2.1 (1992): 13–23.

Warren, S. (1984). *The emergence of dialectical theory.* Chicago: University of Chicago Press.

Critical Pedagogy and Democratic Schooling

Apple, M. (2000). *Official knowledge, democratic education in a conservative age.* New York: Routledge.

Apple, M. (2000). "The Shock of the Real—Critical Pedagogies and Rightist Reconstruction," in *Revolutionary Pedagogies,* edited by Peter Trifonas. New York and London: RoutledgeFalmer.

Apple, M. (1996). *Cultural Politics and Education.* New York and London: Teachers College, Columbia University.

Apple, M. "The Politics of Official Knowledge: Does a National Curriculum Make Sense?" *Teachers College Record,* Vol. 95, No. 2, Winter, 1993, pp. 222–241.

Araujo Freire, A. and Macedo, D. (1998). *The Paulo Freire reader.* New York: Continuum.

Aronowitz, S. and Giroux, H. (1985). *Education under siege.* South Hadley, MA: Bergin & Garvey.

Ayers, W. (1998). *Teaching for social justice: A demoracy and education reader.* New York: New Press.

Barbules, N. (1992). *Dialogue in teaching: Theory and practice.* New York: Teachers College Press.

Boler, M. (2004). *Democratic Dialogue in Education: Troubling Speech, Disturbing Silence.* New York: Peter Lang.

Borg, C., Buttiegieg, J., and Mayo, P. (2002). *Gramsci and education.* Lanham, MD: Rowman & Littlefield.

Carlson, D. and Apple, M. (2003). *Power/Knowledge/Pedagogy: The Meaning of Democratic Education in Unsettling Times.* Colorado: Westview.

Carr, W. and Harnett, A. (1996). *Education and the Struggle for Democracy: The Politics of Educational Ideas.* Buckingham (England) and Bristol, PA: Open University Press.

Carr, W. (1995). *For Education: Towards Critical Educational Inquiry.* Buckingham (England) and Bristol, PA: Open University Press.

Chomsky, N. (2000). *Chomsky on Miseducation.* Lanham, MD: Rowman & Littlefield Publishers.

Cole, M. (2006). *Education, Equality and Human Rights: Issues of Gender, "Race", Sexuality, Disability and Social Class.* London: Routledge.

Darder, A. (1991). *Culture and Power in the Classroom.* Westport, CT: Bergin & Garvey.

Darder, A. (2002). *Reinventing Paulo Freire: A Pedagogy of Love.* Boulder, CO: Westview.

Dewey, J. (1916). *Democracy and Education.* New York: The Free Press.

Fletcher, Scott (2000). *Education and emancipation theory and practice in a new constellation.* New York: Teachers College Press.

Freire, P. (1997). *Pedagogy of the heart.* New York: Continuum.

Freire, P. (1993). *Pedagogy of the city.* New York: Continuum.

Freire, P. (1994). *Pedagogy of the oppressed* (anniversary edition). New York: Continuum.

Freire, P. (1987). *The politics of education: Culture, power and liberation.* South Hadley, MA: Bergin & Garvey.

Freire, P. and Faundez, A. (1989). *Learning to question: A pedagogy of liberation.* New York: Continuum.

Forester, J. (1993). *Critical theory, public policy and planning practice: Toward a critical pragmatism.* New York: SUNY Press.

Gadotti, M. (1994). *Reading Paulo Freire: His life and work.* New York: SUNY.

Giroux, H. (1983). *Theory and resistance in education.* South Hadley, MA: Bergin & Garvey.

Giroux, H. (1981). *Ideology, Culture and the Process of Schooling.* Philadelphia: Temple University Press.

Goodman, J. (1992). *Elementary schooling for critical democracy.* Albany: State University of New York Press.

Holst, J. (2006). "Paulo Freire in Chile, 1964–1969: Pedagogy of the Oppressed in Its Sociopolitical Economic Context," *Harvard Education Review,* vol. 6, no. 2.

Inglis, F. and Carr, W. (2004). *Education and the Good Society.* London: Palgrave Macmillan.

Kanpol, B. (1994). *Critical pedagogy—an introduction.* Westport, CN: Bergin & Garvey.

Kelly, E. (1995). *Education, democracy and public knowledge.* Boulder, CO: Westview Press.

Kinchloe, J. (2004). *The Critical Pedagogy Primer.* New York: Peter Lang.

Kozol, J. and Merrow, J. (2001). *Choosing Excellence.* Lanham, MD: Scarecrow Press, Inc.

Kozol, J. (2001). *Ordinary Resurrections: Children in the Years of Hope.* New York: HarperCollins Publishers.

Kozol, J. (1991). *Savage Inequalities—Children in America's Schools.* New York: Harper Perennial.

Leistyna, P. (1999). *Presence of Mind—Education and the Politics of Deception.* Boulder, CO: Westview Press.

Leistyna, P., Woodrum, A. and Sherblom, S., eds. (1996). *Breaking free. The transformative power of critical pedagogy.* Cambridge, MA: Harvard Educational Review.

Livingstone, D., ed. (1987). *Critical Pedagogy and Cultural Power.* South Hadley, MA: Bergin & Garvey.

McLaren, P. and Kincheloe, J. (2007). *Critical Pedagogy: Where are we now?* New York: Peter Lang.

McLaren, P. (1989). *Life in Schools: An Introduction to Critical Pedagogy and the Foundations of Education.* New York: Longman.

McLaren, P. (1986). *Schooling as Ritual Performance.* London: Routledge and Kegan Paul.

McLaren, P. and Giarelli, J. (1995). *Critical Theory and Educational Research.* New York: SUNY Press.

Simon, R. (1992). *Teaching Against the Grain: A Pedagogy of Possibility.* New York: Bergin and Garvey.

Shor, I. (1992) *Empowering Education: Critical Teaching for Social Change.* Chicago: University of Chicago Press.

Shor, I. and Freire, P. (1987). *A Pedagogy for Liberation.* South Hadley, MA: Bergin and Garvey.

Shor, I. (1980). *Critical Teaching and Everyday Life.* Boston: South End Press.

Sullivan, E. (1990). *Critical Psychology and Pedagogy: Interpretation of the Personal World.* New York: Bergin & Garvey.

Torres, C. A., ed. (2000). *Challenges of Urban Education.* Albany: State University of New York Press.

Part Two

Education and Social Class

Introduction to Part Two

The US economy with its increasing inequalities has failed to challenge the belief in the power of education and the ability of America's economic machine to create prosperity for all. It is even asserted by some that social class inequality is not inherently wrong as long as "everybody has an opportunity to climb up the ladder" and to achieve the American dream. That is, meritocracy works as long as the ladder has enough rungs to climb. Unfortunately, the delusion that we live in a classless society is perpetuated by teachers and embraced uncritically by most students. Like all component elements of what Antonio Gramsci called *common sense*, much of the everyday discourse of the power of schools to create access to quality jobs and personal fulfillment is considered gospel.

This section on education and social class examines the nature of economic inequalities and the problematic role of a market-driven education policy. Inherent to such an examination is the need to critically interrogate the ways in which macroeconomic trends impact life in schools, as well as create sites of resistance. Critical pedagogical principles encourage educators to reclaim class as both an analytical category and political toolkit, in order to effectively unpack the idealist assumptions and social implications of schools as the *great equalizer*, in a system driven by the dictates of profit, rather than those of human need.

This points to an urgent need to question whether educational researchers and policy makers are misguided in focusing exclusively on schools as sites of transformation and potential renewal, while ignoring the wider structural sources of social class and inequality. Within a critical pedagogical context, there is a pressing need to breathe new intellectual life into the debate on the possibilities and limits of democratic school reform. Particular attention must be paid to the manner in which contemporary social and cultural transformations and changing class relations impact the life chances of students in and outside of schools.

Such interrogations have significant implications for educational theory, policy, and classroom practice. For example, there is increasing evidence that a correlation exists between social class origin and educational outcomes. Historically, it has been common-sense that quality education will reduce inequality and social class differences. For most Americans, education is heralded as an indisputably "good thing." Parents frequently mortgage their homes and lives, work inhumanely long hours to finance a "good education" for their children, so that they will be able to compete in the "new economy." Further, schools are viewed as democratic institutions leading to intergenerational mobility, improved life chances, greater economic opportunities, and fulfillment of the so-called American Dream.

This recurrent fantasy of the power of education is firmly embedded in American culture. The belief that reforms in education along with improved teaching and school leadership can counter and overcome differentials in school outcomes and student achievement is the driving force in educational policy. These views persist in the face of gross concentrations of wealth and burgeoning class inequality in the US. In fact, a Congressional Budget Office report released in 2007 revealed that the gap between wealthy Americans and their fellow citizens has now become a chasm—reaching its widest point since the Roaring Twenties. This gap, according to the report, has actually been widening for nearly three decades. Numerous other studies have reached similar conclusions—despite the tremendous wealth generated by the US economy, the wealth does not reach working families nor those most in need who, thanks to neoliberal policies, have been left without an economic safety net.

Due to a series of interlinked developments in the 1980s, a paradigm shift rendered inequality, and especially social class, invisible. Research in education reflected this shift, with classroom practice and issues of race, ethnicity, and gender replacing class—the so-called *death of class*. However, in an era of stagnant wages, decline in job quality, and unbalanced growth—a return to class is more timely than ever before. In an era of growing inequality—with a drop in real wages, decline in job quality, and unbalanced growth—a re-examination of the popular contention, that schools are the miracle panacea capable of solving all our social ills, is sorely needed. But to carry this out requires, more than ever, a critical understanding and engagement with the politics of social class and its relationship to the reproduction of inequality within schools and the larger society.

Summary of Articles

The articles in this section offer, through their diverse interpretive analyses, perspectives of how an unleashed predatory market, driven by global capitalism, shapes the everyday life and culture of schools. For the moment, it should be emphasized that in none of the essays which follow, is it simply asserted that education does not matter. A major theoretical and conceptual underpinning of the articles is that school-based solutions alone are unlikely to improve the school performance, unless material inequalities are tackled as part of a wider set of public social policies. Thus, America's most distinctive features—inequality and class—matter, in and out of schools. Moreover, the authors examine in broad strokes the different ways in which class and inequality are implicated in the so-called crisis in education. As the reader will discover, these critical theorists use the category of class, or social classes, and attach its significance and theoretical ambition in divergent ways; however, the salience of class and traditions of class analysis are embedded in their interrogation of schools.

In the first article, "Against Schooling: Education and Social Class," Stanley Aronowitz speaks to the false promise of education which aims to teach students the world of work. He describes how the structure of schooling embodies and reflects the wider system of class relations. He masterfully debunks the gospel of school reformers—namely, the belief in "education and access." He concludes with a democratic program for the reconstruction of schooling, which includes such reforms as democratizing the curricula and creating spaces of intellectual endeavor, leaving behind the testing mania and cutting school ties with corporate interests. Aronowitz is fully aware of the difficulty of such a project being successful and the possibility of being viewed as *utopian*. However, as critique, his analysis is essential and timely.

Concerns about security dominate public life in the United States. Public education is one important site where the perceived need for greater security has given rise to new formations in school discipline and control. In "The Surveillance Curriculum" Torin Monahan explores how surveillance systems in schools produce sites of social control. He places the emerging relationship between schools, private technology firms, and the police, within a political economy context, to unmask the commodification of fear and the criminalization and containment of students. Further, Monahan argues that the predatory market drives the increasing privatization of surveillance technologies, as well. Such a critique is particularly important as we enter a new era of the fear of the Other, as technologies driven by corporate interests are reproduced by existing disciplinary mechanisms of social control.

The final article, "Confronting Class in the Classroom" by cultural critic bell hooks, utilizes class analysis to examine how class differences are enacted in the classroom. She launches a critique of faculty in higher education who legitimate the predatory market by their, conscious or unconscious, refusal to address social class and their tendency to silence working class voices in the classroom. In so doing, hooks highlights the manner in which educators render invisible class and economic inequality.

Questions for Reflection and Dialogue

1. What does "social class" mean? Why does class matter in and out of school?
2. Explain how the surveillance of schools reproduces class inequality?
3. How would you engage with issues of social class in higher education? In elementary school? In the middle school? In high school? Describe differences and similarities in your approaches.
4. While all uses of the word "class" in social theory invoke, in one way or another, the problem of understanding systems of economic inequality, different uses of the word are embedded in very different theoretical agendas. How did the authors differ in their use of the concept of class?
5. List and evaluate the arguments for (a) an optimistic, and (b) a pessimistic view of the prospects of democratic renewal, as offered in Stanley Aronowitz's outline for school transformation.
6. What is clear from the three articles is that school policies and practices within a market-driven system display many contradictory elements and paradoxical tendencies. What are some of the contradictory elements we are witnessing at the present time with the practice of surveillance in schools?

5

Against Schooling: Education and Social Class

Stanley Aronowitz

> The crisis in American education, on the one hand, announces the bankruptcy of progressive education and, on the other hand, presents a problem of immense difficulty because it has arisen under the conditions and in response to the demands of a mass society.
>
> Hannah Arendt, "Crisis in Education"

At the dawn of the new century no American institution is invested with a greater role to bring the young and their parents into the modernist regime than public schools. The common school is charged with the task of preparing children and youth for their dual responsibilities to the social order: citizenship and, more important, learning to labor. On the one hand, in the older curriculum on the road to citizenship in a democratic, secular society, schools are supposed to transmit the jewels of the Enlightenment, especially literature and science. On the other, students are to be prepared for the work world by means of a loose but definite stress on the redemptive value of work, the importance of family, and, of course, the imperative of love and loyalty to one's country. As to the Enlightenment's concept of citizenship, students are, at least putatively, encouraged to engage in independent, critical thinking.

But the socializing functions of schooling play to the opposite idea: children of the working and professional and middle classes are to be molded to the industrial and technological imperatives of contemporary society. Students learn science and mathematics not as a discourse of liberation from myth and religious superstition but as a series of algorithms, the mastery of which are presumed to improve the student's logical capacities, or with no aim other than fulfilling academic requirements. In most places the social studies do not emphasize the choices between authoritarian and democratic forms of social organization, or democratic values, particularly criticism and renewal, but offer instead bits of information that have little significance for the conduct of life. Perhaps the teaching and learning of world literature where some students are inspired by the power of the story to, in John Dewey's terms, "reconstruct" experience is a partial exception to the rule that for most students school is endured rather than experienced as a series of exciting explorations of self and society.[1]

In the wake of these awesome tasks, fiscal exigency and a changing mission have combined to leave public education in the United States in a chronic state of crisis. For some the main issue is whether schools are failing to transmit the general intellectual culture, even to the most able students. What is at stake in this critique is the fate of America as a global model of civilization, particularly the condition of its democratic institutions and the citizens who are, in the final analysis, responsible for maintaining them. Of course, we may contend that the "global model" is fulfilled by the relentless anti-intellectual bias of schools and by a ruthless regime of the virtual expulsion of the most rebellious students, especially by secondary schools. Hannah Arendt goes so far as to ask whether we "love the world" and our children enough to devise an educational system capable of transmitting to them the salient cultural traditions. Other critics complain that schools are failing to fulfill the promise of equal opportunity for good jobs for working-class students, whether black, Latino, or white. Schools unwittingly reinforce the class bias of schooling by ignoring its content. The two positions, with respect both to their goals and to their implied educational philosophies, may not necessarily be contradictory, but their simultaneous enunciation produces, with exceptions to be discussed below, considerable tension for the American workplace, which has virtually no room for dissent. Individual or collective initiative is not sanctioned by management. The corporate factory, which includes sites of goods and symbolic production alike, is perhaps the nation's most authoritarian institution. But any reasonable concept of democratic citizenship requires an individual who is able to discern knowledge from propaganda, is competent to choose among conflicting claims and programs, and is capable of actively participating in the affairs of the polity. Yet the political system offers few opportunities, beyond the ritual of voting, for active citizen participation.[2]

Even identifying the problem of why and how schools fail has proven to be controversial. For those who define mass education as a form of training for the contemporary workplace, the problem can be traced to the crisis of authority, particularly school authority. That some of the same educational analysts favor a curriculum that stresses critical thinking for a small number of students in a restricted number of sites is consistent with the dominant trends of schooling since the turn of the twenty-first century. In the quest to restore authority, conservative educational policy has forcefully caused schools to abandon, both rhetorically and practically, the so-called child-centered curriculum and pedagogy in favor of measures that not only hold students accountable for passing standardized tests and for a definite quantity of school knowledge—on penalty of being left back from promotion or expelled—but also impose performance-based criteria on administrators and teachers. For example, in New York City the schools chancellor has issued "report cards" to principals and has threatened to fire those whose schools do not meet standards established by high-stakes tests. These tests are the antithesis of critical thought. Their precise object is to evaluate the student's ability to imbibe and regurgitate information and to solve problems according to prescribed algorithms.

On the other side, the progressives—who misread John Dewey's educational philosophy to mean that the past need not be studied too seriously—have offered little resistance to the gradual vocationalizing and dumbing down of the mass education curriculum. In fact, historically they were advocates of making the curriculum less formal, reducing requirements, and, on the basis of a degraded argument that children learn best by "doing," promoting practical, work-oriented programs for high-school students. Curricular deformalization was often justified on interdisciplinary criteria, which resulted in watering down course content and de-emphasizing writing. Most American high-school students, in the affluent as well as the "inner-city" districts, may write short papers that amount to book reviews and autobiographical essays, but most graduate without ever having to perform research and write a paper of considerable length. Moreover, since the late 1960s, in an attempt to make the study of history more "relevant" to students' lives, students have not been required to memorize dates; they may learn the narratives but are often unable to place them in a specific chronological context. Similarly, economics has been eliminated in many schools or is taught as a "unit" of a general social studies course. And if philosophy is taught at all, it is construed in terms of "values clarification," a kind of ethics in which students are assisted to discover and examine their own values.

That after more than a century of universal schooling the relationship between education and class has once more been thrust to the forefront is just one more signal of the crisis in American education. The educational Left, never strong on promoting intellectual knowledge as a substantive demand, clings to one of the crucial precepts of progressive educational philosophy: under the sign of egalitarianism, the idea that class deficits can be overcome by equalizing access to school opportunities without questioning what those opportunities have to do with genuine education. The access question has dominated higher education debates since the early 1970s; even conservatives who favor vouchers and other forms of public funding for private and parochial schools have justified privatizing instruction on access grounds.

The structure of schooling already embodies the class system of society, and, for this reason, the access debate misfires. To gain entrance into schools always entails placement into that system. "Equality of Opportunity" for class mobility is the system's tacit recognition that inequality is normative. In the system of mass education, schools are no longer constituted to transmit the Enlightenment intellectual traditions or the fundamental prerequisites of participatory citizenship, even for a substantial minority. While the acquisition of credentials conferred by schools remains an important prerequisite for many occupations, the conflation of schooling with education is mistaken. Schooling is surely a source of training both by its disciplinary regime and by its credentialing system. But schools do not transmit a "love for the world" or "for our children," as Arendt suggests; contrary to their democratic pretensions, they teach conformity to the social, cultural, and occupational hierarchy. In our contemporary world they are not constituted to foster independent thought, let alone encourage independent action. School knowledge is not the only source of education for students, perhaps not even the most important source. Young people learn, for ill as well as good, from popular culture (especially music), from parents, and, perhaps most important, from their peers. Schools are the stand-in for "society," the aggregation of individuals who, by contract or by coercion, are subject to governing authorities in return for which they may be admitted into the world albeit on the basis of different degrees of reward. To the extent that popular culture, parents, and peers signify solidarity and embody common dreams, they are the worlds of quasi communities that exert more influence on their members.

Access to What?

In the main, the critique of education has been directed to the question of access and its entailments, particularly the idea that greater access presumably opens up the gates to higher learning or to better jobs. Generally speaking, critical education analysis focuses on the degree to which schools are willing and able to open their doors to working-class students, coded in many cities as "black, Asian, and Latino" students, because through the mechanisms of differential access, schools are viewed as, perhaps, the principal reproductive institutions of economically and technologically advanced capitalist societies. With some exceptions, most critics of schooling have paid scant attention to school authority, the conditions for the accumulation of social capital—the intricate network of personal relations that articulate with occupational access—and to cultural capital, the accumulation of the signs, if not the substance, of the kinds of knowledge that are markers of distinction.[3]

The progressives assume that the heart of the class question is whether schooling provides working-class kids equality of opportunity to acquire legitimate knowledge and marketable academic credentials. They have adduced overwhelming evidence that contradicts schooling's reigning doctrine: that despite class, race, or gender hierarchies in the economic and political system, public education provides every individual with the tools to overcome conditions of birth. In reality only about a quarter of people of working-class origin attain professional, technical, and managerial careers through the credentialing system. Many more obtain general diplomas, but as the saying goes, a high-school diploma and $2 gets you a ride on the New York subway. The professional and technical credential implies that students have mastered specialized knowledge and acquired a set of skills associated with the speciality. They find occupational niches, but not at the top of their respective domains. Typically graduating from third-tier, nonresearch colleges and universities, they have not acquired knowledge connected with substantial intellectual work: theory, extensive writing, and independent research. Students leaving these institutions find jobs as line supervisors, computer technicians, teachers, nurses, social workers, and other niches in the social service professions.

A small number may join their better-educated colleagues in getting no-collar jobs, where "no collar"—Andrew Ross's term—designates occupations that afford considerable work autonomy, such as computer design, which, although salaried, cannot be comfortably folded into the conventional division of manual and intellectual labor. That so-called social mobility was a product of the specific conditions of American economic development at a particular time—the first quarter of the twentieth century—and was due, principally, to the absence of an indigenous peasantry during the country's industrial revolution and the forced confinement of millions of blacks to southern agricultural lands, which is conveniently forgotten or ignored by consensus opinion. Nor were the labor shortages provoked by World War II and the subsequent U.S. dominance of world capitalism until 1973 taken into account by the celebrants of mobility. Economic stagnation has afflicted the U.S. economy for more than three decades, and, despite the high-tech bubble of the 1990s, its position has deteriorated in the world market. Yet the mythology of mobility retains a powerful grip on the popular mind. That schooling makes credentials available to anyone regardless of rank or status forms one of the sturdy pillars of American ideology.[4]

In recent years the constitutional and legal assignment to the states and local communities of responsibility for public education has been undermined by what has been termed the "standards" movement that is today the prevailing national educational policy, enforced not so much by federal law—notwithstanding the Bush administration's No Child Left Behind program—as by political and ideological coercion. At the state and district levels the invocation to "tough love" has attained widespread support. We are witnessing the abrogation, both in practice and in rhetoric, of the tradition of social promotion whereby students moved through the system without acquiring academic skills. Having proven unable to provide to most working-class kids the necessary educational experiences that qualify them for academic promotion, the standards movement, more than a decade after its installation, reveals its underlying content: it is the latest means of exclusion, whose success depends on placing the onus for failure to achieve academic credentials on the individual rather than the system. Although state departments of education frequently mandate the teaching of certain subjects and have established standards based on high-stakes tests applicable to all districts, everyone knows that districts with working-class

majorities provide neither a curriculum and pedagogy, nor facilities that meet these standards, because, among other problems, they are chronically underfunded. The state aid
formulas that, since the advent of conservative policy hegemony, reward those districts
whose students perform well on high-stakes tests tend to be unequal. Performance-based
aid policies mean that school districts where the affluent live get more than their share;
they make up for state budget deficits by raising local property taxes and soliciting annual
subventions from parents, measures not affordable by even the top layer of wage workers,
or low-level salaried employees. The result is overcrowded classrooms, poor facilities,
especially libraries, and underpaid, often poorly prepared teachers, an outcome of finan-
cially starved education schools in public universities.

Standards presuppose students' prior possession of cultural capital—an acquisition that
almost invariably entails having been reared in a professional or otherwise upper-class
family. That, in the main, even the most privileged elementary and secondary schools
are ill equipped to compensate for home backgrounds in which reading and writing are
virtually absent has become a matter of indifference for school authorities. In this era of
social Darwinism, poor school performance is likely to be coded as genetic deficit rather
than being ascribed to social policy. Of course, the idea that working-class kids, whatever
their gender, race, or ethnic backgrounds, were selected by evolution or by God to perform
material rather than immaterial labor is not new; this view is as old as class-divided
societies. But in an epoch in which the chances of obtaining a good working-class job have
sharply declined, most kids face dire consequences if they don't acquire the skills needed in
the world of immaterial labor. Not only are 75 percent assigned to working-class jobs, but
in the absence of a shrinking pool of unionized industrial jobs, which often pay more than
some professions such as teaching and social work, they must accept low-paying service-
sector employment, enter the informal economy, or join the ranks of the chronically
unemployed.

The rise of higher education since World War II has been seen by many as a repudiation
of academic elitism. Do not the booming higher education enrollments validate the propositions of social mobility and democratic education? Not at all. Rather than constituting
a sign of rising qualifications and widening opportunity, burgeoning college and university
enrollments signify changing economic and political trends. The scientific and technical
nature of our production and service sectors increasingly requires qualified and creden-
tialed workers (it would be a mistake to regard them as identical). Students who would
have sought good factory jobs in the past now believe, with reason, they need credentials to
qualify for a well-paying job. On the other hand, even as politicians and educators decry
social promotion, and most high schools with working-class constituencies remain aging
vats, mass higher education is, to a great extent, a holding pen: effectively masking
unemployment and underemployment. This may account for its rapid expansion over the
last thirty-five years of chronic economic stagnation, deindustrialization, and the proliferation of part-time and temporary jobs, largely in the low-paid service sectors. Consequently, working-class students are able, even encouraged, to enter universities and
colleges at the bottom of the academic hierarchy—community colleges but also public
four-year colleges—thus fulfilling the formal pledge of equal opportunity for class mobility even as most of these institutions suppress the intellectual content that would fulfill the
mobility promise. But grade-point averages, which in the standards era depend as much as
the Scholastic Aptitude Test on high-stakes testing, measure the acquired knowledge of
students and restrict their access to elite institutions of higher learning, the obligatory
training grounds for professional and managerial occupations. Since all credentials are not

equal, graduating from third- and fourth-tier institutions does not confer on the successful candidate the prerequisites for entering a leading graduate school—the preparatory institution for professional and managerial occupations, or the most desirable entry-level service jobs that require only a bachelor's degree.

Pierre Bourdieu argues that schools reproduce class relations by reinforcing rather than reducing class-based differential access to social and cultural capital, key markers of class affiliation and mobility. Children of the wealthy, professionals, and the intelligentsia, he argues, always already possess these forms of capital. Far from making possible a rich intellectual education, or providing the chance to affiliate with networks of students and faculty who have handles on better jobs, schooling habituates working-class students, through mechanisms of discipline and punishment, to the bottom rungs of the work world or the academic world by subordinating or expelling them.[5] Poorly prepared for academic work by their primary and secondary schools, and having few alternatives to acquiring some kind of credential, many who stay the course and graduate from high school and third- and fourth-tier college inevitably confront a series of severely limited occupational choices—or none at all. Their life chances are just a cut above those who do not complete high school or college. Their school performances seem to validate what common sense has always suspected: given equal opportunity to attain school knowledge, the cream always rises to the top and those stuck at the bottom must be biologically impaired, victimized by the infamous "culture of poverty" or just plain distracted. That most working-class high-school and college students are obliged to hold full- or part-time jobs in order to stay in school fails to temper this judgment, for as is well known, preconceptions usually trump facts.[6] Nor does the fact that the children of the recent 20 million immigrants from Latin America, Russia, and especially Asia speak their native languages at home, in the neighborhood, and to each other in school evoke more than hand-wringing from educational leaders. In this era of tight school budgets, English as a Second Language funds have been cut or eliminated at every level of schooling.

But Paul Willis insists that working-class kids get working-class jobs by means of their refusal to accept the discipline entailed in curricular mastery and by their rebellion against school authority. Challenging the familiar "socialization" thesis—of which Bourdieu's is perhaps the most sophisticated version, according to which working-class kids "fail" because they are culturally deprived or, in the American critical version, are assaulted by the hidden curriculum and school pedagogy that subsumes kids under the prevailing order—Willis recodes kids' failure as refusal of [school] work, which lands them in the world of factory or low level service work. Willis offers no alternative educational model to schooling: his discovery functions as critique. Indeed, as Willis himself acknowledges, the school remains, in Louis Althusser's famous phrase, the main "ideological state apparatus," but working-class kids are not victims. Implicitly rejecting Richard Sennett and Jonathan Cobb's notion that school failure is a "hidden injury" of class insofar as working-class kids internalize poor school performance as a sign of personal deficit, he argues that most early school leavers are active agents in the production of their own class position. While students' antipathy to school authority is enacted at the site of the school, its origins are the working-class culture from which they spring. Workers do not like bosses, and kids do not like school bosses, the deans and principals, but often as well the teachers, whose main job in the urban centers is to keep order. The source of working-class kids' education is not the school but the shop floor, the places where their parents work, the home, and the neighborhood.[7]

In the past half-century the class question has been inflected by race and gender discrimination, and, in the American way, the "race, gender, class" phrase implies that these domains are ontologically distinct, if not entirely separate. Nor have critics theorized the race and gender question as a class issue, but as an attribute of bioidentities. In fact, in the era of identity politics, for many writers class itself stands alongside race and gender as just another identity. Having made the easy, inaccurate judgment that white students—regardless of their class or gender—stand in a qualitatively different relation to school-related opportunities than blacks, class is often suppressed as a sign of exclusion. In privileging issues of access, not only is the curriculum presupposed, in which case Bourdieu's insistence on the concept of cultural capital is ignored, but also the entire question is elided of whether schooling may be conflated with education. Only rarely do writers examine other forms of education. In both the Marxist and liberal traditions, schooling is presumed to remain—over a vast spectrum of spatial and temporal situations—the theater within which life chances are determined.

Education and Immaterial Labor

Education may be defined as the collective and individual reflection on the totality of life experiences: what we learn from peers, parents (and the socially situated cultures of which they are a part), media, and schools. By reflection I mean the transformation of experience into a multitude of concepts that constitute the abstractions we call "knowledge." Which of the forms of learning predominate are always configured historically. The exclusive focus by theorists and researchers on school knowledges—indeed, the implication that school is the principal site of what we mean by education—reflects the degree to which they have, themselves, internalized the equation of education with school knowledge and its preconditions. The key learning is they (we) have been habituated to a specific regime of intellectual labor that entails a high level of self-discipline, the acquisition of the skills of reading and writing, and the career expectations associated with professionalization.

To say this constitutes the self-reflection by intellectuals—in the broadest sense of the term—of their own relation to schooling. In the age of the decline of critical intelligence and the proliferation of technical intelligence, "intellectual" in its current connotation designates immaterial labor, not traditional intellectual pursuits such as literature, philosophy, and art. Immaterial labor describes those who work not with objects or the administration of things and people, but with ideas, symbols, and signs. Some of the occupations grouped under immaterial labor have an affective dimension. The work demands the complete subordination of brain, emotion, and body to the task while requiring the worker to exercise considerable judgment and imagination in its performance. For example, at sites such as "new economy" private-sector software workplaces; some law firms that deal with questions of intellectual property, public interest, or constitutional and international law; research universities and independent research institutes; and small, innovative design, architectural, and engineering firms, the informality of the labor process, close collaborative relationships among members of task-oriented teams, and the overflow of the space of the shop floor with the spaces of home and play evoke, at times, a high level of exhilaration, even giddiness, among members, and at other times utter exhaustion and burnout because the work invades the dreamwork and prohibits relaxation and genuine attention to partners and children.

To be an immaterial worker means, in the interest of having selfgenerated work, surrendering much of one's unfettered time. Such workers are obliged to sunder the conventional separation of work and leisure, to adopt the view that time devoted to creative, albeit commodified labor, is actually "free." Or, to be more exact, even play must be engaged in as serious business. For many the golf course, the bar, the weekend at the beach are workplaces, where dreams are shared, plans formulated, and deals are made. Just as time becomes unified around work, so work loses its geographic specificity. As Andrew Ross shows in his pathbreaking ethnography of a New York new economy workplace during and after the dot-com boom, the headiness for the pioneers of this new work world was, tacitly, a function of the halcyon period of the computer software industry when everyone felt the sky was no longer the limit.[8] When the economic crunch descended on thousands of workplaces, people were laid off, and those who remained, as well as those who became unemployed, experienced a heavy dose of market reality.

It may be argued that among elite students and institutions, schooling not only prepares immaterial labor by transmitting a bundle of legitimate knowledges; the diligent, academically successful student internalizes the blur between the classroom, play, and home by spending a great deal of time in the library or ostensibly playing at the computer. Thus the price of the promise of autonomy, a situation intrinsic to professional ideology, if not always its practice in the context of bureaucratic and hierarchical corporate systems, is to accept work as a mode of life; one lives to work, rather than the reverse. The hopes and expectations of these strata are formed in the process of schooling; indeed, they have most completely assimilated the ideologies linked to school knowledge and to the credentials conferred by the system. Thus whether professional school people, educational researchers, or not, they tend to evaluate people by the criteria to which they, themselves, were subjected. If the child has not fully embraced work as life, he is consigned to the educational nether land. Even the egalitarians (better read *populists*) accept this regime: their object is to afford those for whom work is a necessary evil entry into the social world, where work is the mission.

The Labor and Radical Movements as Educational Sites

The working-class intellectual as a social type precedes and parallels the emergence of universal public education. At the dawn of the public-school movement in the 1830s, the antebellum labor movement, which consisted largely of literate skilled workers, favored six years of schooling in order to transmit to their children the basics of reading and writing, but opposed compulsory attendance in secondary schools. The reasons were bound up with their congenital suspicion of the state, which they believed never exhibited sympathy for the workers' cause. Although opposed to child labor, the early workers' movements were convinced that the substance of education—literature, history, philosophy—should be supplied by the movement itself. Consequently, in both the oral and the written tradition, workers' organizations often constituted an alternate university to that of public schools. The active program of many workers' and radical movements until World War II consisted largely in education through newspapers, literacy classes for immigrants where the reading materials were drawn from labor and socialist classics, and world literature. These were supplemented by lectures offered by independent scholars who toured the country in the employ of lecture organizations commissioned by the unions and radical organizations.[9]

But the shop floor was also a site of education. Skilled workers were usually literate in their own language and in English, and many were voracious readers and writers. Union and radical newspapers often ran poetry and stories written by workers. Socialist-led unions sponsored educational programs; in the era when the union contract was still a rarity, the union was not so much an agency of contract negotiation and enforcement as an educational, political, and social association. In his autobiography, Samuel Gompers, the founding American Federation of Labor president, remembers his fellow cigar makers hiring a "reader" in the 1870s, who sat at the center of the shop floor and read from literary and historical classics as well as more contemporary works of political and economic analysis such as the writings of Marx and Engels. Reading groups met in the back of a bar, in the union hall, or in the local affiliate of the socialist wing of the nationality federations. Often these groups were ostensibly devoted to preparing immigrants to pass the obligatory language test for citizenship status. But the content of the reading was, in addition to labor and socialist newspapers and magazines, often supplemented by works of fiction by Shakespeare, the great nineteenth-century novelists and poets, and Karl Kautsky. In its anarchist inflection, Peter Kropotkin, Moses Hess, and Michael Bakunin were the required texts.[10]

In New York, Chicago, San Francisco, and other large cities where the Socialist, Anarchist, and Communist movements had considerable membership and a fairly substantial periphery of sympathizers, the parties established adult schools that not only offered courses pertaining to political and ideological knowledge but were vehicles for many working- and middle-class students to gain a general education. Among them, in New York, the socialist-oriented Rand School and the Communist-sponsored Jefferson School (formerly the Workers' School) lasted until the mid-1950s when, because of the decline of a Left intellectual culture among workers as much as the contemporary repressive political environment, they closed. But in their heydays, from the 1920s to the late 1940s, for tens of thousands of working-class people—many of them high-school students and industrial workers—these schools were alternate universities. Many courses concerned history, literature, and philosophy, and, at least at the Jefferson School, students could study art, drama, and music, as could their children. The tradition was revived, briefly, by the 1960s New Left that, in similar sites, sponsored free universities where the term *free* designated not an absence of tuition fees but an ideological and intellectual freedom from either the traditional Left parties or the conventional school system. I participated in organizing New York's Free University and two of its successors. While not affiliated with the labor movement or socialist parties, it successfully attracted more than a thousand mostly young students in each of its semesters and offered a broad range of courses taught by people of divergent intellectual and political orientations, including some free-market libertarians attracted to the school's nonsectarianism.[11]

When I worked in a steel mill in the late 1950s, some of us formed a group that read current literature, labor history, and economics. I discussed books and magazine articles with some of my fellow workers in bars as well as on breaks. Tony Mazzocchi, who was at the same time a worker and union officer of a Long Island local of the Oil, Chemical and Atomic Workers Union, organized a similar group, and I knew of several other cases in which young workers did the same. Some of these groups evolved into rank-and-file caucuses that eventually contested the leadership of their local unions; others were mainly for the self-edification of the participants and had no particular political goals.

But beyond formal programs, the working-class intellectual, although by no means visible in the United States, has been part of shop-floor culture since the industrializing era. In almost every workplace there is a person or persons to whom other workers turn for information about the law, the union contract, contemporary politics, or, equally important, as a source of general education. These individuals may or may not have been schooled, but, until the late 1950s, they rarely had any college education. For schools were not the primary source of their knowledge. They were, and are, largely self-educated. In my own case, having left Brooklyn College after less than a year, I worked in various industrial production jobs. When I worked the midnight shift, I got off at 8:00 a.m., ate breakfast, and spent four hours in the library before going home. Mostly I read American and European history and political economy, particularly the physiocrats, Adam Smith, David Ricardo, John Maynard Keynes, and Joseph Schumpeter. Marx's *Capital* I read in high school, and owned the three volumes.

My friend Russell Rommele, who worked in a nearby mill, was also an autodidact. His father was a first-generation German American brewery worker, with no particular literary interests. But Russell had read a wide range of historical and philosophical works as a high-school student at Saint Benedict's Prep, a Jesuit institution. The priests singled out Russell for the priesthood and mentored him in theology and social theory. The experience radicalized him, and he decided not to answer the call but to enter the industrial working class instead. Like me, he was active in the union and Newark Democratic Party politics. Working as an educator with a local union in the auto industry recently, I have met several active unionists who are intellectuals. The major difference between them and those of my generation is that they are college graduates, although none of them claim to have acquired their love of learning or their analytic perspective from schools. One is a former member of a radical organization; another learned his politics from participation in a shop-based study of a group/union caucus. In both instances, with the demise of their organizational affiliations, they remain habituated to reading, writing, and union activity.

Beneath the radar screen, union–university collaborations sprang up in the 1980s. I was among those who founded the Center for Worker Education at City College. It is a bachelor's degree program, begun for union members and their families, but expanded to other working people as well. Worker education meant, in this case, that the emphasis is not on labor studies in the manner of Cornell, UCLA, University of Minnesota's schools of industrial and labor relations, or the Queens College Labor Resource Center. Instead, City College's center offers a liberal arts and professional curriculum as well as a few courses in labor history. While the educational content is often critical, the intention articulates with the recent focus on credentialism of undergraduate institutions. Similar programs have been in operation for two decades in a collaboration between the large New York municipal employees' District Council 37 and the College of New Rochelle, and the Hospital Workers Union's various arrangements with New York-area colleges that offer upgrading, training, and college courses to thousands of its members.

Parents, Neighborhood, Class, Culture

John Locke observes that, consistent with his rejection of innate ideas, even if conceptions of good and evil are present in divine or civil law, morality is constituted by reference to our parents, relatives, and especially the "club" of peers to which we belong:

He who imagines commendation and disgrace not to be strong motives to men to accommodate themselves to the opinions and rules of those with whom they converse seems little skilled in the nature or the history of mankind: the greatest part whereof we shall find govern themselves, chiefly, if not solely by this law of *fashion* [emphasis in the original]; and so they do what keeps them in reputation with their company, [with] little regard for the laws of God or the magistrate.[12]

William James puts the matter equally succinctly:

A man's social self is the recognition which he gets from his mates. We are not only gregarious animals, liking to be in the sight of our fellows, but we have an innate propensity to get ourselves noticed, and noticed favorably, by our kind. No more fiendish punishment could be devised, were such a thing physically possible, than that he should be turned loose in society and remain absolutely unnoticed by all the members thereof.[13]

That the social worlds of peers and family are the chief referents for the formation of the social self, neither philosopher doubted. Each in his own fashion situates the individual in social context, which provides a "common measure of virtue and vice" (Locke) even as they acknowledge the ultimate choice resides with the individual self. These, and not the institutions, even those that have the force of law, are the primary sources of authority.

Hannah Arendt argues that education "by its very nature cannot forego either authority or tradition." Nor can it base itself on the presumption that children share an autonomous existence from adults.[14] Yet schooling ignores the reality of the society of kids at the cost of undermining its own authority. The society of kids is in virtually all classes an alternative and oppositional site of knowledge and of moral valuation. We have already seen how working-class kids get working-class jobs by means of their rebellion against school authority. Since refusal and resistance is a hallmark of that moral order, the few who will not obey the invocation to fail, or to perform indifferently in school, often find themselves marginalized or expelled from the society of kids. While they adopt a rationality that can be justified on eminently practical grounds, the long tradition of rejection of academic culture has proven hard to break, even in the wake of evidence that those working-class jobs to which they were oriented no longer exist. For what is at stake in the resistance of adolescents is their perception that the blandishments of the adult world are vastly inferior to the pleasures of their own. In the first place, the new service economy offers few inducements: wages are low, the job is boring, and the future bleak. And since the schools now openly present themselves as a link in the general system of control, it may appear to some students that cooperation is a form of self-deception.

If not invariably, then in many households parents provide to the young a wealth of knowledges: the family mythologies that feature an uncle or aunt, a grandparent or an absent parent. These are the stories, loosely based on some actual event(s) in which family members have distinguished themselves in various ways that (usually) illustrate a moral virtue or defect, the telling of which constitutes a kind of didactic message. Even when not attached to an overt narrative, parable, or myth, the actions of our parents offer many lessons: How do they deal with adversity? How do they address ordinary, everyday problems? What do they learn from their own trials and tribulations and what do they say to us? What are our parents' attitudes toward money, joblessness, and everyday life disruptions such as sudden, acute illness or accidents? What do they learn from the endless conflicts with their parent(s) over issues of sex, money, and household responsibilities?

The relative weight of parental to peer authority is an empirical question that cannot be decided in advance; what both have in common is their location in everyday life. Parents are likely to be more susceptible to the authority of law and of its magistrates and, in a world of increasing uncertainty, will worry that if their children choose badly, they may be left behind. But the associations with our peers we make in everyday life provide the recognition that we crave, define what is worthy of praise or blame, and confer approbation or disapproval on our decisions. But having made a choice that runs counter to that of "their company" or club, individuals must form or join a new "company" to confer the judgment of virtue on their actions. This company must, of necessity, consist of "peers," the definition of which has proven fungible.

Religion, the law, and, among kids, school authorities face the obstacles erected by the powerful rewards and punishments meted out by the "clubs" to which people are affiliated. At a historical conjunction when—beneath the relentless pressure imposed by capital to transform all labor into wage labor, thereby forcing every adult into the paid labor force— the society of kids increasingly occupies the space of civil society. The neighborhood, once dominated by women and small shopkeepers, has all but disappeared save for the presence of children and youth. As parents toil for endless hours to pay the ever-mounting debts incurred by home ownership, perpetual car and appliance payments, and the costs of health care, kids are increasingly on their own, and this lack of supervision affects their conceptions of education and life.

Some recent studies and teacher observations have discovered a considerable reluctance among black students in elite universities to perform well in school, even among those with professional or managerial family backgrounds. Many seem indifferent to arguments that show that school performance is a central prerequisite to better jobs and higher status in the larger work world. Among the more acute speculations is the conclusion that black students' resistance reflects an anti-intellectual bias and a hesitation, if not refusal, to enter the mainstream corporate world. There are similar attitudes among some relatively affluent white students as well. Although by no means a majority, some students are less enamored by the work world to which they, presumably, have been habituated by school, and especially by the prospect of perpetual work. In the third-tier universities, state and private alike, many students, apparently forced by their parents to enroll, wonder out loud why they are there. Skepticism about schooling still abounds even as they graduate from high school and enroll in postsecondary schools in record numbers. According to one colleague of mine who teaches in a third-tier private university in the New York metropolitan area, many of these mostly suburban students "sleepwalk" through their classes, do not participate in class discussions, and are lucky to get a C grade.[15]

In the working-class neighborhoods—white, black, and Latino—the word is out: given the absence of viable alternatives, you must try to obtain that degree, but this defines the limit of loyalty to the enterprise. Based on testimonies of high-school and community-college teachers, for every student who takes school knowledge seriously there are twenty or more who are timeservers. Most are ill prepared for academic work, and, since the community colleges, four-year state colleges, and "teaching" universities simply lack the resources to provide the means by which such students can improve their school performance, beyond the credential there is little motivation among them to try to get an education.

In some instances, those who break from their club and enter the regime of school knowledge risk being drummed out of a lifetime of relationships with their peers. What has euphemistically been described as "peer pressure" bears, among other moral structures, on the degree to which kids are permitted to cross over the line into the precincts of adult authority. While success in school is not equivalent to squealing on a friend to the cops, or transgressing some sacred moral code of the society of kids, it comes close to committing an act of betrayal. This is comprehensible only if the reader is willing to suspend the prejudice that schooling is tantamount to education and is an unqualified "good," as compared to the presumed evil of school failure, or the decision of the slacker to rebel by refusing to succeed.

To invoke the concept of "class" in either educational debates or any other politically charged discourse generally refers to the white working class. Educational theory and practice treats blacks and Latinos, regardless of their economic positions, as unified categories. That black kids from professional, managerial, and business backgrounds share as much or more with their white counterparts than with working-class blacks is generally ignored by most educational writers, just as in race discourse whites are an undifferentiated racial identity, which refers in slightly different registers to people of African origin and those who migrated from Latin countries of South America and the Caribbean, and are treated as a unified category. The narrowing of the concept of class limits our ability to discern class at all. I want to suggest that, although we must stipulate ethnic, gender, race, and occupational distinction among differentiated strata of wage labor—with the exception of children of salaried professional and technical groups, where the culture of schooling plays a decisive role—class education transcends these distinctions. No doubt there are gradations among the strata that comprise this social formation, but the most privileged professional strata (physicians, attorneys, scientists, professors) and the high-level managers are self-reproducing, not principally through schooling but through social networks. These include private schools, some of which are residential; clubs and associations; and, in suburban public schools, the self-selection of students on the basis of distinctions. Show me a school friendship between the son or daughter of a corporate manager and the child of a janitor or factory worker, and I will show you an anomaly.

Schooling selects a fairly small number of children of the class of wage labor for genuine class mobility. In the first half of the twentieth century, having lost its appeal among middle-class youth, the Catholic Church turned to working-class students as a source of cadre recruitment. In my neighborhood of the East Bronx two close childhood friends, both of Italian background, entered the priesthood. For these sons of construction workers, the Church provided their best chance to escape the hardships and economic uncertainties of manual labor. Another kid became a pharmacist because the local college, Fordham University, offered scholarships. A fourth was among the tiny coterie of students who passed the test for one of the city's special schools, Bronx Science, and became a science teacher. Otherwise, almost everybody else remained a worker or, like my best friend, Kenny, went to prison.

Despite the well-publicized claim that anyone can escape their condition of social and economic birth—a claim reproduced by schools and by the media with numbing regularity—most working-class students, many of whom have some college credits but often do not graduate—end up in low- and middle-level service jobs that do not pay a decent working-class wage. Owing to the steep decline of unionized industrial production jobs, those who enter factories increasingly draw wages substantially below union standards. Those who do graduate find work in computers, although rarely at the professional levels. The relatively low paid become K-12 school teachers and health care professionals, mostly nurses and technicians, or enter the social services field as caseworkers, medical social workers, or nonsupervisory social welfare workers. The question I want to pose is whether these "professional" occupations represent genuine mobility.

During the postwar economic boom that made possible a significant expansion of spending for schools, the social services, and administration of public goods, the public sector workplace became a favored site of black and Latino recruitment, mainly for clerical, maintenance, and entry-level patient care jobs in hospitals and other health care facilities. Within several decades a good number advanced to practical and registered nursing, but not in all sections of the country. As unionization spread to the nonprofit private sector as well as public employment in the 1960s and 1970s, these jobs paid enough to enable many to enjoy what became known as a middle-class living standard, with a measure of job security offered by union security and civil service status. While it is true that "job security" has often been observed in its breach, the traditional deal made by teachers, nurses, and social workers was that they traded higher incomes for job security. But after about 1960, spurred by the resurgent civil rights movement, these "second-level" professionals—white and black—began to see themselves as workers more than professionals: they formed unions, struck for higher pay and shorter hours, and assumed a very unprofessional adversarial stance toward institutional authority. Contracts stipulated higher salaries, definite hours—a sharp departure from professional ideology—and seniority as a basis for layoffs, like any industrial contract, and demanded substantial vacation and sick leave.

Their assertion of working-class values and social position may have been strategic; indeed, it inspired the largest wave of union organizing since the 1930s. But, together with the entrance of huge numbers of women and blacks into the public and quasi-public sector workforces, it was also a symptom of the proletarianization of the second-tier professions. Several decades later, salaried physicians made a similar discovery; they formed unions and struck against high malpractice insurance costs as much as the onerous conditions imposed on their autonomy by health maintenance organizations and government authorities bent on cost containment, often at the physicians' expense. More to the point, the steep rise of public employees' salaries and benefits posed the question of how to maintain services in times of fiscal austerity, which might be due to economic downturn or to probusiness tax policies. The answer has been that the political and public officials told employees that the temporary respite from the classical trade union trade-off was over. All public employees have suffered a relative deterioration in their salaries and benefits. Since the mid-1970s fiscal crises, begun in New York City, they have experienced layoffs for the first time since the Depression. And their unions have been in a concessionary bargaining mode for decades. In the politically and ideologically repressive environment of the last twenty-five years, the class divide has sharpened. Ironically, in the wake of the attacks by legislatures and business against their hard-won gains in the early 1980s, the teachers unions abandoned their militant class posture and reverted to professionalism and a center-right political strategy.

In truth, schools are learning sites, even if only for a handful, of intellectual knowledge. For the most part, they transmit the instrumental logic of credentialism, together with their transformation from institutions of discipline to those of control, especially in working-class districts. Even talented, dedicated teachers have difficulty reaching kids and convincing them that the life of the mind may hold unexpected rewards, though the career implications of critical thought are not apparent. The breakdown of the mission of public schools has produced varied forms of disaffection; if school violence has abated in some places, that does not signify the decline of gangs and other "clubs" that represent the autonomous world of youth. The society of kids is more autonomous because, in contrast to the 1960s, official authorities no longer offer hope; instead, in concert with the doctrine of control, they threaten punishment that includes, but is not necessarily associated with, incarceration. The large number of drug busts of young black and Latino men should not be minimized. With over a million blacks, more than 3 percent of the African American population—most of them young (25 percent of young black men)—within the purview of the criminal justice system, the law may be viewed as a more or less concerted effort to counter by force the power of peers. This may be regarded in the context of the failure of schools. Of course, more than three hundred years ago John Locke knew the limits of the magistrates—indeed, of any adult authority—to overcome the power of the society of kids.[16]

Conclusion

What are the requisite changes that would transform schools from credential mills and institutions of control to sites of education that prepare young people to see themselves as active participants in the world? As my analysis implies, the fundamental condition is to abolish high-stakes tests that dominate the curriculum and subordinate teachers to the role of drillmasters and subject students to stringent controls. By this proposal I do not mean to eliminate the need for evaluative tools. The essay is a fine measure of both writing ability and of the student's grasp of literature, social science, and history. While mathematics, science, and language proficiency do require considerable rote learning, the current curriculum and pedagogy in these fields includes neither a historical account of the changes in scientific and mathematical theory nor a metaconceptual explanation of what the disciplines are about. Nor are courses in language at the secondary level ever concerned with etymological issues, comparative cultural study of semantic differences, and other topics that might relieve the boredom of rote learning by providing depth of understanding. The broader understanding of science in the modern world—its relation to technology, war, and medicine, for example—should surely be integrated into the curriculum; some of these issues appear in the textbooks, but teachers rarely discuss them because they are busy preparing students for the high-stakes tests in which knowledge of the social contexts for science, language, and mathematics is not included.

I agree with Hannah Arendt that education "cannot forgo either authority or tradition." But authority must be earned rather than assumed, and the transmission of tradition needs to be critical rather than worshipful. If teachers were allowed to acknowledge student skepticism to incorporate kids' knowledge into the curriculum by making what they know the object of rigorous study, especially popular music and television, teachers might be treated with greater respect. But there is no point denying the canon; one of the more egregious conditions of subordination is the failure of schools to expose students to the best exemplars, for people who have no cultural capital are thereby condemned to social and political marginality, let alone deprived of some of the genuine pleasures to be derived from encounters with genuine works of art. When the New York City Board of Education (now the Department of Education) mandates that during every semester high-school English classes read a Shakespeare play, and one or two works of nineteenth-century English literature, but afford little or no access to the best Russian novels of the nineteenth century, no opportunities to examine some of the most influential works of Western or Eastern philosophy, and provide no social and historical context for what is learned, tradition is observed in the breach more than in its practice.

Finally, schools should cut their ties to corporate interests and reconstruct the curriculum along the lines of genuine intellectual endeavor. Nor should schools be seen as career conduits, although this function will be difficult to displace: in an era of high economic anxiety, many kids and their parents worry about the future and seek some practical purchase on it. It will take some convincing that their best leg up is to be educated. It is unlikely in the present environment, but possible in some places.

One could elaborate these options; this is only an outline. In order to come close to their fulfillment at least three things are needed. First, we require a conversation concerning the nature and scope of education and the limits of schooling as an educational site. Along with this, theorists and researchers need to link their knowledge of popular culture, culture in the anthropological sense—that is, everyday life—with the politics of education. Teachers who, by their own education, are intellectuals who respect and want to help children obtain a genuine education regardless of their social class are in the forefront of enabling social change and are entrusted with widening students' possibilities in life. For this we need a new regime of teacher education founded on the idea that the educator must be educated well. It would surely entail abolishing the current curricula of most education schools, if not the schools themselves. Teacher training should be embedded in general education, not in "methods," many of which are useless; instruction should include knowledge other than credential and bring the union/movement/organic intellectuals into the classroom. In other words, the classroom should be a window on the world, not a hermetically sealed regime of the imposition of habitus, that is, making the test of academic success equivalent to measuring the degree to which the student has been inculcated with the habit of subordination to school and pedagogic authority.[17] And we need a movement of parents, students, teachers, and labor armed with a political program to force legislatures to adequately fund schooling at the federal, state, and local levels, and boards of education to deauthorize high-stakes tests that currently drive the curriculum and pedagogy.

To outline a program for the reconstruction of schooling does not imply that the chances for its success are good, especially in the current environment. Indeed, almost all current trends oppose the concept of public education as a school of freedom. But if the principle of critique is hope rather than the most rigorous form of nihilism—the suspension of action pending an upsurge from below—we have an obligation to resist but also to suggest alternatives. These will, inevitably, be attacked as Utopian, and, of course, they are. But as many have argued, Utopian thought is the condition for change. Without the "impossible," there is little chance for reform.

Notes

1. John Dewey, *Democracy and Education: An Introduction to the Philosophy of Education* (1916; Glencoe, Ill.: Free Press, 1964).
2. The literature on the limits of democracy in America is vast. For a searing indictment, see the classic critique: Grant McConnell, *Private Power and American Democracy* (New York: Knopf, 1966).
3. Pierre Bourdieu's concepts of cultural and social capital are introduced in Pierre Bourdieu and Jean-Claude Passeron, *Reproduction in Education, Culture, and Society*, trans. Richard Nice (London: Sage, 1977).
4. Andrew Ross, *No-Collar: The Humane Workplace and Its Hidden Costs* (New York: Basic Books, 2003).
5. Bourdieu, *Reproduction*.
6. Aaron V. Cicourel and John I. Kitsuse, *The Educational Decision-Makers* (Indianapolis, Ind.: Bobbs Merrill, 1963). This is one of the most persuasive studies demonstrating the salience of phenomenological investigations of social life. It is a tacit repudiation of the reliance of much of social science, especially sociology and political science, on what people say rather than what they do.
7. The best analysis of the relation of schools to the lives of working-class kids remains Paul Willis, *Learning to Labor: How Working Class Kids Get Working Class Jobs* (New York: Columbia University Press, 1981).
8. Ross, *No-Collar*.
9. Paul C. Mishler, *Raising Reds: The Young Pioneers, Radical Summer Camps, and Communist Political Culture in the United States* (New York: Columbia University Press, 1999).

10. Samuel Gompers, *Seventy Years of Life and Labor: An Autobiography* (New York: E.P. Button, 1925).

11. Marvin Gettleman, "No Varsity Teams: New York's Jefferson School of Social Science, 1943–1956," *Science and Society* (fall 2002), 336–59. My reflections on the Free University and other New Left educational projects may be found in Aronowitz, "When the New Left Was New," in *The Sixties without Apology*, ed. Sohnya Sayres, Anders Stephanson, Stanley Aronowitz, and Fredric Jameson (Minneapolis: University of Minnesota Press, 1984).

12. John Locke, *An Essay concerning Human Understanding* (New York: Dover, 1958), bk. 1, chap. 28, 478.

13. William James, *The Principles of Psychology* (New York: Dover, 1955), 1, 293.

14. Hannah Arendt, "Crisis in Education," *Between Past and Future* (New York: Harcourt, Brace and World, 1961).

15. James H. McWhorter, *Losing the Race: Self-Sabotage in Black America* (New York: Free Press, 2000).

16. Stanley Aronowitz, *False Promises: The Shaping of American Working Class Consciousness*, 2d ed. (Durham, N.C.: Duke University Press, 1992); Henry A. Giroux, *The Abandoned Generation: Democracy beyond the Culture of Fear* (New York: Palgrave, 2003); Stephanie Urso Spina, ed., *Smoke and Mirrors: The Hidden Context of Violence in Schools and Society* (Boulder, Colo.: Rowman and Littlefield, 2001).

17. Bourdieu, *Reproduction.*

6

The Surveillance Curriculum: Risk Management and Social Control in the Neoliberal School

Torin Monahan

On the morning of April 20, 1999, two students walked into Columbine High School in Littleton, Colorado, and opened fire. Armed with shotguns, a rifle, a handgun, and homemade bombs, Eric Harris, age eighteen, and Dylan Klebold, age seventeen, went on a forty-nine minute shooting spree that resulted in the death of fifteen people, including a teacher and the two shooters (who committed suicide), and the injury of twenty-three others (CNN 2000). The activities of Harris and Klebold that day were caught on video surveillance and broadcasted across the major television networks, despite protests from students' parents and school officials (BBC 1999). It is ironic that although the school's surveillance system and an on-site, armed security guard were unable to prevent the killings at Columbine, the terrifying shooting has become a key reference point in justifying increased surveillance and security systems in schools throughout the United States.

This chapter questions the rise of high-tech surveillance systems in public schools and argues that debates over student safety, although important, tend to obscure deeper changes in social relations brought about by surveillance and security regimes. After all, schools continue to be some of the absolutely safest places for youth: with a one in two million chance of dying a violent death in school, "students are safer at school than they are in their own communities, in cars, and even in their own homes" (American Civil Liberties Union [ACLU] 2001). But one would be hard-pressed to believe this fact, given the increased media attention to school violence and the continuing investment of millions of dollars in school surveillance equipment. What might be even more surprising is that independent evaluations of video surveillance systems have found them to be entirely ineffectual at preventing violent crimes (Armitage 2002; Rice-Oxley 2004; Ditton et al. 1999), yet these systems continue to be funded at a record rate.

To say that surveillance systems are ineffectual at preventing violent crimes, however, does not imply that they are without effects. The most profound results from surveillance in schools may be the integration of law enforcement functions into the everyday practices of individuals at schools and the subsequent rise of a culture of control that supplants other social or educational missions of public education. Currently, more than 75 percent of all new schools are being equipped with video surveillance systems (Dillon 2003), and school districts are lobbying for funds from federal and state governments and from the private sector for surveillance in older schools. The most common school surveillance devices are digital or analog cameras for video recording, but others include metal detectors, ID cards, Internet tracking, biometrics, transparent lockers and book bags, electronic gates, and two-way radios.

Thus far, except for words of caution from civil liberties groups, there has been almost no inquiry into the kinds of relationships being produced from this new amalgam of high-tech industry, law enforcement, and public education. By examining several recent high-profile cases, this chapter begins to probe these emergent relations and their wider implications. The argument advanced here is that surveillance systems operate as extensions of the neoliberal state, carving out new markets for high-tech companies and integrating police functions into the social worlds of public education. Neoliberalism, as discussed here, is characterized by a simultaneous retreat from social programs and an advancement of social control over the public (Bourdieu 1998; Monahan 2005a; Katz, Chapter 2, this volume). The mass media advance this process by presenting students as either victims or criminals who can be protected or controlled, respectively, by surveillance systems. As a result, criminalization and victimization may become the primary experiences for students in public education.

The Hummingbird's Song: Biometrics in Public Schools

In late 2003, the sheriff's department of Maricopa County, Arizona, installed a face-recognition surveillance system at the Royal Palm Middle School in Phoenix. As with other biometric systems, such as those based on fingerprinting or retinal scans, the primary objective is not to track the movements or activities of people hut instead to identify them (Van der Ploeg 1999a). Specifically, the data from face scans at the middle school are transmitted straight to the sheriff's department for immediate, automated comparison with national databases of sex offenders, child abductors, and missing children. Should a positive match be found, the sheriff will dispatch officers to the school site, bypassing administrators and teachers, effectively removing school representatives from the intervention process.

As with most schools, Royal Palm Middle School has had no previous (reported) problems with sex offenders, child abductors, or missing children. What, then, are the reasons behind this seemingly sudden and extreme move? The impulse for this system originated with a $350,000 donation of equipment to the sheriff's department by Hummingbird Defense Systems, Inc., a security technology company in Phoenix (Kossan 2003). This donated equipment was earmarked for "pilot programs," presumably to test the efficacy of the systems but also to locate new markets for biometric security systems designed by the company. According to one news source, the "Sheriffs Office and Hummingbird's CEO concocted the idea of using the technology in schools" (Brown 2004). The sheriff, leveraging much more clout than any single high-tech company could on its own, persuaded the superintendent and school board to allow the system to be implemented, on a trial basis, in the school district.[1] And whereas local news stories framed this donation as a "gift" to the schools, press releases from the company's partners put an entirely different spin on the relationship:

> Hummingbird's CEO Steve Greschner said, "This is a great application of technology and a great opportunity to help make schools a safer place for our children. The system is deployed on a school by school basis and should generate recurring revenue of approximately $350,000.00 (USD) per year for Acsys Biometrics."
>
> (Acsys Biometrics 2004)

The press release states quite clearly that the company's goal is to insert these systems into all schools within Maricopa County, not to have Royal Palm Middle School serve as an isolated test case (Acsys Biometrics 2004).

Hummingbird Defense Systems, Inc., is not alone in cultivating or capitalizing on new public markets for security systems post-9/11. In 2002 the industry for biometric systems was already huge, with gross sales in the United States expected "to grow from $400 million in 2000 to $1.9 billion in 2005" (Nieto, Johnston-Dodds, and Simmons 2002:8). In 2004 the U.S. Department of Homeland Security blew that projection out of the water by awarding a 10-year contract of up to $10 billion to the private company Accenture for biometric systems at U.S. ports of entry (Lichtblau and Markoff 2004). A total of $250 billion in U.S. tax dollars has been spent on airline security alone since 9/11 (Mother Jones 2005). Thus, the larger context of public security systems is vast. One can learn much about the assumptions driving surveillance regimes in public schools and beyond by attending to the discourses employed by surveillance and security companies such as Hummingbird.

Hummingbird's website presents the quest for security as a dangerous war against unknown assailants or terrorists. The "solutions" they provide to their potential clients are explicitly militaristic "command and control systems" developed in government laboratories:

> Security technology, specifically command and control systems and environments, have been developed and operated in federal and national government laboratories and environments for the past 10 years. It is this sophisticated and critical-level technology that is now being brought to the commercial business industry.
>
> (Hummingbird Defense Systems, Inc., 2004)

Graphic illustrations on the website depict a centralized environment of surveillance and identification subsystems, networking infrastructures, and alerting mechanisms orbiting around the command and control center of servers and software that run the system. Should one get the impression that such a centralized system is cumbersome or labor intensive, Hummingbird assures clients that their solutions are entirely "flexible" and labor saving, requiring only one operator to manage the entire system and deflect threats in real time (Hummingbird Defense Systems, Inc., 2004).

The intended message is clear: security is achieved through militaristic technical systems of automation, standardization, and centralization. Whether the client is a school, a corporation, or the military, the same command and control systems will provide solutions to its security problems. Hummingbird's argument gains rhetorical force by erasing the social world from its flowchart representation of reality; the mission of "security" is the same even if the threats are wildly divergent across contexts of use or if the threats are entirely manufactured. Indeed, security is something that is never operationalized—it is, instead, assumed to be a universal value and a good that is beyond question. But it is worth asking what happens to the social functions and climates of public schools when they are perceived as urban outposts in need of military-grade protections.

Surveillance systems of the sort designed by Hummingbird and implemented by the Maricopa County sheriff's department signal one dimension of the growing culture of control in public education. In this case, the systems promise to manage a range of risks: the risk that a child molester or abductor will be circulating among schoolchildren without anyone's awareness, the risk that *your* child might be abducted or molested, the risk that an abducted child will never be found, the risk that police will not arrive at the scene in time. All these "risks" are really "fears" that were vague or nonexistent prior to the introduction of the systems and the subsequent media coverage and public conversation. By means of this process of fear cultivation, the surveillance systems become "necessary" interventions, worth any cost, inconvenience, or more profound alteration of educational environments. As the sheriff avers, "If it works one time, locates one missing child or saves a child from a sexual attack, I feel it's worth it" (Rushlo 2003).

In the networks of control being established in Phoenix schools and elsewhere, law enforcement personnel are absorbing more power over school operations, especially those operations concerning risk management and student discipline. Many schools have on-site armed police personnel—typically called school resource officers (SROs)—who handle disciplinary matters, develop relationships with students, and often garner more fear and respect from students than do teachers or principals (McDaniel 2001; Brotherton 1996). Students' ambivalent relationships with SROs are well grounded, because with the advent of zero tolerance policies for drugs or violence at schools, SROs become the primary agents for funneling students into the criminal justice system. Public education and criminal justice systems are overlapping in many places and are initiating youth into disciplinary relationships with the state (Kupchik and Monahan forthcoming). In this context, for schools without SROs, surveillance systems like Hummingbird's give police an open invitation to charge into schools whenever they suspect a positive match, even though face-recognition systems are notorious for delivering false positives (Garfinkel 2002). But because police or security personnel are already present at many school sites,[2] the surveillance system functions as one more hardwired justification for police presence, interaction, and intervention with public education.

Scopophilia and SWAT in Public Schools

Students arriving at Stratford High School in Goose Creek, South Carolina, early on November 5, 2003, were met with an unforgettable experience. As they were socializing in the hallways, stashing lunches and books in their lockers, and using the restrooms before class, teams of uniformed police officers stormed into the building with guns drawn. Seemingly coming from nowhere, the police bore down on students in a SWAT-style paramilitary raid, yelling, "Get on the ground! Get on the ground! Hands on your head, hands on your head, do you understand?" (Associated Press 2003). Students who did not immediately comply were forced down at gunpoint, and plastic ties (similar to those used by police on protesters or by U.S. troops on prisoners in Iraq) were cinched tightly around their wrists behind their backs. Next, a menacing police dog was led down the hallway, barking and grabbing and shaking students' bags with its mouth and periodically jumping as it passed just inches from students' heads in its search for illegal drugs.[3] No drugs were found. Yet as officers left, they threatened students with a repeat of that morning's assault: "If you're an innocent bystander to what has transpired here today, you can thank those people that are bringing dope into this school. Every time we think there's dope in this school, we're going to be coming up here to deal with it, and this is one of the ways we can deal with it" (Associated Press 2003).

This entire event was captured on the school's elaborate video surveillance system and later broadcasted across local and national television news stations. As seen in the school's video playback, one of the officers was brandishing a video camera instead of a gun, recording the scene from yet another perspective. Afterward, the principal gave several media interviews from his office, where he proudly displayed five of his video monitors (each divided into sixteen frames, one per camera), played back the scene of the police raid, and narrated it, seemingly without any compunction or concern that his recorded words might later be used against him in court. But the surveillance system, it turns out, was not simply an objective observer to what happened that day; it helped motivate the raid, because the principal—although he could not see it, and perhaps *because* he could not see it—was certain that somewhere, somehow, students were evading the system to sell large quantities of illegal drugs at the school (Mizzell 2003).

The media broadcasts of the raid solidified the event for the community, becoming a tangible reference point for parents in their anger and outrage. The principal responded to the public by both defending the actions of the police and distancing himself from them: "I have to defend all the trained professionals. If that's how they've been trained and been instructed on what to do. Yes, it was a situation. This was real" (Mizzell 2003). Yet this attempt to separate himself from the police and their training rings somewhat false, because he was the one who planned the raid with the officers, hiding them in closets, offices, and under stairwells so that they could descend stealthily and rapidly on the students (ACLU 2003a). The principal also adopted a hands-on approach of walking the hallways with the police and instructing them to restrain certain black students with plastic ties and subject them to extra scrutiny—orders that the police willingly obeyed (Lewin 2003; ACLU 2003b).

Soon after the raid, the ACLU filed a lawsuit on behalf of 20 of the students, claiming that the police and school officials violated these students' constitutional rights to be safeguarded against unreasonable search and seizure:

> By deploying uniformed police officers with their firearms drawn in the school, by allowing these officers to threaten plaintiffs with a large and aggressive police dog, and by searching the persons and property of the plaintiffs and other students, the defendants terrorized the students and betrayed the promise of a safe, secure learning environment.
>
> (ACLU 2003a)

The community was not soothed by the fact that the police accosted a disproportionate number of black students during the event. According to one report, "While Black students make up less than a quarter of the 2,700 students at Stratford High School, two-thirds of the 107 students caught up in the sweep were Black" (*San Francisco Bay View* 2004). On December 16, 2003, Reverend Jesse Jackson traveled to the school's county to participate in public protests against the aggressive and discriminatory tactics used by police in the drug search.

The school's surveillance system plays an interesting and complex role in this story. Yes, it fostered public awareness about the extreme tactics used on students, most of whom were minors. But it also seems to have facilitated a profound disconnect between the principal and the students under his care in the first place. The surveillance system contributed to the principal's paranoia about illicit activities occurring somewhere *outside* of his almost ubiquitous field of vision yet *inside* the protected territory under his watch. Holed up in his office, cycling through all the video feeds like a cross between a security guard in a war-zone bunker and a channel surfer at home in his living room, he was able to demonize the students and see them as dangerous criminal threats rather than as young people. The video terminals filtered reality in an extremely underdetermined way, inviting him to weave any narrative or impose any biases that he pleased. As he watched the playback on his monitor, he explained to one interviewer that the reason the dogs did not find any drugs was that the students had already dumped them, and the reason why other students did not arrive with drugs was that they received cell-phone tips from others

(ACLU 2003b). Because these (and other) constructed "facts" find no representation in the surveillance monitors, they paradoxically become all the more true for the observer—the cameras do not prove otherwise.

Surveillance systems may not directly create prejudice or fear, but they tend to cultivate extreme voyeuristic impulses (scopophilia) that enforce divisions between subjects and objects and amplify the base qualities of those doing the watching. For example, from 2002 to 2003, administrators at a public middle school in Tennessee illegally used video surveillance to monitor students in locker rooms (Dillon 2003). Records from Internet service providers show that the saved digital recordings, mostly of girls, were accessed 98 times through the Internet at all hours of the night and from multiple states (Riley 2003; National Consumer Coalition 2003). In the example of the police raid at Stratford High School, students under surveillance were marked as criminals in advance, and this encouraged police to adopt paramilitary tactics appropriate to dealing with extreme threats. When no drugs were found, the students were not vindicated but still perceived as criminals; they just happened to be clever enough to evade the system, this time. But even if drugs had been found, the discovery would not have justified the means employed, the assumption of student guilt, or the absence of genuine social relations between administrators and students.

Taking the Media to School

Would that the media were neutral parties in the ongoing transformation of schools into fertile sites for police intervention and profitable markets for private companies.[4] But there is nothing impartial and little factual about news reporting on violence in schools. When shootings such as those at Columbine occur, media outlets such as CNN provide 24-hour coverage, and school violence is declared to be a widespread "epidemic" that demands that policy makers immediately make schools safer. Video surveillance fuels this perception and desire by allowing for continual playback of "real" events, casting all viewers as on-site witnesses, complicit in the events and guilty for their own inaction. Every rebroadcast accretes upon the last, further reinforcing the belief in a widespread "pattern of violence" until the epidemic is taken as truth and fear sets in.

The statistics on school violence tell another story. Contrary to media-generated popular perceptions, violence in schools has steadily *decreased* over the past decade, creating a discernible trend toward safer schools (Lawrence and Mueller 2003). In 1992–93, there were 42 student homicides on school premises throughout the United States, but after steady decline, that figure reached 4 student homicides in 2002–2003 (Youth Violence Project 2003).[5] Serious violent crimes (i.e., rape, sexual assault, aggravated assault, or robbery) also have diminished, starting at 10 per 1,000 in 1992, peaking at 13 per 1,000 in 1994, and dropping to 6 per 1,000 in 2001 (DeVoe et al. 2003). And even before the Columbine shooting and the subsequent rush to equip schools with metal detectors, which only 1 percent of schools currently use (Chandler 2004), gun possession by students had dropped from 6 percent in 1993–94 to 3.8 percent in 1997–98 (Burns and Crawford 1999). Considering that school populations have increased by 19 percent over roughly the same period of time, from 45.4 million in 1988 to 53.9 million in 2001 (Hussar and Gerald 2003), the few occurrences of school violence can hardly be equated with an epidemic of any sort. In fact, school violence does not appear to be a pressing problem at all when compared to the 2,000 to 3,000 children killed each year by parents or guardians (Burns and Crawford 1999). Just as an unjustified fear of increasing crime pushes people into gated communities (Low 2003), this "phantom epidemic" of school violence (Best 2002) nonetheless generates fear-inspired social practices that aggravate social inequalities and arguably give rise to even greater fear of others, whether in schools or in neighborhoods.

The culture of fear generated by the media spills over into a culture of control in schools. When news media continually return to the motif of school violence, they effectively fuse fear with the topic, such that "school violence" elicits an emotional response apart from its specific circumstances or degree of magnitude.[6] Surveillance equipment is one material and symbolic manifestation of this reactionary culture of control that infiltrates social worlds and structures social relations. Not only does surveillance in schools produce a demand for even more surveillance, as with the Columbine case or other high-profile events caught on video, but it also provides a rationale and responsibility for police to involve themselves as agents of discipline and control within schools.

The culture of control produces so-called "victims" and "criminals" and imposes these identities on students, as was seen with the two examples of surveillance in schools presented previously. In the process, school practices mutate into those of risk management. When students are constructed as victims, the radical interventions for the protection of their bodies and for the protection of school districts from liability are seemingly justified. Victimhood, in other words, serves as the motivating logic for the advancement of systems of control in public education. The reason for this is that the production of students as victims—who are "innocent children" or "kids"—engenders moral outrage on a far greater scale than stories about the victimization of the general public by young delinquents or gang members. Childhood is a sacred state, one that society demands be protected by public institutions, until the "children" become "criminals," at which point they are tossed into a moral abyss, perceived as somehow less than human but increasingly held accountable as adults.[7]

Although victimhood is a risk that demands mitigation, (potential) criminals must also be managed (Lyon 2001). Surveillance regimes in schools, police in schools, and zero tolerance laws are overlapping and complementary mechanisms for risk management and the advancement of the culture of control (Kupchik and Monahan forthcoming). As Henry Giroux expounds, these mechanisms "signify a shift away from treating the body as a social investment (i.e., rehabilitation) to viewing it as a threat to security, demanding control, surveillance, and punishment" (cited in T. Lewis 2003:348). The cultivation and imposition of criminal identities are as important as the identities of victimhood to the perpetuation of the system. Public education depends on victims and criminals, potential or actual, to justify its risk management functions, which enmesh industry interests and police actions with educational institutions. The media eagerly meet this need for victims and criminals by manufacturing them and/or elevating them to epidemic proportions in the public imagination. Such media reports are influential in shaping public opinion and policy agendas, whereby policy makers and law enforcement agents feel compelled to respond to the public's augmented concerns about school safety.

The media's production of fear, then, acquires force by transforming particular and idiosyncratic events into universal and absolute threats. Random acts of school violence are presented as evidence of widespread social chaos and moral decay, and the perpetrators of these crimes are viewed as enemies of the social order or the very fabric of society. In this way, "moral panic" is cultivated (Burns and Crawford 1999), increasing both the stakes of any response and the demand for harsh retaliation, because failure to win decisively the battle against criminals (or terrorists) means nothing less than the demise of civilization.

The framing of the debate along these lines should not be seen as specific to school violence; instead, it is the dominant rhetorical modality for repressive social control within neoliberal states and for imperial practices beyond them (Garland 2001; Wacquant 2004; Winner 2004). Discourses of routine exceptional events that carry universal importance (such as police actions in foreign countries) are the contemporary colonizing agents of global capital (Hardt and Negri 2000; Agamben 2000, 2005).

The phrase "taking the media to school" might imply teaching them the real data on school violence or the negative effects of irresponsible reporting, but the larger problem is that the media are already involved with schools and are thoroughly invested in the image of schools that they project. Just as high-tech surveillance companies stand to profit handsomely from the so-called epidemic of school violence or from hypothetical threats to students, so too does the media thrive on fear and control in schools. The media oversaturation of rare school shootings, for instance, attests to the profitability of hyping fear to boost ratings (Burns and Crawford 1999). More often than not, what should be local interest stories about random occurrences of school violence are exported to national or international media audiences, further reinforcing public perceptions that the situation is out of control.

Footage from video surveillance makes some of the best fear-generating news possible. Whether of the shooters at Columbine, the killers of young Jamie Bulger in England,[8] the police beating Rodney King, or the police terrorizing students in Stratford High School in South Carolina, video recordings concurrently personalize and universalize threats. They animate the scenes, providing unclear visual representations that invite replay for further investigation or analysis. The lack of visual quality testifies to the "reality" of the recordings and lures viewers into the scenes, positioning them as agents charged with deciphering the ambiguous text. Replaying surveillance footage or exporting it to other media markets connotes widespread manifestation of the events depicted, where the viewing activity is inflected with the unspoken insinuation that for every event caught on tape, there must be many more not captured. Finally, surveillance footage whets voyeuristic appetites that both shame and titillate viewers, creating a hunger for even more recordings, and thus more surveillance systems, throughout public life.

The media's relationship to the surveillance industry runs deeper than a simple interest in television ratings, however. Because media corporations are megalithic conglomerates with financial ties to many industries, it should not be surprising that they or their sister companies produce surveillance equipment. Although the terrain of corporate mergers and partnerships fluctuates constantly and is therefore difficult to pin down, connections among media and electronics corporations persist, even as the companies' names or owners change. For instance, General Electric presently owns MSNBC, and they produce, in addition to military munitions, an entire line of surveillance technologies for public and private sectors (Think & Ask 2002; General Electric 2004). As another example, General Motors owns Hughes Electronics Corp., which owns DirectTV; and the AOL TimeWarner CNN conglomerate is in partnership with General Motors, Hughes, Philips Electronics, and Raytheon (Regan 2001; Williams 2001; Global Security 2002). Philips produces surveillance equipment of all sorts, from video to radio frequency identification systems, and Raytheon manufactures high-grade surveillance devices, such as thermal-imaging equipment for police, military, or border-control use (Philips 2004; BurleCCTV 2004; Raytheon 2004). These links between media corporations and the surveillance and military industries are just the tip of the iceberg and are worthy of further research, but they do suggest media interest in developing the portfolios of parent companies and corporate partners.

And unfortunately media companies have demonstrated a track record of unabashedly promoting products within their corporate families or shielding their partners from public criticism (Jackson and Hart 2002).

This section has argued that the media are complicit in the unfolding of surveillance regimes and cultures of control in public education. By cultivating fear of school violence, presenting students as victims or criminals, airing surveillance video recordings, and (perhaps unintentionally) promoting the use of surveillance equipment in schools, the media celebrate technological fixes to social problems while ignoring the social relations being produced by those purported fixes. Above all, the media portrayal of school violence as an epidemic supports institutional criminalization of students while effectively diverting attention away from root causes of crime, such as gross inequality, whether in schools or in society at large.

Conclusion

The cases of surveillance in schools presented here illustrate two possible configurations of social relations and material embodiments in the neoliberal state. As Cindi Katz (Chapter 2, this volume) writes about surveillance devices in the child protection industry, the simultaneous elimination of the social wage and rise in social control aggravate inequalities and reinforce fears about others. One result is the displacement of responsibility for care of children (and students) onto individuals, families, and private service companies who promise to meet the social and emotional needs of those who can afford them, whereas others must struggle without much assistance from the state or from employers. Historically, public education has been an institution of social welfare and control, providing civic education for citizens while socializing them into mainstream norms and relations. In this neoliberal climate, public education is a tense and unstable enterprise, rife with new contradictions over obligations to educate and control students with diminishing public resources and for labor markets with fewer viable opportunities. As this chapter has shown, law enforcement and technological encroachments into public education may make victimization and criminalization the primary educational experiences for students in the system.

Even within the stigmatized worlds of public education, however, neoliberalism finds varied and unique expressions as it is mediated by local places and cultures. In Royal Palm Middle School in Phoenix, police and media discourses situate danger and risk outside of the school grounds; biometric surveillance devices serve as high-tech fortification against potentially malicious others in the community at large. Embedded in this rhetoric is the notion that even though these others may look and act like anyone else, should they attempt to infiltrate the school, the face-recognition system will pierce their disguises of normalcy, fix their identities, and initiate a rapid-response law enforcement intervention. Because the school has no reported history of internal crime or verified external threats, social control and police authority are justified in reference to vague and implausible—yet frightening—threats of child abduction. Students are constructed as (potential) victims, and the school becomes a material and metaphorical extension of the private gated communities prevalent in the region. But unlike private communities where individuals willingly sacrifice freedoms and submit to increased scrutiny at their own expense, the social and financial burden of school-based security regimes is placed squarely on the public's shoulders.

In Stratford High School in South Carolina, by contrast, the principal and police construct the criminal threat as internal to the school site. Video surveillance systems actively monitor students in an attempt to collect evidence of criminal activities and then use this intelligence to guide targeted attacks against individuals perceived as delinquents. The surveillance system is employed with the purpose of mitigating risks and controlling the student population; as with police on campus or with gates around schools, surveillance is but one tool for containing (and potentially neutralizing) threats within schools so that they do not overflow into surrounding communities. In this scenario, students—especially black students—are constructed as always-already criminals. This interpretation is supported by the principal's insistence that the students must have cleverly evaded the drug raid. They were not innocent; they were just lucky. If students are seen as criminals and as threats to society, then the effective operation of the school system, beyond containment, is to socialize students to police abuse and escort them into the criminal justice system.

Surveillance regimes in most schools, however, operate somewhere between these two poles of victimization and criminalization. In ethnographic research I conducted with Los Angeles public schools from 2000 to 2001, discourses of security from outside threats prevailed (Monahan 2005a). All the fences with barbed wire, locked gates, student and visitor checkpoints, video cameras, metal detectors, and police presence on school sites were described as necessary insulation against the criminal and gang activity outside. Whereas the *discourses* emphasized outside risks, the *practices* were those of prisonlike containment of poor minority students. It is shocking that it did not seem to matter to most teachers or administrators that students would roam the school grounds all day without ever stepping foot inside a classroom; as long as students were not on the streets, the public education system had fulfilled its social duty. Thus, students were seen as both potential victims and potential criminals, and the two interpretations blurred without any apparent dissonance on the part of school personnel. Either way, the systems of monitoring and control were never called into question.

In most discussions about surveillance in schools, what goes unasked are questions about how emerging relationships among public schools, private technology companies, and the police connect with the larger political economy. One obvious answer is that the implementation of surveillance equipment in schools effectively transfers enormous amounts of sorely needed financial resources from the public education system into the private sector (a similar argument could be made for putting computers in schools). But unlike contentious political movements to privatize public education or establish voucher systems, this transfer of capital occurs under the political radar screen. It meets many of the goals of privatization without the political backlash. It is not a coincidence that the imperative for security systems in schools is propelled by the mass media, who stand to profit both directly and indirectly from this development. Furthermore, inequality drives the neoliberal system, producing both fear of others and individual desires to accumulate capital. Fears can be assuaged temporarily through investment in surveillance systems, and these systems, in turn, feed those fears, as was seen with the biometrics example in Royal Palm Middle School in Phoenix. The criminalization and containment of students serve a dual purpose of safeguarding capital from the marginalized and dispossessed in society while also producing a vast and growing criminal base to justify further social exclusion and inequality (Reiman 2000).

The surveillance systems discussed here shape identity constructions and social interactions. In other words, they produce social relations. In a sense, students have to be seen as victims to justify biometric systems that are tied in with the sheriff's department, and students have to be seen as criminals to warrant the extreme scrutiny of omnipresent monitoring with video surveillance. But the systems, once in place, also invite these constructions of students and resist other uses or interpretations. With the biometric system at Royal Palm Middle School the very presence of the technology conjured fears in parents that were previously remote or nonexistent. And the deployment of surveillance cameras throughout Stratford High School facilitated the principal's social disconnect from students, allowing him to isolate himself in his office and stoke prejudices and fears that would likely be kept in check if he were interacting and socializing directly with students. These surveillance systems engender identity constructions of students that appear radically different: either victims or criminals. But what these constructions share is a view of students as passive, as individuals whose identities are prescripted.

A more empowering role for students would be that of "agents" who are active in their own identity formation. Of course, students are already agents, but the systems being deployed offer very little support for identities outside the dominant binary of victim–criminal. Instead, all student actions are filtered through this conceptual lens by authorities and by the media, and students adapt accordingly to these roles. A corrective to this situation would be to recognize students' agency, accommodate multiple student identities, and provide avenues for students to participate in structuring the material, social, and symbolic conditions of their lives. It could be, however, that modern surveillance regimes preclude these possibilities or that the control society—which they are expressions of—has effectively colonized the lifeworld of the body. To allow individual and communal expressions of agency and equality to flourish may require a radical reconfiguration of surveillance regimes and the neoliberal state.

Acknowledgments

I want to thank David Altheide, Aaron Kupchik, and Jill A. Fisher for their helpful comments on this chapter.

Notes

1. This is the same sheriff—Sheriff Joe Arpaio—who is infamous for his humiliating and dehumanizing treatment of inmates and others under his jurisdiction. Some of his highlights to date include "jail cam," an Internet camera for broadcasting live images from the county detention center (Lynch 2004), and "tent city," where inmates are relocated to un-air-conditioned tents in the sweltering Arizona desert, required to pay for their meals, and forced to dress in pink underwear (Hill 1999).

2. In a 1996–97 survey of U.S. public schools, 39 percent of high schools with 1,000 or more students reported the presence of full-time police officers on campus (Heaviside et al. 1998). That figure has likely increased dramatically since that time.

3. Whether or not the suspects were minors, this use of a police dog is in violation of the Goose Creek Police Department's policy on detecting illegal drugs. The policy states, "Only after the on-scene supervisor has cleared the area of all personnel will the canine enter and conduct an illegal narcotics detection" (cited in Associated Press 2003).

4. The view of public education as a market is nothing new, of course, as can be seen clearly with widespread advertising and the sale of branded products on school grounds. This trend is epitomized perhaps by Channel One, a news program with paid advertisements that is beamed into more than 10,000 schools by satellite, especially into relatively poorer school districts (Bromley 1998). What I am drawing attention to here are some of the ways that the insertion of these market logics into educational domains produces new subject positions and

institutional relations. See Monahan (2004) for focused attention on the role of information technologies, more generally, in the ongoing commodification of public education.

5.   These figures account only for homicides of minors on school premises and do not include death by suicide.

6.   See Altheide (2002, 2006), Glassner (2000), and Furedi (2005) for treatments of media-constructed fear more generally.

7.   See Kupchik (2006) for a superb comparative analysis of children prosecuted as adults in both juvenile and criminal courts.

8.   See Chapter 1 of this volume for a discussion of video surveillance and the Jamie Bulger case in England.

7

Confronting Class in the Classroom
bell hooks

Class is rarely talked about in the United States; nowhere is there a more intense silence about the reality of class differences than in educational settings. Significantly, class differences are particularly ignored in classrooms. From grade school on, we are all encouraged to cross the threshold of the classroom believing we are entering a democratic space—a free zone where the desire to study and learn makes us all equal. And even if we enter accepting the reality of class differences, most of us still believe knowledge will be meted out in fair and equal proportions. In those rare cases where it is acknowledged that students and professors do not share the same class backgrounds, the underlying assumption is still that we are all equally committed to getting ahead, to moving up the ladder of success to the top. And even though many of us will not make it to the top, the unspoken understanding is that we will land somewhere in the middle, between top and bottom.

Coming from a nonmaterially privileged background, from the working poor, I entered college acutely aware of class. When I received notice of my acceptance at Stanford University, the first question that was raised in my household was how I would pay for it. My parents understood that I had been awarded scholarships, and allowed to take out loans, but they wanted to know where the money would come from for transportation, clothes, books. Given these concerns, I went to Stanford thinking that class was mainly about materiality. It only took me a short while to understand that class was more than just a question of money, that it shaped values, attitudes, social relations, and the biases that informed the way knowledge would be given and received. These same realizations about class in the academy are expressed again and again by academics from working-class backgrounds in the collection of essays *Strangers in Paradise* edited by Jake Ryan and Charles Sackrey.

During my college years it was tacitly assumed that we all agreed that class should not be talked about, that there would be no critique of the bourgeois class biases shaping and informing pedagogical process (as well as social etiquette) in the classroom. Although no one ever directly stated the rules that would govern our conduct, it was taught by example and reinforced by a system of rewards. As silence and obedience to authority were most rewarded, students learned that this was the appropriate demeanor in the classroom. Loudness, anger, emotional outbursts, and even something as seemingly innocent as unrestrained laughter were deemed unacceptable, vulgar disruptions of classroom social order. These traits were also associated with being a member of the lower classes. If one was not from a privileged class group, adopting a demeanor similar to that of the group could help one to advance. It is still necessary for students to assimilate bourgeois values in order to be deemed acceptable.

Bourgeois values in the classroom create a barrier, blocking the possibility of confrontation and conflict, warding off dissent. Students are often silenced by means of their acceptance of class values that teach them to maintain order at all costs. When the obsession with maintaining order is coupled with the fear of "losing face," of not being thought well of by one's professor and peers, all possibility of constructive dialogue is undermined. Even though students enter the "democratic" classroom believing they have the right to "free speech," most students are not comfortable exercising this right to "free speech." Most students are not comfortable exercising this right—especially if it means they must give voice to thoughts, ideas, feelings that go against the grain, that are unpopular. This censoring process is only one way bourgeois values overdetermine social behavior in the classroom and undermine the democratic exchange of ideas. Writing about his experience in the section of *Strangers in Paradise* entitled "Outsiders," Karl Anderson confessed:

> Power and hierarchy, and not teaching and learning, dominated the graduate school I found myself in. "Knowledge" was one-upmanship, and no one disguised the fact. . . . The one thing I learned absolutely was the inseparability of free speech and free thought. I, as well as some of my peers, were refused the opportunity to speak and sometimes to ask questions deemed "irrelevant" when the instructors didn't wish to discuss or respond to them.

Students who enter the academy unwilling to accept without question the assumptions and values held by privileged classes tend to be silenced, deemed troublemakers.

Conservative discussions of censorship in contemporary university settings often suggest that the absence of constructive dialogue, enforced silencing, takes place as a by-product of progressive efforts to question canonical knowledge, critique relations of domination, or subvert bourgeois class biases. There is little or no discussion of the way in which the attitudes and values of those from materially privileged classes are imposed upon everyone via biased pedagogical strategies. Reflected in choice of subject matter and the manner in which ideas are shared, these biases need never be overtly stated. In his essay Karl Anderson states that silencing is "the most oppressive aspect of middle-class life." He maintains:

> It thrives upon people keeping their mouths shut, unless they are actually endorsing whatever powers exist. The free marketplace of "ideas" that is so beloved of liberals is as much a fantasy as a free marketplace in oil or automobiles; a more harmful fantasy, because it breeds even more hypocrisy and cynicism. Just as teachers can control what is said in their classrooms, most also have ultra-sensitive antennae as to what will be rewarded or punished that is said outside them. And these antennae control them.

Silencing enforced by bourgeois values is sanctioned in the classroom by everyone.

Even those professors who embrace the tenets of critical pedagogy (many of whom are white and male) still conduct their classrooms in a manner that only reinforces bourgeois models of decorum. At the same time, the subject matter taught in such classes might reflect professorial awareness of intellectual perspectives that critique domination, that emphasize an understanding of the politics of difference, of race, class, gender, even though classroom dynamics remain conventional, business as usual. When the contemporary feminist movement made its initial presence felt in the academy there was both an ongoing critique of conventional classroom dynamics and an attempt to create alternative pedagogical strategies. However, as feminist scholars endeavored to make Women's Studies a discipline administrators and peers would respect, there was a shift in perspective.

Significantly, feminist classrooms were the first spaces in the university where I encountered any attempt to acknowledge class difference. The focus was usually on the way class differences are structured in the larger society, not on our class position. Yet the focus on gender privilege in patriarchal society often meant that there was a recognition of the ways women were economically disenfranchised and therefore more likely to be poor or working class. Often, the feminist classroom was the only place where students (mostly female) from materially disadvantaged circumstances would speak from that class positionality, acknowledging both the impact of class on our social status as well as critiquing the class biases of feminist thought.

When I first entered university settings I felt estranged from this new environment. Like most of my peers and professors, I initially believed those feelings were there because of differences in racial and cultural background. However, as time passed it was more evident that this estrangement was in part a reflection of class difference. At Stanford, I was often asked by peers and professors if I was there on a scholarship. Underlying this question was the implication that receiving financial aid "diminished" one in some way. It was not just this experience that intensified my awareness of class difference, it was the constant evocation of materially privileged class experience (usually that of the middle class) as a universal norm that not only set those of us from working-class backgrounds apart but effectively excluded those who were not privileged from discussions, from social activities. To avoid feelings of estrangement, students from working-class backgrounds could assimilate into the mainstream, change speech patterns, points of reference, drop any habit that might reveal them to be from a nonmaterially privileged background.

Of course I entered college hoping that a university degree would enhance my class mobility. Yet I thought of this solely in economic terms. Early on I did not realize that class was much more than one's economic standing, that it determined values, standpoint, and interests. It was assumed that any student coming from a poor or working-class background would willingly surrender all values and habits of being associated with this background. Those of us from diverse ethnic/racial backgrounds learned that no aspect of our vernacular culture could be voiced in elite settings. This was especially the case with vernacular language or a first language that was not English. To insist on speaking in any manner that did not conform to privileged class ideals and mannerisms placed one always in the position of interloper.

Demands that individuals from class backgrounds deemed undesirable surrender all vestiges of their past create psychic turmoil. We were encouraged, as many students are today, to betray our class origins. Rewarded if we chose to assimilate, estranged if we chose to maintain those aspects of who we were, some were all too often seen as outsiders. Some of us rebelled by clinging to exaggerated manners and behavior clearly marked as outside the accepted bourgeois norm. During my student years, and now as a professor, I see many students from "undesirable" class backgrounds become unable to complete their studies because the contradictions between the behavior necessary to "make it" in the academy and those that allowed them to be comfortable at home, with their families and friends, are just too great.

Often, African Americans are among those students I teach from poor and working-class backgrounds who are most vocal about issues of class. They express frustration, anger, and sadness about the tensions and stress they experience trying to conform to acceptable white, middle-class behaviors in university settings while retaining the ability to "deal" at home. Sharing strategies for coping from my own experience, I encourage students to reject the notion that they must choose between experiences. They must believe they can inhabit comfortably two different worlds, but they must make each space one of comfort. They must creatively invent ways to cross borders. They must believe in their capacity to alter the bourgeois settings they enter. All too often, students from nonmaterially privileged backgrounds assume a position of passivity—they behave as victims, as though they can only be acted upon against their will. Ultimately, they end up feeling they can only reject or accept the norms imposed upon them. This either/or often sets them up for disappointment and failure.

Those of us in the academy from working-class backgrounds are empowered when we recognize our own agency, our capacity to be active participants in the pedagogical process. This process is not simple or easy: it takes courage to embrace a vision of wholeness of being that does not reinforce the capitalist version that suggests that one must always give something up to gain another. In the introduction to the section of their book titled "Class Mobility and Internalized Conflict," Ryan and Sackrey remind readers that "the academic work process is essentially antagonistic to the working class, and academics for the most part live in a different world of culture, different ways that make it, too, antagonistic to working class life." Yet those of us from working-class backgrounds cannot allow class antagonism to prevent us from gaining knowledge, degrees and enjoying the aspects of higher education that are fulfilling. Class antagonism can be constructively used, not made to reinforce the notion that students and professors from working-class backgrounds are "outsiders" and "interlopers," but to subvert and challenge the existing structure.

When I entered my first Women's Studies classes at Stanford, white professors talked about "women" when they were making the experience of materially privileged white women a norm. It was both a matter of personal and intellectual integrity for me to challenge this biased assumption. By challenging, I refused to be complicit in the erasure of black and/or working-class women of all ethnicities. Personally, that meant I was not able just to sit in class, grooving on the good feminist vibes—that was a loss. The gain was that I was honoring the experience of poor and working-class women in my own family, in that very community that had encouraged and supported me in my efforts to be better educated. Even though my intervention was not wholeheartedly welcomed, it created a context for critical thinking, for dialectical exchange.

Any attempt on the part of individual students to critique the bourgeois biases that shape pedagogical process, particularly as they relate to epistemological perspectives (the points from which information is shared) will, in most cases, no doubt, be viewed as negative and disruptive. Given the presumed radical or liberal nature of early feminist classrooms, it was shocking to me to find those settings were also often closed to different ways of thinking. While it was acceptable to critique patriarchy in that context, it was not acceptable to confront issues of class, especially in ways that were not simply about the evocation of guilt. In general, despite their participation in different disciplines and the diversity of class backgrounds, African American scholars and other nonwhite professors have been no more willing to confront issues of class. Even when it became more acceptable to give at least lip service to the recognition of race, gender, and class, most professors and students just did not feel they were able to address class in anything more than a simplistic way. Certainly, the primary area where there was the possibility of meaningful critique and change was in relation to biased scholarship, work that used the experiences and thoughts of materially privileged people as normative.

In recent years, growing awareness of class differences in progressive academic circles has meant that students and professors committed to critical and feminist pedagogy have the opportunity to make spaces in the academy where class can receive attention. Yet there can be no intervention that challenges the status quo if we are not willing to interrogate the way our presentation of self as well as our pedagogical process is often shaped by middle-class norms. My awareness of class has been continually reinforced by my efforts to remain close to loved ones who remain in materially underprivileged class positions. This has helped me to employ pedagogical strategies that create ruptures in the established order, that promote modes of learning which challenge bourgeois hegemony.

One such strategy has been the emphasis on creating in classrooms learning communities where everyone's voice can be heard, their presence recognized and valued. In the section of *Strangers in Paradise* entitled "Balancing Class Locations," Jane Ellen Wilson shares the way an emphasis on personal voice strengthened her.

> Only by coming to terms with my own past, my own background, and seeing that in the context of the world at large, have I begun to find my true voice and to understand that, since it is my own voice, that no pre-cut niche exists for it; that part of the work to be done is making a place, with others, where my and our voices, can stand clear of the background noise and voice our concerns as part of a larger song.

When those of us in the academy who are working class or from working-class backgrounds share our perspectives, we subvert the tendency to focus only on the thoughts, attitudes, and experiences of those who are materially privileged. Feminist and critical pedagogy are two alternative paradigms for teaching which have really emphasized the issue of coming to voice. That focus emerged as central, precisely because it was so evident that race, sex, and class privilege empower some students more than others, granting "authority" to some voices more than others.

A distinction must be made between a shallow emphasis on coming to voice, which wrongly suggests there can be some democratization of voice wherein everyone's words will be given equal time and be seen as equally valuable (often the model applied in feminist classrooms), and the more complex recognition of the uniqueness of each voice and a willingness to create spaces in the classroom where all voices can be heard because all students are free to speak, knowing their presence will be recognized and valued. This does not mean that anything can be said, no matter how irrelevant to classroom subject matter, and receive attention—or that something meaningful takes place if everyone has equal time to voice an opinion. In the classes I teach, I have students write short paragraphs that they read aloud so that we all have a chance to hear unique perspectives and we are all given an opportunity to pause and listen to one another. Just the physical experience of hearing, of listening intently, to each particular voice strengthens our capacity to learn together. Even though a student may not speak again after this moment, that student's presence has been acknowledged.

Hearing each other's voices, individual thoughts, and sometimes associating these voices with personal experience makes us more acutely aware of each other. That moment of collective participation and dialogue means that students and professor respect—and here I invoke the root meaning of the word, "to look at"—each other, engage in acts of recognition with one another, and do not just talk to the professor. Sharing experiences and confessional narratives in the classroom helps establish communal commitment to learning. These narrative moments usually are the space where the assumption that we share a common class background and perspective is disrupted. While students may be open to the idea that they do not all come from a common class background, they may still expect that the values of materially privileged groups will be the class's norm.

Some students may feel threatened if awareness of class difference leads to changes in the classroom. Today's students all dress alike, wearing clothes from stores such as the Gap and Benetton; this acts to erase the markers of class difference that older generations of students experienced. Young students are more eager to deny the impact of class and class differences in our society. I have found that students from upper- and middle-class backgrounds are disturbed if heated exchange takes place in the classroom. Many of them equate loud talk or interruptions with rude and threatening behavior. Yet those of us from working-class backgrounds may feel that discussion is deeper and richer if it arouses intense responses. In class, students are often disturbed if anyone is interrupted while speaking, even though outside class most of them are not threatened. Few of us are taught to facilitate heated discussions that may include useful interruptions and digressions, but it is often the professor who is most invested in maintaining order in the classroom. Professors cannot empower students to embrace diversities of experience, standpoint, behavior, or style if our training has disempowered us, socialized us to cope effectively only with a single mode of interaction based on middle-class values.

Most progressive professors are more comfortable striving to challenge class biases through the material studied than they are with interrogating how class biases shape conduct in the classroom and transforming their pedagogical process. When I entered my first classroom as a college professor and a feminist, I was deeply afraid of using authority in a way that would perpetuate class elitism and other forms of domination. Fearful that I might abuse power, I falsely pretended that no power difference existed between students and myself. That was a mistake. Yet it was only as I began to interrogate my fear of "power"—the way that fear was related to my own class background where I had so often seen those with class power coerce, abuse, and dominate those without—that I began to understand that power was not itself negative. It depended what one did with it. It was up to me to create ways within my professional power constructively, precisely because I was teaching in institutional structures that affirm it is fine to use power to reinforce and maintain coercive hierarchies.

Fear of losing control in the classroom often leads individual professors to fall into a conventional teaching pattern wherein power is used destructively. It is this fear that leads to collective professorial investment in bourgeois decorum as a means of maintaining a fixed notion of order, of ensuring that the teacher will have absolute authority. Unfortunately, this fear of losing control shapes and informs the professorial pedagogical process to the extent that it acts a barrier preventing any constructive grappling with issues of class.

Sometimes students who want professors to grapple with class differences often simply desire that individuals from less materially privileged backgrounds be given center stage so that an inversion of hierarchical structures takes place, not a disruption. One semester, a number of black female students from working-class backgrounds attended a course I taught on African American women writers. They arrived hoping I would use my professorial power to decenter the voices of privileged white students in nonconstructive ways so that those students would experience what it is like to be an outsider. Some of these black students rigidly resisted attempts to involve the others in an engaged pedagogy where space is created for everyone. Many of the black students feared that learning new terminology or new perspectives would alienate them from familiar social relations. Since these fears are rarely addressed as part of a progressive pedagogical process, students caught in the grip of such anxiety often sit in classes feeling hostile, estranged, refusing to participate. I often face students who think that in my classes they will "naturally" not feel estranged and that part of this feeling of comfort, or being "at home," is that they will not have to work as hard as they do in other classes.

These students are not expecting to find alternative pedagogy in my classes but merely "rest" from the negative tensions they may feel in the majority of other courses. It is my job to address these tensions.

If we can trust the demographics, we must assume that the academy will be full of students from diverse classes, and that more of our students than ever before will be from poor and working-class backgrounds. This change will not be reflected in the class background of professors. In my own experience, I encounter fewer and fewer academics from working-class backgrounds. Our absence is no doubt related to the way class politics and class struggle shapes who will receive graduate degrees in our society. However, constructively confronting issues of class is not simply a task for those of us who came from working-class and poor backgrounds; it is a challenge for all professors. Critiquing the way academic settings are structured to reproduce class hierarchy, Jake Ryan and Charles Sackrey emphasize "that no matter what the politics or ideological stripe of the individual professor, of what the content of his or her teaching, Marxist, anarchist, or nihilist, he or she nonetheless participates in the reproduction of the cultural and class relations of capitalism." Despite this bleak assertion they are willing to acknowledge that "nonconformist intellectuals can, through research and publication, chip away with some success at the conventional orthodoxies, nurture students with comparable ideas and intentions, or find ways to bring some fraction of the resources of the university to the service of the ... class interests of the workers and others below." Any professor who commits to engaged pedagogy recognizes the importance of constructively confronting issues of class. That means welcoming the opportunity to alter our classroom practices creatively so that the democratic ideal of education for everyone can be realized.

Suggested Readings for Future Study

Anyon, J. (2005). *Radical Possibilities: Public Policy, Urban Education and a New Social Movement*. New York: Routledge.

Anyon, J. (1997). *Ghetto Schooling: A political economy of urban educational reform*. New York: Teachers College Press.

Apple, M. (2006). *Educating the "Right" Way: Markets, Standards, God, and Inequality*. New York: Routledge.

Apple, M. (2007). *Late to Class: Social Class and Schooling in the New Economy*. State University of New York Press.

Apple, M. (1986). *Teachers and Texts: A Political Economy of Class and Gender Relations in Education*. New York: Routledge & Kegan Paul.

Archer, L. (2003). *Higher Education and Social Class: Issues of Inclusion and Exclusion*. New York: RoutledgeFalmer.

Aronowitz, A. (2001). *The Last Good Job in America: Work and education in the new global technoculture*. New York: Rowman & Littlefield.

Aronowitz, S. (2000). *The Knowledge Factory: Dismantling the corporate university and creating true higher learning*. Boston: Beacon Press.

Aronowitz, S. and Cutler, J. (1998). *Post-work: The wages of cybernation*. New York: Routledge.

Ball S. (2006). *Education Policy and Social Class*. New York: Routledge.

Bowles, S. and Gintis, H. (1976). *Schooling in Capitalist America*. New York: Basic Books.

Brosio, R. (1994). *A Radical Democratic Critique of Capitalist Education*. New York: Peter Lang.

Bourdieu, P. (1987). "What Makes a Social Class? On The Theoretical and Practical Existence of Groups," *Berkeley Journal of Sociology: A Critical Review*, vol. 32, pp. 1–17.

Bourdieu, P. (1986). "The Forms of Capital," in J. G. Richardson (ed.) *Handbook of Theory and Research for the Sociology of Education*, pp. 241–58. New York and London: Greenwood Press.

Burbules, N. C. and Torres, C. A. (2000). *Globalization and Education: Critical perspectives*. New York: Routledge.

Carnoy, M. (1994). *Faded Dreams: The politics and economics of race in America*. Cambridge: Cambridge University Press.

Collins, C., Leondar-Wright, B., and Sklar, H. (1999). *Shifting Fortunes: The perils of the growing American wealth gap*. Boston: United for a Fair Economy.

Evans, A., Evans, R., and Kennedy, W. (1990). *Pedagogies of the Non-Poor*. New York: Orbis Books.

Gabbard, D. A. (2007). *Knowledge and Power in the Global Economy*. New York: Routledge.

Gee, J. P., Hull, G., and Lankshear, C. (1996). *The New Work Order: Behind the language of the new capitalism*. Boulder, CO: Westview.

Greider, W. (1997). *One World Ready or Not: The manic logic of global capitalism*. New York: Simon & Schuster.

Halsey, A. H., ed. (1997). *Education: Culture, Economy, and Society*. New York: Oxford University Press.

Herman, E. and Chomsky, N. (1988). *Manufacturing Consent: The political economy of the mass media*. New York: Pantheon Books.

hooks, b. (2000). *Where We Stand: Class Matters*. New York: Routledge.

Jones, J. and Bomer, R. (2006). *Girls, Social Class, and Literacy: What Teachers Can Do to Make a Difference*. Heinemann.

Kozol, J. (1991). *Savage Inequalities: Children in America's Schools*. New York: Harper Perennial.

Kumar, A. (1997). *Class issues: Pedagogy, cultural studies, and the public sphere*. New York: New York University Press.

Lauder, H. and Hughes, D. (1999). *Trading in Futures: Why markets in education don't work*. Philadelphia: Open University Press.

Lee, V. (2002). *Inequality at the Starting Gate: Social Background Differences in Achievement as Children Begin School*. Washington, DC: Economic Policy Institute.

Martin, E. J. and Torres, R. D. (2004). *Savage State: Welfare Capitalism and Inequality*. Lanham, MD: Rowman & Littlefield.

McChesney, R., Wood, E. M., and Foster, J. B., eds. (1998). *Capitalism and the information age: The political economy of the global communication revolution.* New York: Monthly Review Press.

McLaren, P. and Jaramillo, N. (2006). "Critical Pedagogy, Latino/a Education, and the Politics of Class Struggle," *Critical Methodologies*, vol. 6, no. 1, pp. 73–93.

McLaren, P. (2005). *Capitalist and Conquerors: A Critical Pedagogy Against Empire.* New York: Rowman and Littlefield.

McLaren, P. (1998). "Revolutionary pedagogy in post-revolutionary times: Rethinking the political economy of critical education," *Educational Theory*, 48(4): 431–462.

Michales, W. B. (2006). *The Trouble with Diversity: How We Learned to Love Identity and Ignore Inequality.* New York: Metropolitan Books.

Milner, A. (1999). *Class.* London: Sage.

Molnar, A. (1996). *Giving kids the business: The commercialization of America's Schools.* Boulder, CO: Westview.

Newman, K. and Chan, V. T. (2007). *The Missing Class: Portraits of the Near Poor.* Boston: Beacon Press.

Rothstein, R. (2004). *Class and Schools: Using Social, Economic, and Educational Reform to Close the Black-White Achievement Gap*, Washington, DC: Economic Policy Institute (May).

Sacks, P. (2007). *Tearing Down the Gates: Confronting the Class Divide in American Education.* Berkeley: University of California Press.

Sassen, S. (1998). *Globalization and its discontent: Essays on the new mobility of people and money.* New York: The New York Press.

Spring, J. (2001). *Globalization and educational rights.* New York: Lawrence Erlbaum Associates.

Weis, L. (2007). *The Way Class Works: Readings on School, Family, and the Economy.* New York: Routledge.

Weis, Lois and Fine, Michelle, eds (1993). *Beyond Silenced Voices: Class, Race and Gender in United States Schools.* New York: State University of New York Press.

Willis, P. (1981). *Learning to labor: How working class kids get working class jobs.* New York: Columbia University Press.

Wood, E. M. (1999). *The origin of capitalism.* New York: Monthly Review Press.

Wood, E. M. (1995). *Democracy against capitalism.* New York: Monthly Review Press.

Part Three

Race and Education

Introduction to Part Three

Over the last several decades, race and ethnicity have been the focus of theoretical debates in the social sciences and educational research. Debates concerning their analytical utility have been the subject of conferences and best-selling books. The academic discourse has focused primarily on how best to untangle the race problematic. The articles in this section are inspired by divergent traditions in the social sciences and humanities that address a number of theoretical concerns tied to the interrogation of race and racism and, more specifically, its pedagogical implications in and outside the classroom.

Current intellectual concerns in educational research, which advance a range of theoretical approaches from post-colonial and post-structural critiques of race and racism, reflect broader assumptions that often fail to interrogate the role of capitalism and social class in the reproduction of racialized educational practices. This so-called analytical "death of class" and its limited explanatory ambition has led to a set of diverse claims about the kind of socioeconomic structures and political and cultural forms that have emerged within schools since the 1980s. This is most apparent in the wide proliferation of an eclectic body of critical writings that emerged from the ideas of critical legal scholars. A critical race theory, with its signature idea that "racial power" and "white supremacy" exist as an intractable social phenomenon in U.S. schools, represents a critical educational example of this perspective.

So, although there is no biological basis for dividing the human species into groups based on the idea that certain physical traits, such as skin color, are tied to such attributes as intellect and morality, important debates about the utility and significance of race within a critical pedagogical perspective persist. Thus, while "race" may not be a natural category, as asserted by W. E. B. Du Bois in 1903, many critical theorists vigorously uphold the notion that "race" has social meaning and therefore should be retained. Nevertheless, there are others in the critical tradition that contest the social significance of race and instead argue for the recognition of its historical fabrication and its undeniable connection to economic oppression. The articles included here help to illustrate a few of these competing perspectives and shed light on the major arguments that inform this contested terrain in critical pedagogy.

Summary of Articles

Overall, the essays share a common goal to further develop an oppositional pedagogy of praxis that places anti-racism, social justice, and democracy at the center of teaching and learning in these changing times. This endeavor to untangle the contradictory forces that shape one of the most contested concepts in social science is offered in the spirit of critical collegial exchange and a reminder of the struggle ahead. The authors all place considerable emphasis on the theoretical and conceptual questions put forward in these debates, contributing to the further development of critical pedagogy as an oppositional stronghold in the struggle against racism(s).

In "After Race," Antonia Darder and Rodolfo Torres offer a critical assessment of the contemporary debate on race and racism. The critique of the race problematic and the ways in which the idea of race is conceptualized are explored. Deploying a Marxist informed perspective, they challenge educational activists and theorists to retain racism, rather than "race," as the focus of analysis, grounded in a forthright critique of capitalism. The essay also offers a counter-narrative to the death of the Marxist project in education and asserts the continuing theoretical and political value of the concepts and propositions of historical materialism in the interrogation of the impact of racism and the capitalist political economy on life in schools today.

The seminal essay, *Toward a Critical Race Theory of Education*, by Gloria Ladson-Billings and William F. Tate, first published in 1995, offers a stimulating and important critique of the multicultural paradigm and an articulation of the salience of race as the primary determinant factor in educational and social inequities. Yet, despite the salience of race in US society, the authors contend that the current scholarly literature remains wanting and theoretically underdeveloped. Drawing on the jurisprudential trend of critical race theory, Ladson-Billings and Tate advance propositions that consider property and race as method and critique in the interrogation of race and the multicultural enterprise.

The American Indian question has long been problematic in U.S. scholarly literature, with scant attention to socioeconomic concerns or the cultural histories of the population. Sandy Marie Anglás Grande, in *American Indian Geographies of Identity and Power*, examines the tension between American Indian epistemology and critical pedagogy. She asserts that critical pedagogical perspectives have failed to acknowledge the unique position of the American Indian population, within the ethno-racial landscape of the United States. She concludes with a critical optimism that a new Red Pedagogy, grounded in critical principles, can emerge from a forthright engagement of the historical and socioeconomic conditions that shape the everyday lives of indigenous populations today. However, Grande rightly insists that this will require a paradigm shift, in which analytical specificity of particular histories and imperial practices imposed on American Indians are made central to critical discussion of indigenous knowledge and pedagogy.

Questions for Reflection and Dialogue

1. Darder and Torres assert that, analytically speaking, "race" constitutes a paper tiger; a term that may be commonly used within everyday discourse but presents a serious theoretical concern. Discuss this claim and its implications to the forging of a critical pedagogy committed to the elimination of racism.
2. Identify specific acts of racism in education and consider their causes and consequences, using the three articles as theoretical points of departure.
3. Assess the contention that American Indians are such a unique ethno-racial population that a paradigm shift in critical pedagogy is necessary, in order to realize a new Red Pedagogy.

4. What educational examples can you identify where it is imperative that educators engage with American Indian geographies of identities, histories, and power? Why is this necessary to a critical pedagogical practice?

5. What are the contributions of a critical race theory to pedagogical practices in schools and communities and what are the implications of this approach, within the domain of educational policy?

6. What are the differences in how the articles conceptualize the relationship of race and class, within the ethno-racial landscape of the United States?

8

After Race: An Introduction

Antonia Darder and Rodolfo D. Torres

> The truth is that there are no races. . . . The evil that is done is done by the concept and by—yet impossible—assumptions as to its application. What we miss through our obsession . . . is, simply, reality.
>
> (Appiah 1995, 75)

Over a century ago, W.E.B. Du Bois in *The Souls of Black Folk* proclaimed one of his most cited dictums: "The problem of the 20th Century is the problem of the color line" (1989, 10). In this book we echo his sentiment, but with a radical twist. The problem of the twenty-first century is the problem of "race"—an ideology that has served well to success-fully obscure and disguise class interests behind the smokescreen of multiculturalism, diversity, difference, and more recently, whiteness. Whether the terms of analysis are "race," "racial identity," "race consciousness," or "political race," the category of "race" and its many derivatives function as the lynchpin of racism, which "forbids its objects to be other than members of a race" (Fields 2001, 49). As Barbara Fields has noted with respect to African Americans:

> Afro-Americans themselves have fought successively for different ways of naming themselves as people. . . . Each name, once accepted into the general public vocabulary, has simply become a variant word for Afro-Americans' race. A sense of peoplehood, nationhood, or comradeship in struggle may be available to others; but, for persons of African descent, all reduces to race, a life sentence for them and their issue in perpetuity. (50)

To radically shift directions and speak "against race," as Paul Gilroy (2000) suggests, or "after race" as we attempt to do here, is to uncompromisingly refuse to accept or legitimate any longer the perpetual racialized demarcations of "raced" (Guinier and Torres 2002) or "problem" (Du Bois 1989) populations. Our intention is to contest the notion that the color of a person's skin, and all it has historically come to signify within the sociological, political, or popular imagination, should continue to function as such. We seek to shatter dubious claims that essentialize the responses of populations, whether they exist as objects or subjects of racism; and by so doing, acknowledge the complexity of the world in which we negotiate our daily existence today.

To be clear, we are not arguing in the tradition of the color-blind conservatives or political pundits who would have us believe that the structures and practices that have formidably embedded racism as a way of life for centuries in the United States and around the world have been undone and that the problem of racism has been ameliorated. Our position, in fact, is diametrically opposed to this argument. Instead, the political force of our analysis is anchored in the centrality of "race" as an ideology and racism as a powerful, structuring, hegemonic force in the world today. We argue that we must disconnect from "race" as it has been constructed in the past, and contend fully with the impact of "race" as ideology on the lives of all people—but most importantly on the lives of those who have been enslaved, colonized, or marked for genocide in the course of world history.

Situating the Debate

We have arrived at this position after ten long years of debate and research into the extremely murky, contradictory, and disturbing literature in the field. During this time, a variety of questions have informed our work, questions that the reader will find repeatedly reflected or inferred in the collection of interpretive essays included in this book. Some of these questions include: How has the notion of "race" changed over time? What analytical value or utility does the concept of "race" have in our struggle against racism and economic inequality? What value do contemporary notions of "race" have in our efforts to dismantle the external material structures of oppression that sustain racialized inequalities? Should we jettison the concept of "race" but continue to study racism? Can racism exist without "races"? Does the concept of "race" have any real referent in the social world beyond its link to racism as an ideology? What is the relationship between changing class formations and racialized inequalities? What are the problematics of "white supremacy" arguments in the antiracist struggle for economic democracy? To what extent do retaining black-white dichotomous perceptions of "race relations" render other racialized populations invisible? Is the black-white paradigm of "race relations" able to grasp the new patterns of conflict or racialized inequalities within a changing political economy? What are the implications of questioning the "race relations" paradigm? How can we arrive at a more precise and specific concept with which to analyze both the historical and contemporary social realities and material conditions of racialized inequalities? What new strategies might help us dissolve the historical barriers that interfere with the establishment of antiracism solidarity across populations with quite different histories of integration into the U.S. body politic?

The posing of these difficult questions should not be interpreted to mean that white-on-black racism is not a significant and necessary area of study. Rather, we believe that breaking with the black-white racism problematic can open up new research possibilities in comparative studies of racialized inequalities that could potentially reinvigorate our political efforts to ameliorate human suffering. As we attempt to address different aspects of these questions in this book, we want to state explicitly that our critique of the race problematic goes beyond positing that biological "races" do not exist or the claim that the concept of "race" is socially and culturally constructed. Despite the proverbial caveat of "social construction," the analytical and descriptive (or discursive) categories of "race" lead to some serious theoretical problems, as we suggest in the following chapters. Thus, we contend that the everyday use of "race" for symbolic or political purposes must be uprooted, along with outdated biological assertions. In so doing, our attention will be focused on how best to conceptualize multiple racisms and racialized formations within the context of demographic shifts, changing capitalist class relations, and global socioeconomic dislocations.

The debate over such questions is not new. European and Australian, as well as American social scientists such as Collette Guillaumin, Robert Miles, Paul Gilroy, Stuart Hall, Kenan

Malik, Etienne Balibar, Michael Omi, Howard Winant, Stephen Castles, David Theo Goldberg, Stephen Small, Anthony Appiah, William Julius Wilson, Barbara Fields, and others have been examining questions such as these since the 1980s. Most notable among them is Robert Miles, a British sociologist, who in 1982 first blew open the debate on the analytical utility of "race" as a suitable construct for the sociological analysis of human populations. Miles called into question the "race relations" paradigm that had dominated the field since the 1960s. Importantly, his efforts have assisted Marxist scholars in recovering class analysis as a significant analytical tool in the examination of racism at a time when postmodern theories began to severely curtail and erode the analytical power of this approach in scholarly examinations of culture. In addition, Miles has pointed to the need for scholars to engage the historical specificity, rather than to adhere to a view of singularity, in theorizing racism. He has argued that historically specific racisms possess their own "effectivity" and, as such, could operate as a constitutive (determinant) force in shaping the ideology of the time. Two decades later, this critique remains compelling and instructive but conspicuously missing as we navigate through the contemporary debate.

Along with the writings in the study of "race" and racism, the work of Ellen Meiksins Wood has been significant to our understanding of contemporary capitalism (with its unrelenting project of modernization) and its impact on the de-democratization of public life within nation-states. Wood's (1995) efforts to rethink democracy without capitalism constitute a powerful treatise that unapologetically points to capitalism as the most engulfing system of social relations in the history of humankind. Wood insists that we recognize power as unrelentingly anchored in external material conditions and remain ever cognizant of the social impact of the mode of production upon workers, in this country and abroad. That is, we cannot ignore the increasing significance of class and the specificity of capitalism as a system of social and political relations of power, particularly in light of current struggles to contend with the virulent particularities of globalized racisms. The failure to engage the political economy and its impact on class formations—inherent in all contemporary expressions of racism—is a severe shortcoming in many of the scholarly treatments of "race" during the last fifty years. Moreover, we need greater specificity in the language we use to talk about the complexities of class, the economy, and social power in contemporary formations of racialized inequalities.

The Idea of "Race"

The research on contemporary racism points to an arresting dilemma. Social scientists seem befuddled in their efforts to extend their analysis beyond the traditional "racial" classifications sustained by the idea of "race." This can be briefly articulated in the following manner. "Race" has no scientific basis, yet racial categorization certainly foregrounds social structure and action. The majority of people in this country continue to believe that they belong to a specific race, and this has an impact on the way they conceive of their social identity. Hence, it can be said that for many racism functions to define both Self and Other. This is apparent in racialized discourses of hierarchy, in which members of dominant groups assert their superiority over other groups, and in racialized discourses of solidarity, in which subordinated groups assert their unity and rights. As such, "race may not be a biological fact, but it certainly is a social reality" (Castles 1996, 22)—a social reality kept alive by the relentless use of "race" to construct meaning within both academic and popular culture.

The history of "race" as ideology is equally puzzling. In early writings, categories used to define people were both similar to and different from the way we conceptualize "race" today. For example, it was not unusual for English writers to refer to the Irish as an inferior "race." However, their judgments were not necessarily linked to biological determinism but rather to cultural or social determinants, such as nationality or religion. It was not until the legacy of Darwin seeped into the popular imagination that the belief in "race" as a genetic predisposition of social behavior flourished. The concept of "race" has always been linked to either social or genetic constructions of inferiority or superiority assigned to particular populations, depending on the term's historical usage and reference. The ideology of "race" and its use, whether as a construct in the interest of genocide and colonialism or in the interest of political resistance, has always engendered the seeds of essentialism. So, if "race" is "real," it is only "because we have acted as if certain people, at certain points in time, were inferior based on innate or essentialized characteristics" (Lee, Mountain, and Koenig 2001, 40). Hence, the circularity of "race" logic leaves little possibility outside the realm of determinism. The power that ratifies "race" thinking is, wittingly or unwittingly, grounded in the notion that "race," whether biological or cultural, is immutable—indivisible from the essential character of individuals.

Although today "race" is generally linked to phenotypic characteristics, there is a strong consensus among evolutionary biologists and genetic anthropologists that "biologically identifiable human races do not exist; *Homo sapiens* constitute a single species, and have been so since their evolution in Africa and throughout their migration around the world" (Lee, Mountain, and Koenig 2001, 39). This perspective is similar to that which existed prior to the eighteenth century, when the notion that there were distinct populations whose differences were grounded in biology did not exist. For the Greeks, for example, the term "barbarian" was tied to how civilized a people were considered to be (generally based on language rather than genetics). So how did all this begin?

George Fredrickson (2002), writing on the history of racism, identifies the anticipatory moment of modern racism with the "treatment of Jewish converts to Christianity in fifteenth- and sixteenth-century Spain. *Conversos* were identified and discriminated against because of the belief held by Christians that the impurity of their blood made them incapable of experiencing a true conversion" (31). Fredrickson argues that the racism inherent in the quasi-religious, Spanish doctrine of *limpeza de sangre*, referring to purity of blood, set the stage for the spread of racism to the New World:

> To the extent that it was enforced represented the stigmatization of an entire ethnic group on the basis of deficiencies that allegedly could not be eradicated by conversion or assimilation. Inherited social status was nothing new; the concept of "noble blood" had long meant that the off-spring of certain families were born with a claim to high status. But when the status of large numbers of people was depressed purely and simply because of their derivation from a denigrated *ethnos*, a line had been crossed that gave "race" a new and more comprehensive significance. (33)

Hence, religious notions, steeped in an ideology of "race," played a significant role in the exportation of racism into the Americas, where domination by the superior "race" was perceived as "inevitable and desirable, because it was thought to lead to human progress" (Castles 1996, 21).

The emergence of "race" as ideology can also be traced to the rise of nationalism. Efforts by nation-states to extend or deny rights of citizenship contingent on "race" or "ethnicity" were not uncommon, even within so-called democratic republics. Here, national mythology about those with "the biological unfitness for full citizenship" (Fredrickson 2002, 68) served to sanction exclusionary practices, despite the fact that all people shared "the historical process of migration and intermingling" (Castles 1996, 21). Herein is contained the logic behind what Valle and Torres (2000) term "the policing of race," a condition that results in official policies and practices by the nation-state designed to exclude or curtail the rights of racialized populations. In Germany, the Nazi regime took the logic of "race" to its pinnacle, rendering Jewish and Gypsy populations a threat to the state, thus rationalizing and justifying their demise. This example disrupts the notion that racism occurs only within the context of black-white relations. Instead, Castles (1996) argues that economic exploitation has always been central to the emergence of racism. Whether it incorporated slavery or indentured servitude, racialized systems of labor were perpetrated in Europe against immigrants, including Irish, Jewish, and Polish workers, as well as against indigenous populations around the world.

In the midst of the "scientific" penchant of the eighteenth century, Carolus Linnaeus developed one of the first topologies to actually categorize human beings into four distinct subspecies: *americanus, asiaticus, africanus,* and *europaeus*. Linnaeus's classification, allegedly neutral and scientific, included not only physical features but also behavioral characteristics, hierarchically arranged in accordance with the prevailing social values and the political-economic interests of the times. The predictable result is the current ideological configuration of "race" used to both explain and control social behavior.

Etienne Balibar's (2003) work on racism is useful in understanding the ideological justifications that historically have accompanied the exclusion and domination of racialized populations—a phenomenon heavily fueled by the tensions of internal migration in the current era of globalization.

> [R]acism describes in an abstract idealizing manner "types of humanity," and ... makes extensive use of classifications which allow all individuals and groups to imagine answers for the most immediate existential questions, such as imposition of identities and the permanence of violence between nations, ethnic or religious communities. (3)

Balibar also points to the impact of "symbolic projections and mediations" (in particular, stereotypes and prejudices linked to divine-humanity or bestial-animality) in the construction of racialized formations. "Racial" classification becomes associated with a distinction between the "properly human" and its imaginary (animal-like) "other." Such projections and mediations, Balibar argues, are inscribed with modernity's expansionist rationality—a quasi-humanist conception that suggests that differences and inequalities are the result of unequal access and social exclusion from cultural, political, or intellectual life but also implies that these differences and inequalities represent normal patterns, given the level of "humanity" or "animality" attributed to particular populations. James Baldwin in "A Talk to Teachers" (1988) links this phenomenon of racialization to the political economy and its impact on African Americans.

> The point of all this is that Black men were brought here as a source of cheap labor. They were indispensable to the economy. In order to justify the fact that men were treated as though they were animals, the white republic had to brainwash itself into believing that they were indeed animals and deserved to be treated like animals. (7)

Lee, Mountain, and Koenig (2001) note, "the taxonomy of race has always been and continues to be primarily political" (43). Since politics and economics actually constitute one sphere, it is more precise to say that the ideology of "race" continues to be primarily about political economy. Thus, historians of "race" and racism argue that the idea of immutable, biologically determined "races" is a direct outcome of exploration and coloni- alism, which furnished the "scientific" justification for the economic exploitation, slavery, and even genocide of those groups perceived as subhuman.

Racialized Constructions

The veiled history of racialized taxonomy continues to be at work today, under the aus- pices of the national census system. Since its inception in 1790, the U.S. Census Bureau has gathered information on "race." Criteria utilized over the years have included nationality, tribal affiliation, as well as indicators of "blood" (i.e., mulatto, quadroon, octoroon). This eventually resulted in the current framework mandated by the U.S. Office of Management and Budget (OMB)—a framework inspired by an ideology of "race."

> [This] framework of identifying race focused on lineage and implicitly defined "whiteness" by a standard of genetic "purity," despite physiological markers that may give the appearance of whiteness or blackness. This rule, although no longer embraced officially by the government, reflects a belief in the biological basis for group differences that continues to characterize racial thinking in the United States.
>
> (Lee, Mountain, and Koenig 2001, 43)

In the twentieth century, the U.S. Census Bureau utilized twenty-six distinct classification designs for measuring "race." By the year 2000, all non-European groups had been collapsed into four (nonwhite) categories and two ethnicities, including the category "some other race." In a separate question, all respondents were also asked to identify their "ethnicity." As has been documented by the research related to the 2000 census, respondents often experienced confusion in distinguishing between "race" and ethnicity.

Stephen Castles (1996) argues, "racism chooses its targets according to its own perverse inner logic, rather than on the basis of some fixed hierarchical taxonomy" (28). In response to this inner logic, the state continues to preserve a vested interest in the control and management of diverse populations. Through its power to legislate "race relations"—the social relations between people of different "races"—the reality of "race" is legitimated by law (Guillaumin 1980). To illustrate this point, Manning Marable (2000) cites the emergence of the term "Hispanic":

> The U.S. government's decision in 1971 to create a new "ethnic," but not "racial," category of "Hispanic" on its census form is the best recent example of state manipulation of the politics of difference. The designation of "Hispanic" was imposed on more than fifteen million citizens and resident aliens who had very different nationalities, racial-ethnic identities, cultures, social organizations, and political histories. (B4)

Such machinations by the state to regulate "identities" both fuel and ignite a foundational belief in the unexamined assumption that "race" (or ethnicity) equals "identity." Con- sequently, the strangest political bedfellows result—white right-wing conservatives in bed with black or Chicano nationalists in bed with Latino politicos—all of whom would readily refute any perspective that sought to eliminate "race" as an explanatory category of analysis. Gilroy (2000) argues that for those mired in the immutable belief in "race" as identity, "the idea that priceless, essential identities are in perpetual danger from the difference outside them and that their precious purity is always at risk from the impressible power of heteroculture has certainly supplied the pivot for some unlikely political alliances" (221). The results of such alliances have been well evidenced, for instance, in educational struggles related to standardized testing and charter school initiatives or public policy debates concerning welfare rights, abortion rights, gun control, or gay and lesbian civil rights.

"Race" today continues to exist as part of a commonsense discourse that encompasses the accumulated and often contradictory assumptions used by people to decipher and contend with the complex world around us. This is why the influence of past ideologies and practices makes itself known and felt, directly and indirectly, through the racialized discourse of the media, political officials, and popular culture, even in ostensibly democratic societies. For recent examples, we need only recall the racialized discourse of the Bush administration to justify military action against Afghanistan and Iraq, economic blockades in Venezuela, and threats with weapons of mass destruction against North Korea. From the halls of Congress, we need only summon reports on the segregationist assertions of former majority whip Trent Lott and the racialized justifications of Howard Coble for the use of severe "security" measures to "protect" Japanese citizens during World War II. And even on the pages of *Vanity Fair* (February 2003), Dame Edna (pseudonym for Barry Humphries) is given license, in the spirit of satirical humor, to express racialized wisdom. To "Torn Romantic from Palm Beach," who is agonizing over whether to learn Spanish or French, Dame Edna responds:

> Forget Spanish. There's nothing in that language worth reading except Don Quixote, and a quick listen to the CD of Man of La Mancha will take care of that. There was a poet named Garcia Lorca, but I'd leave him on the intellectual back burner if I were you. As for everyone's speaking it, what twaddle! Who speaks it that you are really desperate to talk to? The help? Your leaf blower? Study French or German, where there are at least a few books worth reading, or, if you're American, try English.

These examples illustrate how the power of racialized discourse "allows elite groups to claim enlightened and meritocratic views, while applying racist definitions of social reality" (Castles 1996, 30). Such forms of racialized discourse effectively perpetuate what Miles (1989) terms racialization—an ideological process of "delineation of group boundaries and of allocation of persons within those boundaries by primary reference to (supposedly) inherent and/or biological (usually phenotypical) characteristics" (74). The use of racialization here encompasses a "dialectical process of signification where those characteristics that are ascribed to define the Other, necessarily elicit a definition of the Self by the same criterion" (75).[1]

It is the process of racialization, with its reified commonsense notions of "race," that sustains the study of "race relations," an approach that has dominated the field for almost half a century. As a consequence of the "race relations" paradigm, U.S. society became further entrenched in the language of "race" as destiny, with an implicit dictum that membership in particular "races" enacted social processes rather than ideology. This approach has effectively fueled the racialization of politics, through which political discourses of many kinds are structured by attaching deterministic meaning to social constructs of physical and cultural characteristics. The outcome is the racialization of all social and political relations, infusing every conflict of interest with an ethnic dimension, so that racism becomes a way of expressing group interests (Ball and Solomos 1990). Fields (2001), an acerbic critic of "race relations," describes its impact on the engagement of the "Negro problem."

The ideological formation of race relations skirted the considerable difficulty of stating the Negro problem within the forms of a purportedly democratic polity and with respect to persons who were nominally citizens in that polity enjoying full political rights. Race relations so suited the liberal thought of the time, and has been so well able to accommodate the internal twists of liberal and neo-liberal thought since, that it remains a vital part of the prevailing public language today. It lingers on to cozen scholars who, instead of investigating it as an ideological device, accept it ingenuously as an empirical datum. (54)

While we argue against attributing explanatory or descriptive value to "race," we do not mean to suggest that races have no social reality—they do. This fiction of "race" is produced in the real world, thus serving to legitimate it and give it conceptual meaning and social life. At its core, the effort to transmute the concept of "race" into an objective reality is limited and, as Appiah (cited in Postal 2002) concludes, a morally dangerous proposition. Hence, there is no need for a distinct (critical) theory of "race"; instead, what is required is an earnest endeavor to theorize the specious concept with its illusory status out of existence and renew our commitment to the interrogation of racism as an ideology of social exclusion (Miles and Brown 2003).

In other words, if "race" is real, it is so only because it has been rendered meaningful by the actions and beliefs of the powerful, who retain the myth in order to protect their own political-economic interests. "Race" as a social construct of resistance comes into play only later, as racialized populations and their advocates embrace the concept in reverse to struggle against material conditions of domination and exploitation. Nevertheless, it cannot be denied that the essentialism inherent in the original epistemological intent of "race" is preserved. At its core, the effort to transmute the concept of "race" into an emancipatory category is a limited and unwise undertaking. Thus, it is high time we disrupt the continued use of a dubious concept that cannot help but render our theorizing ambiguous and problematic.

In its simplest terms, this ambiguity is most visible in the inconsistency with which the term "race" is applied—sometimes meaning ethnicity, at other times referring to culture or ancestry. More often than not, "terms used for race are seldom defined and race is frequently employed in a routine and uncritical manner to represent ill-defined social and cultural factors" (Williams 1994). This explains why in all the writings on "race" there is so little substantive theorizing about the construct itself. The category of "race" is thus suspect with respect to its analytical utility. If "race" is socially constructed and its origins clearly steeped in an ideology of exclusion, domination, exploitation, even genocide, why should we continue to make sense of people's lives based on the legacy of a pseudoscientific distortion from a previous era? Is not racism—as an ideology that exists within a structure of class differentiation and exploitation—rather than "race," the concept that merits our attention, particularly in these perilous times of global upheaval?

Theorizing Racism

Racism has been defined in a variety of ways, but certain points are central to our conceptualization of the term. First, racism is not the result of individual pathology; instead, it is an ideological set of practices and discourses embedded in the project of modernity and capitalist expansion. Second, racism is linked to racialization, a process by which populations are categorized and ranked on the basis of phenotypical traits or cultural signifiers. Economic and political power is implicated because of its explicit (or implicit) purpose of legitimating the exploitation or exclusion of racialized groups. And third, there is no one generic form, but rather multiple, diverse, and historically specific racisms that may vary in intensity, but constitute part and parcel of the larger phenomenon (Goldberg 1993; Castles 1996).

Etienne Balibar and Immanuel Wallerstein (1991) argue that in order to make our studies of racism more specific we must distinguish between two forms of racism. The first refers to those racisms whose primary intent is the exclusion and extermination of racialized populations deemed a threat. The second, termed *"inferiorization,"* is found in modern situations of migrant labor where labor rights are denied, forcing immigrant workers to take menial jobs and low entry positions that all others are unwilling to accept. Generally speaking, these two forms of racism "exist side by side and are linked to class interests. The ruling class is more likely to be interested in the racism of exploitation, while workers may favor exclusion" (Castles 1996, 26). This should come as no surprise, given that economic and political relations have been constructed in concert with the ideology of racism.

The reduction of racism to white racism against nonwhites is usually linked to post-1945 anticolonial and civil rights movements. However, Miles (1989) traces the roots of this process to early colonial life.

> [T]here is a universal dimension to [the] process of spatial segregation in so far as every ruling class usually organises its life in a distinct spatial location, separated from the lives of those whose labour power is exploited. The specificity lies in the conscious and strategic institutionalisation of a particular representational construction, that is, racism. The ideology of racism was used to not only select certain people to fill certain positions in the structure of class relations but class relations were themselves structured in a particular manner to create a large proportion of Africans as suppliers of cheap labour. (111)

This explanation sheds light on the evolution of racism against ethnic minority workers in Europe and against indigenous populations in Latin America, Africa, and Asia. The multiplicity of racisms currently expressed on the international stage in the face of globalization counters singular black-white notions of racism, so prevalent in the United States. Within U.S. cities, changing demographic profiles associated with a rapidly increasing immigrant population also expose the limits of a black-white paradigm. In its place, more complex configurations of racialized populations are evolving, as "the phenotypical, color-based categories of differences that only a generation ago appeared rigid and fixed are being restructured and reconfigured against the background of globalized capitalism and neoliberal government policies worldwide" (Marable 2000, 9). But such change is slow and uneven; and newly arrived immigrants often find themselves confusingly initiated into the rigidity of black-white racialized relations. Nevertheless, Fields (2001) argues that

> the real issue is not how immigrants became white or black, but how persons not born and bred to it, whatever their ancestry, become oriented in the American world of black and white. When the dichotomy was not completely irrelevant in the immigrants' place of origin (as for most European immigrants), it would have been overlaid with other pairs—peasant/landlord, villager/chief, native/colonial, illiterate/educated, indigene/evolue, black/brown (or coloured)—that fundamentally distinguished it from the stark opposition that prevailed in the United States. (52)

Given the complexity of our times, Castles (1996) rightly suggests that any study of racism requires an interdisciplinary approach in order to arrive at a more precise understanding of the different economic, political, and cultural factors which engender its existence.

Theories of racism must be sufficiently comprehensive as to take into account the great diversity among and between populations "without losing sight of their essential unity" (20), anchored in the fact that we are all human beings belonging to one species that descended from Africa. Hence, we must develop theories that can negotiate both the commonality and plurality of racisms, anchored, as Goldberg (1993) suggests, in the "historical alterations and discontinuities" (41) that give rise to their ideological formations and their explicit social practices. Theories of racism must also grapple with the development of strategies and counterpractices for dismantling the hegemonic structures that give rise to its consequences.

As we have suggested, scholars have tended to study "race" rather than racism. New scholarly texts on "race" are released daily, particularly in England, Australia, and the United States. Everywhere scholars seem eager to address "race" with its myriad of racial identities—including whiteness. Indeed, even the media has discovered the currency of "race." For example, on September 18, 2000, *Newsweek* published a special report entitled "Redefining Race in America." On the cover was a photographic collage of a variety of dismembered phenotypic representations, including hair, eyes, lips, and skin color. One of the feature stories, "The New Faces of Race," included a variety of photographs depicting "a gallery of native-born Americans." All those depicted were captioned with no less than three (racial, ethnic, national) labels to connote racial identities. In the text, reference was made to thirty census categories—a scheme that, as suggested earlier, is far more attached to the racialized constructions of the ivory tower and government officials than to what is actually taking place on the streets. Consequently, official labels obscure rather than illuminate the social and political experiences and realities of racialized populations in the United States (Oboler 1995).

This then begs the question as to why so many scholars (and politicians) are willing to speak of "race" as a reified, commonsense category of analysis in the construction of social theories and the development of public policy. Why do class analysis or challenges to capitalism—an overarching material force linked to the survival (or destruction) of people worldwide—not receive the level of treatment and regard accorded to the study of "race"? In today's virtual reality where capital transits the globe at lightning speed, there seems to be little tolerance for serious scholarly or political interrogations of capitalism as an ideology of modernity run amuck. Even many scholars of multiculturalism who solemnly proclaim that the purpose of their work is social justice have failed to critically examine capitalism.

Forthright analyses of racism, as not only one of the most effective hegemonic forces of our time in sustaining the interests of capitalist exploitation and domination but also as the progenitor of one of the greatest fallacies of history—the idea that "races" truly exist— are few and far between. Could it be that scholars worldwide find themselves so deeply entrenched or implicated that close analysis would find us all mired in contradiction, while supporting the very system responsible for so much human suffering in the first place? In response Fields (2001) contrasts the "homier and more tractable notion" of "race" with racism.

> Racism . . . unsettles fundamental instincts of American academic professionals who consider themselves liberal, leftist, or progressive. It is an act of peremptory, hostile, and supremely— often fatally—consequential identification that unceremoniously overrides its objects' sense of themselves. Racism thus unseats both identity and agency, if identity means sense of "self," and agency anything beyond conscious, goal directed activity, however trivial and ineffectual. The targets of racism do not "make" racism, nor are they free to "negotiate" the obstacles it places

in their way. Even as racism exposes the hollowness of agency and identity, it violates the two-sides-to-every-story expectation of symmetry that Americans are peculiarly attached to. There is no voluntary and affirmative side to racism as far as its victims are concerned, and it has no respect for symmetry at all. That is why well-meaning scholars are more apt to speak of race than racism. (48)

This insight calls to mind the problematics of identity politics grounded in the simple and compelling premise that members of particular groups share a greater commonality than those considered outsiders. Although this may sometimes be the case, identity politics always hangs on the edge of essentialism, particularly when social (if not phenotypical) traits are generated as proof of both trustworthiness and political solidarity. Gilroy (2000) cautions against the myth of "short-cut solidarity" that such an approach engenders, particularly when identity and class are decoupled and the promise of identity politics falls flat on its face. Community interests easily become "diverted into middle class campaigns for affirmation, assimilation and 'a piece of the pie' " (Anner 1996, 9), while working-class and poor people see little improvement in the quality of their lives.

Moreover, when questions of identity and agency consistently displace questions of economic and social power, the structures of inequality are cleverly masked and it becomes difficult to change them. It is precisely this irreparable flaw of identity politics that drives Wood (1995) to challenge its validity. "The 'politics of identity' . . . purports to be both more fine-tuned in its sensitivity to the complexity of human experience and more inclusive in its emancipatory sweep than the old politics of socialism. . . . But the 'politics of identity' reveals its limitations, both theoretical and political, the moment we try to situate class differences within its democratic vision" (258).

Wood's critique allows us to segue to the methodological shortcomings of the intersectionality arguments, with its oft-repeated recitation of "race, class, and gender." While we agree with those who argue that racism, sexism, and class oppression are interrelated and intrinsic to modernity, we categorically disagree that a host of oppressions should be afforded equal analytical explanatory power while the unrivaled force of capitalism in the world today is ignored. Both racism and sexism are most certainly implicated in the hegemonic forces that result in class domination. However, it is the *material* domination and exploitation of populations, in the interest of perpetuating a deeply entrenched capitalist system of world dominion, which serves as the impetus for the construction of social formations of inequality. It is this reality that prompts Wood (1995) to ask: "Is it possible to imagine class difference without exploitation and domination?" Her response echoes our own critique of the intersectionality argument.

> The "difference" that constitutes class as an "identity" *is*, by definition, a relationship of inequality and power, in a way that sexual or cultural "difference" need not be. A truly democratic society can celebrate diversities of life styles, culture or sexual preference; but in what sense would it be "democratic" to celebrate class difference? If a conception of freedom or equality adapted to sexual and cultural differences is intended to extend the reach of human liberation, can the same be said of a conception of freedom or equality that accommodates *class* difference? (258; emphasis in original)

Such a critique of the intersectionality argument also raises concerns related to the manner in which scholars define the constitutive force of racism, an issue seldom addressed with any specificity in the literature on "race." So, are we to accept phylogenetic or socially constructed notions of "race" as eternal and, possibly, even as a precondition without which humankind could not evolve (Toynbee 1899 and Keith 1931, cited in Barot and Bird 2001)?

Or should we see racism as a complex ideological apparatus of domination intricately linked to the conservation of power and control over resources and material wealth?

Relatedly, should we accept sexism as a pathology originating in the essentialized misogynist beliefs of men? Or is it a historical outgrowth of both patriarchal conquest and modernity, in the interest of dominance over material resources and the public institutions that govern their control? We are not arguing here against the notion that all forms of oppression are connected and act upon populations simultaneously. Instead, we argue that class, gender, sexuality, and racism do not have the same meaning or constitutive power—a highly significant issue for potentially reshaping political action in the coming years.

> At the very least, class equality means something different and requires different conditions from sexual or racial equality. In particular, the abolition of class inequality would by definition mean the end of capitalism. But is the same necessarily true about the abolition of sexual or racial inequality? Sexual and racial inequality . . . are not in principle incompatible with capitalism. The disappearance of class inequalities, on the other hand, is by definition incompatible with capitalism. At the same time, although class exploitation is constitutive of capitalism as sexual or racial inequality are not, capitalism subjects all social relations to its requirement.
>
> (Wood 1995, 259)

Racism and the Political Economy

Important to our understanding of racism, then, is the manner in which class and capitalism are inextricably linked in ways that do not apply to other categories of oppression. This perspective points to the social and political apparatus of the state that functions systematically to retain widespread control and governance over material wealth and resources. This apparatus operates in conjunction with those ideologies (whether cultural, political, class, gendered, sexual, or racialized) that preserve the hegemony of the modern capitalist state, engendering its capacity to appropriate even revolutionary projects and strip them of their transformative potential.

Such has been the fate of multiculturalism which, falling prey to both the politics of identity and state appropriation, became an effective vehicle for further depoliticizing progressive efforts against inequality rooted in the civil rights era of the 1960s and 1970s. Notwithstanding its original emancipatory intent, the politics of multiculturalism was from its inception flawed by its adherence to the language of "race relations." Moreover, the well-meaning celebrations of difference and the hard-fought battles for representation by a variety of identity movements failed to generate any real or lasting structural change. Thus, liberal proposals such as affirmative action, for instance, more often than not served the interests of the more privileged. In the final analysis, multiculturalism became an effective mechanism of the state, used to manage and preserve racialized class divisions, while in the marketplace the new multiplicity of identities generated new products for consumption. Arun Kundnani (2002) describes the fate of multiculturalism in terms of black culture in England.

> Multiculturalism now meant taking black culture off the streets—where it has been politicised and turned into a rebellion against the state—and putting it in the council chamber, in the classroom and on the television, where it could be institutionalized, managed and reified. Black culture was thus turned from a living movement into an object of passive contemplation, something to be "celebrated" rather than acted on. Multiculturalism became an ideology of conservatism, of preserving the status quo intact, in the face of a real desire to move forward.

> As post-modern theories of "hybridity" became popular in academia, cultural difference came to be seen as an end in itself, rather than an expression of revolt, and the concept of culture became a straitjacket, hindering rather than helping the fight against [racism] and class oppressions. (2)

Large metropolitan areas across the United States have experienced similar events. Most notable in the 1990s was the aforementioned uprising in South Central Los Angeles, where the language of "race relations" coupled with a politics of difference dominated the discourse of the media. Sidestepped were the underlying class tensions, associated with the way in which "globalization, economic restructuring, and automation had transformed the Los Angeles industrial landscape" (Valle and Torres 2000, 61). Instead, the sensationalism of racialized images and "race relations" rhetoric prevailed for days, nonstop, on major television networks.

What was successfully camouflaged in Los Angeles was the fact that racism is not about cultural differences; it is about political economy. By converting racism into a conflict of cultural differences, whether it was between blacks and Latinos, or Latinos and Koreans, or blacks and whites, the commonsense notion of "race" was effectively preserved in Los Angeles and the inequality of class relations normalized. Thus people are socialized to perceive "race" as a matter of cultural (and often individual) differences, when in truth what generally passes under the guise of "race" are deeply entrenched racialized class relations. In the process, the political economy of racism, embedded in capitalism, effectively divides oppressed communities, leaving much of the world's population vulnerable to economic exploitation.

There are many who argue that the prevalent emphasis on cultural differences during the 1980s has brought with it a new wave of racism, unfettered by the old baggage of biological determinism. Balibar (1991), for instance, argues that this "new racism" is actually "racism without race" (23), an ideology that utilizes the covert belief in immutable human differences to assert the impossibility of coexistence. Meanwhile, class concerns are masked, while "the power of the dominant group to proclaim and manage hierarchies of acceptable and unacceptable difference" (Castles 1996, 29) shapes the rhetoric of community development, public policy debates, and global economic interests. In the same vein, Teun van Dijk (1993) argues that the dominance of the "new racism" on the global stage has remained unchanged. "This undeniable progress has only softened the style of dominance of . . . Western nations. Far from abolished are the deeply entrenched economic, social and cultural remnants of past oppression and inequality; the modern prejudices about minorities; the economic and military power or the cultural hegemony of white over black, north over south, majorities over minorities" (cited in Castles 1996, 30).

Undoubtedly, the globalization of the political economy, or rather the *universalization of capital* (Wood 1998), raises new and complex questions related to the changing nature of racism and class formations. However, we do not subscribe to the notion that the process of globalization reflects a grand epochal shift. As Wood argues, what we are seeing is not a major shift in the logic of capitalism but rather "the consequences of capitalism as a comprehensive system . . . capitalism reaching maturity" (47). Historically, then, globalization must be understood within the context of modernization—the process of European colonial expansionism since the fifteenth century. In his writings on the racisms of globalization, Castles (1996) links the Western project of modernity to racism:

> Modernity implies increasingly integrated capitalist production and distribution systems, linked to secular cultures based on the principles of rationality. Modernity has meant colonization of

the rest of the world, not only in the direct sense of political control, but also through diffusion of Western cultural values. Racism—as an ideology which justified European domination—has always been part of modernity. (19)

In agreement, we assert that the constitutive force of most contemporary racisms is closely aligned with labor transformations, systematically initiated by the economic expansionism of globalization. Castles (1996) provides a variety of examples to illustrate this point. These include: the oppression of indigenous peoples as legacies of colonialism; the decolonization and formation of new nation-states which frequently have resulted in the exploitation or exclusion of minority workers; violent struggles linked to the processes of globalization which have resulted in the movement of refugee populations within and outside their countries, resulting in the impoverishment and denial of human rights; the recruitment of migrant labor for the labor market, forcing wages down, with tensions ignited by the racialized conflict between native and immigrant workers; and the racism against old and new minorities which is contributing to the growing complexity of inter-ethnic relations in urban centers and leading to new types of conflict and politicization, particularly on issues linked to culture and ethnicity.

Hence, the economic profiteering of transnational corporations, best illustrated by the Enron scandal,[2] has taken place on the backs of workers everywhere. Previously well-paying jobs in this country have been transferred to regions where cheap labor and little regulation enhances the profit margin of global enterprises. In cities such as Los Angeles, this phenomenon has given rise to high unemployment or underemployment, particularly among African American and Latino workers. The "global city" is now a place where jobs are few and immigration and poverty are high, while urban capital is heavily invested in complex international markets, eroding the political power of urban workers. Consequently, the cityscape continues to reflect previous segregation patterns of class and ethnicity, but in more complex and conflictual ways (Sassen 2001; Davis 1990; Valle and Torres 2000). In the large urban metropolis, the majority of the population is divested of any real opportunities for participation and decision-making, intensifying exclusionary practices. Yet, even in the midst of such entrenched inequalities, communities continue to seek out ways in which to launch antiracist struggles that might potentially impact the quality of their lives. Hence, we cannot ignore the myriad of popular movements that embrace antiracism as a key component of their organizing platform.

There is no question that to recognize racism as a central part of the social and political life of the capitalist state implies the need for radical change—change that would, undoubtedly, portend major shifts in the existing structures of inequality and asymmetrical relations of power. However, since the 1970s, antiracist advocates have blatantly ignored the centrality of class relations in the evolution and persistence of racism in U.S. society. Unwittingly, this neglect has led to the eruption of new racisms worldwide, as provincial attitudes prevailed. Absorbed with doing battle with what many deemed "economic determinism," antiracist advocates lost sight of the unfettered movement of capitalist interests around the globe as they attended to issues of identity and representation. Additionally, this approach prevented the formulation of a more substantive and comparative analysis of racism at the end of the twentieth century.

At this juncture, it seems important to say a few words regarding our approach to the study of racism, which we suspect will be characterized by some as privileging class or simply as economic determinism. If this is all that the reader gleans from our analysis, we certainly do not wish to debate the point; for we make no apologies for the centrality of our critique of capitalism and class formations in our analysis of racism. Furthermore, as we have repeatedly stated, we do not argue against the notion that "race" is a social construction or that all relations of inequality merit examination. As such, our criticism of the black-white problematic is not intended to marginalize the study of white-on-black racism, but rather to recognize the existence of multiple modalities of racisms.

However, instead of falling in line with cultural studies or postmodern renditions of power, we concur with Joanne Naiman that we must rescue the concept of power from its diffused and unmeasurable position, everywhere and nowhere, back to where it holds the promise of collective political action. That is to say, where power is perceived as centered in the external, material world, rather than simply in people's heads. We firmly believe that this task is imperative to any political project that claims to counter racism in the world today. As Naiman (1996) argues:

> In any society where private property and social classes exist, those who own the means of production will dominate. This is most obvious in the economic sphere, where those who own the productive units can decide what to produce, how to produce it, where to produce it, and so on. But the power of ownership goes far beyond mere economic control, and those who own the means of production also come to have power in the political and ideological spheres as well. Indeed, no owning class could maintain its position for long if it did not effectively control all three spheres within a society. (18)

Our work is in concert with those who seek to reclaim the power of working people—who, while less powerful than the owning class, are not powerless. The power of working-class people is embodied in the unequivocal fact that without their labor the capitalist class could not survive. In addition, workers are empowered through their sheer numbers. These are the qualities that along with important characteristics of organization make the working class central to our struggle against racism and for social change. In our view, this has nothing to do with privileging class over other oppressions. Instead, it represents our evolving assessment of structural power, both actual and potential, of different groups within society—and the growing recognition that, no matter how one wishes to theorize "race" and racism, all forms of oppression are ultimately linked to the exploitation and domination of both natural resources and human populations.

As we continue to advance our arguments for a historical materialist approach to the study of racism, we find ourselves especially attentive to new political ideas and emancipatory visions that can advance the struggle for social justice, human rights, and economic democracy. One such possibility is the work currently being developed by U.S. scholars in the area of cultural citizenship. Cultural citizenship, initially advanced by Renato Rosaldo (1994), attempts to engage difficult and often conflicting questions of citizenship with respect to culture, identity, and political participation. Importantly, it seeks to understand differences significant to people along a continuum, in the hope of disrupting the racialized discourse of the "Other." As such, cultural citizenship as a political strategy seeks not only to establish a collectivity in which no one is left outside the system, but also to extend the rights of first-class citizenship to all people. Key to the concept is a critical universalism that fundamentally respects the particularities of populations while working to dismantle structures of inequality that interfere with the exercise of human rights. There is no doubt that many questions still remain to be answered, particularly about the manner in which cultural citizenship can "overcome the limitations of the state and embrace the body of human rights in the context of globalization, transnational movements, and localism" (Delgado-Moreira 1997, 2). But for the moment, it offers in its theoretical infancy a political promise—one that will need to forthrightly challenge capitalism and the ideology of "race" if it is to gain any currency within a world of overwhelming capital excesses and racialized inequalities.

In 1982, Robert Miles courageously did the unthinkable by challenging the utility of "race" in his efforts to construct an effective politics of antiracism. In 1996, Kenan Malik argued, in *The Meaning of Race*, that rather than embracing difference, we should strive to transcend "race" and embrace a human universality that contends with the particularities and differences of our existence. Paul Gilroy (2000) echoes both Miles and Malik, as he proposes a radical humanist project "against race" so that we may free ourselves of its bondage. Along with Miles, Gilroy, and Malik, we now call for a movement "after race," anchored in the radical proposition that we are not distinct "races" but rather, as Renato Rosaldo (1994) posits, cultural citizens—entitled to live in a world where economic, political, and cultural democracy is the birthright of all people, not the thievery of a few.

Notes

1. For a thoughtful critique of the concept of racialization, see Rohit Barot and John Bird (2001), "Racialization: The Genealogy and Critique of a Concept," in *Ethnic and Racial Studies* 24(4) (4 July):601–18.
2. In December 2001, Enron, the transnational energy giant with $62 billion in assets, filed the largest bankruptcy in U.S. corporate history. Enron, the seventh-largest U.S. company, employing 21,000 workers in more than forty countries, lied about its profits and stands accused of a variety of shady investment dealings and concealments of debt through false accounting. The financial scandal, in which the life savings and retirement funds of tens of thousands of workers vanished while Enron executives lined their pockets, came to the public's attention when the company's link with President George W. Bush and Vice President Dick Cheney, among other Washington officials was publicly unveiled—Enron contributed millions of dollars to finance the 2004 Bush–Cheney presidential re-election campaign. Enron's deep financial roots on Capitol Hill served to insulate the company from government attempts to regulate its business dealings.

References

Anner, John. 1996. *Beyond Identity Politics*. Boston: South End Press.
Appiah, K. Anthony. 1995. "The Uncompleted Argument: Du Bois and the Illusion of Race." In Linda Bell and David Blumenfeld, eds., *Overcoming Racism and Sexism*. Lanham, Md.: Rowman and Littlefield.
Baldwin, James. 1988. "A Talk to Teachers." In Rick Simonson and Scott Walker, eds., *Multicultural Literacy*, 3–12. Saint Paul, Minn: Graywolf Press.
Balibar, Etienne. 2003. "Election/Selection." Keynote delivered at Traces: Race, Deconstruction and Critical Theory Conference. University of California, Irvine (April 10):1–19.
Balibar, Etienne, and Immanuel Wallerstein. 1991. *Race, Nation, Class: Ambiguous Identities*. London: Verso.
Ball, Wendy, and John Solomos. 1990. *Race and Local Politics*. New York: Macmillan.
Barot, Rohit, and John Bird. 2001. "Racialization: The Genealogy and Critique of a Concept." *Ethnic and Racial Studies* 24(4) (4 July):601–18.
Castles, Stephen. 1996. "The Racisms of Globalization." In Ellie Vasta and Stephen Castles, eds., *The Teeth Are Smiling: The Persistence of Racism in Australia*, 17–45. St. Leonards, New South Wales: Allen and Unwin.
Davis, Mike. 1990. *City of Quartz*. London: Verso.
Delgado-Moreira, Juan. 1997. "Cultural Citizenship and the Creation of European Identity." *Electronic journal of Sociology* (ISSN 1198) 3655:1–19.
Du Bois, W.E.B. 1989/1903. *The Souls of Black Folk*. New York: Bantam Books.
Fields, Barbara Jean 2001. "Whiteness, Racism, and Identity." In *International Labor and Working Class History* 60 (Fall):48–56.
Fredrickson, George M. 2002. *Racism: A Short History*. Princeton, N.J.: Princeton University Press.
Gilroy, Paul 2000. *Against Race: Imagining Political Culture beyond the Colorline*. Cambridge, Mass: Harvard University Press.

Goldberg, David Theo. 1993. *Racist Culture: Philosophy and the Politics of Meaning.* Oxford: Blackwell.

Guillaumin, Colette. 1980. "The Idea of Race and Its Elevation to Autonomous Scientific and Legal Status in UNESCO." In *Sociological Theories: Race and Colonialism.* Paris: UNESCO.

Guinier, Lani, and Gerald Torres. 2002. *The Miner's Canary: Enlisting Race, Resisting Power, Transforming Democracy.* Cambridge, Mass.: Harvard University Press.

Kundnani, Arun. 2002. "The Death of Multiculturalism." Institute of Race Relations. (Accessed on-line http://www.irr.org.uk)

Lee, Sandra Soo-Jin, Joanne Mountain, and Barbara Koenig. 2001. "The Meaning of 'Race.' " In "The New Genomics: Implications for Health Disparities Research." *Yale Journal of Health Policy, Law, and Ethics* 1:33–75.

Malik, Kenan. 1996. *The Meaning of Race: Race, History, and Culture in Western Society.* New York: New York University Press.

Marable, Manning. 2000. "We Need a New and Critical Study of Race and Ethnicity." *Chronicle of Higher Education* 46(1):25, B4.

Miles, Robert. 1982. *Racism and Migrant Labor.* New York: Routledge and Kegan Paul.

——— . 1989. *Racism.* Key Ideas series. London: Routledge.

Miles, Robert, and Malcolm Brown. 2003. *Racism* (2d ed.). London: Routledge.

Naiman, Joanne. 1996. "Left Feminism and the Return to Class." *Monthly Review* 48(2) (June):12–28.

Oboler, Suzanne. 1995. *Ethnic Labels, Latino Lives: Identity and the Politics of (Re)Presentation in the United States.* Minneapolis: University of Minnesota Press.

Postal, Danny. 2002. "Is Race Real? How Does Identity Matter?" *Chronicle of Higher Education* (April 5):A10.

Rosaldo, Renato. 1989. *Culture and Truth: The Remaking of Social Analysis.* Boston: Beacon Press.

——— . 1994. "Social Justice and the Crisis of National Communities." *Cultural Anthropology* 9(3):402–11.

Sassen, Saskia. 2001. *The Global City.* Princeton, N.J.: Princeton University Press.

Valle, Victor, and Rodolfo D. Torres 2000. *Latino Metropolis.* Minneapolis: University of Minnesota Press.

van Dijk, T.A. 1993. *Elite Discourses on Racism.* Newbury Park, Calif.: Sage.

Williams, David R. 1994. "The Concept of Race in Health Services Research: 1966 to 1990." *Health Services Research* 29:261.

Wood, Ellen M. 1995. *Democracy against Capitalism: Renewing Historical Materialism.* New York: Cambridge University Press.

——— . 1998. "Modernity, Postmodernity, or Capitalism?" In Robert N. McChesney, Ellen Meiksins Wood, and John Bellamy Foster, eds., *Capitalism and the Information Age.* New York: Monthly Review Press.

9

Toward a Critical Race Theory of Education
Gloria Ladson-Billings and William F. Tate IV

This article asserts that despite the salience of race in U.S. society, as a topic of scholarly inquiry, it remains untheorized. The article argues for a critical race theoretical perspective in education analogous to that of critical race theory in legal scholarship by developing three propositions: (1) race continues to be significant in the United States; (2) U.S. society is based on property rights rather than human rights; and (3) the intersection of race and property creates an analytical tool for understanding inequity. The article concludes with a look at the limitations of the current multicultural paradigm.

The presentation of truth in new forms provokes resistance, confounding those committed to accepted measures for determining the quality and validity of statements made and conclusions reached, and making it difficult for them to respond and adjudge what is acceptable.

Derrick Bell,
Faces at the Bottom of the Well

I am not included within the pale of this glorious anniversary! Your high independence only reveals the immeasurable distance between us. The blessings in which you this day, rejoice, are not enjoyed in common. The rich inheritance of justice, liberty, prosperity and independence bequeathed by your fathers, not by me . . .

Frederick Douglass,
My Bondage and My Freedom

In 1991 social activist and education critic Jonathan Kozol delineated the great inequities that exist between the schooling experiences of white middle-class students and those of poor African-American and Latino students. And, while Kozol's graphic descriptions may prompt some to question how it is possible that we allow these "savage inequalities," this article suggests that these inequalities are a logical and predictable result of a racialized society in which discussions of race and racism continue to be muted and marginalized.[1]

In this article we attempt to theorize race and use it as an analytic tool for understanding school inequity.[2] We begin with a set of propositions about race and property and their intersections. We situate our discussion in an explication of critical race theory and attempt to move beyond the boundaries of the educational research literature to include arguments and new perspectives from law and the social sciences. In doing so, we acknowledge and are indebted to a number of scholars whose work crosses disciplinary boundaries.[3] We conclude by exploring the tensions between our conceptualization of a critical race theory in education and the educational reform movement identified as multicultural education.

Understanding Race and Property

Our discussion of social inequity in general, and school inequity in particular, is based on three central propositions:[4]

1. Race continues to be a significant factor in determining inequity in the United States.
2. U.S. society is based on property rights.
3. The intersection of race and property creates an analytic tool through which we can understand social (and, consequently, school) inequity.

In this section we expand on these propositions and provide supporting "meta-propositions" to make clear our line of reasoning and relevant application to educational or school settings.

Race as Factor in Inequity

The first proposition—that race continues to be a significant factor in determining inequity in the United States—is easily documented in the statistical and demographic data. Hacker's look at educational and life chances such as high school dropout rates, suspension rates, and incarceration rates echoes earlier statistics of the Children's Defense Fund.[5] However, in what we now call the postmodern era, some scholars question the usefulness of race as a category.

Omi and Winant argue that popular notions of race as either an ideological construct or an objective condition have epistemological limitations.[6] Thinking of race strictly as an ideological construct denies the reality of a racialized society and its impact on "raced" people in their everyday lives. On the other hand, thinking of race solely as an objective condition denies the problematic aspects of race—how do we decide who fits into which racial classifications? How do we categorize racial mixtures? Indeed, the world of biology has found the concept of race virtually useless. Geneticist Cavalli-Sforza asserts that "human populations are sometimes known as ethnic groups, or 'races.' . . . They are hard to define in a way that is both rigorous and useful because human beings group themselves in a bewildering array of sets, some of them overlapping, all of them in a state of flux."[7]

Nonetheless, even when the concept of race fails to "make sense," we continue to employ it. According to Nobel Laureate Toni Morrison:

> Race has become metaphorical—a way of referring to and disguising forces, events, classes, and expressions of social decay and economic division far more threatening to the body politic than biological "race" ever was.
>
> Expensively kept, economically unsound, a spurious and useless political asset in election campaigns, racism is as healthy today as it was during the Enlightenment. It seems that it has a utility far beyond economy, beyond the sequestering of classes from one another, and has assumed a metaphorical life so completely embedded in daily discourse that it is perhaps more necessary and more on display than ever before.[8]

Despite the problematic nature of race, we offer as a first meta-proposition that race, unlike gender and class, remains untheorized.[9] Over the past few decades theoretical and epistemological considerations of gender have proliferated.[10] Though the field continues to struggle for legitimacy in academe, interest in and publications about feminist theories abound. At the same time, Marxist and Neo-Marxist formulations about class continue to merit consideration as theoretical models for understanding social inequity.[11] We recognize the importance of both gender- and class-based analyses while at the same time pointing to their shortcomings vis-à-vis race. Roediger points out that "the main body of writing by White Marxists in the United States has both 'naturalized' whiteness and oversimplified race."[12]

Omi and Winant have done significant work in providing a sociological explanation of race in the United States. They argue that the paradigms of race have been conflated with notions of ethnicity, class, and nation because

> theories of race—of its meaning, its transformations, the significance of racial events—have never been a top priority in social science. In the U.S., although the "founding fathers" of American sociology ... were explicitly concerned with the state of domestic race relations, racial theory remained one of the least developed fields of sociological inquiry.[13]

To mount a viable challenge to the dominant paradigm of ethnicity (i.e., we are all ethnic and, consequently, must assimilate and rise socially the same way European Americans have), Omi and Winant offer a racial formation theory that they define as "the sociohistorical process by which racial categories are created, inhabited, transformed and destroyed. . . . [It] is a process of historically situated *projects* in which human bodies and social structures are represented and organized." Further, they link "racial formation to the evolution of hegemony, the way in which society is organized and ruled." Their analysis suggests that "race is a matter of both social structure and cultural representation."[14]

By arguing that race remains untheorized, we are not suggesting that other scholars have not looked carefully at race as a powerful tool for explaining social inequity, but that the intellectual salience of this theorizing has not been systematically employed in the analysis of educational inequality. Thus, like Omi and Winant, we are attempting to uncover or decipher the social-structural and cultural significance of race in education. Our work owes an intellectual debt to both Carter G. Woodson and W.E.B. Du Bois, who, although marginalized by the mainstream academic community, used race as a theoretical lens for assessing social inequity.[15]

Both Woodson and Du Bois presented cogent arguments for considering race as *the* central construct for understanding inequality. In many ways our work is an attempt to build on the foundation laid by these scholars.[16] Briefly, Woodson, as far back as 1916, began to establish the legitimacy of race (and, in particular, African Americans) as a subject of scholarly inquiry.[17] As founder of the Association for the Study of Negro Life and History and editor of its *Journal of Negro History*, Woodson revolutionized the thinking about African Americans from that of pathology and inferiority to a multitextured analysis of the uniqueness of African Americans and their situation in the United States. His most notable publication, *The Miseducation of the Negro*, identified the school's role in structuring inequality and demotivating African-American students:

> The same educational process which inspires and stimulates the oppressor with the thought that he is everything and has accomplished everything worthwhile, depresses and crushes at the same time the spark of genius in the Negro by making him feel that his race does not amount to much and never will measure up to the standards of other peoples.[18]

Du Bois, perhaps better known among mainstream scholars, profoundly impacted the thinking of many identified as "other" by naming a "double consciousness" felt by African Americans. According to Du Bois, the African American "ever feels his two-ness—an

American, A Negro; two souls, two thoughts, two unreconciled strivings."[19] In a current
biography of Du Bois, Lewis details the intellectual impact of this concept:

> It was a revolutionary concept. It was not just revolutionary; the concept of the divided self was
> profoundly mystical, for Du Bois invested this double consciousness with a capacity to see
> incomparably further and deeper. The African-American—seventh son after the Egyptian and
> Indian, the Greek and Roman, the Teuton and Mongolian—possessed the gift of "second sight
> in this American world," an intuitive faculty (prelogical, in a sense) enabling him/her to see
> and say things about American society that possessed a heightened moral validity. Because he
> dwelt equally in the mind and heart of his oppressor as in his own beset psyche, the African
> American embraced a vision of the commonweal at its best.[20]

As a prophetic foreshadowing of the centrality of race in U.S. society, Du Bois reminded us
that "the problem of the twentieth century is the problem of the color line."[21]

The second meta-proposition that we use to support the proposition that race continues
to be significant in explaining inequity in the United States is that class- and gender-based
explanations are not powerful enough to explain all of the difference (or variance) in
school experience and performance. Although both class and gender can and do intersect
race, as stand-alone variables they do not explain all of the educational achievement
differences apparent between whites and students of color. Indeed, there is some evidence
to suggest that even when we hold constant for class, middle-class African-American
students do not achieve at the same level as their white counterparts.[22] Although Oakes
reports that "in academic tracking, . . . poor and minority students are most likely to be
placed at the lowest levels of the school's sorting system,"[23] we are less clear as to which
factor—race or class—is causal. Perhaps the larger question of the impact of race on social
class is the more relevant one. Space limitations do not permit us to examine that question.

Issues of gender bias also figure in inequitable schooling.[24] Females receive less attention
from teachers, are counseled away from or out of advanced mathematics and science
courses, and although they receive better grades than their male counterparts, their grades
do not translate into advantages in college admission and/or the work place.[25]

But examination of class and gender, taken alone or together, do not account for the
extraordinarily high rates of school dropout, suspension, expulsion, and failure among
African-American and Latino males.[26] In the case of suspension, Majors and Billson argue
that many African-American males are suspended or expelled from school for what they
termed "non-contact violations"—wearing banned items of clothing such as hats and
jackets, or wearing these items in an "unauthorized" manner, such as backwards or inside
out.[27]

The point we strive to make with this meta-proposition is not that class and gender are
insignificant, but rather, as West suggests, that "race matters," and, as Smith insists,
"blackness matters in more detailed ways."[28]

The Property Issue

Our second proposition, that U.S. society is based on property rights, is best explicated
by examining legal scholarship and interpretations of rights. To develop this proposition it
is important to situate it in the context of critical race theory. Monaghan reports that
"critical race legal scholarship developed in the 1970s, in part because minority scholars
thought they were being overlooked in critical legal studies, a better-known movement that

examines the way law encodes cultural norms."[29] However, Delgado argues that despite the diversity contained within the critical race movement, there are some shared features:

> an assumption that racism is not a series of isolated acts, but is endemic in American life, deeply ingrained legally, culturally, and even psychologically;
>
> a call for a reinterpretation of civil-rights law "in light of its ineffectuality, showing that laws to remedy racial injustices are often undermined before they can fulfill their promise";
>
> a challenge to the "traditional claims of legal neutrality, objectivity, color-blindness, and meritocracy as camouflages for the self-interest of dominant groups in American society";
>
> an insistence on subjectivity and the reformulation of legal doctrine to reflect the perspectives of those who have experienced and been victimized by racism firsthand;
>
> the use of stories or first-person accounts.[30]

In our analysis we add another aspect to this critical paradigm that disentangles democracy and capitalism. Many discussions of democracy conflate it with capitalism despite the fact that it is possible to have a democratic government with an economic system other than capitalism. Discussing the two ideologies as if they were one masks the pernicious effects of capitalism on those who are relegated to its lowest ranks. Traditional civil rights approaches to solving inequality have depended on the "rightness" of democracy while ignoring the structural inequality of capitalism.[31] However, democracy in the U.S. context was built on capitalism.

In the early years of the republic *only* capitalists enjoyed the franchise. Two hundred years later when civil rights leaders of the 1950s and 1960s built their pleas for social justice on an appeal to civil and human rights, they were ignoring the fact that the society was based on *property rights*.[32] An example from the 1600s underscores the centrality of property in the Americas from the beginning of European settlement:

> When the Pilgrims came to New England they too were coming not to vacant land but to territory inhabited by tribes of Indians. The governor of the Massachusetts Bay Colony, John Winthrop, created the excuse to take Indian land by declaring the area legally a "vacuum." The Indians, he said, had not "subdued" the land, and therefore had only a "natural" right to it, but not a "civil right." A "natural right" did not have legal standing.[33]

Bell examined the events leading up to the Constitution's development and concluded that there exists a tension between property rights and human rights.[34] This tension was greatly exacerbated by the presence of African peoples as slaves in America. The purpose of the government was to protect the main object of society—property. The slave status of most African Americans (as well as women and children) resulted in their being objectified as property. And, a government constructed to protect the rights of property owners lacked the incentive to secure human rights for the African American.[35]

According to Bell "the concept of individual rights, unconnected to property rights, was totally foreign to these men of property; and thus, despite two decades of civil rights gains, most Blacks remain disadvantaged and deprived because of their race."[36]

The grand narrative of U.S. history is replete with tensions and struggles over property —in its various forms. From the removal of Indians (and later Japanese Americans) from the land, to military conquest of the Mexicans,[37] to the construction of Africans as property,[38] the ability to define, possess, and own property has been a central feature of power in America. We do not suggest that other nations have not fought over and defined themselves by property and landownership.[39] However, the contradiction of a reified symbolic individual juxtaposed to the reality of "real estate" means that emphasis on the centrality of property can be disguised. Thus, we talk about the importance of the individual, individual rights, and civil rights while social benefits accrue largely to property owners.[40]

Property relates to education in explicit and implicit ways. Recurring discussions about property tax relief indicate that more affluent communities (which have higher property values, hence higher tax assessments) resent paying for a public school system whose clientele is largely non-white and poor.[41] In the simplest of equations, those with "better" property are entitled to "better" schools. Kozol illustrates the disparities: "Average expenditures per pupil in the city of New York in 1987 were some $5,500. In the highest spending suburbs of New York (Great Neck or Manhasset, for example, on Long Island) funding levels rose above $11,000, with the highest districts in the state at $15,000."[42]

But the property differences manifest themselves in other ways. For example, curriculum represents a form of "intellectual property."[43] The quality and quantity of the curriculum varies with the "property values" of the school. The use of a critical race story[44] appropriately represents this notion:

> The teenage son of one of the authors of this article was preparing to attend high school. A friend had a youngster of similar age who also was preparing to enter high school. The boys excitedly poured over course offerings in their respective schools' catalogues. One boy was planning on attending school in an upper-middle-class white community. The other would be attending school in an urban, largely African-American district. The difference between the course offerings as specified in the catalogues was striking. The boy attending the white, middle-class school had his choice of many foreign languages—Spanish, French, German, Latin, Greek, Italian, Chinese, and Japanese. His mathematics offerings included algebra, geometry, trigonometry, calculus, statistics, general math, and business math. The science department at this school offered biology, chemistry, physics, geology, science in society, biochemistry, and general science. The other boy's curriculum choices were not nearly as broad. His foreign language choices were Spanish and French. His mathematics choices were general math, business math, and algebra (there were no geometry or trig classes offered). His science choices were general science, life science, biology, and physical science. The differences in electives were even more pronounced, with the affluent school offering courses such as Film as Literature, Asian Studies, computer programming, and journalism. Very few elective courses were offered at the African-American school, which had no band, orchestra, or school newspaper.

The availability of "rich" (or enriched) intellectual property delimits what is now called "opportunity to learn"[45]—the presumption that along with providing educational "standards"[46] that detail what students should know and be able to do, they must have the material resources that support their learning. Thus, intellectual property must be undergirded by "real" property, that is, science labs, computers and other state-of-the-art technologies, appropriately certified and prepared teachers. Of course, Kozol demonstrated that schools that serve poor students of color are unlikely to have access to these resources and, consequently, students will have little or no opportunity to learn despite the attempt to mandate educational standards.[47]

Critical Race Theory and Education

With this notion of property rights as a defining feature of the society, we proceed to describe the ways that the features of critical race theory mentioned in the previous section can be applied to our understanding of educational inequity.

Racism as Endemic and Deeply Ingrained in American Life

If racism were merely isolated, unrelated, individual acts, we would expect to see at least a few examples of educational excellence and equity together in the nation's public schools. Instead, those places where African Americans do experience educational success tend to be outside of the public schools.[48] While some might argue that poor children, regardless of race, do worse in school, and that the high proportion of African-American poor contributes to their dismal school performance, we argue that the cause of their poverty in conjunction with the condition of their schools and schooling is institutional and structural racism. Thus, when we speak of racism we refer to Wellman's definition of "culturally sanctioned beliefs which, regardless of the intentions involved, defend the advantages Whites have because of the subordinated positions of racial minorities." We must therefore contend with the "problem facing White people [of coming] to grips with the demands made by Blacks and Whites while at the same time *avoiding* the possibility of institutional change and reorganization that might affect them."[49]

A Reinterpretation of Ineffective Civil Rights Law

In the case of education, the civil rights decision that best exemplifies our position is the landmark *Brown* v. *Board of Education of Topeka, Kansas*. While having the utmost respect for the work of Thurgood Marshall and the National Association for the Advancement of Colored People (NAACP) legal defense team in arguing the *Brown* decision, with forty years of hindsight we recognize some serious shortcomings in that strategy. Today, students of color are more segregated than ever before.[50] Although African Americans represent 12 percent of the national population, they are the majority in twenty-one of the twenty-two largest (urban) school districts.[51] Instead of providing more and better educational opportunities, school desegregation has meant increased white flight along with a loss of African-American teaching and administrative positions.[52] In explaining the double-edge sword of civil rights legislation, Crenshaw argued that

> the civil rights community ... must come to terms with the fact that antidiscrimination discourse is fundamentally ambiguous and can accommodate conservative as well as liberal views of race and equality. This dilemma suggests that the civil rights constituency cannot afford to view antidiscrimination doctrine as a permanent pronouncement of society's commitment to ending racial subordination. Rather, antidiscrimination law represents an ongoing ideological struggle in which occasional winners harness the moral, coercive, consensual power of law. Nonetheless, the victories it offers can be ephemeral and the risks of engagement substantial.[53]

An example of Crenshaw's point about the ambiguity of civil rights legislation was demonstrated in a high school district in Northern California.[54] Of the five high schools in the district, one was located in a predominantly African-American community. To entice white students to attend that school, the district funded a number of inducements including free camping and skiing trips. While the trips were available to all of the students, they were attended largely by the white students, who already owned the expensive camping and skiing equipment. However, these inducements were not enough to continuously attract white students. As enrollment began to fall, the district decided to close a school. Not surprisingly, the school in the African-American community was closed and all of its students had to be (and continue to be) bused to the four white schools in the district.

Lomotey and Staley's examination of Buffalo's "model" desegregation program revealed that African-American and Latino students continued to be poorly served by the school system. The academic achievement of African-American and Latino students failed to improve while their suspension, expulsion, and dropout rates continued to rise. On the other hand, the desegregation plan provided special magnet programs and extended day care of which whites were able to take advantage. What, then, made Buffalo a model school desegregation program? In short, the benefits that whites derived from school desegregation and their seeming support of the district's desegregation program.[55] Thus, a model desegregation program becomes defined as one that ensures that whites are happy (and do not leave the system altogether) regardless of whether African-American and other students of color achieve or remain.

Challenging Claims of Neutrality, Objectivity, Color-blindness, and Meritocracy

A theme of "naming one's own reality" or "voice" is entrenched in the work of critical race theorists. Many critical race theorists argue that the form and substance of scholarship are closely connected.[56] These scholars use parables, chronicles, stories, counterstories, poetry, fiction, and revisionist histories to illustrate the false necessity and irony of much of current civil rights doctrine. Delgado suggests that there are at least three reasons for naming one's own reality in legal discourse:

1. Much of reality is socially constructed.
2. Stories provide members of outgroups a vehicle for psychic self-preservation.
3. The exchange of stories from teller to listener can help overcome ethnocentrism and the dysconscious conviction of viewing the world in one way.[57]

The first reason for naming one's own reality is to demonstrate how political and moral analysis is conducted in legal scholarship. Many mainstream legal scholars embrace universalism over particularity.[58] According to Williams, "theoretical legal understanding" is characterized, in Anglo-American jurisprudence, by the acceptance of transcendent, acontextual, universal legal truths or procedures.[59] For instance, some legal scholars might contend that the tort of fraud has always existed and that it is a component belonging to the universal system of right and wrong. This view tends to discount anything that is nontranscendent (historical), or contextual (socially constructed), or nonuniversal (specific) with the unscholarly labels of "emotional," "literary," "personal," or "false."

In contrast, critical race theorists argue that political and moral analysis is situational— "truths only exist for this person in this predicament at this time in history."[60] For the critical race theorist, social reality is constructed by the formulation and the exchange of stories about individual situations.[61] These stories serve as interpretive structures by which we impose order on experience and it on us.[62]

A second reason for the naming-one's-own-reality theme of critical race theory is the psychic preservation of marginalized groups. A factor contributing to the demoralization of marginalized groups is self-condemnation.[63] Members of minority groups internalize the stereotypic images that certain elements of society have constructed in order to maintain their power.[64] Historically, storytelling has been a kind of medicine to heal the wounds of pain caused by racial oppression.[65] The story of one's condition leads to the realization of how one came to be oppressed and subjugated and allows one to stop inflicting mental violence on oneself.

Finally, naming one's own reality with stories can affect the oppressor. Most oppression does not seem like oppression to the perpetrator.[66] Delgado argues that the dominant group justifies its power with stories—stock explanations—that construct reality in ways to maintain their privilege.[67] Thus, oppression is rationalized, causing little self-examination by the oppressor. Stories by people of color can catalyze the necessary cognitive conflict to jar dysconscious racism.

The "voice" component of critical race theory provides a way to communicate the experience and realities of the oppressed, a first step on the road to justice. As we attempt to make linkages between critical race theory and education, we contend that the voice of people of color is required for a complete analysis of the educational system. Delpit argues that one of the tragedies of education is the way in which the dialogue of people of color has been silenced. An example from her conversation with an African-American graduate student illustrates this point:

> There comes a moment in every class when we have to discuss "The Black Issue" and what's appropriate education for Black children. I tell you, I'm tired of arguing with those White people, because they won't listen. Well, I don't know if they really don't listen or if they just don't believe you. It seems like if you can't quote Vygotsky or something, then you don't have any validity to speak about your own kids. Anyway, I'm not bothering with it anymore, now I'm just in it for a grade.[68]

A growing number of education scholars of color are raising critical questions about the way that research is being conducted in communities of color.[69] Thus, without authentic voices of people of color (as teachers, parents, administrators, students, and community members) it is doubtful that we can say or know anything useful about education in their communities.

The Intersection of Race and Property

In the previous sections of this article we argued that race is still a significant factor in determining inequity in the United States and that the society is based on property rights rather than on human rights. In this section we discuss the intersection of race and property as a central construct in understanding a critical race theoretical approach to education.

Harris argues that "slavery linked the privilege of Whites to the subordination of Blacks through a legal regime that attempted the conversion of Blacks into objects of property. Similarly, the settlement and seizure of Native American land supported White privilege through a system of property rights in land in which the 'race' of the Native Americans rendered their first possession right invisible and justified conquest." But, more pernicious and long lasting then the victimization of people of color is the construction of whiteness as the ultimate property. "Possession—the act necessary to lay the basis for rights in property—was defined to include only the cultural practices of Whites. This definition laid the foundation for the idea that whiteness—that which Whites alone possess—is valuable and is property."[70]

Because of space constraints, it is not possible to fully explicate Harris's thorough analysis of whiteness as property. However, it is important to delineate what she terms the "property functions of whiteness," which include: (1) rights of disposition; (2) rights to use and enjoyment; (3) reputation and status property; and (4) the absolute right to exclude. How these rights apply to education is germane to our discussion.

Rights of disposition. Because property rights are described as fully alienable, that is, transferable, it is difficult to see how whiteness can be construed as property.[71] However, alienability of certain property is limited (e.g., entitlements, government licenses, professional degrees or licenses held by one party and financed by the labor of the other in the context of divorce). Thus, whiteness when conferred on certain student performances is alienable.[72] When students are rewarded only for conformity to perceived "white norms" or sanctioned for cultural practices (e.g., dress, speech patterns, unauthorized conceptions of knowledge), white property is being rendered alienable.

Rights to use and enjoyment. Legally, whites can use and enjoy the privileges of whiteness. As McIntosh has explicitly demonstrated, whiteness allows for specific social, cultural, and economic privileges.[73] Fuller further asserts that whiteness is both performative and pleasurable.[74] In the school setting, whiteness allows for extensive use of school property. Kozol's description of the material differences in two New York City schools can be interpreted as the difference between those who possess the right to use and enjoy what schools can offer and those who do not:

> The [white] school serves 825 children in the kindergarten through sixth grade. This is approximately half the student population crowded into [black] P.S. 79, where 1,550 children fill a space intended for 1,000, and a great deal smaller than the 1,300 children packed into the former skating rink.[75]

This right of use and enjoyment is also reflected in the structure of the curriculum, also described by Kozol:

> The curriculum [the white school] follows "emphasizes critical thinking, reasoning and logic." The planetarium, for instance, is employed not simply for the study of the universe as it exists. "Children also are designing their own galaxies," the teacher says. . . .
>   In my [Kozol's] notes: "Six girls, four boys. Nine White, one Chinese. I am glad they have this class. But what about the others? Aren't there ten Black children in the school who could *enjoy* this also?"[76]

Reputation and status property. The concept of reputation as property is regularly demonstrated in legal cases of libel and slander. Thus, to damage someone's reputation is to damage some aspect of his or her personal property. In the case of race, to call a white person "black" is to defame him or her.[77] In the case of schooling, to identify a school or program as nonwhite in any way is to diminish its reputation or status. For example, despite the prestige of foreign language learning, bilingual education as practiced in the United States as a nonwhite form of second language learning has lower status.[78] The term *urban*, the root word of *urbane*, has come to mean black. Thus, urban schools (located in the urbane, sophisticated cities) lack the status and reputation of suburban (white) schools and when urban students move to or are bused to suburban schools, these schools lose their reputation.[79]

The absolute right to exclude. Whiteness is constructed in this society as the absence of the "contaminating" influence of blackness. Thus, "one drop of black blood" constructs one as black, regardless of phenotypic markers.[80] In schooling, the absolute right to exclude was demonstrated initially by denying blacks access to schooling altogether. Later, it was demonstrated by the creation and maintenance of separate schools. More recently it has been demonstrated by white flight and the growing insistence on vouchers, public funding of private schools, and schools of choice.[81] Within schools, absolute right to exclude is demonstrated by resegregation via tracking,[82] the institution of "gifted" programs, honors programs, and advanced placement classes. So complete is this exclusion that black students often come to the university in the role of intruders—who have been granted special permission to be there.

In this section we have attempted to draw parallels between the critical race legal theory notion of whiteness as property and educational inequity. In the final section we relate some of the intellectual/theoretical tensions that exist between critical race theory and multicultural education.

The Limits of the Multicultural Paradigm

Throughout this article we have argued the need for a critical race theoretical perspective to cast a new gaze on the persistent problems of racism in schooling. We have argued the need for this perspective because of the failure of scholars to theorize race. We have drawn parallels between the way critical race legal scholars understand their position vis-à-vis traditional legal scholarship and the ways critical race theory applied to education offers a way to rethink traditional educational scholarship. We also have referred to the tensions that exist between traditional civil rights legislation and critical race legal theory. In this section we identify a necessary tension between critical race theory in education and what we term the multicultural paradigm.

Multicultural education has been conceptualized as a reform movement designed to effect change in the "school and other educational institutions so that students from diverse racial, ethnic, and other social-class groups will experience educational equality."[83] In more recent years, multicultural education has expanded to include issues of gender, ability, and sexual orientation. Although one could argue for an early history of the "multicultural education movement" as far back as the 1880s when George Washington Williams wrote his history of African Americans, much of the current multicultural education practice seems more appropriately rooted in the intergroup education movement of the 1950s, which was designed to help African Americans and other "unmeltable" ethnics become a part of America's melting pot.[84] Their goals were primarily assimilationist through the reduction of prejudice. However, after the civil rights unrest and growing self-awareness of African Americans in the 1960s, the desire to assimilate was supplanted by the reclamation of an "authentic black personality" that did not rely on the acceptance by or standards of white America. This new vision was evidenced in the academy in the form of first, black studies and later, when other groups made similar liberating moves, ethnic studies.[85]

Current practical demonstrations of multicultural education in schools often reduce it to trivial examples and artifacts of cultures such as eating ethnic or cultural foods, singing songs or dancing, reading folktales, and other less than scholarly pursuits of the fundamentally different conceptions of knowledge or quests for social justice.[86] At the university level, much of the concern over multicultural education has been over curriculum inclusion.[87] However, another level of debate emerged over what became known as "multiculturalism."

Somewhat different from multicultural education in that it does not represent a particular educational reform or scholarly tradition, multiculturalism came to be viewed as a political philosophy of "many cultures" existing together in an atmosphere of respect and tolerance.[88] Thus, outside of the classroom multiculturalism represented the attempt to bring both students and faculty from a variety of cultures into the school (or academy) environment. Today, the term is used interchangeably with the ever-expanding "diversity," a term used to explain all types of "difference"—racial, ethnic, cultural, linguistic, ability, gender, sexual orientation. Thus, popular music, clothes, media, books, and so forth, reflect a growing awareness of diversity and/or multiculturalism. Less often discussed are the growing tensions that exist between and among various groups that gather under the umbrella of multiculturalism—that is, the interests of groups can be competing or their perspectives can be at odds.[89] We assert that the ever-expanding multicultural paradigm follows the traditions of liberalism—allowing a proliferation of difference. Unfortunately, the tensions between and among these differences is rarely interrogated, presuming a "unity of difference"—that is, that all difference is both analogous and equivalent.[90]

To make parallel the analogy between critical race legal theory and traditional civil rights law with that of critical race theory in education and multicultural education we need to restate the point that critical race legal theorists have "doubts about the foundation of moderate/incremental civil rights law."[91] The foundation of civil rights law has been in human rights rather than in property rights. Thus, without disrespect to the pioneers of civil rights law, critical race legal scholars document the ways in which civil rights law is regularly subverted to benefit whites.[92]

We argue that the current multicultural paradigm functions in a manner similar to civil rights law. Instead of creating radically new paradigms that ensure justice, multicultural reforms are routinely "sucked back into the system" and just as traditional civil rights law is based on a foundation of human rights, the current multicultural paradigm is mired in liberal ideology that offers no radical change in the current order.[93] Thus, critical race theory in education, like its antecedent in legal scholarship, is a radical critique of both the status quo and the purported reforms.

We make this observation of the limits of the current multicultural paradigm not to disparage the scholarly efforts and sacrifices of many of its proponents, but to underscore the difficulty (indeed, impossibility) of maintaining the spirit and intent of justice for the oppressed while simultaneously permitting the hegemonic rule of the oppressor.[94] Thus, as critical race theory scholars we unabashedly reject a paradigm that attempts to be everything to everyone and consequently becomes nothing for anyone, allowing the status quo to prevail. Instead, we align our scholarship and activism with the philosophy of Marcus Garvey, who believed that the black man was universally oppressed on racial grounds, and that any program of emancipation would have to be built around the question of race first.[95] In his own words, Garvey speaks to us clearly and unequivocally:

> In a world of wolves one should go armed, and one of the most powerful defensive weapons within the reach of Negroes is the practice of race first in all parts of the world.[96]

Notes

1. Jonathan Kozol, *Savage Inequalities* (New York: Crown Publishers, 1991). For further discussion of our inability to articulate issues of race and racism see Toni Morrison, *Playing in the Dark: Whiteness and the Literary Imagination* (Cambridge: Harvard University Press, 1992); Cornel West, "Learning to Talk of Race," *New York Times Magazine*, August 2, 1992, pp. 24, 26; and Beverly Daniel Tatum, "Talking about Race, Learning about Racism: The Application of Racial Identity Development Theory in the Classroom," *Harvard Educational Review* 62 (1992): 1–24.

2. Throughout this article the term *race* is used to define the polar opposites of "conceptual whiteness" and "conceptual blackness" (Joyce King, "Perceiving Reality in a New Way: Rethinking the Black/white Duality of our Time" [Paper presented at the annual meeting of the American Educational Research Association, New Orleans, April 1994]). We do not mean to reserve the sense of "otherness" for African Americans; rather, our discussion attempts to illuminate how discussions of race in the United States position *everyone* as either "white" or "nonwhite." Thus, despite the use of African-American legal and educational exemplars, we include other groups who have been constructed at various time in their history as nonwhite or black. Readers should note that some of the leading legal scholars in the critical race legal theory movement are of Latino and Asian-American as well as African-American heritage.

3. See, for example, Patricia Hill Collins, *Black Feminist Thought* (New York: Routledge, 1991); Joyce King and Carolyn Mitchell, *Black Mothers to Sons: Juxtaposing African American Literature and Social Practice* (New York: Peter Lang, 1990); and Patricia Williams, *The Alchemy of Race and Rights: Diary of a Law Professor* (Cambridge: Harvard University Press, 1991).

4. These propositions are not hierarchical. Rather, they can be envisioned as sides of an equilateral triangle, each equal and each central to the construction of the overall theory.

5. Andrew Hacker, *Two Nations: Black and White, Separate, Hostile, Unequal* (New York: Ballantine Books, 1992); and Marian Wright Edelman, *Families in Peril: An Agenda for Social Change* (Cambridge: Harvard University Press, 1987).

6. Michael Omi and Howard Winant, "On the Theoretical Concept of Race," in *Race, Identity and Representation in Education,* ed. C. McCarthy and W. Crichlow (New York: Routledge, 1993), pp. 3–10.

7. Luigi Luca Cavalli-Sforza, "Genes, People and Languages," *Scientific American,* November 1991, p. 104.

8. Morrison, *Playing in the Dark,* p. 63.

9. This assertion was made forcefully by the participants of the Institute NHI (No Humans Involved) at a symposium entitled "The Two Reservations: Western Thought, the Color Line, and the Crisis of the Negro Intellectual Revisited," sponsored by the Department of African and Afro-American Studies at Stanford University, Stanford, Calif, March 3–5, 1994.

10. See, for example, Nancy Chodorow, *The Reproduction of Mothering* (Berkeley: University of California Press, 1978); Simone DeBeauvoir, *The Second Sex* (New York: Bantam Books, 1961); Vivian Gornick, "Women as Outsiders," in *Women in Sexist Society,* ed. V. Gornick and B. Moran (New York: Basic Books, 1971), pp. 70–84; Nancy Hartsock, "Feminist Theory and the Development of Revolutionary Strategy," *Capitalist Patriarch and the Case for Socialist Feminism,* ed. Z. Eisenstein (London and New York: Monthly Review Press, 1979); and Alison Jagger, *Feminist Theory and Human Nature* (Sussex, England: Harvester Press, 1983).

11. See, for example, Samuel Bowles and Herbert Gintis, *Schooling in Capitalist America* (New York: Basic Books, 1976); Martin Carnoy, *Education and Cultural Imperialism* (New York: McKay, 1974); Michael W. Apple, "Redefining Inequality: Authoritarian Populism and the Conservative Restoration," *Teachers College Record* 90 (1988): 167–84; and Philip Wexler, *Social Analysis and Education: After the New Sociology* (New York: Routledge & Kegan Paul, 1987).

12. David Roediger, *The Wages of Whiteness* (London: Verso, 1991), p. 6.

13. Michael Omi and Howard Winant, *Racial Formation in the United States from the 1960s to the 1990s,* 2nd ed. (New York: Routledge, 1994), p. 9.

14. Ibid., p. 56.

15. Carter G. Woodson, *The Miseducation of the Negro* (Washington, D.C.: Association Press, 1933); and W.E.B. Du Bois, *The Souls of Black Folks* (New York: Penguin Books, 1989; first published in 1903).

16. Our decision to focus on Woodson and Du Bois is not intended to diminish the import of the scores of African-American scholars who also emerged during their time such as George E. Haynes, Charles S. Johnson, E. Franklin Frazier, Abram Harris, Sadie T. Alexander, Robert C. Weaver, Rayford Logan, Allison Davis, Dorothy Porter, and Benjamin Quarles. We highlight Woodson and Du Bois as early seminal thinkers about issues of race and racism.

17. See John Hope Franklin, *From Slavery to Freedom,* 6th ed. (New York: Alfred A. Knopf, 1988).

18. Woodson, *The Miseducation of the Negro,* p. xiii.

19. Du Bois, *The Souls of Black Folks,* p. 5. Other people of color, feminists, and gay and lesbian theorists all have appropriated Du Bois's notion of double consciousness to explain their estrangement from mainstream patriarchal, masculinist U.S. culture.

20. David Levering Lewis, *W.E.B. Du Bois: Biography of a Race, 1868–1919* (New York: Henry Holt, 1993), p. 281.

21. Du Bois, *The Souls of Black Folks,* p. 1.

22. See, for example, Lorene Cary, *Black Ice* (New York: Alfred A. Knopf, 1991); and Jeannie Oakes, *Keeping Track: How Schools Structure Inequality* (New Haven: Yale University Press, 1985).

23. Oakes, *Keeping Track,* p. 67.

24. American Association of University Women, *How Schools Shortchange Girls: A Study of Major Findings on Gender and Education* (Washington, D.C.: Author and National Education Association, 1992).

25. Myra Sadker, David Sadker, and Susan Klein, "The Issue of Gender in Elementary and Secondary Education," in

Review of Educational Research in Education, vol. 19, ed. G. Cerant (Washington, D.C.: American Educational Research Association, 1991), pp. 269–334.

26. Hacker, *Two Nations*, puts the dropout rate for African-American males in some large cities at close to 50 percent.

27. Robert Majors and Janet Billson, *Cool Pose: The Dilemmas of Black Manhood in America* (New York: Lexington Books, 1992).

28. Cornel West, *Race Matters* (Boston: Beacon Press, 1993); and David Lionel Smith, "Let Our People Go," *Black Scholar* (1993): 75–76.

29. Peter Monaghan, " 'Critical Race Theory' Questions the Role of Legal Doctrine in Racial Inequity," *Chronicle of Higher Education, June* 23, 1993, pp. A7, A9.

30. Delgado, cited in Monaghan, "Critical Race Theory." Quotations are from p. A7. For a more detailed explication of the first item in the list, see Bell, *Faces at the Bottom of the Well.*

31. Manning Marable, *How Capitalism Underdeveloped Black America* (Boston: South End Press, 1983).

32. Derrick Bell, *And We Are Not Saved: The Elusive Quest for Racial Justice* (New York: Basic Books, 1987).

33. Howard Zinn, *A People's History of the United States* (New York: Harper & Row, 1980), p. 13.

34. Bell, *And We Are Not Saved.*

35. William Tate, Gloria Ladson-Billings, and Carl Grant, "The *Brown* Decision Revisited: Mathematizing Social Problems," *Educational Policy* 7 (1993): 255–75.

36. Bell, *And We Are Not Saved*, p. 239.

37. Ronald Takaki, *A Different Mirror: A History of Multicultural America* (Boston: Little Brown, 1993).

38. Franklin, *From Slavery to Freedom.*

39. Clearly, an analysis of worldwide tensions reinforces the importance of land to a people—Israel and the Palestinians, Iraq and Kuwait, the former Soviet bloc, Hitler and the Third Reich, all represent some of the struggles over land.

40. Even at a time when there is increased public sentiment for reducing the federal deficit, the one source of tax relief that no president or member of Congress would ever consider is that of denying home (property) owners their tax benefits.

41. See, for example, Howard Wainer, "Does Spending Money on Education Help?" *Educational Researcher* 22 (1993): 22–24; or Paul Houston, "School Vouchers: The Latest California Joke," *Phi Delta Kappan* 75 (1993): 61–66.

42. Kozol, *Savage Inequalities*, pp. 83–84.

43. This notion of "intellectual property" came into popular use when television talk show host David Letterman moved from NBC to CBS. NBC claimed that certain routines and jokes used by Letterman were the intellectual property of the network and, as such, could not be used by Letterman without permission.

44. Richard Delgado, "When a Story Is Just a Story: Does Voice Really Matter?" *Virginia Law Review* 76 (1990): 95–111.

45. See, for example, Floraline Stevens, *Opportunity to Learn: Issues of Equity for Poor and Minority Students* (Washington, D.C.: National Center for Education Statistics, 1993); idem, "Applying an Opportunity-to-learn Conceptual Framework to the Investigation of the Effects of Teaching Practices via Secondary Analyses of Multiple-case-study Summary Data," *The Journal of Negro Education* 62 (1993): 232–48; and Linda Winfield and Michael D. Woodard, "Assessment, Equity, Diversity in Reforming America's Schools," *Educational Policy* 8 (1994): 3–27.

46. The standards debate is too long and detailed to be discussed here. For a more detailed discussion of standards see, for example, Michael W. Apple, "Do the Standards Go Far Enough? Power, Policy, and Practices in Mathematics Education," *Journal for Research in Mathematics Education* 23 (1992): 412–31; and National Council of Education Standards and Testing, *Raising Standards for American Education: A Report to Congress, the Secretary of Education, the National Goals Panel, and the American People* (Washington, D.C.: Government Printing Office, 1992).

47. Kozol, *Savage Inequalities.*

48. Some urban Catholic schools, black independent schools, and historically black colleges and universities have demonstrated the educability of African-American students. As of this writing we have no data on the success of urban districts such as Detroit or Milwaukee that are attempting what is termed "African Centered" or Africentric education. See also Mwalimu J. Shujaa, Ed., *Too Much Schooling, Too Little Education: A Paradox of Black Life in White Societies* (Trenton, N.J.: Africa World Press, 1994).

49. David Wellman, *Portraits of White Racism* (Cambridge, England: Cambridge University Press, 1977). Quotations are from pp. xviii and 42.

50. See, for example, Gary Orfield, "School Desegregation in the 1980s," *Equity and Choice*, February 1988, p. 25; Derrick Bell, "Learning from Our Losses: Is School Desegregation Still Feasible in the 1980s?" *Phi Delta Kappan* 64 (April 1983): 575; Willis D. Hawley, "Why It Is Hard to Believe in Desegregation," *Equity and Choice*, February 1988, pp. 9–15; and Janet Ward Schofield, *Black and White in School: Trust, Tension, or Tolerance?* (New York: Teachers College Press, 1989).

51. James Banks, "Teaching Multicultural Literacy to Teachers," *Teaching Education* 4 (1991): 135–44.

52. See Karl Taeuber, "Desegregation of Public School Districts: Persistence and Change," *Phi Delta Kappan* 72 (1990): 18–24; and H.L. Bisinger, "When Whites Flee," *New York Times Magazine*, May 29, 1994, pp. 26–33, 43,

50, 53–54, 56. On loss of professional positions, see Sabrina King, "The Limited Presence of African American Teachers," *Review of Educational Research* 63 (1993): 115–49; and Jacqueline Irvine, "An Analysis of the Problem of Disappearing Black Educators," *Elementary School Journal* 88 (1988): 503–13.

53. Kimberle Williams Crenshaw, "Race Reform, and Retrenchment: Transformation and Legitimation in Antidiscrimination Law," *Harvard Law Review* 101 (1988): 1331–87.

54. Ibid., p. 1335.

55. Kofi Lomotey and John Statley, "The Education of African Americans in Buffalo Public Schools" (Paper presented at the annual meeting of the American Educational Research Association, Boston, 1990).

56. Richard Delgado, "Storytelling for Oppositionists and Others: A Plea for Narrative," *Michigan Law Review* 87 (1989): 2411–41.

57. See Richard Delgado et al., "Symposium: Legal Storytelling," *Michigan Law Review* 87 (1989): 2073. On dysconsciousness, see Joyce E. King, "Dysconscious Racism: Ideology, Identity and the Miseducation of Teachers," *Journal of Negro Education* 60 (1991): 135. King defines dysconsciousness as "an uncritical habit of mind (including perceptions, attitudes, assumptions, and beliefs) that justifies inequity and exploitation by accepting the existing order of things as given. . . . Dysconscious racism is a form of racism that tacitly accepts dominant White norms and privileges. It is not the *absence* of consciousness (that is, not unconsciousness) but an *impaired* consciousness or distorted way of thinking about race as compared to, for example, critical consciousness."

58. These notions of universalism prevail in much of social science research, including educational research.

59. Williams, *Alchemy of Race and Rights*.

60. Richard Delgado, "Brewer's Plea: Critical Thoughts on Common Cause," *Vanderbilt Law Review* 44 (1991): 11.

61. For example, see Williams, *Alchemy of Race and Rights*; Bell, *Faces at the Bottom of the Well*; and Mari Matsuda, "Public Response to Racist Speech: Considering the Victim's Story," *Michigan Law Review* 87 (1989): 2320–81.

62. Delgado, "Storytelling."

63. Ibid.

64. For example, see Crenshaw, "Race, Reform, and Retrenchment."

65. Delgado, "Storytelling."

66. Charles Lawrence, "The Id, the Ego, and Equal Protection: Reckoning with Unconscious Racism," *Stanford Law Review* 39 (1987): 317–88.

67. Delgado et al., "Symposium."

68. Lisa Delpit, "The Silenced Dialogue: Power and Pedagogy in Educating Other People's Children," *Harvard Educational Review* 58 (1988): 280.

69. At the 1994 annual meeting of the American Educational Research Association in New Orleans, two sessions entitled "Private Lives, Public Voices: Ethics of Research in Communities of Color" were convened to discuss the continued exploitation of people of color. According to one scholar of color, our communities have become "data plantations."

70. Cheryl I. Harris, "Whiteness as Property," *Harvard Law Review* 106 (1993): 1721.

71. See Margaret Radin, "Market-Inalienability," *Harvard Law Review* 100 (1987): 1849–906.

72. See Signithia Fordham and John Ogbu, "Black Student School Success: Coping with the Burden of 'Acting White,'" *The Urban Review* 18 (1986): 1–31.

73. Peggy McIntosh, "White Privilege: Unpacking the Invisible Knapsack," *Independent School*, Winter, 1990, pp. 31–36.

74. Laurie Fuller, "Whiteness as Performance" (Unpublished preliminary examination paper, University of Wisconsin—Madison, 1994).

75. Kozol, *Savage Inequalities*, p. 93.

76. Ibid., p. 96; emphasis added.

77. Harris, "Whiteness as Property," p. 1735.

78. David Spener, "Transitional Bilingual Education and the Socialization of Immigrants," *Harvard Educational Review* 58 (1988): 133–53.

79. H.G. Bissinger, "When Whites Flee," *New York Times Magazine*, May 29, 1994, pp. 26–33, 43, 50, 53–54, 56.

80. Derrick Bell, *Race, Racism, and Ameiican Law* (Boston: Little, Brown, 1980).

81. We assert that the current movement toward African-centered (or Africentric) schools is not equivalent to the racial exclusion of vouchers, or choice programs. Indeed, African-centeredness has become a logical response of a community to schools that have been abandoned by whites, have been stripped of material resources, and have demonstrated a lack of commitment to African-American academic achievement.

82. Oakes, *Keeping Track*.

83. James A. Banks, "Multicultural Education: Historical Development, Dimensions, and Practice," in *Review of Research in Education*, vol. 19, ed. L. Darling-Hammond (Washington, D.C.: American Educational Research Association, 1993), p. 3.

84. George Washington Williams, *History of the Negro Race in America from 1619–1880: Negroes as Slaves, as Soldiers, and as Citizens* (2 vols.) (New York: G.P. Putnam & Sons, 1882–1883). On the intergroup education movement, see, for example, L.A. Cook and E. Cook, *Intergroup Education* (New York: McGraw-Hill, 1954); and

H.G. Traeger and M.R. Yarrow, *They Learn What They Live: Prejudice in Young Children* (New York: Harper and Brothers, 1952).

85. See, for example, Vincent Harding, *Beyond Chaos: Black History and the Search for a New Land* (Black Paper No. 2) (Atlanta: Institute of the Black World, August 1970); J. Blassingame, ed., *New Perspectives in Black Studies* (Urbana: University of Illinois Press, 1971); James A. Banks, ed., *Teaching Ethnic Studies* (Washington, D.C.: National Council for the Social Studies, 1973); and Geneva Gay, "Ethnic Minority Studies: How Widespread? How Successful?" *Educational Leadership* 29 (1971): 108–12.

86. Banks, "Multicultural Education."

87. In 1988 at Stanford University the inclusion of literature from women and people of color in the Western Civilization core course resulted in a heated debate. The university's faculty senate approved this inclusion in a course called Cultures, Ideas, and Values. The controversy was further heightened when then Secretary of Education William Bennett came to the campus to denounce this decision.

88. In the "Book Notes" section of the *Harvard Educational Review* 64 (1994): 345–47, Jane Davagian Tchaicha reviews Donaldo Macedo's *Literacies of Power* (Boulder: Westview Press, 1994) and includes two quotes, one from noted conservative Patrick Buchanan and another from Macedo on multiculturalism. According to Buchanan, "Our Judeo-Christian values are going to be preserved, and our Western heritage is going to be handed down to future generations, not dumped into some landfill called multiculturalism" (quoted in Tchaicha, p. 345). Macedo asserts that "the real issue isn't Western culture versus multiculturalism, the fundamental issue is the recognition of humanity in us and in others" (quoted in Tchaicha, p. 347).

89. In New York City, controversy over the inclusion of gay and lesbian issues in the curriculum caused vitriolic debate among racial and ethnic groups who opposed their issues being linked to or compared with homosexuals. Some ethnic group members asserted that homosexuals were not a "culture" while gay and lesbian spokespeople argued that these group members were homophobic.

90. Shirley Torres-Medina, "Issues of Power: Constructing the Meaning of Linguistic Difference in First Grade Classrooms" (Ph.D. diss., University of Wisconsin-Madison, 1994).

91. Richard Delgado, "Enormous Anomaly? Left-Right Parallels in Recent Writing about Race," *Columbia Law Review* 91 (1991): 1547–60.

92. See Bell, *And We Are Not Saved*

93. See Cameron McCarthy, "After the Canon: Knowledge and Ideological Representation in the Multicultural Discourse on Curriculum Reform," in *Race, Identity and Representation*, ed. C. McCarthy and W. Crichlow (New York: Routledge, 1994), pp. 290; and Michael Olneck, "Terms of Inclusion: Has Multiculturalism Redefined Equality in American Education," *American Journal of Education* 101 (1993): 234–60.

94. We are particularly cognizant of the hard-fought battles in the academy waged and won by scholars such as James Banks, Carlos Cortez, Geneva Gay, Carl Grant, and others.

95. Tony Martin, *Race First: The Ideological and Organizational Struggles of Marcus Garvey and the Universal Negro Improvement Association* (Dover, Mass.: The Majority Press, 1976).

96. Marcus Garvey, cited in ibid., p. 22.

10

American Indian Geographies of Identity and Power: At the Crossroads of Indígena and Mestizaje

Sandy Marie Anglás Grande

> Until Indians resolve for themselves a comfortable modern identity that can be used to energize reservation institutions, radical changes will not be of much assistance.
>
> (Deloria & Lytle, 1984, p. 266)

> Our struggle at the moment is to continue to survive and work toward a time when we can replace the need for being preoccupied with survival with a more responsible and peaceful way of living within communities and with the ever-changing landscape that will ever be our only home.
>
> (Warrior, 1995, p. 126)

Broadly speaking, this article focuses on the intersection between dominant modes of critical pedagogy[1] and American Indian intellectualism.[2] At present, critical theories are often indiscriminately employed to explain the sociopolitical conditions of all marginalized peoples. As a result, many Indigenous scholars view the current liberatory project as simply the latest in a long line of political endeavors that fails to consider American Indians as a unique population.[3] Thus, while critical pedagogy may have propelled mainstream educational theory and practice along the path of social justice, I argue that it has muted and thus marginalized the distinctive concerns of American Indian intellectualism and education. As such, I argue further that the particular history of imperialism enacted upon Indigenous peoples requires a reevaluation of dominant views of democracy and social justice, and of the universal validity of such emancipatory projects—including critical pedagogy. It is not that critical pedagogy is irrelevant to Indigenous peoples, as they clearly experience oppression, but rather that the deep structures of the "pedagogy of oppression" fail to consider American Indians as a categorically different population, virtually incomparable to other minority groups. To assert this is not to advocate any kind of hierarchy of oppression but merely to call attention to the fundamental difference of what it means to be a sovereign and tribal people within the geopolitical confines of the United States.

Previous examinations of the potential for critical theory to inform Indigenous pedagogy (Grande, 1997, 2000) expose significant tensions in their deep theoretical structures. For instance, insofar as critical theorists retain "democracy" as the central struggle concept of liberation, they fail to recognize Indigenous peoples' historical battles to resist absorption into the "democratic imaginary"[4]—and their contemporary struggles to retain tribal sovereignty. In fact, it could be argued that the forces of "democracy" have done more to imperil American Indian nations then they have to sustain them (e.g., the extension of democracy in the form of civil rights and citizenship has acted as a powerful if not lethal colonizing force when imposed on the intricate tribal, clan, and kinship systems of traditional Native communities).

Compounding the tensions between American Indian intellectualism and critical pedagogy is the fact that American Indian scholars have, by and large, resisted engagement with
critical theory,[5] and concentrated instead on the production of historical monographs,
ethnographic studies, tribally centered curricula, and site-based research. Such a focus
stems from the fact that most American Indian scholars feel compelled to address the
political urgencies of their own communities, against which engagement in abstract theory
appears to be a luxury and privilege of the academic elite. While I recognize the need
for practically based research, I argue that the ever-increasing global encroachment on
American Indian lands, resources, cultures, and communities points to the equally urgent
need to build political coalitions and formulate transcendent theories of liberation. Moreover, while individual tribal needs are in fact great, I believe that, unless the boundaries of
coalition are expanded to include non-Indian communities, Indian nations will remain
vulnerable to whims of the existing social order.

The combined effect of internal neglect and external resistance to critical pedagogy has
pushed American Indian intellectualism to the margins of critical discourse. This reality
raises a series of important questions that help form the basis of this discussion:

1. Insofar as critical theory remains disconnected from the work of American Indian
   scholars, how do its language and epistemic frames serve as homogenizing agents
   when interfaced with the conceptual and analytical categories persistent within
   American Indian educational history and intellectualism?
2. How has the resistance of American Indian intellectuals to critical theory contributed to the general lack of analyses on the impact of racism (and, for that matter,
   other "isms") within American Indian communities?
3. How have the marginalization of critical scholarship and the concomitant fascin-
   ation with cultural/literary forms of American Indian writing contributed to the
   preoccupation with parochial questions of identity and authenticity? And, how
   have these obsessions about identity concealed the social-political realities facing
   American Indian communities?

While the above questions provide the foundation for a broad discussion of the intersection of critical theory and American Indian intellectualism, I submit that the main
source of tension is embedded in their competing notions of identity—one rooted in
Western definitions of the civil society and the other in the traditional structures of tribal
society.

In terms of identity, critical theorists aim to explode the concretized categories of race,
class, gender, and sexuality and to claim the intersections—the borderlands—as the space
to create a new culture—*una cultura mestízo,*—in which the only normative standard is
hybridity and all subjects are constructed as inherently transgressive.[6] Though American
Indian intellectuals support the notion of hybridity, they remain skeptical of the new
mestíza as a possible continuation of the colonialist project to fuse Indians into the
national model of the democratic citizen. There is, in other words, an undercurrent
to the postcolonial lexicon of *mestizaje* that seems to undermine the formation of "a
comfortable modern American Indian identity" (Deloria & Lytle, 1984, p. 266). More
specifically, I argue that the contemporary pressures of ethnic fraud, corporate commodification, and culture loss render the critical notion of "transgressive" identity highly
problematic for Indigenous peoples. As such, the primary argument is that critical efforts
to promote mestizaje as the basis of a new cultural democracy does not fully consider

Indigenous struggles to sustain the cultural and political integrity of American Indian communities.

That being said, it is important to note that American Indian critical studies are perceived by both Indigenous and non-Indigenous scholars as a "dangerous discourse" equally threatening to the fields of critical pedagogy and American Indian intellectualism.[7] After all, American Indian critical studies would compel "Whitestream" advocates of critical theory to ask how their knowledge and practices may have contributed and remained blind to the continued exploitation of Indigenous peoples. Specifically, it would require a deeper recognition that these are not postcolonial times, that "globalization" is simply the new metaphor for imperialism, and that current constructions of democracy continue to presume the eventual absorption of Indigenous peoples. For American Indian intellectuals, the infusion of critical studies would require a movement away from the safety of unified, essentialized, and idealized constructions of American Indianness toward more complicated readings of American Indian formations of power and identity, particularly those that take into account the existence of internal oppression. Specifically, it would compel American Indian intellectuals to confront the taboo subjects of racism, sexism, and homophobia within American Indian communities.

Ultimately, however, this article is not a call for American Indian scholars to simply join the conversation of critical theorists. Rather, it is an initiation of an Indigenous conversation that can, in turn, engage in dialectical contestation with the dominant modes of critical theory. In this way, I hope that the development of an Indigenous theory of liberation can itself be a politically transformative practice, one that works to transgress tribal divisions and move toward the development of a transcendent theory of American Indian sovereignty and self-determination. With this in mind, my discussion of the central tension between critical pedagogy and American Indian intellectualism unfolds in four parts. Part one examines formations of identity that have emerged from the dominant modes of critical discourse, paying special attention to the notion of transgression, and the construction of mestizaje as a counter-discourse of subjectivity. Part two examines American Indian formations of identity and the external forces that work to threaten these formations, namely ethnic fraud, cultural encroachment, corporate commodification, and culture loss. Part three examines the intersection between American Indian identity and mestizaje, as well as other models of hybridity generated by American Indian and other scholars of color. The article concludes with a call for the development of a new Red Pedagogy,[8] or one that is historically grounded in American Indian intellectualism, politically centered in issues of sovereignty and tribal self-determination, and inspired by the religious and spiritual[9] traditions of American Indian peoples.

Part I. Identity, Subjectivity and Critical Theory: Mestizaje and the New Cultural Democracy

"Critical pedagogy is the term used to describe what emerges when critical theory encounters education" (Kincheloe & Steinberg, 1997, p. 24). Rather than offer prescriptions, critical pedagogy draws from the structural critique of critical theory, extending an analysis of school as a site of reproduction, resistance, and social transformation. It examines the ways that power and domination inform the processes and procedures of schooling and works to expose the sorting and selecting functions of the institution. As it has evolved into its current form(s), critical pedagogy has emerged as both a rhetoric and a social movement. Critical educators continue to advocate an increasingly sophisticated critique of the social, economic, and political barriers to social justice, as well as to crusade for the transformation of schools to reflect the imperatives of democracy.

Critical scholars have, over time, provided a sustained critique of the forces of power and domination and their relation to the pedagogical (Kincheloe & Steinberg, 1997). As defined here, "the pedagogical" refers to the production of identity or the way one learns to see oneself in relation to the world. Identity is thus situated as one of the core struggle concepts of critical pedagogy, where the formation of self serves as the basis for analyses of race, class, gender, and sexuality and their relationship to the questions of democracy, justice, and community.

By positioning identity in the foreground of their theories, critical scholars have fueled as many theories of identity as they have varieties of critical pedagogy. While there are differences between and among these formulations, critical constructions of identity are distinct from both liberal and conservative theories of identity. Such theories are viewed as problematic by critical scholars because of their use of "essentialist" or reductionistic analyses of difference (Kincheloe & Steinberg, 1997; McCarthy & Crichlow, 1993; McLaren, 1997). "Essentialist" analysis refers to the treatment of racial and social groups as if they were stable and homogeneous entities, or as if members of each group possessed "some innate and invariant set of characteristics setting them apart from each other and from 'Whites'" (McCarthy & Crichlow, 1993, p. xviii). Critical scholars argue that essentialism not only undertheorizes race but can also result in a gross misreading of the nature of difference, opening the door for the proliferation of deeply cynical theories of racial superiority, such as Richard Herrnstein and Charles Murray's The Bell Curve (1994). While conservatives typically invoke essentialist theories, critical scholars acknowledge that some forms of left-essentialism operate in the contemporary landscape to similarly divisive ends.[10]

In response to the undertheorizing of race by both the Left and the Right, critical theorists advocate a theory of difference that is firmly rooted in the "power-sensitive discourses of power, democracy, social justice and historical memory" (McLaren & Giroux, 1997, p. 17). In so doing, they replace the comparatively static notion of identity as a relatively fixed entity that one embodies with the more fluid concept of subjectivity—an entity that one actively and continually constructs. Subjectivity works to underscore the contingency of identity and the understanding that "individuals consist of a decentered flux of subject positions highly dependent on discourse, social structure, repetition, memory, and affective investment" (McLaren & Giroux, 1997, p. 25). In other words, one's "identity" is historically situated and socially constructed, rather than predetermined by biological or other prima facie indicators.

In addition to calling attention to the relational aspects of identity, the critical notion of subjectivity advances a more complex analysis of cultural and racial identity. It shifts race from a passive product of biological endowment to an active "product of human work" (Said, 1993, p. xix). Critical scholars argue that the rupture of previously rigid racial categories reveals contested spaces or borderlands where cultures collide, creating the space to explore new notions of identity in the resulting contradictions, nuances, and discontinuities they introduce into the terrain of racial identity. Thus, where essentialist scholars examine race, class, gender, and sexuality as discrete categories, critical scholars focus on the spaces of intersection between and among these categories.

The emergence of subjectivity as a socially constructed entity spawned a whole new language about identity. Border cultures, border-crossers, mestíza (Anzaldúa, 1987;

Delgado Bernal, 1998); *Xicanisma* (Castillo, 1995); postcolonial hybridities, cyborg identities (Harraway, 1991); and mestizaje (Darder, Torres, & Gutierrez, 1997; McLaren & Sleeter, 1995; Valle & Torres, 1995) are just some of the emergent concepts formulated to explain and bring language to the experience of multiplicity, relationality, and transgression as they relate to identity. Moreover, critical scholars contend that the development of transgressive subjectivity not only works to resist essentialist constructions of identity but also acts to counter the hegemonic notion of Whiteness as the normative standard for all subjects. Such efforts represent the hope and possibility of critical pedagogy as they seek to construct a critical democracy that includes multiple cultures, languages, and voices. Critical pedagogy thus serves both to challenge the existing sociocultural and economic relations of exploitation and to strengthen collective work toward peace and social justice, thereby creating a more equitable democratic order and, by definition, more equitable educational institutions.

From Mestizaje to Mestíza back to Mestizaje

The critical notion of mestizaje (Darder, Torres, & Gutierrez, 1997; McLaren & Sleeter, 1995; Kinchloe & Steinberg, 1997; Valle & Torres, 1995) is arguably among the most widely embraced models of multisubjectivity. Historically speaking, the counterdiscourse of mestizaje is rooted in the Latin American subjectivity of the *mestízo*—literally, a person of mixed ancestry, especially of American Indian, European, and African backgrounds (Delgado Bernal, 1998). Mestizaje is the Latin American term for cultural ambiguity, representative of "the continent's unfinished business of cultural hybridization" (Valle & Torres, 1995, p. 141). With regard to this history, Latin American scholars Victor Valle and Rodolfo Torres write:

> In Latin America the genetic and cultural dialogue between the descendants of Europe, Africa, Asia, and the hemisphere's indigenous populations has been expressed in discourses reflecting and responding to a host of concrete national circumstances. In some cases, mestizaje has risen to the level of a truly critical counter-discourse of revolutionary aspirations, while at other times it has been co-opted by the state (p. 141).

Thus, it could be argued that the political project of mestizaje originated in Latin America, where the cluster of Spanish, Indian, and Afro-Caribbean peoples were ostensibly "fused" through the violence of genocide into the national model of the mestízo.

In the northern hemisphere, Chicana scholar Gloria Anzaldúa's seminal text *Borderlands, la Frontera: The New Mestíza* (1987) reinscribed the cultural terrain with the language and embodiment of mestíza consciousness. Since the book's publication, mestíza has come to embody a new feminist Chicana consciousness that "straddles cultures, races, languages, nations, sexualities, and spiritualities" and the experience of "living with ambivalence while balancing opposing powers" (Delgado Bernal, 1998, p. 561). Anzaldúa (1987) states, "The new mestíza copes by developing a tolerance for contradictions, a tolerance for ambiguity. She learns to be an Indian in Mexican culture [and] to be Mexican from an Anglo point of view" (p. 79). From this base, a variety of Chicana and other border feminisms have emerged, centered on the social histories and epistemologies of women of color.

More recently, the intellectual left, particularly critical scholars, has incorporated the spirit of the Chicana mestíza in its own search for a viable model of subjectivity. It embraces the emergent discourse of mestizaje and its emphasis on the way in which all cultures change in relation to one another as the postcolonial antidote to imperialist notions of racial purity (di Leonardo, 1991). This radically inclusive construct "willfully blurs political, racial, [and] cultural borders in order to better adapt to the world as it is actually constructed" (Valle & Torres, 1995, p. 149) and embodies the mestízo's demonstrated refusal to prefer one language, one national heritage, or one culture at the expense of others. Leading critical scholar Peter McLaren (1997) summarily articulates mestizaje as "the embodiment of a transcultural, transnational subject, a self-reflexive entity capable of rupturing the facile legitimization of 'authentic' national identities through [the] articulation of a subject who is conjunctural, who is a relational part of an ongoing negotiated connection to the larger society, and who is interpolated by multiple subject positionings" (p. 12). In other words, mestizaje crosses all imposed cultural, linguistic, and national borders, refusing all "natural" or transcendent claims that "by definition attempt to escape from any type of historical and normative grounding" (McLaren & Giroux, 1997, p. 117). Ultimately, the critical notion of mestizaje is itself multifunctional, for it signifies a strategic response to the decline of the imperial West, facilitates the decentering of Whiteness, and undermines the myth of the democratic nation-state based on borders and exclusions (Valle & Torres, 1995).

Insofar as the notion of mestizaje disrupts the discourse of jingoistic nationalism, it is indeed crucial to the project of liberation. As McLaren notes, "Educators would do well to consider Gloria Anzaldúa's (1987) project of creating mestizaje theories that create new categories of identity for those left out or pushed out of existing ones" (McLaren, 1997, p. 537). In so doing, however, "care must be taken not to equate hybridity with equality" (McLaren, 1997, p. 46).[11] As Coco Fusco notes, "The postcolonial celebration of hybridity has (too often) been interpreted as the sign that no further concern about the politics of representation and cultural exchange is needed. With ease, we lapse back into the integrationist rhetoric of the 1960's" (Fusco, 1995, p. 46). These words caution us not to lose sight—in the wake of transgressing borders and building postnational coalitions—of the unique challenges presented to particular groups in their distinct struggles for social justice. In taking this admonition seriously, the following discussion moves into an examination of American Indian tribal identity and some of the current pressures facing Indian communities that, I argue, render the notion of mestizaje somewhat problematic. The question remains whether the construction of a transgressive subjectivity-mestizaje—can be reconciled with the pressures of identity appropriation, cultural commodification, culture loss, and, perhaps more importantly, with Indigenous imperatives of self-determination and sovereignty.

Part II. The Formation of Indígena: American Indian Geographies of Power and Identity

Whitestream America has never really understood what it means to be Indian and even less about what it means to be tribal. Such ignorance has deep historical roots and wide political implications of not understanding what it means to be tribal, since the U.S. government determined long ago that to be "tribal" runs deeply counter to the notion of democracy and the proliferation of (individual) civil rights. Throughout the centuries, uncompromising belief in this tenet of democratic order provided the ideological foundation for numerous expurgatory campaigns against Indigenous peoples. The Civilization

Act of 1819, the Indian Removal Act of 1830, the Dawes Allotment Act of 1886, the Indian Citizenship Act of 1924, the Indian Reorganization Act of 1934, and the Indian Civil Rights Act of 1968 are just a few of the legal mechanisms imposed to "further democracy" and concomitantly erode traditional tribal structures.

Although five centuries of continuous contact may have extinguished the traditional societies of the precontact era, modern American Indian communities still resemble traditional societies enough that, "given a choice between Indian society and non-Indian society, most Indians feel comfortable with their own institutions, lands and traditions" (Deloria & Lytle, 1983, p. xii). Despite such significant differences, tribal America remains curiously difficult to articulate. Vine Deloria Jr., one of the preeminent American Indian scholars, has written over eighteen books and one hundred articles defining the political, spiritual, cultural, and intellectual dimensions of American Indian life. His expansive body of work serves as testimony to the difficulty and complexity of defining tribal life and suggests the impossibility of encompassing the multiple dimensions of Indianness in a single article. To do so would not only minimize Deloria's and other scholars' work, but also presume that centuries of ancestral knowledge could be transcribed into a single literary form. Similarly, to tease out, list, name, and assign primacy to a particular subset of defining characteristics of Indianness would not only serve to objectify and oversimplify the diversity of Native cultures, but would also force what is fundamentally traditional, spatial, and interconnected into the modern, temporal, and epistemic frames of Western knowledge. Accordingly, the following is merely a sample of existing legal, prima facie indicators of what it means to be American Indian in U.S. society, rather than some mythic view of a unified Indigenous culture or an objectified view of Indian "identity":

Sovereignty vs. Democracy: American Indians have been engaged in a centuries-long struggle to have what is legally theirs recognized (i.e., land, sovereignty, treaty rights). As such, Indigenous peoples have not, like other marginalized groups, been fighting for inclusion in the democratic imaginary but, rather, for the right to remain distinct, sovereign, and tribal peoples.

Treaty Rights: These rights articulate the unique status of Indian tribes as "domestic dependent nations." A dizzying array of tribal, federal, and state laws, policies, and treaties creates a political maze that keeps the legal status of most tribes in a constant state of flux. Treaties are negotiated and renegotiated in a process that typically reduces tribal rights and erodes traditional structures (Deloria & Lytle, 1984; Fixcio, 1998).

Dual Citizenship: The Indian Citizenship Act of 1924 extends the rights of full citizenship to American Indians born within the territorial United States, insofar as such status does not infringe upon the rights to tribal and other property. It is a dual citizenship wherein American Indians do not lose civil rights because of their status as tribal members and individual tribal members are not denied tribal rights because of their American citizenship (Deloria & Lytle, 1984).[12]

Federal Recognition: Federal law mandates that American Indians prove that they have continued to exist over time as stable, prima facie entities to retain federal recognition as tribes. Acknowledgment of tribal existence by the Department of the Interior is critical, as it is a prerequisite to the protection, services, and benefits of the federal government available to Indian tribes by virtue of their status as tribes. Therefore, a tribe's existence is contingent upon its ability to prove its existence over time, to provide evidence of shared cultural patterns, and to prove "persistence of a named, collective Indian identity" (USD, Bureau of Indian Affairs, n.d., 83.7).

Economic Dependency: American Indians continue to exist as nations within a nation wherein the relationship between the U.S. government and Indian tribes is not the fictive "government to government" relationship described in U.S. documents, but, rather, one that positions tribes as fundamentally dependent.[13]

Reservations: Roughly two-thirds of American Indians continue either to live on or to remain significantly tied to their reservations and, as such, remain predominantly "tribally oriented" as opposed to generically Indian (Joe & Miller, 1997).

The aggregate of the above indicators positions American Indians in a wholly unique and paradoxical relationship to the United States. These indicators further illuminate the inherent contradictions of modern American Indian existence and point to the gross insufficiency of models that treat American Indians as simply another ethnic minority group. Moreover, the paradox of having to prove "authenticity" to gain legitimacy as a "recognized" tribe and of simultaneously having to negotiate a postmodern world in which all claims to authenticity and legitimacy are dismissed as essentialist (if not racist) conscripts American Indians to a gravely dangerous and precarious space. This reality of Indian existence not only deeply problematizes various postmodern theories' insistence that we move beyond concretized categories, but also reveals their colonizing impulse.[14]

In addition to the (legal) prima facie indicators of American Indianness, there are external forces that further impede and complicate the landscape of American Indian identity. More specifically, the forces of ethnic fraud, cultural encroachment, and corporate commodification work in tandem to call into question the ostensibly liberatory effects of transgression. Such forces pressure Indian communities to define American Indian subjectivity in stable, prima facie measures. In other words, the forces of colonialism and imperialism deeply problematize the postmodern notion of transgression in terms of its abandonment of totality and its emphasis on pluralism and discontinuity. As Steven Best (1989) points out, where critical scholars rightly deconstruct essentialist and repressive wholes, they fail to see how crippling the valorization of difference, fragmentation, and agnostics can be. For the American Indian community, the "crippling" effects have been significant. In particular, the struggle to define "comfortable modern American Indian identities" becomes deeply complicated, enmeshed in the impossible paradox of having to respond to the growing pluralism within their own communities and thus the need to define more fluid constructions of Indianness, while also recognizing that the pressures of identity appropriation, cultural encroachment, and corporate commodification require more restrictive constructions of Indianness. In order to better understand the significance of this paradox, the forces of ethnic fraud, cultural encroachment, and corporate commodification are discussed in greater detail.

Identity Appropriation

In *post-Dances with Wolves* America, it has become increasingly popular to be American Indian. Joane Nagel, a sociologist and expert in the politics of ethnicity, attests that between 1960 and 1990 the number of Americans reporting "American Indian" as their racial category in the U.S. Census more than tripled. Researchers attribute this growth to the practice of "ethnic switching," where individuals previously identifying themselves as "non-Indian," now claim "Indian" as their racial affiliation. She identifies three factors promoting ethnic switching: changes in federal Indian policy; changes in American ethnic politics; and American Indian political activism (Nagel, 1995). Those seminal changes in federal policy referred to by Nagel are the Indian relocation policies of the 1960s and 1970s that led to the creation of urban Indian populations, and the various land-claims settlement of the 1980s, which also led to increases in certain tribal populations.[15] The changes in ethnic politics emanate from the civil rights and Red Power movements that made American Indian identification "a more attractive ethnic option" (Nagel, 1995, p. 956). According to Nagel, these factors helped to raise American Indian ethnic consciousness and encouraged individuals to claim or reclaim their Native American ancestry.

While she makes strong arguments for the three factors she identifies, Nagel ignores the possibility that part of the resurgence may also be due to increasing incidents of identity appropriation, or *ethnic fraud*. Ethnic fraud is the term used to describe the phenomenon of Whitestream individuals who, in spite of growing up far removed from any discernible American Indian community, claim an Indian identity based on the discovery of residuals of Indian blood in their distant ancestries. There is nothing categorically wrong with "discovering" one's ancestral background, but when such claims are opportunistically used to cash in on scholarships, set-aside programs, and other affirmative economic incentives, it becomes highly problematic. Furthermore, there is evidence that such "new Indians" discard their new-found identities as soon as they no longer serve them. For example, studies conducted at UCLA in 1988–1989 and 1993 reveal that of the enrolled 179 American Indian students, 125 did not or could not provide adequate documentation of their tribal affiliation, and that, on average, less than 15 percent of American Indian students were enrolled in federally recognized tribes (Machamer, 1997). More importantly, a significant number of students chose to identify as American Indian only to relinquish this identification by the time of graduation, suggesting that, economic incentives aside, "new Indians" chose to reclaim their Whiteness (Machamer, 1997). Such practices indicate that it is not only popular but profitable to be "Indian" in postmodern America.

In addition to outright identity fraud, American Indian communities also endure the more superficial but equally problematic phenomena of ethnic "vogueing." The seasonal influx of tour buses, church groups, and do-gooders discharges a veritable wave of Whiteness into reservation communities. Armed with their own constructions of Indianness, Whitestream individuals appropriate and try on various elements of Native culture and, in the name of religion, multiculturalism, environmentalism, and radicalism, voyeuristically tour reservation communities like cultural predators loose in Indian theme parks. During these visits, they acquire the usual assemblage of trinkets and souvenirs, and afterwards exit dysconscious[16] of the fact that their adventures have conscripted Native culture as fashion, Indian as exotic, and the sacred as entertainment. While there is a measure of complicity on the part of some American Indians who sell their culture, the overlay of colonialism situates these practices more as products of lost culture, lost economic vitality, and a lost sense of being than as crass indicators of Indian capitalism.

All told, the practice of identity appropriation is believed to have become so widespread that some American Indian organizations have felt compelled to devise statements and enact policies against its proliferation.[17] Even the federal government has recognized the occurrence and ill effects of ethnic fraud. The Indian Arts and Crafts Act, for example, stipulates that all products must be marketed truthfully regarding the Indian heritage and tribal affiliation of the artist or craftsperson. Though this act does more to protect consumers against the purchase of "fraudulent" merchandise, it also protects American Indian artisans from unfair competition by "fraudulent Indian" profiteers.

While such tactics appear to be reasonable in theory, in practice they require the employment of equally problematic essentialist ideology. In other words, in the same moment that particular groups work to determine who is and who is not Indian, they also define fixed parameters of authenticity, reducing the question of Indianness to quantifiable variables and objectified models of culture. It is also difficult to reconcile such contemporary measures with the historical memory that quantifying Indianness is a remnant of the Dawes Allotment Act (1887),[18] in which the U.S. government first introduced blood quantum policies and tribal rolls, and the knowledge that, regardless of how they are defined, measures of authenticity will conjure the same political divisiveness they always have. Finally, insofar as compliance with ethnic fraud policies requires the formation of an Indian Identity Police,[19] enforcement also becomes a dubious enterprise, inviting increased scrutiny from outside agencies.

Cultural Encroachment

The fact that nearly two-thirds of American Indians remain closely tied to their reservations not only points to the continued significance of land in the formation of American Indian identity, but also suggests that a large portion of the Indian population remains fairly segregated from the rest of the nation. Clearly, "Indian Country" persists as both a metaphorical and literal place, undoubtedly shaping the subjectivities of all those who call it home. In other words, living in a physically circumscribed space where literal borders distinguish "us" from "them" must, by definition, shape American Indian consciousness and emergent views of identity and difference. More specifically, the relationship between American Indian communities and the predominantly White border towns not only shapes the ways Indians perceive and construct Whites, but also significantly influences their own views of American Indian identity.

Thus, although reservations exist as a vestige of forced removal, colonialist domination, and Whitestream greed, they have also come to serve as protective barriers and defensive perimeters between cultural integrity and wholesale assimilation. They also serve to distinguish American Indians as the only peoples with federally recognized land claims, demarcating the borders of the only domestic sovereign nations. Though the power of this domestic-dependent-nation status is continually challenged in federal courts, Indians have retained a significant portion of their plenary powers, such as the right to establish tribal courts, tribal governments, and tribal police forces. Ultimately, however, the notion of self-government remains a bit of a farce, since most tribes remain entrenched in untenable relationships with the U.S. government and most reservation economies can only maintain stability with the infusion of outside capital (Deloria & Lytle, 1984).

The dependency on outside capital generates a subordinating effect, leaving American Indians at the virtual mercy of venture capitalists and Whitestream do-gooders. As a result, most reservation communities are overrun by emissaries of White justice, private entrepreneurs, and New Age liberals seeking to forge lucrative careers from predatory practices. Bivouacked in internal and external compounds, enterprising members of the Whitestream wield power and broker services by day, and by night retreat back into the comforts of their bourgeois border towns. As a result, most of the businessmen, teachers, principals, doctors, and health-care providers in reservation communities are White, and most of the laborers, minimum-wagers, underemployed, and unemployed are American Indian.

In spite of the pressures of cultural encroachment, reservation communities continue to work toward becoming sites of political contestation and empowerment. They are learning to survive the dangers of imperialistic forces by employing both proactive strategies that emphasize education, empowerment, and self-determination, and defensive tactics that protect against unfettered economic and political encroachment. Thus, whatever else reservation borders may or may not signify, they serve as potent geographic filters of all that is non-Indian—literal dividing lines between the real and metaphoric spaces differentiating Indian Country from the rest of Whitestream America.

Corporate Commodification

The forces of both ethnic fraud and cultural encroachment operate to create a climate ripe for the corporate commodification of American Indianness. While this commodification takes many forms, it is perhaps most visible in the marketing of Indian narratives, particularly publishing, in which literary/cultural forms of Indian intellectualism have been historically favored over critical forms.

For instance, Indigenous scholar Elizabeth Cook-Lynn (1998) questions why the same editors and agents who solicit her "life story" also routinely reject her scholarly work. She writes, "While I may have a reasonable understanding why a state-run university press would not want to publish research that has little good to say about America's relationship to tribes, . . . I am at a loss to explain why anyone would be more interested in my life story (which for one thing is quite unremarkable)" (p. 121). The explanation, of course, is that the marketable narrative is that which subscribes to the Whitestream notion of Indian as romantic figure, and not Indian as scholar and social critic. Such a predisposition works to favor not only cultural/literary forms of American Indian intellectualism over critical forms, but also the work of "fraudulent" Indians over that of "legitimate" American Indian scholars. Cook-Lynn (1998) argues that, just as the rights to our land remain in the hands of the Whitestream government, the rights to our stories remain in non-Indian enclaves. Deloria (1998) similarly contends that what passes in the academic world as legitimate scholarship on American Indians is often the product of average scholars (often White) advocating a predetermined anti-Indian agenda[20] and "fraudulent" Indians. That such work has been allowed to corner the market raises the question of who controls access to the intellectual property of American Indian peoples. Deloria himself asks, "Who is it that has made such people as Adolph Hungry Wolf, Jamake Highwater, Joseph Epes Brown, Su Bear, Rolling Thunder, Wallace Black Elk, John Redtail Freesoul, Lynn Andrews, and Dhyani Ywahoo the spokespeople of American Indians?" (p. 79). He responds by naming Whitestream America as both patron and peddler of the Hollywood Indian. He writes, "They [the fraudulent Indians] represent the intense desire of Whites to create in their own minds an Indian they want to believe in" (p. 79).

As such, the market is flooded with tragic stories of lost cultures, intimate narratives of "frontier life," and quasi-historic accounts of the Native Americans' plight. Such stories are told and retold as part of America's dark and distant past, a bygone era of misguided faith where cultural genocide is depicted as an egregious but perhaps unavoidable consequence of the country's manifest destiny toward democracy. While I would never argue that stories depicting the truth of Native peoples' tragic experiences (e.g., Indian boarding schools, the Trail of Tears) do not deserve a central place in the telling of American history, such accounts become problematic in the wider context of Whitestream consumption of Indian history.

Why are these stories the ones most often presented as the prime-time programs in the commodified literary network of Indian history? What is gained by focusing on these particular aspects of White domination and Indian subjugation? I argue that such stories serve several purposes, none of which contributes to the emancipatory project of American Indians. First, by propagating the romantic image of American Indians and concomitantly marginalizing the work of Indigenous intellectuals and social critics, Whitestream publishers maintain control over the epistemic frames that define Indians, and thus over the fund of available knowledge on American Indians. Second, such control is underwritten by the understanding that American Indian intellectualism exists as a threat to the myth of the ever-evolving democratization of Indian–White relations, and to the notion that cultural genocide is a remnant of America's dark and distant past. Third, the often oversimplified accounts of Indian history, framed in good-v.-bad-guy terms, allow the consumer to fault rogue groups of dogmatic missionaries and wayward military officers for the slow but steady erosion of Indigenous life, thereby distancing themselves and mainstream government from the ongoing project of cultural genocide. Finally, the focus on Indian history allows the Whitestream to avoid issues facing American Indians in the twenty-first century. As a result, Indians as a modern people remain invisible, allowing a wide array of distorted myths to flourish as contemporary reality—for example, that all the "real" Indians are extinct, that the surviving Indians are all alcoholic-drug addicts who have forsaken traditional ways to become budding capitalists, gaming entrepreneurs, and casino owners— and find their way into public discourse. At the same time these images are circulated, the intensive, ongoing court battles over land, natural resources, and federal recognition are ignored, fueling the great lie of twenty-first century democracy—that America's "Indian problem" has long been solved.

Discussion

The forces of identity appropriation, cultural encroachment, and corporate commodification pressure American Indian communities to employ essentialist tactics and construct relatively fixed notions of identity, and to render the concepts of fluidity and transgression highly problematic. It is evident from the examples above that the notion of fluid boundaries has never worked to the advantage of Indigenous peoples: federal agencies have invoked the language of fluid or unstable identities as the rationale for dismantling the structures of tribal life and creating greater dependency on the U.S. government; Whitestream America has seized its message to declare open season on Indians, thereby appropriating Native lands, culture, spiritual practices, history, and literature; and Whitestream academics have now employed the language of postmodern fluidity to unwittingly transmute centuries of war between Indigenous peoples and their respective nation-states into a "genetic and cultural dialogue" (Valle & Torres, 1995, p. 141). Thus, in spite of its aspirations to social justice, the notion of a new cultural democracy based on the ideal of mestizaje represents a rather ominous threat to American Indian communities.

In addition, the undercurrent of fluidity and sense of displacedness that permeates, if not defines, mestizaje runs contrary to American Indian sensibilities of connection to place, land, and the Earth itself. Consider, for example, the following statement on the nature of critical subjectivity by Peter McLaren:

> The struggle for critical subjectivity is the struggle to occupy a space of hope—a liminal space, an intimation of the anti-structure, of what lives in the in-between zone of undecidedability— in which one can work toward a praxis of redemption. . . . A sense of atopy has always been with me, a resplendent placelessness, a feeling of living in germinal formlessness. . . . I cannot

find words to express what this border identity means to me. All I have are what Georges
Bastille (1988) calls mots glissants (slippery words).

(1997, pp. 13–14)

McLaren speaks passionately and directly about the crisis of modern society and the need
for a "praxis of redemption." As he perceives it, the very possibility of redemption is
situated in our willingness not only to accept but to flourish in the "liminal" spaces, border
identities, and postcolonial hybridities that are inherent in postmodern life and subjectivity. In fact, McLaren perceives the fostering of a "resplendent placelessness" itself as the
gateway to a more just, democratic society.

While American Indian intellectuals also seek to embrace the notion of transcendent
subjectivities, they seek a notion of transcendence that remains rooted in historical place
and the sacred connection to land. Consider, for example, the following commentary by
Deloria (1992) on the centrality of place and land in the construction of American Indian
subjectivity:

> Recognizing the sacredness of lands on which previous generations have lived and died is the
> foundation of all other sentiment. Instead of denying this dimension of our emotional lives, we
> should be setting aside additional places that have transcendent meaning. Sacred sites that
> higher spiritual powers have chosen for manifestation enable us to focus our concerns on the
> specific form of our lives. . . . Sacred places are the foundation of all other beliefs and practices
> because they represent the presence of the sacred in our lives. They properly inform us that
> we are not larger than nature and that we have responsibilities to the rest of the natural world
> that transcend our own personal desires and wishes. This lesson must be learned by each
> generation. (pp. 278, 281)

Gross misunderstanding of this connection between American Indian subjectivity and
land, and, more importantly, between sovereignty and land has been the source of numerous injustices in Indian country. For instance, I believe there was little understanding on
the part of government officials that passage of the Indian Religious Freedom Act (1978)
would open a Pandora's box of discord over land, setting up an intractable conflict
between property rights and religious freedom. American Indians, on the other hand,
viewed the act as an invitation to return to their sacred sites, several of which were on
government lands and were being damaged by commercial use. As a result, a flurry of
lawsuits alleging mismanagement and destruction of sacred sites was filed by numerous
tribes. Similarly, corporations, tourists, and even rock climbers filed suits accusing land
managers of unlawfully restricting access to public places by implementing policies that
violate the constitutional separation between church and state. All of this is to point out
that the critical project of mestizaje continues to operate on the same assumption made by
the U.S. government in this instance, that in a democratic society, human subjectivity—
and liberation for that matter—is conceived of as inherently rights-based as opposed to
land-based.

To be fair, I believe that both American Indian intellectuals and critical theorists share a
similar vision—a time, place, and space free of the compulsions of Whitestream, global
capitalism and the racism, sexism, classism, and xenophobia it engenders. But where
critical scholars ground their vision in Western conceptions of democracy and justice that
presume a "liberated" self, American Indian intellectuals ground their vision in conceptions of sovereignty that presume a sacred connection to place and land. Thus, to a large
degree, the seemingly liberatory constructs of fluidity, mobility, and transgression are
perceived not only as the language of critical subjectivity, but also as part of the fundamental lexicon of Western imperialism. Deloria (1999) writes:

Although the loss of land must be seen as a political and economic disaster of the first magnitude, the real exile of the tribes occurred with the destruction of ceremonial life (associated with the loss of land) and the failure or inability of white society to offer a sensible and cohesive alternative to the traditions which Indians remembered. People became disoriented with respect to the world in which they lived. They could not practice their old ways, and the new ways which they were expected to learn were in a constant state of change because they were not a cohesive view of the world but simply adjustments which whites were making to the technology they had invented. (p. 247)

In summary, insofar as American Indian identities continue to be defined and shaped in interdependence with place, the transgressive mestizaje functions as a potentially homogenizing force that presumes the continued exile of tribal peoples and their enduring absorption into the American "democratic" Whitestream. The notion of mestizaje as absorption is particularly problematic for the Indigenous peoples of Central and South America, where the myth of the mestizaje (belief that the continent's original cultures and inhabitants no longer exist) has been used for centuries to force the integration of Indigenous communities into the national mestízo model (Van Cott, 1994). According to Rodolfo Stavenhagen (1992), the myth of mestizaje has provided the ideological pretext for numerous South American governmental laws and policies expressly designed to strengthen the nation-state through incorporation of all "non-national" (read "Indigenous") elements into the mainstream. Thus, what Valle and Torres (1995) previously describe as "the continent's unfinished business of cultural hybridization" (p. 141), Indigenous peoples view as the continents' long and bloody battle to absorb their existence into the master narrative of the mestízo.

While critical scholars do construct a very different kind of democratic solidarity that disrupts the sociopolitical and economic hegemony of the dominant culture around a transformed notion of mestizaje (one committed to the destabilization of the isolationist narratives of nationalism and cultural chauvinism), I argue that any liberatory project that does not begin with a clear understanding of the difference of American Indianness will, in the end, work to undermine tribal life. Moreover, there is a potential danger that the ostensibly "new" cultural democracy based upon the radical mestizaje will continue to mute tribal differences and erase distinctive Indian identities. Therefore, as the physical and metaphysical borders of the postmodern world become increasingly fluid, the desire of American Indian communities to protect geographic borders and employ "essentialist" tactics also increases. Though such tactics may be viewed by critical scholars as highly problematic, they are viewed by American Indian intellectuals as a last line of defense against the steady erosion of tribal culture, political sovereignty, Native resources, and Native lands.

The tensions described above indicate the dire need for an Indigenous, revolutionary theory that maintains the distinctiveness of American Indians as tribal peoples of sovereign nations (border patrolling) and also encourages the building of coalitions and political solidarity (border crossing). In contrast to critical scholars McLaren and Kris Gutierrez (1997), who admonish educators to develop a concept of unity and difference as political mobilization rather than cultural authenticity, I urge American Indian intellectuals to develop a language that operates at the crossroads of unity and difference and defines this space in terms of political mobilization and cultural authenticity, thus expressing both the interdependence and distinctiveness of tribal peoples.

Part III. Mestizaje Revisited: Critical Indígena and a New Red Pedagogy

To their credit, Whitestream critical scholars recognize the potential for their own subject-ivities and locations of privilege to infiltrate the critical discourse, limiting it in ways they cannot see or anticipate. McLaren (1997) writes, "An individual cannot say he or she has achieved critical pedagogy if he or she stops struggling to attain it. Only sincere discontent and dissatisfaction with the limited effort we exercise in the name of social justice can assure us that we really have the faith in a dialogical commitment to others and otherness" (p. 13). It is perhaps this commitment to self-reflexivity and an ever-evolving pedagogy that represents critical pedagogy's greatest strength. Indeed, critical scholars from other marginalized groups such as Gloria Anzaldúa, Hazel Carby, Antonia Darder, Dolores Delgado Bernal, Kris Gutierrez, bell hooks, Rudy Mattai, Cameron McCarthy, Enrique Murillo, Frances V. Rains, and Sofia Villenas have seized upon its openness, transmuting critical theories to fit their own constructions of culturally relevant praxis. Currently, American Indian scholars are also investigating ways to import the message of critical pedagogy without wholesale adoption of its means. While addressing the impact of racism, sexism, and globalization on American Indian communities, some American Indian intel-lectuals share underlying principles of mestizaje like reflexivity, hybridity, and multiplicity. However, this notion of a transgressive mestizaje may ultimately undermine American Indian subjectivity. Recognizing the common ground of struggle is an important first step in working to define the ways that critical pedagogy can inform Indigenous praxis.

The following discussion excerpts work by American Indian and other scholars of color who have taken the next step: to define locally and culturally relevant praxis based on a broader critical foundation. I contend that such work represents the possibility and future of both American Indian intellectualism and critical pedagogy.

Voices from the Margin

As might be expected, Latino, Latina, African American, and feminist riffs on Whitestream critical pedagogy speak more directly to the concerns of American Indian intellectuals. In particular, other scholars of color have recognized that the experience of oppression often requires the assertion of hyperauthenticity, and thus have worked to refine critical theor-ists' hard line against essentialism. For instance, though Chicano scholar Enrique Murillo (1997) rejects the notion of essentialism as a means of recalibrating the balance of power, he employs the term *strategic essentialism* to describe the contradictory experience of many scholars of color caught between the different legitimizing forces of the academy and their own communities. There are times, for example, when scholars of color feel compelled to perform a heightened professional or scholarly identity when seeking legitimacy in the academy, and other times when they feel compelled to perform a hyperauthentic or racialized self to gain or retain legitimacy within their own communities. Murillo's notion of "strategic essentialism" is useful in describing the experience of American Indian intel-lectuals working to balance the fluidity of the postmodern world with the more stable obligations of their tribal communities. In more concrete terms, this means that, as American Indian scholars work to construct and advocate more complex understandings of American Indian identity, such efforts remain haunted by the knowledge that any failure to continually define and authenticate Indianness in stable and quantifiable terms may result in the loss of everything from school funding to tribal recognition. Within this context, strategic essentialism refers not only to choosing multiple subjectivities where power is located in the self, but also to negotiating between chosen and imposed identities where power continues to be located in the oppressor.

Similar to Murillo's variation on the notion of strategic essentialism, Delgado Bernal (1998) defines a culturally relevant theory of knowledge that brings discussions of power and identity into the realm of epistemology. She argues for a model of identity-based epistemology and develops the notion of "cultural intuition" to validate the centrality of cultural knowledge in the processes of research and in the development of a culture's intellectual history. Specifically, Delgado Bernal employs the notion of cultural intuition to legitimate her unique viewpoint as a Chicana researcher conducting research within the Chicana community.[21] Though similar to Anselm Strauss and Juliet Corbin's concept of "theoretical sensitivity" (1990), Delgado Bernal's paradigm extends the realm of cultural intuition to include collective experience and community memory and to stress the importance of participants' inclusion in the research process, particularly in data analysis. She writes, "While I do not argue for an essentialist notion of who is capable of conducting research with various populations based on personal experiences, I do believe that many Chicana scholars achieve a sense of cultural intuition that is different from other scholars" (p. 567). This insightful articulation of the value and power of cultural intuition brings voice and, more importantly, language to the struggles of Chicano and other scholars of color seeking validation, power, and equity in the domain of academic research. Moreover, the notion of cultural intuition buttresses arguments already made by American Indian scholars on behalf of their own communities; specifically, for the right to speak in their own voices, define their own realities, and develop their own intellectual histories.

Voices from Indian Country

While it is important and beneficial to observe the insights of other critical pedagogies, it is crucial to look to one's own intellectual history and sources of cultural intuition in the development of Indigenous theories and praxis. In this effort, the challenge to American Indian scholars is not merely to "resurrect" these histories and sources of cultural intuition, but to construct meaningful bridges and points of intersection between American Indian intellectualism and Whitestream critical pedagogies.

To this end, while American Indian scholars have, by and large, resisted direct engagement with critical theory, many have begun to theorize their own constructions of Indigenous knowledge and American Indian identity.[22] As a collective effort, such work provides increasingly complex views of American Indian history; of the promise and failures of education; of the struggles for language, agency, and sovereignty; and of the need for political and sociocultural coalitions. Their writings strive to achieve interplay between the past, present, and future, and ride the faultline between continuity, resistance, and possibility.

What follows is a sampling of such works, chosen because of their particular relevance to the topic of American Indian identity and identity formation. The selected scholars differ in their methods and approaches, but they share a thematic undercurrent that includes the interplay of coalition, agency, tradition, and identity; the transformation of curriculum and pedagogy; the retention and reinvigoration of Indigenous languages; the intersection of religion and spirituality; and the quest for sovereignty. While each domain merits extensive discussion, such an effort goes beyond the limits of this work. However, insofar as American Indian "identity" is formulated as an aggregate of the above struggles, they will be discussed interdependently with the understanding that, especially for American Indians, religion/spirituality and sovereignty are inextricably woven into the struggles for identity, education, and language, and vice versa.

The Interplay of Coalition, Agency, and Identity

In the first draft of the final report of the Indian Nations at Risk Task Force, Indigenous scholar and activist Michael Charleston (1994) writes of the importance of coalition and its central role in the development of effective American Indian schools and Indian-centered curricula. Rather than the abstract language of critical pedagogy, however, Charleston invokes the Lakota tradition of the Ghost Dance as a metaphor of the need for healing through community, ceremony, sacrifice, and tradition.[23] He writes:

> The new Ghost Dance calls Native and non-Native peoples to join together and take action. It calls us to be responsible for the future of the people of our tribes. It calls us to protect, revive and restore our cultures, our Native languages, our religions and values. It calls us to heal our people, our families, our tribes, and our societies. It calls for harmony and respect among all relations of creation. It offers a future of co-existence of tribal societies with other American societies . . . indeed domination, oppression, and bigotry are exactly what we are overcoming in the new Ghost Dance as we seek to establish harmony and coexistence of tribes with other societies in the modern world. (p. 28)

This spirit of coalition reflects the growing desire among American Indians to work together and form alliances with Native and non-Native forces in a mutual quest for American Indian sovereignty and self-determination. Though Charleston's rendition of coalition reflects the spirit of mestizaje—that is, the blurring of political, racial, and cultural borders in the service of social justice—he carefully relegates such coalition to the realm of sociopolitical action. In other words, the new Ghost Dance calls to Indian and non-Indian peoples to take collective action against U.S. policies that continue the project of colonization and cultural genocide. It is thus not a call for the embodiment, in critical-theoretical terms, of a transcultural, transnational subject that calls into question the very notion of authentic identities (McLaren, 1997), but rather a metaphor for collective political action.

This is not to say that Charleston or other American Indian scholars do not support the notion that identity is constructed through multiple, intersecting, and contradictory elements. Rather, they remain wary of constructionist understandings of identity that, in the process of providing a corrective to static notions of culture, ignore the real possibility of culture loss—that is, the real existing threat of cultural genocide of Indigenous peoples. Hale (2000) is worth quoting at length:

> When (cultural) transformation is conflated with loss . . . the collective trauma is obscured and the brute historical fact of ethnocide is softened. The culprits in this erasure are the Indians' . . . . enemies, but even more centrally . . . elites who embraced classic nineteenth century liberalism cast in the idiom of mestizáje. A homogeneous and individualized notion of citizenship could not be compatible with the rights of Indian communities whose collective histories and identities stood opposed to the dominant mestizo culture. Just beneath the alluring promises to Indians who would accept these individual rights of citizenship was incomprehension, invisibility, and punishing racism for those who would not. (p. 269)

Again, though the contemporary critical project of mestizaje is in many ways antithetical to the Latin American one, both projects ignore the "brute historical fact of ethnocide" and the invisibility of Indians within the broader democratic project. In contradistinction to the critical notion of mestizaje, American Indian scholars seek understandings of identity that not only reflect the multiple and contradictory aspects of contemporary experience, but also maintain a sense of American Indians as historically placed, sovereign peoples. For them, sovereignty is not a political ideology but a way of life (Warrior, 1995). As Charleston (1994) writes, "Our tribes are at a very critical point in our history again. We can stand by and wait for our children and grandchildren to be assimilated into mainstream American society as proud ethnic descendants of extinct tribal peoples. . . . Or, we can protect our tribes, as our ancestors did, and ensure a future for our children and grandchildren as tribal people" (p. 28).

Though it may seem from the above that American Indian intellectuals advocate exclusionary rather than coalitionary tactics, impulses toward isolationism need to be understood in the context of unrelenting threats of cultural appropriation and culture loss. Within this context, it is actually remarkable that American Indian tribal communities remain open and working to define the balance between cultural tradition, cultural shift, and cultural transformation.

Identity Formation and American Indian Tradition(s)

Indigenous scholar Devon Mihesuah (1998) examines the notion of "tradition" in the formation of American Indian identity. Acknowledging that, while traditions are important to maintain, they have always been fluid, she writes:

> An Indian who speaks her tribal language and participates in tribal religious ceremonies is often considered traditional, but that term is applicable only within the context of this decade, because chances are she wears jeans, drives a car and watches television—very "untraditional" things to do. Plains Indians who rode horses in the 1860's are considered traditional today, but they were not the same as their traditional ancestors of the early 1500's who had never seen a horse. (p. 50)

While contemporary life requires most Indians to negotiate or "transgress" between a multitude of subject positions (i.e., one who is Navajo may also be Catholic, gay, and live in an off-reservation urban center), such movement remains historically embedded and geographically placed. Moreover, the various and competing subjectivities remain tied through memory, ceremony, ritual, and obligation to a traditional identity type that operates not as a measure of authenticity, but rather of cultural continuity and survival. For example, current understanding of a traditional Navajo (Diné) woman is that she lives in a hogan, speaks her language, participates in ceremonies, maintains a subsistence lifestyle, nurtures strong clan and kinship ties, serves as a vast repository of cultural and tribal history, participates in tribal governance, wears long hair wrapped in traditional cotton cloth, dresses in long skirts and velvet blouses, and dons the silver jewelry of her family to reside as matriarch of the clan. Such individuals, along with their male counterparts, are typically held in high esteem and are granted a great deal of respect and social power. While the Diné recognize this identity as only one among many accepted as "authentically" Diné, it forms the essence of their tribal identity, serves as the repository of their ancestral knowledge, and roots them as a historically embedded and geographically placed people.

The struggle for American Indian subjectivity is, in part, a struggle to protect this essence and the right of Indigenous peoples to live in accordance with their traditional ways. In other words, regardless of how any individual American Indian may choose to live his or her life as an Indian person, most experience a deep sense of responsibility and obligation to protect the rights of those choosing to live in the ways of their ancestors. The struggle for identity thus also becomes the struggle to negotiate effectively the line between fetishizing traditional identities and recognizing their importance to the continuation of American Indians as distinctive tribal peoples. Insofar as American Indian traditional identities remain tethered to "traditional" practices (such as ceremony) and such practices remain interconnected with the land, the struggle for identity becomes inextricably linked with political struggles for sovereignty and the ongoing battle against cultural encroachment and capitalist desire to control Native land, resources, traditions, and languages. So, while American Indians join the struggle against the kind of essentialism that recognizes only one way of being, they also work to retain a vast constellation of distinct traditions that serve as the defining characteristics of "traditional" ways of being. As Vine Deloria and Clifford Lytle (1983) note, this allegiance to traditional knowledge has protected American Indians from annihilation or its modern counterpart, categoric absorption into the democratic mainstream.

The Transformation of Curriculum and Pedagogy

There is a growing body of work by Indigenous scholars that examines the intersection between the experiences of formal education and tribal culture. Recently, such work has moved away from comparatively simplistic analyses of "learning style" or curriculum content into deeper examination of the interplay between power, difference, opportunity, and institutional structure (see, for example, Deyhle & Swisher, 1997; Haig-Brown & Archibald, 1996; Hermes, 1998; Lipka, 1994; Pewewardy, 1998). Though such work builds upon the efforts of other scholars of color seeking to define culturally relevant pedagogies (Delpit, 1995; Fordham & Ogbu, 1986; Ladson-Billings, 1995; Trueba, 1988; Watahomigie & McCarty, 1994, for example), American Indian scholars rebuff the undercurrent of democratic inclusion and empowerment that undergirds this work, choosing instead to employ sovereignty as the central struggle in defining relevant praxis.[24]

For example, in her work with Lac Courtie Ojibwe (LCO) reservation schools, Indigenous scholar Mary Hermes (1995, 1998) struggles to define a "culturally based curriculum" where both "culture" and "curriculum" are viewed as fluid, "living" constructs that develop in and through relationship. In her own words, Hermes shifts the research question from "What is the role of culture in knowledge acquisition?" to "What is the role of the school as a site of cultural production?" She argues that research focused on the first question often results in essentialized definitions of culture and the subsequent generation of curricular dichotomies distinguishing "academic" curricula from "cultural" curricula. Instead she seeks answers to the more complicated question, "How can we frame our teaching in an Ojibwe epistemology without representing Ojibwe as a static culture?" (Hermes, 2000). Hermes's question represents a paradigm shift, one that decenters the insertion of a static notion of "culture" into "knowledge" and recenters cultural production as an outcome of the schooling process. In practical terms, such a shift means that community interests not only informed but directed her research methods and outcomes. In her work with Ojibwe schools, she implores educators of American Indian students to recognize culture in the classroom at a deeper level than simply adding content or naming learning styles. She writes:

> I am proposing that we begin to view culture as a complex web of relationships, not just material practices, and enact this in our schools in a way that is central to the curriculum. This could mean, for example, directly teaching tribal history, or simply inviting Elders and community members into the school, regardless of the historical knowledge they bring. (p. 389)

Although Hermes is clearly committed to defining a liberatory praxis based upon a trans- formative understanding of Ojibwe identity, a goal reminiscent of critical pedagogies, she remains equally committed to the project of American Indian self-determination and sovereignty. Thus, as she advocates an understanding of identity that reflects the fluidity of mestizaje, she also seeks to define a curriculum that remains grounded in the unfolding relationships of tribalness.

In summary, although the development of culturally relevant pedagogy is an objective shared by many marginalized groups, the goal of such efforts for most non-Indian minor- ities is to ensure inclusion in the democratic imaginary, while the goal for American Indian scholars and educators is to disrupt and impede absorption into that democracy and continue the struggle to remain distinctive, tribal, and sovereign peoples.

The Retention and Reinvigoration of Indigenous Languages

For many American Indian communities, language retention and renewal efforts signify ground zero in the struggle for American Indian sovereignty. Like other aspects of Indigenous experience, there is no single state or uniform condition of Native languages. Some are vibrant like Quechua, which has over one million speakers, and others, like Passamaquoddy, are threatened with extinction. Although ways of speaking and thinking about language shift and language loss may vary within a single community by age, family, life history, gender, and social role, there is a shared sensibility among American Indian peoples that language is inherently tied to cultural continuity—particularly religious and ceremonial continuity—and therefore remains at the core of American Indian identity formation (Anderson, 1998).

Therefore, while many would eschew the oft-implied and "essentialistic" construction of language fluency as a marker of cultural authenticity, there is virtual consensus among American Indian peoples that language loss is tantamount to cultural eradication. Language, in other words, is viewed as a carrier of culture and culture as a carrier of language so that shifts in one reverberate in the other. As such, most tribes work hard to maintain their language through a variety of means, including school, ceremony, com- munity, and family. However, as the traditional structures of community and family erode under the pressures of Whitestream encroachment, tribal members increasingly look to schools to serve as sites of American Indian cultural production and reproduction.

In this effort, American Indian educators looking to develop a critical language of American Indian selfdetermination and intellectual sovereignty are finding that their own Native languages are replete with metaphors of existence that speak to the lived experience of multiplicity, to the sense of interconnection, and to the understanding that American Indians live not only in relationship with each other, but also with the land. In Quechua, for example, the word for being, person, and Andean person is all the same, *Runa*. This root term has the potential to incorporate the many subcategories of beingness while retaining the same basic reference group, as in *llaqtaruna* (inhabitants of the village) and *qualaruna* (foreigner; literally, naked, peeled). It can be used passively as in *yuyay runa* (one who is knowing or understanding), actively as in *runayáchikk* (that which cultivates a person), or reflexively as in *runaman tukuy* (to complete oneself). Hence, the construct speaks to both the group and the individual and distinguishes in-group from out-group while maintaining the fundamental connection between them. Therefore, it is not a static category or limitation to the sense of Runa as the becoming self (Skar, 1994). Border crossing and the idea of a shifting identity is, thus, neither new nor revolutionary to this Indigenous community, but rather the way of life of Quechua peoples for over five hundred years.

Conclusion

The work outlined above suggests that while American Indian scholars share many of the same concerns as mainstream critical scholars' development of critical agency, construction of political coalition, and transformation through praxis, they reject the construction of the radical mestizaje and work instead to balance their community's needs to both cross and patrol borders of identity and location. They also retain as the central and common goal the perseverance of American Indians as distinctive and sovereign peoples.

Defining that balance is perhaps the quintessential struggle of American Indian peoples today. It is a deeply complicated and contradictory struggle that reflects the colonialist past and portends an uncertain future. In short, American Indians face an identity paradox. At the same time that pressures to respond to internal crises of identity formation—including racism, sexism, and homophobia—require more fluid constructions of Indianness, pressures to respond to external threats to identity formation—cultural encroachment, ethnic fraud, corporate commodification, and culture loss—require more restrictive constructions of Indianness. Hence, as American Indian intellectuals struggle to awaken Indian communities to the "challenges and cultural politics of (their) own ever-burgeoning multiculturalism" (Vizenor, 1999, p. 3), they must also work to ground the ever-changing present in the historical memories of the past while searching for links to an American Indian future.

Though, as I have demonstrated, there is good reason to remain cautious of the constructs that emerge from dominant Whitestream discourses, there is also much to be learned from engagement with such discourse. As Indigenous scholar Robert Allen Warrior (1995) notes, American Indian intellectuals have remained caught in "a death dance of dependence between, on the one hand, abandoning ourselves to the intellectual strategies and categories of white, European thought and, on the other hand, declaring we need nothing outside of ourselves and our cultures in order to understand the world and our place in it" (p. 123). He observes that only when American Indian intellectuals remove themselves from this dichotomy that "much becomes possible" (p. 124).

To this end, I argue that critical scholars need to broaden their own theoretical scopes to consider the different and, at times, competing moral visions of American Indian peoples. Critical engagement with the intellectual histories of Indigenous peoples could only serve to inform discussions of revolutionary theory and praxis. Specifically, such histories call into question the ongoing assumption of conservative and radical ideologies that democracy, as presently constructed in liberal, capitalist terms, presumes the continued absorption or colonization of Indigenous peoples. American Indian scholars also need to enter the critical dialogue and help reimagine the political terrain surrounding identity. They need to create the intellectual space for the struggle for sovereignty and for their efforts to renegotiate the relationship between sovereign American Indian tribal nations and the current democratic order. The challenge to Indigenous scholars is to define the same kind of balance between cultural integrity and critical resistance in their own quest for American Indian intellectual sovereignty. As Warrior (1995) notes, just "as many of the poets find their work continuous with but not circumscribed by Native traditions of story-telling or ceremonial chanting, we can find the work of (critical studies) continuous with Native traditions of deliberation and decision making. Holding these various factors (sovereignty, tradition, community, process and so on) in tension while attempting to understand the role of critics in an American Indian future is of crucial importance" (p. 118).

Ultimately, I am confident that American Indian and non-Indian critical scholars devoted to the remapping of the political project can together define a common ground of struggle and construct an insurgent but poetic moral vision of liberty, sovereignty, and social justice. It is my hope that this discussion will also serve as the foundation for a new critical theory of Indigenous identity and the development of a new Red Pedagogy.

Notes

1. The term *critical pedagogy* will be used interchangeably with *critical theory* to refer to the diverse body of critical educational theories (i.e., postcolonial, feminist, postmodern, multicultural, and Marxist) that advocate an increasingly sophisticated critique of the social, economic, and political barriers to social justice, as well as crusade for the transformation of schools to reflect the imperatives of democracy. The totality of these theories are viewed by critical scholars as the foundation of liberatory discourse and the political project of liberation. *Project* refers to a collectivity of critique and action or solidarity.

2. For the purposes of this article, American Indian intellectualism is distinguished from purely literary or cultural forms of writing, and refers to intellectual activity that engages in substantive critical analysis from an Indigenous perspective.

3. I use the term *American Indians* to refer to the tribal peoples of North America and *Indigenous peoples* as a more inclusive term to relate to global Indigenous peoples.

4. *Democratic imaginary* refers to the notion that democracy is a never-ending project and continuous pursuit—an imagined concept.

5. The comprehensive literature reviews of Robert Allen Warrior (1995), *Tribal Secrets: Recovering American Indian Intellectual Traditions*, and of Donna Deyhle and Karen Swisher (1997), "Research in American Indian and Alaska Native Education: From Assimilation to Self-Determination," provide adequate evidence of the lack of participation of American Indian scholars within the broader field of critical studies.

6. In the critical discourse the notion of transgressive identity takes the postmodern notion of identity as a highly fluid construct with intersections among the perceived stable categories of race, class, ethnicity, sexuality, and gender—a step further by indicating that even within categories there is "transgression" or strategies of resistance that work to destabilize identity. In other words, it is not only that the categories of race, class, gender, and sexuality intersect but also that the categories (e.g., Lesbian, African American, upper class) themselves are highly contested spaces. Moreover, "transgression" is viewed as an inherently subversive and destabilizing construct, where there is constant resistance to any fixed notion of identity.

7. By "dangerous discourse" I mean that American Indian critical studies is viewed in the same spirit that Black feminism was once perceived by Whitestream feminists and African American intellectuals. (Adapting from the feminist notion of "malestream," critical scholar Claude Denis [1997] defines Whitestream as the idea that, while American society is not White in sociodemographic terms, it remains principally and fundamentally structured on the basis of White, Anglo-European experience.)

8. Though Marxist-feminist scholar Teresa Ebert employs the term *Red Pedagogy* to refer to her own work toward revitalizing the Marxist critique in feminist discourse, I use the term as a historical reference to such empowering

metaphors as "Red Power" and the "Great Red Road." Moreover, in the spirit of such venerable Indian scholars and activists as Vine Deloria and Winona LaDuke, I reappropriate the signifier *Red* as a contemporary metaphor for the ongoing political project of Indigenous peoples to retain sovereignty and establish self-determination.

9. I wish to be clear that the terms *spiritual* and *spirituality* in this text do not refer to New Age constructions of some mythic pan-Indian spirituality but rather to the historical presence and persistence within Indigenous belief systems of life forces beyond human rationality.

10. For example, various race-centric theories and certain forms of feminism. Joe Kincheloe and Shirley Steinberg (1997) state that "left essentialists tend to focus attention on one form of oppression as elemental, as taking precedence over all modes of subjugation. Certain radical feminists view gender as a central form of oppression, certain ethnic study scholars privilege race, while orthodox Marxists focus on class" (p. 22).

11. Similarly, Cameron McCarthy (1988, 1995), John Ogbu (1978), Chandra Mohanty (1989), and Henry Giroux (1992)—among others—caution against equating hybridity with equality.

12. The very "protection" typically proffered by citizenship rights (i.e., civil liberties) has often worked to erode traditional structures of tribal life, sometimes pitting Indian against Indian and tribe against tribe. For a more complete discussion of the difference between that which is civic and that which is tribal, see Vine Deloria and Clifford Lytle's *The Nations Within: The Past and Future of American Indian Sovereignty*, or Claude Denis's *We Are Not You: First Nations and Canadian Modernity*.

13. As presently constructed, tribal governments retain many powers of nations, some powers greater than those of states, and some governing powers greater than local non-Indian municipalities (Deloria & Lytle, 1984). In spite of their "sovereign" status, Indian tribes currently rely on the federal government for their operating funds, for the right to interpret and renegotiate their own treaty rights, and for access to the natural resources on their own reservations.

14. By "colonizing impulse" I mean the inherent perhaps unconscious impulse to include or conscript Indigenous (tribal) people into the "democratic project."

15. For example, in Maine, with the setting of land claims in the 1970s Carter administration, many people of varying Indian blood quantums "returned" to the reservation since they had a place to call home. The same thing has happened with the Pequot in Connecticut.

16. Joyce King (1991) defines *dysconcious racism* as an uncritical habit of mind; a form of racism that tacitly accepts White norms and privileges. She contends that such unintended racism does not reflect the absence of consciousness, but rather an impaired or distorted way of thinking about race.

17. For example, in response to the growing phenomenon of "ethnic fraud," the Association of American Indian and Alaska Native Professors has issued a position statement urging colleges and universities to follow specific guidelines in their considerations of admissions, scholarships, and hiring practices. Those guidelines are as follows: 1) Require documentation of enrollment in a state or federally recognized nation/tribe, with preference given to those who meet this criterion; 2) Establish a case-by-case review process for those unable to meet the first criterion; 3) Include American Indian/Alaska Native faculty in the selection process; 4) Require a statement from the applicant that demonstrates past and future commitment to American Indian/Alaska Native concerns; 5) Require higher education administrators to attend workshops on tribal sovereignty and meet with local tribal officials, and 6) Advertise vacancies at all levels on a broad scale and in tribal publications. Contrary to the backlash that this statement received, the association does not promote "policing," nor do they employ exclusionary tactics within their own organization, instead relying on self-disclosure.

18. The Dawes Allotment Act (1887) authorized the president of the United States to allot any reservation according to the following formula: 1) To each head of family, one quarter section; 2) To each single person over 18, one-eighth section; 3) To each orphan under eighteen, one-eighth section; 4) To each other single person under eighteen, born prior to the date of the order, one-sixteenth section (Deloria & Lytle, 1983). In order to allot the land, however, government officials required an efficient method by which to determine who was a "legitimate" member of a given community, which resulted in the beginning of widespread use of tribal rolls and blood-quantum policies.

19. The term *Indian Identity Police* is used by M. Annette Jaimes Guerrero (1996).

20. Deloria (1998) includes among such scholars James Clifton, Sam Gill, Elisabeth Tooker, Alice Kehoe, Richard deMille, and Stephen Farca.

21. Dolores Delgado Bernal (1998) identifies four sources of cultural intuition that together provide the epistemological framework for her analysis of Chicana experience: personal experience, knowledge of existing (academic) literature, professional experience, and the analytical research process itself.

22. See, for example, Elizabeth Cook-Lynn (1998), Michael Charleston (1994, 1998); Vine Deloria (1992, 1998); M. Annette Jaimes Guerrero (1996); Mary Hermes (1998); K. Tsianina Lomawaima (1994); Devon Mihesuah (1998); Frances Rains (1998, 1999); Karen Swisher (1998); Gerald Vizenor (1999); Robert Warrior (1995).

23. The Ghost Dance was started in 1890 by Chief Big Foot and his band of Lakota as a means of declaring that the Creator would prevent the total destruction of Native people, alleviate their suffering, and return the people to pre-war days of happiness.

24. The Freirean notion of praxis is best understood as action and reflection upon the world in order to change it or simply as intentional action.

References

Anderson, J. (1998). Ethnolinguistic dimensions of northern Arapaho language shift. *Anthropological Linguistics, 40*(1), 43–108.

Anzaldúa, G. (1987). *Borderlands, la frontera: The new mestíza.* San Francisco: Aunt Lute Books.

Best, S. (1989). Jameson totality and post-structuralist critique: In D. Kellener (Ed.), *Postmodernism/Jameson/critique* (pp. 233–368). Washington, DC: Maisonneuve.

Castillo, A. (1995). *Massacre of dreamers: Essays on Xicanisma.* New York: Plume.

Charleston, G.M. (1994). Toward true native education: A treaty of 1992 (Final Report of the Indian Nations at Risk Task Force, draft 3). *Journal of American Indian Education, 33*(2), 7–56.

Cook-Lynn, E. (1998). American Indian intellectualism and the new Indian story. In D.A. Mihesuah (Ed.), *Natives and academics: Researching and writing about American Indians* (pp. 111–138), Lincoln: University of Nebraska Press.

Darder, A., Torres, R., & Gutiérrez, H. (Eds.). (1997). *Latinos and education: A critical reader.* New York: Routledge.

Delgado Bernal, D. (1998). Using a Chicana feminist epistemology in educational research. *Harvard Educational Review, 68*, 555–582.

Deloria, V. (1992). *God is Red: A Native view of religion.* Golden, CO: North American Press.

Deloria, V., Jr. (1998). Comfortable fictions and the struggles for turf: An essay review of *The invented Indian: Cultural fictions and government policies.* In D.A. Mihesuah (Ed.), *Natives and academics: Researching and writing about American Indians* (pp. 65–83). Lincoln: University of Nebraska Press.

Deloria, V., Jr. (1999). *For this land: Writings on religion in America.* New York: Routledge.

Deloria, V., Jr., & Lytle, C. (1983). *American Indians, American justice.* Austin: University of Texas Press.

Deloria, V., Jr., & Lytle, C. (1984). *The nations within: The past and future of American Indian sovereignty.* Austin: University of Texas Press.

Delpit, L. (1995). *Other people's children; Cultural conflicts in the classroom.* New York: New Press.

Denis, C. (1997). *We are not you.* Toronto: Broadview.

Deyhle, R., & Swisher, K. (1997). Research in American Indian and Alaskan Native education: From assimilation to self-determination. In *Review of Research in Education* (pp. 113–183). Washington, DC: American Educational Research Association.

di Leonardo, M. (1991). *Gender at the crossroads of knowledge: Feminist anthropology in the postmodernist era.* Berkeley: University of California Press.

Fixcio, D.L. (1998). *The invasion of Indian country in the twentieth century: American capitalism and tribal natural resources.* Niwot: University Press of Colorado.

Fordham, S., & Ogbu, J. (1986). Black students and the burden of "acting White." *Urban Review, 18*, 176–203.

Fusco, C. (1995). *English is broken here: Notes on the cultural fusion in the Americas.* New York: New Press.

Giroux, H. (1992). *Border crossings: Cultural workers and the politics of education.* New York: Routledge.

Grande, S. (1997). *Critical multicultural education and the modern project: An exploratory analysis.* Unpublished doctoral dissertation, Kent State University.

Grande, S. (2000). American Indian identity and intellectualism: The quest for a new Red pedagogy. *Journal of Qualitative Studies in Education, 13*, 373–354.

Guerrero, M.A.J. (1996). Academic apartheid: American Indian studies and "multiculturalism." In A. Gordon & C. Newfield (Eds.), *Mapping multiculturalism* (pp. 49–63). Minneapolis: University of Minnesota Press.

Haig-Brown, C., & Archibald, J. (1996). Transforming First Nations research with respect and power. *International Journal of Qualitative Studies in Education, 9*, 245–267.

Hale, C.R. (2000). Book review of *To die in this way: Nicaraguan Indians and the myth of mestizaje 1880–1965. American Society for Ethnohistory, 47*, 268–271.

Harraway, D.J. (1991). *Simians, cyborgs, and women.* New York: Routledge.

Hermes, M. (1995). *Making culture, making curriculum: Teaching through meanings and identities at an American Indian tribal school.* Unpublished doctoral dissertation, University of Wisconsin-Madison.

Hermes, M. (1998). Research methods as a situated response: Towards a First Nation's methodology. *International Journal of Qualitative Studies in Education, 11*, 155–168.

Hermes, M. (2000). The scientific method, Nintendo, and eagle feathers: Rethinking the meaning of "culture based" curriculum at an Ojibwe tribal school. *International Journal of Qualitative Studies in Education, 13*, 387–400.

Herrnstein, R.J., & Murray, C. (1994). *The bell curve: Intelligence and class structure in American life.* New York: Free Press.

Joe, J.R., & Miller, D.L. (1997). Cultural survival and contemporary American Indian women in the city. In C.J. Cohen (Ed.), *Indigenous women transforming politics: An alternative reader* (pp. 137–150). New York: New York University Press.

Kincheloe, J., & Steinberg, S. (1997). *Changing multiculturalism*. Bristol, PA: Open University Press.

King, J. (1991). Dysconcious racism: Ideology, identity and the miseducation of teachers. *Journal of New Education, 60*, 133–146.

Ladson-Billings, G. (1995). "But that's just good teaching!" The case for culturally relevant pedagogy. *Theory Into Practice, 34*, 159–165.

Lipka, J. (1994). Language, power, and pedagogy: Whose school is it? *Peabody Journal of Education, 69*, 71–93.

Lomawaima, K.T. (1994). *They called it prairie light: The story of Chilocco Indian school*. Lincoln: University of Nebraska Press.

Machamer, A.M. (1997). Ethnic fraud in the university: Serious implications for American Indian education. *Native Bruin, 2*, 1–2.

McCarthy, C. (1988). Rethinking liberal and radical perspectives on racial inequality in schooling: Making the case for nonsynchrony. *Harvard Educational Review, 58*, 265–269.

McCarthy, C. (1995). The problem with origins: Race and the contrapuntal nature of the educational experience. In P. McLaren & C. Sleeter (Eds.), *Multicultural education, critical pedagogy and the politics of difference* (pp. 245–268). Albany: State University of New York Press.

McCarthy, C., & Crichlow, W. (1993). *Race and identity and representation in education*. New York: Routledge.

McLaren, P. (Ed.). (1997). *Revolutionary multiculturalism: Pedagogies of dissent for the new millennium*. Boulder, CO: Westview Press.

McLaren, P., & Giroux, H. (1997). Writing from the margins: Geographies of identity, pedagogy and power. In P. McLaren (Ed.), *Revolutionary multiculturalism: Pedagogies of dissent for the new millennium* (pp. 16–41). Boulder, CO: Westview Press.

McLaren, P., & Gutierrez, K. (1997). Global politics and local antagonists: Research and practice as dissent and possibility. In P. McLaren (Ed.), *Revolutionary multiculturalism: Pedagogy of dissent for the new millennium*, (pp. 192–222) Boulder, CO: Westview Press.

McLaren, P., & Sleeter, C. (Eds.). (1995). *Multicultural education, critical pedagogy, and the politics of difference*. Albany: State University of New York Press.

Mihesuah, D. (1998). *Natives and academics: Researching and writing about American Indians*. Lincoln: University of Nebraska Press.

Mohanty, C. (1989). On race and violence: Challenges for liberal education in the 1990s. *Cultural Critique, 14*, 179–208.

Murillo, E.G. (1997, April). *Research under cultural assault: Mojado ethnography*. Paper presented at the annual meeting of the American Educational Studies Association, San Diego.

Nagel, J. (1995). American Indian ethnic renewal: Politics and the resurgence of identity. *American Sociological Review, 60*, 947–965.

Ogbu, J. (1978). *Minority education and caste: The American system in cross-cultural perspective*. New York: Academic Press.

Pewewardy, C. (1998). Fluff and feathers: Treatment of American Indians in the literature and the classroom. *Equity and Excellence in Education, 31*, 69–76.

Rains, F.V. (1998). Is the benign really harmless? Deconstructing some "benign" manifestations of operationalized White privilege. In J. Kincheloe, S.R. Steinberg, & R.E. Chennault (Eds.), *White reign: Deploying Whiteness in America* (pp. 77–101). New York: St. Martin's Press.

Rains, F.V. (1999). Indigenous knowledge, historical amnesia and intellectual authority: Deconstructing hegemony and the social and political implications of the curricular other. In L.M. Semeli & J. Kinchloe (Eds.), *What is Indigenous knowledge? Voices from the academy* (pp. 317–332). New York: Falmer Press.

Said, E. (1985). Orientalism reconsidered. *Race and Class, 26*, 1–15.

Said, E. (1993). *Culture and Imperialism*. New York: Knopf.

Skar, S.L. (1994). *Lives together—worlds apart: Quechua colonization in jungle and city*. New York: Scandinavian University Press.

Stavenhagen, R. (1992). Challenging the nation-state in Latin America. *Journal of International Affairs, 34*, 421–441.

Strauss, A., & Corbin, J. (1990). *Basics of qualitative research: Grounded theory procedures and techniques*. Newbury Park, CA: Sage.

Swisher, K. (1998). Why Indian people should write about Indian education. In D.A. Mihesuah (Ed.), *Natives and academics: Researching and writing about American Indians* (pp. 190–199). Omaha: University of Nebraska Press.

Trueba, E. (1988). Culturally based explanation of minority students' academic achievement. *Minority Achievement, 19*, 270–287.

USD, Bureau of Indian Affairs, 209 manual 8, 83.7. Mandatory Criteria for Federal Recognition. 44 U.S.C. 3501 (et seq.) n.d.

Valle, V., & Torres, R. (1995). The idea of mestizaje and the "race" problematic: Racialized media discourse in a post-Fordist landscape. In A. Darder (Ed.), *Culture and difference: Critical perspectives on the bi-cultural experience in the United States* (pp. 139–153). Westport: Bergin & Garvey.

Van Cott, D.L. (1994). *Indigenous peoples and democracy in Latin America*. New York: St. Martin's Press.

Vizenor, G. (1999). *Postindian conversations*. Lincoln: University of Nebraska Press.

Warrior, R.A. (1995). *Tribal secrets: Recovering American Indian intellectual traditions*. Minneapolis: University of Minnesota Press.

Watahomigie, J., & McCarty, T.L. (1994). Bilingual/bicultural education at Peach Springs: A Hualapai way of schooling. *Peabody Journal of Education, 69*, 26–42.

Suggested Readings for Future Study

Anderson, J. D. and Watkins, W. H. (2005). *Black Protest Thought and Education*. New York: Peter Lang.

Anzaldúa, G. (1987). *Borderlands/La Frontera: The New Mestiza*. San Francisco: Spinster/Aunt Lute.

Bell, D. (1992). *Faces at the Bottom of the Well: The permanence of racism*. New York: Basic Books.

Clark, S., ed. (1992). *Malcolm X: The final speeches, February 1965*. New York: Pathfinder.

Cox, O. (1948). *Caste, Class and Race*. New York: Modern Reader.

Darder, A. and Torres, R. D. (2004). *After Race: Racism After Multiculturalism*. New York: New York University Press.

Darder, A. and Torres, R. (1997). *Latinos and Education: A Critical Reader*. New York: Routledge.

Darder, A. and Torres, R. (1996). *The Latino Studies Reader: Culture, economy and politics*. Boston: Blackwell.

Darder, A. (1995). *Culture and Difference*. Westport, Conn.: Bergin & Garvey.

Dent, G. (1992). *Black Popular Culture*. Seattle: Bay Press.

Dixson, A. D. and Rousseau, C. K., eds. (2006). *Critical Race Theory in Education: All God's Children Got A Song*. New York: Routledge.

Du Bois, W. E. B. (1903). *The Souls of Black Folk*. New York: Gramercy.

Dyer, R. (1993). *The Matter of Images: Essays on representations*. New York: Routledge.

Fanon, F. (1967). *Black Skin, White Masks*. New York: Grove Press.

Ferguson, R., Gever, M., Minh-ha, T., and West, C. (1990). *Out There: Marginalization and contemporary cultures*. Cambridge, MA.: MIT Press.

Fredrickson, George M. (2003). *Racism: A Short History*. New Jersey: Princeton University Press.

Gallegos, B., Villenas, S., and Braybo, B. (2003). *Indigenous Education in the Americas. A Special Issue of Educational Studies*. Lawrence Erlbaum.

Gates, H. L., Jr. (1992). *Loose Canons: Notes on the Culture Wars*. New York: Oxford University Press.

Gillborn, D. (2008). *Conspiracy? Racism and Education*. New York: Routledge.

Gilroy, P. (1993). *Black Atlantic: Modernity and double consciousness*. Cambridge, MA: Harvard University Press.

Giroux, H. (1992). *Border crossings*. New York: Routledge.

Giroux, H. (1993). *Living dangerously: Multiculturalism and the politics of difference*. New York: Peter Lang.

Giroux, H., and McLaren, P., eds. (1994). *Between Borders: Pedagogy and the politics of cultural study*. New York: Routledge.

Goldberg, D. T. (1994). *Multiculturalism: A Critical Reader*. Oxford: Blackwell.

Gordon, A. and Newfield, C. (1996). *Mapping Multiculturalism*. Minneapolis: University of Minnesota Press.

Gutierrez, R. (2004)."Internal Colonialism: An American Theory of Race," *DuBois Review*, 1(2): 281–295.

Hauptman, L. (1995). *Tribes and Tribulations: Misconceptions about American Indians and their histories*. Albuquerque: University of New Mexico Press.

Haymes, S. (1995). *Race, culture and the city: Pedagogy for black urban struggle*. Albany: SUNY Press.

hooks, b. (1992). *Black Looks: Race and Representation*. Boston, MA: South End Press.

hooks, b. and West, C. (1991). *Breaking bread: Insurgent Black intellectual life*. Boston: South End Press.

Johansen, B. (1998). *Debating democracy: Native American legacy of freedom*. Santa Fe, NM: Clear Light.

Karim, M. and Solomos J., eds. (2005). *Racialization: Studies in Theory and Practice*. Oxford: Oxford University Press.

Kelley, R. (1997). *Yo' Mama's DisFUNKtional! Fighting the culture wars in urban America*. Boston: Beacon.

Leonardo, Z. (2005). *Critical Pedagogy and Race*. New York: Blackwell Publishers.

Leistyna, P. (1999). *Presence of Mind: Education and the politics of deception*. Boulder, CO: Westview.

McCarthy, C. (1997). *The Uses of Culture: Education and the Limits of Ethnic Affiliation*. New York: Routledge.

McCarthy, C. and Crichlow, W., eds. (1993). *Race, Identity and Representations in Education*. New York: Routledge.

McLaren, P. (1995). *Critical pedagogy and predatory culture: Oppositional politics in a postmodern era*. New York: Bergin & Garvey.

McLaren, P. (1997). *Revolutionary multiculturalism: Pedagogies of dissent for the new millennium*. Boulder, CO: Westview.

Memmi, A. (1991). *The Colonizer and the Colonized*. Boston: Beacon.

Miles, R. (1993). *Racism after "Race" Relations*. London: Routledge.

Monk, R. (1994). *Taking sides: Clashing views on controversial issues in race and ethnicity*. Guilford, Conn.: The Dushkin Publishing Group.

Morrison, T. (1992). *Playing in the Dark: Whiteness and the literary imagination*. Cambridge, MA: Harvard University Press.

Noguera, P. A. (2008). *The Trouble With Black Boys: And Other Reflections on Race, Equity, and the Future of Public Education*. New York: Jossey-Bass.

Omi, M. and Winant, H. (1994). *Racial Formation in the United States*. New York: Routledge.

Olsen, L. (1997). *Made in America: Immigrant students in our public schools*. New York: The New Press.

Parker, L., Deyhle, D. and Villenas, S. (1999). *Race Is—Race Isn't: Critical Race Theory and Qualitative Studies in Education*. Colorado: Westview.

Rossatto, C. A., Allen, R. L. and Pruyn, M. (2006). *Reinventing Critical Pedagogy: Widening the Circle of Anti-Oppression*. Lanham, MD: Rowman & Littlefield.

Said, E. (1993). *Culture and Imperialism*. New York: Knopf.

Salaita, S. (2006). *Anti-Arab Racism in the USA: Where it Comes from and What it Means for Politics Today*. London: Pluto Press.

Sleeter, C. and McLaren, P. (1995). *Multicultural Education, Critical Pedagogy and the Politics of Difference*. New York: SUNY Press.

Stanton-Salazar, R. (2001). *Manufacturing Hope and Despair: The school and kin support networks of US-Mexican youth*. New York: Teachers College.

Steinberg, S. (2007). *Race Relations: A Critique*. Stanford: Stanford University Press.

Street, P. (2005). *Segregated Schools*. New York: Routledge.

Tai, R. and Kenyatta, M., eds. (1999). *Critical Ethnicity: Countering the waves of identity politics*. Lanham, MD: Rowman and Littlefield.

Takaki, R. (1990). *Iron cages: Race and Culture in 19th Century America*. New York: Oxford University Press.

Takezawa, Y. (1995). *Breaking the Silence: Redress and Japanese American ethnicity*. New York: Cornell University Press.

Torres, R. and Hamamoto, D., eds. (1997). *New American Destinies: A reader in contemporary Asian and Latino immigration*. New York: Routledge.

Torres, R., Miron, L., and Inda, J. X. (1999). *Race, Identity and Citizenship: A Reader*. Boston, Blackwell.

Valenzuela, A. (1999). *Subtractive Schooling: U.S.-Mexican youth and the politics of caring*. New York: SUNY Press.

Wa Thion'o, N. (1986). *Decolonizing the Mind: The politics of language in African Literature*. London: James Curry.

Wacquant, L. (2008). *Urban Outcasts: A Comparative Sociology of Advanced Marginality*. Cambridge: Polity Press.

Watkins, W. H. (2001). *The White Architects of Black Education: Ideology and Power in America, 1865–1954*.

Watkins, W. H., Lewis, J. H. and Chou, V. (2000). *Race and Education: The Roles of History and Society in Educating African American Students*. New York: Allyn & Bacon.

West, C. (1993). *Race Matters*. Boston: Beacon.

Winant, H. (1994). *Racial Conditions*. Minneapolis: University of Minnesota Press.

Woodson, C. G. (2007). *The Mis-education of the Negro*. Book Tree Publisher.

Young, I. (1990). *Justice and the Politics of Difference*. Princeton, N.J.: Princeton University Press.

Part Four

Gender, Sexuality, and Schooling

Introduction to Part Four

In the late 1980s, formidable feminist critiques charged critical pedagogical scholars with both analytical neglect in their engagement of asymmetrical gender relations and deficiency in their classroom practice of empowerment. In response, a flurry of critical pedagogical writings emerged that spoke to feminist questions of gender and sexuality, in important and meaningful ways. Feminist critical scholars and educators sought to interrogate the missing discourse of power and privilege, associated with the deep patriarchal tenets of Western philosophical thought, which they contended undergird critical theoretical discourses. Namely, feminist views challenged masculine notions of technocratic rationality, instrumentalism, efficiency, objectivity, and a privileging of the intellectual domain in the production of knowledge—values considered to permeate the hierarchical structures and pedagogical relationships within schools and society.

In place of these staunchly masculine conceptions of knowledge production and social relations, critical feminist educators have called for a pedagogy that unapologetically centers the voices and lived experiences associated with issues of gender inequalities and heterosexual domination. This entails the creation of counterhegemonic classroom spaces in which students can name their world, while they simultaneously grapple with commonsense notions of gender and sexuality. Linked to this pedagogical intent is the ability of educators to affirm and enable a multiplicity of lived histories, diverse voices, and personal narratives, through creating the conditions for consistent dialogical interaction.

As such, the principle of critical dialogue is imperative in efforts to deconstruct mainstream ideologies associated with social inequalities and exclusions, which can lead students to initiate emancipatory possibilities that integrate the personal, political, and pedagogical. As such, critical feminist educators encourage students to contend rigorously with diverse ways of thinking, feeling, and being, as they undertake the arduous task of challenging the recalcitrant institutional sexism that undermines their humanity and self-determination. In conjunction with efforts to question the larger oppressive conditions of society, a critical feminist approach vigorously affirms the importance of recognizing and nurturing students in negotiating multiple identities and experiences of cultural hybridity. Many feminist educators contend that this is best accomplished through a fluid pedagogy that embraces ambiguities, contradictions and uncertainties, as essential features of democratic life.

Foremost to a feminist understanding of schooling is an acknowledgment that gendered attitudes, practices, and language are inextricably linked to the hierarchical structure of gender relations, which are not biologically defined, but rather naturalized within social relationships that authorize dominant formations of gender and sexuality. Hence, from our arrival into the world, hegemonic and universal notions of gender and sexuality constrain and oppress, systematically silencing alternative ways of being human—rendering moral and commonsense the subordination of women and the enactment of compulsory heterosexuality.

In a similar vein, a queer pedagogy has sought to critique and challenge the silencing of sexual identities, by derailing the plethora of false notions and mistaken beliefs about sexualities—notions and beliefs heavily driven by the hegemony of an essentialized heterosexual identity. This pedagogical approach, in concert with feminist ideals, highlights the significance of critically contending with the politics of gender roles and sexual identities, the pedagogical negation of eroticism, and the homophobic underpinnings of the classroom curriculum. By openly exploring such issues within the classroom, teachers and students can grapple with the impact of repressive notions of sexuality, in context to social relations and the production of knowledge.

For example, openly countering classroom practices in which the sexualities of lesbian, gay, bisexual, transgendered, and queer students (LGBTQ) are silenced and undermined by the representation of heterosexual dominance is imperative in any pedagogy which claims an emancipatory vision of a genuinely pluralistic society. Such a commitment, indeed, requires the courage to transgress the structures of silence that often persist even when students' sexualities are maligned and denigrated, and they are subjected to brutal bullying and harassment within the classroom, the community, and often even at home. Significant to note here is the manner in which the silence of educators regarding diverse sexualities not only silences LGBTQ students, but also reinscribes a homophobic morality that renders taboo diverse sexual desires and inhibits the exercise of freedom.

Hence, a critical queer pedagogy summons teachers to enter the danger zones of transgressive knowledge and risky possibilities, in the name of social justice and human rights. This also carries the expectation that educators begin with an interrogation of their personal beliefs and values associated with gender and sexual formations. To effectively challenge and transform gendered and sexual inequalities produced in schools, teachers must develop a critical understanding of sexual orientation and the suppressed histories, knowledge, and cultural communities of LGBTQ students, whose lives are shaped by the anxieties of repression and resistance to their sexual location at the margins. Hence, critical educators must openly contend with the struggles of lesbian, gay, bisexual, and queer students, who are often marked by a society where "hate speech" is sanctioned and license is given to bully, torment, and endanger those who are deemed outside the heterosexual norm. There is no question then that the degree of powerlessness experienced by many of these students is particularly pervasive during adolescence, given the highly homophobic nature of educational institutions.

Summary of Articles

Kathleen Weiler's essay, "Feminist Analysis of Gender and Schooling," introduces the reader to notions of gender, schooling, and sexuality with a review of the major feminist approaches to education. Her work examines some of the problematic assumptions of traditional and liberal perspectives of gender oppression. Weiler also looks at feminist research of the 1970s and 1980s conducted in response to the all-male-oriented research of the correspondence movement. Following the tradition of other exponents of critical pedagogy, Weiler exposes the weaknesses of correspondence theories, in an effort to address, in a comprehensive manner, how both gender and race are at work in the classroom. In particular, she engages the concept of counterhegemony, as conceptualized by Gramsci, and its utility to an emancipatory feminist pedagogy. Weiler argues that, through providing an analysis of resistance, gender, race, and social class, critical pedagogy can provide a theoretical framework for the transcendence of limitations found in earlier feminist discourses.

In "Sexuality, Schooling, and Adolescent Females: The Missing Discourse of Desire," Michelle Fine crafts an important analysis, in which she effectively integrates feminist concerns within a critical pedagogical perspective. Her groundbreaking ethnography on sex education in New York City public schools exposes the hypocrisy at work in the politics of sex education—a politics that functions to suppress an ever present (but hidden) discourse of desire among female adolescents. In so doing, she illustrates how this phenomenon actually functions to prevent the construction of healthy sexual identities, as it perpetuates a cycle of victimization and poverty among teenage girls.

In "The Tolerance That Dare Not Speak Its Name," Cris Mayo confronts the contradiction of speech and conduct codes in schools, intended to "protect" the rights of LGBTQ students, but that actually stunt open classroom dialogue about sexuality. Consequently, Mayo contends, pedagogical practices and policies meant to enact social justice collude inadvertently with conservative interests, blocking the free public exchange necessary for social transformation. This brings into focus a common phenomenon, where curricular materials celebrated as "tolerance" or expressively emancipatory in intent, fail to uproot the material inequalities at work in schools and communities. This is particularly the case where isolated policies forbidding "hate speech" are enacted, in the absence of curricular representations of sexual diversity in the classroom. Instead, Mayo rightly advocates critical classroom dialogues that dare to speak of homophobia, its prevalence, its meaning, and impact, especially on the lives of lesbian, gay, bisexual, transgendered, and queer students.

Questions for Reflection and Dialogue

1. Describe the historical development of feminist approaches to schooling and education.
2. What are the major distinctions between liberal, radical, and socialist feminisms?
3. What are the shortcomings of reproduction theory in explaining gender oppression and human agency?
4. What are the four major approaches to sex education in public schools in the United States? How distinct are these from the experiences of other industrialized countries?
5. How efficient are these four approaches to alleviating problems of teenage pregnancy, sexual violence, and school dropouts?
6. In what ways can the public's recognition of the role of "desire" in the lives of students contribute to both the development of emancipated subjectivities among female and LGBTQ students and the establishment of critical educational practices within schools?
7. In what ways are the conditions of lesbian, gay, bisexual, transgendered, and queer students different from those of heterosexual teenagers?

8. How are gay, lesbian and bisexual students affected emotionally and socially by the ostracism experienced within the high school classroom? How do you believe this might impact their academic development?

9. What concrete steps can educators take to address the sexuality of their students? How can they help to prevent the harassment or bullying of LGBTQ students by their classmates?

10. Explain Mayo's concerns regarding the effectiveness of "codes of conduct" in altering "hate speech" and the homophobic climate within schools.

11

Feminist Analysis of Gender and Schooling

Kathleen Weiler

Much of the work that has been done to date on the relationship of women and schooling has emerged from liberal feminist analyses of schools. Such work has focused on sex stereotyping and bias. Theorists working from this perspective have outlined and exposed the sexual bias in curricular materials and school practices. Their focus has been on the reform of both texts and practices and on state policies toward education. Both classroom ethnographies and analyses of textbooks have emerged from this tradition.[2]

This liberal feminist work has been extremely important in documenting the biases and distortions of texts and the sexism that underlies such practices as course and career counseling for girls and boys. But it also has significant shortcomings in its narrow focus on texts and institutional structures. It has tended to ignore the depth of sexism in power relationships and the relationship of gender and class. Because this approach fails to place schools and schooling in the context of a wider social and economic analysis, it does not analyze the constraints under which the process of schooling actually takes place. Moreover, the liberal approach omits any class analysis and thus ignores not only differences between middle-class and working-class girls and women, but ignores the oppression and exploitation of working-class boys as well. As Arnot comments:

> This literature does not search too deeply into the class basis or the inequality of opportunity which boys suffer . . . The implication then appears to be that girls should match the class differentials of educational achievement and access to occupations which boys experience. Equality of opportunity in this context therefore appears to mean similar class-based inequalities of opportunity for both men and women. Or, one could say, equal oppression.
> (Arnot, 1982, p. 68)

While the strength of the liberal perspective lies in its documentation of gender discrimination and the analysis of specific sexist texts and practices, its lack of social or economic analysis limits its ability to explain the origins of these practices or the ways in which other structures of power and control affect what goes on within schools. Its lack of class analysis leads to a blurring of what actually happens in schools as individuals are described only in terms of their gender and are not viewed in terms of their class or race location as well.

In the liberal feminist studies of sex-role stereotyping, there has been an implicit assumption that changes of texts and practices will lead to changes in social relationships and that girls and boys will then be equal within capitalist society. Implicit in this view is the concept that sexism exists within the realm of ideas, and that if those ideas are changed, then social relationships will also change. Such a view ignores the constraints of the material world and the various forms of power and privilege that work together in a complex and mutually reinforced process to make up social reality as we know it. It also ignores the complexity of consciousness and the existence of ideology and culture. Thus while liberal feminist critiques of sex-role stereotyping in school texts and descriptions of classroom practices have been very useful, they are of limited analytic value in investigating the complexity of the social construction of gender in the intersection of school, family, and work.

In this chapter, I examine the work of feminists influenced by socialist feminism and by critical educational theory who have investigated the relationship of schooling and gender. This critical feminist educational theory begins with certain assumptions that distinguish it from liberal feminist studies. The first assumption is that schooling is deeply connected to the class structure and economic system of capitalism; thus one focus of this work is on the relationship of women's schooling and women's work. The second assumption, again derived from more general socialist feminist theory, is that capitalism and patriarchy are related and mutually reinforcing of one another. In other words, both men and women exist in interconnected and overlapping relationships of gender and class—and, as feminists of color have increasingly emphasized, of race as well.

These theorists share the difficulties of other socialist-feminist theorists who attempt to fuse Marxism and feminism. They are deeply influenced by traditional Marxist theory, and want to apply that theory to the situation of women. But Marx and Engels were primarily concerned with the mode of production and relationships of production in class and not in gender terms. For Marx and Engels as well as for later Marxist theorists, women's oppression was subsumed within their class position and was analyzed through examining the demands of capital. Socialist-feminist theorists have argued that this traditional Marxist analysis is inadequate to reveal the nature of women's experience and oppression (Jagger, 1983; Hartsock, 1983; Eisenstein, 1979). As Kuhn and Wolpe comment, "much marxist analysis, in subsuming women to the general categories of that problematic—class relations, labour process, the state, and so on—fails to confront the specificity of women's oppression" (Kuhn and Wolpe, 1978, p. 8). This theoretical debate, what Hartmann has called "the unhappy marriage of socialism and feminism," is complex and still being worked out. The immediate task for socialist feminists is to create a synthesis of these two lines of analysis, to create a theory that can relate what Rubin has called "the sex/gender system" and the economic system through an analysis of the sexual division of labor and an understanding of the intersection of these two forms of power (Barrett, 1980; Eisenstein, 1979; Rubin, 1975). As Hartmann puts it:

> Both marxist analysis, particularly its historical and materialist method, and feminist analysis, especially the identification of patriarchy as a social and historical structure, must be drawn upon if we are to understand the development of western capitalist societies and the predicament of women within them.
>
> (Hartmann, 1981, p. 191)

These arguments are complex and as yet incomplete. The historical development of socialist feminism itself has recently come under scrutiny and the question of its future development is hardly clear (Barrett, 1980; Ehrenreich, 1984; Rowbotham, Segal and Wainright, 1981; Tax, 1984). But while the relationship between socialism and feminism, capitalism and patriarchy is filled with tension, as Ehrenreich writes, a socialist and feminist perspective is still needed:

Socialist—or perhaps here I should say Marxist—because a Marxist way of thinking, at its best, helps us understand the cutting edge of change, the blind driving force of capital, the dislocations, innovations, and global reshufflings. Feminist because feminism offers our best insight into that which is most ancient and intractable about our common situation: the gulf that divides the species by gender and, tragically, divides us all from nature and that which is most human in our nature.

(1984, p. 57)

This study of feminist teachers is grounded in this complex and developing tradition of socialist feminist theory. But I have also been influenced by a variety of feminist theorists who have concerned themselves with the relationship of gender and schooling and who have approached these questions from less clearly defined theoretical perspectives.

In discussing ongoing feminist work on the relationship of gender and schooling, I have identified the same two perspectives that I use in discussing critical educational theory in general: theories of social and cultural reproduction and theories of cultural production and resistance. But I want to make clear at the outset of this discussion that this division is in certain ways artificial and should not be taken as connoting a rigid separation of these theorists into competing schools of thought. What I have identified in their work are tendencies, a concern with certain problems, a way of defining what is significant or causal in looking at the relationship of gender and schooling. What I think we can see here is what Althusser calls the "problematique" of theory—that is, the underlying questions that define what is significant and therefore what is to be investigated. I feel this distinction between those concerned with social and cultural reproduction and those concerned with cultural production and resistance is a valid one. But in a field of inquiry as new and fluid as this one, in which feminist scholars are in the process of generating theory, there will be a blurring and shifting of perspectives as the theorists themselves develop and refine their own concerns.[3]

The earliest of these investigations into gender and school from a critical feminist perspective can be found in what I have called feminist reproduction theory. Feminist reproduction theory is concerned with the ways in which schools function to reproduce gender divisions and oppression. In response to this emphasis on reproduction, a smaller but growing body of work has emerged which employs the concepts of resistance and cultural production to look at the lived experience of girls in schools. Most recently, the concept of counter-hegemony has been raised as a way of approaching the politically conscious work of teachers. These theoretical traditions focus on different moments in the experience of girls and women in schools, and as I have emphasized, it should be kept in mind that these categories are a kind of heuristic device, and that the individual theorists themselves may be engaged in their own process of growth and reconceptualization. But trying to clarify and identify their underlying theoretical assumptions can be of help to all of us as we attempt to generate theory and focus our own research.

Feminist Reproduction Theory

Although socialist feminist theory has developed rapidly in the last decade, work that explicitly addresses the role of schools in reproducing gender oppression has been somewhat limited. The most significant work has emerged in England, and has been influenced by the work of both new sociologists of education and Marxist theorists who have focused on the role of schools as ideological state apparatuses. While these feminist reproduction theorists take somewhat different approaches, they all share a common belief in the power of material historical analysis and a focus on the relationship of class and gender. Basic to their approach is the view that women's oppression in the paid workforce and in domestic work is reproduced through what happens in the schools. Thus statistical analyses of women's inferior position in the economy are tied to sexist texts and discriminatory practices in schools. Official state educational policies are examined for their overt and hidden assumptions about women and their "proper" role in the economy. The major focus of this approach is on the connection between sexist practices in the schools and women's oppression in society as a whole.

Feminist reproduction theorists are deeply influenced by traditional Marxist analysis and have been primarily concerned with social reproduction—that is, the reproduction of relationships to and control over economic production and work.[4] These theorists are concerned with the nature of women's work, both within the public sphere and within the domestic or private sphere. Thus the focus of their analysis is on the class-based nature of women's experiences in schools and the ways in which the experience of schooling reproduces gender oppression. But they also emphasize the differences between middle-class and working-class experience of gender. For them, what are being reproduced are not simply "men" and "women," but working-class or bourgeois men and women who have particular relationships to one another and to production which are the result of their class as well as their gender. As Arnot comments, this approach reveals "the diversity of class experience and the nature of class hegemony in education" (Arnot, 1982, p. 69).

The debate about the relationship of gender and class underlies the work of all of these feminist reproduction theorists who concern themselves with schooling. While they recognize the "specificity" of women's oppression and often speak of patriarchal as opposed to class oppression, they remain committed to the primacy of production. Because of the centrality of this sphere of material life and production in their thought, feminist reproduction theorists see the relationship between gender as an ideology and women's role in production as fundamental to any analysis of women and schooling. Thus for them, work, both paid and unpaid, becomes the central focus of analysis. Since they are concerned with the role of schooling in the reproduction of existing society, they focus on the way schools work ideologically to prepare girls to accept their role as low paid or unpaid workers in capitalism.

Several socialist feminist analyses of reproduction and schooling are also deeply influenced by the work of Althusser. This is particularly true of the work of Michelle Barrett. An Althusserian perspective in this case implies an emphasis on the "relative autonomy" of schools as sites of ideological reproduction. The most obvious difficulty of using an Althusserian approach for an analysis of gender is that Althusser is concerned with the category of class, not gender, and there is some question whether it is fruitful or even possible to substitute "gender" for "class" in this analysis. However, Althusser's insistence that ideological apparatuses are "relatively autonomous" from the economic sphere appears to provide the means to raise questions of gender and patriarchal practices apart from, although not unrelated to, questions of class and capitalist practices. Barrett recognizes the complexity of this issue and argues that the method of analysis must include an analysis of gender *within* specific class structures (1980). While feminist theorists of schooling influenced by Althusser provide a more complex view of the role of schools in relation to women's oppression in capitalism, they remain focused on the question of how this oppression is reproduced and, like Althusser, argue at a very abstract level of analysis that leaves little room for human agency or resistance. While a view of schools as ideological state apparatuses "relatively autonomous" from the economic base provides room for the contradictions and disjunctions evident in schools, it still remains within a paradigm of reproduction. The strengths and weaknesses of feminist reproduction theory may be clarified if we look at the work of several representative theorists.

AnnMarie Wolpe was one of the earliest socialist feminists to address the role of gender in schooling. Her work includes both a critique of official government statements on education and a critique of earlier work on sexism in schools for its lack of economic or social analysis. One of the strongest parts of Wolpe's argument is her attack on what she calls "stratification" theories, which look at women's position as the result of innate psychological differences such as lack of aggression, excessive anxiety, or orientation toward "intrinsic" rewards such as nurturing relationships (1978, p. 306). Wolpe argues that such interpretations fail to recognize the powerful forces of the capitalist economy with its need for unpaid domestic work and a reserve army of labor.

Wolpe reveals in detail the ideological assumptions about the role of women in society which underlie the offical British Norwood (1943), Crowther (1959), and Newsom (1963) reports and the later unofficial Conservative Green and Black papers (1977). Wolpe shows clearly the acceptance of the role of women as wives and mothers doing unpaid work in the home and the failure to recognize either that women *do* work in paid jobs or that the paid work that they do is in low-paying and dead-end jobs. Thus by failing to recognize the reality of women's actual work as paid workers and by encouraging girls to see their own work (both paid and unpaid) as insignificant, Wolpe argues that these reports perpetuated and helped to reproduce existing inequality. She argues that in influencing school policies, these reports have played a vital ideological role in reproducing the oppression and subordination of women in the economy.

This kind of analysis is valuable since it points to the connection between hegemonic ideological views (in the consciousness of the groups—primarily men—who wrote these reports) and actual educational policy and practices as they are carried out in the schools. But what Wolpe does not address is precisely *how* these assumptions and views are put into practice in the schools or how students and teachers have accepted, incorporated, or resisted them. This is not to discredit or discount Wolpe's analysis, but to point to the limitations inherent in a view of ideology as the uncontested imposition of a view of reality or set of values. Wolpe's tendency to depict the imposition of ideology as a relatively smooth and almost mechanical process is the result of her focus on reproduction at a very abstract level of economic and structural analysis. It is Wolpe's reliance on reproduction and her failure to address the question of human agency that ultimately limits her work. While she criticizes stratification theories of education for their failure to provide any economic analysis of the role of schooling, she accepts without much criticism social reproduction theories of education. As she says:

> I want to consider the educational system first, as a mechanism of *reproduction* of "agents" in the sense that it operates, more or less successfully, to qualify them both "technically" and ideologically; and second, as a mediating agency in the *allocation* of agents into the division of labour.
>
> (Wolpe, 1978, p. 313)

Since Wolpe is concerned with women and women's oppression, the use of this reproduction paradigm ultimately leads her to depict schools as the means of reproducing women who will accept their role as workers in both paid and unpaid work. The ideology of the school is seen as important in justifying this role both for those who control the educational system and for the girls and women in the schools.

Wolpe's approach shares the limitations and shortcomings of all social reproduction theory, in that it fails to address individual consciousness or the possibilities of resistance, but it also fails to address forms of women's oppression other than those of work. Wolpe later qualifies her early, rather functionalist, view by referring to the "relative autonomy" of schools. Following Althusser, she sees schools as mediating between students and the demands of capital. This "relative autonomy" recognizes the contradictions involved in the relationship between the economic base and the schools. Nonetheless, Wolpe's central concern remains the reproduction of women in relation to work. Thus, Wolpe's analysis has no place for sexuality, human needs, the historical and class-based forms of resistance of women, or the contradictory role of schooling for girls in a system of patriarchy. Ultimately Wolpe's work is valuable in pointing out the need to locate women's oppression and women's experience in schooling within a larger social structure and in making central the role of work in women's lives, but at the same time her work is frustrating in its tendency toward a mechanical form of reproduction theory.

Another early influential feminist analysis of schooling was Rosemary Deem's *Women and Schooling* (1978). In this general overview, Deem combines quantitative information about the percentage of girls in various courses, the numbers of girls taking and passing exams, and the percentage of women in various teaching and administrative jobs. She also writes from the general perspective of social reproduction, arguing that the schools are central to the process of maintaining and reproducing the existing sexual division of labor. This underlying paradigm of social reproduction leads Deem to emphasize the significance of work and the role of schooling in preparing women for certain kinds of work. Thus she emphasizes the domestic nature of working-class girls' curriculum, with its assumption that women's primary work will be unpaid labor in the home. She also points to the small number of girls in mathematics and science, and shows how that in turn excludes women from certain university courses and later technological and professional jobs. Deem points out that the schools do not create this division, but that they reinforce the present arrangement of society through their acceptance of the status quo in both class and gender terms:

> Education does not create the sexual division of labour, nor the kinds of work available in the labour market, nor the class relationships of society, but it rarely does anything to undermine them.
>
> (Deem, 1978, p. 20)

Deem emphasizes that schools, in their expectations of boys and girls and in their authority structures (so heavily dominated by men in positions of power and authority), transmit different cultures to boys and to girls, and that the "choices" made by students in school reproduce the existing sexual division of labor.

One of the strengths of Deem's analysis is her emphasis on the continuity of women's work as mothers in the family and as teachers in the primary schools. As she makes clear, the role of women in doing the unpaid labor of nurturing, feeding, and caring for the material needs of children is not the reflection of some innate "women's nature," but is part of the existing social division of labor in capitalism. This arrangement may not be inevitable in capitalist societies, but in the present organization of capitalism, it is central to the reproduction of the work force. Thus Deem argues that there is a continuum between the rearing and socialization of children within the family, where the primary work is done by mothers, and the socialization that takes place in the early years of schooling, with the work done by women teachers.[5] Deem's grounding in social reproduction theory leads her to reject views of women's nurturing role as either "natural" or the "fault" of women. As she emphasizes, it is the structural organization of capitalist societies that leads to this division of labor and the resulting personal and psychological traits assumed to be natural to men and women. She criticizes the view that women teachers are inadequate because of their feminine qualities or their roles within their own families:

> Furthermore, there is the implicit assumption (in criticizing women teachers) that all these factors are the fault of women and are not attributable to their relationship with men in the sexual division of labour, or to the manner in which capitalist societies organize and reward productive and non-productive work.
>
> (Deem, 1978, p. 116)

This emphasis on the existing division of capitalist societies in gender as well as class terms is one of the strongest elements in Deem's work, since it leads her to see the experiences and struggles of women teachers in the context of larger social dynamics.

Although Deem's book provides a valuable overview of the relationship of women and schooling, its strength—a recognition of the role of schools in reproducing an unequal gender and class system—is at the same time a limitation. Like Wolpe, Deem fails to deal adequately with ideology and the way in which women teachers and students exist within a structure of socially influenced needs and desires—an ideological world of male hegemony, in Arnot's phrase. Moreover, she ignores the struggles and resistance of both teachers and students to this hegemony. While her work is useful in providing specific evidence of discriminatory patterns, the picture it gives of this process is one sided. Again, what is needed here is an examination of the way in which these meanings and forms of power are negotiated and worked out in the actual lived reality of teachers and students in schools.

An interesting analysis of women's schooling from a similar perspective but in the United States context is provided by the recent work of Kelly and Nihlen (1982). Like many other socialist feminists, Kelly and Nihlen argue that an emphasis on paid work as the only meaningful form of work ignores the significance of domestic unpaid labor—a domain that has been defined as "women's sphere" in advanced capitalist societies like the United States. They argue that the ideological assumption that this work is the responsibility (and natural province) of women profoundly shapes women's working lives, making certain jobs "unnatural" for women because of the difficulties involved in doing both paid and unpaid work. Moreover, the assumption that certain characteristics are natural to women —such as nurturance, caring, sensitivity, etc.—leads women into certain jobs and not others. Kelly and Nihlen consider the evidence that links schools to this division of labor, but unlike some of the earlier writers who focus on reproduction, they also raise the question of the extent to which students "do in fact become what the messages of the schools would have them become" (Kelly and Nihlen, 1982, p. 174). Thus, while they work from the perspective of reproduction theory, seeking to delineate the reproductive role of schools in the creation of the sexual division of labor, they also begin to question the adequacy of that perspective in addressing the realities of women's experience in schools.

In looking at the relationship of schooling and women's work, Kelly and Nihlen focus on several areas of schooling. They look first at authority patterns and staffing. Using available statistics and data, they show clearly the unequal representation of women in positions of authority and status and note the *decline* of women in higher paying and higher status jobs since the 1950s. They also examine the formal curriculum, and, citing the numerous studies of curriculum and texts that exist, particularly in the 1970s, show again the sex-stereotyping prevalent in curricular material at both the primary and secondary levels. They then examine the ways in which knowledge is distributed in the classroom itself and in the social relationships of schooling. As they point out, this area is least researched; we know the least about the ways in which girls and boys are treated by male and female teachers. But the studies that do exist point to discrimination and stereotyped expectations based not only on gender, but on race and class as well. Thus working-class girls of color receive the least attention and have the lowest expectations from teachers. On the other hand, there is evidence that teachers tend to prefer white middle-class girls to black working-class boys, for example.

The most interesting part of Kelly and Nihlen's discussion is the final section on the possible resistance of girls. As they make clear, girls do continue to higher education (although disproportionally to two-year colleges as opposed to more elite public and private four-year colleges) despite the ideological message of the school curriculum that their place is at home doing domestic work. As Kelly and Nihlen point out, women do not accept the ideological message of the school unproblematically. Instead, they obviously "negotiate" that knowledge in light of their own emotional, intellectual and material needs:

> While the above suggests that women may not necessarily incorporate all "school knowledge" it should not be taken by any means to deny what school knowledge in fact is or its attempted transmission in the classroom. Rather, it is to point out that within the classroom sets of knowledge renegotiation and/or active filtering occurs that may counter what the schools consider legitimate. How this renegotiation occurs we do not know, yet there is ample evidence to suggest its existence.
>
> (Kelly and Nihlen, 1982, p. 175)

Kelly and Nihlen's work is valuable in pointing to the weaknesses of the reproduction paradigm and in calling for an examination of the ways in which girls appropriate or reject school knowledge about the roles of women in paid and domestic work. They point to evidence that girls do not unproblematically accept the vision of sexual identity transmitted to them through the social relationships, authority patterns, and curriculum of the schools. However, despite their valuable work in recognizing the need to take into account resistance in looking at girls in schools, Kelly and Nihlen's work has certain limitations. First, I think, is their failure to apply or develop the concept of resistance to account for contradictory relationships to schooling on the part of both students and teachers. And second, they are still tied to a theory of work and work value that does not address the sexuality and power in the relationships of men and women which are extremely important in school settings, as in all socially constructed gender relationships.

Certainly the most sophisticated and fully developed theoretical work in the socialist feminist sociology of education can be found in the work of Madeleine Arnot. A sociologist of education versed in the theories of Bernstein and Bourdieu, Arnot has developd a critique of their work and an analysis of traditional reproduction theory from a feminist perspective. Her work combines a thorough knowledge of both reproduction and resistance theory. Her use of these difficult and sometimes contradictory traditions provides a complex analysis of the relationship of gender, class, and schooling. As Arnot defines her own position: "I do not believe that one can disassociate the ideological forms of masculinity and femininity, in their historical specificity, from either the material basis of patriarchy or from the class structure" (1980, p. 60). Underlying all of her work is the central under-standing that social relationships are always in process and are constructed by individual human beings within a web of power and material constraints.

While Arnot has been influenced by reproduction theory and is sympathetic to a materialist analysis, she is critical of feminist reproduction theory for its failure to deal with the question of resistance and the contested nature of the construction of both class and gender identities. Arnot argues that socialist feminist social reproduction theorists, like social reproduction theorists in general, project too total a vision of domination and oppression. In some of these accounts, girls are turned into women through the effects of schooling in a mechanical process in which their humanity and consciousness are simply ignored. Thus Arnot suggests replacing the concept of reproduction with Gramsci's concept of hegemony. As she says:

> By putting the concept of hegemony, rather than "reproduction" at the fore of an analysis of class and gender, it is less easy in research to forget the *active* nature of the learning process, the existence of dialectical relations, power struggles, and points of conflict, the range of alternative practices which may exist inside, or exist outside and be brought into the school.
>
> (1982, p. 66)

In seeking a way to address questions of cultural production, Arnot looks back to the work of Bernstein and Bourdieu. While Arnot criticizes their work for their failure to address gender, she is also deeply influenced by this work, particularly that of Bernstein and his theories of the framing and transmission of knowledge. She uses his concept of a code to suggest that "one can develop a theory of gender codes which is class based and which can expose the structural and interactional features of gender reproduction and conflict in families, in schools and in work places" (1982, p. 80). What this focus on gender codes would allow us, Arnot argues, is to remain conscious of the different moments and crossing structures of power which are negotiated by individuals in social settings. Thus she emphasizes that girls negotiate and construct their own gendered identities through different definitions of what it means to be a woman from their families, their peers, the school, the media, etc., and that this involves both contradictions and conflict. Arnot argues that feminist educational theorists, by emphasizing hegemony, the existence of competing codes of meaning and the continual *process* of social relationships, will be able to unravel the complexities of the effects of both capitalism and patriarchy on individual lives without falling into the mechanical functionalism of reproduction theory or the atheoretical stance of liberal theory.

The work of Arnot and Kelly and Nihlen draws attention to the need to take into account agency and the production of meaning on the part of girls and women in schools. It also reiterates the basic argument of Barrett and other socialist feminists that we must try to understand the construction of gender within specific historical and social sites. While this project is only beginning, the basis for this investigation can be found in the work of feminists who have turned to the lived experience of girls and women in school. The most developed of this work has come from feminists using the concept of resistance to investigate the lived reality of working-class girls in and out of schools. But other work is in process and emerging that considers the lives and work of women teachers as well as students. This new work builds upon the earlier reproduction studies, but its basic focus is quite different. It is to this work that I now want to turn.

Feminist Resistance and Cultural Production Theory

As we have seen, feminist reproduction theory has emphasized the ways in which school-ing *reproduces* existing gender inequalities. This work has focused on the ideological func-tion of texts and classroom practices in reinforcing patriarchal hegemony. And because much of this work is grounded in traditional Marxist class analysis, it has also focused on the connection between schooling and women's work in the paid work force. I have argued that the limitation of this approach lies in its failure to consider human beings as agents who are able to contest and redefine the ideological messages they receive in schools. It is a much too mechanistic and all-encompassing view of social reality. In response to these limitations, some feminists have begun to examine girls' and women's experiences in schools from the perspective of resistance and cultural production theories.

While traditionally the concept of resistance has been used to describe public counter-school or antisocial actions, there is an emerging view that this definition is inadequate to explain or understand the lives of girls or women. Some feminist theorists argue that resistance has different meanings for boys and for girls and that girls' resistance can only be understood in relation to both gender and class position (Connell et al., 1982; Davies, 1983; Kessler et al., 1985). These theorists insist that women as well as men can resist domination and oppression and they as well as men negotiate social forces and possibilities in an attempt to meet their own needs. This is the same dialectic between human needs and human will that we see in other critical studies. Women, as well as men, are enmeshed in social relationships and ideological, as well as material, webs of meaning and power. But because they are oppressed by sexism as well as class, the form of their resistance will be different from that of men. Moreover, schooling may have a different meaning for them than it has for boys of their same class or race. As Gaskell comments:

> . . . schools, operating in their traditional function, do not simply reproduce sex-stereotypes or confirm girls in subordinate positions. Certainly they do that much of the time. But they have also long been a vehicle for women who wish to construct their own intellectual lives and careers.
>
> (1985, p. 35)

Girls and women with different race and class subjectivities will have different experi-ences in schools. Both their resistance and their "reading" of the ideological messages of schools will differ in specific school settings. And of course girls of different class and race subjectivities will be met with varying expectations on the part of white and black, male and female teachers, depending on these teachers' own views of what is gender appropriate. By adding the categories of race and class to that of gender, we can begin to reveal the diversity and complexity of girls' and women's experiences in schools.

Some of the most important work addressing the experiences of working-class girls in schools has come from feminist sociologists of education who have studied groups of antisocial or antischool girls. The work of these theorists has emerged from a wider sociological investigation of youth subcultures as the site of working-class resistance to the hegemonic ideology of capitalism. Much of this research has come from the Centre for Contemporary Cultural Studies at the University of Birmingham in England and the feminist research group there has engaged in a number of valuable projects and critiques (Women's Study Group, 1978). While these feminist sociologists have worked closely with the male sociologists using this perspective, they have also generated sharp criticisms of this male-focused work. In particular, feminist sociologists interested in the question of working-class girls' resistance have been both influenced by and critical of the work of Willis. Willis's study of working-class boys, *Learning to Labour*, made an immediate impact on critical educational theory, and particularly on critical ethnographic studies of schools. However, despite its originality and richness, it shared the weakness of earlier studies in its exclusive examination of the public subcultures of young men. This exclusive interest in men and a subsequent (sometimes subtle, and sometimes not) definition of male counter-culture as working-class culture evoked a feminist response, both in the form of critiques of Willis and also in the sociological investigation of working-class girls' experiences and subcultures on the part of feminist sociologists (McRobbie, 1980; Acker, 1981).

The feminist critique of Willis centers around two general points. First is the fundamental question of the reliability of descriptions of working-class culture by male sociologists. The question raised here is whether Willis has given weight to certain aspects of that culture because of his own ideological valuing of male actions. That is, does Willis, in common with other male sociologists, "see" male activities and spheres as significant, but remain "blind" to the significance of female spheres. This criticism follows the line of argument of feminist anthropologists who have critiqued male anthropologists for their own form of male ethnocentrism (Reiter, 1975).

The second feminist criticism of Willis's work highlights his failure to address the sexist oppression inherent in male working-class culture. As McRobbie puts it:

> Shopfloor culture may have developed a toughness and resilience to deal with the brutality of capitalist productive relations, but these same "values" can be used internally . . . They can also be used, and often are, against women and girls in the form of both wife and girlfriend battering. A fully *sexed* notion of working class culture would have to consider such features more centrally.
>
> (McRobbie, 1980, p. 41)

Thus a failure to recognize the oppressive sexism of male subcultures and an acceptance of the absence of girls in these subcultures are clearly interrelated. In fact, of course, the boys' own sexism reproduces the role of girls in working-class culture as oppressed and subordinate.

While these relationships may in some sense reflect a logic of capitalism, it is not the ideology or state policies of capitalism that directly pressures these working-class girls, but rather the immediate and oppressive sexism of working-class boys. As we will see, feminists argue that the moral failure to condemn or even to see the sexism of male subcultures leads in turn to a failure to understand the full dynamics of working-class culture and life.

In response to this feminist critique of Willis and other male work on boys' public subcultures, feminists have turned to an examination of girls' antisocial and counter-school groups. While studies of girls' subcultures are still relatively few in comparison to studies of boys', McRobbie, Fuller and others in England, and Thomas in Australia have contributed ethnographic studies that raise new questions about the intersection of gender, race, and class in the lives of working-class girls.

Studies of white working-class girls have been undertaken by McRobbie and her associates at the Centre for Contemporary Cultural Studies in England and by Thomas in Australia. These studies have been deeply influenced by the cultural production theories of Willis and others at the CCCS and provide an alternative approach to similar problems. McRobbie worked with a group of 14–16 year-old-girls at a Birmingham youth club for six months, while Thomas studied two groups of antischool or antiacademic girls—one group in a middle-class and one in a working-class school—for an academic year. In both cases, there was a clear and stated recognition that the experiences and actions of girls could not be explained solely through an analysis of class, but that, as McRobbie put it, "their culture would be linked to and partly determined by, although not mechanically so, the material position occupied by the girls in society" (1978, p. 97). Thus, unlike comparable studies of male subcultures, McRobbie and Thomas begin with an awareness of the dual oppression of working-class girls through both capitalism and patriarchy. And in looking at the gender-specific nature of their oppression and their resistance, they focus on the private, domestic world of sexuality and the family as well as the public world of the street and paid work.

Both McRobbie and Thomas studied girls who rejected the values of school and official state institutions. In both cases, these girls rejected school values of propriety and behavior. They challenged dominant views of what a "proper girl" should be like by asserting the values of their own sexuality in sites where that sexuality was deemed inappropriate. Both McRobbie and Thomas emphasize the ways in which these girls use sexuality as opposition to the authority of the school or to middle-class definitions of femininity. As McRobbie comments:

> One way in which girls combat the class-based and oppressive features of the school is to assert their "femaleness," to introduce into the classroom their physical maturity in such a way as to force the teachers to take notice. A class instinct then finds expression at the level of jettisoning the official ideology for girls in the school (neatness, diligence, appliance, femininity, passivity, etc.) and replacing it with a *more* feminine, even sexual one.
>
> (1978, p. 104)

Thomas found that counterculture girls in opposition to school authority vacillated between aggressive defiance and an assertive and sometimes coy sexuality, particularly toward younger men teachers (Thomas, 1980, p. 148). What these girls appear to be doing, then, is using their sexuality as an act of resistance to accepted norms of female behavior. They take what society tells them is their most significant characteristic and exaggerate it as an assertion of their own individuality. Thus their aggressive use of sexuality becomes a form of power. This use of sexuality, however, is particularly true of working-class girls, and only in the context of situations defined by school or state authorities. Thomas found that antischool middle-class girls were much more likely to be immersed in the ideology of romance, and to view marriage as a way out of the boring and irrelevant world of school and the dead-end world of work (Thomas, 1980, p. 152). And working-class girls, although they would flaunt their sexuality in such sites as schools, were in fact very cautious in entering into sexual relationships, since they were very much aware of the dangers of becoming labeled "loose" in the context of their own working-class culture.

This attitude toward sexuality among working-class girls is supported by Wilson's study of "delinquent" or "semi-delinquent" girls in a northern England working-class community (Wilson, 1978). She found that girls categorized themselves into three groups based on sexual activity—virgins, one-man girls, and lays. Most of the girls categorized themselves as one-man girls, which meant they engaged in sex, but with an ideology of romance and the intention of marriage. For them, marriage seemed the only possible future. Thomas points out that in the groups of antischool girls she studied, working-class girls, although committed to marriage and in particular to motherhood, had far fewer illusions about what married life would be like. Middle-class girls, on the other hand, were immersed in an ideology of heterosexual romance (Thomas, 1980, p. 152). In fact, for working-class girls with no education and no skills, marriage is virtually an economic necessity. Thus what the girls have to oppose to the dominant-class culture and ideology of the school and the state is the assertion of their own exploited and submissive role in working-class culture. Just as Willis's lads emphasize their masculinity as manual workers and thus end up in dead-end and exploited unskilled jobs, so these girls emphasize their femininity in a traditional sense and end up exploited both in their unpaid labor in the home as well as in the marginal and low paying jobs they can get as waged workers. As Thomas comments:

> In this way, counter-school youth subcultures serve to reproduce working-class culture in the new generation; by providing a vehicle for the expression of opposition to the school's central academic purpose, they help to ensure the perpetuation of a voluntary labouring class under capitalism.
>
> (1980, p. 131)

In the case of girls, this reproduction is achieved not only through the conflict of class cultures, but within the context of patriarchal definitions of sexuality and exploitative sexual relationships that *appear* to provide girls with their only source of personal power.

Feminists have argued that a definition of working-class culture that only considers the public world of paid labor and public sites such as the pub or the street corner in fact ignores the domestic world of unpaid labor, sexuality, and childcare that is found in the private world of the family. They call for studies of girls and women that can reveal the ways in which their lives reflect the forces of production and reproduction and the ways in which they experience the social world and negotiate within it. Such studies should reveal the ways in which women's lives also reflect and are shaped by the forces of production and reproduction in different configurations but just as powerfully as men's. In this way, a more complete picture of working-class culture and of the process that Willis calls cultural production would be illuminated. Such studies would approach both public and private sites, definitions of work that include both waged and nonwaged work, and an analysis of sexuality and deep human needs as they are mediated in all aspects of class culture, for both men and women.

In order to understand the totality of working-class life both for men and women it is necessary to realize that culture is produced in *both* public and private sites and that social relationships, the production of culture, and the values given to both work and individual experience are profoundly influenced by both capitalism and patriarchy in both sites. This is not to argue that the public and private are unrelated. Quite the contrary. They are deeply related and intertwined as they make up a whole cultural world. But because boys and girls, men and women, are associated in sometimes very rigid ways with one sphere or the other, they work out individual and collective cultural responses that are quite different, though at the same time complementary. The central argument here is that to ignore the cultural world of women is to distort any understanding of the *totality* of working-class culture or resistance. A focus solely on the public male world of waged work and public oppositional culture is inadequate to come to grips with the ways in which the logics of both capitalism and patriarchy structure the individual experiences of working-class men and women and their common class culture as well as their separate men's and women's cultures.

The emphasis on the production of meaning and culture in public and private sites is, I think, instructive when we turn back to the question of schooling and the nature of the resistance of girls to the school. As both McRobbie and Thomas make clear, while the official ideology of schooling for girls sometimes reinforces the messages of working-class culture, at other times it is in opposition to that culture. But the working-class girls studied by McRobbie and Thomas fall back on an exaggerated form of the definitions of gender from wider working-class culture (as well as the ideological messages of the dominant culture as expressed in advertisements and the media). Their resistance thus simply embeds them more deeply in the culture of domination and submission, of double work, both waged and nonwaged.

The concept of resistance is used by McRobbie and Thomas to address the complexity of class and gender experience of working-class girls. But that concept is also useful in examining the nature of race and its relation to gender and class. The work of Fuller is particularly interesting in raising questions about the nature and implications of girls' resistance. Fuller studied groups of Afro-Caribbean, Indo-Pakistani, and white British girls in a London comprehensive school (Fuller, 1980; 1983). By making the category of race central to her work, she brings the realities of racism and the need to consider racial identity as well as gender and class position into her work in a fundamental way.[6]

Thus the question of cultural production and resistance takes on a more complex meaning, since these girls have to negotiate structures of what Amos and Parmar have called "triple oppression" (Amos and Parmar, 1981). Fuller explores the strategies these girls of color employ to try to gain some control over their lives. She points to three areas of control that emerged from her observation and interviews with these girls: "Firstly, their being controlled by others in and out of school; secondly, their wish for control for themselves at some time in the future; and lastly (and perhaps paradoxically) their need to exercise forms of self-control and resentment now in order to achieve self-determination later" (1983, p. 127). While Fuller has been influenced by the work of Willis and male sociological theorists of resistance, her work is more concerned with the ways in which girls, both individually and collectively, make sense of and try to negotiate oppressive social relationships and structures in order to gain more control over their own lives.

Fuller's work calls into question certain qualities of the concept of resistance that are relatively unquestioned in work that has focused on counter-school girls' subcultures. Basic to Fuller's analysis is the idea that critical understanding (what Willis would call "penetration") and the formation of an oppositional subcultural view of society is not necessarily tied to public antiauthority and counter-school groups. Instead, she argues in the case of black British girls in particular that they can combine a critical view of schools with an ability to manipulate and succeed within the school system of examinations and certification. She sees these girls' ability to combine two apparently contradictory perspectives as the result of their own social identities as black girls in a racist and sexist society. In their negotiation of these double or triple forms of oppression, the girls create complex responses. As Fuller points out:

> Indeed in regard to many aspects of their current and likely future lives some of the fifth-year girls were markedly *more* critical and politically sophisticated than most of the boys. Yet in terms of overt "symptoms" within the school the girls' opposition to what was actually and what in the future they thought was likely to be happening to them, did not come across as obviously oppositional or troublesome in the terms that others describe "troublesome" male pupils.
>
> (1983 p. 125)

Thus while the black girls were conscious of the racism and sexism they faced, they did not express that criticism as opposition to the school and the system of certification that the school represented. Instead, they overtly conformed to school mores (although in a way that was often on the edge of overt rejection of the rules) and more specifically saw the school as the means to resist the sexism of black British culture and the racism of white British culture. As Fuller puts it:

> I would suggest that in concentrating on pupils rather than on opposition we can get away from seeing pupils' cultural criticism as residing solely or even mainly in overt resistance to schooling. It may be that girls are too busy resisting other aspects of their life for resistance to schooling to have a high priority for them.
>
> (1983, p. 140)

Fuller argues that black girls saw the obtaining of academic qualifications as an assertion of their own sense of competence and intelligence that was denied them in black culture as girls. In her interviews, Fuller cites the girls' consciousness of and rejection of the sexist and sometimes sexually violent attitudes of black boys. In the face of this they asserted their own toughness and, in particular, their ability to work for wages and thus have a basis for their own identity and autonomy. They were also conscious of the double standard within their own families in which they were expected to do unpaid domestic work while their brothers were allowed and even expected to be out of the house. The success of black girls in state schools caused resentment among black boys, who saw this as a challenge to accepted women's roles. Here is Marcia, a black fifteen-year-old girl:

> I've always got my head in a book. I don't think they like it because they [black boys] are always commenting on it and they say, "You won't get anywhere," and sometimes I think they don't want me to learn or something like that, you know, but I spoke to my mum about it, and she said I shouldn't listen and I should keep working hard.
>
> (Fuller, 1983, p. 131)

This is not to argue that the sexism these black girls face is unique to black culture, or that they are not equally or more affected by racism. Fuller argues that it is in fact the conjunction of these two forms of oppression along with their assertion of their value as girls and as blacks that gives them the anger and power to resist dominant definitions of themselves and to assert their own control over their futures by taking control of the educational system of certification and examinations:

> The conjunction of all these—their positive identity as black but knowledge of racial discrimination in Britain, their positive identity as female but belief that both in Britain and in the Caribbean women were often accorded less than their due status—meant that the girls were angry at the foreclosing of options available to them as blacks and as women.
>
> (Fuller, 1980, p. 57)

Fuller's work raises important issues not only for the study of resistance and cultural production, but also about the nature of subcultures in general. First of all, the combination of critical consciousness and an apparent acceptance of the official ideology of school success needs to be examined. Fuller argues that these girls have achieved a certain "penetration" of the ideology of certification, in that they consciously intend to use school examinations to gain some control over their lives. However, this might also be viewed as a form of individual accommodation to existing social conditions rather than a collective cultural pattern that can be called resistance. I think the question that is not addressed in Fuller's work concerns the nature of class in capitalist societies. By positing only race and gender as relationships of oppression, Fuller's black girls fail to critique the nature of work in class society and thus in one sense oppose one relationship of oppression to another in just the way Willis's lads do. That is, just as the lads use racial and sexual domination to assert themselves and thus obscure their own class oppression and the nature of the work that they will do, so these black girls use "success" in school and an acceptance of the dominant definitions of work in capitalism to oppose the racism and sexism they experience in both black and white culture. The individual manipulation of school and certification may allow them to oppose oppressive aspects of their own lives, but without a more political and public expression, it may be more individual accommodation than collective resistance.

The other question raised by Fuller's work is about the nature of subcultures in general. Because, as we have seen, girls are usually excluded from the public arena of the street, the subcultural groups they form are private and exist in the domestic sphere of the home or in friendship groups among girls. While the black boys in the school in which Fuller worked joined a wider Rastafarian culture and adopted the style and clothes of that subculture, the girls were excluded. Thus what Fuller calls a subculture in fact was based on a kind of common understanding and attitude toward both whites and boys and an assertion of a common pride in being black and female. While this common understanding was very significant as the girls struggled to assert their own autonomy and to gain some measure of control over their lives, it did not have the weight of more public male subcultures. What Fuller does not address is the need for a more public and politically conscious assertion of black women's identity and strength that could be the basis for more organized resistance. As Amos and Parmar state:

> Existing political organizations cannot always incorporate all these struggles and although we feel that as black women we should organize with other black people against the racism in this society, and as part of the working class we should organize around the issues of work and non-work, and as women we should organize with other women, as black women we also need to organize separately around the issues that are particular to our experience as black women, experiences which come out of the triple oppression we face.
>
> (Amos and Parmar, 1981, p. 146)

Resistance is an important concept in looking at the lives of girls and women in schools, because it highlights their ability as human agents to make meaning and to act in social situations as well as to be acted upon. However, resistance must be used with some caution and careful definition if it is to help us understand social processes. We can see some of the difficulties involved in the use of the term resistance in Anyon's work on girls in fifth-grade classrooms. Anyon's research rests on a more general and shallow study of the cultural life of younger girls. She studied one hundred students in five different schools and depended on one seemingly quite structured interview with each child. Anyon's data is rather weak in comparison with the work of Fuller, McRobbie, and Thomas, but she does raise similar issues in her theoretical discussion. Like the cultural production theorists, Anyon questions the view of ideology as complete and uncontested. Instead, she argues that girls and women do not passively accept the dominant ideology of sexism, but rather negotiate ideology and needs. She argues that "gender development involves not so much passive imprinting as active response to social contradictions" (Anyon, 1984, p. 26).

Like Fuller, Anyon questions the depiction of resistance as solely found in public anti-social or counter-school actions. Instead, and following Genovese in his work on black slavery, she argues that women employ a "simultaneous process of accommodation and resistance" in their negotiation of social relationships. However, the line between accommodation and resistance is somewhat blurred in Anyon's discussion and it is not always clear when exaggerated feminine behavior or acquiescence to school authority can be viewed as accommodation or resistance. What is lacking in this work is a more rigorous discussion of what resistance might mean in complex and overlapping relationships of domination and oppression. Because Anyon does not locate the girls she interviews in a more complete social world, she is left with a description of attitudes or actions in school and must interpret them outside of a social totality. In this use, terms like resistance and accommodation become convenient categories into which observed behavior or beliefs can be slotted. Anyon's work is frustrating in this regard. Consider, for example her analysis of this incident in one of the working-class fifth-grade classrooms she observed:

> She told me that she wanted to be a veterinarian, and that she did not want to work in a factory like her mother did. I watched her persist at her desk to do her school work as the teacher screamed at the other children and gave confusing directions, and as belligerent boys roamed the classroom. Thus, I interpret her hard work not only as an accommodation to expectations that she do what is demanded in school, but also that through this accommodation she can resist both present and future social discomfort.
>
> (Anyon, 1984, p. 41)

There is something in this picture of a hostile school world ("screaming" teacher, "belligerent" boys) and the obedient, hardworking girl that smooths over the complexity of the competing forms of social power that this girl (not to mention the teacher and boys) negotiates in order to make sense of the world and to try to assert herself. I think the problem here rests ultimately in the lack of depth in our understanding of this girl, the school, the class and gender ideology that is embodied in the texts and social relationships of the school and among school chidren and in the dynamics of the girl's own family. In this case, the terms accommodation and resistance feel like empty generalities that can, in fact, be applied to any social action.

Anyon does make some valuable points about the need to make "resistance" cultural and public if it is to serve as the basis for social change. Like McRobbie, McCabe, and Garber, Anyon points out that individual resistance to sexism and the negotiation of existing concepts of femininity lead to an acceptance of the status quo: "While accommodation and resistance as modes of daily activity provide most females with ways of negotiating individually felt social conflict or oppression, this individual activity of everyday life remains just that: individual, fragmented, and isolated from group effort" (Anyon, 1984, p. 45). It has been argued that the failure of girls and women to participate in public antisocial groups and activities is the result of a certain psychological tendency to turn opposition and anger inward in private, self-destructive activities (Cloward and Piven, 1979). However, it may be that girls and women resist dominant and oppressive patriarchal values and relationships, though in different ways from men. But the question for women is how the human ability to create meaning and resist an imposed ideology can be turned to praxis and social transformation.

The work of Gaskell (1985) and Kessler, Ashenden, Connell, and Dowsett (1985) develops the question of women's relationships to schooling by examining the activities and choices of girls and women in particular school settings. Both of these studies argue that schools are contradictory sites for girls and women and, despite the existence of sexist texts and practices, provide the possibility of resistance to male hegemony on the part of both students and teachers. Kessler et al. argue:

> Yet the central fact, perhaps the most important point our interviews have demonstrated, is that the complex of gender inequality and patriarchal ideology is not a smoothly function-ing machine. It is a mass of tensions, contradictions, and complexities that always have the potential for change.
>
> (1985, p. 47)

By looking at girls and women teachers in both a working-class public school and an elite private school, Kessler et al. show the need to analyze power relations and the intersec-tion of family and school in each particular site. They argue that we need to understand the intersection of the family, the workplace, and the state in terms of sexual ideology and structural constraints on girls and women. Thus the struggles of elite girls will be quite different from those of working-class women teachers. To ignore class and racial difference in studying gender is to distort both the realities of their experience and the possibilities for resistance in each site.

Gaskell argues along similar lines. In studying working-class girls' course choices, Gaskell argues that girls were not simply "reproduced" by male hegemony, but that they made choices according to what their own understanding of the world was like:

> They knew, for their own good reasons, what the world was like, and their experience acted as a filter through which any new message was tested, confirmed, rejected, challenged, and reinterpreted. Changing their minds would have meant changing the world they experienced, not simply convincing them of a new set of ideals around equality of opportunity and the desirability of a different world.
>
> (1985, p. 58)

Gaskell emphasizes the need to hear the girls' own stories. She argues that reproduction theories that view women as simply the creation of male hegemony or sexist institutions obscure and fail to see the realities of women's strengths and agency.

> There is . . . a tradition in feminist scholarship that has emphasized that women's conscious-ness is not simply an internalization of male forms but contains its own alternative inter-pretations, commitments and connections . . . The relation between women's consciousness and man's world is complex and involves accommodation, resistance, and self-imposed and externally imposed silences. Correspondence does not account for their relationship.
>
> (1985, p. 58)

These studies point out and analyze oppressive practices and ideology, but at the same time insist that the schooling of girls is a complex process that contains contradictions and points of resistance which must be analyzed in each particular historical instance.

Throughout the feminist studies of resistance and cultural production certain themes are illuminated. First is the assertion that all people have the capacity to make meaning of their lives and to resist oppression. This is expressed in Giroux's remark that "inherent in a radical notion of resistance is an expressed hope, an element of transcendence" (1983, p. 108). Second, that that capacity to resist and to understand is limited and influenced by class, race, and gender position. People will use the means at hand, the power that they can employ to meet their needs and assert their humanity. This is clear in the work of Fuller, Gaskell, and Kessler, Ashenden, Connell, and Dowsett. Third, as is clear from the work of Willis, McRobbie, and Thomas in particular, the various "solutions" sought by people embedded in sexist, racist, and classist society can lead in fact to deeper forms of domin-ation and the oppression of others. Willis's lads "partially penetrate" the logic of capital-ism, but that rejection leads them to a rejection of mental work and to the celebration of a masculinity defined by sexism and racism. McRobbie's and Thomas's girls' rejection of school ideology leads them to a definition of their own sexuality that leads back to the oppressive sexism of working-class culture. And Fuller's girls, in succeeding in school and gaining certification, assert their abilities and value as black women, but accept the logic of work in capitalism. For women, who are so often excluded from the public sphere, the question of whether resistance can lead to change if it is only expressed in individual critique or private opposition is a very real one. And this leads back to the schools. Can schools become a possible "public sphere" for the encouragement of resistance and the building of a critical counter-hegemony for girls?

Feminist Teaching as Counter-Hegemony

I have argued that the concept of resistance has been used as a heuristic device to explore the possibilities of human agency. But various theorists have argued that we need to expand our view of agency to include not only resistance in the form of various kinds of opposition to oppressive beliefs and practices, but also to include more critical and politicized work in the form of organized and conscious collective oppositional actions. This kind of opposition has been called counter-hegemony. By this is meant the creation of a self-conscious analysis of a situation and the development of collective practices and organization that can oppose the hegemony of the existing order and begin to build the base for a new understanding and transformation of society. Feminist counter-hegemonic teaching has been developed and refined at the university level in a variety of women's studies programs (Bunch and Pollack, 1983; Spanier, Bloom and Borovak, 1984). In these programs both feminist theory and methods have been developed to provide a counter-hegemonic vision and critique (Bunch, 1983; Schniedewind, 1983). Teaching in public schools, although more profoundly bounded by institutional constraints, also con-tains the possibility of transformative work. This does not imply that this work will be achieved without enormous and sometimes overpowering opposition. As Freire says, critical teaching in dominant institutions means that teachers are constantly living a con-tradiction. But possibilities for critical work exist within that very contradiction. It is vital that teachers recognize not only the structural constraints under which they work, but also the potential inherent in teaching for transformative and political work. As Connell comments:

> The doctrine that tells teachers the schools are captive to capitalism and exhorts them to get on with the revolution outside, could not be more mistaken; it is teachers' work as teachers that is central to the remaking of the social patterns investing education.
>
> (1985, p. 4)

If the work of critical teachers can be viewed as counter-hegemonic work, the latent and unarticulated resistance of students can in turn become the focus of critical teaching. As Giroux points out, "the concept of resistance highlights the need for classroom teachers to decipher how modes of cultural production displayed by subordinate groups can be analyzed to reveal both their limits and their possibilities for enabling critical thinking, analytic discourse, and new modes of intellectual appropriation" (1983, p. 111). Thus the ability of students to resist and the forms of subcultural resistance become the focus of critical teaching, which can be part of the creation of a counterhegemony.

As several feminist educational theorists have argued, the schools can provide the site for feminist teachers to raise issues of sexism and gender oppression. Kelly and Nihlen, for example, mention the potential significance of the women's movement in legitimating an alternative vision of gender. As they comment, "It well may be—and more research is needed—that the presence of a woman's movement provides a means of making resistance 'count' and sets the tenor for the renegotiation of knowledge within the classroom" (1982, p. 176). McRobbie and Garber have argued along the same lines that the school can be a progressive force if it can serve as a site for feminist teachers to introduce the ideas of the women's movement to girls and to open up a discussion of the structural limitations and oppression they face (McRobbie, 1978, p. 102). Kessler et al. argue the need to "democratize the curriculum by reorganizing knowledge to advantage the disadvantaged; and to mobilize support for democratization of the schools in relation to gender, as much as other structures of power" (1985, p. 46).

This view of teaching as critical work leads us to see the resistance of students as an important basis for the building of a counter-hegemony, as teachers and students together struggle to understand the forces acting upon their lives. Many feminists have argued that feminist teaching can contribute to the building of this alternative vision of social reality and morality (Hartsock, 1979; Lather, 1984). The outline of this kind of argument can be found in the work of Lather (1984). Lather's work has focused on the impact of feminism and women's studies courses on the education of teachers. She has argued that while male critical educational theorists speak of the need for critical teaching, they have overlooked the power of feminism to challenge the status quo through the creation of women's studies courses and critiques of sexist texts and practices. Looking back to Gramsci for a theoretical perspective to understand the work of feminist teachers, she argues that his call for a progressive social group who can create what he calls a new historical bloc can be found in the women's movement.

> Adopting gender as a basic analytic tool will enable critical theory to see what is right under its nose: the possibilities for fundamental social changes that open up when we put women at the center of our transformation.
>
> (Lather, 1984, p. 52)

In Gramsci's view, revolutionary theory had to be grounded in the struggles of everyday life. Lather argues that feminist theory and the women's movement are grounded in precisely these struggles to make the personal political. A critical, materialist feminism could illuminate these relationships of personal and public and begin to create a new politics that would be truly revolutionary. Lather applies the Gramscian concept of counter-hegemony to this feminist work. She emphasizes the difference between counter-hegemony and the more commonly used term of *resistance*. *Resistance* is "usually informal, disorganized, and apolitical," but *counter-hegemony* implies a more critical theoretical understanding and is expressed in organized and active political opposition. As Lather defines it:

> The task of counter-hegemonic groups is the development of counter-institutions, ideologies, and cultures that provide an ethical alternative to the dominant hegemony, a lived experience of how the world can be different.
>
> (1984, p. 55)

While the starting point of counter-hegemonic work is the world of students, both their oppression and their opposition, it must move beyond that point to provide more democratic relationships, an alternative value system and a critique of existing society.[7]

While feminist teaching has focused on gender oppression, we need to remember that feminists in teaching and outside of it tend to be middle class and white. Thus although they share with working-class girls the common oppression of being female in a patriarchal and sexist society, they are divided from them by class and, in the case of girls of color, by race as well. Nonetheless, the work of conscious feminists *is* important in building counter-hegemony; schools can be sites for critical teaching and work in specific sites and under certain conditions. What we need to do is to be very clear about the specific meanings of class, race, and gender for people in differing relationships of control and power in a society dominated by capitalism, racism, and patriarchy. We need to locate ourselves in these complex webs of relationships and then attempt to act at whatever sites we find ourselves, in ways that will encourage both resistance to oppression and the building of a counter-hegemony through critical understanding.

Notes

1. See Jagger (1983) for the clearest and most accessible discussion of the differences among radical feminism, liberal feminism, and socialist feminism in terms of feminist theory in general.

2. Significant examples of this approach are Frazier and Sadker (1973); Levy (1974); Chetwynd and Harnett (1978); Byrne (1978); and Delamont (1980). See Acker (1982) for an overview of various feminist approaches to the question of the relationship of gender and schooling from the perspective of the early 1980s, particularly with reference to British studies.

3. Feminist inquiry into the relation of gender and schooling has continued in recent British works which have addressed the existence of sex bias in schools and have begun to focus on potential strategies to redress those practices from a variety of theoretical perspectives. *Girl-friendly schooling* (1985), a selection of papers from the 1984 conference on girl-friendly schooling, provides both studies of sexist practices and discussions of feminist intervention and policy suggestions. Weiner's *Just a bunch of girls* (1985) contributes a valuable perspective on race that has been missing from most accounts. Mahony's *Schools for the boys* (1985) presents a powerful indictment of co-education from a radical feminist perspective. Like Walkerdine (1981) Mahony raises significant questions about the nature of male sexual power and privilege that have not been adequately addressed in either liberal or socialist feminist studies.

4. Representative theorists in this tradition are Barrett (1980); David (1980); Deem (1978; 1980); Kelly and Nihlen (1982); and Wolpe (1978; 1981).

5. As Mannicom has shown, this shared nurturing role of mothers and primary teachers does not necessarily lead to mutual understanding and cooperation between mothers and primary teachers, even though sexist assumptions about the "natural" nurturing qualities of women are at work in both instances (Mannicom, 1984).

6. See also the recent articles by Brak and Mihas (1985), Foster (1985) and Riley (1985).

7. Examples of curriculum and teaching can be found that begin to bring together feminist and critical thinking. For example, a group of radical teachers at the Group School in Cambridge, Mass. created various curricula with working-class girls. This work has been published as *Changing learning, changing lives* (Gates, Klaw, and Steinberg, 1979). These teachers used the life experiences of working-class girls to draw out themes of race, class, and gender for critical analysis. Schneidewind and Davidson have provided a feminist curriculum for public schools in *Open minds to equality* (1983). McRobbie and her associate Trisha McCabe have published *Feminism for girls*, directed at both students and teachers and youth workers. McRobbie and McCabe raise questions of the transmission of images and values through the media and texts, both in school and outside of school. Articles in this collection critique such areas as the depiction of girls in the literature curriculum, the nature of secretarial work, and the overt and hidden meanings of *Jackie*, the British equivalent of *Seventeen*. In providing analyses and critiques of sites and texts that make up the cultural world of teenage girls, McRobbie and McCabe hope to provide these girls with the kind of critical vision that will lead them to see their experiences critically as socially created and thus open to resistance and change.

References

Acker, Sandra. No-woman's land: British sociology of education 1960–1979. *The Sociological Review* (1981) 29, 1.

Amos, Valerie and Parmar, Pratibha. Resistances and responses: The experiences of black girls in Britain. In Angela McRobbie and Trisha McCabe, eds., *Feminism for girls.* London and Boston: Routledge and Kegan Paul, 1981.

Anyon, Jean. Intersections of gender and class: Accommodation and resistance by working class and affluent females to contradictory sex-role ideologies. *Journal of Education* (1984) 166, 1, 25–48.

Arnot, Madeleine. Male hegemony, social class and women's education. *Journal of Education* (1982) 164, 1, 64–89.

Barrett, Michele. *Women's oppression today.* London: Virago Press, 1980.

Bunch, Charlotte. Not by degrees: Feminist theory and education. In Charlotte Bunch and Sandra Pollack, eds. *Learning our way.* Trumansburg, N.Y.: Crossing Press, 1983.

Bunch, Charlotte and Pollack, Sandra, eds. *Learning our way.* Trumansburg, N.Y.: Crossing Press. 1983.

Cloward, Richard and Piven, Frances Fox. Hidden protest: The channeling of female innovation and resistance. *Signs* (1979) 4, 4, 651–669.

Connell, R. W. *Teachers' work.* London: George Allen and Unwin, 1985.

Connell, R. W., Dowsett, G. W., Kessler, S., and Aschenden, D. J. *Making the difference.* Boston: Allen and Unwin, 1982.

Davies, Lynn. Gender, resistance and power. In Stephen Walker and Len Barton, eds. *Gender class and education.* Lewes, Sussex: The Falmer Press, 1983.

Deem, Rosemary. *Women and schooling.* London and Boston: Routledge and Kegan Paul, 1978.

——— . ed. *Schooling for women's work.* London and Boston: Routledge and Kegan Paul, 1980.

Ehrenreich, Barbara. Life without father: Reconsidering socialist-feminist theory. *Socialist Review* (Jan.–Feb., 1984) 73, 48–58.

Eisenstein, Zillah. ed. *Capitalist patriarchy and the case for socialist feminism.* New York and London: Monthly Review Press, 1979.

——— , Qualified criticism, critical qualifications. In Jane Purvis and Margaret Hales. *Achievement and inequality in education.* London: Routledge and Kegan Paul, 1983.

Fuller, Mary. Black girls in a London comprehensive school. In Rosemary Deem, ed. *Schooling for women's work.* London and Boston: Routledge and Kegan Paul, 1980.

——— . Qualified criticism, critical qualifications. In Jane Purvis and Margaret Hales. *Achievement and inequality in education.* London: Routledge and Kegan Paul, 1983.

Gaskell, Jane. Course enrollment in the high school: The perspective of working class females. *Sociology of Education* (1985) 58, 1, 48–59.

Giroux, Henry. *Theory, resistance, and education.* South Hadley, Mass.: Bergin and Garvey, 1983.

Hartsock, Nancy. Feminist theory and the development of revolutionary strategy. In Zillah Eisenstein, ed. *Capitalist patriarchy and the case for socialist feminism.* London and New York: Monthly Review Press, 1979.

Hartsock, Nancy. *Money, Sex, and Power: Toward a Feminist Historical Materialism.* New York: Longman, 1983.

Hartmann, Heidi. The unhappy marriage of socialism and feminism. In Lydia Sargent, ed. *Women and Revolution.* Boston: South End Press, 1981.

Jagger, Alison. *Feminist theory and human nature.* Sussex: Harvester Press, 1983.

Kelly, Gayle and Nihlen, Ann. Schooling and the reproduction of patriarchy: Unequal workloads, unequal rewards. In Michael Apple, ed. *Cultural and economic reproduction in education.* London and Boston: Routledge and Kegan Paul, 1982.

Kessler, S., Ashenden, R., Connell, R., and Dowsett, G. Gender relations in secondary schooling. *Sociology of Education* (1985) 58, 1, 34–48.

Kuhn, Annette and Wolpe, AnnMarie, eds. *Feminism and materialism.* London and Boston: Routledge and Kegan Paul, 1978.

Lather, Patti. Critical theory, curricular transformation and feminist mainstreaming. *Journal of Education* (1984) 166, 1, 49–62.

McRobbie, Angela. Working class girls and the culture of femininity. In Centre for Contemporary Cultural Studies Women's Group. *Women take issue.* London: Hutchison, 1978.

——— . Settling accounts with subcultures, *Screen Education* (1980) 34, 37–51.

Reiter, Rayna, ed. *Toward an anthropology of women.* New York and London: Monthly Review Press, 1975.

Rowbotham, Sheila, Segal, Lynne, and Wainwright, Hilary. *Beyond the fragments: Feminism and the making of socialism.* Boston: Alyson Publications, 1981.

Rubin, Gayle. The traffic in women: Notes on the political economy of sex. In Rayna Reiter, ed. *Toward an anthropology of women.* New York and London: Monthly Review Press, 1975.

Schniedewind, Nancy. Feminist values: Guidelines for teaching methodology in women's studies. In Charlotte Bunch and Sandra Pollack, eds. *Learning our way: Essays in feminist education.* Trumansburg, N.Y.: Crossing Press, 1983.

Spanier, Bonnie, Bloom, Alex, and Boroviak, Darlene. *Toward a balanced curriculum.* Cambridge, Mass.: Schenkman Publishing Company, 1984.

Tax, Meredith. Learning how to bake. *Socialist Review* (Jan.–Feb. 1984) 73, 36–41.

Thomas, Claire. Girls and counter-school culture. *Melbourne Working Papers.* Melbourne, 1980.

Wilson, Deirdre. Sexual codes and conduct: A study of teenage girls. In Carol Smart and Barry Smart, eds. *Women, sexuality and social control.* London and Boston: Routledge and Kegan Paul, 1978.

Wolpe, AnnMarie. Education and the sexual division of labour. In Annette Kuhn and AnnMarie Wolpe, eds. *Feminism and materialism.* Boston and London: Routledge and Kegan Paul, 1978.

Women's Study Group. *Women take issue.* London: CCCS/Hutchison, 1978.

12

Sexuality, Schooling, and Adolescent Females: The Missing Discourse of Desire

Michelle Fine

Since late 1986, popular magazines and newspapers have printed steamy stories about education and sexuality. Whether the controversy surrounds sex education or school-based health clinics (SBHCs), public discourses of adolescent sexuality are represented forcefully by government officials, New Right spokespersons, educators, "the public," feminists, and health-care professionals. These stories offer the authority of "facts," insights into the political controversies, and access to unacknowledged fears about sexuality (Foucault, 1980). Although the facts usually involve the adolescent female body, little has been heard from young women themselves.

This article examines these diverse perspectives on adolescent sexuality and, in addition, presents the views of a group of adolescent females. The article is informed by a study of numerous current sex education curricula, a year of negotiating for inclusion of lesbian and gay sexuality in a citywide sex education curriculum, and interviews and observations gathered in New York City sex education classrooms.[1] The analysis examines the desires, fears, and fantasies which give structure and shape to silences and voices concerning sex education and school-based health clinics in the 1980s.

Despite the attention devoted to teen sexuality, pregnancy, and parenting in this country, and despite the evidence of effective interventions and the widespread public support expressed for these interventions (Harris, 1985), the systematic implementation of sex education and SBHCs continues to be obstructed by the controversies surrounding them (Kantrowitz et al., 1987; Leo, 1986). Those who resist sex education or SBHCs often present their views as based on rationality and a concern for protecting the young. For such opponents, sex education raises questions of promoting promiscuity and immorality, and of undermining family values. Yet the language of the challenges suggests an affect substantially more profound and primitive. Gary Bauer, Undersecretary of Education in the U.S. Department of Education, for example, constructs an image of immorality littered by adolescent sexuality and drug abuse:

> There is ample impressionistic evidence to indicate that drug abuse and promiscuity are not independent behaviors. When inhibitions fall, they collapse across the board. When people of any age lose a sense of right and wrong, the loss is not selective. . . . [T]hey are all expressions of the same ethical vacuum among many teens. . . . (1986)

Even Surgeon General C. Everett Koop, a strong supporter of sex education, recently explained: "[W]e have to be as explicit as necessary. . . . You can't talk of the dangers of snake poisoning and not mention snakes" (quoted in Leo, 1986, p. 54). Such commonly used and often repeated metaphors associate adolescent sexuality with victimization and danger.

Yet public schools have rejected the task of sexual dialogue and critique, or what has been called "sexuality education." Within today's standard sex education curricula and many public school classrooms, we find: (1) the authorized suppression of a discourse of female sexual desire; (2) the promotion of a discourse of female sexual victimization; and (3) the explicit privileging of married heterosexuality over other practices of sexuality. One finds an unacknowledged social ambivalence about female sexuality which ideologically separates the female sexual agent, or subject, from her counterpart, the female sexual victim. The adolescent woman of the 1980s is constructed as the latter. Educated primarily as the potential victim of male sexuality, she represents no subject in her own right. Young women continue to be taught to fear and defend in isolation from exploring desire, and in this context there is little possibility of their developing a critique of gender or sexual arrangements.

Prevailing Discourses of Female Sexuality inside Public Schools

> If the body is seen as endangered by uncontrollable forces, then presumably this is a society or social group which fears change—change which it perceived simultaneously as powerful and beyond its control.
>
> (Smith-Rosenberg, 1978, p. 229)

Public schools have historically been the site for identifying, civilizing, and containing that which is considered uncontrollable. While evidence of sexuality is everywhere within public high schools—in the halls, classrooms, bathrooms, lunchrooms, and the library—official sexuality education occurs sparsely: in social studies, biology, sex education, or inside the nurse's office. To understand how sexuality is managed inside schools, I examined the major discourses of sexuality which characterize the national debates over sex education and SBHCs. These discourses are then tracked as they weave through the curricula, classrooms, and halls of public high schools.

The first discourse, *sexuality as violence*, is clearly the most conservative, and equates adolescent heterosexuality with violence. At the 1986 American Dreams Symposium on education, Phyllis Schlafly commented: "Those courses on sex, abuse, incest, AIDS, they are all designed to terrorize our children. We should fight their existence, and stop putting terror in the hearts and minds of our youngsters." One aspect of this position, shared by women as politically distinct as Schlafly and the radical feminist lawyer Catherine MacKinnon (1983), views heterosexuality as essentially violent and coercive. In its full conservative form, proponents call for the elimination of sex education and clinics and urge complete reliance on the family to dictate appropriate values, mores, and behaviors.

Sexuality as violence presumes that there is a causal relationship between official silence about sexuality and a decrease in sexual activity—therefore, by not teaching about sexuality, adolescent sexual behavior will not occur. The irony, of course, lies in the empirical evidence. Fisher, Byrne, and White (1983) have documented sex-negative attitudes and contraceptive use to be negatively correlated. In their study, sex-negative attitudes do not discourage sexual activity, but they do discourage responsible use of contraception. Teens who believe sexual involvement is wrong deny responsibility for contraception. To accept responsibility would legitimate "bad" behavior. By contrast, Fisher et al. (1983) found that adolescents with sex-positive attitudes tend to be both more consistent and more positive about contraceptive use. By not teaching about sexuality, or by teaching sex-negative attitudes, schools apparently will not forestall sexual activity, but may well discourage responsible contraception.

The second discourse, *sexuality as victimization*, gathers a much greater following. Female adolescent sexuality is represented as a moment of victimization in which the dangers of heterosexuality for adolescent women (and, more recently, of homosexuality for adolescent men) are prominent. While sex may not be depicted as inherently violent, young women (and today, men) learn of their vulnerability to potential male predators.

To avoid being victimized, females learn to defend themselves against disease, pregnancy, and "being used." The discourse of victimization supports sex education, including AIDS education, with parental consent. Suggested classroom activities emphasize "saying no," practicing abstinence, enumerating the social and emotional risks of sexual intimacy, and listing the possible diseases associated with sexual intimacy. The language, as well as the questions asked and not asked, represents females as the actual and potential victims of male desire. In exercises, role plays, and class discussions, girls practice resistance to trite lines, unwanted hands, opened buttons, and the surrender of other "bases" they are not prepared to yield. The discourses of violence and victimization both portray males as potential predators and females as victims. Three problematic assumptions underlie these two views:

— First, female subjectivity, including the desire to engage in sexual activity, is placed outside the prevailing conversation (Vance, 1984).
— Second, both arguments present female victimization as contingent upon unmarried heterosexual involvement—rather than inherent in existing gender, class, and racial arrangements (Rubin, 1984). While feminists have long fought for the legal and social acknowledgment of sexual violence against women, most have resisted the claim that female victimization hinges primarily upon sexual involvement with men. The full range of victimization of women—at work, at home, on the streets—has instead been uncovered. The language and emotion invested in these two discourses divert attention away from structures, arrangements, and relationships which oppress women in general, and low-income women and women of color in particular (Lorde, 1980).
— Third, the messages, while narrowly anti-sexual, nevertheless buttress traditional heterosexual arrangements. These views assume that as long as females avoid premarital sexual relations with men, victimization can be avoided. Ironically, however, protection from male victimization is available primarily through marriage—by coupling with a man. The paradoxical message teaches females to fear the very men who will ultimately protect them.

The third discourse, *sexuality as individual morality*, introduces explicit notions of sexual subjectivity for women. Although quite judgmental and moralistic, this discourse values women's sexual decisionmaking as long as the decisions made are for premarital abstinence. For example, Secretary of Education William Bennett urges schools to teach "morality literacy" and to educate towards "modesty," "chastity," and "abstinence" until marriage. The language of self-control and self-respect reminds students that sexual immorality breeds not only personal problems but also community tax burdens.

The debate over morality in sex education curricula marks a clear contradiction among educational conservatives over whether and how the state may intervene in the "privacy of families." Non-interventionists, including Schlafly and Onalee McGraw, argue that educators should not teach about sexuality at all. To do so is to take a particular moral position which subverts the family. Interventionists, including Koop, Bennett, and Bauer, argue that schools should teach about sexuality by focusing on "good values," but disagree about how. Koop proposes open discussion of sexuality and the use of condoms, while Bennett advocates "sexual restraint" ("Koop AIDS Stand Assailed," 1987). Sexuality in this discourse is posed as a test of self-control; individual restraint triumphs over social temptation. Pleasure and desire for women as sexual subjects remain largely in the shadows, obscured from adolescent eyes.

The fourth discourse, a *discourse of desire*, remains a whisper inside the official work of U.S. public schools. If introduced at all, it is as an interruption of the ongoing conversation (Snitow, Stansell, & Thompson, 1983). The naming of desire, pleasure, or sexual entitlement, particularly for females, barely exists in the formal agenda of public schooling on sexuality. When spoken, it is tagged with reminders of "consequences"—emotional, physical, moral, reproductive, and/or financial (Freudenberg, 1987). A genuine discourse of desire would invite adolescents to explore what feels good and bad, desirable and undesirable, grounded in experiences, needs, and limits. Such a discourse would release females from a position of receptivity, enable an analysis of the dialectics of victimization and pleasure, and would pose female adolescents as subjects of sexuality, initiators as well as negotiators (Golden, 1984; Petchesky, 1984; Thompson, 1983).

In Sweden, where sex education has been offered in schools since the turn of the twentieth century, the State Commission on Sex Education recommends teaching students to "acquire a knowledge . . . [which] will equip them to experience sexual life as a source of happiness and joy in fellowship with other [people]" (Brown, 1983, p. 88). The teachers' handbook goes on, "The many young people who wish to wait [before initiating sexual activity] and those who have had early sexual relations should experience, in class, [the feeling] that they are understood and accepted" (p. 93). Compare this to an exercise suggested in a major U.S. metropolitan sex education curriculum: "Discuss and evaluate: things which may cause teenagers to engage in sexual relations before they are ready to assume the responsibility of marriage" (see Philadelphia School District, 1986; and New York City Board of Education, 1984).

A discourse of desire, though seldom explored in U.S. classrooms, does occur in less structured school situations. The following excerpts, taken from group and individual student interviews, demonstrate female adolescents' subjective experiences of body and desire as they begin to articulate notions of sexuality.

In some cases young women pose a critique of marriage:

> I'm still in love with Simon, but I'm seeing Jose. He's OK but he said, "Will you be my girl?" I hate that. It feels like they own you. Like I say to a girlfried, "What's wrong? You look terrible!" and she says, "I'm married!"
>
> (Millie, a 16-year-old student from the Dominican Republic)

In other cases they offer stories of their own victimization:

> It's not like last year. Then I came to school regular. Now my old boyfriend, he waits for me in front of my building every morning and he fights with me. Threatens me, gettin' all bad. . . . I want to move out of my house and live 'cause he ain't gonna stop no way.
>
> (Sylvia, age 17, about to drop out of twelfth grade)

Some even speak of desire:

> I'm sorry I couldn't call you last night about the interview, but my boyfriend came back from [the] Navy and I wanted to spend the night with him, we don't get to see each other much.
>
> (Shandra, age 17, after a no-show for an interview)

In a context in which desire is not silenced, but acknowledged and discussed, conversations with adolescent women can, as seen here, educate through a dialectic of victimization and pleasure. Despite formal silencing, it would be misleading to suggest that talk of desire never emerges within public schools. Notwithstanding a political climate organized around the suppression of this conversation, some teachers and community advocates continue to struggle for an empowering sex education curriculum both in and out of the high school classroom.

Family life curricula and/or plans for a school-based health clinic have been carefully generated in many communities. Yet they continue to face loud and sometimes violent resistance by religious and community groups, often from outside the district lines (Boffey, 1987; "Chicago School Clinic," 1986; Dowd, 1986; Perlez, 1986a, 1986b; Rohter, 1985). In other communities, when curricula or clinics have been approved with little overt confrontation, monies for training are withheld. For example, in New York City in 1987, $1.7 million was initially requested to implement training on the Family Life education curriculum. As sex educators confronted community and religious groups, the inclusion of some topics as well as the language of others were continually negotiated. Ultimately, the Chancellor requested only $600,000 for training, a sum substantially inadequate to the task.[2]

In this political context many public school educators nevertheless continue to take personal and professional risks to create materials and foster classroom environments which speak fully to the sexual subjectivities of young women and men. Some operate within the privacy of their classrooms, subverting the official curriculum and engaging students in critical discussion. Others advocate publicly for enriched curricula and training. A few have even requested that community-based advocates *not* agitate for official curricular change, so "we [teachers] can continue to do what we do in the classroom, with nobody looking over our shoulders. You make a big public deal of this, and it will blow open."[3] Within public school classrooms, it seems that female desire may indeed be addressed when educators act subversively. But in the typical sex education classroom, silence, and therefore distortion, surrounds female desire.

The blanketing of female sexual subjectivity in public school classrooms, in public discourse, and in bed will sound familiar to those who have read Luce Irigaray (1980) and Helene Cíxous (1981). These French feminists have argued that expressions of female voice, body, and sexuality are essentially inaudible when the dominant language and ways of viewing are male. Inside the hegemony of what they call The Law of the Father, female desire and pleasure can gain expression only in the terrain already charted by men (see also Burke, 1980). In the public school arena, this constriction of what is called sexuality allows girls one primary decision—to say yes or no—to a question not necessarily their own. A discourse of desire in which young women have a voice would be informed and generated out of their own socially constructed sexual meanings. It is to these expressions that we now turn.

The Bodies of Female Adolescents: Voices and Structured Silences

If four discourses can be distinguished among the many positions articulated by various "authorities," the sexual meanings voiced by female adolescents defy such classification. A discourse of desire, though absent in the "official" curriculum, is by no means missing from the lived experiences or commentaries of young women. This section introduces their sexual thoughts, concerns, and meanings, as represented by a group of Black and Latina female adolescents—students and dropouts from a public high school in New York City serving predominantly low-income youths. In my year at this comprehensive high school I had frequent opportunity to speak with adolescents and listen to them talk about sex. The comments reported derive from conversations between the young women and their teachers, among themselves, and with me, as researcher. During conversations, the young women talked freely about fears and, in the same breath, asked about passions. Their struggle to untangle issues of gender, power, and sexuality underscores the fact that, for them, notions of sexual negotiation cannot be separated from sacrifice and nurturance.

The adolescent female rarely reflects simply on sexuality. Her sense of sexuality is informed by peers, culture, religion, violence, history, passion, authority, rebellion, body, past and future, and gender and racial relations of power (Espin, 1984; Omolade, 1983). The adolescent woman herself assumes a dual consciousness—at once taken with the excitement of actual/anticipated sexuality and consumed with anxiety and worry. While too few safe spaces exist for adolescent women's exploration of sexual subjectivities, there are all too many dangerous spots for their exploitation.

Whether in a classroom, on the street, at work, or at home, the adolescent female's sexuality is negotiated by, for, and despite the young woman herself. Patricia, a young Puerto Rican woman who worried about her younger sister, relates: "You see, I'm the love child and she's the one born because my mother was raped in Puerto Rico. Her father's in jail now, and she feels so bad about the whole thing so she acts bad." For Patricia, as for the many young women who have experienced and/or witnessed sexual violence, discussions of sexuality merge representations of passion with violence. Often the initiator of conversation among peers about virginity, orgasm, "getting off," and pleasure, Patricia mixed sexual talk freely with references to force and violence. She is a poignant narrator who illustrates, from the female adolescent's perspective, that sexual victimization and desire coexist (Benjamin, 1983).

Sharlene and Betty echo this braiding of danger and desire. Sharlene explained: "Boys always be trying to get into my panties," and Betty added: "I don't be needin' a man who won't give me no pleasure but take my money and expect me to take care of him." This powerful commentary on gender relations, voiced by Black adolescent females, was inseparable from their views of sexuality. To be a woman was to be strong, independent, and reliable—but not too independent for fear of scaring off a man.

Deirdre continued this conversation, explicitly pitting male fragility against female strength: "Boys in my neighborhood ain't wrapped so tight. Got to be careful how you treat them. . . ." She reluctantly admitted that perhaps it is more important for Black males than females to attend college, "Girls and women, we're stronger, we take care of ourselves. But boys and men, if they don't get away from the neighborhood, they end up in jail, on drugs or dead . . . or wack [crazy]."

These young women spoke often of anger at males, while concurrently expressing a strong desire for male attention: "I dropped out 'cause I fell in love, and couldn't stop thinking of him." An equally compelling desire was to protect young males—particularly Black males—from a system which "makes them wack." Ever aware of the ways that institutional racism and the economy have affected Black males, these young women seek pleasure but also offer comfort. They often view self-protection as taking something away from young men. Lavanda offered a telling example: "If I ask him to use a condom, he won't feel like a man."

In order to understand the sexual subjectivities of young women more completely, educators need to reconstruct schooling as an empowering context in which we listen to and work with the meanings and experiences of gender and sexuality revealed by the adolescents themselves. When we refuse that responsibility, we prohibit an education which adolescents wholly need and deserve. My classroom observations suggest that such education is rare.

Ms. Rosen, a teacher of a sex education class, opened one session with a request: "You should talk to your mother or father about sex before you get involved." Nilda initiated what became an informal protest by a number of Latino students: "Not our parents! We tell them one little thing and they get crazy. My cousin got sent to Puerto Rico to live with her religious aunt, and my sister got beat 'cause my father thought she was with a boy." For these adolescents, a safe space for discussion, critique, and construction of sexualities was not something they found in their homes. Instead, they relied on school, the spot they chose for the safe exploration of sexualities.

The absence of safe spaces for exploring sexuality affects all adolescents. It was paradoxical to realize that perhaps the only students who had an in-school opportunity for critical sexual discussion in the comfort of peers were the few students who had organized the Gay and Lesbian Association (GALA) at the high school. While most lesbian, gay, or bisexual students were undoubtedly closeted, those few who were "out" claimed this public space for their display and for their sanctuary. Exchanging support when families and peers would offer little, GALA members worried that so few students were willing to come out, and that so many suffered the assaults of homophobia individually. The gay and lesbian rights movement had powerfully affected these youngsters, who were comfortable enough to support each other in a place not considered very safe—a public high school in which echoes of "faggot!" fill the halls.

In the absence of an education which explores and unearths danger and desire, sexuality education classes typically provide little opportunity for discussions beyond those constructed around superficial notions of male heterosexuality (see Kelly, 1986, for a counterexample). Male pleasure is taught, albeit as biology. Teens learn about "wet dreams" (as the onset of puberty for males), "erection" (as the preface to intercourse), and "ejaculation" (as the act of inseminating). Female pleasures and questions are far less often the topic of discussion. Few voices of female sexual agency can be heard. The language of victimization and its underlying concerns—"Say No," put a brake on his sexuality, don't encourage—ultimately deny young women the right to control their own sexuality by providing no access to a legitimate position of sexual subjectivity. Often conflicted about self-representation, adolescent females spend enormous amounts of time trying to "save it," "lose it," convince others that they have lost or saved it, or trying to be "discreet" instead of focusing their energies in ways that are sexually autonomous, responsible, and pleasurable. In classroom observations, girls who were heterosexually active rarely spoke, for fear of being ostracized (Fine, 1986). Those who were heterosexual virgins had the same worry. And most students who were gay, bisexual, or lesbian remained closeted, aware of the very real dangers of homophobia.

Occasionally, the difficult and pleasurable aspects of sexuality were discussed together, coming either as an interruption, or because an educational context was constructed. During a social studies class, for example, Catherine, the proud mother of two-year-old Tiffany, challenged an assumption underlying the class discussion—that teen motherhood devastates mother and child; "If I didn't get pregnant I would have continued on a downward path, going nowhere. They say teenage pregnancy is bad for you, but it was good for me. I know I can't mess around now, I got to worry about what's good for Tiffany and for me."

Another interruption came from Opal, a young Black student. Excerpts from her hygiene class follow.

Teacher: Let's talk about teenage pregnancy.
Opal: How come girls in the locker room say, "You a virgin?" and if you say "Yeah" they laugh and say "Ohh, you're a virgin. . . ." And some Black teenagers, I don't mean to be racial, when they get ready to tell their mothers they had sex, some break on them and some look funny. My friend told her mother and she broke all the dishes. She told her mother so she could get protection so she don't get pregnant.
Teacher: When my 13-year-old (relative) asked for birth control I was shocked and angry.
Portia: Mothers should help so she can get protection and not get pregnant or diseases. So you was wrong.
Teacher: Why not say "I'm thinking about having sex?"
Portia: You tell them after, not before, having sex but before pregnancy.
Teacher (now angry):   Then it's a fait accompli and you expect my compassion? You have to take more responsibility.
Portia: I am! If you get pregnant after you told your mother and you got all the stuff and still get pregnant, you the fool. Take up hygiene and learn. Then it's my responsibility if I end up pregnant. . . .
                                        Field Note, October 23, Hygiene Class

Two days later, the discussion continued.

Teacher: What topics should we talk about in sex education?
Portia: Organs, how they work.
Opal: What's an orgasm?
             [laughter]
Teacher: Sexual response, sensation all over the body. What's analogous to the male penis on the female?
Theo: Clitoris.
Teacher: Right, go home and look in the mirror.
Portia: She is too much!
Teacher: Why look in the mirror?
Elaine: It's yours.
Teacher: Why is it important to know what your body looks like?
Opal: You should like your body.
Teacher: You should know what it looks like when it's healthy, so you can recognize problems like vaginal warts.
                                        Field Note, October 25, Hygiene Class

The discourse of desire, initiated by Opal but evident only as an interruption, faded rapidly into the discourse of disease—warning about the dangers of sexuality.

It was in the spring of that year that Opal showed up pregnant. Her hygiene teacher, who was extremely concerned and involved with her students, was also quite angry with

Opal: "Who is going to take care of that baby, you or your mother? You know what it costs to buy diapers and milk and afford child care?"

Opal, in conversation with me, related, "I got to leave [school] 'cause even if they don't say it, them teachers got hate in their eyes when they look at my belly." In the absence of a way to talk about passion, pleasure, danger, and responsibility, this teacher fetishized the latter two, holding the former two hostage. Because adolescent females combine these experiences in their daily lives, the separation is false, judgmental, and ultimately not very educational.

Over the year in this high school, and in other public schools since, I have observed a systematic refusal to name issues, particularly issues that caused adults discomfort. Educators often projected their discomfort onto students in the guise of "protecting" them (Fine, 1987). An example of such silencing can be seen in a (now altered) policy of the school district of Philadelphia. In 1985 a student informed me, "We're not allowed to talk about abortion in our school." Assuming this was an overstatement, I asked an administrator at the District about this practice. She explained, "That's not quite right. If a student asks a question about abortion, the teacher can define abortion, she just can't discuss it." How can definition occur without discussion, exchange, conversation, or critique unless a subtext of silencing prevails (Greene, 1986; Noddings, 1986)?

Explicit silencing of abortion has since been lifted in Philadelphia. The revised curriculum now reads:

Options for unintended pregnancy:

(a) adoption
(b) foster care
(c) single parenthood
(d) teen marriage
(e) abortion

A footnote is supposed to be added, however, to elaborate the negative consequences of abortion. In the social politics which surround public schools, such compromises are apparent across cities.

The New York City Family Life Education curriculum reads similarly (New York City Board of Education, 1984, p. 172):

List: The possible options for an unintended pregnancy. What considerations should be given in the decision on the alternatives?

— adoption
— foster care
— mother keeps baby
— elective abortion

Discuss:

— religious viewpoints on abortion
— present laws concerning abortion
— current developments in prenatal diagnosis and their implication for abortion issues
— why abortion should not be considered a contraceptive device

List: The people or community services that could provide assistance in the event of an unintended pregnancy.

Invite: A speaker to discuss alternatives to abortion; for example, a social worker from the Department of Social Services to discuss foster care.

One must be suspicious when diverse views are sought only for abortion, and not for adoption, teen motherhood, or foster care. The call to silence is easily identified in current political and educational contexts (Fine, 1987; Foucault, 1980). The silence surrounding contraception and abortion options and diversity in sexual orientations denies adolescents information and sends the message that such conversations are taboo—at home, at church, and even at school.

In contrast to these "official curricula," which allow discussion and admission of desire only as an interruption, let us examine other situations in which young women were invited to analyze sexuality across categories of the body, the mind, the heart, and of course, gender politics.

Teen Choice, a voluntary counseling program held on-site by non-Board of Education social workers, offered an instance in which the complexities of pleasure and danger were invited, analyzed, and braided into discussions of sexuality. In a small group discussion, the counselor asked of the seven ninth graders, "What are the two functions of a penis?" One student responded, "To pee!" Another student offered the second function: "To eat!" which was followed by laughter and serious discussion. The conversation proceeded as the teacher asked, "Do all penises look alike?" The students explained, "No, they are all different colors!"

The freedom to express, beyond simple right and wrong answers, enabled these young women to offer what they knew with humor and delight. This discussion ended as one student insisted that if you "jump up and down a lot, the stuff will fall out of you and you won't get pregnant," to which the social worker answered with slight exasperation that millions of sperm would have to be released for such "expulsion" to work, and that of course, it wouldn't work. In this conversation one could hear what seemed like too much experience, too little information, and too few questions asked by the students. But the discussion, which was sex-segregated and guided by the experiences and questions of the students themselves (and the skills of the social worker), enabled easy movement between pleasure and danger, safety and desire, naiveté and knowledge, and victimization and entitlement.

What is evident, then, is that even in the absence of a discourse of desire, young women express their notions of sexuality and relate their experiences. Yet, "official" discourses of sexuality leave little room for such exploration. The authorized sexual discourses define what is safe, what is taboo, and what will be silenced. This discourse of sexuality mis-educates adolescent women. What results is a discourse of sexuality based on the male in search of desire and the female in search of protection. The open, co-ed sexuality discussions so many fought for in the 1970s have been appropriated as a forum for the primacy of male heterosexuality and the preservation of female victimization.

The Politics of Female Sexual Subjectivities

In 1912, an education committee explicitly argued that "scientific" sex education "should . . . keep sex consciousness and sex emotions at the minimum" (Leo, 1986). In the same era G. Stanley Hall proposed diversionary pursuits for adolescents, including hunting, music, and sports, "to reduce sex stress and tension . . . to short-circuit, transmute it and turn it on to develop the higher powers of the men [sic]" (Hall, 1914, pp. 29, 30). In 1915 Orison Marden, author of *The Crime of Silence*, chastised educators, reformers, and public health specialists for their unwillingness to speak publicly about sexuality and for relying inappropriately on parents and peers, who were deemed too ignorant to provide sex instruction (Imber, 1984; Strong, 1972). And in 1921 radical sex educator Maurice Bigelow wrote:

> Now, most scientifically-trained women seem to agree that there are no corresponding phenomena in the early pubertal life of the normal young woman who has good health (corresponding to male masturbation). A limited number of mature women, some of them physicians, report having experienced in the pubertal years localized tumescence and other disturbances which made them definitely conscious of sexual instincts. However, it should be noted that most of these are known to have had a personal history including one or more such abnormalities such as dysmenorrhea, uterine displacement, pathological ovaries, leucorrhea, tuberculosis, masturbation, neurasthenia, nymphomania, or other disturbances which are sufficient to account for local sexual stimulation. In short such women are not normal. . . . (p. 179)

In the 1950s public school health classes separated girls from boys. Girls "learned about sex" by watching films of the accelerated development of breasts and hips, the flow of menstrual blood, and then the progression of venereal disease as a result of participation in out-of-wedlock heterosexual activity.

Thirty years and a much-debated sexual revolution later (Ehrenreich, Hess, & Jacobs, 1986), much has changed. Feminism, the Civil Rights Movement, the disability and gay rights movements, birth control, legal abortion with federal funding (won and then lost), and reproductive technologies are part of these changes (Weeks, 1985). Due both to the consequences of, and the backlashes against, these movements, students today do learn about sexuality—if typically through the representations of female sexuality as inadequacy or victimization, male homosexuality as a story of predator and prey, and male hetero-sexuality as desire.

Young women today know that female sexual subjectivity is at least not an inherent contradiction. Perhaps they even feel it is an entitlement. Yet when public schools resist acknowledging the fullness of female sexual subjectivities, they reproduce a profound social ambivalence which dichotomizes female heterosexuality (Espin, 1984; Golden, 1984; Omolade, 1983). This ambivalence surrounds a fragile cultural distinction between two forms of female sexuality: *consensual* sexuality, representing consent or choice in sexuality, and *coercive* sexuality, which represents force, victimization, and/or crime (Weeks, 1985).

During the 1980s, however, this distinction began to be challenged. It was acknowledged that gender-based power inequities shape, define, and construct experiences of sexuality. Notions of sexual consent and force, except in extreme circumstances, became compli-cated, no longer in simple opposition. The first problem concerned how to conceptualize power asymmetries and consensual sexuality. Could *consensual* female heterosexuality be said to exist within a context replete with structures, relationships, acts, and threats of female victimization (sexual, social, and economic) (MacKinnon, 1983)? How could we speak of "sexual preference" when sexual involvement outside of heterosexuality may seriously jeopardize one's social and/or economic well-being (Petchesky, 1984)? Diverse female sexual subjectivities emerge through, despite, and because of gender-based power asymmetries. To imagine a female sexual self, free of and uncontaminated by power, was rendered naive (Foucault, 1980; Irigaray, 1980; Rubin, 1984).

The second problem involved the internal incoherence of the categories. Once assumed fully independent, the two began to blur as the varied practices of sexuality went public. At the intersection of these presumably parallel forms—coercive and consensual sexualities—lay "sexual" acts of violence and "violent" acts of sex. "Sexual" acts of violence, including marital rape, acquaintance rape, and sexual harassment, were historically considered consensual. A woman involved in a marriage, on a date, or working outside her home "naturally" risked receiving sexual attention; her consent was inferred from her presence. But today, in many states, this woman can sue her husband for such sexual acts of violence; in all states, she can prosecute a boss. What was once part of "domestic life" or "work" may, today, be criminal. On the other hand, "violent" acts of sex, including consensual sadomasochism and the use of violence-portraying pornography, were once considered inherently coercive for women (Benjamin, 1983; Rubin, 1984; Weeks, 1985). Female involvement in such sexual practices historically had been dismissed as nonconsensual. Today such romanticizing of a naive and moral "feminine sexuality" has been challenged as essentialist, and the assumption that such a feminine sexuality is "natural" to women has been shown to be false (Rubin, 1984).

Over the past decade, understandings of female sexual choice, consent, and coercion have grown richer and more complex. While questions about female subjectivities have become more interesting, the answers (for some) remain deceptively simple. Inside public schools, for example, female adolescents continue to be educated as though they were the potential *victims* of sexual (male) desire. By contrast, the ideological opposition represents only adult married women as fully consensual partners. The distinction of coercion and consent has been organized simply and respectively around age and marital status—which effectively resolves any complexity and/or ambivalence.

The ambivalence surrounding female heterosexuality places the victim and subject in opposition and derogates all women who represent female sexual subjectivities outside of marriage—prostitutes, lesbians, single mothers, women involved with multiple partners, and particularly, Black single mothers (Weitz, 1984). "Protected" from this derogation, the typical adolescent woman, as represented in sex education curricula, is without any sexual subjectivity. The discourse of victimization not only obscures the derogation, it also transforms socially distributed anxieties about female sexuality into acceptable, and even protective, talk.

The fact that schools implicitly organize sex education around a concern for female victimization is suspect, however, for two reasons. First, if female victims of male violence were truly a social concern, wouldn't the victims of rape, incest, and sexual harassment encounter social compassion, and not suspicion and blame? And second, if sex education were designed primarily to prevent victimization but not to prevent exploration of desire, wouldn't there be more discussions of both the pleasures and relatively fewer risks of disease or pregnancy associated with lesbian relationships and protected sexual inter-course, or of the risk-free pleasures of masturbation and fantasy? Public education's con-cern for the female victim is revealed as deceptively thin when real victims are discredited, and when nonvictimizing pleasures are silenced.

This unacknowledged social ambivalence about heterosexuality polarizes the debates over sex education and school-based health clinics. The anxiety effectively treats the female sexual victim as though she were a completely separate species from the female sexual subject. Yet the adolescent women quoted earlier in this text remind us that the female victim and subject coexist in every woman's body.

Toward a Discourse of Sexual Desire and Social Entitlement: In the Student Bodies of
Public Schools

I have argued that silencing a discourse of desire buttresses the icon of woman-as-victim.
In so doing, public schooling may actually disable young women in their negotiations as
sexual subjects. Trained through and into positions of passivity and victimization, young
women are currently educated away from positions of sexual self-interest.

If we re-situate the adolescent woman in a rich and empowering educational context,
she develops a sense of self which is sexual as well as intellectual, social, and economic. In
this section I invite readers to imagine such a context. The dialectic of desire and victimization—across spheres of labor, social relations, and sexuality—would then frame schooling.
While many of the curricula and interventions discussed in this paper are imperfect, data
on the effectiveness of what *is* available are nevertheless compelling. Studies of sex education curricula, SBHCs, classroom discussions, and ethnographies of life inside public high
schools demonstrate that a sense of sexual and social entitlement for young women *can* be
fostered within public schools.

Sex Education as Intellectual Empowerment

Harris and Yankelovich polls confirm that over 80 percent of American adults believe that
students should be educated about sexuality within their public schools. Seventy-five
percent believe that homosexuality and abortion should be included in the curriculum,
with 40 percent of those surveyed by Yankelovich et al. (N = 1015) agreeing that 12-year-
olds should be taught about oral and anal sex (see Leo, 1986; Harris, 1985).

While the public continues to debate the precise content of sex education, most parents
approve and support sex education for their children. An Illinois program monitored
parental requests to "opt out" and found that only 6 or 7 of 850 children were actually
excused from sex education courses (Leo, 1986). In a California assessment, fewer than
2 percent of parents disallowed their children's participation. And in a longitudinal 5-year
program in Connecticut, 7 of 2,500 students requested exemption from these classes
(Scales, 1981). Resistance to sex education, while loud at the level of public rhetoric and
conservative organizing, is both less vocal and less active within schools and parents'
groups (Hottois & Milner, 1975; Scales, 1981).

Sex education courses are offered broadly, if not comprehensively, across the United
States. In 1981, only 7 of 50 states actually had laws against such instruction, and only one
state enforced a prohibition (Kirby & Scales, 1981). Surveying 179 urban school districts,
Sonnenstein and Pittman (1984) found that 75 percent offered some sex education within
senior and junior high schools, while 66 percent of the elementary schools offered sex
education units. Most instruction was, however, limited to 10 hours or less, with content
focused on anatomy. In his extensive review of sex education programs, Kirby (1985)
concludes that less than 10 percent of all public school students are exposed to what might
be considered comprehensive sex education courses.

The progress on AIDS education is more encouraging, and more complex (see Freudenberg, 1987), but cannot be adequately reviewed in this article. It is important to note,
however, that a December 1986 report released by the U.S. Conference of Mayors
documents that 54 percent of the 73 largest school districts and 25 state school agencies
offer some form of AIDS education (Benedetto, 1987). Today, debates among federal

officials—including Secretary of Education Bennett and Surgeon General Koop—and among educators question *when* and *what* to offer in AIDS education. The question is no longer *whether* such education should be promoted.

Not only has sex education been accepted as a function of public schooling, but it has survived empirical tests of effectiveness. Evaluation data demonstrate that sex education can increase contraceptive knowledge and use (Kirby, 1985; Public/Private Ventures, 1987). In terms of sexual activity (measured narrowly in terms of the onset or frequency of heterosexual intercourse), the evidence suggests that sex education does not instigate an earlier onset or increase of such sexual activity (Zelnick & Kim, 1982) and may, in fact, postpone the onset of heterosexual intercourse (Zabin, Hirsch, Smith, Streett, & Hardy, 1986). The data for pregnancy rates appear to demonstrate no effect for exposure to sex education alone (see Dawson, 1986; Marsiglio & Mott, 1986; Kirby, 1985).

Sex education as constituted in these studies is not sufficient to diminish teen pregnancy rates. In all likelihood it would be naive to expect that sex education (especially if only ten hours in duration) would carry such a "long arm" of effectiveness. While the widespread problem of teen pregnancy must be attributed broadly to economic and social inequities (Jones et al., 1985), sex education remains necessary and sufficient to educate, demystify, and improve contraceptive knowledge and use. In conjunction with material opportunities for enhanced life options, it is believed that sex education and access to contraceptives and abortion can help to reduce the rate of unintended pregnancy among teens (Dryfoos, 1985a, 1985b; National Research Council, 1987).

School-Based Health Clinics: Sexual Empowerment

The public opinion and effectiveness data for school-based health clinics are even more compelling than those for sex education. Thirty SBHCs provide on-site health care services to senior, and sometimes junior, high school students in more than 18 U.S. communities, with an additional 25 communities developing similar programs (Kirby, 1985). These clinics offer, at a minimum, health counseling, referrals, and follow-up examinations. Over 70 percent conduct pelvic examinations (Kirby, 1985), approximately 52 percent prescribe contraceptives, and 28 percent dispense contraceptives (Leo, 1986). None performs abortions, and few refer for abortions.

All SBHCs require some form of general parental notification and/or consent, and some charge a nominal fee for generic health services. Relative to private physicians, school-based health clinics and other family planning agencies are substantially more willing to provide contraceptive services to unmarried minors without specific parental consent (consent in this case referring explicitly to contraception). Only one percent of national Planned Parenthood affiliates require consent or notification, compared to 10 percent of public health department programs and 19 percent of hospitals (Torres & Forrest, 1985).

The consequences of consent provisions for abortion are substantial. Data from two states, Massachusetts and Minnesota, demonstrate that parental consent laws result in increased teenage pregnancies or increased numbers of out-of-state abortions. The Reproductive Freedom Project of the American Civil Liberties Union, in a report which examines the consequences of such consent provisions, details the impact of these statutes on teens, on their familial relationships, and ultimately, on their unwanted children (Reproductive Freedom Project, 1986). In an analysis of the impact of Minnesota's mandatory parental notification law from 1981 to 1985, this report documents over

7,000 pregnancies in teens aged 13–17, 3,500 of whom "went to state court to seek the right to confidential abortions, all at considerable personal cost." The report also notes that many of the pregnant teens did not petition the court, "although their entitlement and need for confidential abortions was as strong or more so than the teenagers who made it to court.... Only those minors who are old enough and wealthy enough or resourceful enough are actually able to use the court bypass option" (Reproductive Freedom Project, p. 4).

These consent provisions, with allowance for court bypass, not only increase the number of unwanted teenage pregnancies carried to term, but also extend the length of time required to secure an abortion, potentially endangering the life of the teenage woman, and increasing the costs of the abortion. The provisions may also jeopardize the physical and emotional well-being of some young women and their mothers, particularly when paternal consent is required and the pregnant teenager resides with a single mother. Finally, the consent provisions create a class-based health care system. Adolescents able to afford travel to a nearby state, or able to pay a private physician for a confidential abortion, have access to an abortion. Those unable to afford the travel, or those who are unable to contact a private physician, are likely to become teenage mothers (Reproductive Freedom Project, 1986).

In Minneapolis, during the time from 1980 to 1984 when the law was implemented, the birth rate for 15- to 17-year-olds increased 38.4 percent, while the birth rate for 18- and 19-year-olds—not affected by the law—rose only 3 percent (Reproductive Freedom Project, 1986). The state of Massachusetts passed a parental consent law which took effect in 1981. An analysis of the impact of that law concludes that "... the major impact of the Massachusetts parental consent law has been to send a monthly average of between 90 and 95 of the state's minors across state lines in search of an abortion. This number represents about one in every three minor abortion patients living in Massachusetts" (Cartoof & Klerman, 1986). These researchers, among others, write that parental consent laws could have more devastating effects in larger states, from which access to neighboring states would be more difficult.

The inequalities inherent in consent provisions and the dramatic consequences which result for young women are well recognized. For example, twenty-nine states and the District of Columbia now explicitly authorize minors to grant their own consent for receipt of contraceptive information and/or services, independent of parental knowledge or consent (see Melton & Russo, 1987, for full discussion; National Research Council, 1987; for a full analysis of the legal, emotional, and physical health problems attendant upon parental consent laws for abortion, see the Reproductive Freedom Project report). More recently, consent laws for abortion in Pennsylvania and California have been challenged as unconstitutional.

Public approval of SBHCs has been slow but consistent. In the 1986 Yankelovich survey, 84 percent of surveyed adults agree that these clinics should provide birth control information; 36 percent endorse dispensing of contraceptives to students (Leo, 1986). In 1985, Harris found that 67 percent of all respondents, including 76 percent of Blacks and 76 percent of Hispanics, agree that public schools should establish formal ties with family planning clinics for teens to learn about and obtain contraception (Harris, 1985). Mirroring the views of the general public, a national sample of school administrators polled by the Education Research Group indicated that more than 50 percent believe birth control should be offered in school-based clinics; 30 percent agree that parental permission should be sought, and 27 percent agree that contraceptives should be dispensed, even if parental consent is not forthcoming. The discouraging news is that 96 percent of these respondents indicate that their districts do not presently offer such services (Benedetto, 1987; Werner, 1987).

Research on the effectiveness of SBHCs is consistently persuasive. The three-year Johns Hopkins study of school-based health clinics (Zabin et al., 1986) found that schools in which SBHCs made referrals and dispensed contraceptives noted an increase in the percentage of "virgin" females visiting the program as well as an increase in contraceptive use. They also found a significant reduction in pregnancy rates: there was a 13 percent decrease at experimental schools after 10 months, versus a 50 percent increase at control schools; after 28 months, pregnancy rates decreased 30 percent at experimental schools versus a 53 percent increase at control schools. Furthermore, by the second year, a substantial percentage of males visited the clinic (48 percent of males in experimental schools indicated that they "have ever been to a birth control clinic or to a physician about birth control," compared to 12 percent of males in control schools). Contrary to common belief, the schools in which clinics dispensed contraceptives showed a substantial postponement of first experience of heterosexual intercourse among high school students and an increase in the proportion of young women visiting the clinic prior to "first coitus."

Paralleling the Hopkins findings, the St. Paul Maternity and Infant Care Project (1985) found that pregnancy rates dropped substantially in schools with clinics, from 79 births/1,000 (1973) to 26 births/1,000 (1984). Teens who delivered and kept their infants had an 80 percent graduation rate, relative to approximately 50 percent of young mothers nationally. Those who stayed in school reported a 1.3 percent repeat birth rate, compared to 17 percent nationally. Over three years, pregnancy rates dropped by 40 percent. Twenty-five percent of young women in the school received some form of family planning and 87 percent of clients were continuing to use contraception at a 3-year follow-up. There were fewer obstetric complications; fewer babies were born at low birth weights; and prenatal visits to physicians increased relative to students in the control schools.

Predictions that school-based health clinics would advance the onset of sexual intimacy, heighten the degree of "promiscuity" and incidence of pregnancy, and hold females primarily responsible for sexuality were countered by the evidence. The onset of sexual intimacy was postponed, while contraception was used more reliably. Pregnancy rates substantially diminished and, over time, a large group of males began to view contraception as a shared responsibility.

It is worth restating here that females who received family planning counseling and/or contraception actually postponed the onset of heterosexual intercourse. I would argue that the availability of such services may enable females to feel they are sexual agents, entitled and therefore responsible, rather than at the constant and terrifying mercy of a young man's pressure to "give in" or of a parent's demands to "save yourself." With a sense of sexual agency and not necessarily urgency, teen girls may be less likely to use or be used by pregnancy (Petchesky, 1984).

Nontraditional Vocational Training: Social and Economic Entitlement

The literature reviewed suggests that sex education, access to contraception, and opportunities for enhanced life options, in combination (Dryfoos, 1985a, 1985b; Kirby, 1985; Select Committee on Children, Youth and Families, 1985), can significantly diminish the likelihood that a teenager will become pregnant, carry to term, and/or have a repeat pregnancy, and can increase the likelihood that she will stay in high school through graduation (National Research Council, 1987). Education toward entitlement—including a sense of sexual, economic, and social entitlement—may be sufficient to affect adolescent girls' views on sexuality, contraception, and abortion. By framing female subjectivity within the context of social entitlement, sex education would be organized around dialogue and critique, SBHCs would offer health services, options counseling, contraception, and abortion referrals, and the provision of real "life options" would include nontraditional vocational training programs and employment opportunities for adolescent females (Dryfoos, 1985a, 1985b).

In a nontraditional vocational training program in New York City designed for young women, many of whom are mothers, participants' attitudes toward contraception and abortion shifted once they acquired a set of vocational skills, a sense of social entitlement, and a sense of personal competence (Weinbaum, personal communication, 1986). The young women often began the program without strong academic skills or a sense of competence. At the start, they were more likely to express more negative sentiments about contraception and abortion than when they completed the program. One young woman, who initially held strong antiabortion attitudes, learned that she was pregnant midway through her carpentry apprenticeship. She decided to abort, reasoning that now that she has a future, she can't risk losing it for another baby (Weinbaum, paraphrase of personal communication, 1986). A developing sense of social entitlement may have transformed this young woman's view of reproduction, sexuality, and self.

The Manpower Development Research Corporation (MDRC), in its evaluation of Project Redirection (Polit, Kahn, & Stevens, 1985) offers similar conclusions about a comprehensive vocational training and community-based mentor project for teen mothers and mothers-to-be. Low-income teens were enrolled in Project Redirection, a network of services designed to instill self-sufficiency, in which community women served as mentors. The program included training for what is called "employability," Individual Participation Plans, and peer group sessions. Data on education, employment, and pregnancy outcomes were collected at 12 and 24 months after enrollment. Two years after the program began, many newspapers headlined the program as a failure. The data actually indicated that at 12 months, the end of program involvement, Project Redirection women were significantly *less likely* to experience a repeat pregnancy than comparison women; *more likely* to be using contraception; *more likely* to be in school, to have completed school, or to be in the labor force; and twice as likely (20 percent versus 11 percent, respectively) to have earned a Graduate Equivalency Diploma. At 24 months, however, approximately one year out of the program, Project and comparison women were virtually indistinguishable. MDRC reported equivalent rates of repeat pregnancies, dropout, and unemployment.

The Project Redirection data demonstrate that sustained outcomes cannot be expected once programs have been withdrawn and participants confront the realities of a dismal economy and inadequate child care and social services. The data confirm, however, the effectiveness of comprehensive programs to reduce teen pregnancy rates and encourage study or work as long as the young women are actively engaged. Supply-side interventions—changing people but not structures or opportunities—which leave unchallenged an inhospitable and discriminating economy and a thoroughly impoverished child care/social welfare system are inherently doomed to long-term failure. When such programs fail, the social reading is that "these young women can't be helped." Blaming the victim obscures the fact that the current economy and social welfare arrangements need overhauling if the sustained educational, social, and psychological gains accrued by the Project Redirection participants are to be maintained.

In the absence of enhanced life options, low-income young women are likely to default to early and repeat motherhood as a source of perceived competence, significance, and pleasure. When life options are available, however, a sense of competence and "entitlement to better" may help to prevent second pregnancies, may help to encourage education, and, when available, the pursuit of meaningful work (Burt, Kimmich, Goldmuntz, & Sonnenstein, 1984).

Femininity May Be Hazardous to Her Health: The Absence of Entitlement

Growing evidence suggests that women who lack a sense of social or sexual entitlement, who hold traditional notions of what it means to be female—self-sacrificing and relatively passive—and who undervalue themselves, are disproportionately likely to find themselves with an unwanted pregnancy and to maintain it through to motherhood. While many young women who drop out, pregnant or not, are not at all traditional in these ways, but are quite feisty and are fueled with a sense of entitlement (Fine, 1986; Weinbaum, personal communication, 1987), it may also be the case that young women who do internalize such notions of "femininity" are disproportionately at risk of pregnancy and dropping out.

The Hispanic Policy Development Project reports that low-income female sophomores who, in 1980, expected to be married and/or to have a child by age 19 were disproportionately represented among nongraduates in 1984. Expectations of early marriage and childbearing correspond to dramatic increases (200 to 400 percent) in nongraduation rates for low-income adolescent women across racial and ethnic groups (Hispanic Policy Development Project, 1987). These indicators of traditional notions of womanhood bode poorly for female academic achievement.

The Children's Defense Fund (1986) recently published additional data which demonstrate that young women with poor basic skills are three times more likely to become teen parents than women with average or above-average basic skills. Those with poor or fair basic skills are four times more likely to have more than one child while a teen; 29 percent of women in the bottom skills quintile became mothers by age 18 versus 5 percent of young women in the top quintile. While academic skill problems must be placed in the context of alienating and problematic schools, and not viewed as inherent in these young women, those who fall in the bottom quintile may nevertheless be the least likely to feel entitled or in control of their lives. They may feel more vulnerable to male pressure or more willing to have a child as a means of feeling competent.

My own observations, derived from a year-long ethnographic study of a comprehensive public high school in New York City, further confirm some of these conclusions. Six months into the ethnography, new pregnancies began showing. I noticed that many of the girls who got pregnant and carried to term were not those whose bodies, dress, and manner evoked sensuality and experience. Rather, a number of the pregnant women were those who were quite passive and relatively quiet in their classes. One young woman, who granted me an interview anytime, washed the blackboard for her teacher, rarely spoke in class, and never disobeyed her mother, was pregnant by the spring of the school year (Fine, 1986).

Simple stereotypes, of course, betray the complexity of circumstances under which young women become pregnant and maintain their pregnancies. While U.S. rates of teenage sexual activity and age of "sexual initiation" approximate those of comparable developed countries, the teenage pregnancy, abortion, and childbearing rates in the United States are substantially higher. In the United States, teenagers under age fifteen are at least five times more likely to give birth than similarly aged teens in other industrialized nations (Jones et al., 1985; National Research Council, 1987). The national factors which correlate with low teenage birthrates include adolescent access to sex education and contraception, and relative equality in the distribution of wealth. Economic and structural conditions which support a class-stratified society, and which limit adolescent access to sexual information and contraception, contribute to inflated teenage pregnancy rates and birthrates.

This broad national context acknowledged, it might still be argued that within our country, traditional notions of what it means to be a woman—to remain subordinate, dependent, self-sacrificing, compliant, and ready to marry and/or bear children early—do little to empower women or enhance a sense of entitlement. This is not to say that teenage dropouts or mothers tend to be of any one type. Yet it may well be that the traditions and practices of "femininity" as commonly understood may be hazardous to the economic, social, educational, and sexual development of young women.

In summary, the historic silencing within public schools of conversations about sexuality, contraception, and abortion, as well as the absence of a discourse of desire—in the form of comprehensive sex education, school-based health clinics, and viable life options via vocational training and placement—all combine to exacerbate the vulnerability of young women whom schools, and the critics of sex education and SBHCs, claim to protect.

Conclusion

Adolescents are entitled to a discussion of desire instead of the anti-sex rhetoric which controls the controversies around sex education, SBHCs, and AIDS education. The absence of a discourse of desire, combined with the lack of analysis of the language of victimization, may actually retard the development of sexual subjectivity and responsibility in students. Those most "at risk" of victimization through pregnancy, disease, violence, or harassment—all female students, low-income females in particular, and non-heterosexual males—are those most likely to be victimized by the absence of critical conversation in public schools. Public schools can no longer afford to maintain silence around a discourse of desire. This is not to say that the silencing of a discourse of desire is the primary root of sexual victimization, teen motherhood, and the concomitant poverty experienced by young and low-income females. Nor could it be responsibly argued that interventions initiated by public schools could ever be successful if separate from economic and social development. But it is important to understand that by providing education, counseling, contraception, and abortion referrals, as well as meaningful educational and vocational opportunities, public schools could play an essential role in the construction of the female subject—social and sexual.

And by not providing such an educational context, public schools contribute to the rendering of substantially different outcomes for male and female students, and for male and female dropouts (Fine, 1986). The absence of a thorough sex education curriculum, of school-based health clinics, of access to free and confidential contraceptive and abortion services, of exposure to information about the varieties of sexual pleasures and partners, and of involvement in sustained employment training programs may so jeopardize the educational and economic outcomes for female adolescents as to constitute sex discrimination. How can we ethically continue to withhold educational treatments we know to be effective for adolescent women?

Public schools constitute a sphere in which young women could be offered access to a language and experience of empowerment. In such contexts, "well-educated" young women could breathe life into positions of social critique and experience entitlement rather than victimization, autonomy rather than terror.

Notes

1. The research reported in this article represents one component of a year-long ethnographic investigation of students and dropouts at a comprehensive public high school in New York City. Funded by the W.T. Grant Foundation, the research was designed to investigate how public urban high schools produce dropout rates in excess of 50 percent. The methods employed over the year included: in-school observations four days/week during the fall, and one to two days/week during the spring; regular (daily) attendance in a hygiene course for twelfth graders; an archival analysis of more than 1200 students who compose the 1978–79 cohort of incoming ninth graders; interviews with approximately 55 recent and long-term dropouts; analysis of fictional and autobiographical writings by students; a survey distributed to a subsample of the cohort population; and visits to proprietary schools, programs for Graduate Equivalency Diplomas, naval recruitment sites, and a public high school for pregnant and parenting teens. The methods and preliminary results of the ethnography are detailed in Fine (1986).
2. This information is derived from personal communications with former and present employees of major urban school districts who have chosen to remain anonymous.
3. Personal communication.

References

Bauer, G. (1986). *The family: Preserving America's future*. Washington, DC: U.S. Department of Education.
Benedetto, R. (1987, January 23). AIDS studies become part of curricula. *USA Today*, p. D1.
Benjamin, J. (1983). Master and slave: The fantasy of erotic domination. In A. Snitow, C. Stansell, & S. Thompson (Eds.), *Powers of desire* (pp. 280–299). New York: Monthly Review Press.
Bennett, W. (1987, July 3). Why Johnny can't abstain. *National Review*, pp. 36–38, 56.
Bigelow, M. (1921). *Sex-Education*. New York: Macmillan.
Boffey, P. (1987, February 27). Reagan to back AIDS plan urging youths to avoid sex. *New York Times*, p. A14.
Brown, P. (1983). The Swedish approach to sex education and adolescent pregnancy: Some impressions. *Family Planning Perspectives, 15*(2), 92–95.
Burke, C. (1980), Introduction to Luce Irigaray's "When our lips speak together." *Signs, 6*, 66–68.
Burt, M., Kimmich, M., Goldmuntz, J., & Sonnenstein, F. (1984). *Helping pregnant adolescents: Outcomes and costs of service delivery*. Final Report on the Evaluation of Adolescent Pregnancy Programs. Washington, DC: Urban Institute.
Cartoof, V., & Klerman, L. (1986). Parental consent for abortion: Impact of the Massachusetts law. *American Journal of Public Health, 76*, 397–400.
Chicago school clinic is sued over birth control materials. (1986, October 16). *New York Times*, p. A24.
Children's Defense Fund. (1986). *Preventing adolescent pregnancy: What schools can do*. Washington, DC: Children's Defense Fund.
Children's Defense Fund. (1987). *Adolescent pregnancy: An anatomy of a social problem in search of comprehensive solutions*. Washington, DC: Children's Defense Fund.
Cixous, H. (1981). Castration or decapitation? *Signs, 7*, 41–55.
Dawson, D. (1986). The effects of sex education on adolescent behavior. *Family Planning Perspectives, 18*, 162–170.
Dowd, M. (1986, April 16). Bid to update sex education confronts resistance in city. *New York Times*, p. A1.
Dryfoos, J. (1985a). A time for new thinking about teenage pregnancy. *American Journal of Public Health, 75*, 13–14.
Dryfoos, J. (1985b). School-based health clinics: A new approach to preventing adolescent pregnancy? *Family Planning Perspectives, 17*(2), 70–75.
Ehrenreich, B., Hess, E., & Jacobs, G. (1986). *Re-making love*. Garden City, NY: Anchor Press.

Espin, O. (1984). Cultural and historical influences on sexuality in Hispanic/Latina women: Implications for psycho-therapy. In C. Vance (Ed.), *Pleasure and danger* (pp. 149–164). Boston: Routledge & Kegan Paul.

Fine, M. (1986). Why urban adolescents drop into and out of high school. *Teachers College Record, 87,* 393–409.

Fine, M. (1987). Silencing in public school. *Language Arts, 64,* 157–174.

Fisher, W., Byrne, D., & White, L. (1983). Emotional barriers to contraception. In D. Byrne & W. Fisher (Eds.), *Adolescents; sex, and contraception* (pp. 207–239). Hillsdale, NJ: Lawrence Erlbaum.

Foucault, M. (1980). *The history of sexuality* (Vol.1). New York: Vintage Books.

Freudenberg, N. (1987). The politics of sex education. *Health PAC Bulletin.* New York: HealthPAC.

Golden, C. (1984, March). *Diversity and variability in lesbian identities.* Paper presented at Lesbian Psychologies Conference of the Association of Women in Psychology.

Greene, M. (1986). In search of a critical pedagogy. *Harvard Educational Review, 56,* 427–441.

Hall, G. S. (1914). Education and the social hygiene movement. *Social Hygiene, 1* (1 December), 29–35.

Harris, L., and Associates. (1985). *Public attitudes about sex education, family planning and abortion in the United States.* New York: Louis Harris and Associates, Inc.

Hispanic Policy Development Project. (1987, Fall). *1980 high school sophomores from poverty backgrounds: Whites, Blacks, Hispanics look at school and adult responsibilities,* Vol. 1, No. 2. New York: Author.

Hottois, J., & Milner, N. (1975). *The sex education controversy.* Lexington, MA: Lexington Books.

Imber, M. (1984). Towards a theory of educational origins: The genesis of sex education. *Educational Theory, 34,* 275–286.

Irigaray, L. (1980). When our lips speak together. *Signs, 6,* 69.

Jones, E., Forrest, J., Goldman, N., Henshaw, S., Lincoln, R., Rosoff, J., Westoff, C., & Wulf, D. (1985). Teenage pregnancy in developed countries. *Family Planning Perspectives, 17*(1), 55–63.

Kantrowitz, B., Hager, M., Wingert, S., Carroll, G., Raine, G., Witherspoon, D., Huck, J., & Doherty, S. (1987, February 16). Kids and contraceptives. *Newsweek,* pp. 54–65.

Kelly, G. (1986). *Learning about sex.* Woodbury, NY: Barron's Educational Series.

Kirby, D. (1985). *School-based health clinics: An emerging approach to improving adolescent health and addressing teenage pregnancy.* Washington, DC: Center for Population Options.

Kirby, D., & Scales, P. (1981, April). An analysis of state guidelines for sex education instruction in public schools. *Family Relations,* pp. 229–237.

Koop, C. E. (1986). *Surgeon General's report on acquired immune deficiency syndrome.* Washington, DC: Office of the Surgeon General.

Koop's AIDS stand assailed. (1987, March 15). *New York Times,* p. A25.

Leo, J. (1986, November 24). Sex and schools. *Time,* pp. 54–63.

Lorde, A. (1980, August). *Uses of the erotic: The erotic as power.* Paper presented at the Fourth Berkshire Conference on the History of Women, Mt. Holyoke College.

MacKinnon, C. (1983). Complicity: An introduction to Andrea Dworkin's "Abortion," Chapter 3, "Right-Wing Women." *Law and Inequality, 1,* 89–94.

Marsiglio, W., & Mott, F. (1986). The impact of sex education on sexual activity, contraceptive use and premarital pregnancy among American teenagers. *Family Planning Perspectives, 18*(4), 151–162.

Melton, S., & Russo, N. (1987). Adolescent abortion. *American Psychologist, 42,* 69–83.

National Research Council. (1987). *Risking the future: Adolescent sexuality, pregnancy and childbearing* (Vol. 1). Washington, DC: National Academy Press.

New York City Board of Education. (1984). *Family living curriculum including sex education. Grades K through 12.* New York City Board of Education, Division of Curriculum and Instruction.

Noddings, N. (1986). Fidelity in teaching, teacher education, and research for teaching. *Harvard Educational Review, 56,* 496–510.

Omolade, B. (1983). Hearts of darkness. In A. Snitow, C. Stansell, & S. Thompson (Eds.), *Powers of desire* (pp. 350–367). NY: Monthly Review Press.

Perlez, J. (1986a, June 24). On teaching about sex. *New York Times,* p. C1.

Perlez, J. (1986b, September 24). School chief to ask mandatory sex education. *New York Times,* p. A36.

Petchesky, R. (1984). *Abortion and woman's choice.* New York: Longman.

Philadelphia School District. (1986). Sex education curriculum. Draft.

Polit, D., Kahn, J., & Stevens, D. (1985). *Final impacts from Project Redirection.* New York: Manpower Development Research Center.

Public/Private Ventures. (1987, April). *Summer training and education program.* Philadelphia: Author.

Reproductive Freedom Project. (1986). *Parental consent laws on abortion: Their catastrophic impact on teenagers.* New York: American Civil Liberties Union.

Rohter, L. (1985, October 29). School workers shown AIDS film. *New York Times,* p. B3.

Rubin, G. (1984). Thinking sex: Notes for a radical theory of the politics of sex. In C. Vance (Ed.), *Pleasure and danger* (pp. 267–319). Boston: Routledge & Kegan Paul.

St. Paul Maternity and Infant Care Project. (1985). *Health services project description*. St. Paul, MN: Author.

Scales, P. (1981). Sex education and the prevention of teenage pregnancy: An overview of policies and programs in the United States. In T. Ooms (Ed.), *Teenage pregnancy in a family context: Implications for policy* (pp. 213–253). Philadelphia: Temple University Press.

Schlafly, P. (1986). Presentation on women's issues. American Dreams Symposium, Indiana University of Pennsylvania.

Selected group to see original AIDS tape. (1987, January 29). *New York Times*, p. B4.

Smith-Rosenberg, C. (1978). Sex as symbol in Victorian purity: An ethnohistorical analysis of Jacksonian America. *American Journal of Sociology, 84,* 212–247.

Snitow, A., Stansell, C., & Thompson, S. (Eds.). (1983). *Powers of desire*. New York: Monthly Review Press.

Sonnenstein, F., & Pittman, K. (1984). The availability of sex education in large city school districts. *Family Planning Perspectives, 16*(1), 19–25.

Strong, B. (1972). Ideas of the early sex education movement in America, 1890–1920. *History of Education Quarterly, 12,* 129–161.

Thompson, S. (1983). Search for tomorrow: On feminism and the reconstruction of teen romance. In A. Snitow, C. Stansell, & S. Thompson (Eds.), *Powers of desire* (pp. 367–384). New York: Monthly Review Press.

Torres, A., & Forest, J. (1985). Family planning clinic services in the United States, 1983. *Family Planning Perspectives, 17*(1), 30–35.

Vance, C. (1984). *Pleasure and danger*. Boston: Routledge & Kegan Paul.

Weeks, J. (1985). *Sexuality and its discontents*. London: Routledge & Kegan Paul.

Weitz, R. (1984). What price independence? Social reactions to lesbians, spinsters, widows and nuns. In J. Freeman (Ed.), *Women: A ferminist perspective* (3rd ed.). Palo Alto, CA: Mayfield.

Werner, L. (1987, November 14). U.S. report asserts administration halted liberal "anti-family agenda." *New York Times*, p. A12.

Zabin, L., Hirsch, M., Smith, E., Streett, R., & Hardy, J. (1986). Evaluation of a pregnancy prevention program for urban teenagers. *Family Planning Perspectives, 18*(3), 119–126.

Zelnick, M., & Kim, Y. (1982). Sex education and its association with teenage sexual activity, pregnancy and contraceptive use. *Family Planning Perspectives, 14*(3), 117–126.

13

The Tolerance that Dare Not Speak Its Name

Cris Mayo

Recently I have been asking queer college students to recall their public school experiences. I have received a pattern of oddly contradictory responses that turn out not to be contradictions at all. I ask, "Have you ever experienced harassment of any kind because you were queer?" Many of the respondents begin their answers with something like "No, I didn't experience harassment, what happened was no big deal, nothing out of the ordinary." They then, having framed their experience as ordinary, recount harassment from teachers and students, harassment from students in front of teachers who did nothing, and physical harassment. Surprisingly, though they emphasize that they expected that kind of behavior, and even if, on further reconsideration, they acknowledge that it is unacceptable, they understand it to have been normal and unremarkable. As one young man put it, "No one really frowned upon it [homosexuality], but no one talked about it." He then said he remembered "maybe one bad thing." It turned out that he had had his head smashed into a locker because other students thought he was gay, but he said "I felt it wasn't that bad of an action." In addition to what other students did to them, respondents point out the official silence, the lack of information, and the lack of teacher and administrator attention to the homophobic speech and action. All their schools, of course, had policies intent on protecting students from harassment. However, none of the schools had policies that specifically protected sexual minority students. Thus, part of the problem was that the kind of speech that harassed sexual minority students was not understood by the school community to be harassment. Homophobic speech was just what queer kids should expect. I contend in this paper that because the structure of social institutions and practices fuels homophobia, that even with policies to protect them, homophobia is still what queer people can expect. Even policies and rules that purport to protect sexual minority students will not work because they are still guided by institutions intent on maintaining a veneer of acceptance of sexual minorities through the establishment of conduct codes centralizing individual agency. Though individual acts are sanctioned, schools as institutions continue to engage in substantially discriminatory practices.

The policies that I examine in this chapter are indicative of the intentional shortsightedness that maintains dominance while appearing to protect sexual minority students, as well as other students, in public schools. I will argue that policies are written to prevent substantive change by focusing on simple, reactive rules rather than large-scale changes in curricula or social practices. To examine how adding rules is meant to limit larger changes, I analyze nondiscrimination policies in Massachusetts and Maryland that curtail curricular representation of sexual minority issues. I then turn to an examination of the decision in *Saxe v. State College Area School District* that cancelled a broadly protective speech code in Pennsylvania. In each of these cases I will show that policies are more intent on regulating speakers of words than encouraging learning and community. Rules and rulings about rules continue the intentional silencing and trivializing of sexual minority students. Even the anti-homophobia demonstration most popular in public schools, "Day of Silence" requires silencing. While the intentional silence required by the "Day of Silence" does pose some difficulties for imagining what a vibrant community of sexual diversity would look *like*, I will argue that the intentional self-silencing draws productive attention to the unproductive silences policies attempt to enforce.

Civil Speech and Curricular Silence

While the damage done by hateful speech is considerable, we need to think more broadly about the context in which that speech takes place as well as the tendency for codes of conduct to focus on individual action. While it may be tempting to say that all laws and rules ultimately require that individuals control themselves for the good of the community, laws and rules also cover over the situation in which individuals act. The particular acts of harassment that occur in public schools are so damaging because they occur in contexts that are pervasively homophobic, not only because of individual action but institutional arrangement. Schools do not address issues of concern to sexual minority students or to students at all curious about sexuality. Sexual minority students are simultaneously damaged by official silence and harassing talk. Official silence in curricula gives them no way to adequately address the homophobic words from other students and school professionals. Harassing talk appears to be the source of their problems, but attention to harassment only leaves most official silence in place. In contrast to quick fixes such as speech codes, lack of representation in curricula and lack of advocacy by authority figures are harder to solve by rules that govern individual conduct. So while prohibiting disrespectful speech is the quickest way for school districts to do something, those codes in and of themselves are insufficient. More problematically, policies purportedly intent on protecting sexual minorities from harassment are increasingly being used and interpreted to exclude gay and lesbian issues from public schools. Too often the careful choreography of civil speech is the only action taken to change the school environment. While some speech is stifled, exclusions in curricula, educational and social resources, continue to be clearly heard, felt, and experienced by students of all sexualities.

Because codes of civility and conduct are so closely linked with the practice of propriety, these codes maintain relations of dominance by shifting the focus on structural inequities to matters of social interaction. I am not arguing that structural inequities and social interaction are disconnected but rather that codes of conduct sidestep the material inequalities and install instead a civil place where the difficulties of inequality purportedly do not matter as much as they do in other spaces. Uncivil speech becomes the site of inequalities and thus the place where policy directs its attention. Policies make the individual's speech the focus of concern and thus lodge agency fully within the speaker. As Butler argues, "Such a reduction of the agency of power to the actions of the subject may well seek to compensate for the difficulties and anxieties produced in the course of living a contemporary cultural predicament in which neither the law nor hate speech are uttered exclusively by a singular subject" (1997, p. 80). While it may be difficult to trace the multiple workings of power through a variety of institutions and relations that form bias, it is not so difficult to find the representation of bias within a single speech act. So codes are intent on finding and stopping uncivil speech and also intent on establishing a civil community by removing that offensive speech.

The civility installed by speech codes and other school conduct policies maintain the individual speaker as a source of inequalities and, by suggesting alternative forms of engagement for all participating in the school community, essentially advocate not only fighting speech with speech. Policies intent on forming civil subjects advocate fighting the representation of political inequalities by the practice of social propriety. Civility, then, is a practice that masks differences, not a practice that enables discourse across difference. Further, practices of civility, such as using the correct words to address minority groups and using sensitive language, enable dominant people to protect their own property interest in the source of their dominance. By keeping up the appearance of being cultivated and sensitive, they seem less culpable for inequalities. By gaining a sense of themselves as having currency with issues of diversity, they maintain the veneer of a cosmopolitan person in the know, a kind of tourist of inequality who need never fully engage with the degree to which their own property and investment in saying the right words maintains the inequalities they can converse their way around. In short, speech and conduct codes only keep up the appearance of equality and encourage people to believe that they have, in fact, challenged inequality by using the right words, but not substantially altering their practices. Antidiscrimination policies and speech codes, then, shut down more than offensive speech; these policies prevent education on contentious issues. Further, if the individual agent fails to behave correctly, the power to adjudicate disturbances falls to the state. As Butler argues, "the state produces hate speech" and thus that speech becomes regulated by the state in ways that reinforce the relations of power between the individual and the state in problematic ways (1997, p. 83). The state will not only not act in the best interests of those harassed, its power will create categories of protection and identity, and conditions for that protection that will be difficult to negotiate.

In at least two states, Massachusetts and Maryland, laws attempting to protect gay and lesbian students from harassment have been crafted specifically to prohibit using those laws as an impetus to bring curricular materials positively representing gays and lesbians into public schools. In other words, both states want harassment to be prevented through a kind of tolerance that dare not speak its name in curricula. In Maryland, the State School Board's lawyers have raised concerns that school antidiscrimination policies may bring too much information on homosexuality into public schools because of a "technical glitch" in the text of the policy. When an antidiscrimination bill was approved by the General Assembly in 2001 that banned bias against gays and lesbians, the bill emphasized that public schools are "not required to promote any form of sexuality or include any sexual orientation in the curriculum" (Desmond, 2002, p. 2B). Like the Helms Amendment of the 1980s that prohibited federal funds from supporting AIDS education that promoted homosexuality but was only used to keep funding from gay organizations, the Maryland law uses the language of fairness to suggest that no sexual orientation will find a place in the curriculum. Of course, family life classes continue to advocate heterosexual marriage. School board members are caught between trying to protect gay and lesbian students from harassment, as they must do in order to follow the state antidiscrimination policy, and also trying to avoid opening a loop hole that might allow the introduction of gay and lesbian issues into the curricula. As of the summer of 2002, they are working together with lawyers to ensure that their policy does replicate this "glitch" that might bring gay and lesbian issues into the classroom (Desmond, 2002, p. 2B).

The Massachusetts legislature also simultaneously sought to prevent antilesbian, gay, and bisexual discrimination and limit curricular representations of sexual minorities. When it passed an antidiscrimination policy including protection for sexual orientation to its equal educational opportunity law, the legislature included clauses minimizing the degree to which curricula could represent gay and lesbian issues. The state now calls for schools to start "active efforts" to address and prevent discrimination on the basis of sexual orientation. While original drafts of the law called for schools to "counteract" bias found in curricular materials, the state board revised the law to require that schools "provide balance and context" for bias and stereotypes about sexual orientation (Gehring, 2000, p. 23). In other words, although the schools are required to protect students from anti-gay bias, they are also required to provide school time for explanations for that bias. In criticizing the call for making sexual orientation a special form of protection requiring opponents of homosexuality to have voice in the curriculum, one advocate for sexual minorities argued, "We don't hear people say we need balanced views of racism" (LaFontaine quoted in Gehring, 2000, p. 23). Further, changes made to the draft of regulations, now state law, removed a requirement for sexual orientation that is still in place for racial minorities and gender: Curricula should "depict individuals of both sexes and from minority groups in 'a broad variety of positive roles' " (Gehring, 2000, p. 23). While curricula must, for instance, use racially, ethnically, and gender diverse examples and representations, there is no requirement that representation of gays, lesbians, bisexuals, or transgender people be incorporated into curricula. If schools do decide to represent sexual minorities, they are also required to represent those who oppose homosexuality. So, despite the policy's intention to be proactive against bias, Massachusetts actually opens school curricula to representations of bias against sexual minorities in order to appear fair. At the very least, these examples show a high level of ambivalence among policy makers who understand schools are open to liability for discrimination against sexual minority youth. At the worst, even inclusive policies reflect a continuing desire to minimize the protections and representations of sexual minorities. Further, by making discrimination against sexual minorities against the rules, but not part of curricula, schools do not need to engage in substantial discussion of why homophobia is so prevalent, what it means to be a sexual minority, and so on. Official silence can continue to do the work of homophobic harassment by trivializing the experiences of sexual minorities and minimizing representation of sexual minority issues.

Bias as Mere Discourtesy

Even school policies fully committed to protecting and representing a broad range of student diversity have run into problems with the courts. A recent decision indicates that concerns about liability in harassment cases will not easily be solved by installing restrictive antiharassment policies that limit speech. In *Saxe v. State College Area School District*, a broadly conceived school antiharassment policy and speech code that protected sexual minority students, among others, was disallowed by a court that construed the range of things considered by the policy to be harassment as too broad. While the court was concerned that the school district had overstepped its power in circumscribing free speech, the complainant in the case was more specifically concerned with curricular representation of homosexuality. Saxe has been quite candid that his intention was to prevent respect for homosexuality from becoming a school issue. Saxe began his case against the school district when he realized they "were trying to promote homosexuality" and the school used a video that was "a positive look at how teachers deal with homosexuality" (Zernike, 2001, p. A10). As his complaint to the court explains, he and his sons "openly and sincerely identify themselves as Christians. They believe, and their religion teaches, that homosexuality is a sin. Plaintiffs further believe that they have a right to speak out about the sinful nature and harmful effects of homosexuality" (Saxe quoted in United States Court of Appeals for the Third District, *Saxe v. State College*, 2001, p. 2). So any code that attempted to regulate community by excluding speech would necessarily exclude Saxe's sons because their religious commitment requires them to speak out against homosexuality.

The *Saxe* case is part of a larger trend of conservative challenges to multiculturalism, gay-inclusive nondiscrimination policies, and representations of a variety of minority concerns in school and after-school programs. Character education, for instance, has been embraced by conservatives who argue that the historical/political specificity of multicultural education emphasizes social fractures over commonalities. Rather than educating students about oppression, conservatives want to see all children taught values that have no particular context and respect that has no particular aim. Increasingly, conservative groups have begun challenging public school policies that teach tolerance. They claim, "Programs to teach tolerance in public schools are actually being used to promote and encourage homosexuality." In the name of tolerance, "homosexual activists have hijacked our schools. If we don't take a stand, were going to lose this battle" (McCain, 2002, p. A6).

Regardless of Saxe's particular intentions or the conservative backlash against anti-discrimination policies, the court ruled against the conduct code because it lacked a distinction between harassing speech and the sort of uncomfortable speech that was not protected by law. As Judge Samuel A. Alito Jr. argued, "previous courts had ruled that harassment statutes were not violated by epithets that injured someone's feelings, or mere 'discourtesy and rudeness' " (United States Court of Appeals for the Third District, *Saxe v. State College*, 2001, p. 7). In other words, the school district had attempted to limit its liability by preventing speech that made students uncomfortable and in the process had extended the definition of discomfort beyond the legal definition of harassment. While the court supported the school district's concern for liability, it argued that school codes cannot be broader than laws against harassment. Thus the court decided that concerns over liability would have been handled by a narrower conduct policy that did conform to already existing harassment law.

The district argued that it was doing more than attempting to avoid liability and that its policy was attempting to encourage the development of a just and equitable school community. The conduct code was meant to go beyond harassment and liability concerns and into more substantial protections for all students. Judge Alito argued that the code "ignores Tinker's requirement that a school must reasonably believe that speech will cause actual, material disruption before prohibiting it." In addition, because the policy covers speech that has both "the purpose and effect" of "interfering with educational performance or creating a hostile environment," it potentially punishes speech that intends to disrupt, but does not actually disrupt (United States Court of Appeals for the Third District, *Saxe v. State College*, 2001, p. 8). Policy cannot punish an intention, only an effect, according to the court. Further,

> because the Policy's "hostile environment" prong does not, on its face, require any threshold showing of severity or pervasiveness, it could conceivably be applied to cover any speech about

some enumerated personal characteristics the content of which offends someone. This could include much "core" political and religious speech: the Policy's "Definitions" section lists as examples of covered harassment "negative" or "derogatory" speech about such contentious issues as "racial customs," "religious tradition," "language," "sexual orientation," and "values." Such speech, when it does not pose a realist threat of substantial disruption, is within a student's First Amendment rights.

(U.S. Court of Appeals for the Third District, *Saxe v. State College*, 2001, pp. 11–12)

Even granting that the policy in question is quite broad (though its makers argue it is modeled after state and federal policies), "substantial disruption" means that many people would have to take offense before speech could be regulated by school policy. At the moment, homophobia is pervasive in public schools but not yet thought to be sufficient enough disruption that most faculty and administrators do anything at all about it. For sexual minority youth and those perceived to be sexual minority youth, these disruptions are problematic not because they are widely understood to be disruptive but because they are such perfectly normal situations.

While speech codes are the only answer to homophobia and bias, nonetheless, what students learn from codes is that there are some things worth the protections of codes and other things not worthy. Even giving codes their due as ceremonial markers of importance, though, codes themselves are not enough. Codes also, perhaps against the intention of those who design them, teach that following the code is equivalent to negotiating the difficulties of community and diversity. The code stands for the kind of interactions that might take place under the code and thus can encourage the lazy to go no further than installing a code. In Maryland and Massachusetts, as I described earlier, antidiscrimination policies not only stand in for more substantial education of the school community, but also prohibit more substantial curricular coverage of gay and lesbian issues. Simply providing a policy of protection from discrimination does not, after all, end discrimination. There is a loud silence in curricula that indicates to all students that there are some people in the school who do not deserve to be spoken about and that even some interested in protecting sexual minority youth appear willing to use a community agreement on civil silence as protection.

While educational environments should be challenging and contentious places, it remains striking that opponents to the inclusion of anti-gay discrimination clauses in school policies are not interested in making schools easier for sexual minority youth or places where bias is critically examined. The attempted inclusions I have described require as much exclusion as they attempt to prevent. The *Saxe* decision helps provide justification for further exclusions by conceiving of homophobia as trivial rudeness. Calling oppression rudeness and discourtesy misses the historical fact that exclusions are the stuff of courtesy, not rudeness. Civility has historically and contemporarily meant "not saying all that one wishes to say" or not raising difficult issues in a context where there will be disagreement. Under civility's dulling practice, social fractures continued unabated under a watchful process of removing what can be said. Indeed the conservative right's turn away from tolerance and civility in recent years has been in response to the left's attempt to refigure tolerance and civility as inclusion of issues that would previously have been considered inappropriate for polite company. So trying to untangle oppression from public interactions via civility and speech codes uses a tool inappropriate to the task of inclusion and definitely a tool that makes difference, even contentiously debated and intentionally provocative forms of difference, the domesticated stuff of deracinated interaction.

The problem for schools attempting to avoid liability for sexual minority students' (or any students') harassment means that schools must forge codes that do not upset the schools' usual silence on lesbian, gay, bisexual and transgender people. The bind is a difficult one largely because tolerance or civility, if unspecified by class or target, provide no particular coverage. However, as the school district found in *Saxe*, an overspecification may mean that school policy extends coverage for students beyond what is reflected in law. The school attempted to argue that this overextension is a good thing because schools are particularly fragile places whose mixture of diversity and youth requires a higher standard of conduct than antiharassment laws. Still, concern with liability or desire to stop harassment through simple codes do not fully educate about and against bias. It is not enough to stop bad words, education is also about explaining and exploring why homophobic bias has so prominent a place in public schools. Covering over the simmering homophobia by making sure students stop using homophobic language in front of teachers would be an improvement, of course, but it is not a solution to the problem of near total official silence on sexuality in public schools.

Say the Magic Words

Official silence makes schools hostile places for sexual minority youth and any youth perceived to be a sexual minority. The 2001 Gay Lesbian and Straight Educators Network survey on school climate has found that 99.9% of students surveyed reported hearing homophobic remarks in school (Kosciw & Cullen, 2001, p. 7). Further, homophobic words also damage students of all sexualities, making them cautious about their behavior for fear of being called lesbian or gay. According to the American Association of University Women, being called gay is the only form of harassment that affects boys and girls nearly equally, with 74% of boys and 73% of girls reporting that being called gay or lesbian would make them feel "very upset" (American Association of University Women, 2001, p. 1). What should be clear from these examples is that official silence on lesbian, gay, bisexual, and transgender youth occurs in a climate of constant harassment and speech. Unfortunately, though, the seriousness of that speech or understanding of its nuances is often lost on school authorities.

In a survey I did of school administrators about the school climate for sexual minority students, one principal reported that he had heard anti-gay comments but that they were usually among redneck friends insulting one another, so could hardly be the sort of speech that could be prevented. In addition, he indicated that these words were also not the sort of words anyone would consider insulting because they were clearly directed at friends, even if the intention was to tease those friends. Later, in an interview, another school administrator made a similar comment about the context of "homophobic" slurs at his school. The words "faggot" and "homo" were frequently tossed about among friends, but like the earlier comments on the survey he contended that no one would take them to be serious insults because they were directed only at friends. However, whether the words were directed at friends or not, students know which words to choose to inflict harm. Even if friends use the words to tease one another, other students may understand the content of that teasing differently.

It is not difficult to imagine that a sexual minority student overhearing comments made among friends insulting one another and getting a fairly clear sense that being a "faggot" or "homo" was not something to which one should aspire. Add to that situation the fact that teachers and administrators stop students from using some terms of derision, but allow (and even use themselves) words that insult sexual minorities, and all students learn that some insults are appropriate. When "insults" are appropriate, in fact, they are no longer insults, but rather acceptable ways of describing people one does not like. Banning the use of a word or even broadly suggesting in a code that all students should be tolerated does not guarantee that the experience of the school climate improves, especially if nothing else really changes. If teachers and administrators remain uncomfortable bringing issues affecting sexual minority youth (and any youth who may be interested, which seems likely to be all) into the curricula or if they continue practices that discriminate, restricting speech only masks the degree to which the context has not changed. Suppose that teachers, administrators, and students very earnestly police one another's speech without a full understanding of the complexity and diversity of sexual minority youth. One can imagine a situation in a school with a strict speech code where one young gay man could affectionately call another young gay man a "faggot" and be found to have violated the code. It may be the case, in this imaginary scenario, that the students are punished because of the possibility that other listeners may not have understood the affection with which the term was used. At that point, one rather imagines that the code was doing far too much work and other members of the school community far too little.

In other words, focusing too much on what a nondiscrimination policy or conduct code "does" and not enough on what one might want one's school community to become means that the play of meanings and spaces for different kinds of communication will be diminished. Further, codes with strict and concretized categories of protection may impede the ability of members of the school community to understand variations and innovations that exceed categories they have only tentatively begun to understand. When a gay student at a Chicago school put on high heels for a few minutes, he was told to dress appropriately for his gender or to leave school. While the school has a policy protecting gay students from discrimination, it also has a gender-specific dress code. While the student appears not to identify as transgender, nor does the school have a policy protecting transgender students, it is not fully clear that a policy in and of itself would support this student. Further, the situation raises the question of what sort of policy would best protect this student who clearly understands himself to be more complex than the categories that might protect or expel him. As he explains, "I identify as whatever I put on in the morning" (anonymous student quoted in Barlow, 2002, p. 2). By guaranteeing protection via categories, then, codes allow people to avoid having to fully understand the complexity of their world and consider how categories are constantly complicated by the variety of practice.

Codes also allow people the comfort of falling back on a few conversational techniques to make up for their loss of experience. When asked what they would do if an elementary school child called another child "faggot," my preservice teachers quickly fall back on, "I would tell them that word is inappropriate." They cannot easily say why the word is inappropriate and can, after a little prodding, recall that being told something they were doing was "inappropriate" really did not settle the issue for them when they were kids. However, they are more comfortable dealing with difficult issues if there is a rule to back them up because the rule gets them off the hook for providing an explanation. In short, following a very good understanding of cultural attitudes about homosexuality, students combine their desire to squelch homophobia with a desire to curtail any discussion of queer people. "Inappropriate" is as closely linked to homophobia as it is to homosexuality.

Further, "inappropriate" means that the less said about the insulting words, the better. Homophobic incidents become unremarkable in the sense that they will not be remarked upon. Students also say, "the kids don't even know what those words mean," but they also do not want to be the people who provide meaning to the words. They just want the words to be stopped, as if the context for speaking those words is challenged by challenging a speaker without explanation.

Knowing the right rule or the right term replaces fuller discussions of why words cause problems in the first place. A few of my students have, in all seriousness, asked me if it is acceptable to call a Jewish person a Jew because they have only ever heard the word "Jew" as an insult. Likewise, students forced to sit through antihomophobia workshops have often asked if it is OK for them to refer to gays and lesbians as "queers" because they have heard the word used among sexual minorities as a positive term. While I usually say something overly simplistic like, "as long as you don't shout it out of a pick-up truck while tossing a beer bottle, sure, it's OK," the question still sets up the problem of how much context, speaker, and intention go into making words mean something. And even then, the meaning still is not certain. What may set one person's teeth on edge, whoever says it, however it is said, may cause another person no trouble at all. However, students who have little experience with a variety of people from a variety of different groups and background have no way, in their own limited experience, to navigate the complexity and possibility of language. "Experience," of course, is no less complicated than tolerance or meaning, and having the experience of understanding that some things are worthy of being covered by codes and that other things are not are in themselves instructive experiences, whether one rebels, assents, or continues oneself to grapple with the possibilities.

In these examples of students looking for the right words to say to others, one gets the feeling that the correct words have a magical quality that will heal the social fractures that maintain difference. In discussions with preservice teachers trying to strategize how they would handle a range of bias-related harassment, many students explained that they would be afraid to say the wrong words and thus be mistaken for a racist or a homophobe. They said they would be reluctant to intervene in conflicts between students and even more reluctant to say anything to an overtly biased colleague because their own inexperience with words would indict them as well. The upshot of the discussions has been that until preservice teachers feel comfortable using words associated with diversity, they claim they will not intervene. This dodging of responsibility often travels with exasperated comments like, "I don't know what 'they' want to be called now, it seems like it's always changing and if you call 'them' the wrong thing, 'they'll' get mad." In other words, preservice teachers know what not to say, but because they have likely lived under codes, but not had substantial engagement with diversity or education about diversity, they cannot add to a situation. They can only frustratedly subtract words or phrases that presumably they used to use (or they would not be frustrated) but have now found out are taboo.

Most troubling, like the old "What is a kike? A Jewish gentleman who has left the room," the desire to use the right words only comes up in examples where the group being described is present. The etiquette implied by the necessary presence of the other contains within its restraint the continued presence of suppressed bias. Finding the right words only requires a momentary abatement of the business as usual bias. Part of the frustration of majority students who feel they are being unreasonably asked to curtail their speech or alter their word choice is that they cannot see any real change in not saying all they would like to say. Perhaps because they have lived under school codes and relatively silent curricula, students have learned that changing the words one calls another person counts as sufficient.

Answering Silence with Silence

Sexual minority youth and their allies have used the climate of silence to their own advantage in the most popular antihomophobia demonstration in public schools, the "Day of Silence." Annually, on or about April 9, participants in the "Day of Silence" take a nine-hour vow of silence. They use this time to mark the institutional and personal silences that frame their lives by handing out cards that explain their silence:

> Please understand my reasons for not speaking today. I support lesbian, gay, bisexual, and transgender rights. People who are silent today believe that laws and attitudes should be inclusive of people of all sexual orientations. The Day of Silence is to draw attention to those who have been silenced by hatred, oppression, and prejudice. Think about the voices you are not hearing.
>
> (Day of Silence Project, 2001, p. 1)

Information on the Day of Silence suggests that activism is not enough because "actions are too detached from students' daily life. Homophobes can just avoid rallies. Educational events end up preaching to the converted" (Day of Silence Project, 2001, p. 2). However, by being visible about their silence, organizers explain that "everywhere participants go, they are silent in a visible manner to show that they will no longer stand for the silencing of queer people" (Day of Silence Project, 2001, p. 3). While a cynical response to the popularity of this demonstration might be that it is about the least disruptive demonstration one can think of, there is more going on than silence as usual. Intentional silence with the clear purpose of pointing out the normal silencing of sexual minorities seems to raise quite a bit of ire. At my university, the student queer group received numerous claims of harassment from non ally straight people. Apparently being reminded that lesbian, gay, bisexual, and transgender people were specifically deciding not to talk was just too much for a few straight people who had gotten used to not thinking about the fact that queer people were usually silent. One student said she felt "bombarded" by the queer students handing out cards explaining why they were not talking. The effects of silence, then, can be just as troubling as effects of speech. On the one hand, the student was disturbed and thus presumably thinking differently about homophobia. At the same time, though, she had converted the disruption back into a self-centered response. However, that is the danger with using passive aggressive techniques to make a substantive point.

Still, the demonstration gets people thinking and talking about why they had not previously noticed the silence of sexual minorities. In some schools, teachers and nonsilent students have spontaneously engaged in discussions about homophobia. Although one might also be troubled by the fact that the absence of sexual minority voices spurs this conversation on, the Day of Silence action requires that those who normally ignore the situation take more responsibility for their ignorance. Because I am of the generation that preferred yelling in the streets to silence, I worry that the lack of speech allows for a queer-sanctioned "homophobia as usual" and allows too many people to dodge behind the silence as if nothing were happening. Even so, the action does generate response. Media coverage uses the opportunity to provide balanced coverage of conservatives, interviewing protestors, or even seeking out representatives of conservative organizations who had never heard of the protest but, wryly, approve. As one conservative explained to a reporter, "We figured if they're going to be silent, it's a chance for us to speak up even more" (Ovadal quoted in Williams, 2002, p. 1).

Media coverage also takes the opportunity to run its fair share of humorous headlines, like "Shutting Up to Get a Point Across," "Day of Silence Makes Noise," and "Day of Silence Speaks Volumes." In Salt Lake City, where years of court battles ended with the official recognition of the right of Gay Straight Alliances to meet in public schools, coverage of the event mimics homophobic prejudice. "In the past 24 hours, a group of Highland High School students may have heard classmates use such words as 'gay' or 'ghetto' in derogatory ways, make sexist jokes or shun others for their clothing. They didn't say a word to stop it. And that's a good thing." The article goes on to explain that the silence is an action against oppression (May, 2002, p. 1). So one odd effect of the Day of Silence is that non allies are startled to see a silenced minority using passive aggressive techniques to counter its silencing. Whereas the silent treatment may seem initially trivial, the discomfort of students who are not silent grows throughout the day. Silence, in effect, does get their ire up and eventually, like anyone enduring the silent treatment, they have to start asking questions. More than a few participants have explained that their vow does not last long because inevitably someone around them will say something that needs to be answered. The silence of queers then becomes something that nonsilent students have to request an end to.

While I do not think one action is the answer to homophobia, in contrast to codes that limit speech in exchange for limited representation, the Day of Silence highlights institutional, cultural and personal practices that allow people to remain ignorant of the homophobia structuring their lives. In effect, the intentionality of silence disturbs people who are used to having silence on sexual minorities be the seemingly unintentional norm. If they get to the point where the disruption of homophobia as usual bothers them, they start asking questions of people with whom they may never have spoken or whom they may never have thought might be critical of homophobia. Silence itself is not the whole point of the day, though students do begin to get an idea of the discomforting pervasiveness of silence on sexual minorities. Unlike the tendency of codes to concentrate on individual speech acts as the site of bias, silence shows the pervasiveness of bias, the way silences structure the lives of people, which many policies appear on protecting through limitations on speech. The greater point may be that silence has to be addressed and that realization reminds all involved that they are to some degree involved in one another's lives and need to examine uncomfortable and too comfortable silences.

References

American Association of University Women. (2001). *Hostile hallways: Bullying, teasing, and sexual harassment in school.* Accessed at http://www.aauw.org/2000/hostile.html.

Barlow, G. (2002, July 31). Principal gives high heels on boys the boot. *Chicago Free Press.* Accessed at http://www.glsen.org/templates/news/record.html?section=12&record=1386.

Butler, J. (1997). *Excitable speech: A politics of the performative.* New York: Routledge. Day of silence project. (2001). Accessed at www.glsen.org/templates/student/record.htmt?section=108&record=636

Desmond, S. (2002, 27 June). School board defers vote on policy to protect gay students. *Baltimore Sun, 27,* p. 28.

Gehring, J. (2000, 17 May). Mass stance on anti-gay bias in schools stirring debate. *Education Week,* p. 23.

Kosciw, J.G., & Cullen, M.K. (2001). *The GLSEN 2001 national school climate survey: The school-related experiences of our nation's lesbian, gay, bisexual, and transgender youth.* New York: Gay, Lesbian, and Straight Educators Network.

May, H. (2002, May 30). Highland students use silence to speak out against oppression. *Salt Lake Tribune*. Accessed at http://www.glsen.org/templates/news/record.html?section=12&recordt=1341.

McCain, R.S. (2002). Tolerance in schools a homosexual ploy, conservatives say. *The Washington Times*, p. A6.

United States Court of Appeals for the Third District. (2001). *David Warren Saxe v. State College Area School District*, No 99–4081.

Williams, S. (2002, April 11). Day of silence disrupted by protests. *Journal Sentinel*. Accessed at: http://www.glsen.org/templates/news/record.html?section=12&record=1296.

Zernike, K. (2001, February 16). Free-speech ruling voids school districts harassment policy. *New York Times*, A10.

Suggested Readings for Future Study

Abelove, H., Barale, M., and Halperin, D. (1993). *Lesbian and gay studies reader*. New York: Routledge.

Anzaldúa, G., ed. (1990). *Haciendo caras: Creative and critical perspectives by feminists of color*. San Francisco: Aunt Lute Books.

Azzarito, L. and Solmon, M. (2006). "A Feminist Poststructuralist View on Student Bodies in Physical Education: Sites of Compliance, Resistance, and Transformation," *Journal of Teaching Physical Education*, 25: 200–225.

Beasley, C. (2005). *Gender and Sexuality: Critical Theories, Critical Thinkers*. Thousand Oaks, CA: Sage.

Boler, M. (2007). *Feeling Power: Emotions and Education*. New York: Taylor & Francis.

Boler, M. (2004). *Democratic Dialogue in Education: Troubling Speech, Disturbing Silence*. New York: Peter Lang.

Butler, J. (1990). *Gender trouble: Feminism and the subversion of identity*. New York: Routledge.

Butler, J. and Scott, J. (1992). *Feminists theorize the political*. New York: Routledge.

de Beauvoir, Simone. 1953. *The second sex*. New York: Vintage Books.

Delgado Bernal, D., Elenes, C. A., Godinez, F. E. and Villenas, S. (2006). *Chicana/Latina Education in Everyday Life: Feminista Perspectives on Pedagogy and Epistemology*. New York: SUNY Press.

Ellsworth, E. (1989). "Why Doesn't This Feel Empowering? Working Through the Repressive Myths of Critical Pedagogy," *Harvard Education Review* 59(3): 297–324.

Fischman, G. (2000). *Imagining teachers: Rethinking gender dynamics in teacher education*. Lanham, MD: Rowman and Littlefield.

Fields, J. and Tolman, D. L. (2006). "Risky Business: Sexuality Education and Research in U.S. Schools," *Sexuality Research and Social Policy*, Vol. 3, No. 4, pp. 63–76.

Forrest, S. (2006). "Straight Talking: Challenges in teaching and learning about sexuality and homophobia in schools," in Cole, M. (ed.), *Education, Equality and Human Rights: Issues of Gender, 'Race', Sexuality, Disability and Social Class*, pp. 111–133. London: Routledge.

Fuss, D. (1991). *Inside/outside: Lesbian theories, gay theories*. New York: Routledge.

Garcia, A., ed. (1997). *Chicana feminist thought*. New York: Routledge.

Gore, Jennifer (1998). "On the limits to empowerment through critical and feminist pedagogies," in *From power, knowledge, and pedagogy: The meaning of democratic education in unsettling time*, ed. Dennis Carlson and Michael W. Apple, 271–288. Boulder, CO and Oxford: Westview Press.

Gore, J. (1993). *The struggle for pedagogies: Critical and feminist discourses as regimes of truth*. New York: Routledge.

Giroux, H., ed. (1991). *Postmodernism, feminism, and cultural politics*. Albany: SUNY Press.

Grace, A. P. & Benson, F. J. (2000). "Using autobiographical queer life narratives of teachers to connect personal, political and pedagogical spaces." *International Journal of Inclusive Education* 4(2): 89–109.

Grumet, M. (1988). *Bitter Milk*. Cambridge, MA: University of Massachusetts Press.

Guillaumin, C. (1995). *Racism, sexism, power and ideology*. London: Routledge.

Hernandez, A. (1987). *Pedagogy, democracy, and feminism: Rethinking the public sphere*. Albany: SUNY Press.

Hill, R. J. (1995). "Gay discourse in adult education: A critical review," *Adult Education Quarterly* 45(3): 142–158.

Hill, R. J. (1996). "Learning to transgress: A social-historical conspectus of the American gay lifeworld as a site of struggle and resistance," *Studies in the Education of Adults* 28(2): 253–279.

hooks, b. and Shapiro, E. P. (2000). *Feminist Theory: From Margin to Center*. Boston, MA: South End Press.

hooks, b. (1990). *Yearning: Race, gender and cultural politics*. Boston: South End Press.

hooks, b. (1999). *Talking back: Thinking feminist, thinking black*. Boston: South End Press.

Irvine, J. (1994). *Sexual cultures and the construction of adolescent identity*. Philadelphia: Temple University Press.

Kameda, Atsuko (1995). *Sexism and gender stereotyping in schools. Japanese women: New feminist perspectivs on the past, present, and future*, ed. Kumiko Fujimura-Fanselow and Atsuko Kameda, pp. 107–124. New York: The Feminist Press.

Kehily, M. J. (2002). *Sexuality, Gender and Schooling: Shifting Agendas in Social Learning.* New York: Routledge.

Keohane, N., et al. (1982). *Feminist theory: A critique of ideology.* Chicago: University of Chicago Press.

Kumashiro, K. (2002). *Troubling Education: Queer Activism and Anti-Oppressive Pedagogy.* New York: RoutledgeFalmer.

Lancaster, R. and Di Leonardo, M., eds. (1997). *The gender sexuality reader.* New York: Routledge.

Lather, P. (1995). "Post-critical pedagogies: A feminist reading," in P. McLaren (ed.), *Postmodernism, post-colonialism and pedagogy.* Albert Park, Australia: James Nicholas Publishers.

Letts, W., IV, and Sears, T. (1999). *Queering elementary education: Advancing the dialogue about sexuality and schooling.* Lanham, MD: Rowman and Littlefield.

Lewis, M. (1993). *Without a Word: Teaching Beyond Women's Silence.* New York: Routledge.

Lewis, M. (1992). "Interrupting Patriarchy: Politics, Resistance and Transformation in the Feminist Classroom," in C. Luke (ed.) *Feminisms and Critical Pedagogy.* New York: Routledge.

Luke, C. (1996) "Feminist pedagogy theory: reflections on power and authority," *Educational Theory,* 46: 283–302.

Luke, C. and Gore, J. (1992). *Feminism and critical pedagogy.* New York: Routledge.

Luker, K. (1997). *Dubious Conceptions: The Politics of Teenage Pregnancy.* Harvard University Press.

Lutrell, W. (2003). *Pregnant Bodies, Fertile Minds: Gender, Race, and the Schooling of Pregnant Teens.* New York: Routledge.

Maher, F. (1999). "Progessive Education and Feminist Pedagogies: Issues in Gender, Power, and Authority," *Teachers College Record,* 101(1) (Fall): 35–39.

Mason, Gail (2001). *The Spectacle of Violence: Homophobia, Gender and Knowledge.* New York: Routledge.

Mayo, C. (2007). *Disputing the Subject of Sex: Sexuality and Public School Controversies.* Lanham, MD: Rowman and Littlefield.

Macdonald, A. & Sanchez-Casal, S. (2002). *Twenty-First Century Feminist Classrooms: Pedagogies of Identity and Difference.* New York: Palgrave Macmillan.

McRobbie, A. (1991). *Feminism and Youth Culture: From Jackie to Just Seventeen.* London: Macmillan.

Minh-ha, T. (1989). *Woman native other: Writing Postcoloniality and feminism.* Bloomington: Indiana University Press.

Mohanty, C., Russo, A., and Torres, L. (1991). *Third world women and the politics of feminism.* Bloomington: Indiana University Press.

Ng, R., Staton, P., and Scane, J. (1995). *Anti-racism, Feminism, and Critical Approaches to Education.* Westport, CN: Bergin & Garvey.

Parmeter, S., Reti, I., Hart, E.L., and Rosa, M.E. (1988). *The Lesbian in Front of the Classroom: Writings by Lesbian Teachers.* Santa Cruz, CA: HerBooks.

Perumal, J. (2007). *Identity, diversity and teaching for social justice.* New York: Peter Lang.

Pillow, W. (2004). *Unfit Subjects: Educational Policy and the Teen Mother.* New York: Routledge.

Pinar, W. (1988). *Queer Theory in Education.* New York: Lawrence Erlbaum.

Rasmussen, M.L., Rofes, E., and Talburt, S. (2004). *Youth and Sexualities: Pleasure, Subversion, and Insubordination In and Out of Schools.* London: Palgrave Macmillan.

Rhoads, R. (1994). *Coming Out in College: The Struggle for a Queer Identity.* Connecticut: Bergin & Garvey.

Rosaldo, Michelle and Lamphere, Louise, eds. (1974). *Women, Culture, and Society.* Stanford: Stanford University Press.

Segal, L. (1997). "Sexualities," in Woodward, K. (ed.), *Identity and Difference,* pp. 183–238. London: Sage Publications.

Shapiro, S. (1999). *Pedagogy and the Politics of the Body: A Critical Praxis.* New York and London: Garland Publishing.

Simon, R. I. (1992). *Teaching against the grain: Texts for a pedagogy of possibility.* New York: Bergin & Garvey.

Stromquist, N. (2004). "The Educational Nature of Feminist Action," in G. Foley (ed.), *Dimensions of Adult Learning. Adult Education and Training in a Global Era.* Sydney: Allen & Unwin; Maidenhead: Open University Press/McGraw-Hill.

Sudbury, J. (1998). *Other kinds of dreams.* New York: Routledge.

Talburt, S. and Steinberg, S. (2000). *Thinking Queer: Sexuality, Culture, and Education (Counterpoints: Studies in the Postmodern Theory of Education,* vol. 118). New York: Peter Lang.

Thompson, J. (1983). *Learning liberation: Women's response to men's education.* London: Croom Helm.

Thompson, J. (2000). *Women, class, and education.* London: Routledge.

Tierney, W. G. (1997). *Academic outlaws: Queer Theory and Cultural Studies in the Academy.* Sage Publications.

Tisdell, E. J. (1993). "Feminism and adult learning: Power, pedagogy, and praxis," in Merriam, S. B. (ed.), *An Update on Adult Learning Theory,* pp. 91–103. San Francisco: Jossey-Bass Publishers.

Tisdell, E. J. (1998). "Poststructural feminist pedagogies: The possibilities and limitations of feminist emancipatory adult learning theory and practice." *Adult Education Quarterly,* 48: 139–156.

Tisdell, E. L. (2000). "Feminist pedagogies," in Hayes, E. and Flannery, D.D. (eds.), *Women as learners: The significance of gender in adult learning,* pp. 155–83. San Francisco, CA: Jossey-Bass.

Trujillo, C. (1998). *Living Chicana theory.* Berkeley, CA: Third Woman Press.

Unks, G., ed. (1995). *The gay teen. Educational practice and theory for lesbian, gay and bisexual adolescents.* New York: Routledge.

Valadez, G. and Elsbree, A. (2005). "Queer Coyotes: Transforming Education To Be More Accepting, Affirming, and Supportive of Queer Individuals," in Cline, Z., Reyes, M., and Necochea, J. (eds.), *Journal of Latinos and Education*, 4(3): 171–192.

Wallace, M. (1990). *Invisibility blues: From pop to theory*. New York: Routledge.

Warren, K., ed. (1997). *Ecofeminism: Women, culture, nature*. Bloomington: Indiana University Press.

Weedon, C. (1987). *Feminist practice and poststructuralist theory*. Oxford, UK: Blackwell.

Weeks, B. (1995). "The Body and Sexuality," in Hall, S., Held, D., Hubert, D., and Thompson, K. (eds.), *Modernity: An Introduction to Modern Societies*, pp. 363–388. Cambridge: Polity.

Weiler, K. (2001). *Feminist engagements: Reading, resisting, and reinventing male theorists in education and cultural studies*. New York: Routledge.

Weiler, K. (1998). *Women teaching for change: Gender, class and power*. South Hadley, MA: Bergin & Garvey.

Weiler, K. (1994). "Freire and a feminist pedagogy of difference," in McLaren, P.L. and Lankshear, C. (eds.), *Politics of liberation: Paths from Freire*, pp. 12–40. New York: Routledge.

Weis, L. and Fine, M. (2005). *Beyond Silenced Voices: Class, Race, And Gender In United States Schools*. New York: SUNY Press.

Welton, D. (1998). *Body and flesh*. Boston: Blackwell.

Part Five

Language, Literacy, and Pedagogy

Introduction to Part Five

In concert with Paulo Freire's integrated vision of language, literacy, and pedagogy, critical literacy does not constitute a subfield or a different approach to literacy, but rather, is one of the major pillars of critical pedagogy. For Freire, an emancipatory education is founded on an evolving capacity to read the world critically and effectively problematize the assymetrical relations of power, which structurally reproduce inequalities and social exclusions within schools and society. Moreover, the tradition of emancipatory education is firmly rooted in the teaching and learning of literacy and orality in its multiple forms, as vehicles for the development of conscientization.

Given the eminently political nature of education, literacy cannot simply be reduced to the mastery of decoding and encoding skills, or to the neutral and technical teaching of language symbols, nor to the adoption of simple "fetish methods." Critical literacy, instead, is the vehicle through which critical pedagogy is implemented and enacted. It encompasses a pedagogical process of teaching and learning, by which students and teachers interrogate the world, unmask ideological and hegemonic discourses, and frame their actions, in the interest of the larger struggle for social justice. As such, teachers and students together deconstruct and demystify the curriculum, challenging the fragmentation, instrumentalism, and absolute nature of official knowledge. This is actualized, in part, through the use of a political economic framework that helps to unveil how education serves the interests of the marketplace. Critical literacy, true to its pedagogical roots, employs the principles of dialogue and conscientization in the development of critical discourse. Thus, encoding and decoding skills, spelling, comprehension, and writing, all function as critical tools that facilitate the awakening process of social consciousness.

Accordingly, the articles included in this section are informed by a critical pedagogical view of literacy. Exposed is the value-laden, political nature of education, and more specifically in the teaching of literacy. Fundamental to this understanding of schooling is awareness that the teaching of literacy and orality can either function as a mechanism to perpetuate asymmetries of power and privilege in the larger society or emancipatory opportunities for transformative education. Proposed here is a liberatory vision of literacy that is intrinsically linked to the diverse identities, languages, and cultural meanings that students bring to the classroom. Thus, what emerges is a pedagogical analysis of what constitutes critical pedagogy, in the form of critical literacy.

Summary of Articles

The articles examine a variety of key questions, related to the teaching of literacy. How is literacy and orality taught? What are teachers' expectations and interactions with students? What is the goal of literacy? What kind of curriculum is being used in the classroom? How is student experience incorporated in lessons? How conducive for learning is the classroom environment? How are issues of power and discipline addressed? What is the hierarchy of diverse knowledge and languages at work in the classroom? What are the assumptions, stereotypes and ideologies that teachers bring to their teaching? In sum, the authors address the cultural politics that undergird traditional notions of reading and writing.

In *What is Critical Literacy?*, Ira Shor provides a variety of definitions of emancipatory literacy. All of them allude to the awakening experience, proposed by Freire, of reading the world and the word. In those definitions, critical literacy is visualized as a project of dissension where, over the last twenty years, the act of teaching has been steadily undermined by the "culture wars" of the New Conservative Right. To counter the oppressive nature of this context, critical literacy also draws on John Dewey's proposition that student experiences be incorporated into schools, in order to support the development of "reflective, democratic citizens." Further, Shor contends that both Lev Vygotsky's notion of social learning, in which the incorporation of language and culture are vital components for the development of cognition, and Freire's vision of teachers as knowledgable, political, and rigorous educators are at work. Shor provides examples of critical literacy, through multiple modalities of writing, including composition, autoethnography, and other writing programs.

In the article, *Teaching How to Read the World and Change It*, Robert Peterson explains how the teaching of the world and the word happens. This article provides an excellent example of how critical pedagogy is enacted in the classroom, even under the heavy constraints of a powerful conservative movement in schools. Peterson's account offers a variety of practical applications, from thematic teaching—or generative themes as Freire calls them—to experiential learning for second language students. He provides excellent examples of how to teach using a problem-posing pedagogy, and how to use dialogue and conscientization as a vehicle for the development of voice and participation within a middle-school classroom.

Lisa Delpit's article, *Language Diversity and Learning*, examines the role of language in the construction of literate identities, as defined by the dominant society. She offers important insights into the manner in which language form, language use, language performance, language competency, cultural communication styles, and linguistic knowledge play significant roles in how teachers both perceive and teach literacy in their classroom. More important, she extends this insightful analysis to the development of low expectations among teachers of second language learners and speakers of "nonstandard" forms of English. Delpit reveals the way in which speakers of non-mainstream forms of English are systematically disabled from reading, as a consequence of debilitating reading intervention programs, which dismiss students' existing literacy skills when these fail to conform to the authoritative usage of "standard" English.

In *Beyond the Methods Fetish*, Lilia Bartolomé examines the common and persistent demands of classroom teachers for appropriate methods to assist them in the teaching of culturally diverse students. In response, she warns against the reification of instructional approaches designed to help teachers to deal (or cope) with the assumed exceptionality of diverse, working-class students. Bartolomé's research reveals the manner in which an obsessive focus on instructional methods, inadvertently, becomes an obstacle to the critical development of the very students that teachers propose to serve. Instead, she encourages educators to embrace a humanizing pedagogy that centers students as subjects, rather than dehumanized objects upon which instruction is applied. Bartolomé reaffirms, here, the significance of process writing, language experience, cooperative learning, strategic teaching and whole language activities—but only when implemented within the context of a liberating educational process.

Questions for Reflection and Dialogue

1. In what ways is Ira Shor's definition of critical literacy grounded in the philosophical ideas of John Dewey, Lev Vygotsky, and Paulo Freire?
2. What classroom suggestions does Robert Peterson offer to counterbalance the debilitating impact of teacher-proof reading programs (i.e., Open Court, Reading First)?
3. How does Peterson incorporate dialogue, reflection, political action, and critical literacy in his middle-school teaching?
4. In what ways do teachers legitimate and reward the communication styles of the dominant society?
5. What are the implications of dominant literacy approaches to the accumulation of cultural capital and the education of working-class students?
6. What does Lilia Bartolomé mean by the phrase "teachers' political clarity"?
7. How do you understand the role and importance of political clarity within critical pedagogy?
8. What approach would you take to teach critical literacy to second language learners and speakers of "non-standard" English? Explain why.
9. Given the critical views of literacy included in this section, provide an analysis of traditional reading intervention programs in public schools today.

14

What is Critical Literacy?

Ira Shor

Introduction

We are what we say and do. The way we speak and are spoken to help shape us into the people we become. Through words and other actions, we build ourselves in a world that is building us. That world addresses us to produce the different identities we carry forward in life: men are addressed differently than are women, people of color differently than whites, elite students differently than those from working families. Yet, though language is fateful in teaching us what kind of people to become and what kind of society to make, discourse is not destiny. We can redefine ourselves and remake society, if we choose, through alternative rhetoric and dissident projects. This is where critical literacy begins, for questioning power relations, discourses, and identities in a world not yet finished, just, or humane.

Critical literacy thus challenges the status quo in an effort to discover alternative paths for self and social development. This kind of literacy—words rethinking worlds, self dissenting in society—connects the political and the personal, the public and the private, the global and the local, the economic and the pedagogical, for rethinking our lives and for promoting justice in place of inequity. Critical literacy, then, is an attitude towards history, as Kenneth Burke (1984) might have said, or a dream of a new society against the power now in power, as Paulo Freire proposed (Shor and Freire, 1987), or an insurrection of subjugated knowledges, in the ideas of Michel Foucault (1980), or a counter-hegemonic structure of feeling, as Raymond Williams (1977) theorized, or a multicultural resistance invented on the borders of crossing identities, as Gloria Anzaldua (1990) imagined, or language used against fitting unexceptionably into the status quo, as Adrienne Rich (1979) declared.

From this perspective, *literacy* is understood as social action through language use that develops us as agents inside a larger culture, while *critical literacy* is understood as "learning to read and write as part of the process of becoming conscious of one's experience as historically constructed within specific power relations" (Anderson and Irvine, 82). Consequently, my opening question, "What is critical literacy?," leads me to ask, "How have we been shaped by the words we use and encounter? If language use is one social force constructing us ('symbolic action' as Kenneth Burke, 1966, argued), how can we use and teach oppositional discourses so as to remake ourselves and our culture?"

Essentially, then, critical literacy is language use that questions the social construction of the self. When we are critically literate, we examine our ongoing development, to reveal the subjective positions from which we make sense of the world and act in it. All of us grow up and live in local cultures set in global contexts where multiple discourses shape us.

Neighborhood life and schooling are two formidable sites where the local and the global converge. In my case, until I left home for an elite university in 1962, I grew up in a Jewish working-class neighborhood in the South Bronx of New York City. In this treeless, teeming area, moms and dads held steady jobs but always spoke of needing money; chimneys coughed out garbage smoke daily yet few people complained; abundant ethnic food with names like "kishke" and "kugel" were occasions for passionate conviviality in kitchens filled with talk and stories; Eastern European accents were common and sometimes ridiculed, while non-Standard English was typical even among the native-born; televisions were always on and newspapers were delivered daily to our doors, teaching us the world beyond the neighborhood; and the N-word was spoken casually on gray blocks where only whites lived and only whites operated the small stores (except for one Asian family that slept and cooked in the back room of the Chinese laundry run by a mom and a dad who spoke little English, unlike the African-Americans I heard who had lots of English but no stores).

In that alleged Golden Age, black families and their own English were quarantined across the Bronx River Parkway in a housing project built in 1953 along with a junior high that straddled the racial border and became home to gangs divided by color and ethnicity. My first September day there in 1957 was made memorable by seeing a knife fight at dismissal time. For the next two years, I never went to the bathroom in that building. This was a coming attraction for the even more aggressive senior high nearby, which could have been the set for "Blackboard Jungle," a famous urban flick in that decade.

Like many American places then and now across the country, these gritty streets were a suburb of Hollywood. We kids went weekly to the local Skouras movie house under the roaring Pelham Bay el, paid 40 cents to see a John Wayne cowboy or war saga along with 20 cartoons, and devoured teeth-destroying candy, like a chocolate treat we called "nigger babies." It was a time when John D. Rockefeller's grandson Nelson first ran for Governor of New York, and my young ears noticed a change in one of my favorite jingles—Chock Full of Nuts, the heavenly coffee, stopped saying that "better coffee Rockefeller's money can't buy" and suddenly crooned that "better coffee a millionaire's money can't buy." Could such a change help the famous grandson get elected? Were words that important?

Rockefeller took the state house in Albany while I was in junior high, but before I got to that gang-divided territory and the accelerated "special progress" section that creamed off the most scholastic working-class kids, I patiently made my way up the "one" track in my all-white elementary school (1–1, 2–1, 3–1, 4–1, etc.) set aside for supposedly "smart" kids who were being divided from their "ordinary" peers very early in life. I soon learned that a handful of chosen white working-class kids were supposed to leave the others behind, which I happily did with the push of my mother who insisted I stop cursing like my friends and speak proper English ("he doesn't" not "he don't").

Racially, in the desegregation 1950s, my elementary school changed ever so slightly when a single perfect black girl mysteriously appeared—Olivia was her name. One day, our third grade teacher asked us how many of our fathers went to work in suits and ties. Few hands went up, not mine or Olivia's. The teacher's question confused and embarrassed me because my dad—a sheet-metal worker and high-school drop-out—wore his only suit for special occasions, perhaps as did Olivia's father. Suits in my neighborhood were for bar mitzvahs, weddings, funerals, lodge gatherings, high holidays, or union meetings. The teacher's question that morning invited me to be ashamed of my family and our clothes which, like our thick urban accents and bad table manners, marked us as socially inferior, despite the white skin which gave us some decisive privileges over Olivia's family, such as my dad's union wages, living on the "better" side of the Parkway, segregated classes for us white kids in junior high (internal tracking), and moms who could hire black cleaning ladies on Saturdays while they went off to the local beauty parlors to get a perm.

Perms were a small weekly luxury in this neighborhood, where suits, "proper" English, and good table manners were rare. Still, I did see in those days a grownup wearing a tie and jacket to work—the elementary school principal. One morning, this suit called me to his office to let me know he was banning the little school newspaper I had started with my best friend Barry. (We called it "The Spirit of '93" to play on "the spirit of '76" we had read about vis-à-vis the American Revolution, and to honor our public school that had a number but no name.) When the principal abruptly ended our literate venture, I learned that 11-year-olds in our democracy can't publish a paper without prior official approval. The suit's word was power and law. Our kid's word vanished.

Thirty years later, unfortunately, the Supreme Court confirmed the right of public schools to censor student publications, in the Hazelwood decision. More recently, my memory of childhood censorship was stirred again when a New Jersey principal stopped my colleague Maria Sweeney's class from performing its original anti-sweatshop play (Nieves, 1997; Karp, 1997). The suit this time was worn by a female who suggested that fifth-graders can't really understand such issues as sweatshops, and besides, the kids weren't being fair to Nike and Disney. Maria with some parents and theater professionals stood by the 11-year-olds and their script, which the kids eventually performed onstage in Manhattan, so there was a happy ending to this story.

I could have used Maria Sweeney and activist parents in the '50s. Students of all ages need adult coalitions to help them win language rights to free speech and to social criticism (the presidents at two City University of New York campuses recently nullifed student government elections when dissident slates won). Adult support can keep restrictive authorities at bay, not only when a Broadway cause célèbre erupts like the sweatshop play, but also for the low-profile, everyday forms of silencing that researchers like John Goodlad (1984) and Michelle Fine (1987, 1993) found in mass schooling. Administrative rule-making and top-down curricula mean that authority is unilateral not democratic, featuring standardized tests, commercial textbooks, mandated syllabi, oneway teacher-talk, and fill-in-the-blank exams. As teachers well know, silenced students find ways to make lots of noise, in the unofficial spaces of halls, toilets, lunchrooms, yards, and streets, as well as during class when teachers attempt their lesson plans. At many sites of mass education including public colleges, a culture war of discourses is apparently underway. In wars of words, can language and literacy be innocent? Can education be neutral?

Innocent or Neutral? Literacy and Pedagogy

If language and education were non-partisan, I suppose my school principal would have allowed the "Spirit of '93" to circulate in the building. (Why didn't he campaign against the circulation of the N-word among us kids and our parents?) If words and schooling were free from conventional politics, I suppose Maria's class would have been able to perform its sweatshop play for classes at their Jersey school instead of crossing the Hudson River to do an exile gig. (Why didn't their principal support the campaign against sweatshop apparel instead of declaring the students unfair to corporate America?) All in all, if classroom discourse was not partisan, this nation's schools and colleges would display different stories than the conflicted accounts rendered by various scholars (Ravitch, 1974,

1983; Karabel and Brint, 1989; Dougherty, 1994; Tyack and Cuban, 1995; Berliner and Biddle, 1995). Consider, for example, the case of the Boston authorities in 1826, who decided to open an all-girls high school to match the all-boys one started a few years earlier. So many girls applied that the brahmin city fathers chose to kill the project rather than to meet the demand for female equality. For the time being, patriarchy was protected. If education were indeed neutral, boys and girls of all colors and classes would have had equal access as well as equal monies invested in their development, something this democratic nation never provided and still doesn't (*Quality Counts*, 20–21, 54). Racially, in fact, schools have become resegregated since the 1954 decision, according to recent studies (Orfield, 1993; Orfield and Easton, 1996; Orfield, et al., 1997).

While segregation and unequal funding remain fixtures in American education, a partisan inequality rules daily life as well. For example, the Hunger Action Network and Food First group estimate that 5 million senior citizens and upwards of 4 million children go to bed hungry every day in this food-rich country (Lieberman, 1998). Can anyone doubt that hungry students are at a disadvantage in the classroom? The response of a humane society would be to simply feed everyone with the vast food surplus already available, but distribution in a market-driven society is based on income, not need. ("Marketplace" on National Public Radio for June 25, 1998 reported a "problem" for farmers in the Northwest—"too much wheat and too few customers.") This sorry saga of separating hungry kids from plentiful food includes a bizarre attempt during the Reagan Administration to declare ketchup a vegetable to save money on school lunch programs. You don't need a PhD to know that ketchup is a condiment and not a vegetable, but such irrational claims mark conservative politics in recent decades (Bracey, 1994). When it comes to the disgraceful fact of hungry kids in a food-rich nation, all we can claim for critical literacy is that this discourse and pedagogy is food for thought and feeling (symbolic nourishment), not real calories needed by real people. Critical education cannot feed the hungry or raise the minimum wage; it can only invite people into action to achieve these and other humane goals. The moral core of critical literacy, then, should be put in high profile, exspecially in the wealthy U.S., where General Electric reported a record $8.2 billion profit (Smart, 1998) and General Motors sits on $14 billion in cash (Moody, 1998). The consequences of corporate power make it necessary for dissidents to say the obvious: Real food must be guaranteed each child to support her or his academic learning.

Food-rich America has the highest child poverty rate in the industrialized world, 20.8% (*Statistical Abstract*, Table 739, 1997). Here, black and Hispanic kids are more than twice as likely to live in poverty as are white kids (*Statistical Abstract*, Table 737, 1997). Conversely, in a high-tech age, white students are three times more likely to have computers at home than are black or Hispanic youth (*Technology Counts*, 1997; Zehr, 1998). A child whose parents earn $70,000 or more (top quartile) has an 80% chance to graduate college by age 24, while a child whose family earns $22,000 or less (bottom quartile) has about an 8% chance (Mortenson, 1995; Viadero, 1998). White median family income is about $41,000, remarkably higher than that of blacks ($24,698) or Hispanics ($24,318), indicating that white supremacy is still firmly in the saddle (*Statistical Abstract*, Table No. 727, 1997). Education and literacy are situated in these larger conditions, where the economy is the "decisive" factor influencing school policy and outcomes, as John Kenneth Galbraith (1967) suggested some time ago.

The good news is that from the 1970s to mid-1980s, black students substantially narrowed test score gaps between them and their white peers (*Digest of Education Statistics*, Table 128, 1997; Williams and Ceci, 1997). The bad news is that these gains slowed or stopped by the 1990s, as economic and educational policies that increased inequality gained momentum (*Quality Counts*, 10–13). Further, black unemployment has remained about twice the white rate, virtually unchanged through boom and bust periods (*Statistical Abstract*, Table 656, 1997), despite the black achievement of near-parity with whites in average levels of education (*Digest of Education Statistics*, Table 8, 1997). Similarly, the income advantage of white families over minority households mentioned above has also remained steady during this recent period of improving non-white educational achievement (Henwood, 1997). Additionally, in higher education, black and Hispanic graduation rates severely lag white student rates despite a notable narrowing of the racial gap in high school completion and test scores (Gose, 1998). Further, in higher education, only 3% of full professors are black and only 2% of all faculty are Hispanic (Schneider, 1998a). While the racial gap in wages has not narrowed, inner cities have become more segregated and minority families there more impoverished and isolated (*Quality Counts*, 14–15; Anyon, 1998).

Like black students' test score gains, females made historic advances in college attendance and degrees, yet have not been able to translate their higher credentials into wage parity. As the Department of Education (1996) noted, "despite large gains in educational attainment and labor force participation, significant differences in earnings persist between females and males, even at similar levels of education" (18). Female high school grads earn about a third less than male grads the same age; female college grads earn about 80% of what their male counterparts receive. Further, women are not getting PhDs in the high-paying fields of science and technology still dominated by white men, who also continue to dominate the high-salaried professions of medicine and law. Instead, women collect in low-wage doctorates and "helping" professions such as education, social work, and library science (*Digest of Education Statistics*, Tables 272, 299–304, 1997). Finally, women hold only 18% of high-wage full professorships but about 70% of low-salary schoolteacher jobs (Schneider, 1998a).

Besides the race and gender divides, mass education has also not equalized the widening gaps between social classes (Hershey, 1996; Perez-Pena, 1997). People of all colors and genders have gained more educational credentials every decade, yet the bottom 80% of wage-earners saw no growth in their share of national income since the 1970s while the top 20% take home higher wages (Holmes, 1996; "Wealthiest Americans," *New York Times*, 1997). In a single year, 1996–1997, the number of billionaires in the U.S. increased from 135 to 170, according to Forbes magazine's annual report on the richest Americans (Sklar and Collins, 1997). The top 1% now control about 40% of the country's wealth, the highest percentage in our history, even though high-school diplomas and college degrees are more widely distributed today than ever (Boutwell, 1997). What Lester Faigley (1997) called "the revolution of the rich" means that class inequity is growing, not declining, at a moment when mass education is at its greatest reach.

Such inequities in school and society have been constant sources of critique as well as conflict. For example, Christopher Jencks (1972) concluded in a landmark study that progress towards equality would be at the speed of *glaciers* [his metaphor], if we depended on education to level disparities. What would move equality faster? Jencks proposed reducing wage differences and rotating jobs within occupations to give all people access to all competencies in a field or industry. An income/employment policy plus progressive taxation to redistribute wealth would be far swifter equity mechanisms than mass education, he argued, because they would directly create more wages from the bottom up. A quarter of a century later, Jencks's analysis still holds, I would say, insofar as economic inequality is the primary problem needing change to build community foundations for school achievement (Anyon, 1998; Mickelson and Smith, 1998).

All in all, perhaps these are a few good reasons to question the status quo, including the myth of education as a "great equalizer" (Horace Mann's hope, discussed further shortly). Critical literacy is a pedagogy for those teachers and students morally disturbed by the above "savage inequalities" as Jonathan Kozol (1991) named them, for those who wish to act against the violence of imposed hierarchy and forced hunger.

Literacy for Equity: Transforming Words in the World

In many ways, the project of critical literacy fits the savage and contentious time in which it emerged. In recent decades, America has been moving left and right at the same time though not in the same way or at the same speed, I would say. In this long period of polarization, when the liberal "center" declined dramatically, Democrats and Republicans virtually fused on the right. Humane hope has resided in challenges to inequality made on various fronts of the left-challenges which have been met by powerful reactionary efforts to maintain tradition and privilege (Faludi, 1991; Ingalls, 1998; Morris, 1998; Shepard, 1998). To state the obvious, the past thirty years have witnessed monumental culture wars in school and society over gender, race, class, and sexual preference. Since the 1960s, these culture wars—a long-term questioning of the unequal status quo—have disturbed traditional language arts (phonics, the 5-paragraph essay, and grammar drills) and mainstream discourse (like the practice of only using the masculine pronoun "he" to refer to people in general). A familiar response to egalitarian pressures from below has been the "political correctness" campaign and other conservative education projects which have attempted to turn back the clock through various school policies: career education, back-to-basics, the literacy crisis, steep tuition increases, public sector budget cuts, more standardized testing at all levels, restrictions on open access to higher education, "cultural literacy" proposals steeped in Eurocentric facts and didactic lecturing (Hirsch, 1987, 1989; Hirsch, Kett, and Trefil, 1988), and "bell curve" arguments justifying the subordination of minorities (Herrnstein and Murray, 1994; Gould, 1995; Williams and Ceci, 1997). This counter-offensive to defend the status quo—which I call "the conservative restoration" against the democratic opening of the 1960s (see *Culture Wars*)—included corporate conglomeration of the mass media as well as high-profile attempts to muzzle criticism, such as progressive Jim Hightower's removal from national talk-radio, *Time* magazine's refusal to run essays on welfare reform, militarism, and the death penalty by its own columnist Barbara Ehrenreich, Oprah Winfrey's famous "free speech" beef case in Texas, and the industry lawsuit against Cornell researcher Prof. Kate Bronfenbrenner who publicly criticized labor-law violations by Beverly Enterprises, a health-care provider. The broad defense of the status quo also brought attacks on affirmative action (begun in earnest with the 1978 Bakke case in California; see Sandman, 1998, and Hill, 1998, for more recent events); on welfare (epitomized by the punitive "W-2" program in Wisconsin and cheap-labor "workfare" in New York; see Conniff, 1998, on the "mirage" of welfare reform and Gordon, 1994, on "how welfare became a dirty word"); on labor unions (like the 1998 corporate attempt to end labor financing of political campaigns through Proposition 226 in California); on abortion rights (restrictive access sanctioned by the Supreme Court; shooting of doctors, murders and bombings at clinics); on school-equity (the refusal of states like New Jersey and Texas to equalize student funding despite three decades of lawsuits and one court order after another); and on gay rights (like the banning of Indigo Girls from some high school concerts because of their lesbian identification, Strauss, 1998, and the attempt to drive Terrence McNally's new play *Corpus Christi* out of the Manhattan Theater Club, Blumenthal, 1998).

In this embattled period, when the status quo mobilized to defend tradition and hierarchy, culture wars have been particularly sharp in the field of English. Consider the bitter conflict fought by Linda Brodkey (1996) at Austin when she tried to redesign freshman comp with diversity issues; Maxine Hairston's (1992a) denunciation of critical theorists in composition and the responses it provoked; the growing dispute between entrenched literary study and subordinated writing instruction (the "comp-lit split," Schneider, 1998b); the rescue of the SAT as a tool for measuring literacy despite 20 years of criticism against its cultural bias (Weissglass, 1998); and the long-term contention between phonics and whole-language (Daniels, Zemelman, and Bizar, 1998).

The specific area of culture wars which I address in this essay involves literacy and pedagogy in writing instruction. What methods help develop students as critically thinking citizens who use language to question knowledge, experience, and power in society? This social context for education joins a long discussion dating back to John Dewey and in some ways to Horace Mann before him.

Looking Back: Reform and Reformers

In the year John Dewey was born in Vermont, 1859, an ailing 63-year-old Horace Mann delivered his final commencement address as President of Antioch, which he had helped found six years earlier as the first co-ed college in the country (also admitting blacks as well as whites, though Oberlin broke the race barrier a decade before). Mann, known as the Father of the Common School for his prodigious efforts to set up free public schooling in Massachusetts from 1837–1849, had helped rescue Antioch from near-bankruptcy soon after it opened (Williams, 1937). Now, on a June day in Ohio, he ended his last address with an extraordinary call to students, "Be ashamed to die until you have won some victory for humanity." A zealous reformer, he succumbed to illness that August, ending a controversial career devoted to mass education which he hoped, in part, would solve growing class divisions in 19th century America. If education remained private, Mann thought, "Intellectual castes would inevitably be followed by castes in privilege, in honor, in property" (Williams, 188).

Dewey, more secular than Mann, argued in *Democracy and Education* (1916) that the curricular split between elite and mass education was passed down from the class divisions of ancient Greece, where leisured rulers could study philosophy and evade useful labor, supported by the majority who were marked inferior precisely because they worked with their hands. Subject matters dealing with utility and labor were deemed lesser than those relating to philosophy. Dewey thus saw the new mass curriculum of his time (the three R's and job-training) deriving from class inequities, where the study of abstract liberal arts remained a leisure class privilege while basic skills and occupationalism were relegated to society's subordinates: "The idea still prevails that a truly cultural or liberal education cannot have anything in common, directly at least, with industrial affairs, and that the education which is fit for the masses must be a useful or practical education in a sense which opposes useful and practical to nurture of appreciation and liberation of thought ... The notion that the 'essentials' of elementary education are the three R's, mechanically treated, is based upon ignorance of the essentials needed for realization of democratic ideals" (*Democracy and Education*, 257, 192). Education separated from experience and usefulness on the one hand, and from philosophy on the other, was a dead-end for learning in a democracy, he argued. Dewey thus affirmed a holistic curriculum based simultaneously in experience and philosophy, in working and thinking, in action and reflection.

Accordingly, from such an integrated curriculum, Deweyan education seeks the construction of a reflective democratic citizen. In this curriculum, the class-based division between the ideal and the real, the liberal arts and the vocations, is collapsed into a unified learning field. Language use in such an egalitarian field is the vehicle for making knowledge and for nurturing democratic citizens through a philosophical approach to experience. For Dewey, language use is a social activity where theory and experience meet for the discovery of meaning and purpose. In this curricular theory and practice, discourse in school is not a one-way, teacher-centered conduit of class-restricted materials while "language arts" is not a separate subject for the transfer of correct usage or grammar skills to students. "Think of the absurdity of having to teach language as a thing by itself," Dewey proposed in *The School and Society* (1900). To him, children are born language-users, naturally and eagerly talking about the things they do and are interested in. "But when there are no vital interests appealed to in the school," he continued,

> when language is used simply for the repetition of lessons, it is not surprising that one of the chief difficulties of school work has come to be instruction in the mother-tongue. Since the language taught is unnatural, not growing out of the real desire to communicate vital impressions and convictions, the freedom of children in its use gradually disappears.
>
> (*The School and Society*, 55–56)

With vital interests disconnected from classroom discourse, the students lose touch with the purpose of human communication. When they lose touch with purpose in speaking or writing, they struggle to mobilize their inherent language competencies. They lose their articulateness along with their motivation, Dewey suggested, compelling the teacher "to invent all kinds of devices to assist in getting any spontaneous and full use of speech" (56).

Dewey's hundred-year-old observations remain relevant today for the ongoing campaign against drilling in grammar and rhetorical forms (like comparison and contrast, description, narration, the 5-paragraph essay, etc.), and against "cultural literacy" transmission models (see also Stunkel, 1998, for a traditional defense of "the lecture"). Since the 1960s, dialogic and student-centered methods from expressivist, feminist, and other critical teachers have foregrounded the personal and the social as the subject matters Dewey called for in his reference to "vital impressions and convictions." The remarkable growth of composition studies in the last decades has led to substantial options to skill drills, such as writing-across-the-curriculum, ethnography-as-syllabus, writing process methods, service learning, journal writing, community literacy approaches, literacy narratives, mainstreaming basic writers, portfolio assessment, and collaborative learning, with many classrooms redesigned as writing workshops. These forward-looking developments in language arts coexist with the regressive dominance of grammars and workbooks, and the rise of more standardized testing and more mandated syllabi in public schools, as well as the greater exploitation of adjunct teachers in higher education (Shor, 1997). Top-down authority in school and society has aggressively reasserted itself against bottom-up efforts for democratic language arts.

In this conflicted milieu, recent developments include the emergence of critical literacy as one approach to pedagogy and language use. Critical literacy can be thought of as a social practice in itself and as a tool for the study of other social practices. That is, critical literacy is reflective and reflexive: Language use and education are social practices used to critically study all social practices including the social practices of language use and education. Globally, this literate practice seeks the larger cultural context of any specific situation. "Only as we interpret school activities with reference to the larger circle of social activities to which they relate do we find any standard for judging their moral significance," Dewey wrote (*Moral Principles in Education*, 13). Critical literacy involves questioning received knowledge and immediate experience with the goal of challenging inequality and developing an activist citizenry. The two foundational thinkers in this area are certainly Dewey and Freire, but the work of Lev Vygotsky is also central. Some contemporary critical educators have made exceptional contributions: theorists and practitioners like Elsa Auerbach, Jim Berlin, Bill Bigelow, Patricia Bizzell, Stephen Brookfield, Linda Christensen, Jim Cummins, Nan Elsasser, Marilyn Frankenstein, Henry Giroux, Patricia Irvine, Donaldo Macedo, Peter Mayo, Peter McLaren, Richard Ohmann, Bob Peterson, Arthur Powell, Roger Simon, and Nina Wallerstein; feminists like Carmen Luke, Jennifer Gore, and Kathleen Weiler; and multiculturalists like Jim Banks, Antonia Darder, Deborah Menkart, Sonia Nieto, Nancy Schniedewind, and Christine Sleeter.

The diverse paths to critical literacy represent it as a discourse and pedagogy that can be configured in feminist, multicultural, queer, and neo-Marxist approaches. As mentioned earlier, critical teaching invites students to consider options to fitting quietly into the way things are. Disturbing the socialization of students and teachers into the system is certainly not easy, transparent, or risk-free (try questioning Nike's use of sweatshop labor to students who are Nike'd from head to toe and for whom Michael Jordan is an airborne god; try questioning such ventures as the Gulf War of 1991 among students with military relatives ordered to the front in Iraq). Coming to critical literacy is a rather unpredictable and even contentious process filled with surprises, resistances, breakthroughs, and reversals (Shor, 1996). It's no easy or open road for a number of reasons I've been defining in various books. The forces that need questioning are very old, deeply entrenched, and remarkably complex, sometimes too complicated for the interventions of critical pedagogy in a single semester. But, as Horton and Freire (1990) put it, we make the road by walking, and for teachers who report their experiences so far, the critical road has produced some interesting results and some still unresolved problems.

Do *Not* Walk Gently Into That Status Quo: Alternative Roads for Development

As I've been arguing, critical literacy belongs to Deweyan constructivist education which has also been associated with *activity theory*. As David Russell (1995) defined it in a masterful essay:

> Activity theory analyzes human behavior and consciousness in terms of *activity systems:* goal-directed, historically situated, cooperative human interactions, such as a child's attempt to reach an out-of-reach toy, a job interview, a "date," a social club, a classroom, a discipline, a profession, an institution, a political movement, and so on. The activity system is the basic unit of analysis for both cultures' and individuals' psychological and social processes . . . Activity systems are historically developed, mediated by tools, dialectically structured, analyzed as the relationship of participants and tools, and changed through *zones of proximal development.* (54–55)

Activity theory in general, and the "zone of proximal development" (ZPD) specifically, derive from cognitivist Lev Vygotsky (1962, 1978) who proposed that such zones exist when a less-developed individual or student interacts with a more-advanced person or teacher, allowing the student to achieve things not possible when acting on her or his own. The relationship with the more-developed person pulls the less-developed forward, a dynamic similar to the way Dewey understood curriculum that began from student experience and was structured forward into organized reflective knowledge of the kind teachers have. In posing experience as the starting point of a reflective process, Dewey asked: "What is the place and meaning of subject-matter and of organization within experience? How does subject-matter function? Is there anything inherent in experience which tends towards progressive organization of its contents?" (*Experience and Education*, 19).

A critical writing class is a zone where teachers invite students to move into deepening interrogations of knowledge in its global contexts. The main differences between critical literacy as I propose it here and Vygotsky's zone of proximal development are first that critical literacy is an activity that reconstructs and develops ALL parties involved, pulling teachers forward as well as students (whereas Vygotsky focused on student development), and second that dissident politics is foregrounded in a critical literacy program, inviting democratic relations in class and democratic action outside class (whereas Vygotsky did not foreground power relations as the social context for learning). I want here to emphasize the mutual and dissident orientations of critical literacy's zone compared to the ZPD of Vygotsky. Again, one key departure is that all participants in a critical process become redeveloped as democratic agents and social critics. Critical teaching is not a one-way development, not "something done for students or to them" for their own good (Freire, 1989, 34). It's not a paternal campaign of clever teachers against defenseless students. Rather, a critical process is driven and justified by mutuality. This ethic of mutual development can be thought of as a Freirean addition to the Vygotskian zone. By inviting students to develop critical thought and action on various subject matters, the teacher herself develops as a critical-democratic educator who becomes more informed of the needs, conditions, speech habits, and perceptions of the students, from which knowledge she designs activities and into which she integrates her special expertise. Besides learning in-process how to design a course *for* the students, the critical teacher also learns how to design the course *with* the students (co-governance). A mutual learning process develops the teacher's democratic competence in negotiating the curriculum and in sharing power. Overall, then, vis-à-vis the Freirean addition to the Vygotskian zone, the mutual develop-ment ethic constructs students as authorities, agents, and unofficial teachers who educate the official teacher while also getting educated by each other and by the teacher.

Though he highlighted mutuality in his two foundational works, Freire (1970, 1973) was not a libertarian educator of the "Summerhill" kind. He believed in rigor, structure, and political contention in society at large. For Freire, critical education as a group process rather than as an individualist one, was neither permissive nor agnostic (*A Pedagogy for Liberation*, "Chapter Three," 75–96). That is, on the one hand, students and teachers were not free to do whatever they wanted whenever they wanted, and on the other hand, the conceptual knowledge of the teacher was not denied but rather posed as a necessary element. The teacher must be expert and knowledgeable to be a responsible critical educator, Freire thought.

Yet, teacher knowledge and authority could also contradict dialogue and thus destroy mutuality in this critical process. A central problem for Freirean mutuality is how and when a teacher should use authority and expertise to promote rather than to silence student agency. Saying too much or too little, too soon or too late, can damage the group process. The problem of adjusting to dialogic practice is complicated because students and teachers have already been deeply socialized by prior "banking" models, that is, by one-way teacher-talk and non-negotiable syllabi. Critical literacy has to develop mutual inquiry in a field already crowded with anti-critical monologue. No wonder, then, that in Freire's "culture circle," the first problem of education was reconciling the student–teacher dichotomy (*Pedagogy of the Oppressed*, 57–60). Freire complained early on that "liberatory" educators were themselves too often poor practitioners of dialogue and too infected with the old habits of one-way communication:

> A major problem in setting up the program is instructing the teams of coordinators. Teaching the purely technical aspects of the procedure is not difficult. The difficulty lies rather in the creation of a new attitude—that of dialogue, so absent in our upbringing and education.
> (*Education for Critical Consciousness*, 52; see also *Empowering Education*, Chapter 4, 85–111)

While distributing democratic authority is a teacher's challenge in a dialogic program, there is also the opposite dilemma, that is, of the teacher *not having enough authority*. In some cases, the *lack* of authority interferes with a teacher's ability to initiate a critical and power-sharing process. On the one hand, there are classrooms where some students' disruptive behavior overwhelms other students and the teacher, making control the issue instead of knowledge-making or power-sharing. On the other hand, the authority teachers bring to class varies according to the teacher's gender, race, age, condition of employment (full or part-time), physical stature and ability, regional location, grade level, discipline or subject matter, type of institution (elite or mass), and other factors. Similarly, the students' varying ages, genders, races, classes, ethnicities, etc., equally affect their authority as well as that of the teacher. Students who develop socially subordinate identities can possess too little authority for them to feel secure in joining an unfamiliar critical process. Put simply, there is simply no universal teacher authority uniformly empowered in front of standard students. Teachers, students, and settings differ. The same teacher can have more authority in one class and less in another because few classes are alike. In sum, identity differences in an unequal society mean that teachers possess uneven authority when they address students and students possess uneven and unequal authority when they encounter a critical process. Consequently, while all teachers need to establish and distribute authority in critical classrooms, some are at a distinct advantage both in taking charge and in sharing power: white males who are tall, older, full-time, long-employed, and able-bodied, though teachers of color tend to have more authority than whites in inner-city schools with minority populations.

These differences complicate the mutual ethic of critical literacy. The risk and difficulty of democratizing education should be apparent to those who read these lines or to those who have attempted critical literacy, perhaps encountering the awkward position of distributing authority to students who often do not want it or know how to use it. Still, the long history of this mutual ethic makes it a landmark responsibility of democratic teachers. Mutuality certainly goes back to Dewey, who was preoccupied with the cooperative development of social feeling and with the democratic involvement of students:

> There is, I think, no point in the philosophy of progressive education which is sounder than its emphasis upon the importance of the participation of the learner in the formation of the purposes which direct his activities in the learning process, just as there is no defect in

traditional education greater than its failure to secure the active cooperation of the pupil in construction of the purposes involved in his studying.

(*Experience and Education*, 67)

Dewey saw cooperative relations as central to democratizing education and society. To him, any social situation where people could not consult, collaborate, or negotiate was an activity of slaves rather than of a free people. Freedom and liberty are high-profile "god-words" in American life, but, traditionally, teachers are trained and rewarded as unilateral authorities who transmit expert skills and official information, who not only take charge but stay in charge. At the same time, students are trained to be authority-dependent, waiting to be told what things mean and what to do, a position that encourages passive-aggressive submission and sabotage.

In this and other difficult settings for critical pedagogy, I knew Freire as an optimist in touch with the limits of his own interventions. His pedagogy was hopeful but historical, Utopian but situated, that is, aware of the limits in any specific situation yet aimed to question and overcome restrictions. Freire proposed that critical pedagogy was one form of cultural action for freedom whose goal was to bring a humane future to life against and within an unjust present (*A Pedagogy for Liberation*, 184–187). Freire's social hopefulness and concrete practice stood on the shoulders of John Dewey, whose impact Freire openly acknowledged. Dewey was himself optimistically focused on pragmatic "agencies for doing" (*Democracy and Education*, 38), by which he meant concrete methods for enacting a project in a specific setting. Dewey proposed that a curriculum must have a social ethic at its core: "the intention of improving the life we live in common so that the future shall be better than the past" (*Democracy and Education*, 191). As did Freire, who emphasized "generative themes" taken from everyday life as the starting points for problem-posing, Dewey recognized the power of experience as a curricular resource for critical learning. Dewey even quantified this everyday thematic power with a metaphor by saying that "An ounce of experience is better than a ton of theory" (*Democracy and Education*, 144), certainly a strong statement for this Vermont native of sober words. Only by relating to experience, Dewey argued, does theory have any "vital and verifiable significance." Reflection on experience, he thought, could yield extensive theory while theory alone was "a mere verbal formula, a set of catchwords" that obscured critical thinking. Freire later referred to theory-based action/action-based theorizing as "praxis."

The notion of praxis/reflective action which so preoccupied these two thinkers could be understood in the difference between *theorizing practice* and *theorizing theory*. Consider the phrase "theorizing practice" and how it can be reversed to "practicing theory." This is what praxis meant to Freire and reflective action to Dewey, a close relationship between discourse and action, between symbolic analysis and concrete action, using language as a tool to enhance our understanding of experience—theorizing practice/practicing theory. However, while theorizing practice can be reversed to practicing theory without doing violence to the concept, if we try this same linguistic reversal with the phrase "theorizing theory," we lose praxis; we wind up with the same phrase we began with, "theorizing theory," because the participle and the noun in that phrase have the same root, referring to the same thing, theory alone, symbolic analysis, words without the world (as Freire might have said). Theorizing theory produces abstract discourse whose reference to experience and history gets lost. Yet, in academic life, as we know, the more abstract a spoken or written discourse, the more prestige the speaker or the text represents. Herein lies the immense problem of the elite discourses already dominating academic work in classrooms, conferences, and professional publications (see Peter Elbow's, 1991, provocative and sensible essay on the students' need to use their own language for writing development).

To do praxis through pedagogy, imagine the joint process of theorizing experience and experientializing theory. Critical teaching is a praxis that begins from student generative themes and then invites unfamiliar reflection and unfamiliar connection of the local to the global. In doing so, this special discourse evolves what I have called "the third idiom," that is, a local critical discourse synthesized in the immediate setting for the purposes undertaken there, different from the everyday language of students and from the academic language of the teacher (see *Empowering Education*, Chapter 7). The third idiom is thus an invented medium that emerges from the conflicts and collaborations of teacher and students. The emergence of a situated third idiom can suggest that some of the power conflicts between students and teacher are being worked through, because the participants are co-constructing a new code not identical to the ones they brought to class. In this regard, Patricia Bizzell's work in "hybrid discourses" is helpful in clarifying this new idiom as an egalitarian option to traditional academic discourse.

Working Through the Writing Class

As I have argued, human discourse in general, education in particular, and literacy classes specifically are forces for the making of self in society. On the one hand, we make ourselves in the world according to the way we have learned to think about society and our place in it. On the other hand, human thought, language, and action are never fully under singular control, never monolithically determined by a status quo. The opposite to monolithic discourse that sets the agenda from the top down is dialogic discourse that evolves an agenda from the bottom up. Human agency is rarely erased in even the most controlled settings where people find ways to cope with, push against, and sabotage authority (what Scott called "the weapons of the weak"). The more space open or won for critical action, the more we can speak and act critically to change ourselves and the world. We can critique the way things are, imagine alternatives, hypothesize ways to get there, act from these plans, evaluate and adjust our actions (Dewey's problem-solving method, 1933; Stephen Brookfield's, 1987, social theory of critical thinking).

Critical writing classes test the open space available in any setting for questioning the status quo. Because these kinds of writing classes propose alternatives to the dominant culture, the stakes are high. Some indication of just how high the stakes are in doing critical teaching can be seen in the enormous official attention devoted to questions of reading, writing, and the canon. So much controlling administration and testing directed to regulating literacy makes language use and instruction into pillars of the status quo. Power is obviously involved in the "sponsorship of literacy," as Deborah Brandt (1998) wrote:

> . . . everybody's literacy practices are operating in differential economies, which supply different access routes, different degrees of sponsoring power, and different scales of monetary worth to the practices in use. In fact, the interviews I conducted are filled with examples of how economic and political forces, some of them originating in quite distant corporate and government policies, affect people's day-to-day ability to seek out and practice literacy.
>
> ("Sponsors of Literacy," 172)

The power issues specifically circulating in language education were described like this by John Rouse (1979):

... language learning is the process by which a child comes to acquire a specific social identity. What kind of person should we help bring into being? ... [E]very vested interest in the community is concerned with what is to happen during those years, with how language training is to be organized and evaluated, for the continued survival of any power structure requires the production of certain personality types. The making of an English program becomes, then, not simply an educational venture but a political act.

("The Politics of Composition," 1)

Rouse noted that a writing program can help produce people "acceptable to those who would maintain things as they are, who already have power," which Richard Ohmann (1976, 1987) saw as the official function of composition. Ohmann and Rouse anticipated Jim Berlin's idea that when we teach writing we are teaching a version of the world and the students' places in it. Berlin (1996) said that a curriculum "is a device for encouraging the production of a certain kind of graduate, in effect, a certain kind of person. In directing what courses will be taken in what order, the curriculum undertakes the creation of consciousness. The curriculum does not do this on its own, free of outside influence. It instead occupies a position between the conditions of the larger society it is serving—the economic, political, and cultural sectors—and the work of teacher-scholars within the institution" (17). Berlin's orientation was concretely tied to a pedagogy for critical consciousness by Tom Fox (1993), who proposed a composition class that

... interrogates cultural and political commonplaces ... refuses to repeat cliched explanations for poverty, racism, sexism, homophobia ... explores and embodies conflicts ... critiques institutional inequities, especially in the immediate context of the classroom, the writing program, the department, the university, but also in the institutions that have played an important role in students' lives ... demonstrates successful practices of resistance, that seeks historical evidence for possibilities and promise ... that self-consciously explores the workings of its own rhetoric ... that seeks to reduce the deafening violence of inequality.

("Standards and Access," 43–44)

While Fox stipulated goals for questioning the status quo, Robert Brooke (1987) defined writing, per se, as an act of resistance:

[Writing] necessarily involves standing outside the roles and beliefs offered by a social situation—it involves questioning them, searching for new connections, building ideas that may be in conflict with accepted ways of thinking and acting. Writing involves being able to challenge one's assigned roles long enough that one can think originally; it involves living in conflict with accepted (expected) thought and action.

("Underlife and Writing Instruction," 141)

Brooke offered an intelligent argument that writing itself was synonymous with divergent thinking. Still, I question the direct link of composing with resisting. Some kinds of writing and pedagogy consciously disconfirm the status quo, but not composing and instruction in general. Think of all the books written from and for the status quo. Further, it is also easy to find composition classes that reflect traditional values and encourage status quo writing ("current-traditional rhetoric," see Ohmann, as well as Crowley, 1996). Human beings are certainly active when writing, and all action involves development and agency of some kinds, but not all agency or development is critical. Critical agency and writing are self-conscious positions of questioning the status quo and imagining alternative arrangements for self and society (Brookfield, 1987).

This perspective on literacy for questioning society is markedly different from Erika

Lindemann's (1995) definition of writing as ". . . a process of communication that uses a conventional graphic system to convey a message to a reader" (11). From a different point of view than Lindeman's rhetorical functionalism, Louise Phelps (1988) acknowledged writing as a rich cultural activity, not a set of basic skills: "the potential for composing becomes the principle of reflection . . . and especially the critical spirit" (67, echoing Brooke above and endorsing Shirley Brice Heath's, 1983, idea of writing as complex social activity). Phelps also embraced Ann Berthoff s notion (taken up as well by Knoblauch and Brannon, 1984, and John Mayher, 1990) that "Writing is an act of making meaning for self and for others" (70). Related to activity theory and to cultural context, Marilyn Cooper and Michael Holtzman (1989) proposed that "Writing is a form of social action. It is part of the way in which some people live in the world. Thus, when thinking about writing, we must also think about the way that people live in the world" (xii). They reflected Brian Street's (1984) and Harvey Graff's (1987) arguments that all language use is socially situated, against what Street called the myth of autonomous literacy, that is, language falsely posed as independent of its social context.

The social context and making-of-meaning schools of literacy go back not only to Vygotsky's activity theory but also to Dewey's definition of "education" as increasing the ability to perceive and act on meaning in one's society (*Democracy and Education*, 76ff). To Dewey, the goal of education was to advance students' ability to understand, articulate, and act democratically in their social experience. This definition of education as meaning-making in culture prefigures the epistemic approach to composition, which Kenneth Dowst (1980) described as "the activity of making some sense out of an extremely complex set of personal perceptions and experiences of an infinitely complex world . . . A writer (or other language-user), in a sense, composes the world in which he or she lives" (66). Maxine Hairston (1992b) also featured the epistemic nature of "writing as a way of learning," reiterating Brooke's ideal that writing per se is a critical activity: "Writing helps us absorb new information . . . discover new information. . . [and] promotes critical thinking" (1).

Berlin, Ohmann, and Fox would agree with the epistemic definition of writing as a way of making meaning, but they distinguish their critical position by foregrounding and historicizing the power relations at any site where meaning is made. Specifying the political forces in any rhetorical setting is a key distinction of critical literacy separating it from other writing-to-learn proponents and epistemic rhetoricians. Critical literacy as a discourse that foregrounds and questions power relations was called "social-epistemic rhetoric" by Berlin (1988, 1996). The orientation to foreground and question the ideologies in any setting links critical educators of diverse persuasions—feminists, multiculturalists, queer theorists, and neo-Marxists. Even though each dissident approach uses a different identity lens, they all expose and disconfirm dominant ideologies in the rhetorical settings which construct identity in society. Because there are multiple ideologies at the root of the social experiences which make us into who we are (for example, male supremacy, white supremacy, corporate supremacy, heterosexism), the positions or identities for contesting the status quo also need to be appropriately multiple. Critical literacy thus crosses identity boundaries because it is a discourse and pedagogy for counter-hegemonic resistance. This resistance occasionally becomes a common cause against dominant culture when diverse insurgent groups coalesce, but much stands in the way of coalitions in a society where *every difference is used against us* by an elite minority maintaining power by divide-and-conquer among other mechanisms.

Identity, Difference, and Power: Literacy in Contact Zones

Critical literacy classes focused on identity differences have also been construed as "contact zones" by Mary Louise Pratt (1991): "... social spaces where cultures meet, clash, and grapple with each other, often in contexts of highly asymmetrical relations of power ..." (34). Pratt proposed some rhetorical arts for a critical pedagogy that profiles differences while resisting dominant culture, including two useful alternatives to mimicking elite discourse in writing classes. These two alternatives for producing texts offer students and teachers options to assimilating uncritically into academic discourse:

> Autoethnography: a text in which people undertake to describe themselves in ways that engage with representations others have made of them ...
>
> Transculturation: the processes whereby members of subordinated or marginal groups select and invent from materials transmitted by a dominant or metropolitan culture ... While subordinate peoples do not usually control what emanates from the dominant culture, they do determine to varying extents what gets absorbed into their own and what it gets used for.
>
> ("Arts of the Contact Zone," 35, 36)

These literate practices ask students to take critical postures towards their own language uses as well as towards the discourses dominating school and society, such as mainstream news media. Further, from Pratt's contact zone theory, we can extract and summarize more pedagogical advice for questioning power relations and encouraging critical literacy:

1. Structure the class around "safe houses" (group caucuses within the larger class where marginalized "others" can develop their positions).
2. Offer exercises in oral and written storytelling and in identifying with the ideas, interests, histories, and attitudes of "others."
3. Give special attention to the rhetorical techniques of parody, comparison, and critique so as to strengthen students' abilities to speak back to their immersion in the literate products of the dominant culture.
4. Explore suppressed aspects of history (what Foucault referred to as "disqualified" or "unqualified" narratives relating popular resistance).
5. Define ground rules for communication across differences and in the midst of existing hierarchies of authority.
6. Do systematic studies of cultural mediation, or how cultural material is produced, distributed, received, and used.

Finally, Pratt enumerated other "critical arts" of the contact zone that could encourage a rhetoric of resistance: doing imaginary dialogues (to develop student ability to create subjectivities in history), writing in multiple dialects and idioms (to avoid privileging one dominant form), and addressing diverse audiences with discourses of resistance (to invite students to imagine themselves speaking to both empowered and disempowered groups). Pratt's pedagogy for producing critical discourse has been deployed for writing classes by Patricia Bizell and Bruce Herzberg (*Negotiating Difference*, 1996). In general, contact zone theory has a friendly fit with the critical literacy I defined elsewhere as

> Habits of thought, reading, writing, and speaking which go beneath surface meaning, first impressions, dominant myths, official pronouncements, traditional cliches, received wisdom, and mere opinions, to understand the deep meaning, root causes, social context, ideology, and

> personal consequences of any action, event, object, process, organization, experience, text, subject matter, policy, mass media, or discourse.
>
> (*Empowering Education*, 129)

My definition is also consistent with Aronowitz's and Giroux's (1985) notion that "critical literacy would make clear the connection between knowledge and power. It would present knowledge as a social construction linked to norms and values, and it would demonstrate modes of critique that illuminate how, in some cases, knowledge serves very specific economic, political and social interests. Moreover, critical literacy would function as a theoretical tool to help students and others develop a critical relationship to their own knowledge" (132). With this kind of literacy, students "learn how to read the world and their lives critically and relatedly . . . and, most importantly, it points to forms of social action and collective struggle" (132). This activist agenda was also central to Joe Kretovics' (1985) definition: "Critical literacy . . . points to providing students not merely with functional skills, but with the conceptual tools necessary to critique and engage society along with its inequalities and injustices. Furthermore, critical literacy can stress the need for students to develop a collective vision of what it might be like to live in the best of all societies and how such a vision might be made practical" (51).

Critical Literacy For Envisioning Change

Envisioning and realizing change was a key goal of Freire's literacy teams in Brazil before they were destroyed by the military coup of April, 1964:

> From the beginning, we rejected . . . a purely mechanistic literacy program and considered the problem of teaching adults how to read in relation to the awakening of their consciousness . . . We wanted a literacy program which would be an introduction to the democratization of culture, a program with human beings as its subjects rather than as patient recipients, a program which itself would be an act of creation, capable of releasing other creative acts, one in which students would develop the impatience and vivacity which characterize search and invention.
>
> (*Education for Critical Consciousness*, 43)

Freire's original method included trisyllabic exercises for decoding and encoding words. Even though this project had explicit political intentions, Freire's practical pedagogy focused on writing, reading, and dialogue from generative themes based in student life, not on didactic lectures based in teacherly discourse. Freire thus developed pragmatic "agencies for doing," to use Dewey's phrase. The students' literacy skills emerged through concrete exercises on generative themes displayed in drawings ("codifications") from their lives (Dewey's vital subject matter as the context for developing reflective habits and language abilities).

Freire's much-read reports of dialogic pedagogy for illiterate Brazilian peasants and workers offer an instructive comparison to the literacy narrative of Mike Rose (1990) who chronicled his life and work among basic writers at UCLA and elsewhere. Rose, based at a high-profile campus dominated by academic discourse, developed and taught a rhetorical form of critical literacy: "framing an argument or taking someone else's argument apart, systematically inspecting a document, an issue, or an event, synthesizing different points of view, applying theory to disparate phenomena . . . comparing, synthesizing, analyzing . . . summarizing, classifying . . ." (188, 194, 138). Rose's definition of critical literacy reiterates

Mina Shaughnessy's (1977) earlier advice for teaching rhetorical habits to basic writers. By naming these literate habits and by asking students to learn them through complex cases drawn from across the curriculum, Rose responded to the academic needs of basic writers at a flagship campus, UCLA. In Freire's original culture circles, the situation was not academic but rather informal adult basic education offered where the students lived or worked, certainly not on a campus. Later in his career, when Freire became Secretary of Education for the City of Sao Paulo in 1989, responsible for an impoverished school system of about 700,000 students, he proposed that standard forms should be taught to non-elite Brazilian students in the context of democratizing schools and integrating the themes of their lives:

> Finally, teachers have to say to students, Look, in spite of being beautiful, this way you speak also includes the question of *power*. Because of the political problem of power, you need to learn how to command the dominant language, in order for you to survive in the struggle to transform society.
>
> (*A Pedagogy for Liberation*, 73)

Freire reiterated this point a few years later in *Pedagogy of the City* (1993): "The need to master the dominant language is not only to survive but also better to fight for the transformation of an unjust and cruel society where the subordinate groups are rejected, insulted, and humiliated" (135). In these remarks, Freire foregrounds ideology and education for changing society, activist positions typical of critical literacy.

Freire's remarks just above involve an inflammatory issue of language education in the U.S. and elsewhere: Should all students be taught standard usage and initiated into academic discourses used in traditional disciplines, or should students be encouraged to use the language they bring to class (called *students' rights to their own language* in a controversial policy statement by the Conference on College Composition and Communication in 1973)? In the U.S., the argument for teaching standard usage to black youth has been taken up strenuously by Lisa Delpit (1995). Yet, despite her stance in favor of standard usage for all, Delpit produced a special anthology defending "ebonics" in the classroom (with co-editor Theresa Perry, *The Real Ebonics Debate*, 1998). This anthology includes a strong essay by Geneva Smitherman, the long-time proponent of black students using African-American English for writing and teaching. A bidialectal or contrastive rhetoric approach is being suggested here, for honoring and using the students' community language while also studying standard English. Freire would likely agree with the bidialectal approach, but he would insist on ethical and historical foundations for such a program: standard usage, rhetorical forms, and academic discourse make democratic sense only when taught in a critical curriculum explicitly posing problems about the status quo based in themes from the students' lives. In a program clearly against inequality, many tools and resources can be useful, including standard usage, bidialectalism, bilingualism, contrastive translations of texts from community language into academic discourse, etc. In a critical program, the teaching of standard form is thus embedded in a curriculum oriented towards democratic development. By themselves, correct usage, paragraph skills, rhetorical forms like narrative, description, or cause and effect, are certainly not foundations for democratic or critical consciousness, as Bizzell (1992) recognized after her long attempt to connect the teaching of formal technique with the development of social critique.

Another oppositional approach merging technique and critique is Gerald Graff's (1992) "teach the conflicts" method, which has been developed thoughtfully for writing classes by Don Lazere (see his chapter in *Critical Literacy in Action*, Shor and Pari, 1999). Lazere provides rhetorical frameworks to students for analyzing ideologies in competing texts and media sources. The specific rhetorical techniques serve social critique here, insofar as the curriculum invites students to develop ideological sophistication in a society that mystifies politics, a society in fact where "polities" has become a repulsive "devil-word." Lazere uses problem-posing at the level of topical and academic themes (social issues chosen by the teacher and subject matters taken from expert bodies of knowledge and then posed to students as questions) rather than generative themes (materials taken from student thought and language). (See *Empowering Education*, 2–5, 46–48, 73–84.) My own Deweyan and Freirean preference is to situate critical literacy in student discourse and perceptions as the starting points, but the "teach the conflicts" method of Graff and Lazere is indeed a critical approach worthy of study, especially because it teaches us a way to pose academic subject matters as problems, questions, and exercises rather than merely lecturing them to students.

Merging the study of formal technique with social critique is not simple but this project is no more and no less "political" than any other kind of literacy program. The position taken by critical literacy advocates is that no pedagogy is neutral, no learning process is value-free, no curriculum avoids ideology and power relations. To teach is to encourage human beings to develop in one direction or another. In fostering student development, every teacher chooses some subject matters, some ways of knowing, some ways of speaking and relating, instead of others. These choices orient students to map the world and their relation to it.

Every educator, then, orients students towards certain values, actions, and language with implications for the kind of society and people these behaviors will produce. This inevitable involvement of education with developmental values was called "stance" by Jerome Bruner (1986):

> ... the medium of exchange in which education is conducted—language—can never be neu-tral ... [I]t imposes a point of view not only about the world to which it refers but toward the use of mind in respect of this world. Language necessarily imposes a perspective in which things are viewed and a stance toward what we view ... I do not for a minute believe that one can teach even mathematics or physics without transmitting a sense of stance toward nature and toward the use of the mind ... The idea that any *humanistic* subject can be taught without revealing one's stance toward matters of human pith and substance is, of course, nonsense ... [T]he language of education, if it is to be an invitation to reflec-tion and culture creating, cannot be the so-called uncontaminated language of fact and "objectivity."
>
> (*Actual Minds, Possible Worlds*, 121, 128, 129)

Also denying the neutrality of language and learning, poet Adrienne Rich (1979) said of her work in the Open Admissions experiment attacked by conservative authorities at the City University of New York that "My daily life as a teacher confronts me with young men and women who had language and literature used against them, to keep them in their place, to mystify, to bully, to make them feel powerless" (61). Rich ended her tribute to the cultural democracy of Open Admissions by connecting the writing of words to the changing of worlds:

> [L]anguage is power and ... those who suffer from injustice most are the least able to articulate their suffering ... [T]he silent majority, if released into language, would not be content with a perpetuation of the conditions which have betrayed them. But this notion hangs on a special conception of what it means to be released into language: not simply learning the jargon of an

elite, fitting unexceptionably into the status quo, but learning that language can be used as a means for changing reality.

(*On Lies, Secrets, and Silences*, 67–68)

Thus, to be for critical literacy is to take a moral stand on the kind of just society and democratic education we want. This is an ethical center proposed many years ago by the patron saint of American education, John Dewey, who insisted that school and society must be based in cooperation, democratic relations, and egalitarian distribution of resources and authority. Progressive educators since Dewey, such as George Counts, Maxine Greene, and George Wood, have continued this ethical emphasis. Freire openly acknowledged his debt to Dewey and declared his search "for an education that stands for liberty and against the exploitation of the popular classes, the perversity of the social structures, the silence imposed on the poor—always aided by an authoritarian education" (Cox, 94).

Many teachers reject authoritarian education. Many strive against fitting students quietly into the status quo. Many share the democratic goals of critical literacy. This educational work means, finally, inventing what Richard Ohmann (1987) referred to as a "literacy-from-below" that questions the way things are and imagines alternatives, so that the word and the world may meet in history for a dream of social justice.

References

Anderson, Gary L., and Patricia Irvine. 1993. Informing critical literacy with ethnography. In *Critical literacy: Politics, praxis, and the postmodern*. Eds. Colin Lankshear and Peter L. McLaren. Albany, NY: SUNY Press, 81–104.

Anzaldua, Gloria. 1990. *Borderlands/La frontera: The new mestiza*. San Francisco: Spinsters/Aunt Lute.

Anyon, Jean. 1998. *Ghetto schooling: A political economy of urban educational reform*. New York: Teachers College Press.

Applebome, Peter. 1997. Schools see re-emergence of "separate but equal." *New York Times* (April 8), A10.

Aronowitz, Stanley, and Henry Giroux. 1985. *Education under siege*. South Hadley, MA: Bergin-Garvey.

Berlin, James A. 1987. *Rhetoric and reality: Writing instruction in American colleges, 1900–1985*. Carbondale: SIU Press.

——. 1988. Rhetoric and ideology in the writing class. *College English*, 50.5(September): 477–494.

——. 1996. *Rhetorics, poetics, and cultures*. Urbana, IL: NCTE.

Berliner, David, and Steven Biddle. 1995. *The manufactured crisis*. New York: AddisonWesley/Longman.

Bernstein, Aaron. 1996. Is America becoming more of a class society? New data show that, increasingly, workers at the bottom are staying there. *Business week* (February 26), 86–91.

Berthoff, Ann. 1981. *The making of meaning*. Upper Montclair, NJ: Boynton-Cook.

Bizzell, Patricia. 1992. *Academic discourse and critical consciousness*. Pittsburgh: University of Pittsburgh Press.

Bizzell, Patricia, and Bruce Herzberg. 1996. *Negotiating difference*. Boston: Bedford.

Blumenthal, Ralph. 1998. Discord mounts after play is canceled. *New York Times*, May 27: E1, E3.

Boutwell, Clinton E. 1997. *Shell game: Corporate America's agenda for the schools*. Bloomington, IN: Phi Delta Kappa.

Bracey, Gerard. 1995. The right's data-proof ideologues. *Education week*, January 25: 48.

Brandt, Deborah. 1998. Sponsors of literacy. *College Composition and Communication*, 49.2(May): 165–185.

Brodkey, Linda. 1996. *Writing permitted in designated areas only*. Minneapolis: University of Minnesota Press.

Brooke, Robert. 1987. Underlife and writing instruction. *College Composition and Communication*, 38.2(May): 141–153.

Brookfield, Stephen D. 1987. *Developing critical thinkers*. San Francisco: Jossey-Bass.

——. 1995. *Becoming a critically reflective teacher*. San Francisco: Jossey-Bass.

Brookfield, Stephen D., and Stephen Preskill. 1999. *Discussion as a way of teaching; Tools and techniques for democratic classrooms*. San Francisco: Jossey-Bass.

Bruner, Jerome. 1986. *Actual minds, possible worlds*. Cambridge, MA: Harvard University Press.

Burke, Kenneth. 1966. *Language as symbolic action*. Berkeley: University of California Press.

——. 1984. *Attitudes toward history*. Berkeley: University of California Press.

Conniff, Ruth. 1998. Welfare miracle, or mirage? *New York Times*, March 7: A29.

Cooper, Marilyn, and Michael Holtzman. 1989. *Writing as social action*. Portsmouth, NH: Heinemann, Boynton-Cook.

Counts, George. 1932. *Dare the schools build a new social order?* New York: John Day.

Cox, Murray. 1990. Interview with Paulo Freire. *Omni*, 12.7(April): 90–95.

Crowley, Sharon. 1996. Around 1971: Current-traditional rhetoric and process models of composing. In *Composition in the twenty-first century: Crisis and change*. Eds. Lynn Z. Bloom, Donald A. Daiker, and Edward M. White. Carbondale, IL: Southern Illinois University Press, 64–74.

Daniels, Harvey, Steven Zemelman, and Marilyn Bizar. 1998. Teacher alert! Phonics fads sweep nation's schools. *Rethinking schools*, 12.4(Summer): 3, 13.

Delpit, Lisa. 1995. *Other people's children: Cultural conflict in the classroom*. New York: The New Press.

Delpit, Lisa, and Theresa Perry. 1998. *The real ebonics debate*. Boston: Beacon.

Dewey, John, 1900 (1971). *The school and society*. Chicago: University of Chicago Press.

——— . 1900 (1971). *The child and the curriculum*. Chicago: University of Chicago Press.

——— . 1909 (1975). *Moral principles in education*. Carbondale: Southern Illinois University Press.

——— . 1933 (1971). *How we think: A restatement of the relation of reflective thinking to the educative process*. Chicago: Regnery.

——— . 1916 (1966). *Democracy and education*. New York: Free Press.

——— . 1938 (1963). *Experience and education*. New York: Collier.

Digest of education statistics. 1997. Washington, DC: Office of Educational Research and Improvement, U.S. Department of Education.

Dougherty, Kevin J. 1994. *The contradictory college: The conflicts, origins, impacts, and futures of the community colleges*. Albany: SUNY Press.

Dowst, Kenneth. 1980. The epistemic approach: Writing, knowing and learning. In *Eight Approaches to Teaching Composition*, Ed. Timothy R. Donovan and Ben W. McClelland. Urbana, IL: NCTE, 65–85.

Education Week. *Technology counts*. 1997. *Education Week* (November 10, Special Issue).

Elbow, Peter. 1991. Reflections on academic discourse: How it relates to freshmen and colleagues. *College English*, 53.1 (February): 135–155.

Faigley, Lester. 1997. Literacy after the revolution. *College Composition and Communication*, 48.1 (February): 30–43.

Faludi, Susan. 1991. *Backlash: The undeclared war against American women*. New York: Anchor.

Fine, Michelle. 1987. Silencing in public schools. *Language arts*, 64(February): 157–164.

——— . 1993. *Framing dropouts*. Albany: SUNY Press.

Foucault, Michel. 1980. *Power/knowledge*. Ed. C. Gordon. New York: Pantheon.

Fox, Tom. 1993. Standards and access. *Journal of basic writing*, 12.1 (Fall): 37–45.

Freire, Paulo. 1970. *Pedagogy of the oppressed*. New York: Seabury.

——— . 1973. *Education for critical consciousness*. New York: Seabury.

——— . 1978. *Pedagogy-in-process*. New York: Continuum.

——— . 1985a. Reading the world and reading the word: An interview with Paulo Freire (with David Dillon). *Language arts*, 62(January): 15–21.

——— . 1985b. *The politics of education*. Westport, CT: Greenwood.

——— . 1990. Interview. *Omni*, 12(April): 74–94.

——— . 1993. *Pedagogy of the city*. New York: Continuum.

——— . 1996. *Letters to Cristina*. New York: Routledge.

Freire, Paulo, and Antonio Faundez. 1989. *Learning to Question*. New York: Continuum.

Galbraith, John K. 1967. *The new industrial state*. Boston: Houghton-Mifflin.

Goodlad, John. 1984. *A place called school*. New York: McGraw-Hill.

Gordon, Linda. 1994. How "welfare" became a dirty word. *Chronicle of Higher Education*, July 20: B1–B2.

Gose, Ben. 1998. Minority enrollment rose by 3.2% in 1996. *Chronicle of Higher Education*, June 5: A32–A41.

Gould, Stephen Jay. 1995. Ghosts of bell curves past. *Natural history*, February: 12–19.

Graff, Gerald. 1992. *Beyond the culture wars: How teaching the conflicts can revitalize American education*. New York: Norton.

Graff, Harvey J. 1987. *The labyrinths of literacy*. London: Falmer.

Greene, Maxine. 1988. *The dialectic of freedom*. New York: Teachers College Press.

Hairston, Maxine. 1992a. Diversity, ideology, and teaching writing. *College Composition and Communication*, 43.2(May): 179–193. See also "Counterstatement" (1993) by John Trimbur, Robert G. Wood, Ron Strickland, William H. Thelin, William J. Rouster, Toni Mester, and "Reply" by Hairston in CCC, 44.2(May): 248–256.

——— . 1992b. *Successful writing* (3rd edition). New York: Norton.

Heath, Shirley Brice. 1983. *Ways with words*. Cambridge: Cambridge University Press.

Henwood, Doug. 1997. Trashonomics. In *White trash: Race and class in America*. Eds. Matt Wray and Annalee Newitz. New York: Routledge, 177–197.

Herrnstein, Richard, and Charles Murray. 1994. *The bell curve*. New York: Free Press.

Hershey, Robert D. Jr. 1996. In turnabout for workers, wages grow more slowly. *New York Times*, October 30: D1.

Hill, Heather C. 1997. The importance of a minority perspective in the classroom. *Chronicle of Higher Education*, November 7: A60.

Hirsch, E.D. 1987. *Cultural literacy: What every American needs to know.* Boston: Houghton-Mifflin.

———. 1989. *A first dictionary of cultural literacy: What our children need to know.* Boston: Houghton-Mifflin.

Hirsch, E.D., Joseph F. Kett, and James Trefil. 1988. *The dictionary of cultural literacy: What every American needs to know.* Boston: Houghton-Mifflin.

Holmes, Steven A. 1996. Income disparity between poorest and richest rises. *New York Times* (June 20), A1.

Horton, Myles, with Judith Kohl and Herb Kohl. 1990. *The long haul.* New York: Doubleday.

Horton, Myles, and Paulo Freire. 1990. *We make the road by walking.* Philadelphia: Temple University Press.

Ingalls, Zoe. 1998. The eye of the storm at New Paltz. *Chronicle of Higher Education*, May 8: A10.

Jencks, Christopher, et al. 1972. *Inequality: A reassessment of the effects of family and schooling in America.* New York: Basic.

Karabel, Jerome, and Steven Brint. 1989. *The diverted dream: Community colleges and the promise of educational opportunity in America, 1900–1985.* New York: Oxford University Press.

Karp, Stan. 1997/1998. Banned in Jersey, welcomed on Broadway. *Rethinking schools*, 12.2: 14–15.

Knoblauch, C.H., and Lil Brannon. 1984. *Rhetorical traditions and the teaching of writing.* Upper Montclair, NJ: Boynton-Cook.

Kozol, Jonathan. 1991. *Savage inequalities: Children in America's schools.* New York: Crown.

Kretovics, Joseph R. 1985. Critical literacy: challenging the assumptions of mainstream educational theory. *Journal of Education*, 167.2: 50–62.

Lazere, Donald. 1992. Teaching the rhetorical conflicts. *College Composition and Communication*, 43.2(May): 194–213.

Lieberman, Trudy. 1998. Hunger in America. *The Nation.* March 30: 11–16.

Lindemann, Erika. 1995. *A rhetoric for writing teachers.* New York: Oxford University Press.

Mayher, John. 1990. *Uncommon sense: Theoretical practice in language education.* Portsmouth, NH: Boynton-Cook, Heinemann.

Mickelson, Roslyn Arlyn, and Stephen Samuel Smith. 1998. Can education eliminate race, class, and gender inequality? In *Race, class and gender* (3rd edition). Eds. Margaret L. Andersen and Patricia Hill Collins, New York: Wadsworth, 328–340.

Moody, Kim. 1998. On the line in Flint. *The Nation.* July 13: 6.

Morris, Bonnie J. 1998. Women's studies: Prejudice and vilification persist. *Chronicle of Higher Education*, June 19: A56.

Mortenson, Thomas G. 1995. *Post-secondary education opportunity: The Mortenson report on public policy analysis of opportunity for post-secondary education.* November. Iowa City: Mortenson Research Letter.

National Center for Education Statistics. *The educational progress of black students.* 1995. Washington, DC: National Center for Education Statistics.

National Center for Education Statistics. *The educational progress of women.* 1996. Washington, DC: National Center for Education Statistics.

Nieves, Evelyn. 1997. Pupils' script on workers is ruled out. *New York Times*, June 26: B1.

Ohmann, Richard. 1996 (1976). *English in America.* Middletown, CT: Wesleyan University Press.

———. 1987. *Politics of Letters.* Middletown, CT: Wesleyan UP.

Orfield, Gary. 1993. *The growth of segregation in American schools: Changing patterns of separation and poverty since 1968.* A report of the Harvard Project on School Desegregation to the National School Boards Association. Washington, DC.

Orfield, Gary, and Susan Easton. 1996. *Dismantling desegregation: The quiet reversal of Brown v. Board of Education.* New York: The New Press.

Orfield, Gary, et al. 1997. *Deepening segregation in American public schools.* Cambridge, MA: Civil Rights Project, Harvard Graduate School of Education.

Perez-Pena, Richard. 1997. Study shows New York has the greatest income gap. *New York Times*, December 12: A1.

Phelps, Louise Wetherbee. 1988. *Composition as a human science.* New York: Oxford University Press.

Pratt, Mary Louise. 1991. Arts of the contact zone. *Profession '91.* New York: MLA, 33–40.

Quality counts: The urban challenge—public education in the 40 states. 1998. *Education Week*, 17.17(January 8).

Ravitch, Diane. 1974. *The great school wars: New York City, 1805–1973.* New York: Basic.

———. 1983. *The troubled crusade: American education, 1945–1980.* New York: Basic.

Rich, Adrienne. 1979. *On lies, secrets, and silences.* New York: Norton.

Rose, Mike. 1990. *Lives on the boundary.* New York: Penguin.

Rouse, John. 1979. The politics of composition. *College English*, 41.1 (September): 1–12.

Russell, David R., "Activity Theory and Writing Instruction." In *Reconceiving Writing, Rethinking Writing Instruction.* Ed. Joseph Petraglia, Mahwah, NJ: Lawrence Erlbaum, 1995, 51–77.

Sandman, Jessica L. 1998. California colleges going all out to woo minority students. *Education Week*, April 29: 6.

Schneider, Alison. 1998a. More professors are working part time, and more teach at 2 year colleges. *Chronicle of Higher Education* (March 13), A14–A15.

——— . 1998b. Bad blood in the English Department: The rift between composition and literature. *Chronicle of Higher Education*, (February 13), 14–15.

Shaugnessy, Mina. 1977. *Errors and expectations*. New York: Oxford University Press.

Shepard, Scott. 1998. In civil rights shift, EEOC helps white people most. *Atlanta Journal-Constitution*. March 4: A13.

Shor, Ira, 1992. *Culture wars: School and society in the conservative restoration, 1969–1991*. Chicago: University of Chicago Press.

——— . 1992. *Empowering education: Critical teaching for social change*. Chicago: University of Chicago Press.

——— . 1996. *When students have power: Negotiating authority in a critical pedagogy*. Chicago: University of Chicago Press.

——— . 1997. Our apartheid: Writing instruction and inequality. *Journal of Basic Writing*. 16.l (Spring): 91–104.

Shor, Ira, and Paulo Freire. 1987. *A pedagogy for liberation*. Westport, CT: Greenwood.

Sklar, Holly, and Chuck Collins. 1997. Forbes 400 world series. *The Nation*. October 20: 5–6.

Smart, Tim. 1998. GE '97 profit hits a record $8.2 billion. *Washington Post*. January 23: G3.

Statistical Abstract of the United States. 1997. Washington, DC: Bureau of the Census, U.S. Department of Commerce.

Strauss, Neil. 1998. Girl power is squelched. *New York Times*, May 27: E3.

Street, Brian. 1984. *Literacy in theory and practice*. New York: Cambridge UP.

Stunkel, Kenneth R. 1998. The lecture: A powerful tool for intellectual liberation. *Chronicle of Higher Education*, June 26: A52.

Tyack, David, and Larry Cuban. 1995. *Tinkering toward utopia: A century of public school reform*. Cambridge: Harvard University Press.

Viadero, Debra. 1998. ETS study tracks worrisome trend in rate of college completion. *Education Week.*, February 25: 12.

Vygotsky, Lev. 1962. *Thought and language*. Cambridge, MA: MIT Press.

——— . 1978. *Mind in society*. Cambridge, MA: Harvard University Press.

Wealthiest Americans getting an even larger slice of the pie. 1997. *New York Times*, September 30: A26.

Weissglass, Julian. 1998. The SAT: Public spirited or preserving privilege? *Education Week*, April 15: 60.

Williams, E.I.F. 1937. *Horace Mann: Educational statesman*. New York: Macmillan.

Williams, Raymond. 1977. *Marxism and literature*. New York: Oxford University Press.

Williams, Wendy M., and Stephen J. Ceci. 1997. Are Americans becoming more or less alike? Trends in race, class, and ability differences in intelligence. *American Psychologist*, 52.11 (November): 1226–1235.

Zehr, Mary Anne. 1998. Black students found less likely to access the internet. *Education Week*, April 29:9.

15

Teaching How to Read the World and Change It: Critical Pedagogy in the Intermediate Grades

Robert E. Peterson

Introduction

Monday morning a child brings a stray dog into the classroom.

The traditional teacher sees that it is removed immediately.

The progressive teacher builds on the students' interest; perhaps measures and weighs the animal with the children, has the children draw and write about the dog, and eventually calls the humane society.

The Freirian teacher does what the progressive teacher does but more. She asks questions, using the dog as the object of reflection. "Why are there so many stray dogs in our neighborhood?" "Why are there more here than in the rich suburbs?" "Why do people have dogs?" "Why doesn't the city allocate enough money to clean up after the dogs and care for the strays?" While accepting stray animals into a classroom isn't the bellwether mark of an elementary Freiran teacher, engaging children in reflective dialogue on topics of their interest is.

Not surprisingly, the classroom of an elementary teacher applying a Freirian method is markedly different than that of a traditional teacher. What perhaps is not as expected is that a Freirian approach also differs significantly from the methods of many progressive teachers, that is, those who organize their classes in child-centered and holistic ways.

Going to public school in the 1960s I became a proponent of progressive education as a student, but it was only when I read Freire as a junior in high school, that I realized education could be more than just "relevant" and "student-centered." However, the political reality of being a high school student activist in the late 1960s and early 1970s made me doubt the likelihood of a Freiran method being used in the public schools.

It wasn't until a decade later, that I came back to Freire and reexamined his applicability to the public school setting. I was on the other side of the teacher's desk, now looking at things as an educator rather than a student. I had traveled to Nicaragua and observed the week-long celebration that concluded the National Literacy Campaign in August of 1980, and the experience convinced me that I should look again at Freire's work. I knew that the conditions of teaching and learning in the United States differed greatly from those encountered by Freire in the Third World, and yet I felt that the essence of Freire's approach would be appropriate for an urban school setting.

Throughout the 1980s, I worked on applying Freire's ideas in my fourth and fifth grade bilingual inner-city classrooms. My approach contrasted sharply with the numerous "educational reforms" being tried elsewhere. These mainstream proposals were often state and system mandates; their goal was to "teacher-proof" the curricula through the use of basal reader programs, direct instruction, the methods of Madeline Hunter and an expansion of standardized testing (Fairtest, 1988; Gibboney, 1988; Levine, 1988). Under the banners of "back to the basics" and "improving student achievement" these efforts further reinforced and strengthened what Freire calls the "banking" method of education, whereby the teacher puts periodic deposits of knowledge into the students' heads. Such classrooms are very teacher- and text-centered. Little discussion and reflection take place. While the relevance of a banking-type approach appears to go counter to what recent research on literacy suggests (Calkins, 1983; Goodman 1986; Goodman, Smith, Meredith, & Goodman, 1987; Graves, 1983; Smith 1985) this model continues to be the most prevalent method in public school classrooms. Goodlad (1984), for example, found that not even 1 percent of the instructional time in high schools was devoted to discussion that "required some kind of open response involving reasoning or perhaps an opinion from students." As he notes, "the extraordinary degree of student passivity stands out" (p. 229).

Freire posits a dialogic "problem posing" method of education as an alternative. Here, teachers and students both become actors in figuring out the world through a process of mutual communication. In the banking method of education the teacher and the curricular texts have the "right answers" which the students are expected to regurgitate periodically onto criterion referenced tests. However in Freire's model, questions and not answers are the core of the curriculum; open-ended questions prod students to critically analyze their social situation and encourage them to ultimately work towards changing it.

To apply Freire's approach in the elementary classroom one has to have a perspective about the learners and learning which runs counter to the dominant educational ideology. A Freirian approach relies on the experience of the students and implies a respect and use of the students' culture, language, and dialect. It values dialogue and reflection over lecture and repetition. It means constructing a classroom in which students have the maximum amount of power that is legally permitted and that they can socially handle. It means challenging the students to reflect on the social nature of knowledge and the curriculum, to get them to think about why they think and act the way they do.

Ultimately a Freirian approach means moving beyond thought and words to action. This is done on the one hand by teachers themselves modeling social responsibility and critical engagement in community and global issues. On the other hand it means constructing with the students an atmosphere in the classroom and the school where students feel secure and confident enough to interrogate their own realities, see them in a different light, and act on their developing convictions to change their own social reality. In order to do all this, the teachers themselves have to go through a transformative process, breaking the ideological chains of their own formal education, of past training, and the inertia of habit of past teaching.

Teaching Organically

Freire uses generative words and themes in his teaching, words that invoke passion and feeling among his students. In North American jargon this is sometimes called a "language experience" approach for it utilizes students' own language and experiences as the basis of instruction. An example from European literature and from the experience of a New Zealand teacher illustrate the significance of this approach.

In Bertolt Brecht's (1978) famous play *The Mother*, which takes place during the 1905 revolution in Czarist Russia, the mother and a metal worker go to ask a professor to teach them to read and write. The professor, begrudgingly and condescendingly, agrees and proceeds to write two words on a slate board: "Branch" and "nest." The two workers immediately become frustrated by the irrelevance of the situation and demand to know how to spell "worker," "class struggle," and "exploitation." Not clear as to why his initial words were inappropriate, the professor obligingly changes his plans. And, thus, through the power of their own words, the workers learn how to read and write rapidly.

In her work with Maori children in New Zealand, Sylvia Ashton-Warner (1965) developed an educational approach very similar to that of Freire. She understood that the failure of the Aborigine children in New Zealand schools was mainly due to their cultural clash with the Anglicized system. She drew on the interests and experience of her students, within the context of the culture they brought to school. Her use of "organic vocabulary" to teach reading, spelling, and writing was based on the belief that words significant to the learner would motivate the learner into learning. As she explained:

> Pleasant words won't do. Respectable words won't do. They must be words organically tied up, organically born from the dynamic life itself. They must be words that are already part of the child's being.
>
> (1965, p. 33)

The proof of her method was in the students themselves. While it took four months for them to learn words like "come, look, and," in four minutes they could learn words like "police, bulldog, knife, cry, yell, fight, Daddy, Mummy, ghost, kiss, and frightened."

The meaningfulness of these words stands in sharp contrast to the first words taught to many children in urban school settings in the United States. One widely used basal company chose eight words as the primary starting point for reading: "red, yellow, blue, girl, boy, the, a, has." In fact, an entire kindergarten workbook is devoted to the word "the." The Commission on Reading of the National Council of Teachers of English (1988) documents how basal reading programs control vocabulary and syntax to such an extent as to make the initial exposure to reading irrelevant and boring to most children.

Children's learning should be centered in their own experience, language, and culture. For this to happen, the classroom environment should be "language rich," allowing the children to develop their language and thinking abilities in as natural a setting as possible. This applies equally to first and second language learning (Krashen & Terrell, 1983; Goodman, 1986). A generative theme approach fosters the development of such an environment.

Practical application

A generative theme is an issue or topic that catches the interest of students in such a way that discussion, study, and project work can be built around it. Themes may come from an incident in a particular student's life, a problem in the community, or an idea that a student latched onto from the media, the news, or a classroom activity. Writing, reading, talking, acting, and reflecting are the key ways through which generative themes develop. I start the year with a unit on the child's own family and background—placing their birthdates on the class timeline. The second day we place their parents' dates on the timeline, the third, their grandparents. We put pins in a world map indicating the places of birth. I ask them to talk to their parents or other family members and collect at least one story, joke, or memory from their family and either write it down or prepare to tell it orally.

The first day of school I also have the students in my class write a book. Inspired by Ashton-Warner's (1965) continual construction of books based on her children's writings and drawings, I do the same. Quality is not important on the first day. I want to show students that we can write, draw, and accomplish things they would not have dreamed of. We choose a topic or topics together, write, draw, and put the unedited papers into a plastic theme binder creating an instant book. This action of collaboratively producing a book based on the students' own experiences provides both a model of what can be accomplished the rest of the year and a benchmark upon which the teacher and the students can judge growth in their abilities. "If we can accomplish this in only one day by working together," I tell my students, "just imagine what we can do in an entire year!"

Throughout the year I use the "writing process" approach (Graves 1983, Calkins, 1986) which focuses on production of student generated and meaningful themes. Students write for a purpose, whether it is for publication, a pen pal or display. We publish in the school newsletter, the city newspaper, children's magazines,[1] or our own books. Never have I seen students think so much about a piece of writing than when they know it is to be published.

The most ambitious writing we do is for the publication of our own books. Usually this is in the form of anthologies of students' prose, poetry, and drawings—*Kid Power, Colors Laugh, Splashing in Action* are the titles of a few that we have produced. I especially encourage writings on the students' own communities and families (Wigginton, 1989). At times children have written entire booklets—legends, adventures, autobiographies—that they may give to a parent or sibling as a gift for a birthday or holiday. These booklets validate the children's lives, give them self-confidence in their ability to do projects, help focus reflection on our common field trips and areas of study, provide an inspiration to write and a motivation to read. They are also useful for me, not only as the basis for future writing lessons, but because I learn more about my students and their communities.

Generative themes can be discovered and reflected upon not only through writing in the classroom but through a variety of other language and performance arts activities. Mime, drama, role playing, reading aloud from their own writings, chants, and oral story telling allow students to describe and reflect on their world while improving their basic first language and second language abilities.

Even when standardized curricula must be used, a teacher can utilize the life experiences of their students. For example, if by state law or local decree a teacher must use a basal reader, approaches can be taken that downplay its segmented skills orientation. A student could: Write or tell about what would happen if she were to take the main character home for dinner; write a letter to the main character comparing the student's life to that of the main characters; or write a version of the story that draws on some comparable situation in their school community. Teachers can also supplement basals by having students read quality children's literature in decent anthologies[2] or in whole books. My experience has shown that if children shelve the basal a few times a week and instead read classroom sets of entire novels, they are more likely to think longer and more deeply about a piece of literature and how it relates to their lives.

But there are some problems with this organic style of teaching. Given class oppression in our society, poor children usually have a narrower range of experiences than those from more affluent homes. This does not mean they are culturally or experientially deprived— as spending the summer in Mexico or the Mississippi delta or even playing in the back alleys of one of our big cities can be a rich experience. Their culture and experience is just different than that of many teachers; it is also in discordance with the texts of the dominant curricula. I believe though that we should stretch what is organic in the children's lives by taking them out into the world and by bringing the world into the classroom (Searle, 1977). Field trips, speakers, movies, and current events studies are obvious ways to do this.

Poetry and music can also bring the world into the classroom. For example, Langston Hughes' poems "Colored Child at the Carnival" or "The Ballad of the Landlord," speak to the experience of many African-Americans and poor people and spark critical discussions. I have had similar success with songs such as "Harriet Tubman" and "I Cried" sung by Holly Near, "Lives in the Balance" and "Lawless Avenue" by Jackson Browne, "Sambo Lando" sung by Inti Illimani, "El Pueblo Unido Jamas Sera Vencido" by Quilapayun. Whenever I use poems or songs I reproduce the words so that each student can follow along and keep a copy.

As we delve deeper into the nature of students' experiences in urban America, new problems with the application of Freire's theory confront us. Freire (1970) assumes that what will most inspire the learner is discussion and reflection on his or her own experiences, particularly his or her own oppression. In my eyes, many children in urban America are oppressed by a few key institutions: school, family, and community.

For an elementary teacher to apply Freire by focusing on such oppression raises difficult problems. The degree to which a teacher can "deviate" from the standard curriculum depends on a number of factors—the amount of peer and parental support, the political situation in the school and district, and the sophistication and maturity of the particular group of students, to name a few. But there is deviation and there is deviation. To study the Plains Indians instead of the Pilgrims is one thing. To help students become aware and critical about how they are being oppressed in society can be quite another. I have found two ways to approach this problem. First is to deal with power relationships and "oppression" within my own classroom. The second way is to bring the world into the classroom, so that children start reflecting on their own lives. I will first explain the latter.

One year I showed my students the video *The Wrath of Grapes* (United Farm Workers, 1987) about the current grape boycott and followed it up with a field trip to see Cesar Chavez speak at the local technical college. All sorts of good things came out of this activity, but the most interesting was that on the Monday after our trip my students came to school and the first thing they yelled was "Mr. Peterson, Sixth Street is on strike."

"What?" I replied.

"Sixth and National Ave. is on strike!"

Now the streets in Milwaukee have a lot of pot holes after the long winter but I had never heard of a street being on strike. What had in fact occurred was a strike by workers at a local factory. Later that week during art period I took six students armed with a tape recorder over to the company so they could interview the workers. I believe they learned more during their half-hour interview than they had in years of social studies lessons. We debriefed in the teachers' lounge. When we were reviewing the reason for the strike—a wage cut from $7.00 down to $4.00—Cecilia said rather unemotionally, "That's more money than my mom makes now." We examined where each of the children's parents worked and if they were in a union. "Grievance" became a spelling word the next week and pretty soon there seemed to be grievances about all sorts of things in the children's lives. By bringing the world into the classroom they were better able to reflect upon their own lives.

But as I enlarge the world in which my students operate through sharing of such experiences, always tying issues to and building upon the students' own realities, I habitually confront another problem. The "generative themes" of many media-saturated children often seem to have more to do with life on the cathode ray tube than life in our community. During writing workshop or group discussions I sometimes feel I am in another world of professional wrestlers, super heros, and video games. The average child watches television six hours a day and in one year sees 800 war toy commercials, 250 episodes of war cartoons; the violent commercials and episodes being the equivalent of 22 days of school (Liebert & Sprafkin, 1988).[3]

One consequence of this television addiction is physical atrophy, but the deadening of the child's imagination and the imposition of a violent, consumerist ideology are other results that have a direct effect on a "generative theme"-based classroom. When my kids moan about the President their solution is to kill him. A child doesn't like gangs—solve the problem by machine gunning them down or by sending them to the electric chair. There is no simple or short-term solution to this problem, and certainly a single classroom teacher is not going to solve this problem alone. I challenge these ideas through dialogue attempting to get children to think about why they think the way they do (which I explain in more detail in the section on critiquing curriculum and the media). I take what I hear and try to rework it from a different angle—codify it to use Freire's term—and bring it up again in the future in the context of other curricular areas.

In a generative theme-oriented classroom, the tendency is often to try to cover too much too fast. My most successful experiences have been when I've had the class concentrate on one thing in depth. The concept of "less is more" (Coalition of Essential Schools, 1984) applies equally well to a single classroom as it does to an entire school curricula. I have ensured this by using a variety of methods: a word for the day, a quotation of the week, a short poem, a graphic, a cartoon, story, or news article.

When I have a special word for the day it often relates to a topic the children have been discussing or studying. I or one of the students present it in both English and Spanish, explain its epistemology, teach the others how to sign it in American Sign Language, discuss its significance and use it as a "password" as we move through the day's activities. Sometimes the word comes from the conversations I hear, or from a topic of interest that we have discussed in our studies. The focus on one word, particularly in a bilingual setting, helps students become aware of language in a metacognitive sense. Through word webbing or semantic mapping I help connect this word again to the life experiences of the students.

Regardless of whether it's a word, a scripted dialogue, a story, or a discussion which serves to organize classroom dialogue, the focus of instruction and locus of control is learner- rather than teacher-centered. The essence of an organic theme-based approach thus lies in the connections it builds between the topic at hand, the students' lives and broader world around them (Ellwood, 1989).

The Empowerment of Students

Since students have so few rights, they rarely develop responsibility. By fifth grade I get children who are so damaged by society that they are only able to behave if they are given no rights—even going to the pencil sharpener without having to ask permission is too much for some to handle. This irresponsibility is rooted in the teacher-centered and textbook-driven curriculum which serves to disempower children. Because students are denied rights and kept from decision making throughout their school life and subjected to tedious worksheets and boring curriculum, school life prevents them from developing the responsibility and self-discipline necessary to be independent thinkers and actors in our society.[4] Freire (1970) maintains that through this subjugation students become *objects* acted upon by the authoritarian school system and society. He argues, instead, for a pedagogical process of dialogue, reflection, dramatization, and interaction, whereby students move towards being *subjects* capable of understanding the world and their social context, and ultimately engaging in activity based on this new understanding. Again, the realization of students as subjects is not always easily attained.

I want my students to take responsibility for their own learning, but when I begin to encourage this many see it as license to goof off. Shor and Freire (1987) speak of the need to develop transitionary models and activities to train people to be more responsible. In making the transition to empower students, one must therefore be prepared for a sometimes enormous struggle.

The first step in this transition is to enhance the students' self-esteem and reduce the anxiety level. This is done through creating an overall positive atmosphere in the classroom and by planning very specific activities which stress self-awareness, respect, and cooperation. Activities like those suggested by Canfield and Wells (1976), Prutzman, Stern, Burger, and Bodenhamer (1988), and Schniedewind (1987) help students become more aware of their own attitudes about themselves and others while developing skills of listening, speaking, and cooperating.

I have children interview each other at the begining of the year and report on it to the whole class. This shows them that they should take each other seriously and it practices public speaking and careful listening. I play circle games involving drama, storytelling, and physical activity as well as small group activities which stress brainstorming, problem solving, and creative writing and dramatics. Instead of segregating affective education activities off into an afternoon corner of the curriculum I try as much as possible to integrate group process and self-esteem-building activities into the curriculum as a whole. No matter where such activities are during the day, however, I have found that I need to model, role play, and teach many of these social skills. I model something, involve a small group of students with me doing the activity in front of the class, then have another small group do it again in front without my participation. Finally, after a short dicussion with the whole class everyone becomes involved in the activity. Later, it is important for the class to discuss both the content and the process of the activity, with both strengths and short-comings being highlighted. Modeling and discussing with students how to manage their time and to stay organized—from one's desk to one's three-ring binder—are also very powerful tools for the development of independence and high self-esteem.

Finally, I have found that I can reach even more students by linking my attempts at developing self-confidence and responsibility to history. For example, each year I make sure to focus for a while on the fact that in our nation's past females were not allowed to attend many schools, not allowed to speak at political meetings or vote. Through role play, storytelling, discussion, and project work about the past, some students are inspired to take a stronger and more self-conscious role in the classroom.

Beyond the building of self-esteem, students need to be involved with establishing and periodically reviewing the rules and curriculum of the classroom. Students' ability to do this depends on several factors including their maturity and previous schooling experience. At the beginning of the year, I carefully plan lessons which give students a taste of what it would mean to have a large say over what happens in the class. At the same time I am quick to restrict student decision making at the first signs that students are using the increased power as a license to goof off. As I restrict it, I go through a long process of explanation: discussion, role playing, and a lessening of the restrictions. After several cycles of this process, students usually become better able to take on increased responsibility and freedom. Sometimes such restrictions must be done on an individual level. For example, if the desks are arranged in clusters, those students who demonstrate they are capable of sitting close to their classmates and yet still listen to class discussions are permitted to stay in the clusters, while those who are disruptive have as a logical consequence their desk being place in a "row."

Empowerment does not mean "giving" someone their freedom. Nor does it mean creating a type of surface "empowerment" in which one gives the students the impression that they are "equal" to the teacher. The challenge for the teacher who believes in student empowerment is to create an environment which is both stimulating and flexible in which students can exercise increasing levels of power while regularly reflecting upon and evaluating the new learner–teacher relationship.

One element of this environment is class organization. We arrange our classroom according to our needs: rows for presentations, a circle of chairs for large group discussion, and clusters of desks for small group discussion and work.

For class meetings, for instance, desks are pushed to the walls and the chairs are placed in a big circle. Such meetings form the basis of democraticizing the classroom (Glasser, 1969, 1986; Schmuck & Schmuck, 1983) through discussions, voting, and class problem solving. At the beginning of each school year, I chair the meetings but eventually the students take over. One person takes notes each session into a spiral notebook that we keep hung on the wall. I have a special rock which is passed from person to person so we know whose turn it is to speak. The first part of the year is often spent just improving our listening skills so that we can have an interactive dialogue instead of a series of monologues. I do this through modeling what a good listener does and playing listening games, such as having each person repeat one thing or the main idea of the person who spoke immediately before them prior to them speaking.

I start the class meetings with a circle game and then pass the rock and let people state the concern or problem they would like to discuss. I note these and then decide what will be discussed that day, usually starting off with a smaller, solvable problem and then moving into the hot and heavy ones. We use a five-step plan:

1. What is the problem?
2. Are you sure about it?
3. What can we do about it?
4. Try it.
5. How did it work?

Through this five-step process, students begin to work collectively, reflecting upon the problem and together seeking solutions. While many of the problems poor and minority children and communities face cannot be easily or immediately "solved" a "problem-posing" pedagogy can encourage a questioning of why things are the way they are and the identification of actions, no matter how small, to begin to address them. Inherent is a recognition of the "complexity and time needed for solutions with individuals and communities" (Wallerstein & Bernstein, 1988).

A Dialogical Instructional Method

If "student empowerment" is going to be meaningful, students not only need to be involved in some of the problem-solving and posing practices outlined above, but teachers must fundamentally change their methods. Education should not be viewed as the transmission of knowledge by trained technicians, but rather as an interactive process through which problems are posed and answers collaboratively sought. Dewey (1916) felt similarly and spoke of a conception of instruction for knowledge as opposed to instruction for habit. Like Freire, he saw education as an interactive process based on the history, experience, and culture of the student. Dewey said a mechanic taught mechanically would not be able to solve a new problem that might arise, but one taught to understand the whole machine and machines in general would be able to adapt to the new situation. The difference between Dewey and Freire is in part defined by the kinds of activities they advocate as ways for students to gain knowledge. Dewey took a deliberate apolitical stance. The practical educational activities he advocated usually involved students transforming the natural world, that is, gardening or laboratory experiments. Freire, on the other hand, defines practical education activities as critical discussion and collective action aimed at solving political and social problems.

The centerpiece of Freire's method, and what distinguishes it so sharply from the dominant practices in classrooms of most of North America, is its emphasis on dialogue. *Dialogue*, as Freire defines it, is not just permissive talk, but *conversation with a focus and a purpose*. Dialogue shows that the object of study is not the exclusive property of the teacher; knowledge is not produced somewhere in textbook offices and then transferred to the student. By discussion and extensive use of open-ended questioning by the teacher, students begin to think about the object or topic under study. Freire (Shor & Freire, 1987) is not opposed to lectures per se and in fact suggests the use of a variety of formats in the classroom. Since factual knowledge is the foundation upon which many discussions and opinions should be based, short lectures are sometimes important even at the elementary level. However, with the recent trend towards direct instruction, teachers too often demonstrate an overreliance on lecture to convey knowledge, even though only a small amount of such information is retained.

To initiate dialogue, I may use a motivating drawing, photo, cartoon, poem, written dialogue, oral story, or piece of prose. These dialogue "triggers" are useful for full classroom or small group discussions. Wallerstein and Bernstein (1988) have used a simple acronym "SHOWED" as a way to help students systematically respond to such a trigger.

S   what do you *See*?
H   what's *Happening* to your feelings?
O   relate it to your *Own* lives
W   *Why* do we face these problems?
E
D   what can we *Do* about it?

The students are encouraged to use this format to help facilitate their dialogue. It helps to direct students away from spontaneous conversation to a progression that moves from personal reactions to social analysis to consideration of action. A few examples from my class serve to illustrate this process.

One year as my class played at recess, a student slipped and fell on a broken bottle, putting a ghastly wound into the back of her thigh—over 50 stitches. After the police and ambulance had carried her off on a stretcher, we tearfully retreated back into the safety of our classroom and I thought, "What the heck should I do now?" I sent two kids out to retrieve the guilty piece of glass. We put the piece in an open box and passed it around. The rest of the afternoon we discussed everything from the high school students who share our playground, to the bottle manufacturing companies who have prevented the Wisconsin state legislature from passing a bottle deposit law. One of my students, Fernando Valadez, put his thoughts to poetry:

Pig Pen
Nobody likes to live
in the pigpen of broken bottles,
muddy papers and squished cans.
In our neighborhood of
lonely streets, messy parks,
dirty alleys and dangerous playgrounds
you might get hurt like a friend
of mine who got a big cut on the back
of her leg when she was running
by the swings and fell on some glass.
The ambulance came
and took her away.
Who's going to take the junk
away?

At times the triggers I use are more explicitly value-laden and often cut across the curricula integrating language arts, history, and other subject areas. Some of the best dialogue in my class has come from discussions following the reading of poems or short historical pieces. Will Fisher's poem, for instance, helped initiate discussion of history and justice. The context is ice cream cones and mud, one that a child can relate to and understand:

A Command to Drive Horse Recklessly

The first warm day in May, a line of common folk in front of the Dairy Queen shop. A carriage dashes by, spraying mud. Women curse and shake their fists. Two men rush after the carriage. It has been stopped by a traffic light. The men angrily threaten the coachman. Clutching his fifty-cent cone, a child catches up and, ignoring the others, flings the cone through the open window into the face of the nobleperson.

Utilizing the "SHOWED" question format with this simple poem has enabled my students to discuss a wide variety of topics ranging from racial and class discrimination, inflation, splashing each other on the playground, to the invention of traffic lights and cars.

Critique the Curriculum and Society

There is more to Freire than generative themes of the learners' lives and a dialogic style. He speaks of the need to illuminate reality to the student, as opposed to the standard curriculum which obscures reality. Freire (1985) suggests that the "question is a different relationship to knowledge and society and that the only way to truly understand the curriculum of the classroom is to go beyond its walls into the society."

In most schools, facts are presented as value-free. Conceptual analysis—to the degree it exists—does not make contact with the real world. History is presented as a series of nonrelated sequential facts. Scientific "truths" are presented without historical context with little regard to the ramifications such matters have on the learners' environment or global ecology. Students are expected to learn—usually memorize and occasionally "discover"—such facts without regard to the values or interests which inform such perspectives (Shor, 1980, 1987).

As stated previously, teachers should help students draw connections between their own lives, communities, and environment. But we must also *help them reflect upon why they think the way they do; to discover that knowledge is socially constructed, that truth is relative not only to time and place but to class, race, and gender interests as well.* Students need to know that what they have before them in their textbooks, in the newspapers, or on the television is not always true. We should thus engage our students in thinking about the validity of texts (Bigelow, 1989). In fact, this is one of the few uses I have found for them in my classroom.

The third-grade basal reader, *Golden Secrets* (Scott Foresman, 1980), for example, has a story on inventions. The anonymous author states that the traffic light was invented by an anonymous policeman. Actually it was invented by the African-American scientist Garrett A. Morgan. I give my students a short piece on Morgan that is from a black history book (Adams, 1969) and we compare and question. Some of my classes decided to write to Scott Foresman and complain.

The problem with textbooks is also what they omit (Council on Interracial Books for Children, 1977a). The Silver Burdett Social Studies Series, *The World and Its People* (Helmus, Arnsdorff, Toppin, & Pounds, 1984), used in over two-thirds of the nation's school districts, has a 502-page reader on U.S. History. Only five paragraphs of this text mention unions and working-class struggle, only one labor leader, Samuel Gompers, is mentioned and most of the text is written in the passive voice. "Why?" I ask the students, as I provide interesting stories and we role-play the history of working-class struggle in our country. I connect this to local history, like the several-day general strike for the eight-hour day in 1886 which ended with the massacre of seven people including a 13-year-old boy. I have the students survey their parents and neighbors as to knowledge of this strike and other important events in our community's history and then we reflect on why people do not know such things. We recreate such history through readers' theater, role plays, simulations, dramas, and special projects.

Similarly, a Heath science text book (Barufaldi, Ladd, & Moses, 1981) has a short biography on an African-American scientist Charles Drew, who pioneered blood transfusions and plasma research. Omitted is the fact that Dr. Drew died after a car accident in the south when a southern hospital refused to treat him and give him a blood transfusion because of his skin color.

One example that I particularly like to use in my bilingual class is the story of Sequoyah and the Cherokees. Most history books mention Sequoyah's creation of the alphabet and the Trail of Tears, but few mention that the Cherokee nation had a bilingual weekly newspaper and a bilingual school system with over 200 of their own schools including a normal school—that is, until the early 1900s when the federal government stepped in and disbanded it.[5] I tell the children this story of the Cherokees and say, "Let's see what the history books and encyclopedias say." Usually there are gross omissions and we proceed to discuss why and what impact these omissions have on how we view the world. I ask, "Why didn't the government want the Cherokees to maintain their language?" This is a crucial question in my classroom since, by fifth grade, many of the students have already developed negative attitudes toward their native Spanish language.

There are many stories from the untold history of the oppressed that expose the social nature of knowledge and nurture civic courage and a sense of social justice. I find the history of Shea's Rebellion and the Seminole Wars particularly worthwhile because not only was there a struggle for a just cause but a key ingredient was unity among nationalities, a persistent problem in our nation's history.

Another important way to deal with the socially constructed nature of knowledge is to directly deal with racist and sexist stereotypes.[6] Around Thanksgiving time I show my students the filmstrip, *Unlearning "Indian" Stereotypes* (Council on Interracial Books for Children, 1977b). It is narrated by Native American children who visit a public library and become outraged at the various stereotypes of Indians in the books.

One year after viewing the filmstrip the students seemed particularly outraged at what they had learned. They came the next day talking about how their siblings in first grade had come home with construction paper headdresses with feathers. "That's a stereotype," the students proudly proclaimed. "What did you do about it?" I responded. "I ripped it up." "I slugged him," came the chorus of responses. As we continued the discussion, I asked why their brothers and sisters had the objects and interrogated them as to how children learn about such things. Finally they decided there were more productive things they could do. They first scoured the school library for books with stereotypes but since they found few, they decided to investigate their sibling's first grade room and look for stereotypes there. They wrote a letter to the teacher asking permission and then went in armed with clipboards, paper, and pens. Results were a picture of an Indian next to the letter "I" in the alphabet strip on the wall. They came back and decided they wanted to teach the first graders about stereotypes. I was skeptical but agreed and after much rehearsal they entered the first grade classroom to give their lesson—rather unsuccessfully I am afraid. But, they reflected on it and later Paco Resendez and Faviola Alvarez wrote in our school newspaper:

> We have been studying stereotypes on Native Americans. What is a stereotype? It's when somebody says something that's not true about another group of people. For example, it is a stereotype if you think all Indians wear feathers or say "HOW!" Or if you think that all girls are delicate. Why? Because some girls are strong.

Another way to show students that knowledge is socially constructed is to get different newspaper or magazine articles about the same subject, from different points of view. Subscribe to newspapers from another country, like *La Barricada*, or use excerpts from papers such as *The Nation, In These Times, Food and Justice*, or the *Guardian* to contrast the reporting from the established press. Or videotape a children's cartoon or tape record lyrics of a popular tune and then watch or play it, analyze it as a class, and draw out its values. I watch for outrageous stories or advertisements in the paper—these can be real thought provokers—or invite in guests who will shock the students out of their complacency. I also use posters, quotations, and maps.

I place a "poster of the week" on a special moveable bulletin board on my classroom wall. By using dramatic, historical, and/or controversial posters I encourage writing, discussion, and critique.[7] I also use a quotation of the week—in English, Spanish, or both. I begin the year providing the quotations myself, but as time passes children offer ones that they have found or created. Some quotations in particular, lend themselves to comparison, analysis and critique:

> When the missionaries first came to Africa they had bibles and we had the land. They said, "Let us pray." We closed our eyes. When we opened them we had the bibles and they had the land.
> (Bishop Desmond Tutu, Nobel Peace Prize Recipient)

Pointing out the biases in maps is also particularly thought provoking. The Mercator projection map, for example, places the equator two-thirds of the way down and depicts Europe as larger than South America although the area of the latter is approximately (6.9 million square miles) double that of Europe (3.8). The newly created Peters Projection may correct this. Another map challenges the conception that Argentina is on the bottom and North America is on top, by reversing the North and South Poles. Such media invokes considerable dialogue and thinking, including who makes maps, why they are the way they are, and how maps shape our thinking about the world.[8]

Teaching Social Responsibility

As students develop the interest and ability to discuss and reflect on their lives, communities, and the broader world, questions inevitably arise as to how people change the world. This concern and interest in social change can be encouraged by consciously fostering what Giroux (1985) calls "civic courage": stimulating "their passions, imaginations, and intellects so that they will be moved to challenge the social, political and economic forces that weigh so heavily upon their lives" (p. 201). In other words, students should be encourage to act *as if* they were living in a democracy.

One way this can be done is through class meetings and positive reinforcement of socially responsible actions in the classroom. In other words, the first way to build social responsibility is to try to democratize and humanize the educational setting. In my classroom, for example, there is a small quartz rock which is given to the student who has helped someone else. At the beginning of each day, the student who had been awarded for her or his social responsibility the day before chooses the next recipient.

The central theme in my classroom is that the quest for social justice is a neverending struggle in our nation and world; that the vast majority of people have benefited by this struggle; that we must understand this struggle; and that we must make decisions about whether to be involved in it. The academic content areas can be woven around this theme. In reading poetry and literature to children, social issues can be emphasized through books that specifically empower children (Peterson, 1987). Contemporary struggles can be highlighted through curricular materials and readings on Central America, apartheid, and on racism at home.[9] And pictures of real people who have worked for social justice can help children see these struggles as human. In my classroom there is a gallery of freedom fighters, the "luchadores por la justicia" or strugglers for justice that we have studied in social studies and current events. The large portraits—some commercially purchased and others drawn by the children—serve as reminders that women and men of all races have made important contributions to society and serve as keys to unlock our past discussions and studies about people and their struggles. A few years ago one of my students reflected on Cesar Chavez in this way:

> Cesar Chavez is a good man. He is very famous but he is poor. I thought that if people are famous they have to be rich. But this man is poor because he has a group of people and the money he earns he gives to them.

In most curricula, struggle is omitted and conflict forgotten. History is not of social movements or eras but rather the succession of rulers from the earliest Egyptian pharaohs to the most recent presidential administration. It has been fragmented, distorted, and rewritten. With our common history of struggle denied us, the past rewritten, the rulers of our society find the present much easier to manipulate. When Nixon said, "History will absolve our roles in Vietnam," he knew what he was talking about, for corporate textbook companies continue to write and rewrite our history—at least for the immediate future.

In contrast, Freire points to the positive role of struggle in history. He calls conflict the "midwife of real consciousness" and says it should be the focus of learning (Freire, 1970). The cynic might say that with all the conflict in our schools our students must be of very high consciousness. The key point here is to reflect on and critique conflict, in our daily lives, classrooms, and communities, as well as in history.[10]

Focusing on societal conflict—both historic and contemporary—is not only highly motivating and educational but also helps children, even the very young, to analyze and evaluate different points of view and express opinions as to what they think is just. The study of conflicts can be integrated into social studies units, for example, personal conflicts like Fredrick Douglass's struggle to learn to read; historic conflicts like the wars to take the land from American Indians, slave rebellions, worker strikes, bus boycotts, civil rights marches, antiwar movements; and contemporary conflicts like the United Farm Worker grape boycott, the war in El Salvador, apartheid, the antitoxin "Not in My Back Yard Movement." In my classroom, each conflict studied and any other historical event encountered in the normal course of our school day, is recorded on a 3 × 5 file card with a word description and the date. This card is hung on the class time line which circles three sides of the room. This process provides students with a visual representation of time, history, and sequence while fostering the understanding that everything is interrelated.

Historical conflict is best understood through engaging students in participatory activities. Often I will read or tell a story about a conflict and have children role-play parts of it either during or after the story. Occasionally such stories lead to small group or whole class drama presentations. I also use readers theater, that is, scripted plays written so that no acting needs to take place.[11] Sometimes I also encourage students to draw a conflict either together as a mural on large sheets of paper for display or separately for publication.

In addition, each student builds a people's textbook—a three-ring binder in which they put alternative materials. There are sections for geography, history, science, songs, poetry, and quotations. One year after *Rethinking Schools* printed an article on an important Milwaukee event of 1854 when 5,000 people stormed the county jail to free a runaway slave the students used the information to write their own bilingual book about the historic incident. By examining local history in which European Americans fought alongside African-Americans for the abolition of slavery, my students began to understand that social responsibility in a race-divided society means working together on issues that might not necessarily be deemed as in one's immediate self-interest.[12]

Freire takes liberating education even one step further—to action or praxis. He believes learners should use their newfound analysis to transform the world. In the school setting transforming-type activities depend on the nature of the group of students, the community, and the school system, and the courage and seniority of the teacher. My students have gone with me to marches that protested police brutality, demanded that King's birthday be made a national holiday, asked that Congress not fund the Contras, and requested nuclear disarmament. Two of my students testified before the City Council, asking that a Jobs with Peace referendum be placed on the ballot. In another instance, the students went to observe the court proceedings in the case of a police killing of an African-American man. Obviously teachers need to be involved in the community in order to know what's happening and what possibilities exist for involvement of children.

Projects that are less overtly political can also stimulate critical thinking: Joining Amnesty International as a class and adopting a political prisoner, adopting a section of beach on a lake or river and keeping it clean, interviewing people involved in a local strike or community struggle, raising money for earthquake or famine relief, writing letters to governmental representatives, having such representatives or social activists visit the class-room, or corresponding with children in other parts of the USA, Puerto Rico, the USSR, El Salvador and Mozambique.[13] Discussion, writing, and critical reflection on these activities, however, are crucial so these are not to be just "interesting" field trips or projects.

One year we studied the underground railroad as part of the fifth grade U.S. history curriculum. We also studied the second underground railroad, the sanctuary movement. I invited a speaker to my class who had lived in El Salvador for several years. He showed slides of the people. My children at first laughed at the distended bellies of the starving Salvadoran children, but their chuckles turned to horror and then anger as they began to understand that U.S. bombs are being dropped on these children. The class meeting after the presentation was quite informative. The kids asked "Why?" Why was the U.S. govern-ment doing this? Why did Reagan do it?" We asked them "Why do you think?" "Because Reagan supports the rich," said one. "Yeah," agreed the others. But others were still not satisfied. "Why? Why does he support the rich?" Finally the speaker responded. "Because it is the job of the president in this country to support the rich." Paco's hand shot up. "If that's the case," he argued, "what about Kennedy?" The bell rang before the speaker could answer. As I drove him home he said the discussion was better than many he had had on university campuses.

In a group meeting the following day the children decided to write letters to our representatives and the President on the issue. The next day one boy, Michael, came in and said, "Mr. Peterson, we have to send weapons down to Central America or else the Russians will take over and no one will believe in God anymore." I said, "Michael, you've been talking to your mom . . . Great. Keep it up. We'll talk about that later." But that day we didn't get to it and as he left I gave him some *Food First* leaflets about hunger in Central America being the real enemy and asked him to read them with his mom. The following day he did not show up for school—I was a bit concerned. The day after he was back and we talked in detail about the various perspectives on Nicaragua, El Salvador, the USSR and the United States of America. The children decided that even if the Sandinistas received money and weapons from aliens from Saturn they had that right because all they wanted to do was run their own country.

A week later at a group meeting, Emma announced that we had to discuss the letters we wrote to the President. "They won't do any good," she lamented, "I bet he just tore them up." She then proposed we go on a field trip to Washington DC to meet the President in person and that I, the teacher, finance it. I politely declined. At that point there was what Freire (Shor & Freire 1987) would call an inductive moment—when the students are stalled and need direction—I said that sometimes people protested in Washington DC but often people protested right here in Milwaukee, as the Pledge of Resistance was doing regularly. The kids immediately said they wanted to go, and before I knew it I was sending home letters to the parents explaining that although it was not part of the official curric-ulum, if they consented, I would supervise a public bus trip after school up to the Federal

Building to protest U.S. aid to the contras. I bought tag board and markers from the local bookstore careful not to use the school's supplies. Half the class—12 children—brought back signed notes. The next Monday the students stayed after school and made their signs. At first they asked me what they should say, but I responded that if they were going on a protest march they had better know what they were protesting. They could make the signs themselves. They did. Their signs included:

> Let them run their land!
> Support the Poor! Not the "freedom fighters." They're the Rich.
> Help Central America Don't Kill Them
> Give the Nicaraguans their Freedom
> Let Nicaragua Live!
> Give Nicaragua Some Food Instead of Weapons
> We want Freedom and Peace
> Stop spending money to make bombs.

When they were finished making their signs we walked two blocks to the public bus stop and during a steady drizzle headed downtown to the Federal Building. They were the only Hispanics at the march of 150 people and were welcomed with open arms. We walked, marched, chanted, and finally went home wet and exhausted.

The next day we had a panel discussion and the kids talked and listened like they were on top of the world. Paula Martinez wrote about it later in our magazine, *Kid Power*:

> On a rainy Tuesday in April some of the students from our class went to protest against the contras. The people in Central America are poor and being bombed on their heads. When we went protesting it was raining and it seemed like the contras were bombing us. A week before we had visitor, Jim Harney. He had been to El Salvador. He talked to our class about what was going on in El Salvador. He said it was terrible. A lot of people are dying. He showed us slides of El Salvador and told us its bad to be there. He hoped that our government will give them food and money and not bombs.

Michael, the boy who had come back from home concerned about the Russians and God did not go to the march. He said he had to babysit his little brother. Parent conferences were a week later and I was a bit apprehensive to see his mother—a socially mobile Puerto Rican studying to become a nurse. She walked into the room, sat down and said, "Mr Peterson, I want to thank you. Michael has become interested in everything. He watches the news, he talks to me about what's going on, he knows more about things than me sometime. I don't know what you did. But thanks." As our conversation progressed it was clear her conservative political views on Central America had not changed, but our differences were secondary, because what was central to both of us was that her son had started to read the world.

Notes

1. Publications which accept children's writings include: *Children's Album*, PO Box 6086, Concord, CA 94524 ($10/year); *Rethinking Schools*, 1001 E. Keefe Ave., Milwaukee, WI 53212 ($10/year); *Stone Soup*, PO Box 83, Santa Cruz, CA 95063 ($17.50/year); *Reflections*, Box 368, Ducan Falls, OH 43734 ($3/year); *The McGuffy Writer*, 400A McGuffey Hall, Miami University, Oxford, OH 45056 ($3/year); *Chart Your Course*, PO Box 6448, Mobile, AL, 36660 ($20/year); *Creative Kids*, PO Box 637, 100 Pine Ave., Holmes, PA 19043 ($10/year.); *A Young Author's Guide*

to Publishing lists submission guidelines for children's magazines; send $2.50 to Dr. Nicholas Spennato, Delaware County Reading Council, 6th and Olive St., Media, PA 19063.

2. One excellent anthology is called *Embers: Stories for a Changing World* edited by Meyers, Banfield, and Colon J. (1983) distributed by the Council on Interracial Books for Children, 1841 Broadway, New York, NY, 10023. For a bibliography of children's books that have young people as protagonists who are working for social justice see Peterson (1987). Books to empower young people. *Rethinking Schools*, Vol. 1, No. 3, pp. 9–10, available from *Rethinking Schools*, 1001 E., Keefe Ave., Milwaukee, WI 53212.

3. Marie Winn (1987) offers some innovative ideas to both parents and teachers to help children kick the television habit, including plans for classroom and school wide television turnoff campaigns.

4. This generalization ignores the class, race, and gender factors which profoundly affect school structure and student self-esteem. For example, Wodtke (1986) found discrepancies between instructional approaches received by suburban kindergarten and those in poor, working-class settings. The suburban kindergartens tended to encourage children to participate in show-and-tell and speak in front of the class, while the predominantly poor and working-class kindergartens rarely utilized such activities, instead relying more heavily on worksheets and drill because of the pressures to cover standardized curriculum and the emphasis put on direct instruction. This differentiated approach tends to inculcate certain habits and outlooks in children based on class and race factors.

5. In 1838, the United States government forced the Cherokee people and other southeastern tribes to abandon their land in Georgia and move to Oklahoma. The Indians suffered such hardships along the way that the path they followed became known as the Trail of Tears. For more information on the bilingual education system established by the Cherokees see Payne (1984) and Weinberg (1977).

6. The recognition of the importance of dealing with racism among children leads some educators (ALTARE, 1984) to argue that multicultural education is limited if not accompanied by an anti-racist component.

7. High-quality, politically progressive posters can be found through a number of outlets. Particularly good sources are the Syracuse Cultural Worker, Box 6367, Syracuse, NY 13217 and Northern Sun Merchandising, 2916 E. Lake St., Minneapolis, MN 55406. A source for excellent posters of Native American leaders is the Perfection Form Company, Logan, Iowa and for women posters contact: TABS, 438 Fourth St., Brooklyn, NY 11215 (718) 788–3478.

8. The Peters Projection Map can be ordered from Friendship Press, PO Box 37844, Cincinnati, Ohio 45237. The Turnabout map is distributed by Laguna Sales, Inc., 7040 Via Valverde, San Jose, CA 95135.

9. I collect and weave into our class curricula parts of progressive curricula such as *Winning "Justice for All"* (Racism & Sexism Resource Center, 1981), *Open Minds to Equality* (Schniedewind & Davidson, 1983) *Food First Curriculum* (Rubin, 1984), *Cooperative Learning, Cooperative Lives* (Schniedewind, 1987), and a variety of curriculum on contemporary issues such as Central America (contact Network of Educators' Committees on Central America, PO Box 43509, Washington DC 20010–9509. 202–667–2618); apartheid (Bigelow, 1985); U.S. labor struggles (Bigelow & Diamond, 1988); women (contact National Women's History Project, PO Box 316 Santa Rosa CA 95402 (707)526–5974; peace (contact the Wilmington College Peace Resource Center, Pyle Center Box 1183, Willmington, OH 45177; and racism (see the "Unlearning Stereotypes" filmstrips and guides from the CIBC, 1977b, 1982a, 1982b).

10. Simulating classroom and interpersonal conflict through trigger cartoons, scripted dialogues, and role plays helps students to develop the skills and responsibility to analyze and resolve their own interpersonal problems. In classroom conflict, such reflection helps children understand the purposes behind the "misbehavior" and allows them to develop strategies and skills to diffuse and mediate such conflict. For a theoretical and practical approach to helping children understand the reasons for misbehavior see Dreikurs, Grunwald, and Pepper (1982) and for additional ways to mediate conflict see Prutzman et al. (1988), Schniedewind (1987), and the curriculum produced by teachers and administrators in NYC Community School District 15 in collaboration with the New York Chapter of Educators for Social Responsibility (New York City Board of Education, 1988).

11. Dozens of high-quality reader theaters which deal with a host of conflicts in the history of labor, women, and racial minorities are available from Stevens and Shea, Dept. S, PO Box 794, Stockton, CA 95201.

12. The pamphlet *Joshua Glover: The freeing of a runaway slave in Milwaukee—La liberación de un esclavo fugitivo en Milwaukee* is available from Communicate! Rural Route 2, Pulaski, WI 54162.

13. One such telecommunications linkup is De Orilla a Orilla (from Shore to Shore) which can be contacted by writing to Dennis Sayers, De Orilla a Orilla, N.E. MRC, University of Massachusetts, 250 Stuart St., Rm 1105, Boston, MA 02116. Additional information about communication linkups can be obtained from the book, *School Links International: A New Approach to Primary School Linking Around the World*, by Rex Deddis and Cherry Mares (1988), published by the Avon County Council, Tidy Britain Group Schools Research Project.

References

Adams, R. (1969). *Great Negroes: Past and present.* Chicago: Afro-Am Publishing Co.

All London Teachers Against Racism and Fascism (ALTARF). (1984). *Challenging racism.* Nottingham, UK: Russell Press. Available from ALTARF, Room 216, Panther House, 38 Mount Pleasant, London WCIX OAP.

Ashton-Warner, S. (1965). *Teacher.* New York: Simon and Schuster.

Barufaldi, J., Ladd, G., & Moses, A. (1981). *Heath Science.* Lexington, MA: D.C. Heath.

Bigelow, W. (1985). *Strangers in their own land: A curriculum guide to South Africa.* New York: Africa World Press.

Bigelow, W. (1989, October/November). Discovering Columbus: Re-reading the past. *Rethinking Schools*, 4(1), 1, 12–13.

Bigelow, W., & Diamond, N. (1988). *The power in our hands: A curriculum on the history of work and workers in the United States.* New York: Monthly Review Press.

Brecht, B. (1978). *The mother.* New York: Grove Press.

Calkins, L. (1983). *Lessons from a child.* Portsmouth, NH: Heinemann.

Calkins, L. (1986). *The art of teaching writing.* Portsmouth, NH: Heinemann.

Canfield, J., & Wells, H. (1976). *100 ways to enhance self-concept in the classroom: A handbook for teachers and parents.* Englewood Cliffs, NJ: Prentice-Hall.

Coalition of Essential Schools. (1984). *Prospectus: 1984–1994.* Providence, RI: Brown University.

Commission on Reading by the National Council of Teachers of English. (1988). *Report card on basal readers.* Katonah, NY: Richard C. Owen.

Council on Interracial Books for Children (CIBC). (1977a). *Stereotypes, distortions and omissions in U.S. history textbooks.* New York: Racism and Sexism Resource Center for Educators.

Council on Interracial Books for Children. (1977b). *Unlearning "Indian" stereotypes.* New York: Racism and Sexism Resource Center for Educators.

Council on Interracial Books for Children. (1982a). *Unlearning Chicano and Puerto Rican stereotypes.* New York: Racism and Sexism Resource Center for Educators.

Council on Interracial Books for Children. (1982b). *Unlearning Asian American stereotypes.* New York: Racism and Sexism Resource Center for Educators.

Dewey, J. (1916). *Democracy and education.* New York: MacMillan.

Dreikurs, R. Grunwald, B., & Pepper, F. (1982). *Maintaining sanity in the classroom.* New York: Harper & Row.

Ellwood, C. (1989). Making connections: Challenges we face, *Rethinking Schools*, 3(3), 1, 12–13.

Fairtest (National Center for Fair and Open Testing). (1988). *Fallout from the testing explosion: How 100 million standardized exams undermine equity and excellence in American's public schools.* Available from P.O. Box 1272, Harvard Square Station, Cambridge MA 02238.

Freire, P. (1970). *Pedagogy of the oppressed.* New York: Seabury.

Freire, P. (1985). *The politics of education.* South Hadley, MA: Bergin & Garvey.

Gibboney, R. A. (1988). Madeline Hunter's teaching machine. *Rethinking Schools*, 2(3), 10–11.

Giroux, H. (1985). *Theory and resistance in education.* South Hadley, MA: Bergin and Garvey.

Glasser, W. (1969). *Schools without failure.* New York: Harper & Row.

Glasser, W. (1986). *Control theory in the classroom.* New York: Harper & Row.

Goodlad, J. (1984). *A place called school: Prospects for the future.* New York: McGraw-Hill.

Goodman, K. (1986). *What's whole in whole language?* Richmond Hill, Ontario; Canada Scholastic TAB. (Distributed in the United States by Heinemann.)

Goodman, K., Smith, E. B., Meredith, R., & Goodman, Y. (1987). *Language and thinking in school: A whole language curriculum.* New York: Richard C. Owen.

Graves, D. H. (1983). *Writing: Teachers and children at work.* Portsmouth, NH: Heinemann.

Helmus, T., Arnsdorf, V., Toppin, E., & Pounds, N. (1984). *The United States and its neighbors.* Atlanta: Silver Burdett Co.

Krashen, S., & Terrell, T. (1983). *The natural approach: Language acquisition in the classroom.* Hayward, CA: Alemany Press.

Levine, D. (1988). Outcome based education: Grand design or blueprint for failure? *Rethinking Schools*, 2(2), 1, 12–13.

Liebert, R., & Sprafkin, J. (1988). *The early window: Effects of television on children and youth.* New York: Pergamon Press.

Meyers, R., Banfield, B., & Colon, J. (Eds.). (1983). *Embers: Stories for a changing world.* Old Westbury, NY: The Feminist Press.

New York City Board of Education. (1988). *Resolving conflict creatively: A draft teaching guide for grades Kindergarten through six.* New York: Board of Education.

Payne, C. (1984). Multicultural education and racism in American schools. *Theory into Practice*, 33 (2), 124–131.

Peterson, R. (1987). Books to empower young people. *Rethinking Schools*, 1(3), 9–10.

Prutzman, P., Stern, L., Burger, M. L., & Bodenhamer, G. (1988). *The friendly classroom for a small planet: A handbook on creative approaches to living and problem solving for children.* Philadelphia, PA: New Society Publishers.

Racism & Sexism Resource Center. (1981). *Winning justice for all: A supplementary curriculum unit on sexism and racism, stereotyping and discrimination*. New York: Council on Interracial Books for Children.

Rubin, L. (1984). *Food first curriculum*. San Francisco: Food First.

Schmuck P. A., & Schmuck, R. A. (1983). *Group process in the classroom*. Dubuque, IA: Wm. C. Brown Company.

Schniedewind, N. (1987). *Cooperative learning, cooperative lives: A sourcebook of learning activities for building a peaceful world*. Somerville, MA: Circle Press.

Schniedewind, N., & Davidson, E. (1983). *Open minds to equality: A sourcebook of learning activities to promote race, sex, class, and age equity*. Englewood Cliffs, NJ: Prentice-Hall.

Scott, Foresman & Co. (1981). *Scott Foresman reading*. New York.

Searle, C. (1977). *The world in a classroom*. London: Writers and Readers Publishing Cooperative.

Shor, I. (1980). *Critical teaching and everyday life*. Boston: South End Press.

Shor, I. (1987). *Freire for the classroom: A sourcebook for liberatory teaching*. Portsmouth, NH: Heinemann.

Shor, I., & Freire, P. (1987). *A pedagogy for liberation: Dialogues on transforming education*. South Hadley, MA: Bergin and Garvey.

Smith, F. (1985). *Reading without nonsense*. New York: Teachers College Press.

United Farm Workers. (1987). *The wrath of grapes* (video). Keene, CA: The United Farm Workers.

Wallerstein, N., & Bernstein, E. (1988). Empowerment education: Freire's ideas adapted to health education. *Health Education Quarterly*, 15 (4), 379–394.

Weinberg, M. (1977). *A chance to learn: The history of race and education in the United States*. New York: Cambridge University Press.

Wigginton, E. (1989). Foxfire grows up. *Harvard Educational Review*, 59 (1), 24–49.

Winn, M. (1987). *Unplugging the plug-in drug*. New York: Penguin.

Wodtke, K. (1986). Inequality at Age Five? *Rethinking Schools*, 1 (1), 7.

16

Language Diversity and Learning

Lisa Delpit

A brand-new black teacher is delivering her first reading lesson to a group of first-grade students in inner-city Philadelphia. She has almost memorized the entire basal-provided lesson dialogue while practicing in front of a mirror the night before.

"Good morning, boys and girls. Today we're going to read a story about where we live, in the city."

A small brown hand rises.

"Yes, Marti."

Marti and this teacher are special friends, for she was a kindergartner in the classroom where her new teacher taught.

"Teacher, how come you talkin' like a white person? You talkin' just like my momma talk when she get on the phone!"

I was that first-year teacher many years ago, and Marti was among the first to teach me the role of language diversity in the classroom. Marti let me know that children, even young children, are often aware of the different codes we all use in our everyday lives. They may not yet have learned how to produce those codes or what social purposes they serve, but children often have a remarkable ability to discern and identify different codes in different settings. It is this sensitivity to language and its appropriate use upon which we must build to ensure the success of children from diverse backgrounds.

One aspect of language diversity in the classroom—*form* (the code of a language, its phonology, grammar, inflections, sentence structure, and written symbols)—has usually received the most attention from educators, as manifested in their concern about the "nonstandardness" of the code their students speak. While form is important, particularly in the context of social success, it is considerably less important when concern is lodged instead in the area of cognitive development. This area is related to that aspect of language diversity reflected in Marti's statement—language *use*—the socially and cognitively based linguistic determinations speakers make about style, register, vocabulary, and so forth, when they attempt to interact with or achieve particular goals within their environments. It is the purpose of this paper to address a broad conception of language diversity as it affects the learning environments of linguistically diverse students; it focuses on the development of the range of linguistic alternatives that students have at their disposal for use in varying settings.

Acquiring One Language Variety and Learning Another

The acquisition and development of one's native language is a wondrous process, drawing upon all of the cognitive and affective capacities that make us human. By contrast, the successful acquisition of a second form of a language is essentially a rote-learning process brought to automaticity. It is, however, a process in which success is heavily influenced by highly charged affective factors. Because of the frequency with which schools focus unsuccessfully on changing language form, a careful discussion of the topic and its attendant affective aspects is in order.

The Affective Filter in Language Learning

Learning to orally produce an alternate form is not principally a function of cognitive analysis, thereby not ideally learned from protracted rule-based instruction and correction. Rather, it comes with exposure, comfort level, motivation, familiarity, and practice in real communicative contexts. Those who have enjoyed a pleasant interlude in an area where another dialect of English is spoken may have noticed a change in their own speech. Almost unconsciously, their speech has approached that of those native to the area. The evidence suggests that had these learners been corrected or drilled in the rules of the new dialect, they probably would not have acquired it as readily.

Stephen Krashen, in his work on second-language acquisition, distinguishes the processes of conscious *learning* (rule-based instruction leading to the monitoring of verbal output) from unconscious *acquisition* ("picking up" a language through internalizing the linguistic input-derived immersion in a new context—what happens, say, when the North American enjoys a visit to the Caribbean).[1] Krashen found unconscious acquisition to be much more effective. In further studies, however, he found that in some cases people did not easily "acquire" the new language. This finding led him to postulate the existence of what he called the "affective filter." The filter operates "when affective conditions are not optimal, when the student is not motivated, does not identify with the speakers of the second language, or is overanxious about his performance, . . . [causing] a mental block . . . [which] will prevent the input from reaching those parts of the brain responsible for language acquisition."[2] Although the process of learning a new dialect cannot be completely equated with learning a new language, some processes seem to be similar. In this case, it seems that the less stress attached to the process, the more easily it is accomplished.

The so-called affective filter is likely to be raised when the learner is exposed to constant correction. Such correction increases cognitive monitoring of speech, thereby making talking difficult. To illustrate with an experiment anyone can try, I have frequently taught a relatively simple new "dialect" in my work with preservice teachers. In this dialect, the phonetic element "iz" is added after the first consonant or consonant cluster in each syllable of a word. (*Teacher* becomes tiz-ea-chiz-er and *apple*, ap-piz-le-iz.) After a bit of drill and practice, the students are asked to tell a partner why they decided to become teachers. Most only haltingly attempt a few words before lapsing into either silence or into "Standard English," usually to complain about my circling the room to insist that all words they utter be in the new dialect. During a follow-up discussion, all students invariably speak of the impossibility of attempting to apply rules while trying to formulate and express a thought. Forcing speakers to monitor their language for rules while speaking, typically produces silence.

Correction may also affect students' attitudes toward their teachers. In a recent research project, middle-school, inner-city students were interviewed about their attitudes toward their teachers and school. One young woman complained bitterly, "Mrs. ——— always be interrupting to make you 'talk correct' and stuff. She be butting into your conversations when you not even talking to her! She need to mind her own business."

In another example from a Mississippi preschool, a teacher had been drilling her three- and four-year-old charges on responding to the greeting, "Good morning, how are you?" with "I'm fine, thank you." Posting herself near the door one morning, she greeted a four-year-old black boy in an interchange that went something like this:

Teacher: Good morning, Tony, how are you?
Tony: I be's fine.
Teacher: Tony, I said, How *are* you?
Tony: (with raised voice) I be's *fine.*
Teacher: No, Tony, I said *how are you?*
Tony: (angrily) I done told you *I be's fine* and I ain't telling you no more!

Tony must have questioned his teacher's intelligence, if not sanity. In any event, neither of the students discussed above would be predisposed, as Krashen says, to identify with their teachers and thereby increase the possibility of unconsciously acquiring the latter's language form.

Ethnic Identity and Language Performance

Issues of group identity may also affect students' oral production of a different dialect. Nelson-Barber, in a study of phonologic aspects of Pima Indian language found that, in grades 1-3, the children's English most approximated the standard dialect of their teachers.[3] But surprisingly, by fourth grade, when one might assume growing competence in standard forms, their language moved significantly toward the local dialect. These fourth graders had the *competence* to express themselves in a more standard form, but chose, consciously or unconsciously, to use the language of those in their local environments. The researcher believes that, by ages 8–9, these children became aware of their group membership and its importance to their well-being, and this realization was reflected in their language. They may also have become increasingly aware of the school's negative attitude toward their community and found it necessary—through choice of linguistic form—to decide with which camp to identify.

A similar example of linguistic *performance* (what one does with language) belying linguistic *competence* (what one is capable of doing) comes from researcher Gerald Mohatt (personal communication), who was at the time teaching on a Sioux reservation. It was considered axiomatic among the reservation staff that the reason these students failed to become competent readers was that they spoke a nonstandard dialect. One day Mohatt happened to look, unnoticed, into a classroom where a group of boys had congregated. Much to his surprise and amusement, the youngsters were staging a perfect rendition of his own teaching, complete with stance, walk, gestures, *and* Standard English (including Midwestern accent). Clearly, the school's failure to teach these children to read was based on factors other than their inability to speak and understand Standard English. They could do both; they did not often choose to do so in a classroom setting, however, possibly because they chose to identify with their community rather than with the school.

Appreciating Linguistic Diversity in the Classroom

What should teachers do about helping students acquire an additional oral form? First, they should recognize that the linguistic form a student brings to school is intimately connected with loved ones, community, and personal identity. To suggest that this form is "wrong" or, even worse, ignorant, is to suggest that something is wrong with the student and his or her family. On the other hand, it is equally important to understand that students who do not have access to the politically popular dialect form in this country, that is, Standard English, are less likely to succeed economically than their peers who do. How can both realities be embraced?

Teachers need to support the language that students bring to school, provide them input from an additional code, and give them the opportunity to use the new code in a non-threatening, real communicative context. Some teachers accomplish this goal by having groups of students create bidialectal dictionaries of their own language form and Standard English. Others have had students become involved with standard forms through various kinds of role-play. For example, memorizing parts for drama productions will allow students to "get the feel" of speaking Standard English while not under the threat of correction. Young students can create puppet shows or role-play cartoon characters. (Many "superheroes" speak almost hypercorrect Standard English!) Playing a role eliminates the possibility of implying that the *child's* language is inadequate, and suggests, instead, that different language forms are appropriate in different contexts. Some other teachers in New York City have had their students produce a news show every day for the rest of the school. The students take on the persona of some famous newscaster, keeping in character as they develop and read their news reports. Discussions ensue about whether Walter Cronkite would have said it that way, again taking the focus off the child's speech.

Activities for Promoting Linguistic Pluralism

It is possible and desirable to make the actual study of language diversity a part of the curriculum for all students. For younger children, discussions about the differences in the ways television characters from different cultural groups speak can provide a starting point. A collection of the many children's books written in the dialects of various cultural groups can also provide a wonderful basis for learning about linguistic diversity, as can audiotaped stories narrated by individuals from different cultures.[4] Mrs. Pat, a teacher chronicled by Shirley Brice Heath, had her students become language "detectives," interviewing a variety of individuals and listening to the radio and television to discover the differences and similarities in the ways people talked.[5] Children can learn that there are many ways of saying the same thing, and that certain contexts suggest particular kinds of linguistic performances.

Inevitably, each speaker will make his or her own decision about the appropriate form to use in any context. Neither teachers nor anyone else will be able to force a choice upon an individual. All we can do is provide students with the exposure to an alternate form, and allow them the opportunity to practice that form *in contexts that are nonthreatening, have a real purpose, and are intrinsically enjoyable.* If they have access to alternative forms, it will be their decision later in life to choose which to use. We can only provide them with the knowledge base and hope they will make appropriate choices.

Ethnic Identity and Styles of Discourse

Thus far, we have primarily discussed differences in grammar and syntax. There are other differences in oral language of which teachers should be aware in a multicultural context, particularly in discourse style and language use. Michaels and other researchers identified differences in children's narratives at "sharing time."[6] They found that there was a tendency among young white children to tell "topic-centered" narratives—stories focused on one event—and a tendency among black youngsters, especially girls, to tell "episodic" narratives—stories that include shifting scenes and are typically longer. While these differences are interesting in themselves, what is of greater significance is adults' responses to the differences. Cazden reports on a subsequent project in which a white adult was taped reading the oral narratives of black and white first graders, with all syntax dialectal markers removed.[7] Adults were asked to listen to the stories and comment about the children's likelihood of success in school. The researchers were surprised by the differential responses given by black and white adults.

In responding to the retelling of a black child's story, the white adults were uniformly negative, making such comments as "terrible story, incoherent" and "[n]ot a story at all in the sense of describing something that happened." Asked to judge this child's academic competence, all of the white adults rated her below the children who told "topic-centered" stories. Most of these adults also predicted difficulties for this child's future school career, such as, "This child might have trouble reading," that she exhibited "language problems that affect school achievement," and that "family problems" or "emotional problems" might hamper her academic progress.[8]

The black adults had very different reactions. They found this child's story "well formed, easy to understand, and interesting, with lots of detail and description." Even though all five of these adults mentioned the "shifts" and "associations" or "nonlinear" quality of the story, they did not find these features distracting. Three of the black adults selected the story as the best of the five they had heard, and all but one judged the child as exceptionally bright, highly verbal, and successful in school.[9]

When differences in narrative style produce differences in interpretation of competence, the pedagogical implications are evident. If children who produce stories based in differing discourse styles are expected to have trouble reading, and viewed as having language, family, or emotional problems, as was the case with the informants quoted by Cazden, they are unlikely to be viewed as ready for the same challenging instruction awarded students whose language patterns more closely parallel the teacher's. It is important to emphasize that those teachers in the Cazden study who were of the same cultural group as the students recognized the differences in style, but did not assign a negative valence to those differences. Thus, if teachers hope to avoid negatively stereotyping the language patterns of their students, it is important that they be encouraged to interact with, and willingly learn from, knowledgeable members of their students' cultural groups. This can perhaps best become a reality if teacher education programs include diverse parents, community members, and faculty among those who prepare future teachers, and take seriously the need to develop in those teachers the humility required for learning from the surrounding context when entering a culturally different setting.

Questioning Styles

Heath has identified another aspect of diversity in language use which affects classroom instruction and learning.[10] She found that questions were used differently in a southeastern town by young black students and their teachers. The students were unaccustomed to responding to the "known-answer" test questions of the classroom. (The classic example of such questions is the contrast between the real-life questioning routine: "What time is it?" "Two o'clock." "Thanks." and the school questioning routine: "What time is it?" "Two o'clock." "*Right!*"[11]) These students would lapse into silence or contribute very little information when teachers asked direct factual questions which called for feedback of what had just been taught. She found that when the types of questions asked of the children were more in line with the kinds of questions posed to them in their home settings—questions probing the students' own analyses and evaluations—these children responded very differently. They "talked, actively and aggressively became involved in the lesson, and offered useful information about their past experiences."[12] The author concludes not only that these kinds of questions are appropriate for all children rather than just for the "high groups" with which they have typically been used, but that awareness and use of the kinds of language used in children's communities can foster the kind of language and performance and growth sought by the school and teachers.

Oral Styles in Community Life

It would be remiss to end this section without remarking upon the need to draw upon the considerable language strengths of linguistically diverse populations. Smitherman and many others have made note of the value placed upon oral expression in most African-American communities.[13] The "man (person) of words," be he or she preacher, poet, philosopher, huckster, or rap song creator, receives the highest form of respect in the black community. The verbal adroitness, the cogent and quick wit, the brilliant use of metaphorical language, the facility in rhythm and rhyme, evident in the language of preacher Martin Luther King, Jr., boxer Muhammad Ali, comedienne Whoopi Goldberg, rapper L. L. Cool J., singer and songwriter Billie Holiday, and many inner-city black students, may all be drawn upon to facilitate school learning.

Other children, as well, come to school with a wealth of specialized linguistic knowledge. Native American children, for example, come from communities with very sophisticated knowledge about storytelling, and a special way of saying a great deal with a few words. Classroom learning should be structured so that not only are these children able to acquire the verbal patterns they lack, but they are also able to strengthen their proficiencies, and to share these with classmates and teachers. We will then all be enriched.

The Demands of School Language—Orality and Literacy

There is little evidence that speaking another dialectal form per se, negatively affects one's ability to learn to read.[14] For commonsensical proof, one need only reflect on nonstandard-dialect-speaking slaves who not only taught themselves to read, but did so under threat of severe punishment or death. But children who speak nonmainstream varieties of English do have a more difficult time becoming proficient readers. Why?

One explanation is that, where teachers' assessments of competence are influenced by the dialect children speak, teachers may develop low expectations for certain students and subsequently teach them less.[15] A second explanation, which lends itself more readily to observation, rests in teachers' confusing the teaching of reading with the teaching of a new dialect form.

Cunningham found that teachers across the United States were more likely to correct reading miscues that were dialect related ("Here go a table" for "Here is a table") than those that were nondialect related ("Here is the dog" for "There is the dog").[16] Seventy-eight percent of the dialect miscues were corrected, compared with only 27 percent of the nondialect miscues. He concludes that the teachers were acting out of ignorance, not realizing that "here go" and "here is" represent the same meaning in some black children's language.

In my observations of many classrooms, however, I have come to conclude that even when teachers recognize the similarity of meaning, they are likely to correct dialect-related miscues. Consider a typical example:

Text: Yesterday I washed my brother's clothes.
Student's rendition: Yesterday I wash my bruvver close.

The subsequent exchange between student and teacher sounds something like this:

T: Wait, let's go back. What's that word again? [Points at *washed.*]
S: Wash.
T: No. Look at it again. What letters do you see at the end? You see "e-d." Do you remember what we say when we see those letters on the end of a word?
S: "ed"
T: OK, but in this case we say wash*ed.* Can you say that?
S: Wash*ed.*
T: Good. Now read it again.
S: Yesterday I wash*ed* my bruvver . . .
T: Wait a minute, what's that word again? [Points to *brother.*]
S: Bruvver.
T: No. Look at these letters in the middle. [Points to *th.*] Remember to read what you see. Do you remember how we say that sound? Put your tongue between your teeth and say /*th*/ . . .

The lesson continues in such a fashion, the teacher proceeding to correct the student's dialect-influenced pronunciations and grammar while ignoring the fact that the student had to have comprehended the sentence in order to translate it into her own dialect. Such instruction occurs daily and blocks reading development in a number of ways. First, because children become better readers by having the opportunity to read, the overcorrection exhibited in this lesson means that this child will be less likely to become a fluent reader than other children who are not interrupted so consistently. Second, a complete focus on code and pronunciation blocks children's understanding that reading is essentially a meaning-making process. This child, who understands the text, is led to believe that she is doing something wrong. She is encouraged to think of reading not as something you do to get a message, but something you pronounce. Third, constant corrections by the teacher are likely to cause this student and others like her to resist reading and to resent the teacher.

Robert Berden reports that, after observing the kind of teaching routine described above in a number of settings, he incorporated the teacher behaviors into a reading instruction exercise that he used with students in a college class.[17] He put together sundry rules from a number of American social and regional dialects to create what he called the "language of Atlantis." Students were then called upon to read aloud in this dialect they did not know. When they made errors he interrupted them, using some of the same statements/comments he had heard elementary school teachers routinely make to their students. He concludes:

> The results were rather shocking. By the time these Ph.D. candidates in English or linguistics had read 10–20 words, I could make them sound totally illiterate. By using the routines that teachers use of dialectally different students, I could produce all of the behaviors we observe in children who do not learn to read successfully. The first thing that goes is sentence intonation: they sound like they are reading a list from the telephone book. Comment on their pronunciation a bit more, and they begin to subvocalize, rehearsing pronunciations for themselves before they dare to say them out loud. They begin to guess at pronunciations . . . They switch letters around for no reason. They stumble; they repeat. In short, when I attack them for their failure to conform to my demands for Atlantis English pronunciations, they sound very much like the worst of the second graders in any of the classrooms I have observed.
>
> They also begin to fidget. They wad up their papers, bite their fingernails, whisper, and some finally refuse to continue. They do all the things that children do while they are busily failing to learn to read. Emotional trauma can result as well. For instance, once while conducting this little experiment, in a matter of seconds I actually had one of my graduate students in tears.[18]

The moral of this story is not to confuse dialect intervention with reading instruction. To do so will only confuse the child, leading her away from those intuitive understandings about language that will promote reading development, and toward a school career of resistance and a lifetime of avoiding reading. For those who believe that the child has to "say it right in order to spell it right," let me add that English is not a phonetically regular language. There is no particular difference between telling a child, "You may *say* /bruvver/, but it's spelled b-r-o-*t*-*h*-e-r," and "You say /com/, but it's spelled c-o-m-*b*."

For this and other reasons, writing may be an arena in which to address standard forms. Unlike unplanned oral language or public reading, writing lends itself to editing. While conversational talk is spontaneous and must be responsive to an immediate context, writing is a mediated process which may be written and rewritten any number of times before being introduced to public scrutiny. Consequently, writing is amenable to rule application—one may first write freely to get one's thoughts down, and then edit to hone the message and apply specific spelling, syntactical, or punctuation rules. My college students who had such difficulty talking in the "iz" dialect, found writing it, with the rules displayed before them, a relatively easy task.

Styles of Literacy

There are other culturally based differences in language use in writing as well. In a seminal article arguing for the existence of "contrastive rhetoric," Robert Kaplan proposes that different languages have different rhetorical norms, representing different ways of organizing ideas.[19]

Such style differences have also been identified in public school classrooms. Gail Martin, a teacher-researcher in Wyoming, wrote about her work with Arapaho students:

> One of our major concerns was that many of the stories children wrote didn't seem to "go anywhere." The stories just ambled along with no definite start or finish, no climaxes or conclusions. I decided to ask Pius Moss [the school elder] about these stories, since he is a master Arapaho storyteller himself. I learned about a distinctive difference between Arapaho stories and stories I was accustomed to hearing, reading, and telling. Pius Moss explained that Arapaho stories are not written down, they're told in what we might call serial form, continued night after night. A "good" story is one that lasts seven nights . . .
>
> When I asked Pius Moss why Arapaho stories never seem to have an "ending," he answered that there is no ending to life, and stories are about Arapaho life, so there is no need for a conclusion. My colleagues and I talked about what Pius had said, and we decided that we would encourage our students to choose whichever type of story they wished to write: we would try to listen and read in appropriate ways.[20]

Similarly, Native Alaskan teacher Martha Demientieff has discovered that her students find "book language" baffling. To help them gain access to this unfamiliar use of language, she contrasts the "wordy," academic way of saying things with the metaphoric style of Athabaskan. The students discuss how book language always uses more words, but how in Heritage language, brevity is always best. Students then work in pairs, groups, or individually to write papers in the academic way, discussing with Martha and with each other whether they believe they have said enough to "sound like a book." Next they take those papers and try to reduce the meaning to a few sentences. Finally, students further reduce the message to a "saying" brief enough to go on the front of a T-shirt, and the sayings are put on little paper T-shirts that the students cut out and hang throughout the room. Sometimes the students reduce other authors' wordy texts to their essential meanings as well. Thus, through winding back and forth through orality and literacy, the students begin to understand the stylistic differences between their own language and that of standard text.

Functions of Print

Print may serve different functions in some communities than it does in others, and some children may be unaccustomed to using print or seeing it used in the ways that schools demand. Shirley Brice Heath, for example, found that the black children in the community she called Trackton engaged with print as a group activity for specific real-life purposes, such as reading food labels when shopping, reading fix-it books to repair or modify toys, reading the names of cars to identify a wished-for model, or reading to participate in church. There was seldom a time anyone in the community would read as a solitary recreational activity; indeed, anyone who did so was thought to be a little strange.[21]

The children in Trackton, in short, read to learn things, for real purposes. When these children arrived in school they faced another reality. They were required, instead, to "learn to read," that is, they were told to focus on the *process* of reading with little apparent real purposes in mind other than to get through a basal page or complete a worksheet—and much of this they were to accomplish in isolation. Needless to say, they were not successful at the decontextualized, individualized school reading tasks.

Researchers have identified other differences in the use of language in print as well. For example, Ron Scollon and Suzanne Scollon report that, in the Athabaskan Indian approach to communicative interaction, each individual is expected to make his or her own sense of a situation and that no one can unilaterally enforce one interpretation. Consequently, they were not surprised when, in a story-retelling exercise intended to test reading comprehension, Athabaskan children tended to modify the text of the story in their retellings.[22] The school, however, would be likely to interpret these individually constructed retellings as evidence that the students had not comprehended the story.

Talk across the Curriculum

A debate over the role of language diversity in mathematics and science education was fueled recently by the publication of a book by Eleanor Wilson Orr titled *Twice as Less: Black English and the Performance of Black Students in Mathematics and Science.*[23] Orr is a teacher of math and science who, as director of the elite Hawthorne School, worked out a cooperative program with the District of Columbia to allow several Washington, D.C., public high school students to attend the prestigious school. Orr and her colleagues were dismayed to find that despite their faithfully following time-tested teaching strategies, and despite the black D.C. students' high motivation and hard work, the newcomers were failing an alarming percentage of their math and science courses.

Noting the differences in the language the black students used, Orr decided to investigate the possibility that speaking Black English was preventing these students from excelling in math and science. In a detailed argument she contends that the students' nonstandard language is both the cause and the expression of the real problem—their "nonstandard *perceptions.*"[24] She cites student statements such as "So the car traveling *twice as faster* will take *twice as less* hours" to support her thesis, and suggests that it is the difference between Black English and Standard English forms in the use of prepositions, conjunctions, and relative pronouns that is the basis for the students' failures.

It is important to critique this position in order that the failures of those responsible for teaching mathematics and science to poor and black students not be attributed to the students themselves, that is, so that the victims not be blamed. There are many problems with the Orr argument. One is her assumption that black students, by virtue of speaking Black English, do not have access to certain concepts needed in mathematical problem solving. For example, she makes much of the lack of the "as-as" comparison, but I have recorded Black English-speaking six- to eleven-year-olds frequently making such statements as, "She big as you" and "I can too run fast as you."

A second problem is that Orr compares the language and performance of low-income, ill-prepared students with upper-income students who have had superior scholastic preparation. I contend that it was not their language which confused the D.C. students, but mathematics itself! Any students with a similar level of preparation and experience, no matter what their color or language variety, would probably have had the same difficulties.

The most basic problem with the Orr argument, however, is Orr's apparent belief that somehow mathematics is linked to the syntactical constructions of standard English:

"[T]he *grammar* of standard English provides consistently for what is *true mathematically*."[25] What about the grammar of Chinese or Arabic or German? Orr's linguistic naïve determinist position can only lead to the bizarre conclusion that speakers of other languages would be equally handicapped in mathematics because they, too, lacked standard English constructions!

Even though Orr asserts that the cause of the problem is the speaking of Black English, she seems unaware that her proposed solution is not linked to this conceptualization. She does not recommend teaching Standard English, but rather, teaching *math* through the use in instruction of irregular number systems which force students to carefully work out concepts and prevent their dependence on inappropriate rote memorized patterns. One can surmise that as students and teachers work through these irregular systems, they create a shared language, developing for the students what they truly lack, a knowledge of the *content* of the language of mathematics, not the form.

Interviews with black teachers who have enjoyed longterm success teaching math to black-dialect-speaking students suggest that part of the solution also lies in the kind and quality of talk in the mathematics classroom. One teacher explained that her black students were much more likely to learn a new operation successfully when they understood to what use the operation might be put in daily life. Rather than teach decontextualized operations, she would typically first pose a "real-life" problem and challenge the students to find a solution. For example, she once brought in a part of a broken wheel, saying that it came from a toy that she wished to fix for her grandson. To do so, she had to reconstruct the wheel from this tiny part. After the students tried unsuccessfully to solve the problem, she introduced a theorem related to constructing a circle given any two points on an arc, which the students quickly assimilated.

Another black math teacher spoke of putting a problem into terms relevant to the student's life. He found that the same problem that baffled students when posed in terms of distances between two unfamiliar places or in terms of numbers of milk cans needed by a farmer, were much more readily solved when familiar locales and the amount of money needed to buy a leather jacket were substituted. I discovered a similar phenomenon when my first-grade inner-city students did much better on "word problems" on standardized tests when I merely substituted the names of people in our school for the names in the problems.

All of these modifications to the language of instruction speak to Heath's findings in Trackton: some youngsters may become more engaged in school tasks when the language of those tasks is posed in real-life contexts than when they are viewed as merely decontextualized problem completion. Since our long-term goal is producing young people who are able to think critically and creatively in real problem-solving contexts, the instructional—and linguistic—implications should be evident.

Conclusion

One of the most difficult tasks we face as human beings is communicating meaning across our individual differences, a task confounded immeasurably when we attempt to communicate across social lines, racial lines, cultural lines, or lines of unequal power. Yet, all U.S. demographic data points to a society becoming increasingly diverse, and that diversity is nowhere more evident than in our schools. Currently, "minority" students represent a majority in all but two of our twenty-five largest cities, and by some estimates, the turn of the century will find up to 40 percent nonwhite children in American classrooms. At the same time, the teaching force is becoming more homogeneously white. African-American, Asian, Hispanic, and Native American teachers now comprise only 10 percent of the teaching force, and that percentage is shrinking rapidly.

What are we educators to do? We must first decide upon a perspective from which to view the situation. We can continue to view diversity as a problem, attempting to force all differences into standardized boxes. Or we can recognize that diversity of thought, language, and worldview in our classrooms can not only provide an exciting educational setting, but can also prepare our children for the richness of living in an increasingly diverse national community. (Would any of us really want to trade the wonderful variety of American ethnic restaurants for a standard fare of steak houses and fast-food hamburgers?)

I am suggesting that we begin with a perspective that demands finding means to celebrate, not merely tolerate, diversity in our classrooms. Not only should teachers and students who share group membership delight in their own cultural and linguistic history, but all teachers must revel in the diversity of their students and that of the world outside the classroom community. How can we accomplish these lofty goals? Certainly, given the reality of the composition of the teaching force, very few educators can join Martha Demientieff in taking advantage of her shared background with her culturally unique students and contrasting "*our* Heritage language" or "the way *we* say things" with "Formal English." But teachers who do not share the language and culture of their students, or teachers whose students represent a variety of cultural backgrounds, can also celebrate diversity by making language diversity a part of the curriculum. Students can be asked to "teach" the teacher and other students aspects of their language variety. They can "translate" songs, poems, and stories into their own dialect or into "book language" and compare the differences across the cultural groups represented in the classroom.

Amanda Branscombe, a gifted white teacher who has often taught black students whom other teachers have given up on, sometimes has her middle-school students listen to rap songs in order to develop a rule base for their creation. The students would teach her their newly constructed "rules for writing rap," and she would in turn use this knowledge as a base to begin a discussion of the rules Shakespeare used to construct his plays, or the rules poets used to develop their sonnets.[26]

Within our celebration of diversity, we must keep in mind that education, at its best, hones and develops the knowledge and skills each student already possesses, while at the same time adding new knowledge and skills to that base. All students deserve the right both to develop the linguistic skills they bring to the classroom and to add others to their repertoires. While linguists have long proclaimed that no language variety is intrinsically "better" than another, in a stratified society such as ours, language choices are not neutral. The language associated with the power structure—"Standard English"—is the language of economic success, and all students have the right to schooling that gives them access to that language.

While it is also true, as this chapter highlights, that no one can force another to acquire an additional language variety, there are ways to point out to students both the arbitrariness of designating one variety over another as "standard," as well as the political and economic repercussions for not gaining access to that socially designated "standard." Without appearing to preach about a future which most students find hard to envision, one teacher, for example, has high school students interview various personnel officers in actual workplaces about their attitudes toward divergent styles in oral and written language and report their findings to the entire class. Another has students read or listen to a variety of oral and written language styles and discuss the impact of those styles on the message and the likely effect on different audiences. Students then recreate the texts or talks, using different language styles appropriate for different audiences (for example, a church group, academicians, rap singers, a feminist group, politicians, and so on).

Each of us belongs to many communities. Joseph Suina, a Pueblo Indian scholar, has proposed a schematic representation of at least three levels of community membership. He sets up three concentric circles. The inner circle is labeled "home/local community," the middle circle is "national community," and the outer circle represents the "global community."[27] In today's world it is vital that we all learn to become active citizens in all three communities, and one requisite skill for doing so is an ability to acquire additional linguistic codes. We can ignore or try to obliterate language diversity in the classroom, or we can encourage in our teachers and students a "mental set for diversity." If we choose the latter, the classroom can become a laboratory for developing linguistic diversity. Those who have acquired additional codes because their local language differs significantly from the language of the national culture may actually be in a better position to gain access to the global culture than "mainstream" Americans who, as Martha says, "only know one way to talk." Rather than think of these diverse students as problems, we can view them instead as resources who can help all of us learn what it feels like to move between cultures and language varieties, and thus perhaps better learn how to become citizens of the global community.

Notes

1. Stephen D. Krashen, *Principles and Practice in Second Language Acquisition* (New York: Pergamon, 1982).
2. Ibid., p. 22.
3. S. Nelson-Barber, "Phonologic Variations of Pima English," in R. St. Clair and W. Leap, eds., *Language Renewal among American Indian Tribes: Issues, Problems and Prospects* (Rosslyn, Va.: National Clearinghouse for Bilingual Education, 1982).
4. Some of these books include Lucille Clifton, *All Us Come 'Cross the Water* (New York: Holt, Rinehart, and Winston, 1973); Paul Green (aided by Abbe Abbott), *I Am Eskimo-Aknik My Name* (Juneau, Alaska: Alaska Northwest Publishing, 1959); Howard Jacobs and Jim Rice, *Once upon a Bayou* (New Orleans, La.: Phideaux Publications, 1983); Tim Edler, *Santa Cajun's Christmas Adventure* (Baton Rouge, La.: Little Cajun Books, 1981); and a series of biographies produced by Yukon-Koyukkuk School District of Alaska and published by Hancock House Publishers in North Vancouver, British Columbia, Canada.
5. Shirley Brice Heath, *Ways with Words* (Cambridge, Eng.: Cambridge University Press, 1983).
6. S. Michaels and C. B. Cazden, "Teacher-Child Collaboration on Oral Preparation for Literacy," in B. Schieffer, ed., *Acquisition of Literary: Ethnographic Perspectives* (Norwood, N.J.: Ablex, 1986).
7. C. B. Cazden, *Classroom Discourse* (Portsmouth, N.H.: Heinemann, 1988).
8. Ibid., p. 18.
9. Ibid.
10. Heath, *Ways with Words.*
11. H. Mehan, "Asking Known Information," *Theory into Practice* 28 (1979), pp. 285–94.
12. Ibid., p. 124.
13. G. Smitherman, *Talkin and Testifyin* (Boston: Houghton Mifflin, 1977).
14. R. Sims, "Dialect and Reading: Toward Redefining the Issues," in J. Langer and M. T. Smith-Burke, eds., *Reader Meets Author/Bridging the Gap* (Newark, Dela.: International Reading Association, 1982).
15. Ibid.
16. P. M. Cunningham, "Teachers' Correction Responses to Black-Dialect Miscues Which Are Nonmeaning-Changing," *Reading Research Quarterly* 12 (1976–77).
17. Robert Berdan, "Knowledge into Practice: Delivering Research to Teachers," in M. F. Whiteman, ed., *Reactions to Ann Arbor: Vernacular Black English and Education* (Arlington, Va.: Center for Applied Linguistics, 1980).
18. Ibid., p. 78.
19. R. Kaplan, "Cultural Thought Patterns in Intercultural Education," *Language Learning* 16 (1966), pp. 1–2.

20. Cazden, *Classroom Discourse*, p. 12.
21. Heath, *Ways with Words*.
22. Ron Scollon and Suzanne B. K. Scollon, "Cooking It Up and Boiling It Down: Abstracts in Athabaskan Children's Story Retellings," in D. Tannen, ed., *Spoken and Written Language* (Norwood, NJ.: Ablex, 1979).
23. Eleanor Wilson Orr, *Twice as Less: Black English and the Performance of Black Students in Mathematics and Science* (New York: W.W. Norton, 1987).
24. Ibid., p. 30.
25. Ibid., p. 149 (emphasis added).
26. Personal communication, 1988.
27. Personal communication, 1989.

17

Beyond the Methods Fetish: Toward a Humanizing Pedagogy

Lilia I. Bartolomé

Much of the current debate regarding the improvement of minority student academic achievement occurs at a level that treats education as a primarily technical issue (Giroux, 1992).[1] For example, the historical and present-day academic underachievement of certain culturally and linguistically subordinated student populations in the United States (e.g., Mexican Americans, Native Americans, Puerto Ricans) is often explained as resulting from the lack of cognitively, culturally, and/or linguistically appropriate teaching methods and educational programs.[2] As such, the solution to the problem of academic underachievement tends to be constructed in primarily methodological and mechanistic terms dislodged from the sociocultural reality that shapes it. That is, the solution to the current underachievement of students from subordinated cultures is often reduced to finding the "right" teaching methods, strategies, or prepackaged curricula that will work with students who do not respond to so-called "regular" or "normal" instruction.

Recent research studies have begun to identify educational programs found to be successful in working with culturally and linguistically subordinated minority student populations (Carter & Chatfield, 1986; Lucas, Henze, & Donato, 1990; Tikunoff, 1985; Webb, 1987). In addition, there has been specific interest in identifying teaching strategies that more effectively teach culturally and linguistically "different" students and other "disadvantaged" and "at-risk" students (Knapp & Shields, 1990; McLeod, 1994; Means & Knapp, 1991; Tinajero & Ada, 1993). Although it is important to identify useful and promising instructional programs and strategies, it is erroneous to assume that blind replication of instructional programs or teacher mastery of particular teaching methods, in and of themselves, will guarantee successful student learning, especially when we are discussing populations that historically have been mistreated and miseducated by the schools.

This focus on methods as solutions in the current literature coincides with many of my graduate students' beliefs regarding linguistic minority education improvement. As a Chicana professor who has taught anti-racist multicultural education courses at various institutions, I am consistently confronted at the beginning of each semester by students who are anxious to learn the latest teaching methods—methods that they hope will somehow magically work on minority students.[3] Although my students are well-intentioned individuals who sincerely wish to create positive learning environments for culturally and linguistically subordinated students, they arrive with the expectation that I will provide them with easy answers in the form of specific instructional methods. That is, since they (implicitly) perceive the academic underachievement of subordinated students as a technical issue, the solutions they require are also expected to be technical in nature (e.g., specific teaching methods, instructional curricula and materials). They usually assume that: 1) they, as teachers, are fine and do not need to identify, interrogate, and change their biased beliefs and fragmented views about subordinated students; 2) schools, as institutions, are basically fair and democratic sites where all students are provided with similar, if not equal, treatment and learning conditions; and 3) children who experience academic difficulties (especially those from culturally and linguistically low-status groups) require some form of "special" instruction since they obviously have not been able to succeed under "regular" or "normal" instructional conditions. Consequently, if nothing is basically wrong with teachers and schools, they often conclude, then linguistic minority academic underachievement is best dealt with by providing teachers with specific teaching methods that promise to be effective with culturally and linguistically subordinated students. To further complicate matters, many of my students seek *generic* teaching methods that will work with a variety of minority student populations, and they grow anxious and impatient when reminded that instruction for any group of students needs to be tailored or individualized to some extent. Some of my students appear to be seeking what Maria de la Luz Reyes (1992) defines as a "one size fits all" instructional recipe. Reyes explains that the term refers to the assumption that instructional methods that are deemed effective for mainstream populations will benefit *all* students, no matter what their backgrounds may be.[4] She explains that the assumption is

> similar to the "one size fits all" marketing concept that would have buyers believe that there is an average or ideal size among men and women ... Those who market "one size fits all" products suggest that if the article of clothing is not a good fit, the fault is not with the design of the garment, but those who are too fat, too skinny, too tall, too short, or too high-waisted. (p. 435)

I have found that many of my students similarly believe that teaching approaches that work with one minority population should also fit another (see Vogt, Jordan, & Tharp, 1987, for an example of this tendency). Reyes argues that educators often make this "one size fits all" assumption when discussing instructional approaches, such as process writing. For example, as Lisa Delpit (1988) has convincingly argued, the process writing approach that has been blindly embraced by mostly White liberal teachers often produces a negative result with African-American students. Delpit cites one Black student:

> I didn't feel she was teaching us anything. She wanted us to correct each other's papers and we were there to learn from her. She didn't teach anything, absolutely nothing.
>
> Maybe they're trying to learn what Black folks knew all the time. We understand how to improvise, how to express ourselves creatively. When I'm in a classroom, I'm not looking for that, I'm looking for structure, the more formal language.
>
> Now my buddy was in a Black teacher's class. And that lady was very good. She went through and explained and defined each part of the structure. This [White] teacher didn't get along with that Black teacher. She said she didn't agree with her methods. But *I* don't think that White teacher *had* any methods. (1988, p. 287)

The above quote is a glaring testimony that a "one size fits all" approach often does not work with the same level of effectiveness with all students across the board. Such assumptions reinforce a disarticulation between the embraced method and the sociocultural realities within which each method is implemented. I find that this "one size fits all" assumption is also held by many of my students about a number of teaching methods currently in vogue, such as cooperative learning and whole language instruction. The students imbue the "new" methods with almost magical properties that render them, in and of themselves, capable of improving students' academic standing.

One of my greatest challenges throughout the years has been to help students to understand that a myopic focus on methodology often serves to obfuscate the real question—which is why in our society, subordinated students do not generally succeed academically in schools. In fact, schools often reproduce the existing asymmetrical power relations among cultural groups (Anyon, 1988; Gibson & Ogbu, 1991; Giroux, 1992; Freire, 1985). I believe that by taking a sociohistorical view of present-day conditions and concerns that inform the lived experiences of socially perceived minority students, prospective teachers are better able to comprehend the quasi-colonial nature of minority education. By engaging in this critical sociohistorical analysis of subordinated students' academic performance, most of my graduate students (teachers and prospective teachers) are better situated to reinterpret and reframe current educational concerns so as to develop pedagogical structures that speak to the day-to-day reality, struggles, concerns, and dreams of these students. By understanding the historical specificities of marginalized students, these teachers and prospective teachers come to realize that an uncritical focus on methods makes invisible the historical role that schools and their personnel have played (and continue to play), not only in discriminating against many culturally different groups, but also in denying their humanity. By robbing students of their culture, language, history, and values, schools often reduce these students to the status of subhumans who need to be rescued from their "savage" selves. The end result of this cultural and linguistic eradication represents, in my view, a form of dehumanization. Therefore, any discussion having to do with the improvement of subordinated students' academic standing is incomplete if it does not address those discriminatory school practices that lead to dehumanization.

In this article, I argue that a necessary first step in reevaluating the failure or success of particular instructional methods used with subordinated students calls for a shift in perspective—a shift from a narrow and mechanistic view of instruction to one that is broader in scope and takes into consideration the sociohistorical and political dimensions of education. I discuss why effective methods are needed for these students, and why certain strategies are deemed effective or ineffective in a given sociocultural context. My discussion will include a section that addresses the significance of teachers' understanding of the political nature of education, the reproductive nature of schools, and the schools' continued (yet unspoken) deficit views of subordinated students. By conducting a critical analysis of the sociocultural realities in which subordinated students find themselves at school, the implicit and explicit antagonistic relations between students and teachers (and other school representatives) take on focal importance.

As a Chicana and a former classroom elementary and middle school teacher who encountered negative race relations that ranged from teachers' outright rejection of subordinated students to their condescending pity, fear, indifference, and apathy when confronted by the challenges of minority student education, I find it surprising that little minority education literature deals explicitly with the very real issue of antagonistic race relations between subordinated students and White school personnel (see Ogbu, 1987, and Giroux, 1992, for an in-depth discussion of this phenomenon).

For this reason, I also include in this article a section that discusses two instructional methods and approaches identified as effective in current education literature: culturally responsive education and strategic teaching. I examine the methods for pedagogical underpinnings that—under the critical use of politically clear teachers—have the potential to challenge students academically and intellectually while treating them with dignity and respect. More importantly, I examine the pedagogical foundations that serve to humanize the educational process and enable both students and teachers to work toward breaking away from their unspoken antagonism and negative beliefs about each other and get on with the business of sharing and creating knowledge. I argue that the informed way in which a teacher implements a method can serve to offset potentially unequal relations and discriminatory structures and practices in the classroom and, in doing so, improve the quality of the instructional process for both student and teacher. In other words, politically informed teacher use of methods can create conditions that enable subordinated students to move from their usual passive position to one of active and critical engagement. I am convinced that creating pedagogical spaces that enable students to move *from object to subject position* produces more far-reaching, positive effects than the implementation of a particular teaching methodology, regardless of how technically advanced and promising it may be.

The final section of this article will explore and suggest the implementation of what Donaldo Macedo (1994) designates as an

> anti-methods pedagogy that refuses to be enslaved by the rigidity of models and method-ological paradigms. An anti-methods pedagogy should be informed by a critical understanding of the sociocultural context that guides our practices so as to free us from the beaten path of methodological certainties and specialisms. (p. 8)

Simply put, it is important that educators not blindly reject teaching methods across the board, but that they reject uncritical appropriation of methods, materials, curricula, etc. Educators need to reject the present methods fetish so as to create learning environments informed by both action and reflection. In freeing themselves from the blind adoption of so-called effective (and sometimes "teacher-proof") strategies, teachers can begin the reflective process, which allows them to recreate and reinvent teaching methods and materials by always taking into consideration the sociocultural realities that can either limit or expand the possibilities to humanize education. It is important that teachers keep in mind that methods are social constructions that grow out of and reflect ideologies that often prevent teachers from understanding the pedagogical implications of asymmetrical power relations among different cultural groups.

The Significance of Teacher Political Clarity[5]

In his letter to North American educators, Paulo Freire (1987) argues that technical expert-ise and mastery of content area and methodology are insufficient to ensure effective instruction of students from subordinated cultures. Freire contends that, in addition to possessing content area knowledge, teachers must possess political clarity so as to be able to effectively create, adopt, and modify teaching strategies that simultaneously respect and challenge learners from diverse cultural groups in a variety of learning environments.

Teachers working on improving their political clarity recognize that teaching is not a politically neutral undertaking. They understand that educational institutions are social-izing institutions that mirror the greater society's culture, values, and norms. Schools reflect both the positive and negative aspects of a society. Thus, the unequal power rela-tions among various social and cultural groups at the societal level are usually reproduced at the school and classroom level, unless concerted efforts are made to prevent their reproduction. Teachers working toward political clarity understand that they can either maintain the status quo, or they can work to transform the sociocultural reality at the classroom and school level so that the culture at this micro-level does not reflect macro-level inequalities, such as asymmetrical power relations that relegate certain cultural groups to a subordinate status.

Teachers can support positive social change in the classroom in a variety of ways. One possible intervention can consist of the creation of heterogeneous learning groups for the purpose of modifying low-status roles of individuals or groups of children.[6] Elizabeth Cohen (1986) demonstrates that when teachers create learning conditions where students, especially those perceived as low status (e.g., limited English speakers in a classroom where English is the dominant language, students with academic difficulties, or those perceived by their peers for a variety of reasons as less able), can demonstrate their possession of knowledge and expertise, they are then able to see themselves, and be seen by others, as capable and competent. As a result, contexts are created in which peers can learn from each other as well.

A teacher's political clarity will not necessarily compensate for structural inequalities that students face outside the classroom; however, teachers can, to the best of their ability, help their students deal with injustices encountered inside and outside the classroom. A number of possibilities exist for preparing students to deal with the greater society's unfairness and inequality that range from engaging in explicit discussions with students about their experiences, to more indirect ways (that nevertheless require a teacher who is politically clear), such as creating democratic learning environments where students become accustomed to being treated as competent and able individuals. I believe that the students, once accustomed to the rights and responsibilities of full citizenship in the classroom, will come to expect respectful treatment and authentic estimation in other contexts. Again, it is important to point out that it is not the particular lesson or set of activities that prepares the student; rather, it is the teacher's politically clear educational philosophy that underlies the varied methods and lessons/activities she or he employs that makes the difference.

Under ideal conditions, competent educators simultaneously translate theory into practice *and* consider the population being served and the sociocultural reality in which learning is expected to take place. Let me reiterate that command of a content area or specialization is necessary, but it is not sufficient for effectively working with students. Just as critical is that teachers comprehend that their role as educators is a political act that is never neutral (Freire, 1985, 1987, 1993; Freire & Macedo, 1987). In ignoring or negating the political nature of their work with these students, teachers not only reproduce the status quo and their students' low status, but they also inevitably legitimize schools' discriminatory practices. For example, teachers who uncritically follow school practices that unintentionally or intentionally serve to promote tracking and segregation within school and classroom contexts continue to reproduce the status quo. Conversely, teachers can become conscious of, and subsequently challenge, the role of educational institutions and their own roles as educators in maintaining a system that often serves to silence students from subordinated groups.

Teachers must also remember that schools, similar to other institutions in society, are influenced by perceptions of socioeconomic status (SES), race/ethnicity, language, and gender (Anyon, 1988; Bloom, 1991; Cummins, 1989; Ogbu, 1987). They must begin to question how these perceptions influence classroom dynamics. An important step in increasing teacher political clarity is recognizing that, despite current liberal rhetoric regarding the equal value of all cultures, low SES and ethnic minority students have historically (and currently) been perceived as deficient. I believe that the present methods-restricted discussion must be broadened to reveal the deeply entrenched deficit orientation toward "difference" (i.e., non-Western European race/ethnicity, non-English language use, working-class status, femaleness) that prevails in the schools in a deeply "cultural" ideology of White supremacy. As educators, we must constantly be vigilant and ask how the deficit orientation has affected our perceptions concerning students from subordinated populations and created rigid and mechanistic teacher–student relations (Cummins, 1989; Flores, Cousin, & Diaz, 1991; Giroux & McLaren, 1986). Such a model often serves to create classroom conditions in which there is very little opportunity for teachers and students to interact in meaningful ways, establish positive and trusting working relations, and share knowledge.

Our Legacy: A Deficit View of Subordinated Students

As discussed earlier, teaching strategies are neither designed nor implemented in a vacuum. Design, selection, and use of particular teaching approaches and strategies arise from perceptions about learning and learners. I contend that the most pedagogically advanced strategies are sure to be ineffective in the hands of educators who implicitly or explicitly subscribe to a belief system that renders ethnic, racial, and linguistic minority students at best culturally disadvantaged and in need of fixing (if we could only identify the right recipe!), or, at worst, culturally or genetically deficient and beyond fixing.[7] Despite the fact that various models have been proposed to explain the academic failure of certain subordinated groups—academic failure described as *historical, pervasive,* and *disproportionate*—the fact remains that these views of difference are deficit-based and deeply imprinted in our individual and collective psyches (Flores, 1982, 1993; Menchaca & Valencia, 1990; Valencia, 1986, 1991).

The deficit model has the longest history of any model discussed in the education literature. Richard Valencia (1986) traces its evolution over three centuries:

> Also known in the literature as the "social pathology" model or the "cultural deprivation" model, the deficit approach explains disproportionate academic problems among low status students as largely being due to pathologies or deficits in their sociocultural background (e.g., cognitive and linguistic deficiencies, low self-esteem, poor motivation) ... To improve the educability of such students, programs such as compensatory education and parent-child intervention have been proposed. (p. 3)

Barbara Flores (1982, 1993) documents the effect this deficit model has had on the schools' past and current perceptions of Latino students. Her historical overview chronicles descriptions used to refer to Latino students over the last century. The terms range from "mentally retarded," "linguistically handicapped," "culturally and linguistically deprived," and "semilingual," to the current euphemism for Latino and other subordinated students: the "at-risk" student.

Similarly, recent research continues to lay bare our deficit orientation and its links to discriminatory school practices aimed at students from groups perceived as low status (Anyon, 1988; Bloom, 1991; Diaz, Moll, & Mehan, 1986; Oaks, 1986). Findings range from teacher preference for Anglo students, to bilingual teachers' preference for lighter skinned Latino students (Bloom, 1991), to teachers' negative perceptions of working-class parents as compared to middle-class parents (Lareau, 1990), and, finally, to unequal teaching and testing practices in schools serving working-class and ethnic minority students (Anyon, 1988; Diaz et al., 1986; Oaks, 1986; U.S. Commission on Civil Rights, 1973). Especially indicative of our inability to consciously acknowledge the deficit orientation is the fact that the teachers in these studies—teachers from all ethnic groups—were themselves unaware of the active role they played in the differential and unequal treatment of their students.

The deficit view of subordinated students has been critiqued by numerous researchers as ethnocentric and invalid (Boykin, 1983; Diaz et al., 1986; Flores, 1982; Flores et al., 1991; Sue & Padilla, 1986; Trueba, 1989; Walker, 1987). More recent research offers alternative models that shift the source of school failure away from the characteristics of the individual child, their families, and their cultures, and toward the schooling process (Au & Mason, 1983; Heath, 1983; Mehan, 1992; Philips, 1972). Unfortunately, I believe that many of these alternative models often unwittingly give rise to a kinder and more liberal, yet more concealed version of the deficit model that views subordinated students as being in need of "specialized" modes of instruction—a type of instructional "coddling" that mainstream students do not require in order to achieve in school. Despite the use of less overtly ethnocentric models to explain the academic standing of subordinated students, I believe that the deficit orientation toward difference, especially as it relates to low socioeconomic and ethnic minority groups, is very deeply ingrained in the ethos of our most prominent institutions, especially schools, and in the various educational programs in place at these sites.

It is against this sociocultural backdrop that teachers can begin to seriously question the unspoken but prevalent deficit orientation used to hide SES, racial/ethnic, linguistic, and gender inequities present in U.S. classrooms. And it is against this sociocultural backdrop that I critically examine two teaching approaches identified by the educational literature as effective with subordinated student populations.

Potentially Humanizing Pedagogy: Two Promising Teaching Approaches

Well-known approaches and strategies such as cooperative learning, language experience, process writing, reciprocal teaching, and whole language activities can be used to create humanizing learning environments where students cease to be treated as objects and yet receive academically rigorous instruction (Cohen, 1986; Edelsky, Altwerger, & Flores, 1991; Palinscar & Brown, 1984; Pérez & Torres-Guzmán, 1992; Zamel, 1982). However, when these approaches are implemented uncritically, they often produce negative results, as indicated by Lisa Delpit (1986, 1988). Critical teacher applications of these approaches and strategies can contribute to discarding deficit views of students from subordinated groups, so that they are treated with respect and viewed as active and capable subjects in their own learning.

Academically rigorous, student-centered teaching strategies can take many forms. One may well ask, is it not merely common sense to promote approaches and strategies that respect, recognize, utilize, and build on students' existing knowledge bases? The answer would be, of course, yes, it is. However, it is important to recognize, as part of our effort to increase our political clarity, that these practices have *not* typified classroom instruction for students from marginalized populations. The practice of learning from and valuing student language and life experiences *often* occurs in classrooms where students speak a language and possess cultural capital that more closely matches that of the mainstream (Anyon, 1988; Lareau, 1990; Winfield, 1986).[8]

Jean Anyon's (1988) classic research suggests that teachers of affluent students are more likely than teachers of working-class students to utilize and incorporate student life experiences and knowledge into the curriculum. For example, in Anyon's study, teachers of affluent students often designed creative and innovative lessons that tapped students' existing knowledge bases; one math lesson, designed to teach students to find averages, asked them to fill out a possession survey inquiring about the number of cars, television sets, refrigerators, and games owned at home so as to teach students to average. Unfortunately, this practice of tapping students' already existing knowledge and language bases is not commonly utilized with student populations traditionally perceived as deficient. Anyon reports that teachers of working-class students viewed them as lacking the necessary cultural capital, and therefore imposed content and behavioral standards with little consideration and respect for student input. Although Anyon did not generalize beyond her sample, other studies suggest the validity of her findings for ethnic minority student populations (Diaz et al., 1986; Moll, 1986; Oaks, 1986).

The creation of learning environments for low SES and ethnic minority students, similar to those for more affluent and White populations, requires that teachers discard deficit notions and genuinely value and utilize students' existing knowledge bases in their teaching. In order to do so, teachers must confront and challenge their own social biases so as to honestly begin to perceive their students as capable learners. Furthermore, they must remain open to the fact that they will also learn from their students. Learning is not a one-way undertaking.

It is important for educators to recognize that no language or set of life experiences is inherently superior, yet our social values reflect our preferences for certain language and life experiences over others. Student-centered teaching strategies such as cooperative learning, language experience, process writing, reciprocal teaching, and whole language activities (if practiced consciously and critically) can help to offset or neutralize our deficit-based failure and recognize subordinated student strengths. Our tendency to discount these strengths occurs whenever we forget that learning only occurs when prior knowledge is accessed and linked to new information.

Beau Jones, Annemarie Palinscar, Donna Ogle, and Eileen Carr (1987) explain that learning *is* the act of linking new information to prior knowledge. According to their framework, prior knowledge is stored in memory in the form of knowledge frameworks. New information is understood and stored by calling up the appropriate knowledge framework and then integrating the new information. Acknowledging and using existing student language and knowledge makes good pedagogical sense, and it also constitutes a humanizing experience for students traditionally *de*humanized and disempowered in the schools. I believe that strategies identified as effective in the literature have the potential to offset reductive education in which "the educator as *the one who knows* transfers existing knowledge to the learner as *the one who does not know*" (Freire, 1985, p. 114, emphasis added). It is important to repeat that mere implementation of a particular strategy or approach identified as effective does not guarantee success, as the current debate in process writing attests (Delpit, 1986, 1988; Reyes, 1991, 1992).

Creating learning environments that incorporate student language and life experiences in no way negates teachers' responsibility for providing students with particular academic content knowledge and skills. It is important not to link teacher respect and use of student knowledge and language bases with a laissez-faire attitude toward teaching. It is equally necessary not to confuse academic rigor with rigidity that stifles and silences students. The teacher is the authority, with all the resulting responsibilities that entails; however, it is not necessary for the teacher to become authoritarian in order to challenge students intellectually. Education can be a process in which teacher and students mutually participate in the intellectually exciting undertaking we call learning. Students *can* become active subjects in their own learning, instead of passive objects waiting to be filled with facts and figures by the teacher.

I would like to emphasize that teachers who work with subordinated populations have the responsibility to assist them in appropriating knowledge bases and discourse styles deemed desirable by the greater society. However, this process of appropriation must be additive, that is, the new concepts and new discourse skills must be added to, not subtracted from, the students' existing background knowledge. In order to assume this additive stance, teachers must discard deficit views so they can use and build on life experiences and language styles too often viewed and labeled as "low class" and undesirable. Again, there are numerous teaching strategies and methods that can be employed in this additive manner. For the purposes of illustration, I will briefly discuss two approaches currently identified as promising for students from subordinated populations. The selected approaches are referred to in the literature as culturally responsive instructional approaches and strategic teaching.

Culturally Responsive Instruction: The Potential to Equalize Power Relations

Culturally responsive instruction grows out of cultural difference theory, which attributes the academic difficulties of students from subordinated groups to cultural incongruence or discontinuities between the learning, language use, and behavioral practices found in the home and those expected by the schools. Ana Maria Villegas (1988, 1991) defines culturally responsive instruction as attempts to create instructional situations where teachers use teaching approaches and strategies that recognize and build on culturally different ways of learning, behaving, and using language in the classroom.

A number of classic ethnographic studies document culturally incongruent communication practices in classrooms where students and teachers may speak the same language but use it in different ways. This type of incongruence is cited as a major source of academic difficulties for subordinated students and their teachers (see Au, 1980; Au & Mason, 1983; Cazden, 1988; Erickson & Mohatt, 1982; Heath, 1983; Philips, 1972). For the purposes of this analysis, one form of culturally responsive instruction, the Kamehameha Education Project reading program, will be discussed.

The Kamehameha Education Project is a reading program developed as a response to the traditionally low academic achievement of native Hawaiian students in Western schools. The reading program was a result of several years of research that examined the language practices of native Hawaiian children in home and school settings. Observations of native Hawaiian children showed them to be bright and capable learners; however, their behavior in the classroom signaled communication difficulties between them and their non-Hawaiian teachers. For example, Kathryn Hu-Pei Au (1979, 1980) reports that native Hawaiian children's language behavior in the classroom was often misinterpreted by teachers as being unruly and without educational value. She found that the children's preferred language style in the classroom was linked to a practice used by adults in their homes and community called "talk story." She discusses the talk story phenomenon and describes it as a major speech event in the Hawaiian community, where individuals speak almost simultaneously and where little attention is given to turn taking. Au explains that this practice may inhibit students from speaking out as individuals because of their familiarity with and preference for simultaneous group discussion.

Because the non-Hawaiian teachers were unfamiliar with talk story and failed to recognize its value, much class time was spent either silencing the children or prodding unwilling individuals to speak. Needless to say, very little class time was dedicated to other instruction. More important, the children were constrained and not allowed to demonstrate their abilities as speakers and possessors of knowledge. Because the students did not exhibit their skills in mainstream accepted ways (e.g., competing as individuals for the floor), they were prevented from exhibiting knowledge via their culturally preferred style. However, once the children's interaction style was incorporated into classroom lessons, time on task increased and, subsequently, students' performance on standardized reading tests improved. This study's findings conclude that educators can successfully employ the students' culturally valued language practices while introducing the student to more conventional and academically acceptable ways of using language.

It is interesting to note that many of the research studies that examine culturally congruent and incongruent teaching approaches also inadvertently illustrate the equalization of previous asymmetrical power relations between teachers and students. These studies describe classrooms where teachers initially imposed participation structures upon students from subordinated linguistic minority groups and later learned to negotiate with them rules regarding acceptable classroom behavior and language use (Au & Mason, 1983; Erickson & Mohatt, 1982; Heath, 1983; Philips, 1972). Thus these studies, in essence, capture the successful negotiation of power relations, which resulted in higher student academic achievement and increased teacher effectiveness. Yet there is little explicit discussion in these studies of the greater sociocultural reality that renders it perfectly normal for teachers to automatically disregard and disrespect subordinated students' preferences and to allow antagonistic relations to foment until presented with empirical evidence that legitimizes the students' practices. Instead, the focus of most of these studies rests entirely on the cultural congruence of the instruction and not on the humanizing effects of a more democratic pedagogy. Villegas (1988) accurately critiques the cultural congruence literature when she states:

> It is simplistic to claim that differences in languages used at home and in school are the root of the widespread academic problems of minority children. Admittedly, differences do exist, and they can create communication difficulties in the classroom for both teachers and students. Even so, those differences in language must be viewed in the context of a broader struggle for power within a stratified society. (p. 260)

Despite the focus on the cultural versus the political dimensions of pedagogy, some effort is made to link culturally congruent teaching practices with equalization of classroom power relations. For example, Kathryn Au and Jana Mason (1983) explain that "one means of achieving cultural congruence in lessons may be to *seek a balance between the interactional rights of teachers and students*, so that the children can participate in ways comfortable to them" (p. 145, emphasis added). Their study compared two teachers and showed that the teacher who was willing to negotiate with students either the topic of discussion or the appropriate participation structure was better able to implement her lesson. Conversely, the teacher who attempted to impose both topic of discussion *and* appropriate interactional rules was frequently diverted because of conflicts with students over one or the other.

Unfortunately, as mentioned earlier, interpretations and practical applications of this body of research have focused on the *cultural* congruence of the approaches. I emphasize the term *cultural* because in these studies the term "culture" is used in a restricted sense devoid of its dynamic, ideological, and political dimensions. Instead, culture is treated as synonymous with ethnic culture, rather than as "the representation of lived experiences, material artifacts and practices *forged within the unequal and dialectical relations* that different groups establish in a given society at a particular point in historical time" (Giroux, 1985, p. xxi, emphasis added). I use this definition of culture because, without identifying the political dimensions of culture and subsequent unequal status attributed to members of different ethnic groups, the reader may conclude that teaching methods simply need to be ethnically congruent to be effective—without recognizing that not all ethnic and linguistic cultural groups are viewed and treated as equally legitimate in classrooms. Interestingly enough, there is little discussion of the various socially perceived minority groups' subordinate status vis-à-vis White teachers and peers in these studies. All differences are treated as ethnic cultural differences and not as responses of subordinated students to teachers from dominant groups, and vice versa.

Given the sociocultural realities in the above studies, the specific teaching strategies may not be what made the difference. Indeed, efforts to uncritically export the Kamehameha Education Project reading program to other student populations resulted in failure (Vogt et al., 1987). It could well be that the teacher's effort to negotiate and share power by treating students as equal participants in their own learning is what made the difference in Hawaii. Just as important is the teachers' willingness to critically interrogate their deficit views of subordinated students. By employing a variety of strategies and techniques, the Kamehameha students were allowed to interact with teachers in egalitarian and meaningful ways. More importantly, the teachers also learned to recognize, value, use, and build upon students' previously acquired knowledge and skills. In essence, these strategies succeeded in creating a comfort zone so students could exhibit their knowledge and skills and, ultimately, empower themselves to succeed in an academic setting. Teachers also benefited from using a variety of student-centered teaching strategies that humanized their perceptions of treatment of students previously perceived as deficient. Ray McDermott's (1977) classic research reminds us that numerous teaching approaches and strategies can be effective, so long as trusting relations between teacher and students are established and power relations are mutually set and agreed upon.

Strategic Teaching: The Significance of Teacher–Student Interaction and Negotiation

Strategic teaching refers to an instructional model that explicitly teaches students learning strategies that enable them consciously to monitor their own learning. This is accomplished through the development of reflective cognitive monitoring and metacognitive skills (Jones, Palinscar, Ogle, & Carr, 1987). The goal is to prepare independent and metacognitively aware students. This teaching strategy makes explicit for students the structures of various text types used in academic settings and assists students in identifying various strategies for effectively comprehending the various genres. Although text structures and strategies for dissecting the particular structures are presented by the teacher, a key component of these lessons is the elicitation of students' knowledge about text types and their own strategies for making meaning before presenting them with more conventional academic strategies.

Examples of learning strategies include teaching various text structures (i.e., stories and reports) through frames and graphic organizers. *Frames* are sets of questions that help students understand a given topic. Readers monitor their understanding of a text by asking questions, making predictions, and testing their predictions as they read. Before reading, frames serve as an advance organizer to activate prior knowledge and facilitate understanding. Frames can also be utilized during the reading process by the reader to monitor self-learning. Finally, frames can be used after a reading lesson to summarize and integrate newly acquired information.

Graphic organizers are visual maps that represent text structures and organizational patterns used in texts and in student writing. Ideally, graphic organizers reflect both the content and text structure. Graphic organizers include semantic maps, chains, and concept hierarchies, and assist the student in visualizing the rhetorical structure of the text. Beau Jones and colleagues (1987) explain that frames and graphic organizers can be "powerful tools to help the student locate, select, sequence, integrate and restructure information—both from the perspective of understanding and from the perspective of producing information in written responses" (p. 38).

Although much of the research on strategic teaching focuses on English monolingual mainstream students, recent efforts to study linguistic minority students' use of these strategies show similar success. This literature shows that strategic teaching improved the students' reading comprehension, as well as their conscious use of effective learning strategies in their native language (Avelar La Salle, 1991; Chamot, 1983; Hernandez, 1991; O'Malley & Chamot, 1990; Reyes, 1987). Furthermore, these studies show that students, despite limited English proficiency, were able to transfer or apply their knowledge of specific learning strategies and text structure to English reading texts. For example, Jose Hernandez (1991) reports that sixth-grade limited English proficient students learned, in the native language (Spanish), to generate hypotheses, summarize, and make predictions about readings. He reports:

> Students were able to demonstrate use of comprehension strategies even when they could not decode the English text aloud. When asked in Spanish about English texts the students were able to generate questions, summarize stories, and predict future events in Spanish. (p. 101)

Robin Avelar La Salle's (1991) study of third- and fourth-grade bilingual students shows that strategic teaching in the native language of three expository text structures commonly found in elementary social studies and science texts (topical net, matrix, and hierarchy) improved comprehension of these types of texts in both Spanish and English.

Such explicit and strategic teaching is most important in the upper elementary grades, where students are expected to focus on the development of more advanced English literacy skills. Beginning at about third grade, students face literacy demands distinct from those encountered in earlier grades. Jeanne Chall (1983) describes the change in literacy demands in terms of stages of readings. She explains that at a stage three of reading, students cease to "learn to read" and begin "reading to learn." Students in third and fourth grade are introduced to content area subjects such as social studies, science, and health. In addition, students are introduced to expository texts (reports). This change in texts, text structures, and in the functions of reading (reading for information) calls for teaching strategies that will prepare students to comprehend various expository texts (e.g., cause/effect, compare/contrast) used across the curriculum.

Strategic teaching holds great promise for preparing linguistic minority students to face the new literacy challenges in the upper grades. As discussed before, the primary goal of strategic instruction is to foster learner independence. This goal in and of itself is laudable. However, the characteristics of strategic instruction that I find most promising grow out of the premise that teachers and students must interact and negotiate meaning as equals in order to reach a goal.

Teachers, by permitting learners to speak from their own vantage points, create learning contexts in which students are able to empower themselves throughout the strategic learning process. Before teachers attempt to instruct students in new content or learning strategies, efforts are made by the teacher to access student prior knowledge so as to link it with new information. In allowing students to present and discuss their prior knowledge and experiences, the teacher legitimizes and treats as valuable student language and cultural experiences usually ignored in classrooms. If students are encouraged to speak on what they know best, then they are, in a sense, treated as experts—experts who are expected to refine their knowledge bases with the additional new content and strategy information presented by the teacher.

Teachers play a significant role in creating learning contexts in which students are able to empower themselves. Teachers act as cultural mentors of sorts when they introduce students not only to the culture of the classroom, but to particular subjects and discourse styles as well. In the process, teachers assist the students in appropriating the skills (in an additive fashion) for themselves so as to enable them to behave as "insiders" in the particular subject or discipline. Jim Gee (1989) reminds us that the social nature of teaching and learning must involve apprenticeship into the subject's or discipline's discourse in order for students to do well in school. This apprenticeship includes acquisition of particular content matter, ways of organizing content, and ways of using language (oral and written). Gee adds that these discourses are not mastered solely through teacher-centered and directed instruction, but also by "apprenticeship into social practices through scaffolded and supported interaction with people who have already mastered the discourse" (p. 7). The apprenticeship notion can be immensely useful with subordinated students if it facilitates the acceptance and valorization of students' prior knowledge through a mentoring process.

Models of instruction, such as strategic teaching, can promote such an apprenticeship. In the process of apprenticing linguistic minority students, teachers must interact in meaningful ways with them. This human interaction not only assists students in acquiring new knowledge and skills, but it also often familiarizes individuals from different SES and racial/ethnic groups, and creates mutual respect instead of the antagonism that so frequently occurs between teachers and their students from subordinated groups. In this learning environment, teachers and students learn from each other. The strategies serve, then, not to "fix" the student, but to equalize power relations and to humanize the teacher–student relationship. Ideally, teachers are forced to challenge implicitly or explicitly held deficit attitudes and beliefs about their students and the cultural groups to which they belong.

Beyond Teaching Strategies: Towards a Humanizing Pedagogy

When I recall a special education teacher's experience related in a bilingualism and literacy course that I taught, I am reminded of the humanizing effects of teaching strategies that, similar to culturally responsive instruction and strategic teaching, allow teachers to listen, learn from, and mentor their students. This teacher, for most of her career, had been required to assess her students through a variety of closed-ended instruments, and then to remediate their diagnosed "weaknesses" with discrete skills instruction. The assessment instruments provided little information to explain why the student answered a question either correctly or incorrectly, and they often confirmed perceived student academic, linguistic, and cognitive weaknesses. This fragmented discrete skills approach to instruction restricts the teacher's access to existing student knowledge and experiences not specifically elicited by the academic tasks. Needless to say, this teacher knew very little about her students other than her deficit descriptions of them.

As part of the requirements for my course, she was asked to focus on one Spanish-speaking, limited English proficient special education student over the semester. She observed the student in a number of formal and informal contexts, and she engaged him in a number of open-ended tasks. These tasks included allowing him to write entire texts, such as stories and poems (despite diagnosed limited English proficiency), and to engage in "think-alouds" during reading.[9] Through these open-ended activities, the teacher learned about her student's English writing ability (both strengths and weaknesses), his life experiences and world views, and his meaning-making strategies for reading. Consequently, the teacher constructed an instructional plan much better suited to her student's academic needs and interests. And even more important, she underwent a humanizing process that allowed her to recognize the varied and valuable life experiences and knowledge her student brought into the classroom.

This teacher was admirably candid when she shared her initial negative and stereotypic views of the student and her radical transformation. Despite this teacher's mastery of content area, her lack of political clarity blinded her to the oppressive and dehumanizing nature of instruction offered to linguistic minority students. Initially, she had formed an erroneous notion of her student's personality, worldview, academic ability, motivation, and academic potential on the basis of his Puerto Rican ethnicity, low SES background, limited English proficiency, and moderately learning-disabled label. Because of the restricted and closed nature of earlier assessment and instruction, the teacher had never received information about her student that challenged her negative perceptions. Listening to her student and reading his poetry and stories, she discovered his loving and sunny personality, learned his personal history, and identified academic strengths and weaknesses. In the process, she discovered and challenged her deficit orientation. The following excerpt from this student's writing exemplifies the power of the student voice for humanizing teachers:

My Father

I love my father very much. I will never forget what my father has done for me and my brothers and sisters. When we first came from Puerto Rico we didn't have food to eat and we were very poor. My father had to work three jobs to put food and milk on the table. Those were hard times and my father worked so hard that we hardly saw him. But even when I didn't see him, I always knew he loved me very much. I will always be grateful to my father. We are not so poor now and so he works only one job. But I will never forget what my father did for me. I will also work to help my father have a better life when I grow up. I love my father very much.

The process of learning about her student's rich and multifaceted background enabled this teacher to move beyond the rigid methodology that had required her to distance herself from the student and to confirm the deficit model to which she unconsciously adhered. In this case, the meaningful teacher–student interaction served to equalize the teacher–student power relations and to humanize instruction by expanding the horizons through which the student demonstrated human qualities, dreams, desires, and capacities that closed-ended tests and instruction never captured.

I believe that the specific teaching methods implemented by the teacher, in and of themselves, were not the significant factors. The actual strengths of methods depend, first and foremost, on the degree to which they embrace a humanizing pedagogy that values the student's background knowledge, culture, and life experiences, and creates learning contexts where power is shared by students and teachers. Teaching methods are a means to an end—humanizing education to promote academic success for students historically underserved by the schools. A teaching strategy is a vehicle to a greater goal. A number of vehicles exist that may or may not lead to a humanizing pedagogy, depending on the sociocultural reality in which teachers and students operate.

The critical issue is the degree to which we hold the moral conviction that we must humanize the educational experience of students from subordinated populations by eliminating the hostility that often confronts these students. This process would require that we cease to be overly dependent on methods as technical instruments and adopt a pedagogy that seeks to forge a cultural democracy where all students are treated with respect and dignity. A true cultural democracy forces teachers to recognize that students' lack of familiarity with the dominant values of the curriculum "does not mean . . . that the lack of these experiences develops in these children a different 'nature' that determines their absolute incompetence" (Freire, 1993, p. 17).

Unless educational methods are situated in the student's cultural experiences, students will continue to show difficulty in mastering content area that is not only alien to their reality, but is often antagonistic toward their culture and lived experiences. Further, not only will these methods continue to fail students, particularly those from subordinated groups, but they will never lead to the creation of schools as true culturally democratic sites. For this reason, it is imperative that teachers problematize the prevalent notion of "magical" methods and incorporate what Macedo (1994) calls an anti-methods pedagogy, a process through which teachers 1) critically deconstruct the ideology that informs the methods fetish prevalent in education, 2) understand the intimate relationships between methods and the theoretical underpinnings that inform these methods, and 3) evaluate the pedagogical consequences of blindly and uncritically replicating methods without regard to students' subordinate status in terms of cultural, class, gender, and linguistic difference. In short, we need

> an anti-methods pedagogy that would reject the mechanization of intellectualism . . . [and] challenge teachers to work toward reappropriation of endangered dignity and toward reclaiming our humanity. The anti-methods pedagogy adheres to the eloquence of Antonio Machado's poem, "Caminante, no hay camino, se hace camino al andar." (Traveler, there are no roads. The road is created as we walk it [together]).
>
> (Macedo, 1994, p. 8)

Notes

1. The term "technical" refers to the positivist tradition in education that presents teaching as a precise and scientific undertaking and teachers as technicians responsible for carrying out (preselected) instructional programs and strategies.

2. "Subordinated" refers to cultural groups that are politically, socially, and economically subordinate in the greater society. While individual members of these groups may not consider themselves subordinate in any manner to the White "mainstream," they nevertheless are members of a greater collective that historically has been perceived and treated as subordinate and inferior by the dominant society. Thus it is not entirely accurate to describe these students as "minority" students, since the term connotes numerical minority rather than the general low status (economic, political, and social) these groups have held and that I think is important to recognize when discussing their historical academic underachievement.

3. "Chicana" refers to a woman of Mexican ancestry who was born and/or reared in the United States.

4. "Mainstream" refers to the U.S. macroculture that has its roots in Western European traditions. More specifically, the major influence on the United States, particularly on its institutions, has been the culture and traditions of White, Anglo-Saxon Protestants (WASP) (Golnick & Chinn, 1986). Although the mainstream group is no longer composed solely of WASPs, members of the middle class have adopted traditionally WASP bodies of knowledge, language use, values, norms, and beliefs.

5. "Political clarity" refers to the process by which individuals achieve a deepening awareness of the sociopolitical and economic realities that shape their lives and their capacity to recreate them. In addition, it refers to the process by which individuals come to better understand possible linkages between macro-level political, economic, and social variables and subordinated groups' academic performance at the micro-level classroom. Thus, it invariably requires linkages between sociocultural structures and schooling.

6. Elizabeth Cohen (1986) explains that in the society at large there are status distinctions made on the basis of social class, ethnic group, and gender. These status distinctions are often reproduced at the classroom level, unless teachers make conscious efforts to prevent this reproduction.

7. For detailed discussions regarding various deficit views of subordinated students over time, see Flores, Cousin, and Diaz, 1991; also see Sue and Padilla, 1986.

8. "Cultural capital" refers to Pierre Bourdieu's concept that certain forms of cultural knowledge are the equivalent of symbolic wealth in that these forms of "high" culture are socially designated as worthy of being sought and possessed. These cultural (and linguistic) knowledge bases and skills are socially inherited and are believed to facilitate academic achievement. See Lamont and Lareau, 1988, for a more in-depth discussion regarding the multiple meanings of cultural capital in the literature.

9. "Think-alouds" refers to an informal assessment procedure where readers verbalize all their thoughts during reading and writing tasks. See J. A. Langer, 1986, for a more in-depth discussion of think-aloud procedures.

References

Anyon, J. (1988). Social class and the hidden curriculum of work. In J.R. Gress (Ed.), *Curriculum: An introduction to the field* (pp. 366–389). Berkeley, CA: McCutchan.

Au, K. H. (1979). Using the experience text relationship method with minority children. *The Reading Teacher, 32,* 677–679.

Au, K. H. (1980). Participant structures in a reading lesson with Hawaiian children: Analysis of a culturally appropriate instructional event. *Anthropology and Educational Quarterly, 11,* 91–115.

Au, K. H., & Mason, J. M. (1983). Cultural congruence in classroom participation structures: Achieving a balance of rights. *Discourse Processes, 6,* 145–168.

Avelar La Salle, R. (1991). *The effect of metacognitive instruction on the transfer of expository comprehension skills: The interlingual and cross-lingual cases.* Unpublished doctoral dissertation, Stanford University.

Bloom, G. M. (1991). *The effects of speech style and skin color on bilingual teaching candidates' and bilingual teachers' attitudes toward Mexican American pupils.* Unpublished doctoral dissertation, Stanford University.

Boykin, A. W. (1983). The academic performance of Afro-American children. In J. T. Spence (Ed.), *Achievement and achievement motives: Psychological and sociological approaches* (pp. 322–369). San Francisco: W. H. Freeman.

Carter, T. P., & Chatfield, M. L. (1986) Effective bilingual schools: Implications for policy and practice. *American Journal of Education, 95,* 200–232.

Cazden, C. (1988). *Classroom discourse: The language of teaching and learning.* Portsmouth, NH: Heinemann.

Chall, J. (1983). *Stages of reading development.* New York: McGraw-Hill.

Chamot, A. U. (1983). How to plan to transfer curriculum from bilingual to mainstream instruction. *Focus, 12.* (A newsletter aviable from The George Washington University National Clearinghouse for Bilingual Education, 1118 22nd St. NW, Washington, DC 20037).

Cohen, E. G. (1986). *Designing groupwork: Strategies for the heterogeneous classroom.* New York: Teachers College Press.

Cummins, J. (1989). *Empowering minority students.* Sacramento: California Association of Bilingual Education.

Delpit, L. (1986). Skills and other dilemmas of a progressive black educator. *Harvard Educational Review, 56,* 379–385.

Delpit, L. (1988). The silenced dialogue: Power and pedagogy in educating other people's children. *Harvard Educational Review, 58,* 280–298.

Diaz, S., Moll, L. C., & Mehan, H. (1986). Sociocultural resources in instruction: A context-specific approach. In *Beyond language: Social and cultural factors in schooling language minority students* (pp. 187–230). Los Angeles: California State University, Evaluation, Dissemination and Assessment Center.

Edelsky, C., Altwerger, B., & Flores, B. (1991). *Whole language: What's the difference?* Portsmouth, NH: Heinemann.

Erickson, F., & Mohatt, G. (1982). Cultural organization of participation structures in two classrooms of Indian students. In G. Spindler (Ed.), *Doing the ethnography of schooling: Educational anthropology in action* (pp. 133–174). New York: Holt, Rinehart and Winston.

Flores, B. M. (1982). *Language interference or influence: Toward a theory for Hispanic bilingualism.* Unpublished doctoral dissertation, University of Arizona at Tucson.

Flores, B. M. (1993, April). *Interrogating the genesis of the deficit view of Latino children in the educational literature during the 20th century.* Paper presented at the American Educational Research Association Conference, Atlanta.

Flores, B., Cousin, P. T., & Diaz, E. (1991). Critiquing and transforming the deficit myths about learning, language and culture. *Language Arts, 68,* 369–379.

Freire, P. (1985). *The politics of education: Culture, power and liberation.* South Hadley, MA: Bergin & Garvey.

Freire, P. (1987). Letter to North-American teachers. In I. Shor (Ed.), *Freire for the classroom* (pp. 211–214). Portsmouth, NJ: Boynton/Cook.

Freire, P. (1993). *A pedagogy of the city.* New York: Continuum Press.

Freire, P., & Macedo, D. (1987). *Literacy: Reading the word and the world.* South Hadley, MA: Bergin & Garvey.

Gee, J. P. (1989). Literacy, discourse, and linguistics: Introduction. *Journal of Education, 171,* 5–17.

Gibson, M. A., & Ogbu, J. U. (1991). *Minority status and schooling: A comparative study of immigrant and involuntary minorities.* New York: Garland.

Giroux, H. (1985). Introduction. In P. Freire, *The politics of education: Culture, power and liberation* (pp. xi–xxv). South Hadley, MA.: Bergin & Garvey.

Giroux, H. (1992). *Border crossing: Cultural workers and the politics of education.* New York: Routledge.

Giroux, H., & McLaren, P. (1986). Teacher education and the politics of engagement: The case for democratic schooling. *Harvard Educational Review, 56,* 213–238.

Golnick, D. M., & Chinn, P. C. (1986). *Multicultural education in a pluralistic society.* Columbus, OH: Merrill.

Heath, S. B. (1983). *Ways with words.* New York: Cambridge University Press.

Hernandez, J. S. (1991). Assisted performance in reading comprehension strategies with non-English proficient students. *Journal of Educational Issues of Language Minority Students, 8,* 91–112.

Jones, B. F., Palinscar, A. S., Ogle, D. S., & Carr, E. G. (1987). *Strategic teaching and learning: Cognitive instruction in the content areas.* Alexandria, VA: Association for Supervision and Curriculum Development.

Knapp, M. S., & Shields, P. M. (1990). *Better schooling for the children of poverty: Alternatives to conventional wisdom: Vol. 2. Commissioned papers and literature review.* Washington, DC: U.S. Department of Education.

Lamont, M., & Lareau, A. (1988). Cultural capital-allusions, gaps and glissandos in recent theoretical developments. *Sociological Theory, 6,* 153–168.

Langer, J. A. (1986). *Children reading and writing: Structures and strategies.* Norwood, New Jersey: Ablex.

Lareau, A. (1990). *Home advantage: Social class and parental intervention in elementary education.* New York: Falmer Press.

Lucas, T., Henze, R., & Donato, R. (1990). Promoting the success of Latino language-minority students: An exploratory study of six high schools. *Harvard Educational Review, 60,* 315–340.

Macedo, D. (1994). Preface. In P. McLaren & C. Lankshear (Eds.), *Conscientization and resistance* (pp. 1–8). New York: Routledge.

McDermott, R. P. (1977). Social relations as contexts for learning in school. *Harvard Educational Review, 47,* 198–213.

McLeod, B. (Ed.). (1994). *Language and Learning: Educating Linguistically Diverse Students.* Albany: State University of New York Press.

Means, B., & Knapp, M. S. (1991). *Teaching advanced skills to educationally disadvantaged students.* Washington, DC: U.S. Department of Education.

Mehan, H. (1992). Understanding inequality in schools: The contribution of interpretive studies. *Sociology of Education, 65*(1), 1–20.

Menchaca, M., & Valencia, R. (1990). Anglo-Saxon ideologies in the 1920s–1930s: Their impact on the segregation of Mexican students in California. *Anthropology and Education Quarterly, 21,* 222–245.

Moll, L. C. (1986). Writing as communication: Creating learning environments for students. *Theory Into Practice, 25,* 102–110.

Oaks, J. (1986). Tracking, inequality, and the rhetoric of school reform: Why schools don't change. *Journal of Education, 168,* 61–80.

Ogbu, J. (1987). Variability in minority responses to schooling: Nonimmigrants vs. immigrants. In G. Spindler & L. Spindler (Eds.), *Interpretive ethnography of education* (pp. 255–280). Hillsdale, NJ: Lawrence Erlbaum Associates.

O'Malley, J., & Chamot, A. U. (1990). *Learning strategies in second language acquisition.* New York: Cambridge University Press.

Palinscar, A. S., & Brown, A. L. (1984). Reciprocal teaching of comprehension fostering and comprehension-monitoring activities. *Cognition and Instruction, 1*(23), 117–175.

Pérez, B., & Torres-Guzmán, M. E. (1992). *Learning in two worlds: An integrated Spanish/English biliteracy approach.* New York: Longman.

Philips, S. U. (1972). Participant structures and communication competence: Warm Springs children in community and classroom. In C. B. Cazden, V. P. John, & D. Hymes (Eds.), *Functions of language in the classroom* (pp. 370–394). New York: Teachers College Press.

Reyes, M. de la Luz. (1987). Comprehension of content area passages: A study of Spanish/English readers in the third and fourth grade. In S. R. Goldman & H. T. Trueba (Eds.), *Becoming literate in English as a second language* (pp. 107–126). Norwood, NJ: Ablex.

Reyes, M. de la Luz. (1991). A process approach to literacy during dialogue journals and literature logs with second language learners. *Research in the Teaching of English, 25,* 291–313.

Reyes, M. de la Luz. (1992). Challenging venerable assumptions: Literacy instruction for linguistically different students. *Harvard Educational Review, 62,* 427–446.

Sue, S., & Padilla, A. (1986). Ethnic minority issues in the U.S.: Challenges for the educational system. In *Beyond language: Social and cultural factors in schooling language minority students* (pp. 35–72). Los Angeles: California State University, Evaluation, Dissemination and Assessment Center.

Tikunoff, W. (1985). *Applying significant bilingual instructional features in the classroom.* Rosslyn, VA: National Clearinghouse for Bilingual Education.

Tinajero, J. V., & Ada, A. F. (1993). *The power of two languages: Literacy and biliteracy for Spanish-speaking students.* New York: Macmillan/McGraw-Hill.

Trueba, H. T. (1989). Sociocultural integration of minorities and minority school achievement. In *Raising silent voices: Educating the linguistic minorities for the 21st century* (pp. 1–27). New York: Newbury House.

U.S. Commission on Civil Rights. (1973). *Teachers and students: Report V. Mexican-American study: Differences in teacher interaction with Mexican-American and Anglo students.* Washington, DC: Government Printing Office.

Valencia, R. (1986, November 25). *Minority academic underachievement: Conceptual and theoretical considerations for understanding the achievement problems of Chicano students.* Paper presented to the Chicano Faculty Seminar, Stanford University.

Valencia, R. (1991). *Chicano school failure and success: Research and policy agendas for the 1990s.* New York: Falmer Press.

Villegas, A. M. (1988). School failure and cultural mismatch: Another view. *Urban Review, 20,* 253–265.

Villegas, A. M. (1991). *Culturally responsive pedagogy for the 1990s and beyond.* Paper prepared for the Educational Testing Service, Princeton, NJ.

Vogt, L. A., Jordan, C., & Tharp, R. G. (1987). Explaining school failure, producing school success: Two cases. *Anthropology & Education Quarterly, 18,* 276–286.

Walker, C. L. (1987). Hispanic achievement: Old views and new perspectives. In H. T. Trueba (Ed.), *Success or failure: Learning and the language minority student* (pp. 15–32). New York: Newbury House.

Webb, L. C. (1987). *Raising achievement among minority students.* Arlington, VA: American Associates of School Administrators.

Winfield, L. F. (1986). Teachers beliefs toward academically at risk students in inner urban schools. *Urban Review, 18,* 253–267.

Zamel, V. (1982). Writing: The process of discovering meaning. *TESOL Quarterly, 16,* 195–209.

Suggested Readings for Future Study

Bartolomé, L. (1998). *The Misteaching of Academic Discourses: The Politics of Language in the Classroom.* Boulder, CO: Westview.

Bizell, P. (1992). *Academic Discourse and Critical Consciousness.* Pittsburgh: University of Pittsburgh Press.

Cameron, D. (1990). *The Feminist Critique of Language: A Reader.* New York: Routledge.

Chomsky, N. (1977). *Language and Responsibility.* New York: Pantheon.

Courts, P. (1991). *Literacy and Empowerment.* Westport, CT: Bergin & Garvey.

Crawford, J. (1992). *Hold your Tongue: Bilingualism and the Politics of "English only."* New York: Addison-Wesley.

Crawford-Lange, Linda M. (1981). "Redirecting foreign language curricula: Paulo Freire's contribution," *Foreign Language Annals* 14: 257–273.

Crookes, Graham (1993). "Action research for SL teachers—going beyond teacher research." *Applied Linguistics* 14(2): 130–144.

Cummins, J. (1996). *Negotiating Identities: Education for Empowerment in a Diverse Society.* Ontario, CA: California Association for Bilingual Educators.

Davis, K. (1995). "Qualitative theory and methods in applied linguistics research." *TESOL Quarterly* 29(3): 427–453.

Delpit, L. (1995). *Other Peoples' Children: Cultural Conflict in the Classroom.* New York: The New Press.

Diaz-Soto, L. (1997). *Language, Culture and Power.* Albany: SUNY Press.

Fairclough, N. (1995). *Critical Discourse Analysis: The Critical Study of Language.* New York: Longman.

Freire, P. and Macedo, D. (1987). *Literacy, Reading the Word and the World.* South Hadley, MA: Bergin & Garvey.

Fowler, R., Hodge, B., Kress, G., and Trew, T. (1979). *Language and Control.* Boston: Routledge.

Frederickson, J. and Ada, A., eds. (1995). *Reclaiming our Voices: Bilingual Education, Critical Pedagogy and Praxis.* Ontario, CA: California Association for Bilingual Education.

Gallego, M. and Hollingsworth, S., eds. (2000). *What Counts as Literacy: Challenging the School Standard.* New York: Teachers College.

Gee, J. (1992). *The Social Mind: Language, Ideology and Social Practice.* Westport, CT: Bergin & Garvey.

Giroux, H. (2005). "Literacy, Critical Pedagogy and Empowerment," in *Schooling and the Struggle for Public Life: Democracy's Promise and Education's Challenge*, pp. 147–172. Boulder, CO: Paradigm Publishers.

Holquist, M. (1981). *The Dialogic Imagination: Four Essays by M. M. Bakhtin.* Austin: University of Texas Press.

Illich, I. and Sanders, B. (1988). *ABC: The Alphabetization of the Popular Mind.* New York: Vintage.

Macedo, D. (1994). *Literacies of Power.* Boulder, CO: Westview.

McCarty, T. L. (2002). *A place to be Navajo: Rough Rock and the struggle for self determination in indigenous schooling.* Mahwah, NJ: Lawrence Erlbaum.

Mayo, P. (2004). "Critical Literacy, Praxis and Emancipatory Politics," in *Liberating Praxis: Paulo Freire's legacy for radical education and politics.* Westport, CT: Praeger Publishers.

Mitchell, C. and Weiler, K. (1991). *Rewriting Literacy.* New York: Bergin & Garvey.

Nettle, D. and Romaine, S. (2000). *Vanishing Voices: The Extinction of the World's Languages.* New York: Oxford University Press.

Pruyn, M. (1999). *Discourse wars in Gotham-West: A Latino immigrant urban tale of resistance and agency.* Boulder, CO: Westview.

Shannon, P. (1989). *Broken Promises: Reading Instruction in Twentieth-Century America.* South Hadley, MA: Bergin & Garvey.

Skutnabb-Kangas, T. (2000). *Linguistic Genocide in Education or Worldwide Diversity and Human Rights?* Mahwah, NJ: Lawrence Erlbaum.

Talbot, Mary (1998). *Language and gender: An introduction.* New York: Polity Press.

Verplaetse, L. S. and Migliacci, N. (2007). *Inclusive Pedagogy for English Language Learners.* New York: Routledge.

Part Six

Critical Issues in the Classroom

Introduction to Part Six

The current conservative educational climate in the United States is reflected in the violent imposition of high-stakes testing and test-prep curriculum in schools across the nation. These practices resoundingly echo the "banking" approach to education at the center of Freire's critique of traditional schooling. Accountability measures, standardized curriculum, and instrumentalized teaching approaches have all worked to strip education of its democratic ideals and transformative potential. Conservative educational policies, such as "No Child Left Behind" (NCLB), have effectively derailed the development of critical abilities among poor and working-class students, by aligning the school curriculum with the imperatives of a grossly stratified labor market. Rather than creating educational opportunities, as advocates claim, NCLB's privatization agenda imposes teaching regimes that deskill teachers, corrupt classroom practice, and reduce learning to rote memorization—all factors that contribute to poor academic achievement.

The consequence of such neoliberalism is the intensification of a deeply stratified society, where wealthier students are guaranteed opportunities at the top, while the majority of poor and working-class public school students are educated to enter the vast pool of low skilled, poorly paid workers, at the bottom. This phenomenon persists despite NCLB rhetoric to the contrary, for it fails to address fundamentally the most significant reason why children are left behind—namely, rampant economic inequalities. When the quality of education is reduced to test scores and credentials, emancipatory classroom practices that support the development of voice, participation, and community self-determination easily slip by the wayside. In place of open democratic exchange and pedagogical vitality, teachers face mountains of paperwork, teacher-proof curriculum, low teacher morale, increased surveillance, and the unbridled corporate colonization of every aspect of schooling.

This constitutes the contemporary arena in which educators struggle to keep alive the principles of a critical pedagogical practice. These teachers often seek both a clear understanding of the institutional dynamics at work, as well as classroom strategies to help them enact their commitment to democratic schooling. The articles in the section capture three important facets of classroom life. These include an analysis of the detrimental effect of testing policies on schools, the examination of the silencing of disability in K-16 education, and an effective revisiting of Freire's *Pedagogy of the Oppressed*, to gleam strategies for transforming the insidious and alienating conditions at work in schools today.

Summary of Articles

In Pauline Lipman's article, *Beyond Accountability*, she maintains that the invasive politics of the accountability and standardization movement is ravaging public schools, by pushing out teachers committed to an emancipatory education. Lipman insists that the mandates of NCLB have robbed public education of the democratic possibilities that Dewey envisioned at an earlier time. She contends that the politics of globalization have entered school life and appropriated its discourses. So, *equity* has now become *meritocracy*; while *knowledge* has been converted to *rational information and efficiency*. Along the same lines, *equal opportunity* has been reduced to *tracking*; *access* defined by the *needs of labor*; and *literacy* has been reduced to *functional skills*, necessary for menial employment. Lipman further argues that "*good schools*" has become NCLB's euphemism for colonial education, where social control and accountability, as surveillance, impose a "stratified knowledge for a stratified society." However, despite these dismal conditions, Lipman offers concrete examples of counterhegemonic education and inspiring school practices. She presents three case studies: the Citizen School Project in Brazil, the Milwaukee-based Teacher Journal *Rethinking Schools*, and the Culturally Relevant Pedagogy for African-American students, as popularized by Lisa Delpit, Michele Foster, Gloria Ladson-Billings, and others.

In *Standardized Defensive Teaching and the Problem of Control*, Linda McNeil focuses on the detrimental effects of standardization on the quality of teaching. She exposes the fallacious claim that standardization narrows the achievement gap. Instead, McNeil contends that standardization widens the achievement gap and increases schooling inequalities, through fragmenting the curriculum, lowering teacher and student expectations, and undermining the validity of expressly democratic educational ideals. Similar to Lipman's finding, McNeil concludes that neoliberal education reform efforts are undermining the liberatory potential of public schooling in the US.

Linda Ware's article, *Writing, Identity, and the Other: Dare We do Disability Studies*, addresses one of the most silenced and pathologized issues in primary, secondary, and tertiary education—namely, disability. Ware argues that disability is a social construction, in the same way that gender and race have been created to mask political economic forms of domination. She proposes to move the discussion of disability from a biological construct to a cultural signifier, calling for the development of a field of disability studies within critical pedagogy that can challenge the oppressive educational discourses and practices tied to disablism.

Paula Allman asserts in *Paulo Freire's Contribution to Radical Adult Education* that Freire not only developed a philosophy of education, but more importantly provided a strategizing platform from which to carry out emancipatory educational projects, in the face of difficult conditions faced daily by oppressed populations. Allman's analysis, illuminated by her understanding of historical materialism, examines the seminal tenets of Freire's philosophy, among them dialectical theory, praxis, dialogue, conscientization, and cultural action. She reaffirms Freire's vision that all social transformation is necessarily educational, and that all emancipatory education implies a redefinition of teaching and learning and a redefinition of our relationship with knowledge. Lastly, Allman reminds us that Freire's utmost concern with any transformative project is that it should be, above all, eminently humanizing.

Questions for Reflection and Dialogue

1. What are the hidden values and ideas that inform the accountability and standardization movement? What are its implications for the future of public education?
2. In what ways is the neoliberal discourse of accountability and standardization reforms propelled by globalization? Explain.
3. What kinds of changes would have to be made in public schools in order to implement an emancipatory vision of disability?
4. How might you apply Linda Ware's vision of disability in your own classroom practices? In your personal life?
5. Did Paula Allman's analysis of Paulo Freire clarify your understanding of a critical pedagogical vision of schooling? If yes, how? If no, why not?
6. In what ways might Allman's analysis assist teachers in their implementation of critical pedagogy in the classroom? Explain.

18

Beyond Accountability: Toward Schools that Create New People for a New Way of Life

Pauline Lipman

In February 2003, I was having dinner with several friends, all Chicago Public Schools (CPS) teachers. As I looked around the table, I saw stress etched into everyone's face. One friend, who teaches sixth grade, described going to the opera for the first time and being shocked at her own lack of analytical keenness. "And that's something I'm really good at, literary analysis." With all the constant monitoring and test preparation, she said, she just has no time to think. "I want to do those creative things in the classroom, but there's just no space. What happened to the intellectual excitement? I feel like I'm operating on a low 6th grade level." Another teacher talked about feeling schizophrenic. She is active in Teachers for Social Justice, but in her school she finds herself doing things against her beliefs in order to manage a situation in which the pressures of accountability are worse than ever and the social stress on kids rebounds on the classroom. A new high school teacher, also a social activist, with two master's degrees, said, "If it's going to be like this, more mandates every day and no time, I don't think I can do this job for more than three or four years. And this is what I want to do." These are some of the most thoughtful, committed, critically minded teachers I know.

January 2003: At a meeting of CPS students and teachers, a student at one of the city's regular high schools (I'll call him Manuel) described his school. It is so overcrowded they are on double shifts. There are forty kids in a class, and his math class shares a classroom with an English class. It is hard to concentrate on math with the English teacher right next to him. There are lockers for only one third of the students, and the students are not allowed to wear coats and backpacks in school (CPS discipline policy). It is winter, so lots of kids just do not go to school because they do not have lockers. He missed school for two weeks in the fall for this reason. Finally he found a friend who let him share his locker. There are three kids and all their stuff is in one narrow locker. Half of his chemistry lab is roped off because there is a big hole in the floor. Some of his teachers are not teaching in their subject area, and the curriculum provides no space for his voice; nor is it relevant to the serious issues he and his friend grappled with in their lives. Manuel is a senior, and he has been bombarded by military recruiters promising him training, job skills, free college tuition. That is the only recruitment he has seen. He has received no college counseling and does not think he has a future in college. There are few true college prep classes in his high school expect for the small, selective IB program. Manuel is a leader of a citywide student activist organization.

These stories capture a slice of life in Chicago's mostly nonselective public schools eight years after the introduction of a regime of accountability that, in many respects, has become national policy with George W. Bush's *No Child Left Behind* (NCLB) (2001).

NCLB crystallizes neoliberal, business-oriented education policy.[1] Business rhetoric of efficiency, accountability, and performance standards and the redefinition of education to serve the labor market have become the common vocabulary of educational policies across the United States, and increasingly, globally. Chicago embodies this agenda in action, with its high stakes testing and penalties for failure and its differentiated schools (a variant on neoliberal school choice). Under NCLB, every school district and every school will be measured, driven, and sanctioned or rewarded on the basis of its students' performance on standardized tests. Test-driven, standardized teaching is one product of this agenda, except in selective or high-scoring schools that negotiate or are exempted from it.[2] In practice, having served as a stalking horse for NCLB, Chicago is now ironically circumscribed by it even as some officials talk about new teaching initiatives. In a NCLB world of state regulation, deviation from this agenda has become even more difficult. In my last interview with Ms. Grimes, Westview's principal, she defined the power of the national policy context: "If they're not able to master what's on that Iowa, I don't care what other things you're taught. Looking at it from what Bush is looking for, you're not taught. You are a failing school" (January 2001). What we can learn from accountability, centralized regulation, standardization, and differentiated schools in Chicago has implications for what is meant to be the national norm.

Chicago has a specific history and the school district has its own particularities. And the four schools in this study have their own institutional characters, micropolitics, and histories. What happens behind their brick facades is only partially determined by dominant policies. Moreover, my research is just a brief look at each school. I do not suggest that Chicago and these four schools are representative of U.S. schools or urban school systems. Yet I have attempted, through an overview of CPS policies and an examination of how they play out in four different contexts, to tell stories not told about a hegemonic national education agenda. Thus I hope to say something of what might be expected in other contexts, particularly in relation to issues of educational and social equity, the agency of adults and children, the valuing of cultures and languages, and possibilities for making schools places where children develop tools to critique authorized knowledge and challenge social injustice. In this chapter I summarize some main insights from the school case studies and analysis of districtwide policies and their implications in relation to processes of globalization. I counterpose this emphasis with an outline for an alternative educational agenda and three powerful examples of doing education very differently. These examples challenge hegemonic discourses about education by showing that teachers, administrators, students, and families can create schools and school systems that prepare children to be empowered subjects and critical actors for social change. These examples also concretize the strategic role of education in reconstructing the state and challenging neoliberal hegemony. I conclude by commenting on what these policies mean in a post-9/11 world and possibilities for linking education change with emerging, critically conscious social movements.

Lessons from Chicago

I have argued that the regime of accountability supports processes of economic and social dualization linked to globalization. Education policies concretely and symbolically produce a highly segmented and economically polarized labor force and the reconstitution of urban space as the cultural and material province of real estate developers, corporate headquarters, and the new urban gentry. Accountability language, practices, social relations, and ways of valuing and thinking constitute a discourse of social discipline and subjugation that is highly racialized. They legitimate and produce the regulation and control of youth of color and support the eviction and criminalization of communities of color. In this section, I review these arguments and draw out their implications in the present political context.

Changing the Discourse of, and about, Education

Aligned with a broad social agenda that is retrenching on every social gain wrung from the state in the post-World War II era, neoliberal education discourses shift responsibility for inequality produced by the state onto parents, students, schools, communities, and teachers. Chicago's policies bring these discourses to life. *Equity* ("ending the injustice of social promotion," "holding all students to the same high standards," expanding "a variety of education opportunities") is tied to *individual responsibility* (students who progress are those who "work hard"; failure is publicly penalized through grade retention, assignment to remedial high schools, and school probation). *Technical rationality and efficiency* (educational processes are standardized, centrally prescribed and scripted, and subject to accounting measures) are substituted for the complex ethical and social processes and goals of education. This is lived through test-prep drills, educational triage, and semi-scripted curricula. *Business metaphors* of quality control, accountability, and standards replace any notion of democratic participation in education as a public good in a democratic society. The purpose of education is redefined to develop the skills and dispositions necessary for the labor market of a post-Fordist, globalized capitalism.

The four case studies demonstrate the power of the dominant policy agenda to change educational discourse at the level of the classroom and school. In all four schools, to varying degrees, accountability redefined what it means to be a "good school" in technical and narrowly instrumental terms (Ball, 1997a). The practices induced by accountability and centralized regulation created and exacerbated contradictions between substantive long-term projects to change teaching and learning and short-term accountability-driven goals. This process was illustrated by dropping rich mathematics curricula at Grover and Brewer; undermining a budding process of collective, critical reflection at Brewer; channeling Westview teachers' commitment to their students into raising test scores; and chipping away at Farley teachers' sense of professional efficacy.

In this discourse, teachers who were "good" according to multidimensional and complicated criteria, including those constructed by families and communities, became less so. Teachers recognized for their commitment to children and the community, their determination to help students become people who could "read" and "write" the world (Freire & Macedo, 1987), and their defense of children's language and home culture were ultimately judged by a single, instrumental measure. Students, as well as teachers, with all their varied talents and challenges, were reduced to a test score. And schools, as well as their communities, in all their complexity—their failings, inadequacies, strong points, superb and weak teachers, ethical commitments to collective uplift, their energy, demoralization, courage, potential, and setbacks—were blended, homogenized, and reduced to a stanine score and a narrow business model of "success" or "failure." In the process, brilliant spots in the schools were rubbed out rather than cultivated and extended. A few uncommitted and unprepared teachers were driven out, and others were upgraded to standardized teaching. Instead of inducing schools to develop their curricular and pedagogical strengths, accountability policies promoted or reinforced a narrow focus on specific skills and on test-taking techniques. Instead of supporting and extending the strengths of culturally relevant, critical teachers at Grover and Brewer, the policies drove them out or forced them to accommodate. Even when accountability exposed weaknesses, such as racial disparities in achievement at Farley, the policies did little to help address them and may have reinforced conservatism, out of fear of not drawing attention to issues of race. Despite a vocabulary of excellence that clothes school accountability, this is a discourse that produces mediocrity, conservatism, and narrowly instrumental conceptions of people, learning, and the purposes of education. The policies are given life through social practices in specific contexts. The four schools provide a glimpse of how the "ethical retooling of the public sector to emphasize excellence, effectiveness and quality that can be measured" (Ball, 1990, p. 259) is actually *lived* inside the discourses of accountability in schools.

Reproducing and Extending Inequality

I have also demonstrated that Chicago's education policies reproduce existing educational and social inequalities and create new ones. In the name of "choice" of educational "opportunities," Chicago has superimposed new forms of educational tracking on an already tracked system. This differentiated system illustrates the strategic relationship between new forms of educational tracking and the production of a stratified labor force for the new economy. Carlson's (1997) outline of this trend is remarkably close to Chicago's policies: The academic track is becoming more differentiated from other tracks and more spatially separate through magnet and specialty schools and separate academic programs within schools, thus stripping academic track students from the general high school. These selective programs, employing more constructivist and "higher-order-thinking" curricula, as well as advanced course offerings, prepare students to be knowledge producers in the new economy. The new vocationalism of Education-to-Career Academies creates a closer link between applied vocationalism and academics. At the same time, general high schools provide the new basic literacies (i.e., better than eighth grade reading and math skills and compliant and amiable social dispositions) that correspond to the skills required for the large number of low-skill, low-wage service jobs. Because of the fairly low level of these skills and the emphasis on test-driven practices, the new functional literacies are not conducive to critical literacy. As a whole this system constructs new "selective mechanisms within a system that claims inclusivity" (Ozga, 2000, p. 104). As I have argued, this stratified education produces identities for a stratified labor force, stratified city, and stratified society. Gee, Hull, and Lankshear (1996) point to the social logic of these policies in the context of the capitalist informational economy:

> "Education reform" in terms of ensuring quality schools for everyone is deeply paradoxical, because if everyone were educated there would be no servants. The new capitalism is in danger of producing and reproducing an even steeper pyramid than the old capitalism did. And, just as in the old capitalism, it will need institutions—like schools, first and foremost—to reproduce that social structure. (p. 47)

At the school level, although accountability has pushed some schools, such as Grover, to focus more on curriculum coordination and planning of instruction, my data suggest that it reinforces, even extends inequalities. I observed Farley, a high-scoring multiracial, mixed-class school, to be much less oriented to test-prep than the other three schools that served low-income and working-class African American and Latino/a children. There is virtually no evidence in the data from Grover, Westview, and Brewer that accountability policies helped them develop rich literacies, rigorous curriculum, or challenging intellectual experiences for students. The new policies also created a schism between the professional culture of these three schools, which became more regulated, and that of Farley, whose teachers were able to maintain some independent professional judgment. Particularly at Grover, probation and the school's array of external supervisors promoted technical and routinized approaches to improving instruction, deskilling teachers rather than enriching their thinking and knowledge. Accountability undermined the collective self-study at Brewer and practices and orientations that promoted bilingualism and biculturalism. It worked against critical literacy practices and drove out some of the strongest teachers at Brewer and Grover.

In short, the technical and routinized practices promoted by accountability policies have not helped Grover, Brewer, and Westview acquire the strengths of Farley's rich culture of literacy. Nor have they helped teachers to develop the professional competencies and independent professional judgment of some Farley teachers. These strengths are important elements to ensure that all children have access to an intellectually rigorous and multi-faceted literacy curriculum. If anything, accountability has made them more routinized and pushed out teachers who embodied this professional culture making these schools less like Farley. (See McNeil, 2000; Valenzuela, 1999, for similar findings.) However, the other important issue is that accountability-as-surveillance is likely to promote conservatism in high-scoring schools, reinforcing existing tendencies to avoid controversy and in-depth analysis of politically charged issues of race, culture, educational disparities, as well as critical pedagogies. Taking up these issues is a central challenge, but it is made even more difficult in a coercive climate in which public attention might produce closer monitoring and thus pressures to conform to the dominant agenda.

Education for Social Control

The Chicago example demonstrates how accountability and centralized regulation of schools constitute a regime of social control. This is a system that robs principals, teachers, students, and communities of agency. Through accountability the state shifts responsibility for "success" and "improvement" to the school but gives it less control over its evaluation and less room to maneuver. As a Grover teacher said, "You really don't have too much power or say-so in what goes on." The four schools illustrate concretely how regulation of teaching through direct external oversight, standards, and assessment by high stakes tests strips teachers of opportunities for professional and ethical judgment, further eroding whatever agency teachers, principals, and communities have in relation to their schools. As a result of mandated curricula, imposed standards, and the exigencies of preparing for standardized tests, teachers and communities are losing control of knowledge, to the extent they ever had any. This trend was reflected in the thirteen weeks of test preparation at Westview, the instructional routines dictated by Grover's probation partner, the pressure to teach children English at the expense of their Spanish at Brewer, and the curricular compromises pressed on Farley teachers.

This is a complex set of issues because some teachers need more content and pedagogical knowledge, and in its absence, routines and semiscripted curricula fill this gap, as they did for teaching interns at Grover. But no middle-class school would be likely to accept these technical fixes as a substitute for thoughtful pedagogical decisions. Nor is this an acceptable substitute for the pedagogical judgment, sociopolitical knowledge, and cultural sensitivity of teaching that is culturally and politically relevant to students and their communities. Moreover, imposed standardization negates the contested nature of what should constitute common knowledge (Apple, 1996, 2001; Bohn & Sleeter, 2000) and of what constitutes a good school and good teaching (e.g., Darder, 1995; Delpit, 1988; Ladson-Billings, 1994).

In the schools I studied, teachers faced a moral crisis as they were, to paraphrase one teacher, forced to compromise their beliefs. The public display of individual and school failure and the meting out of punishment by the state remind students, teachers, and communities that they have little power, that they are all "on probation" or in danger of being put there. Accountability becomes a totalizing system that infiltrates all aspects of school life and demands that each level of authority, each classroom, each school, and each grade level capitulate more or less, even if a given class or school is not immediately threatened with sanctions. This process is undergirded by a logic of inevitability. "There will always be tests, each grade needs to prepare students to be tested at the next grade, and if we don't comply, we too may be under tighter surveillance"—so goes the refrain. However, this system is deployed differentially. In the four schools in this study there was a continuum of enforcement, from near-total supervision of Grover to relative flexibility at Farley. This mirrors citywide patterns of race and class differentiation as revealed by the pattern of schools on probation—all enrolling predominantly low-income African Americans or Latinos/as. Thus, although everyone is swallowed up in this system, the accrued race and class advantages of some schools versus others mean that there are different constraints and that policies are "read" and accommodated differently in different contexts with different consequences for human agency.

Accountability works as a panoptic system of surveillance that teaches people to comply and to press others into compliance. This works, in part, because "deficiency" is made visible, individual, easily measured, and highly stigmatized within a hierarchical system of authority and supervision. By holding individuals all along the line—students, teachers, parents—responsible for their own "failure," the system and culture of accountability encourage both self-blame (as with Brewer students who failed the eighth grade ITBS) and passing on of the blame to others in a pecking order that originates in the CPS central office and ends at the student's and teacher's desk and parent's living room. This individualization of blame reinforces race-, ethnicity-, and class-based ideologies of deficient "others."

The four case studies illustrate that accountability, centralized regulation, and differentiated schools are (collectively) a system of social discipline that works through everyday practices in schools to shape student and teacher identities. The policies create actual material conditions—military discipline, routines of Direct Instruction, classroom language of accountability, unending test preparation, privileging of English over students' home language, challenging intellectual discussions, International Baccalaureate programs of study—"that construct the truth of who we are" (Ferguson, 2000, p. 59). Within this continuum, routinized, basic skills and highly regulated and assimilationist practices—delivered without critique—produce docile subjectivities:

> These are forms of power that are realized and reproduced through social interaction within the everyday life of institutions. They play upon the insecurities of the discipline subject. . . .

They do not so much bear down upon but take shape within the practices of the institution itself and construct individuals and their social relations through direct interaction.

(Ball, 1997b, p. 261)

Education Policy as a Racialized System of Regulation

Although all Chicago public schools are subject to surveillance and control by the state, patterns of racial subjugation are clear. Schools in low-income neighborhoods of color are the least in charge of their own destiny. (This is clear from the demographics of schools on probation and is illustrated by the differential regulation of the four schools in this study.) These are schools where both students and teachers are disciplined by the routines and frameworks of standardized tests and external supervision. As Ms. Dupree, a Grover teacher, said: "I don't think their [CPS leaders] children are going through this. And they need to realize that these are human beings. And what kind of effects are you having on the students?" (March 2000). School accountability is not a policy of public engagement in the improvement of schooling. Without any real public discussion or participation of teachers, school administrators, students, and parents, powerful city and school officials have held up these schools in Black and Latino/a neighborhoods, and by implication, their communities, as examples of failure, dictated what will happen in their schools; and undermined Local School Councils. As these policies are "rolled out" nationally, through state accountability systems under *No Child Left Behind*, this trend has serious implications for African Americans and Latinos/as, who are most likely to attend schools with low test scores and thus are most likely to be subject to a model of education as social regulation.

This is a form of colonial education governed by powerful (primarily white) outsiders. It signals that the communities affected have neither the knowledge nor the right to debate and act together with educators to improve their children's education. At Grover and Brewer this process also drove out some of the most committed, critical, and culturally relevant teachers. The loss of these teachers and the consolidation of a technical, instrumental version of education disarm African American and Latino/a students, particularly in a context of growing economic polarization, racial repression, and marginalization. Ladson-Billings's argument (1994) is important here:

> Parents, teachers, and neighbors need to help arm African American children with the knowledge, skills, and attitude needed to struggle successfully against oppression. These, more than test scores, more than high grade point averages, are the critical features of education for African Americans. If students are to be equipped to struggle against racism, they need excellent skills from the basics of reading, writing, and math, to understanding history, thinking critically, solving problems, and making decisions; they must go beyond merely filling in test sheet bubbles with Number 2 pencils. (pp. 139–40)

Accountability is also a highly racialized discourse of deficits. The separation of "good" and "bad" schools, of "failing" and "successful" students, that is accomplished through the testing, sorting, and ordering processes of standardized tests, distribution of stanine scores, retention of students, and determination of probation lists constructs categories of functionality and dysfunctionality, normalcy and deviance. In this sense, the test is, in Foucault's language, "a ritual of power." It embodies the power of the state to sort and define students and schools, creating and reinforcing oppressive power relations (Carlson, 1997) of race and class. "Failing" schools and "failing" students (and by implication, "failing" communities), most African American and Latino/a, are measured against the "success" of schools that are generally more white, more middle-class. Low-income schools of color that are defined as relatively successful in this scheme (Brewer is an example) are marked as exceptions, models of functionality in a sea of dysfunctional "others," much as the military high schools demarcate disciplined youth from undisciplined "others." Policies that regulate and punish especially African American, and to some extent Latino/a, students and schools also contribute to the pathologizing of African American and Latino/a communities. In this way, education policy contributes to the construction of consciousness about race in the city and justifies the containment and eviction of African American and Latino/a communities.

Education Policy and Global Transformations

Education policy in Chicago is strategically linked to the restructured economy, urban development and gentrification, transnational migrations, and the politics of race, ethnicity, and racial exclusion in the city. The social, economic, spatial, and cultural changes in Chicago are both products of and responses to transformations in the global economy since the 1970s. The contradictions and tensions of globalization play out on the streets of the city. Here we see a new urban geography—sweeping contrasts of wealth and poverty, centrality and marginality, blatant corporate and financial power, and growing masses of people of color and immigrants whose labor is essential but whose presence (language, culture, place-making practices, and demands for justice) is unwelcome. These tensions and contradictions also play out in the city's public schools. The story of urban education policy today is embedded in this larger narrative of globalization with its social and economic polarization, urban displacement and exclusion, and the salience of race and ethnicity as well as class. The significance of Chicago's education policies lies in their intersection with these economic, political, and cultural processes.

When we say education policy is another front in the struggle over the direction of globalization (Lipman, 2002), this is not a rhetorical flourish but a statement about material and cultural survival and space for agency and transformation. The policy regime I have described is producing stratified knowledge, skills, dispositions, and identities for a deeply stratified society. Under the rubric of standards, the policies impose standardization and enforce language and cultural assimilation to mold the children of the increasingly linguistically and culturally diverse workforce into a more malleable and governable source of future labor. This is a system that treats people as a means to an end. The "economizing of education" and the discourse of accounting reduce people to potential sources of capital accumulation, manipulators of knowledge for global economic expansion, or providers of the services and accessories of leisure and pleasure for the rich. Students are reduced to test scores, future slots in the labor market, prison numbers, and possible cannon fodder in military conquests. Teachers are reduced to technicians and supervisors in the education assembly line—"objects" rather than "subjects" of history. This system is fundamentally about the negation of human agency, despite the good intentions of individuals at all levels.

The nature of this regime is to produce the docile subjectivities necessary for the maintenance of a world of nearly unfathomable contrasts of wealth and poverty. As Gee, Hull, and Lankshear point out, this is a world "in which a small number of countries and a small number of people within them will benefit substantively from the new capitalism, while a large number of others will be progressively worse off and exploited" (1996, p. 44). Such a polarized world requires the sort of domestication of critical thought and agency that is integral to the regime of accountability and discourses of high stakes testing and central-ized regulation of schooling. It also requires intensified policing, nationally and locally, as well as internationally. The militarization of schooling and regimentation, policing, and criminalization of youth of color become increasingly useful as some African American and Latino/a communities, and especially the youth, are becoming a "fourth world" inside the United States. Again, Gee, Hull and Lanshear (1996): "[I]t has become possible for vast tracts of humanity to be dismissed now as simply having nothing of relevance to contribute to the new world economy" (p. 149). These are key targets of social control.

As global economic processes make gentrification "the cutting edge of urban change" (Smith, 1996, p. 8), education policies become a material force supporting the displace-ment of working-class and low-income communities, the transformation of others into urban ethnic theme parks, and the consolidation of the city as a space of corporate culture, middle-class stability, and whiteness. This is what Neal Smith calls the "class conquest" of the city. New forms of selectivity within and among schools are an important quality of life factor in attracting the high-paid knowledge workers central to globalization and the global city.

At the other end of the spectrum, specialized schooling, such as military schools, that discipline and regulate African Americans and some other people of color also mark them as requiring special forms of social control. This is particularly significant in the context of the global city, with its simultaneous dependence on low-paid labor of people of color, exclusion of those superfluous to the labor force, and need to recruit high-paid, primarily white knowledge workers who want to appropriate the city—neatly boulevarded, gated, and skyscrapered—as their own. Although the racialized policing of youth is nothing new, this has become a vastly expanded social policy and practice as the economy excludes whole sectors and as transnational migrations create a more diverse population of youth. The criminalization of some is related to the assimilation of others as part of the process of differentiated racialization. Schools are central to this process. The ideological force of these policies is deeply implicated in struggles over representation and power in increasingly racially and ethnically diverse urban contexts.

Toward an Alternative Educational Agenda

There is good reason why people back tough measures to ensure that when their children are sent to school, they are taught. That these policies resonate with families and com-munities is a measure of the persistent and urgent need to act immediately and decisively to address the abysmal material and intellectual conditions in too many urban schools. Support for accountability also reflects the absence of a viable alternative that grasps this urgency *and* makes a liberatory agenda concrete. In schools, as well as in the broader public, there is an absence of counterhegemonic discourses that capture the gravity of the current situation in urban schools and press for rich intellectual experiences, cultural and social relevance, democratic participation, and critical thought. More equitable, humane, and liberatory schooling can only grow out of a rich dialogue that includes the multiple perspectives of committed educators and students, families, and communities about what is in the best interest of their children (Delpit, 1988). Specifically, this requires the broad participation and cultural resources of the diverse racially, ethnically, and economically marginalized communities most failed by public schools in the United States. A central problem in Chicago is that city and school officials have captured the common sense about school reform. There an absence of public debate and there is no public forum for fundamentally different perspectives. Moreover, some of the best, most committed teachers who might provide leadership in a more democratic process at the school level, whose practices might be the basis for a liberatory educational program, are being driven out by the current policies.

In part, neoliberal education programs and the drive to accountability and standardization have won out because they have captured the national, even international conversation about education as the only alternative for the "failure" of public schooling. Their hegemonic project has succeeded in redefining education as job preparation, learning as standardized skills and information, educational quality as measurable by test scores, and teaching as the technical delivery of that which is centrally mandated and tested. By defining the problem of education as standards and accountability they have made simply irrelevant any talk about humanity, difference, democracy, culture, thinking, personal meaning, ethical deliberation, intellectual rigor, social responsibility, and joy in education. Challenging the dominant discourse and posing alternative frameworks are strategic aspects of reversing the present direction. Parents, students, and committed teachers—especially those in the communities most affected—can provide a new language of critique and possibility that is grounded in their own knowledge, experiences, and commitments. Critics of current policies need to work together with them, and their perspectives need to be injected into discussions about education. The power of such a participatory process is illustrated by the development of Citizen Schools in Brazil, which I discuss in this chapter.

In the spirit of dialogue, I have suggested (Lipman, 2002) several premises of an alternative agenda. First, all students need an education that is intellectually rich and rigorous and that instills a sense of personal, cultural, and social agency. Students need both the knowledge and skills traditionally associated with academic excellence and a curriculum that is meaningfully related to their lives. They need an education that teaches them to think critically about knowledge and social institutions and locate their own history and cultural identity within broader contexts. Students need an education that instills a sense of hope and possibility that they can make a difference in their own family, school, and community and in the broader national and global community while it prepares them for multiple life choices.

Second, a commitment to educate all students requires the deployment of significant resources. This point almost seems a hollow joke at a moment when the U.S. government spends billions of tax dollars on global military domination and corporate enrichment while there are cutbacks in education funding. But what is needed is nothing short of a massive reconstruction and renewal project. Without new intellectual, cultural, material, and ideological resources, urban schools cannot overcome long-standing problems rooted in racism and a history of neglect. In most urban schools, if not most school systems, there is a compelling need to reduce class size substantially; to provide consistent high-quality professional development and time for teachers to plan and reflect in order to transform the nature of teaching, learning, and assessment; to recruit and retain expert committed teachers in schools in the poorest communities; to provide up-to-date science labs, current and well-stocked school libraries, arts and foreign language programs, state of the art and well-run computer labs. The failure to marshal these resources leads to blaming of communities and democratic policy itself for educational failure. This was the case in Chicago when business leaders and political officials declared that Local School Councils were not "working." Failure due to lack of resources provides a justification for the state to impose controls (Apple, 1991) to overcome the "failed policies of the past," as in Chicago, or to privatize public education, as in Philadelphia. In a period of retrenchment of social benefits at home and squandering of billions in military conquest abroad, the lack of political will for such an investment is self-evident. With huge local and state budget deficits, the necessity to reprioritize federal funding for education is obvious. Although reversing historical inequities requires reciprocal responsibility and participation of educators, students, parents, school leaders, and policy makers, political officials should be held accountable to ensure necessary resources. Obviously, this is a question of political priorities, and will require a social movement to enforce the reallocation of resources from militarism and support of corporate profit to these human needs.

Third, transforming urban schools entails a protracted cultural campaign directed against deficit notions about the potential of low-income children and children of color (Lipman, 1998). Changing entrenched discourses of "ability" and of children and communities as "problems" is obviously complex, long-term, and multifaceted. Clearly it requires the active involvement of parents and children as well as committed educators of children of color and others. The work of urban educators has provided a wealth of knowledge about rich, culturally relevant, critical pedagogies. The beginning process of collective reflection about some of these issues at Brewer hints at possibilities for examining assumptions and ideologies at the school level, as do more developed and systematic programs of preparing teachers to teach in diverse classrooms (e.g., Cochran-Smith, 1995; Ladson-Billings, 2001). There is also a substantial body of research that outlines pedagogical theories that build on the experience, language, and cultural identity of students as a basis for learning and that support the development of critical consciousness and the agency of students of color in particular (e.g., Cummins, 1996; Darder, 1995; Delpit, 1988; Ladson-Billings, 1994).

Finally, the state of urban education is deeply embedded in the state of cities and national and global economic and social priorities. Although much needs to be done in schools, putting the onus on them overlooks the impact of the social-economic context. Although much can be done by committed, culturally relevant, critical educators, the state of education at schools like Grover and Westview cannot be separated from the reality of life in deeply impoverished neighborhoods. Nor can it be addressed without addressing the documented history of inequality and racism that has permeated public schooling in the United States, and urban education in particular. Thus, any serious effort to transform public schools ultimately can only succeed as part of a larger local and global social struggle for material redistribution and cultural recognition (Fraser, 1997).

Policy Borrowing from Below—Three Strategic Models of Counter Hegemonic Education

One effect of globalization has been rapid international policy borrowing among states (Blackmore, 2000). As I noted earlier, this policy borrowing *from above* is reflected in the convergence of neoliberal education policies in Western Europe, the United States, New Zealand, and elsewhere, and in the role of the World Bank in setting educational standards to promote market-driven economies in "developing countries" (Jones, 2000). But as globalization strives to bend all nations, all peoples, all economic sectors and organizations of civil society to the discipline of international capital, the ensuing economic and cultural dislocations and generalized immiseration have given rise to new solidarities and links between disparate social movements across the globe. This is globalization from below. The dialogue among social movements, embodied in the World Social Forum, provides a model of policy borrrowing *from below* (Coates, 2002). Examples of counterhegemonic practices drawn from disparate social contexts can deepen our understanding of how to proceed in a period in which discourses of inevitability preach every day that there is no alternative to the existing social order. Here I want to discuss three quite different, but theoretically linked examples and what we might learn from them.

The first are the Citizen Schools being created by the Workers Party Municipal Government in Porto Alegre, Brazil. In a powerful chapter, Luís Armando Gandin and Michael Apple (2003) describe ways in which these schools concretely challenge neoliberal conceptions of education and their role in the struggle for radical democracy in Brazil. My summary is drawn from their discussion, Gandin's research (2002), and my own investigation in Porto Alegre. The Citizen Schools Project was initiated by the Workers Party not only to create better schools for those students who have been excluded from education in Brazil, particularly the children of the *favelas* (the most impoverished neighborhoods), but also to initiate a pedagogical project in radical democracy. Gandin and Apple outline three aspects of this unfolding project. One, the schools respond to the historical exclusion, failure, and dropping out of poor students by reorganizing the structure of schooling to eliminate the mechanisms that have contributed to the problem in the past. New "cycles of formation" challenge notions of "failure" by assigning students to classes with children of their own age while providing a challenging environment in which they can fill in gaps in their development. Two, the schools reconstitute official knowledge by centering the curriculum on interdisciplinary "thematic complexes" grounded in the central issues facing the favela community. The new epistemological perspective is meant to ensure that students learn Brazilian "high culture," *but through new perspectives* grounded in their sociopolitical reality. A stated goal of the new curriculum is to move the culture and history of Afro-Brazilians to the center to openly challenge racism, a central issue in Brazilian society and a principal form of oppression.[3] Three, Citizen Schools are run by councils of teachers, school staff, parents, students, and one member of the school administration. The responsibility of the council to define the aims and direction of the school, allocate economic resources, and ensure implementation makes them schools of democratic participation and collective governance in their own right. The community power and democracy of these councils are redefining neoliberal notions of accountability, reframing it as collective responsibility to ensure that the school serves the community. These three aspects of the project are captured in the idea of democratization of access, knowledge, and management (Gandin, 2002).

While the schools are attempting to productively address the very serious issues of educational exclusion, most important, their goal is to generate a new way of thinking about society as a whole and who should run it. Gandin and Apple report that the schools—their structure, curriculum, and governance—are part of the creation of a movement that "contains as a real social process, the origins of a new way of life" (p. 196). The Citizen Schools provide a powerful example that education projects can be part of a conscious strategy to challenge dominant discourses about schooling and citizenship. Gandin and Apple (2003) emphasize this point:

> . . . there is a constant struggle to legitimize the experience of the Citizen School, to make it socially visible, to pose the discussion over education in terms other than those of neoliberalism, to pull education from the technical economistic realm favored by neoliberal assumptions

and to push it to a more politicized one that has as its basic concern the role of education in social emancipation. (p. 200)

The democratic participatory experiences of creating and running the schools redefine the relationship of communities to schools and of communities to the state. "They develop the collective capacities among people to enable them to continue to engage in the democratic administration and control of their lives" (p. 195). By reconstructing school knowledge to draw on the experiences of the community and developing the democratic leadership of the councils, Citizen Schools are also attempting to transform the "separation between the ones who 'know' and . . . ones who 'don't know' " (p. 211).

The Citizen School Project clarifies strategic relationships between educational change and the protracted process of concretely transforming society. This is an important theoretical foundation for conceptualizing education reform and its relationship to a larger liberatory social project. The schools embody reforms that build up democratic participation, reconceptualize school knowledge around the perspectives and experiences of the oppressed, and create conditions for poor and marginalized people to see themselves as people with the capacity to run society and experiences in doing so. Although the actual practice is fraught with challenges, this framework is a powerful lens through which to assess the liberatory potential of specific educational policy agendas. It provides an orientation for both the process and the content of policies that move in a liberatory direction. The Citizen Schools also challenge neoliberal educational frameworks by rearticulating elements of the dominant agenda to a liberatory educational framework. This insight helps us think about the ways in which neoliberalism articulates equity to accountability, for example, and how we might rearticulate it to a democratic agenda. In short, the Citizen Schools give us new tools to think and act in the field of education in more strategic ways in the context of neoliberalism.

The second example is the Rethinking Schools project anchored in the Milwaukee-based teacher journal *Rethinking Schools*. Since 1986 the editors of *Rethinking Schools*, most of them teachers, have provided a space for educators to read about social justice curriculum in action as well as educational issues from a critical, antiracist perspective. Articles about teaching, from kindergarten through high school, demonstrate that teachers can develop pedagogies that help children grapple with issues of racism, sexism, homophobia, social inequality, destruction of the environment, globalizaton, war, militarism, repressive discipline, community disinvestment, and more. The power of this journal is that it presents the writing of real teachers going against the grain in real schools, working under real ideological and material constraints. The classrooms they describe provide concrete examples of what critical, antiracist, participatory education looks like. They make possibility tangible, concretely challenging discourses of inevitability and disempowerment. Taken as a whole and over time, the journal constructs a counterhegemonic educational discourse grounded in critical social praxis. *Rethinking Schools* books on topics of curriculum and classroom practice (*Rethinking Our Classrooms*, 1994, 2001), *Rethinking Columbus* (Bigelow & Peterson, 1998), *The Real Ebonics Debate* (Perry & Delpit, 1998), *Reading, Writing, and Rising Up* (Christensen, 2000), and *Rethinking Globalization* (Bigelow & Peterson, 2002, among others), provide a powerful knowledge base for teaching that is grounded in critical social theory, thus directly challenging neoliberal assumptions of teachers as technicians.

These publications and the Rethinking Schools critical listserv are nodes of a national network of critical educational praxis. They establish a community across distance, a center at a time when discourse of inevitability drives out all notions that there are others who also dare to think and act differently. A central insight from the Rethinking Schools project is the strategic importance of social justice teachers' creating public spaces for dialogue and presentation of theoretically grounded alternative practices. These concrete models of practice are an important aspect of building up schools and classrooms that instantiate a counternarrative about schooling, ideologically and practically.

The third example is the practice of culturally relevant, liberatory teachers of African American students. Since the late 1980s, an important body of literature by African American scholars (e.g., Delpit, 1988, 1992b; Foster, 1997; Irvine, 1991; King, 1991; Ladson-Billings, 1994, 2001) has made visible the practices of teachers who draw on the culture of African American students to promote their academic competence and sociopolitical awareness. From studies of the practices of these teachers and the history of Black education in the United States, these scholars have constructed an ensemble of theories of culturally relevant, culturally responsive, emancipatory education for African American students. Drawing on students' African American cultural frame of reference, teachers who are the subjects and collaborators in these studies link literacy with students' social identities. Academic success is connected with developing tools to resist racism and oppression and with social analysis of community issues such as homelessness and global issues such as the Gulf War. Students are encouraged to see themselves as African American intellectual leaders. These theories have made their way into some teacher education programs, into scholarly journals, and onto the programs of national education conferences and have become a fashionable part of conversations among educational researchers. Yet, teaching remains largely color-blind (i.e., white-centered) and disconnected from the sociopolitical realities and psychic experiences of children of color, and the practice of liberatory education for African American students is disconnected from the discourse about education as a whole, including some critical discourse. Yet, these practices and the historically grounded philosophy underpinning them constitute a powerful counterhegemonic discourse.

In an extended essay on African American education, Teresa Perry (2003) explains the philosophy of African American education as "freedom for literacy and literacy for freedom" (see also Murrell, 1997). Perry argues that this philosophy is grounded in African Americans' existential necessity to assert their humanness, their very existence as intellectual beings, in a white supremacist context that historically negated Black intellectual capacity as a central tenet. Literacy from this perspective is a means of personal and collective emancipation and is essential to develop leadership for liberation:

> Read and write yourself into freedom! Read and write to assert your identity as human! Read and write yourself into history! Read and write as an act of resistance, as a political act, for racial uplift, so you can lead your people well in the struggle for liberation! (p. 19)

Thus education is inherently an act of resistance, a political act, and a collective responsibility (see also Anderson, 1988).

I see this philosophy at work in the practices of eight culturally relevant teachers in Ladson-Billings's study (1994) who ground teaching in students' cultural identity, are connected with the students' community, and aim to foster their students' intellectual leadership and critical consciousness about their role in fighting injustice. Despite the restrictive public school settings in which they work, they deliberately go against the grain because they understand education as political. This philosophy is also at work in the narratives of Black teachers (Foster, 1997) who describe challenging racism as central to their work. An Oakland teacher, Carrie Secret (Miner, 1997), exemplifies pedagogy rooted in the centrality of culture and the intersection of culture and power. Secret's culturally responsive classroom foregrounds African American intellectual and creative production and the power of Ebonics as a literary language while developing students' linguistic and cultural competence in the dominant code.

As did Black schools during segregation as described by Perry (2003) and Delpit (1992a), these pedagogies create spaces of resistance, organized to counter the myth of Black inferiority. Perry describes segregated Black schools as " 'figured universes'—or more precisely counterhegemonic figured communities" (p. 91) where African Americans forged a collective identity as literate and achieving people. I would argue that the present-day examples of culturally relevant, liberatory pedagogy fit this description and stand as examples of a fundamentally subversive notion of education for African American students—one we can draw upon in general. Not just academic, education in these classrooms is described as social, cultural, and political—directly counter to the narrow test-driven, technical notions of neoliberal accountability oriented schooling. As a whole, this pedagogical discourse challenges the education-for-work agenda that dominates discussions of education and education reform, particularly for "low-achieving" students of color. This is a praxis that rearticulates equity (framed as test scores in the dominant accountability discourse) to its roots in liberation. Although localized and operating sometimes behind closed doors and in narrow spaces, it is like the Brazilian Citizen Schools that work to transform consciousness about one's subject position in society. In this sense, the practices of culturally relevant emancipatory teachers and the philosophy they embody are challenging the dominant discourse about education and are resources with which concretely to demonstrate a liberatory vision of education. Along with the other two, this is an example of an educational project that can concretize an alternative way of thinking about and doing education that embodies liberatory social processes and specifically challenges the dominant discourse.

Education Policy in a Post-9/11, Preemptive-War Era

When we sort through all the nuances, differences, and complexities, the essence of educational accountability, centralized regulation, policing of youth of color, and standards is the imposition of the authority of the state on the work and consciousness of adults and children in schools. I have argued throughout that the new authoritarianism is both material and ideological, disciplining bodies and minds. In some respects it is hardly new at all. The neoliberal project of recent decades has been the steady erosion of the social welfare functions of the state and expansion of its policing functions. The responsibility of the state to educate children and provide educators and communities with the necessary resources to do so has fully morphed into the role of overseer, judge, and dispenser of rewards and punishments—as well as subcontractor to corporations and supplier for the armed services. But education policies that legislate the policing of schools and schooling take on new and ominous implications in a post-September 11 present of militarism and repression at home and war abroad. School policies that teach people to be docile subjects and that undermine critical thought, imposing a reign of surveillance, coercion, and intimidation, are magnified when we look at them through the lens of the U.S. Patriot Act, Total Information Awareness, legalized merger of the spying functions of the Central

Intelligence Agency (CIA) with the domestic "investigation" functions of the Federal Bureau of Investigation (FBI), proposals to recruit ordinary people to spy on their neighbors,
unlimited secret detention without civil liberties of several thousand people, racial profiling as national policy, and an orgy of jingoistic patriotism in what passes for the nightly
newscast. This new political landscape justifies the criminalization and surveillance that
have been a fact of life for some communities of color in the United States and extends it to
everyone, targeting specific immigrant groups in particular.

The state's repressive response to September 11 and the Bush doctrine of preemptive
war have ushered in, at mind boggling speed, the retrenchment of basic civil liberties. We
are living in a dangerous historical moment when state repression is openly being bartered
for supposed security from enemies within and without—in fact, the majority of the
world's people. As I write this, the devastation wrought by the war against Iraq and threats
of other U.S. military aggressions loom as a monstrous storm cloud on our global horizon,
school districts all around announce they are forced to lay off teachers and eliminate
programs, CPS has announced 15 percent budget cuts, and high school students have
walked out of their classes in protest at these deeply interrelated disasters. A historical
dialectic is beginning to unfold. A nascent social movement is building as the full ideological and material force of the state and the avaricious goals of transnational capital bear
down on us.

Adjusting our lenses to align dual images of authoritarianism in the schools and in the
streets puts in focus the political implications of education policies that impose a tight
regulatory and surveillance regime. They have dangerous implications for the suppression
of critical thought and agency just when we need them most. Despite the truism that there
are multiple, potent pedagogical sites beyond schools, schools remain important ideological institutions and spaces for the construction of identities. What we need most right
now are "problem posing pedagogies" (Freire, 1970/1994) that help students question and
investigate questions such as, Why did September 11 happen? Why does so much of the
world hate "us"? What is the history of the Middle East and U.S. involvement in it? How
can the United States change its actions in the world to address the resentments so many
peoples feel toward its policies? What is the relationship between U.S. militarism and
racism in the U.S.?

Instead, accountabilty policies expand the state's function to police knowledge and
educational practices and intensify the repression of critical thought and action. High
stakes tests (with all their accoutrements) take on a whole new meaning as "rituals of
power" in the present context when docile subjectivities serve not only new labor force
demands and global city images but the politics of state repression. Education policies
that sort students and schools into neat, simplified opposites of "failures" and "successes"
also promote a kind of binary thinking that serves the new official discourse of "good"
and "evil" countries, nationalities, and people. Policies that obscure the richly textured
strengths and weaknesses of schools, teachers, students, and communities not only erase
the possibility of addressing in complex ways the process of educational improvement and
transformation. They impose definitions of winners and losers and teach us to identify
quickly and absolutely those who are deviant and must be controlled.

The containment and policing of communities of color take on new dimensions in this
political context. Black and Latino/a communities that have faced repression all along are
now more vulnerable as national security legitimates police raids and singling out of
individuals based solely on nationality. Just at the moment when racial profiling had begun
to be subjected to national scrutiny and critique, the state's response to 9/11 made it

official policy. At the same moment, in a sinister reversal, African Americans and Latinos/as are expected to join in the demonization of people of Arab descent and certain immigrant groups. And in a zero-tolerance world, zero-tolerance discipline policies in schools fit a new common sense of militarism and repression to crack down on dangerous "others." Intense surveillance in urban schools becomes one more part of a commonsense national agenda that allows the state to monitor every facet of private life in the name of national security. If the merger of the military and public schools might have been problematic for some before 9/11, it is now national policy writ large. A provision of No Child Left Behind gives military recruiters access to all high school juniors and seniors. We can be sure that those being recruited are not primarily at the select magnet schools. They are the graduates of general high schools in Chicago and elsewhere, mainly African American and Latino/a youth, eighteen-year-olds whose substandard education and subzero options make them prime candidates for what has been called an unofficial "poverty draft." Indeed the general high school may truly be a "military prep track" as U.S. plans for global military domination require expansion of the military ranks.

Education Change and Social Movements

What is to be done? One source of insight is the history of school reforms since the 1950s that pressed for equity and justice. Desegregation struggles, campaigns by African American communities and others for community control of schools, challenges to the Eurocentric and male-centric curriculum, and demands for bilingual education, equal education for children with disabilities, and equal funding for school programs for girls and women—all were born of, and sustained by, broad social justice movements. The educational demands they proposed were concrete expressions of these social movements and at the same time helped to build and extend them. At a moment when accountability has become a new regime of truth, the history of these movements provides an important counterdiscourse and an alternative perspective on the role of democratic participation and activism in shaping social policy. Although only partially successful in achieving their aims, these movements linked education reforms to wider social change and challenged existing power relations. This relationship was captured by African American parents in Chicago in their 1968 call for an education organizing conference titled "Judgment Day for Racism in West Side Schools" (Danns, 2002).

This is a language that names the political nature of education. Its challenges a system that treats people as a means to an end. There are kernels of organized resistance in Chicago Public Schools today. In fall 2002, twelve teachers at Curie High School refused to give the high stakes Chicago Academic Standards Exam; actions of "The Curie 12" and their support from others around the city led the district to drop the test. The Youth First *Youth Summit*, also in fall 2002, and subsequent public actions have injected the voice of several hundred high school youth into school policies affecting their lives. The high school student walk out against war on Iraq in March 2003 demonstrated heightened political consciousness. An alternative assessment proposal developed by a coalition of local school councils and school reform groups (LSC Summit, 2000) introduced an element of debate to the heretofore narrow discourse of high stakes tests in Chicago.

The three counter-hegemonic education projects that I describe above were born of social movements and the participation of educators in those movements. Educational projects grounded in critical social theories and democratic participation (especially by those who have been most marginalized) help make the emancipatory visions of social movements concrete. Culturally relevant, critical, democratic education can help develop "new people" and new social organization to challenge the existing social order. In the recent past, appeals (including my own, Lipman, 1998) to link education change with social and economic reconstruction have been largely rhetorical in the context of fragmented and largely quiescent social movements. But that may be changing. As globalization increasingly divides the world into a small number of super-rich countries and people on one side and literally billions of increasingly impoverished and dislocated people on the other, it is sowing the seeds of its own destruction. There are new solidarities manifested in a worldwide antiglobalization movement that is perhaps most sharply reflected in the diverse social movements that make up the Porto Alegre World Social Forum and its agenda of "globalization from the bottom": economic, social, and cultural justice and opposition to neoliberalism, war, and militarism (see Coates, 2002). The true face of the "neoliberal miracle" in economically developing countries is being exposed in the intensified exploitation of workers, displacement of peasants and small farmers, destruction of the environment, growing national debt, and regulation by transnational lending institutions. Voters in Latin America are rejecting these policies from Brazil to Bolivia to Venezuela, another sign of the times. This is coupled with a massive worldwide showing of opposition to the U.S.-U.K. war on Iraq. From a historical perspective, the world significance of these gathering social forces as a counter to the global hegemony of transnational capital and U.S. militarism should not be underestimated.

As the effects of globalization have also come home to roost in low-wage jobs, lack of health care and retirement security, a crisis in affordable housing, and homelessness they have begun to awaken the U.S. labor movement and infuse it with the energy of immigrant and women workers in new alliances with African American and white workers. The slogan *Si Se Puede* heard from Chicago's hotel workers signals the rumblings of a new labor militance fortified by new Asian, Latino/a, African, Arab, and Eastern European voices. As I write, the Bush doctrine of preemptive, unilateral military action has begun to give rise to an antiwar, antimilitarization movement with a scope not seen since the Vietnam era. Today's activists are beginning to make critical connections between militarism abroad and racism, economic crisis, labor exploitation, and lack of high-quality education, housing, and health care at home.

These connections bear seeds of a significant new, socially conscious movement in education. It is also quite transparent that those who will fight on the front lines in the U.S. military are overwhelmingly African American and Latino/a, products of the general high schools and the military prep tracks. There is a new hopefulness in a socially conscious, hip hop generation represented by Chicago's Youth First Campaign (September 2002) that says: "We are the generation who asks the question: *Why?* Why do things have to be the way they are? We *challenge the system* by organizing *direct action* to gain respect and have our *opinions heard*, so that we can *make change!*"

Notes

1. This agenda has a long history, going back to the free market proposals of Milton Friedman (1962), Chubb and Moe's (1990) argument for the introduction of market forces and school choice, *A Nation at Risk* (National Commission, 1983), and the business-centered reforms advocated under President Reagan.
2. New York's Board of Education mandated a standard curriculum for all its 1,291 schools but then exempted 208, five-sixths of which are in middle- or upper-income neighborhoods (Hoff, 2003).

3.   Racism is deeply entrenched in Brazilian society and in schooling, but one hopeful development is the initiative of
     the municipal education department (SMED) racial justice working group to make racism visible through the
     Citizen Schools (personal communications, SMED official, July 2003).

References

Anderson, J.D. (1988). *The education of blacks in the South, 1860–1935*. Chapel Hill: University of North Carolina Press.
Apple, M.W. (1991) Conservative agendas and progressive possibilities: Understanding the wider politics of curriculum
     and teaching. *Education and Urban Society, 23*(3), 279–291.
Apple, M.W. (1996). *Cultural politics and education*. New York: Teachers College Press.
Apple, M.W. (2001). *Educating the "Right way."* New York: Routledge.
Apple, M.W. et al. (2003). *The state and the politics of knowledge*. New York: Routledge.
Ball, S.J. (1990). *Politics and policy making in education*. London: Routledge.
Ball, S.J. (1997a). Good school/bad school: Paradox and fabrication. *British Journal of Sociology of Education,
     18*(3), 317–336.
Ball, S.J. (1997b). Policy sociology and critical social research: A personal review of recent education policy and policy
     research. *British Educational Research Journal, 23*, 257–274.
Bigelow, B., & Peterson, B. (Eds.). (1998). *Rethinking Columbus: The next 500 years*. Milwaukee: Rethinking Schools.
Bigelow, B., & Peterson, B. (Eds.). (2002). *Rethinking globalization: Teaching for justice in an unjust world*. Milwaukee:
     Rethinking Schools.
Blackmore, J. (2000). Warning signals or dangerous opportunities? Globalization, gender, and educational policy shifts.
     Education Theory, 50(4), 467–486.
Bohn, A.P., & Sleeter, C.E. (2000). Multicultural education and the standards movement. *Phi Delta Kappan, 82*(2),
     156–159.
Carlson, D. (1997). *Making progress: Education and culture in new times*. New York: Teachers College Press.
Christensen, L. (2000). *Reading, writing, and rising up: Teaching about social justice and the power of the written word*,
     Milwaukee: Rethinking Schools.
Chubb, J.M. & Moe, T.E. (1990). *Politics, markets, and America's schools*. Washington, D.C.: Brookings Institution.
Coates, K. (Ed.). (2002). A better world is possible. *The Spokesman, 74*.
Cochran-Smith, M. (1995). Uncertain allies: Understanding the boundaries of race and teaching. *Harvard Educational
     Review, 65*(4), 541–570.
Cummins, J. (1996). *Negotiating identities: Education for empowerment in a diverse society*. Ontario, CA: California
     Association for Bilingual Education.
Darder, A. (1995). Buscando America: The contribution of critical Latino educators to the academic development and
     empowerment of Latino students in the U.S. In C.E. Sleeter & P.L. McLaren (Eds.), *Multicultural education, critical
     pedagogy, and the politics of difference* (pp. 319–348). Albany, NY: SUNY Press.
Delpit, L. (1988). The silenced dialogue: Power and pedagogy in educating other people's children. *Harvard
     Educational Review, 58*, 280–298.
Delpit, L.D. (1992a). Acquisition of literate discourse: Bowing before the master? *Theory into Practice, 31*, 296–302.
Delpit, L.D. (1992b). Education in a multicultural society: Our future's greatest challenge. *Journal of Negro Education,
     61*, 237–249.
Ferguson, A.A. (2000). *Bad boys: Public schools in the making of Black masculinity*. Ann Arbor: University of Michigan
     Press.
Foster, M. (1997). *Black teachers on teaching*. New York: New Press.
Fraser, N. (1997). *Justice interruptus: Critical reflections on the "postsocialist" condition*. New York: Routledge.
Freire, P. (1970/94). *Pedagogy of the oppressed* (Trans. M.B. Ramos). New York: Continuum.
Freire, R. & Macedo, D. (1987). *Literacy: Reading the word and the world*. Westport, CT: Bergin & Garvey.
Friedman, M. (1962). *Capitalism and Freedom*. Chicago: University of Chicago Press.
Gandin, L.A. (2002). *Democratizing access, governance, and knowledge: The struggle for educational alternatives in Porto
     Alegre, Brazil*. Unpublished doctoral dissertation, University of Wisconsin, Madison.
Gandin, L.A., & Apple, M.W. (2003). Educating the state, democratizing knowledge: The Citizen School Project
     in Porto Alegre, Brazil. In M.W. Apple, *The state and the politics of knowledge* (pp. 193–219). New York:
     Routledge.
Gee, J.P., Hull, G., & Lankshear, C. (1996). *The new work order: Behind the language of the new capitalism*. Boulder, CO:
     Westview Press.
Hoff, D.J. (2003, March 9). Complaints pour in over NYC curriculum exemptions. *Education Week*. Retrieved
     March 14, 2003, from http://www.edweek.org
Irvine, J.J. (1991). *Black students and school failure: Policies, practices, and prescriptions*. New York: Praeger.

Jones, P.W. (2000). Globalization and internationalism: Democratic prospects for world education. In N.P. Stromquist & K. Monkman (Eds.), *Globalization and education.* Lanham, MD: Rowman & Littlefield.

King, J.E. (1991). Unfinished business: Black student alienation and Black teachers' emancipatory pedagogy. In M. Foster (Ed.), *Readings in equal education: Qualitative investigations into schools and schooling* (Vol. 11, pp. 245–271). New York: AMS Press.

Ladson-Billings, G. (1994). *Dreamkeepers: Successful teachers of African American students.* San Francisco: Jossey Bass.

Ladson-Billings, G. (2001). *Crossing over to Canaan: The journey of new teachers in diverse classrooms.* San Francisco: Jossey Bass.

Lipman, P. (1998). *Race, class, and power in school restructuring.* Albany: State University of New York Press.

Lipman, P. (2002). Making the global city, making inequality. Political economy and cultural politics of Chicago school policy. *American Educational Research Journal, 39*(2), 379–419.

LSC Summit. (2000). *The new ERA plan.* Chicago: Author. Contact: Parents United for Responsible Education. Retrieved October 21, 2000 from http://www.pureparents.org

McNeil, L.M. (2000). *Contradictions of school reform: Educational costs of standardized testing.* New York: Routledge.

Miner, B. (1997, Fall). Embracing Ebonics and teaching standard English: An interview with Oakland teacher Carrie Secret. *Rethinking Schools, 12*(1), 18–19, 34.

Murrell, P.C., Jr. (1997). Digging again the family wells: A Freirian literacy framework for emancipatory pedagogy for African American children. In P. Freire (Ed.), *Mentoring the mentor: A critical dialogue with Paulo Freire* (pp. 19–58). New York: Peter Lang.

National Commission on Excellence in Education (1983). *A nation at risk: The imperative for educational reform.* Washington, DC: Government Printing Office.

Ozga, J. (2000). *Policy research in educational settings.* Buckingham, England: Open University Press.

Perry, T. (2003). Up from the parched earth: Toward a theory of African American achievement. In T. Perry, C. Steele, & A. Hilliard III (Eds.), *Young, gifted and Black: Promoting high achievement among African-American students* (pp. 1–108). Boston: Beacon Press..

Perry, T., & Delpit, L. (Eds.), (1998). *The real Ebonics debate: Power, language and the education of African-American children.* Boston: Beacon Press.

Rethinking Columbus (2001). Milwaukee: Rethinking Schools..

Rethinking our classrooms (Vol. 1) (1994). Milwaukee: Rethinking Schools.

Rethinking our classrooms (Vol. 2) (2001). Milwaukee: Rethinking Schools.

Smith, N. (1996). *The new urban frontier: Gentrification and the revanchist city.* New York: Routledge.

Valenzuela, A. (1999). *Subtractive schooling: U.S. Mexican youth and the politics of caring.* Albany: State University of New York Press.

19

Standardization, Defensive Teaching, and the Problems of Control

Linda McNeil

Standardization reduces the quality and quantity of what is taught and learned in schools. This immediate negative effect of standardization is the overwhelming finding of a study of schools where the imposition of standardized controls reduced the scope and quality of course content, diminished the role of teachers, and distanced students from active learning.

The long-term effects of standardization are even more damaging: *over the long term, standardization creates inequities, widening the gap between the quality of education for poor and minority youth and that of more privileged students.* The discriminatory effects of standardization are immediately evident in the reduction in both the quality and quantity of educational content for students who have historically scored low on standardized assessments. Over time, the longer standardized controls are in place, the wider the gap becomes as the system of testing and test preparation comes to substitute in minority schools for the curriculum available to more privileged students. These new structures of discrimination are being generated by the controls that began in the schools documented in this study and that in the succeeding years have become the dominant model of schooling in one of the nation's largest and most diverse states, Texas.

In the name of improving educational quality and holding schools and school personnel more accountable for their professional practice, the state government enacted a set of standardized controls to monitor children's learning and teachers' classroom behavior. These controls arose outside the educational system, derived from pressures from the business establishment to fund only those educational expenses that contributed to measurable outcomes. They were implemented from the top of the state bureaucracy, through the district bureaucracies, and subsequently imposed on schools. The controls were set forth as "reforms." The activities they mandated were to be uniform, and the means of monitoring the activities were standardized scoring instruments. In the name of "equity," these reforms imposed a sameness. In the name of "objectivity" they relied on a narrow set of numerical indicators. These hierarchical reform systems seem upon first reading to be extreme, but over time they have become the model for increasingly hierarchical and prescriptive systems being promoted as improving education. More seriously, they have legitimated "accountability" as the presiding metaphor in shifting the power relations governing public education.

The research did not begin as a study of the effects of state-level educational standardization. The findings are all the more powerful because, in fact, they were not expected. Nor were they sought. This research began as a search for organizational models of schooling that provided structural support for authentic, engaged teaching and learning. The research was designed to study schools in which school knowledge was credible, in which teachers brought their own personal and professional knowledge into the classroom, and in which teachers and students entered into shared, authentic study of significant topics and ways of knowing. Analyzing such teaching and learning in its organizational context could shed light on the ways the structures of schooling can enhance, rather than impede, educational quality.

Teaching and learning widely regarded to be authentic, to be meaningful to the students and to their experiences beyond school, was found in a series of urban magnet schools. As exemplars of authentic teaching and learning, the magnet schools carry special importance because their students were predominantly minority, African American and Latino. These schools had been established to be of such high quality that they would serve a city as the vehicle for desegregation through voluntary cross-city student transfers. This research was intended to document the ways that curriculum and learning are constructed and made meaningful in schools whose organizational structure subordinates the credentialing function and other procedural and behavioral controls to teaching and learning. The magnet schools proved to be schools where teachers and students, free of the constraints of the state textbook adoption list and from state and local prescriptive rules governing curriculum, co-constructed rich academic environments in a multiracial setting.

During the collection of observational data in these magnet schools, while the data on authentic teaching and learning were quite persuasively accruing, the state enacted policies meant to "reform" all schools.[1] These policies brought all schools in the state under a centralized system of prescriptive rules and standardized procedures for monitoring compliance. These exemplary magnet schools, serving racially diverse and in many cases poor students, were not exempt from the centralized controls.

As the controls were imposed, and the regulations increasingly standardized, the quality of teaching and learning at even these exemplary schools began to suffer. Teaching, curriculum, and students' roles in classrooms were transformed by the standardizations and by the categories of compliance they imposed. Within the observational data there began to emerge phony curricula, reluctantly presented by teachers in class to conform to the forms of knowledge their students would encounter on centralized tests. The practice of teaching under these reforms shifted away from intellectual activity toward dispensing packaged fragments of information sent from an upper level of the bureaucracy. And the role of students as contributors to classroom discourse, as thinkers, as people who brought their personal stories and life experiences into the classroom, was silenced or severely circumscribed by the need for the class to "cover" a generic curriculum at a pace established by the district and the state for all the schools.

The magnet teachers and their students did not comply thoughtlessly with the new standardizations. Instead they struggled to hold onto school lessons that held credibility in the world outside schools, to lessons that sprang from teachers' passions and children's curiosities, to lessons that built a cumulative base of new understandings for these students, many of whom were counting on the magnet schools to open previously closed doors to college and careers. The work of resistance itself, however, took a toll on time, energies, and the activities that could not be salvaged as the controls became more tightly monitored.

Controlling Myths

The myth of such controls is that they "bring up the bottom," that they are aimed at the lowest levels of performance. The myth further promotes the idea that "good schools" will not be affected and, conversely, that any school that is adversely affected by centralized controls must not have been a "good" school. The corollary holds for teachers: if teachers are negatively affected by standardized reforms, then they must have been the "weak" or "bad" teachers in need of reforming.

The following analysis shatters the myth that standardization improves education. It challenges the widespread notion that standardization equals, or leads to, "standards." What will be clear from a close-up analysis of the effects of standardization is that, in fact, *standardization undermines academic standards* and seriously limits opportunities for children to learn to a "high standard."

The issue of the confusion between standardization and "standards" is of critical importance because increasingly scores on individual students' standardized tests of academic skills and of the mastery of subject content carry with them serious consequences both for the students and for those who teach them. "High-stakes" decisions, such as grade placement and promotion (or retention), placement in highly stratified academic tracks, and even graduation are increasingly determined by students' scores on centrally imposed, commercial standardized tests. When they are used in "accountability systems," individual and aggregate student test scores are used as indirect measures of teachers' work, principals' "performance," and even of the overall quality of the school. Such practices are highly questionable and are prompting serious scrutiny by policymakers and testing professionals of the possible misuses of student tests (Heubert and Hauser 1999).

The ethical questions raised among testing experts regarding the use of standardized student tests for other purposes such as employee (teacher, principal) performance and school quality tend to be regarded by policymakers in heavily centralized states and districts as points requiring fine-tuning and, in fact, are often used as justification for extending tests to additional grade levels and subjects to "assure that the testing is as comprehensive as possible."[2]

The Texas case is important to study and to analyze at each level of implementation because it demonstrates the wide gulf between academic "standards" and the curricular content to which students have access under a highly centralized system of standardized testing. It is crucial to understand because it provides the first opportunity to examine how issues of quality and "high standards" become so easily co-opted by the similar language— but oppositional philosophy and opposite consequences—of standardization. The "high stakes" to the students, in the use of their scores to regulate an entire system, appear at first to be merely the decisions made about them individually—their promotion or graduation, for example. The schools described here in some detail demonstrate that what is ultimately at stake is the capacity to provide a substantive education that is not driven by, not stratified by, and not reduced by the kinds of standardized tests being increasingly adopted across the states under the guise of "raising standards."

That standardization is harmful to teaching and learning is not a new idea. Critique of the embodiment of technical mechanisms for transforming the power relations within schools and reordering the power relations that govern the larger role of school in society is the subject of a now comprehensive body of theory (Apple 1979, 1995, 1996; Apple and Oliver 1998; Beyer and Apple 1998a; Freire 1970, 1985, 1995; Giroux 1983, 1996; Greene 1978; McLaren and Gutierrez 1998; Sarason 1971, 1996; Wise 1979; Wrigley 1982; and others). Such critical scholarship, including critical cultural studies, studies in the political economy of schools, and critical analyses of pedagogy have emerged as bases upon which to examine the increasing technicizing of public education. At the macrolevel of theorizing, there is, within this body of scholarship, increased attention to and understanding of the conservative transformation of American public education through the use of technicist forms of power. In addition, fine-grained classroom studies, particularly in the area of the sociocultural linguistics and critical race studies, are documenting the linguistic and culturally subtractive effects of generic models of schooling on Spanish-dominant and other immigrant and minority children (Fordham and Ogbu 1986; Gutierrez and Larson 1994; Gutierrez, Rymes, and Larson 1995; Romo and Falbo 1996; Suarez-Orozco 1991; Valenzuela 1999).

This scholarship has been essential in creating frameworks for questioning the power relations that shape the role of the school in the larger society. In addition, through critical scholarship we have now an established tradition for examining the social and cultural origins of school knowledge, for raising questions about whose interests are served by educational institutions and whose interests and cultures are represented by the knowledge and ways of knowing institutionalized in schools. Critical studies have insisted that our understandings of schools and the educational practices within them not be limited to technical representations of the schools, their programs, or their students' performance. Our conceptualizations of the ways race, social class, social "place," gender, conflicting community histories, and competing definitions of schooling that all shape "schooling" for us are enriched by this growing literature.

Even within an increasingly complex and international body of scholarship, however, there are serious gaps. One of these is the absence of critical scholarship that carries theory into, or builds theory from, what goes on inside schools. And even more glaringly and ironically absent, given the role of critical scholarship in raising issues of power and power inequities, is the lack of up-close studies of systems of schooling. Jean Anyon's powerful book, *Ghetto Schooling: A Political Economy of Urban Educational Reform* (1997), stands as an exception. This extraordinarily complex study examines the interrelation of race, local politics, local economics, and even the global economic forces that have over time "pauperized" urban education in a major U.S. city, Newark, New Jersey. Her study is exemplary for situating both the "problems" of urban schools and their potential to become educational for poor and minority children not merely in their internal structures ("Do they 'work'?"), but in the sociocultural contexts of their communities and in the economic and political forces beyond those communities that have over the years come to dominate the resources and political power available in support of these schools. Her analysis is especially powerful because it does not leave these forces at an abstract level, but rather concretizes particular groups, particular legislation, particular individuals' roles in the destruction and rebuilding of the civic capacity of a community to act on behalf of its schools.

Yet even this very detailed study stops at the classroom door. Its analysis of the factors inside schools that have over the years been damaged by increasingly racist and class-based resourcing of schools is descriptive of both the organizational factors (leverage over resources, teacher preparation, administrative authority) and programmatic components (availability of kindergarten, creation of alternative programs for children not well served by traditional schools). But this description and analysis are seen more from an organizational perspective and from the perspective of community constituencies working to reclaim the power to improve schools, rather than from children's experience of these and other aspects of schooling. We still have serious need of studies that not only get inside classrooms but also document from the inside out the ways increasingly differentiated power relations are changing systems of schooling and the ways those systems are shaping what is taught and learned.

It is critical scholarship, then, which gives us a lens for going beyond the appearance, slogans, and indicators, to examine the forces such as standardization that are increasingly shifting both school practice and the power relations shaping that practice. What has been missing from both the global theorizing and the microlevel studies from a critical perspective is an analysis of *how these standardizing forces play out through the system of schooling:* from the political forces shaping the policies, through the bureaucratic systems enacting the policies, to what children are taught and what they experience in the classrooms under these policy mandates. *Contradictions of Reform* (Apple, ed., 2000) provides the first such comprehensive analysis of a system of standardization and its educational consequences. It overcomes the silence in the critical literature about how standardization comes about, how the innocuous-sounding language of standardization ("high standards" and "accountability") comes to mask the reductions in academic quality, and how technical indicators ("objective measures") transform what is valued in teaching and curriculum. The analysis further fills the gap in the critical literature by situating the voices and experiences of particular teachers and students within a particular system, overcoming the tendency of global theorizing to portray a picture that, even if essentially correct, remains at such an abstract level that it lacks credibility to a broader public trying to understand its schools.

Contradictions of Reform looks firsthand at "best case" schools where teachers and highly diverse students, despite serious resource shortages, had been able within the context of a supportive organizational structure, to co-construct authentic educational experiences.

These schools are recorded here in extensive detail to demonstrate the complexity of creating and sustaining such educational programs and to give tangible evidence of the educational value to students when their classroom knowledge is credible and when the educational process involves the minds and knowledge base of the teachers and the minds and experiences of the students. The study then traces the ways standardized controls directly and negatively impact the teaching, curriculum, and role of students in those schools. These standardized controls are traced from their origins in the business leadership outside schools, through political trade-offs with the governor and legislature that silenced educators and forced them to accept a highly complex system of controls over their work in exchange for even very modest pay increments. The analysis then tracks the bureaucratic implementation of these controls, into "instruments of accountability," to measure teachers' classroom practice and the "outcomes" of children's learning. This systemic analysis, from corporate pressure to legislature to school bureaucracy to classroom, sheds new light on the harmful effects of policies that on the surface seem to be benign attempts to monitor educational quality and to assure that schools are run in a cost-effective manner. In reality these policies of standardization are decreasing the quality of teaching and learning in our schools, especially in the schools of poor and minority children. The analysis concludes with an examination of the longer-term effects of such systems of accountability; there is growing evidence that the institutionalization of standardization is widening the gap between poor and minority youth and their peers in more privileged schools.

The language of accountability seems, on a commonsense level, to be about professional practice that is responsible to the children and to the public. The language of standardization appears to denote equity, of assuring that all children receive the same education.

Behind the usages of these terms in educational policy, however, is a far different political and pedagogical reality. "Accountability" reifies both a resource dependency and a hierarchical power structure which maintains that dependency. It further undermines both the public voice in public schooling and the public role of schools in democratic life. "Standardization" equates sameness with equity in ways that mask pervasive and continuing inequalities. Taken together, the increasing use of *standardization*, prescriptive of educational programs, and *accountability*, equating educational accomplishment with outcomes measures, are restructuring public education in two critical ways. First is the shifting of decisions regarding teaching and learning away from communities and educational professionals and into the hands of technical experts following a political agenda to reduce democratic governance of schooling. Second (and particularly serious in its consequences for children in light of the success of the magnet schools in educating highly diverse students) is the restratification by class and race through highly technical systems governing the content and means of evaluation. The forms of control, which have their origins in the 1980s reforms, are now deeply entrenched and are not only reducing the overall quality of education but also dramatically widening the gap between poor and minority children's education and the education of more privileged youth.

Standardization in the form of legislated controls over testing and curriculum is an externalization of management controls arising from the bureaucratizing of schooling early in the twentieth century. Its derivations from within the organizational structures of schooling, rather than from theories of child development and learning, have traditionally signaled a separateness from teaching, learning, and curriculum. The perceived separateness between school organization and teaching and learning has been shown, however, to be misleading. Even where there are not in place formal controls over curriculum and teaching, there are, within bureaucratic school structures, imbedded controls. These bureaucratic controls are not separate from the educational purposes of schooling; rather, they play an active role in determining the quality of teaching and the nature of what is taught.

Defensive Teaching; and the Contradictions of Control

The public will to provide an education to all the citizens in a democracy carries with it issues of cost (Who will pay for such an education?) and governance (How will so many schools be organized and overseen?). It is one of the great ironies of American education that in order to provide a free public education to all its children, schools were created along the model of factory assembly lines in order to reduce the cost of schooling per child and assure millions of children of a diploma, a credential of school completion (Callahan 1962; Kliebard 1986; McNeil 1986). A school that is designed like a factory has a built-in contradiction: running a factory is tightly organized, highly routinized, and geared for the production of uniform products; educating children is complex, inefficient, idiosyncratic, uncertain, and open-ended. Historically, the two purposes of schooling, that is, educating children and running large-scale educational institutions, have been seen as separate domains. The one is aimed at nurturing individual children and equipping them with new knowledge and skills; the other focuses on processing aggregates of students through regularized requirements of the credentialing process. A bureaucratic school, or a school that is part of a bureaucratic system, is thus structured to be in conflict with itself (McNeil 1986, 3). And at the point of the tension—where the two oppositional forces intersect—are the children, the teacher, and the curriculum. How the tension is resolved will in large measure shape the quality of what is taught and learned in the school.

"When the school's organization becomes centered on managing and controlling, teachers and students take school less seriously." With this statement I summed up the analysis of schools and classrooms I wrote as the book, *Contradictions of Control: School Structure and School Knowledge*. To elaborate, I added, "They [teachers and students] fall into a ritual of teaching and learning that tends toward minimal standards and minimal effort. This sets off a vicious cycle. As students disengage from enthusiastic involvement in the learning process, administrators often see the disengagement as a control problem. They then increase their attention to managing students and teachers rather than supporting their instructional purpose" (McNeil 1986, xviii).

That earlier research study, an ethnographic analysis of the factors shaping what is taught in schools (McNeil 1986), revealed that the effects of bureaucratic controls on teaching and learning were not vague influences, but rather very concrete and visible transformations of course content and classroom interaction. That study, conducted in four high schools in the midwestern United States, revealed that behind overt symptoms of poor educational quality lie complicated organizational dynamics (McNeil 1988). The nature of teachers' practice, the quality of course content and the level of students' engagement may not themselves be weaknesses, but may be symptoms that reflect teachers' and students' accommodations to priorities built into the organizational structure of the school.

Where teachers feel that they have no authority in the structure of the school, or where they see the school as emphasizing credentialing over the substance of schooling, they tend to create their own authority or their own efficiencies within the classroom by tightly controlling course content. They begin to teach a course content that I termed *school knowledge*, which serves the credentialing function of the school but which does not provide students with the rich knowledge of the subject fields nor with opportunities to build their own understandings of the subject.

As background for examining the authentic teaching and learning in the magnet schools, it is important to understand the very concrete ways in which teachers in the midwestern schools shaped school content in reaction to the schools' subordination of the educational goals to the goals of control and credentialing. Teachers who wanted their students to comply with course requirements often did so by reducing those requirements in order to gain minimal participation with minimal resistance. I termed this *defensive teaching* (McNeil 1986, ch. 7). Teachers who taught defensively, asking little from their students in order to satisfy institutional requirements with as little resistance and with as few inefficiencies as possible, tended to bracket their own personal knowledge from the treatment of the subject of the lesson. And they used strategies to silence student questions or (inefficient) discussions. These strategies bear reviewing because it is in part their absence from the magnet classrooms that so starkly shows the differences between teaching in a supportive organizational structure and teaching in a controlling environment.

First, teachers controlled content by *omission*. They tended to omit topics that were difficult to understand and/or contemporary topics that would invite student discussion. They especially tended to omit subjects, or treatments of subjects, that were potentially controversial. Controversy, and passionate student discussion, might threaten the teacher's interpretation; interpretations that differed from the teacher's were seen as threatening teacher authority. One teacher even said he had eliminated student research papers because at a time of volatile political debate he found that students doing their own research could become "self-indoctrinated," that is, they came to their own interpretations of the subject (McNeil 1986, 172). At the least, controversy could disrupt the pacing of the coverage of the course material, causing the third-period class, for example, to lag behind the less talkative fourth-period class.

Teachers also maintained a controlling environment in their classes by *mystifying* course content. They mystified a topic by making it seem extremely important, but beyond the students' understanding. It was to be written in the notes for the test, but not understood. In economics class, topics like the Federal Reserve system or international monetary policies would be subjected to mystification; they would be mentioned but not elaborated upon, with the message that students need to recognize the term but leave the understanding of the subject to "the experts." (At times teachers also mystified topics about which *they* had little knowledge, willingly obscuring their students' access to the topic, rather than to learn on behalf of or in collaboration with their students.)

The information that was important to the content of the course, the content that teachers did want their students to learn, would be presented in the form of a list of facts (or names or dates or formulas or terminologies) to be memorized and repeated on tests. Complex subjects that were too essential to the course to be omitted (the Civil War, for example, in a history class; cell processes in biology; the effects of reagents in chemistry) would be reduced to lists and fragments of fact and transmitted by the teacher. In most cases, the lists were presented in a format that condensed and structured the course content into a consensus curriculum. One teacher explained that her job was to read the scholarly literature (in her case, "the historians") and distill the information into a list on which "all historians now agree." This *fragmentation* of course content tended to disembody the curriculum, divorcing it from the cultures and interests and prior knowledge of the students, from the teachers' knowledge of the subject, and from the epistemologies, the ways of knowing, within the subject itself. It also placed barriers between the knowledge as packaged for use in school and its relation to understandings of that subject within the cultural and practical knowledge outside schools. The origins of ideas, the shaping of interpretations, the possibility of inquiry into where this knowledge came from and how it was shaped by human experience were all absent from the curriculum. "School knowledge" was a priori what the teacher conveyed and students received to satisfy school requirements.

A fourth strategy these teachers used to control course content, and with it classroom interactions, was what I have termed *defensive simplification*. When teachers perceived that students had little interest in a lesson or that the difficulty in studying the lesson might cause students to resist the assignment, they made both the content of the assignment and the work students were to do as simple as possible. They minimized *anticipated* student resistance by simplifying course content and demanding little of students. This strategy was used when the topic was complex and in need of multiple explanations if all students were to understand; labor history might be reduced to a list of famous strikes, labor laws, management policies, and key labor leaders. The connections among these would go unexplained; they would simply be names on a list. Student assignments were reduced to taking notes on lectures, copying lists from the blackboard, filling in blanks on worksheets, and reading one or two pages on the subject. Extensive writing that called for student interpretations, for student research beyond the classroom, for engagement with text was absent from these classes—in stark contrast to the responsibilities that, as will be demonstrated, the magnet students assumed on a regular basis.

The thin academic content in these classes, surprising because these were known as "good schools," gave the impression that the teachers were undereducated in their subjects. Interviews with the teachers, however, revealed that they were well read, that they kept up in their fields, that they discussed literature and current events and new discoveries with their friends. They frequently talked with adults, in the teacher's lounge or over lunch, about complex ideas and about what they were learning from their personal reading and travels. When they came into the classroom, however, the subject they had discussed outside the classroom would be rendered unrecognizable when presented to their students as lists and facts. They rarely brought their personal knowledge, or their professional knowledge of their subjects, into the classroom (Shulman 1987); personal knowledge and school knowledge were for them quite separate. In interviews teachers explained that they feared that if the assignments (and treatment of course topics) were too complex, then students would not do the work. In addition, they feared that if students knew how complex the world is, particularly our economic institutions, then they would become cynical and discouraged about their futures and about "the system." They mistook their students' compliance for acceptance of what they were being taught.

Although most of the students in these middle-class, White schools sat quietly and appeared to be absorbing the information provided by their teachers (most of them passed the subjects), interviews with students at all achievement levels revealed that the students did not find the school knowledge credible. School was far from their only source of information; they had televisions, jobs, grandparents, and peers. They did not necessarily have sophisticated understandings of various subjects, but they knew that for some reason "they only tell you here what they want you to know." I had been in the schools for so many months before interviewing students that when we did sit down to talk, several expressed their concern that I might be taken in by the content of the lessons. They advised, "Don't believe what they tell you here," and then each would go on to tell of a school-supplied fact that was directly contradicted by a personal experience or by something learned from a job or a parent. (Some of the school-supplied information was more reliable than what they learned at their jobs or from their friends, but not having the opportunity in school to examine and to come to understandings of what was being taught, they assumed a greater credibility on the part of what they learned outside school.)

The students and teachers in these schools were meeting in an exchange to satisfy the bureaucratic requirements of schooling. The teachers recognized full well that if the school were smooth-running and few students failed their courses, then the administration would be pleased, and that any extra efforts—to develop an interesting curriculum, to assign and grade student research papers, to stay late to meet with students wanting extra help— would not only not be rewarded but also be disdained as unnecessary. The students knew that if they exerted at least minimum effort, then they would pass their required courses; if they ventured opinions and tried to start discussions, then they would be viewed as disruptive. (*Contradictions of Control* includes examples of student attempts to bring their own ideas into the classroom; one teacher lowered "class participation" grades if students tried to discuss.)

In response to impersonal bureaucratic schools that emphasized the controlling and credentialing functions at the expense of the educative goals of schooling, teachers and students were engaged in a vicious cycle of lowering expectations. When teachers tightly controlled the curriculum, the students mentally disengaged; teachers saw student disengagement as the reason to tighten controls. When administrators saw teachers and students exerting so little effort, they saw the school as "out of control," and in response they tightened up administrative controls, issuing new directives and increasingly formalizing the hierarchical distances between the administration and the classroom. Within this cycle of lowering expectations, the school, for both teachers and students, begins to lose its legitimacy as a place for serious learning.

The *Contradictions of Control* schools held within them the potential for authentic teaching and learning. It was to be found not in merely changing the dispositions of individual teachers, but in breaking the cycle of lowering expectations set up when teachers teach defensively and students find school knowledge not worthy of their effort. Breaking this cycle within the traditional bureaucratic school structure, in which the credentialing and controlling processes of schooling so easily came to dominate the educational purposes of schooling, can be difficult. The teachers in the midwestern schools were not under legislated curriculum directives, nor was their pay tied to student test scores or compliance with standardized mandates. These teachers were not directly de-skilled by a regulatory context. They were participating in their own de-skilling by bracketing their personal knowledge when they entered the classroom and by using on their students the controlling practices they so resented from administrators.

One school stood out from the others as a school whose administrative structure was organized not to enforce rules and credentialing procedures, but to support teaching. That school (McNeil 1986, ch. 6) demonstrated that when the professional roles, resource allocations, and procedures of a school are organized in support of academics (rather than oppositional to "real teaching"), teachers feel supported to bring their best knowledge into the classroom. They are willing to take risks in incorporating into lessons their questions and uncertainties as well as their deep understandings of their subject. They are willing to let their students see them learning and asking questions (rather than controlling all discussion) and, in turn, they invite their students to make their own questions, interpretations, and partial understandings a vital part of the learning process. Seeing that school, where curriculum content was not "school knowledge," but was congruent with the knowledge that teachers held and with the subject as it is encountered in the world outside schools, raised the question of what other structures of schooling might foster authentic teaching and learning. Observing that school where scarce resources went first to instruction in a variety of imaginative ways, and where administrative personnel put their own time and efforts at the disposal of their faculties, raised the possibility of identifying other examples of schools structured to support educating children in ways consistent with their need to be nurtured and with their need to learn content whose purpose went far beyond building a record of grades and school credentials.

Contradictions of Control cut new theoretical ground for understanding the complex relationships between school organization and what is taught and learned. The wisdom that school administration and instruction are loosely linked domains was challenged by the clear evidence that a controlling administrative environment undermined teaching and learning by the responses it evoked in teachers and students.

The analysis presented here began with the selection of the magnet schools as counterexamples to the organizational de-skilling of teachers. These schools proved that schools can be organized in ways that do not put teachers in conflict with administrative purposes when they do their best teaching. They show that in a supportive environment, teachers will work alone and collaboratively to develop complex and up-to-date curricula, that they will tackle complex and controversial topics essential to their students' understandings, that they will struggle to find ways to make learning possible for all their students. The magnet schools carried many agendas as they were established and as they came to be the chief conduits to college for hundreds of minority youth in a city with a long history of discriminatory school practices. For this analysis, their benefit is in exemplifying the possibilities for authentic teaching and learning when schools are structured to foster learning rather than to process students or control them.

The success of the magnet schools in providing a substantive education for diverse urban students was jeopardized when a layer of organizational controls became state law. These controls, centralized and highly standardized, threatened the educational programs by imposing on the magnet school curricula magnified versions of the simplifications used by the midwestern teachers to limit their students' access to knowledge. The magnet teachers refused to be de-skilled, but the costs of new standardization policies fell heavily on their curricula and on their students and threatened to drive them out of public classrooms when remaining meant participating in the de-skilled teaching of "school knowledge."

The experiences of the students and teachers in the magnet schools under increasingly standardized controls raise serious questions about the purposes behind these controls. For educators, they also raise serious questions about the long-term effects of students whose entire educational experience is dominated by standardization. When standardization becomes institutionalized, and student testing comes to be used for monitoring "accountability" throughout a state's educational system, the negative effects fall most heavily on the poorest children, minority children whose entire school experience comes to be dominated by an attempt to raise their (historically low) test scores at any cost. Standardization, when it begins to shape a whole system, in effect creates a new system of discrimination.

Notes

1. A note on methodology: this study began as an analysis of the factors shaping curriculum in schools whose organizational and administrative structures were designed to support, rather than control, teaching and learning. For that analysis, daily observations in classrooms over the course of at least a semester in each school formed the primary data on curriculum and teaching. Interviews with teachers, students, administrators, and parents, and historical research into the schools and their programs, were conducted formally and informally at strategic points before, during, and following classroom observations. Interviews with central office administrators in the offices of curriculum, gifted-and-talented programs, magnet services, and evaluation and research provided key information on the administrative and legal contexts of the magnet schools during their formation and in the years leading up to and inclusive of the time of the study.

    Once the state-mandated reforms under House Bill 72 and related state education agency directives began to affect the schools, subsequent investigation was made into the role of the SCOPE committee, Perot's use of advisors, state implementation of the legislation, and the offices and structures through which these policies were implemented within the school district. Reviews of legislative and committee documents, correspondence, initial evaluation reports, administrative documents, and related materials from a wide range of observers and participants in the state-level reforms and district implementation were essential to the understanding of not only the content of the reforms but also the rationale being used at each level to justify their implementation. Interviews with several key shapers of these policies, both from outside and from within SCOPE and the state government, were extremely helpful in tracking how decisions were being made, and the assumptions of schooling on which they were based. (None of these sources was available to or known to the teachers being observed, who were receiving the directives as rules emanating from a higher but undesignated level in the bureaucracy.) Copies of district and state standardized tests and test-driven curricula and teacher assessment instruments from a number of years were examined. The schools have been followed for several years following the initial implementation of the curriculum directives and teacher assessment instruments, through the successive state test-driven programs, which have followed from the proficiencies, with site visits to the schools, periodic interviews with teachers and administrators, and information gathered through a wide association with these schools.

The contemporary legacy of these early standardizations is analyzed here on the basis of extensive work with urban teachers and administrators through the teacher enhancement programs of the Rice University Center for Education, school visits and observations, analysis of TAAS-related materials from the state and the testing companies, interviews with teachers, conversations with a wide range of teachers and administrators, parents, and students, regarding the impact of the TAAS on classrooms, press coverage and district administrative bulletins related to the TAAS, and a variety of other formal and informal sources.

To counter any tendency to generalize from an in-depth but relatively small data sample, or from individual occurrences, several correctives were built into the research. First, any outlier occurrences, for which there was not a pattern beyond those occurrences, were not deemed as "data" for the purpose of the overall analysis. (Individual occurrences held significance in themselves, but are not reported in this analysis unless they indicate a *pattern of teaching and of the effects of standardization* that go beyond that any one occurrence.) There is no reliance on "horror stories" for this analysis, in other words, or exceptional events. Second, at each step of data collection and interim analysis, counter examples to trends in the data have been actively sought. For example, when it became apparent that biology teachers were having to eliminate many of their lessons, particularly those that integrated biological concepts around hands-on phenomena such as student-built marine aquaria or a natural habitat, interviews were scheduled with biology teachers at other schools to determine whether this problem was specific to the magnet schools, or even these teachers, or whether these curricular deletions were widespread. Also, counter interpretations were investigated; for example, if a teacher was having to delete a portion of the curriculum, further research was conducted to see if factors other than the prescriptive testing had had an effect, perhaps a less visible effect.

The search for counter examples and counter interpretations is significant because this analysis is not a mere listing of problems or "unintended consequences" of an otherwise sanguine set of policies. The negative effects of the standardizing policies have been their primary effects on classrooms and teaching, and their effects on the locus of control over schooling have become visible as, in fact, intended consequences, not circumstantial by-products.

2. This perspective has been reiterated by proponents of state testing, and the Texas Accountability System specifically, in public meetings and private discussions at which this researcher was present.

Works Cited

Anyon, Jean. (1997). *Ghetto Schooling: A Political Economy of Urban Educational Reform.* New York and London: Teachers College Press.

Apple, Michael W. (1979). *Ideology and Curriculum.* London: Routledge & Kegan Paul.

Apple, Michael W. (1992). *Education and Power.* Boston and London: Routledge & Kegan Paul.

Apple, Michael W. (1993). *Official Knowledge: Democratic Education in a Conservative Age.* New York: Routledge.

Apple, Michael W. (1995). *Education and Power,* 2d ed. New York: Routledge.

Apple, Michael W. (1996). *Cultural Politics and Education.* New York and London: Teachers College Press.

Apple, Michael W., and Anita Oliver. (1998). "Becoming Right: Education and the Formation of Conservative Movements." In Dennis Carlson and Michael W. Apple (eds.), *Power/Knowledge/Pedagogy: The Meaning of Democratic Education in Unsettling Times.* Boulder: Westview Press.

Beyer, Landon E., and Michael W. Apple (eds.) (1998a). *The Curriculum: Problems, Politics, and Possibilities,* 2d ed. Albany: State University of New York Press.

Callahan, Raymond. (1962). *Education and the Cult of Efficiency.* Chicago: University of Chicago Press.

Fordham, S., and J. Ogbu. (1986). "Black Students' School Success: Coping with the Burden of 'Acting White?'" *Urban Review* 18: (176–206).

Freire, Paulo. (1970). *Pedagogy of the Oppressed.* Translated by Myra Bergman Ramos. New York: Seabury.

Freire, Paulo. (1985). *The Politics of Education: Culture, Power and Liberation.* Translated by Donaldo Macedo. South Hadley, Mass.: Bergin and Garvey.

Freire, Paulo. (1995). *A Pedagogy of Hope.* New York: Continuum.

Giroux, Henry A. (1983). *Critical Theory and Educational Practice.* Geelong, Victoria, Australia: Deakin University Press.

Giroux, Henry A. (1996). *Pedagogy and the Politics of Hope.* Boulder: Westview Press.

Greene, Maxine. (1978). *Landscapes of Learning.* New York: Teachers College Press.

Gutierrez, Kris, and J. Larson. (1994). "Language Borders: Recitation as Hegemonic Discourse." In *International Journal of Educational Reform* 3, no. 1: 22–36.

Gutierrez, K., B. Rymes, and J. Larson. (1995). "Script, Counterscript, and Underlife in the Classroom: *James Brown v. the Board of Education*" *Harvard Educational Review* 65, no.3: 445–71.

Heubert, Jay P., and Robert M. Hauser (eds.) (1999). *High Stakes: Testing for Tracking, Promotion, and Graduation.* Committee on Appropriate Test Use, Board on Testing and Assessment, Commission on Behavioral and Social Sciences and Education, and National Research Council. Washington, D.C.: National Academy Press.

Kliebard, Herbert M. (1986). *The Struggle for an American Curriculum.* New York and London: Routledge.

McLaren, Peter L., and Kris Gutierrez. (1998). "Global Politics and Local Antagonisms: Research and Practice as Dissent and Possibility." In Dennis Carlson and Michael W. Apple (eds.), *Power/Knowledge/Pedagogy: The Meaning of Democratic Education in Unsettling Times.* Boulder: Westview Press.

McNeil, Linda M. (1986). *Contradictions of Control: School Structure and School Knowledge.* New York and London: Routledge.

McNeil, Linda M. (1988). "Teacher Knowledge and the Organization of the School." A paper prepared for presentation at the "School Organization and Climate" session of the Annual Meeting of the American Educational Research Association, New Orleans.

Romo, Harriet D., and Toni Falbo. (1996). *Latino High School Graduation: Defying the Odds.* Austin: University of Texas Press.

Sarason, Seymour B. (1971). *The Culture of School and the Problem of Change.* Boston: Allyn and Bacon.

Sarason, Seymour B. (1996). *Revisiting the Culture of School and the Problem of Change.* New York and London: Teachers College Press.

Shulman, Lee. (1987). "Knowledge and Teaching: Foundations of the New Reform." *Harvard Education Review,* 57, no. 1 (February): 1–22.

Suarez-Orozco, Marcelo M. (1991). "Hispanic Immigrant Adaptation to Schooling." In Margaret A. Gibson and John U. Ogbu (eds.), *Minority Status and Schooling: A Comparative Study of Immigrant and Involuntary Minorities.* New York: Garland Publishing.

Valenzuela, Angela. (1999). *Subtractive Schooling: U.S.-Mexican Youth and the Politics of Caring.* Albany: State University of New York Press.

Wise, Arthur. (1979). *Legislated Learning: The Bureaucratization of the American Classroom.* Berkeley and Los Angeles: University of California Press.

Wrigley, Julia. (1982). *Class Politics and Public Schools: Chicago, 1900–1950.* New Brunswick, N.J.: Rutgers University Press.

20

Writing, Identity, and the Other: Dare We Do Disability Studies?

Linda Ware

I can't ignore my disability, why would you?
Karen (high school student Writing, Identity, and the Other)

The messages we receive are very strong and clear and we have little access to different values, which may place a more positive value on our bodies, our lives and ourselves. Our self-image is thus dominated by the non-disabled world's reaction to us.
Jenny Morris (1991)

Cultural perceptions of disability do not emerge in a vacuum; they accrue slowly and over time, informed by normalizing discourses in medicine and psychology and reinforced by institutions and unchallenged beliefs of deficiency and need. Historically, disability has been the exclusive domain of the biological, social, and cognitive sciences that shape practice in education, rehabilitative medicine, and social work. As a consequence of this limited understanding, disabled people are generally stereotyped as weak, pitiful, dependent, passive, tragic, and many times deserving of their predicament (Gilman, 1985). With the medical lens fixed on the Individual and his or her disability, the larger political, economic, and material forces at play in an able-ist society fall somewhere outside the frame. Despite claims to the contrary, public education, higher education, and teacher education are likewise guilty of ignoring the complexity of disability in our society. Tensions remain when attempting to consider disability as a concept or a constituency in educational settings. In higher education, when disability moves beyond the diversity category to include pedagogical issues, status as an emerging field of study, and a civil rights mandate, "teachers, administrators, and students recognize the pedagogical, scholarly, and practical implications of integrating disability fully into all aspects of academe" (Longmore & Garland-Thomson, 1999, p. 2). Thus, when the context responds to disability as more than a diversity category, concept and constituency merge to create important opportunities for learning. In K-12 settings, disability has typically been defined as constituency—special education students who receive educational services in separate settings. As a consequence of the Individuals With Disabilities Education Act (IDEA, 1987), the inclusion of students with disabilities into general education classrooms now challenges both the constituency and concept of disability. However, there remains much to learn about understanding disability as part of the larger human experience. At large, policies and practices that have a direct impact on the material reality of living with disability are rarely examined by society, as many believe that disabled people have already won their rights. In much the same way that racism is believed to have been resolved by civil rights legislation, similar unexamined beliefs hold that the Americans With

Disabilities Act of 1990 ended injustice for the disabled. However, disabled people and those who research the lived experience of disability know that "the fundamental issue is not one of an individual's inabilities or limitations, but rather, a hostile and unadaptive society" (Barton, 1999, xi). How is it that society can still be cast as hostile and unadaptive despite three decades of important social policy reform for people with disabilities? (1) There are several ways to respond to this question. From a historical perspective, disability has been a specialized field limited to analysis within medicine, rehabilitation, special education, and social work. From a sociological perspective, others suggest that because many of the legal battles for disability access were won in the courts, with little involvement of nondisabled people, the assumption follows that people with disabilities have long since won their rights (Peters & Chimedza, 2000). The media have played a critical role in perpetuating hostility toward disability in numerous ways, including the negative portrayals of disability on television, in films (Longmore, 1987; Longmore & Umansky, 2001; Norden, 1994; Shakespeare, 1999) and in broadcast media depictions that reify unexamined assumptions about disability culture. Consider for example the recent newspaper accounts of the 10-year anniversary of the Americans With Disabilities Act (ADA) of 1990. Of the many variations on the triumph-over-disability theme of America's overcoming narrative (e.g., "Just Keep Moving" in The Atlanta Constitution, "Keep the 'able' in disabled" in The Kansas City Star, and "Improved Access for All, thanks to the ADA" in the Minneapolis Star Tribune), few made mention of the Alabama v. Garrett case before the Supreme Court. Garrett was the latest in a series of cases in which states challenged congressional power to enact legislation regulating state conduct—in this example, its authority specific to Title II of the ADA. Despite its obvious threat to dismantle the ADA, the Garrett case was cast as a states rights issue rather than a disability rights issue in both the courts and the media. Although this is not intended to suggest a media conspiracy, one has to wonder how naivete plays into complicity with societal hostility when the public relies on an ill-informed media.

Scholars in the field of humanities-based disability studies begin with the view of disability as a cultural signifier to problematize a range of unexamined attitudes, beliefs, and assumptions (L.J. Davis, 1995, 1998; Garland-Thomson, 1997; Linton, 1998; Longmore & Umansky, 2001; Mitchell & Snyder, 1997, 2000). Finally, education is just coming to name the inherent hostility to disability in education policy and practice as an evolution of its ongoing internal critique of special education (Brantlinger, 1997; Danforth & Gabel, 2000; Erevelles, 2000; D. Gallagher, 1998; Heshusius, 1989, 1995; Skrtic, 1991, 1995; Ware, 2000b, 2000f). Critical special education theorists interrogate teacher preparation, special education, educational administration, and educational and social policy. Among the questions raised are those that implicate the organizational pathology of schools; for example, Skrtic (1991) asks if special education is a rational system. D. Gallagher (1998) challenges the scientific knowledge base of special education by asking if we know what we think we know. And, borrowing from Foucault (cited in Philip, 1985), my research asks, "What have we done to ourselves by doing these things to them?" (Ware, 2000b). This question interrogates teacher practice that ignores its own complicity in perpetuating exclusion as well as the administrative practice of "meaning-management" (Anderson, 1990), which casts disability as a nonissue in general education in both secondary and postsecondary settings.

Critical special education, now in its "fourth wave" according to Heshusius (2000), provides an increasingly sophisticated range of issues beyond behaviorism. Included here are considerations of postmodern and poststructuralist reimaginings of disability

(Erevelles, 2000; Gabel, 1998, 2001; Peters, 1996, 2000; Smith, 1999a, 1999b, 2000; Ware, 1999, 2000a), reinvigorated calls for open inquiry motivated by concerns for equity and recovery of the original moral grounding of special education's roots (Brantlinger, 1997; Danforth & Gabel, 2000; Heshusius, 2000; Kleiwer, 2000; Ware, 2000b), and research in comparative contexts that makes linkages to international critical special education theory (Gabel, 2001, 2002; Peters, 1995, 1996, 2000; Ware, 1995, 1998, 1999, 2000b, 2000c).

Regardless of the origin of the critique, when unexamined attitudes, beliefs, and assumptions about disability are challenged, multiple perspectives prove more useful than any one field's perspectives. This is particularly important for teacher educators who seek to interrupt the contradictory subtexts in pedagogy and practice when special education's core concerns of cure, care, and remediation are contrasted with the reflection, transgression, and emancipation that lie at the center of liberatory praxis.

In the first part of this article, I consider two important critiques that have emerged to challenge status quo assumptions about disability. The first is the Disability Rights Movement (DRM), and the second is the emerging field of humanities-based disability studies. Each of these critiques is useful alone, but when taken together, they provide a strong argument for educators' considering disability through a cultural lens, one that interrogates the medicalized view that has powerfully shaped both general and special education and, more important, public perceptions of disability.

The DRM

> Historically, the only choice people with disabilities had in their personal struggle to survive was to individually resist isolation, even death, by relying on others. This meant, practically speaking, begging and becoming dependents of family or charities. That has begun to change. Now there is a movement of empowered people that seeks control of these necessities for themselves and their community.
>
> (Charlton, 1998, p. 165)

> There are 43 million of us in this country. But we're as invisible as Casper the Ghost.
> (Billy Golfus, cited in Golfus & Simpson, 1994)

According to Longmore and Umansky (2001), disability has been "present in penumbra if not in print, on virtually every page of American history" (p. 2), yet history has failed to include disability other than in medical case histories. In an effort to fill in the "historical gaps" of disability in American history, Longmore and Umansky have edited a collection of essays that capture the social, cultural, and political history of disability and disability rights activism. For example, during the Great Depression, the League of the Physically Handicapped staged actions in protest of job discrimination resulting from the medical model of disability that had begun to shape policy, professional practices, and social arrangements of the early 20th century (Longmore & Goldberger, 2000). Most Americans, including historians, will be surprised at the rich documentation supporting the essays in this collection, given the commonly held belief that only a "small fraction of the population appears to be disabled" (L J. Davis, 1995, p. 6). The origin of the DRM is typically associated with the late 20th century, from the 1960s through the present. Activism erupted in simultaneous waves in Berkeley, Boston, and Houston, giving rise to the DRM and paving the way for important legislation and social policy for disabled Americans. During this time, civil rights protests for accessible housing, transportation, employment, and education invited new conversations about self-determination and the real meaning of access. Through well-planned actions, disability advocates challenged public perceptions and raised consciousness about social justice and living conditions for the millions of Americans who live with disabilities (e.g., Block, 1997; Brock, 1998; Charlton, 1998; Golfus & Simpson, 1994; Shapiro, 1993). A recent show at the Smithsonian National Museum of American History titled The Disability Rights Movement captures much of the history of this era with original protest placards, footage of activism, and reform legislation documents among the objects on display. According to the curator, Katherine Ott (2000), the social progress of this era is most evident when contrasted with an earlier show, Triumph Over Disability (A.B. Davis, 1973), which displayed various medical instruments, devices, and aids that signaled the rise and development of physical and rehabilitation medicine in the United States. Consistent with the new disability history outlined by Longmore and Umansky (2001), the Smithsonian exhibit departs from the medical model of disability to instead relocate the disability experience in social rather than biological constructs.

The DRM characterizes a rich history of liberation by individuals claiming rights and staging actions that should have earned a more central place in the history of American life. Because DRM history has been elided from common understanding, its reintroduction into the collective consciousness will prove timely as it informs humanities-based disability studies and liberatory praxis in teacher education.

Humanities-Based Disability Studies

> Humanities-based disability studies is grounded in the desire to challenge our collective stories about disability, to renarrate disability, [and] to reimagine it as an integral part of all human experience and history.
>
> (Longmore & Garland-Thomson, 1999, p. 2)

Recent efforts to problematize disability through a cultural analysis are found in the emerging multidisciplinary scholarship and research in humanities-based disability studies. (2) History, literature, philosophy, anthropology, religion, medical history, and rhetoric rooted in the humanities rather than in the social sciences and rehabilitative medicine inform this scholarship. With an emphasis on understanding disability as discursively and materially created, the medical model is problematized such that questions of civil rights and social justice are privileged over those cast as personal problems. Among the critical issues in humanities-based disability studies are those related to identity, education, representation, sexuality, personal meanings of disability, access, employment, religion and spirituality, and strategies for empowerment and activism. Representing an unprecedented shift from the modernist project of biological determinism and the medicalization of disability, the new disability studies defines disability as a way of thinking about bodies rather than as something that is wrong with bodies (Longmore & Garland-Thomson, 1999; Mitchell & Snyder, 1997). In sum, disability studies "takes as its domain the intricate interaction among cultural values, social arrangements, public policy, and professional practice regarding disability" (Longmore & Umansky, 2001, pp. 15–16). This interpretation of human differences draws from postmodernist and poststructuralist analyses in which the person with disabilities becomes the "ultimate example, the universal image, the modality through whose knowing the postmodern subject can theorize and act"

(L.J. Davis, 1997, p. 5). Although this scholarship is infinitely broad in topic and scope and beyond an adequate presentation in this artide, (3) a key strand that cuts across this burgeoning literature is the problematizing of the ability–disability binary. That is, when disability is considered through a cultural lens, ability is interrogated in much the same way that gender is interrogated by feminist studies scholars and Whiteness is interrogated by ethnic studies scholars. The instance of the normal–abnormal binary is central to the problematization of disability, particularly as it has morphed into the ability–disability binary central to the invention of categorical systems institutionalized by society (e.g., education, medicine, law, and social policy). Given that many cultures (primarily Western) maintain disability as alterity through the ideology of assigning value to the normal able body and its functioning parts, stigmata are often equated with impairment and the disabled body. How we "other" the disabled body, according to L.J. Davis (1995), is determined by society:

> We tend to group impairments into the categories of either "disabling" (bad) or just "limiting" (good). . . . Wearing a hearing aid is seen as much more disabling than wearing glasses, although both serve to amplify a deficient sense. . . . Loss of hearing is associated with aging in a way that nearsightedness is not. (p. 130)

The subtle yet pervasive practice of assigning value to the body is most evident in cultural representations of disability, wherein, according to Thomson (1997), disability exists in opposition to the "normate." (4) This neologism characterizes the socially constructed identity of those who by way of the "bodily configurations and [the] cultural capital they assume, can step into a position of authority and wield the power it grants them" (Thomson, 1997, p. 8). In her analysis of the cultural representation of disability, Thomson reveals how disability operates in texts to expose the tensions between people who assume the normate position and those "assigned" the disabled position. Incomplete, prototypical disabled characters are more common than are dynamic and complex individuals, and for the most part, representations rely on cultural assumptions to fill in the missing details of personhood (e.g., agency, subjectivity, desire, sexuality, etc.). With respect to cognitive disabilities, moral philosophers have begun to reimagine reason as the center of what makes us human. The moral philosopher Eva Feder Kittay (1997, 1999a, 1996b) draws from her experience parenting her adult daughter with significant disabilities to pose provocative questions about independence, dependence, and interdependence in pursuit of developing a radical theory of equality that extends to both political and social life. Similarily, MacIntyre (1999), in his discussion of who contributes to the common good, suggests that many children in schools experience "too constrained and impoverished [a] view of future possibilities" (p. 75), bound as educators often are by systems that extinguish imagination. Finally, Carlson (1997, 1998) contends that given the ambiguities and intricacies of classification systems of cognitive impairment, to more fully consider the social nature of disability, questions about cognitive ability must move "beyond the boundaries of bioethics" (1997, p. 283). She urges that when feminists theorize physical disability, many "connections can and should be applied to persons with cognitive disabilities" (1997, p, 280).

Intersecting issues for educators

The cultural analyses emerging from disability studies scholarship offer challenging theoretical insights for educators to examine societal attitudes, beliefs, assumptions, and more
fundamentally, the lived experience of disability. For example, McRuer (2001) analyzes a
fundamental ideological cultural demand he terms compulsory able-bodiedness, borrowing from Adrienne Rich, Judith Butter, and a memoir by Michael Berube (1996), who
writes about life with his son Jamie, who has Down's syndrome. According to McRuer
(2001),

> Berube writes of how he "sometimes feel[s] cornered by talking about Jamie's intelligence, as if
> the burden of proof is on me, official spokesman on his behalf" (p. 180). The subtext of these
> encounters always seems to be the same: "In the end, aren't you disappointed to have a retarded
> child? . . . Do we really have to give this person our full attention?" (p. 180)

In his analysis, McRuer (2001) suggests two related questions drawn from Berube's experience and bound by "able-bodied consciousness" to tease out important subtext at play in
interactions between able-bodied and disabled people. These often-unarticulated questions are juxtaposed to make a critical point. In the end, wouldn't you rather be hearing? In
the end, wouldn't you rather not be HIV positive? Although two seemingly different
questions, the former typifies the subtext of the "thinly veiled desire for Deafness not to
exist . . . and the latter [is] more obviously genocidal" (p. 8). By his analysis, these questions are more alike than they are different and more reflective of the able-bodied culture
posing the question than about the "bodies being interrogated" (p. 8). The dialectic is one
in which ableist culture uncritically assumes an "affirmative answer to the unspoken
question; yes, but in the end, wouldn't you rather be more like me?" (p. 8). The significance
of these questions is that of the compulsory able-bodied desire for neither people who are
deaf nor those with AIDS to exist. Although educational researchers have just begun to
challenge these unarticulated questions and their relationship to the hostility and unadaptive structures in society previously cited by Barton (1999), they parallel the issues of
critical race theorists and feminists who seek to move beyond the essences and the
unvoiced in policies and practices. However, these conversations are not easily had in
schools or in teacher development. In my own research with preservice and practicing
teachers, there is sometimes a general sense of relief as we begin to unpack ableist assumptions in education and society, or just the opposite occurs, resulting in defensiveness and
denial. Initially, teachers cite the lack of resources, training, parental support, and administrative vision that reinforces the hegemony of ableist assumptions, as if to say, "That's
just the way it is." Others, upon reflection, acknowledge that they have ignored disability
issues, confident that systems and specialists were better able to address these issues.
And a few recount personal experiences with disability, which serves as the catalyst for
moving beyond the normalizing discourse of disability. Regardless of the response, each is
marked by emotions similar to those outlined by Tatum (1992) in her efforts to teach
race and racism in college classrooms. The parallels are more obvious when considered
against the larger meaning of social inclusion and the value of creating a shared responsibility for teaching all children. In the section that follows, I suggest that analyses offered by
humanities-based disability studies can inform educators about educational and social
inclusion.

Disability Studies in Education

> At stake here is the necessity for progressive educators' studies to provide some common ground in which traditional binarisms of margin/center, unity/difference, local/national, public/private can be reconstituted through more complex representations of identification, belonging, and community.
>
> (Giroux, 1996, p. 53)

Critical educational discourse informed by critical theory and critical pedagogy has, for more than two decades, inspired many activist educators to form alliances in pursuit of educational and social justice. With social transformation at the center of mutual reform efforts, this legacy of morally driven activism has its roots in Freirean efforts to promote justice, equality, democracy, and freedom through liberatory praxis—"conscientization" (Freire, 1970). However, in a recent special issue of Educational Theory (1998), the success of this reform project was challenged. Given its failure to disrupt the inequities in society related to race, class, gender, and ethnicity, critical pedagogy was problematized from several perspectives. The discussion included concerns, criticism, and solutions as in the example of Peter McLaren's (1998) 10-step manifesto for critical pedagogy in the age of globalization—a revivalist revolutionary project "performed in the streets . . . [and] public spaces of potential political, cultural, and economic transformation" (pp. 452–453). In this same issue, Patti Lather (1998, cited in Ellsworth, 1997, pp. xi, 9) voiced concerns that the "big tent" of critical educational discourse had come up against a "stuck place"—thus her calls for praxis informed by Derrida's question, "What must now be thought and thought otherwise?" (p. 495). In response to this challenge, I would answer that disability must now be thought and thought otherwise. By that I mean disability is a long overdue conversation among critical theorists, pedagogues, and educationalists who fail to recognize disability as a cultural signifier; nor do they include disability as a meaningful category of oppression (Erevelles, 2000; Gabel, 2001; Ware, 2000f). This silence on disability issues suggests the typical societal absorption of cultural stereotypes related to disability. Of equal significance is the unexamined assumption about the taken-for-granted category of disability in educational discourse—one shaped by ideologies, history, medicine, and social and political assumptions whose central binary is ability–disability. In an argument informed by the previously cited disability studies literature, I suggest that this binary is the root of all binarisms that inform social formations such as race, class, gender, ethnicity, sexuality, and disability.

Finding Alliances

Although critical theory might seem useful in this analysis, there exists a substantial body of critical special education literature that is readily positioned to merge with humanities-based disability studies. For more than three decades, critical special education literature has challenged the traditional normative paradigm of special education. This literature is doused with references to critical theorists and pedagogues in an effort to integrate the big tent discourse into critical special education scholarship. However, critical special education research has yet to be acknowledged by critical educationalists. In practice, critical special education literature has earned little more than sideshow status in education even though this work represents an exhaustive list of interdisciplinary and international theorists and researchers. With the exception of a handful of teacher preparation programs in the United States, alternative special education theory remains on the margins in both special and general teacher education, and it is off the page among critical theorists.

In fact, it is often the case that among general education audiences, critical issues in special education from an alternative paradigm of analysis must be contextualized to ensure general educators' understanding. In her discussion of inclusion in a mainstream education research journal, Brantlinger (1997) felt it necessary to provide a "brief background of the trends and issues in special education in order to place the debate about inclusion in context" (p. 427). Although the boundaries between general and special education evolved as an unintended consequence of IDEA (see Education for the Handicapped Children Act of 1975), why is it that these exclusionary structures remain? Given the legacy of critical theory in education and contemporary practice with multicultural issues at the forefront, the preservation of a dual and separate system of teacher training with categorical divisions and a clinical orientation to disability can no longer remain unchallenged. However, critical theorists avert their gaze from both the disabled subject and the dual system of education, as if to suggest that liberatory praxis would naturally exclude the disabled. Exclusionary practices such as these suggest clear complicity when teachers and teacher educators unwittingly preserve and prop up "cycles of oppression that operate in our courses, our universities, our schools, and our society" (Lawrence & Tatum, cited in Cochran-Smith, 2000), In sum, general ignorance about issues of disability as a category of educational and social oppression, evidenced by its absence from professional meetings, scholarly journals, and texts devoted to critical pedagogy, prompts me to ask, "Why does the academic nod to diversity morph to cringe at disability?" (Ware, 2000e).

In the absence of purposeful alliances among critical theorists and critical special education theorists, I suggest a new avenue for solidarity through humanities-based disability studies in education and the involvement of colleagues in humanities. (5) That is, if, as Giroux (1996) suggests, cultural studies promises "new spaces for collaborative work" (p. 43), then disability studies in education would invite many important opportunities to provide students with the opportunity to "study larger social issues through multidisciplinary perspectives" (p. 43).

In the section that follows, I describe one aspect of such a project situated in a high school creative writing class in which the teacher and I created a curriculum informed by humanities-based disability studies. This research builds on previous research with secondary teachers in general and special education, many of whom questioned why, despite compliance with IDEA, greater numbers of students remain excluded from the educational mainstream (Ware, 1995, 1998, 2000d). Although the official data report otherwise, the fact remains that although students may be relocated into the educational mainstream in a rush to inclusion, they often remain excluded in many complex ways that defy a simple body count for compliance purposes. The section that follows describes how one teacher realized the subtle contradictions at play in his own inclusive classroom.

Writing, Identity, and the Other(6)

> As I understand the concept of the "other," it involves two essential processes: When we make people "Other," we group them together as the objects of our experience instead of regarding them as subjects of experience with whom we might identify, and we see them primarily as symbolic of something else—usually, but not always, something we reject and fear and project on to them. To the non-disabled, people with disabilities and people with dangerous or

incurable illnesses symbolize, among other things, imperfection, failure to control the body, and everyone's vulnerability to weakness, pain, and death.

(Griffin, cited in Wendell, 1996, p. 60)

With an emphasis on identity and "othering," a veteran language arts teacher, Tom Painting, and I developed a curriculum unit we titled Writing, Identity, and the Other for his ninth grade creative writing class. The class consisted of typical students and those with learning, emotional, and physical disabilities (ages 13 to 15). The unit aimed to promote understanding of disability as part of the human experience, drawing from disability studies literature and first-person accounts of living with disability. Having had no prior awareness of disability studies, Tom hoped the content would cohere with his year-long theme for the class, writing for self-discovery. After several meetings and the exchange of selected excerpts from the literature (e.g., Hockenberry, 1995; Mairs, 1986, 1996; Shapiro, 1993; Shaw, 1994), we discussed the value and applicability of this content for his students. Together we identified selections from the readings each of us was drawn to, including two disability studies film standards, When Billy Broke His Head (Golfus & Simpson, 1994), and Breathing Lessons (Yu, 1996). Tom relied on me to propose a structure for the content, and I relied on him to develop the writing activities that would address the following goals for instruction and research.

- What can I understand about the identity of others who appear different from myself?
- What can I learn about my own identity through understanding the identities of others?
- Can disability ever represent anything other than a negative image?

Although there were many questions we might have focused on, these three represented our initial interests in reimagining disability in the context of a high school language arts class.

Teaming With Tom

Tom is a veteran teacher who has taught for 17 years in the same district: a large, urban, upstate New York system. Throughout our teaming, his tenacity and intuitive sense of his students amazed and intrigued me. His teaching is difficult to script, as he seems never to miss a beat. Each morning, prior to the class, we met over coffee, and based on the previous day's instruction, set a general target for our teaching. Classroom interactions were something akin to "trading fours," as I played sideman to Tom and his students. I learned early to follow their lead and when necessary, to move completely out of the way. The students (ages 13 to 15), having declared creative writing their major at this arts magnet high school, were in their second year with Tom. This familiarity provided an easy atmosphere in the classroom, one that did not begin with roll call or end at the sound of the bell. Early in my classroom observations (prior to co-teaching), a group of his students described their teacher as suffering from "HPD."

"HPD?" I asked with hesitancy, fearing I lacked the vernacular for navigating urban New York schools—or that the DSM-IV had conjured yet another diagnostic category.

"Haiku psychosis disorder," the students laughed, given Tom's intense appreciation and collection of haiku—a simple, image-driven poetry form. True to his diagnosis, on Day 2 of our teaching, Tom arrived with an overstuffed folder full of haiku, beaming with the comment, "I found some really great stuff on disability that I didn't even know I had!"

Throughout our teaming, Tom remarked on his growing disability consciousness informed by both personal history and his professional practice. He described his awkward encounters in the gym with a disabled man and his own uncertainty about engaging in conversation—a phenomenon that was quite uncommon for Tom. He also recalled experiences from his childhood and youth growing up with a twin brother who was physically disabled. Tom recalled these events in a stream of consciousness fashion, as though these prior experiences had long since been reflected on until we began teaming. His growing understanding about the cultural and material conditions of disability reminded me of the historian Douglas Baynton (2001), who asserts that "disability is everywhere in history, once you begin looking for it, but conspicuously absent in the histories we write" (p. 46).

Day 1. We began the unit (7) with a quick review of the previously explored writing genres (e.g., autobiographical writing, poetry, and science fiction). Tom revisited the general goals he had developed for the class and invited student responses as he wrote on the board.

> Writing for Self-Discovery
> To know about ourselves. The use of language how it convinces us to see things a certain way.
> To think about where we came from, like the Day of the Dead Stuff and the deaths we've experienced.
> Culture.
> The future.
> The past.
> Paying attention to dialogue.
> Writing new plots from our lives.
> Experiences—imagined & real!

After summarizing what he wrote, Tom asked the students to hang onto these goals for their writing, as in our upcoming unit we would address these targets from a slightly different perspective. While still at the board, he marked nine points in a three-by-three array with directions to the students to connect the dots without touching any point more than once. This activity is often used in workshops to depict the value of thinking outside the box as a means to creativity. When the only solution to seemingly complex issues is thinking outside the box, Tom engaged the students with the challenge, bribing those who knew the solution to allow their classmates to solve the puzzle on their own. Following an excited discussion of the task, Tom wrote "the Other" beside the image of the box. In the closing minutes of the class, Tom directed the students to "write a brief definition of the Other. What do we mean by the Other? Who is the Other?" The following are examples of student responses:

> When I hear the word Other, I think of the bad. Not the norm. I don't try to think inside of the box but its easier to sometimes. The Other to me is the parts of life and society that people don't want to think about. Maybe because its harder. The other is unwantable.

> Different, not the same, something else to choose or pick. Not including one.

> To me the Other means all the stuff that I've never seen before or all the stuff that has a different opinion than me. The other is outside my arms length, outside my space and outside my habits. The other son, the other boy, the other tree outside of the "box," the other room outside of the box.

Days 2 and 3. Building off their definitions of the Other, we led a whole-class discussion of the freewrite responses that extended over two class periods. Among the key comments raised were those of identity that reflected cultural trends such as body piercing and tattoos as well as issues related to sexuality. The exchange was difficult to predict, as topics cut across a range of issues and levels of awareness. Comments specific to homosexuality tended toward sensationalizing until one student offered, "I have an uncle who's gay, but in my family, he's not outside of us. I can honestly say that he's one of the best uncles I have." Another student, in response to the disdain expressed by some of his peers, raised the ante when he expressed concerns about human rights and social justice, insisting that "if being gay is who you are, no one should have the right to make you feel bad about it." Another student wondered, "Is self-knowing sometimes about not wanting to know?" Although there was no explicit reference to disability, the students demonstrated the capacity to probe complex meanings ascribed to the Other. The students' writing began with personal definitions that later shifted to society and who has the ultimate authority to define and judge normalcy. The term normal was their original descriptor, but given its attendant medicalized notions of the normal–abnormal binary, I introduced the term normalcy (L.J. Davis, 1995) to underscore thinking about social justice. The students appreciated the distinction and were quick to grasp the hegemony of normalcy in a democracy. Our discussion of normalcy led easily into locating the influences on cultural awareness they had previously considered. We closed the day by summarizing where we get our ideas about normalcy. The students' list included "those closest to me—my family, my friends, church, schools, TV—and what I tell myself." Hegemony was thus easy to examine in the context of those judged to be outside normalcy, those we "other" in society.

Pedagogically, Tom's enthusiasm for the topic was significant, as it complemented the disability studies material I introduced and it complicated the issues of disability and society. His willingness to include his own experiences in the conversation provided students the opportunity to consider multilayered and problematic analyses of "local histories and subjugated memories" and to express "open and honest concern for human suffering, values, and the legacy of the often unrepresented or misrepresented" (see Giroux, 1996, pp. 50–52). However, it is important to stress that it was not our intention to lead students to any particular position as much as it was to consider experiences that might support ways to reimagine disability. Working from specific disability studies materials and first-person accounts of disability, the students approached the task as writers might—through images, language, and expression. By the end of the first week, we were able to introduce the lived experience of disability through poetry, as is illustrated in the examples that follow.

Days 4 and 5.
My Place
I don't want to live in bungalow land
On the outer edges of the urban sprawl
In the places designed for people-like-us
Kept safely separate, away from it all,
I want to live in the pulse-hot-thick-of it,
Where the nights jive, where the streets hum.
Amongst people and politics, struggles and upheaval,
I'm a dangerous woman and my time has come,
                              Sue Napolitano (1998)

After providing a few minutes to read the poem in silence, Tom asked the class to read in rounds, with each student reading one half of a line aloud and overlapping into the voice of the next student in a round of voices that read as one. The class repeated this for several readings. Then, without discussion about the poem, Tom asked the students to "attend to the language of the poem" and write at the board the word or words that "really fix your attention—what captured your imagination as you listened to the poem?"

Pulse-hot-thick-of-it   outer edges

safely separate sprawl

amongst   urban sprawl bungalow land

nights jive

a dangerous woman and my time has come

Students discussed the poem in small groups as we fielded questions about the seemingly archaic language (e.g., upheaval, amongst, bungalow land, jive). The language of the poem and its juxtaposition to more contemporary language (e.g., urban sprawl, pulse-hot-thick-of-it, nights jive, dangerous woman) led many to speculate about the time period and its setting. Guessing whether the setting was England, Australia, or Ireland seemed for some to be the sole purpose of the exercise. However, others began to speculate about the speaker, and their curiosity slowly replaced the animated conjecture about the setting. "I think the woman wants to get back into a place she's been pushed out of," one student offered.

"I think she's just getting freedom—like for the first time, or something," said another.

With an air of insistence, another explained, "She could still be struggling to get free—it's not like she won't go back to the other place."

The students were perplexed by the poem and unable to make much sense of the actual lived context of the speaker until Tom posed a few questions.

"Let's think about this for a minute—who lives in places for 'people-like-us?' " Pausing, he continued, "In our society, who do we keep 'safely separate?' "

The elderly?"

"Crazy people?"

"Or maybe developmentally disabled people—people who can't live on their own—they're kept separate."

Before we could bring the lesson to closure, the bell signaled the end of class—but many of the students lingered over the question, Who do we keep safely separate in our society? One student paused on his way out of class to redraw the box that Tom had drawn to enclose their responses. "Hey, Mr. Painting," he teased as he erased the box that encased the words, "a dangerous woman and my time has come." With a laugh, he said, "Don't you think this woman is probably outside the box?" Tom paused by the board and, with a wide smile, raised both hands wide open to the air and with approval replied, "That's it, isn't it, Jose?"

When Tom and I met the next morning, he explained his hunch about where we might go after these first few days of introductory material. "Let's not try to tie everything up too neatly for them. Let's give them the space to enter where they feel comfortable." According to his analysis, the students seemed anxious—perhaps unclear about the purpose of the work or anxious to begin the holiday break. Regardless, he did not want them to feel pressured. Tom then acknowledged his growing unease with the content, remarking, "I hope I know how to stay with them on this—it's hard stuff." His comments were quite unexpected. My sense was that the students were holding their own, and I thought Tom was too. I would later learn from Tom that the content provoked personal issues—some he thought he had dealt with and others he knew still needed his attention.

Later, in class, we did not return to the Napolitano poem but instead began with a focused freewrite. Tom asked the students to define disability, leading with the following prompt: "Disability is . . ." Everyone began writing at once, but when the designated time elapsed, several students asked for additional time. Before inviting the responses, Tom asked, "Did anyone feel frozen at first? I was surprised at how difficult it was to come up with the right words." Many students agreed and commented about having written too many words or too few words. One student explained, "It's weird because it's something you know you know but just don't really think about it." Others offered the following definitions:

> Disability is many things. It can be when you cannot work parts of your body or it can mean you cannot read well. To me, everyone can have a disability in some way even if you don't see it.

> Disability is a problem that some people have that prevents them from living a life like able-bodied people. They may need a wheelchair, a walker, a cane, a seeing-eye dog, a tutor, or captioning and interpreting for all spoken words, or artificial machine-assistance to help them carry on their body's normal functions. A disability may weaken a person physically, but their thoughts and emotions are just like all peoples [sic].

> Something that causes a person to become unable to function the same way other people do. They may still be able to function normally, but in different way [sic] than people without a disability do.

Overall, the students' responses were a mix of objective and subjective descriptions that tied into the earlier conversations about normalcy and the range of visible and invisible disabilities. The exchange prompted Tom's memory of a summer job in his college days as a home health care provider for a disabled adult—something he admitted he had not thought about in years. Tom recalled his reluctance to perform the job requirements and his inability to contend with personal feelings about dependency so starkly contrasted to his own youth and athletic accomplishments that framed his identity. All of these emotions so complicated the job that he resigned from the position in less than a week. The intersections of these very critical issues proved to be of great interest to the students, as the tables were turned and they probed their teacher's emotions and attitudes. As a researcher, I observed Tom's easy exchange with the students despite his prior concerns about the emotional demands of the content. It is interesting that when Tom and I initially planned the unit, he made no mention of his personal experiences with disability. However, because we both participated in the writing assignments along with the students, recounting our personal experiences was a given. On one hand, it was valuable that Tom located himself in this inquiry with the same desire to understand disability differently, as did his students. Conversely, in his role as the teacher, his vulnerability led to concerns about where our teaching would ultimately lead us. The challenge of teaching in the zone of the unknown was clearly becoming burdensome as we neared the Christmas break.

Earlier that day, we had wondered how much could be accomplished given that we were at the end of the last full week of instruction prior to the holiday break. Knowing the following week would be marred by interruptions with holiday programs, early dismissals, and the general frenzy in high schools prior to a holiday, Tom made a quick decision to assign weekend homework. Despite the students' groans of protest, they were assigned an essay describing their first experience with disability. When the students returned on Monday, they had written varied accounts of family members and classmates with a range of disabilities; many provided loving descriptions of grandparents whose aging led to disability, and others wrote about themselves. Karen, a student with physical disabilities, titled her essay "Telling About Disability, Telling About Me." Her essay began with the following:

> My first encounter with disability was when I was born with spina bifida that affected my spinal chord [sic]. I wear leg braces (you probably noticed this). When I was little I didn't walk "I was 3 years old. My parents are very protective of me.

Reflecting With Tom

Although I felt that the first two weeks of instruction were a great success, the experience left Tom with new doubts about his teaching. He wondered why, prior to this unit, Karen and some of the other students had never written about disability. He was unable to recall a single student in all his years teaching who had ever written about disability. He wondered if he had somehow failed to create a place in which it was safe to examine this issue. As a consequence, he expressed doubts about whether the class, now halfway through their second year together, was really a community of writers. More important, Tom wondered if he had unconsciously avoided the topic of disability. His concerns surprised me, but they also provided the opportunity to discuss how schools silence particular discourses. Specifically, race, class, and sexuality are often cited in the educational literature as silenced discourses, but rarely is disability considered among the inequities resulting from the normalizing discourses of schooling. I explained that only certain professionals are sanctioned to broach the topic of disability. That is, although conversations about disability occur in schools every day, for the most part they are restricted to procedural issues of identification, referral, and placement in special education, or they focus on related problems of staffing, curriculum, and inappropriate student and parent behavior. This discourse of containment and control has failed to consider disability through a cultural lens and what it might mean to live with a disability over a lifetime.

As our teaching progressed, Tom recognized his reticence growing from a number of sources. He acknowledged his lack of familiarity with the materials I provided on disability and was surprised to find so many sources available to support disability studies. In addition, he was discomforted by the fact that he had not previously considered disability an identity category. Relatedly, his lack of vocabulary to discuss disability with his students was discomforting. More important, he was slowly coming to realize that students with disabilities would not be likely to find themselves anywhere in the curriculum.

The final two weeks. When we reconvened after the break, we began with Tom's package of haiku. In small group discussion, the students were asked to speculate beyond the moment depicted in the haiku and to flesh out a character with details of physicality and history by locating him or her in a scene. "Envision human attributes—a voice, a look, a story to tell," Tom urged.

a girl is wheeled into
chatter ceases
in the ladies' room
    Jocelyne Villenueve

MEN ONLY
door too narrow
for his wheelchair
    Rebecca M. Osborn

Among their examples are the following:

> The girl is about 23, but why is she called "girl?" She has just been in a car accident and is paralyzed. She is hooked up to all sorts of devices attached to the back of the wheelchair.

> I see a little girl in a wheelchair that cannot go to the bathroom by herself. I think she *is* small and has brown eyes and is embarrassed a little too. I know how she feels too in some ways because I have a disability and sometimes I get a reaction similar to that.

> This man has been handicapped for a while now. He's depressed but still tries to get out of the house. He's alone and has a hard time. Even though he's a man he can't get in the men's room so it's like since he's handicapped he's not a human being. I picture he's overweight, 40 years old, tight blue shirt, messy hair, jeans.

Reviewing their writing, I noted patterns that might be characterized by themes of empathy/compassion, pity/knowing, self-knowing, and rescue/saving. I prepared a handout with excerpts from their writing along with the list of themes and asked the students to confirm these themes and to identify other emotions I may have missed. The students added "anger" and "resentment" and then realized the list comprised only negative emotions. In a discussion about why this occurred, some students seemed at a loss to explain. Others, like Jose, seized the opportunity to remind everyone about his earlier analysis of the cultural messages we receive about disability when the class discussed the Napolitano poem. This time, he expounded on the negative portrayals of disabled people in films:

> I still dislike the way they're portrayed as angry, vengeful people like in films—Davros in Dr. Who or the phantom in The Phantom of the Opera, but this story I like because it showed at the end that the phantom had human emotions.

In response, another student insisted she had really heard many adults describe other adults with disabilities as girls or boys instead of women or men—as she had written in her characterization. She challenged Jose's analysis, explaining that she had borrowed language from how people really talk about the disabled and not how they talk in the movies. Students contributed to both sides of the debate, raising issues about how we infantilize disabled people, how fear frames difference, and how, without thinking, we perpetuate negative media stereotypes. It was remarkable how much the students raised in their criticism generated by two haiku. From this point, it was easy to revisit an earlier conversation on the social construction of disability and the acknowledgment that they lacked sufficient experience with disability to aptly portray characters with disabilities. One student explained, "It's funny that we don't really talk about disability in school. If it is just another way to live, then why don't we know more about that way?" As part of our final activity, we viewed the documentary When Billy Broke His Head . . . and Other Tales of

Wonder (Golfus & Simpson, 1994). This award-winning film introduces more than 20 activists who live with disability and view the experience as central to their identity. The narrator, Billy Golfus, a former radio journalist who was brain damaged after a motor scooter accident, introduces the film saying, "This ain't exactly your inspirational cripple story." The students' final writing assignment was to develop characters informed by the individuals in the film. In contrast to their earlier writing, their characters—informed by the lives of the individuals they came to know in the documentary—were markedly more witty, complex, and humane.

Implications for Teachers

This research was designed to explore K-12 curriculum approaches informed by humanities-based disability studies, as described in the first section of this article. Although I reported only a fraction of this classroom research, in this final section I will focus on the implications for teachers when attempting similar content to promote new understanding of disability. In many ways, one of the greatest challenges to teaching this content will be for teachers as they contend with personal issues that surface as they confront unexamined attitudes, assumptions, and beliefs about disability. Consider, for example, Tom's realization of the absence of disability issues in his general teaching for more than 17 years. Obviously, this was a surprise and a disappointment, given his espoused ideology and daily practice. That is, Tom attended individualized education plan meetings and worked individually with counselors, social workers, special education teachers, and other team members on behalf of his students with disabilities. Among his colleagues, he was known to be an inclusive practitioner; yet disability-related topics were nowhere to be found in his curriculum. He explained this in an interview after we completed the unit: "I felt that I lacked the authority to talk about disability; that was someone else's job." In fact, because the discourse on disability in public education and society is so entrenched in the medical model, by most standards Tom did lack the credential to address disability in his teaching. Professionals from medicine, rehabilitation, psychology, psychiatry, social work, and special education inform the discursive community on disability, which results in a normalizing discourse that informs the collective view of the disabled as diseased, weak, tragic, and too often deserving of their fate.

However, by introducing disability as a cultural construct with the purposeful goal of re-imagining disability, Tom was more than qualified to introduce these issues. By examining disability through a cultural lens, he tapped into prior experiences to inform his insights and practice in a reflective teaching approach. Curiously, this aspect of our teaching was not addressed when we planned the unit. I shared my background as a parent of an adult son with physical disabilities and as a former special education teacher and administrator. However, at the time, Tom did not realize the importance of his personal experiences to his teaching of this content, and I did not assume it was necessary to inquire about his lived experience. In retrospect, this proved to be somewhat ironic in that my work with preservice and practicing teachers is focused on acknowledging prior experience in the formulation of our constructs about ability and disability. As our teaching evolved, the importance of personal reflection when teaching this content became readily apparent. Now that I have expanded this project to include five new teachers along with Tom, the project teachers began with a journal assignment similar to that which I use in my teaching and workshops, titled My First Memory of Disability.

Conclusion

If teacher educators accept the challenge of reimagining disability, we must begin by problematizing disability through a cultural lens. This approach will necessitate new alliances with colleagues in the humanities and new conversations informed by humanities-based disability studies. Teacher education must recognize that purposeful links between general and special education have failed to occur in most teacher education programs. Although some universities have taken the lead in this enterprise, notably Syracuse University (Blanton, Griffin, Winn, & Pugach, 1997) and the University of South Florida (Paul, Duchnowski & Danforth, 1993), many teacher preparation programs are institutionally sanctioned to perpetuate educational apartheid. Turf wars and age-old disputes about professional credentials for educating students with special needs remain unresolved and serve to silence more important conversations about disability as a political and discursive entity. Among these issues are those Tom and I addressed in his class, including identity, education, representation, access, employment, strategies for empowerment and activism, and most significantly, personal meanings of disability. By no means is this list exhaustive, as important related concerns include issues of sexuality, spirituality, religion, and the genocidal aspects of the human genome project. In sum, consideration of these topics would dislodge the silence buried deep inside the uninspired curriculum that restricts teacher and student imagination about disability in both secondary and postsecondary education.

Notes

1. The reforms include, principally, the Americans With Disabilities Act of 1990, and the Individuals With Disabilities Education Act (1990), and the reauthorization of the Individuals With Disabilities Education Act (1997).
2. See Longmore and Umansky (2001) for a more thorough discussion of this history in the United States and Campbell and Oliver (1996) for a discussion of the context of the United Kingdom. In academia, Berube (1997) and Cassuto (1999) provide abbreviated accounts of humanities-based disability studies.
3. Overviews can be found in Corker and French (1999), L.J. Davis (1995), Linton (1998), Longmore and Umansky (2001), Mitchell and Snyder (1997), Shapiro (1993), and Wendell (1996).
4. The term normate was originally coined by Daryl Evans (see Thomson, 1997).
5. One such project is under way at the University of Rochester and is funded by the National Endowment for the Humanities. The project, "A Collaborative Inquiry on understanding Disability in Secondary and Post-Secondary Settings," is attempting purposeful linkages with education, the humanities, and medicine.
6. This research served as a pilot project for a National Endowment for the Humanities collaborative project that will now include six new secondary humanities classrooms.
7. Because Tom had extended the invitation to work with his class in mid-year, we were forced to work around the Christmas break, resulting in a noncontinuous block of 22 teaching days.

Acknowledgment

I would like to acknowledge the participants of the First Summer Institute on Disabilities Studies (July 2000), sponsored by the National Endowment for the Humanities and co-directed by Paul K. Longmore and Rosemarie Garland-Thomson of San Francisco State University.

References

Americans with Disabilities Act, 42 U.S.C. [subsections] 12101–12213 (1990).

Anderson, G.L. (1990). Toward a critical constructivist approach to school administration: Invisibility, legitimization, and the study of non-events. Educational Administration Quarterly, 26(1), 38–59.

Barton, L. (1999). Series editor's preface. In M. Corker & S. French (Eds.), Disability and discourse (p. xi). Buckingham, UK: Open University Press.

Baynton, D. (2001). Disability and the justification of inequality in American history. In P. Longmore & L. Umansky (Eds.), The new disability history: American perspectives (pp. 33–57). New York: New York University Press.

Berube, M. (1996). Life as we know it: A father, a family, and an exceptional child. New York: Vintage-Random House.

Berube, M. (1997, May). On cultural representations of disabilities. Chronicle of Higher Education, 43(38), B4–5.

Blanton, L.P., Griffin, C.C., Winn, J.A., & Pugach, M.C. (1997). Teacher education in transition: Collaborative programs to prepare general and special education educators. Denver, CO: Love.

Block, L. (1997). Beyond affliction: The disability history project [Audiotape series]. Washington, DC: Corporation for Public Broadcasting.

Brantlinger, E. (1997). Using ideology: Cases of nonrecognition of the politics of research and practice in special education. Review of Educational Research, 67, 425–459.

Brock, W. (Producer/Director). (1998). If I can't do it [Videotape]. (Available from Fanlight Productions: www.fanlight.com)

Campbell, J., & Oliver, M. (1996). Disability politics: Understanding our past, changing our future. London: Routledge.

Carlson, A.L. (1997). Beyond bioethics: Philosophy and disability studies. Disability Studies Quarterly, 17(4), 277–283.

Carlson, A.L. (1998). Mindful subjects: Classification and cognitive disability. Unpublished doctoral dissertation, University of Toronto, Canada.

Cassuto, L. (1999, March 19). Whose field is it anyway? Disability studies in the academy. Chronicle of Higher Education, 45(28), A60.

Charlton, J.I. (1998). Nothing about us without us: Disability oppression and empowerment. Berkeley: University of California Press.

Cochran-Smith, M. (2000). Blind vision: Unlearning racism in teacher education. Harvard Education Review, 70, 157–190.

Corker, M., & French, S. (Eds.). (1999). Disability and discourse. Buckingham, UK: Open University Press.

Danforth, S., & Gabel, S. (2000, April). Disability studies in education. Meeting of the American Educational Research Association, New Orleans, LA.

Davis, A.B. (1973). Triumph over disability: The development of rehabilitation medicine in the USA. Washington, DC: Smithsonian Institution, National Museum of History and Technology.

Davis, L.J. (1995). Enforcing normalcy: Disability, deafness and the body. London: Verso.

Davis, L.J. (1997). The disability studies reader. New York: Routledge.

Davis, L.J. (1998, Summer). Who put the the in the novel? Identity politics and disability in novel studies. Novel, 31(3), 317–334.

Ellsworth, E. (1997). Teaching positions: Difference, pedagogy and the power of address. New York: Teachers College Press.

Erevelles, N. (2000). Educating unruly bodies: Critical pedagogy, disability studies, and the politics of schooling. Educational Theory, 50(1), 25–47.

Freire, P. (1970). Pedagogy of the oppressed. New York: Continuum.

Gabel, S. (1998). Depressed and disabled: Some discursive problems with mental illness. In M. Crocker & S. French (Eds.), Disability discourse (pp. 38–46). Buckingham, UK: Open University Press.

Gabel, S. (2001). Problems of conceptual translation in cross-cultural disability studies: A South Asian immigrant example. In B. Altman & S. Barthart (Eds.), Research in social science and disability (Vol. 2). Thousand Oaks, CA: Sage.

Gabel, S. (2002). Some conceptual problems with critical pedagogy. Journal of Curriculum Inquiry.

Gabel, S.L. (2001). "I wash my face with dirty water": Narratives of disability and pedagogy. Journal of Teacher Education, 52.

Gallagher, D. (1998). The scientific knowledge base of special education: Do we know what we think we know? Exceptional Children, 64, 493–502.

Garland-Thomson, R. (1997). Extraordinary bodies: Figuring physical disability in American culture and literature. New York: Columbia University Press.

Gilman, S. (1985). Difference and pathology: Stereotypes of sexuality, race, and madness. Ithaca, NY: Cornell University Press.

Giroux, H. (1996). Is there a place for cultural studies in colleges of education? In H.A. Giroux, C. Lankshear, P. McLaren, & M. Peters (Eds.), Counter-narratives: Cultural studies and critical pedagogies in postmodern spaces (pp. 41–58). London: Routledge.

Golfus, B., & Simpson, D.E. (Producers). (1994). When Billy broke his head . . . and other tales of wonder [Film]. (Available from Fanlight Productions: www.fanlight.com)

Heshusius, L. (1989). The Newtonian mechanistic paradigm, special education, and contours of alternatives: An overview. Journal of Learning Disabilities, 22, 403–415.

Heshusius, L. (1995). Holism and special education: There is no substitute for real life purposes and processes. In T.M. Skrtic (Ed.), Disability and democracy: Reconstructing (special) education (pp. 166–189). New York: Teachers College Press.

Heshusius, L. (2000, April). Breaking the silence: Disability, education, and critical methods. Paper presented at the annual meeting of the American Education Association, New Orleans, LA.

Hockenbury, J. (1995). Moving violations. New York: Hyperion.

Individuals with Disabilities Education Act, 20 U.S.C. [subsections] 1400 et seq. (1997).

Kittay, E.F. (1997). Human dependency and Rawlsian equality. In D.T. Meyers (Ed.), Feminists rethink the self (pp. 219–266). Boulder, CO: Westview.

Kittay, E.F. (1999a). Love's labor: Essays on women, equality, and dependency. London: Routledge.

Kittay, E.F. (1999b). "Not my way, Sesha, your way, slowly": "Maternal thinking" in the raising of a child with profound intellectual disabilities. In J.E. Hanigsberg & S. Ruddick (Eds.), Mother troubles: Rethinking contemporary maternal dilemmas (pp. 3–25). Boston: Beacon.

Kleiwer, C. (2000). The collected papers of Burton Blatt: In search of the promised land [Book review]. Journal of the Association for Severe Handicaps, 25(1), 59–63.

Lather, P. (1998). Critical pedagogy and its complicities: A praxis of stuck places. Educational Theory, 48, 487–497.

Linton, S. (1998). Claiming disability: Knowledge and identity. New York: New York University Press.

Longmore, P. (1987). Screening stereotypes: Images of disabled people in television and motion pictures. In A. Gartner & T. Joe (Eds.), Images of the disabled, disabling images (pp. 65–78). New York: Praeger.

Longmore, P., & Garland-Thomson, R.G. (1999). National Endowment for the Humanities Institute on Disability Studies proposal. July-August, 2000. San Francisco: San Francisco State University.

Longmore, P., & Goldberger, D. (2000). The league of the physically handicapped and the Great Depression: A case study in the new disability history. Journal of American History, 87, 888–922.

Longmore, P., & Umansky, L. (2001). Disability history, from the margins to the mainstream. In P. Longmore & L. Umansky (Eds.), The new disability history: American perspectives (pp. 1–31). New York: New York University Press.

Mairs, N. (1986). On being a cripple. In N. Mairs (Ed.), Plaintext: Essays. Tucson: University of Arizona Press.

Mairs, N. (1996). Waist-high in the world: A life among the non-disabled. Boston: Beacon.

McIntyre, A. (1999). Dependent rational animals: Why human beings need virtue. La Salle, IL: Open Court.

McRuer, R. (2001). Compulsory able-bodiedness and queer/disabled existence. In B. Bruggerman, R. Garland-Thomson, & S.L. Snyder (Eds.), Enabling the humanities: A sourcebook in disability studies. New York: Modern Language Association.

Mitchell, D., & Snyder, S. (Eds.). (1997). The body and physical difference: Discourse of disability. Ann Arbor: University of Michigan Press.

Mitchell, D., & Snyder, S. (Eds.), (2001). Representation and its discontents: The uneasy home of disability in art and literature. In M. Bury, G. Albrecht, & K. Seelman (Eds.), The disability studies handbook. Thousand Oaks, CA: Sage.

Morris, J. (1991). Pride against prejudice: Transforming attitudes to disability. London: Women's Press.

Napolitano, S. (1998). In D. McLean, Beyond barriers: A consultation paper on arts and disability policy. Available: http://ndaf.org.pages/beyondbarriers

Norden, M. F. (1994). The cinema of isolation: A history of physical difference in the movies. New Brunswick, NJ: Rutgers University Press.

Ott, K. (2000, July). History: Disability and medical history. Paper presented at the National Endowment for the Humanities Summer Institute on Disability Studies, San Francisco State University.

Paul, J.L., Duchnowski, A., & Danforth, S. (1993). Changing the way we do business: One department's story of collaboration with schools. Teacher Education and Special Education, 16(2), 95–109.

Peters, S. (1995). Disability baggage: Changing the educational research terrain. In P. Clough & L. Barton (Eds.), Making difficulties: Research & the construction of special educational needs (pp. 59–74). London: Paul Chapman.

Peters, S. (1996). The politics of disability identity. In L. Barton (Ed.), Disability and society: Emerging issues and insights (pp. 215–234). London: Longman.

Peters, S. (2000). Is there a disability culture? A syncretisation of three possible world views. Disability & Society, 15, 583–601.

Peters, S.J., & Chimedza, R. (2000). Conscientization and the cultural politics of education: A radical minority perspective. Comparative Education Review, 44, 245–271.

Philip, M. (1985). Michel Foucault. In Q. Skinner (Ed.), The return of grand theory in the human science. Cambridge, UK: Cambridge University Press.

Shakespeare, T. (1999). Art and lies? Representations of disability on film. In M. Corker & S. French (Eds.), Disability discourse. Buckingham, UK: Open University Press.

Shapiro, J.P. (1993). No pity: People with disabilities forging a new civil rights. New York: Times Books/Random House.

Shaw, B. (Ed.). (1994). The ragged edge. Louisville, KY: Avocado Press.

Skrtic, T. (1991). Behind special education: A critical analysis of professional culture and school organization. Denver, CO: Love.

Skrtic, T. (Ed.). (1995). Disability and democracy: Reconstructing (special) education for postmodernity. New York: Teachers College Press.

Smith, P. (1999a), Drawing new maps: A radical cartography of developmental disabilities. Review of Educational Research, 69(2), 117–144.

Smith, P. (1999b). Food truck's party hat. Qualitative Inquiry, 5, 244–261.

Smith, P. (2000, October). MAN.i.f.e.s.t..: A poetics of d(eviL)op[mental] {dos}ability. Paper presented at Desegregating Disability Studies: An Interdisciplinary Discussion, Syracuse, NY.

Tatum, B. (1992). Talking about race, learning about racism: The application of racial identity development theory in the classroom. Harvard Educational Review, 62(1), 1–24.

Thomson, R.G. (1997). Extraordinary bodies: Figuring physical disability in American culture and literature. New York: Columbia University Press.

Ware, L. (1995). The aftermath of the articulate debate: The invention of inclusive education. In C. Clark, A. Dyson, & A. Millward (Eds.), Towards inclusive schools? (pp. 127–146). New York: Teachers College Press.

Ware, L. (1998). I kinda wonder if we're fooling ourselves? In T. Booth & M. Ainscow (Eds.), From them to us: An international study of inclusion in education (pp. 21–42). London: Routledge.

Ware, L. (1999). My kid and kids kinda like him. In K. Ballard (Ed.), Inclusive education: International voices on disability and justice (pp. 43–66). London: Falmer.

Ware, L. (2000a, April). A collaborative inquiry on understanding disability in secondary and post-secondary settings. Research proposal to the National Endowment for the Humanities. (Available from Linda L. Ware, University of Rochester, P.O. Box 270425, Rochester, NY 14627–0425)

Ware, L. (2000b). Inclusive education. In D.A. Gabbard (Ed.), Education in the global economy: Politics and the rhetoric of school reform (pp. 111–120). Hillsdale, NJ: Lawrence Erlbaum.

Ware, L. (2000c, June-July). Products producing subjectivities: Disability studies in education. Paper presented at the eighth annual meeting of the International Research Colloquium on Inclusive Education, Hamar, Norway.

Ware, L. (2000d). Sunflowers, enchantment, and empires: Reflections on inclusive education in the United States. In F. Armstrong, D. Armstrong, & L. Barton (Eds.), Inclusive education: Policy, contexts and comparative perspectives (pp. 42–59). London: David Fulton Press.

Ware, L. (2000e, April). There's no easy way to say/hear this, "As a cripple, I swagger." Paper presented at the annual meeting of American Education Association, New Orleans, LA.

Ware, L. (2000f, February). What the literature tells us about inclusion: What literature? Who was listening? Presentation to the Greece Central School Board of Education special study session on inclusion, Greece, NY.

Wendell, S. (1996). The rejected body: Feminist philosophical reflections on disability. New York: Routledge.

Yu, J. (Producer), (1996). Breathing lessons: The life of Mark O'Brien [Film]. (Available from Fanlight Productions: www.fanlight.com)

21

Paulo Freire's Contributions to Radical Adult Education

Paula Allman

Your eyes have not deceived you; this article offers yet another discussion of the thinking of Paulo Freire. My intention is that it might be a discussion with a difference, which speaks meaningfully to those who are committed to radical adult education. I will attempt to discuss the essential ideas in their inter-relationships, which constitute Freire's approach to working with adults in radical ways for radical objectives. I also will try, as far as space permits, to explicate the radical theoretical foundations which underpin Freire's thought and practice, i.e. praxis (Allman and Wallis, 1990).

In the following discussion a very specific idea of radical education is used. This idea is linked to a strategy aimed at a revolutionary transformation of our current social formation, an idea of transformation culled from the writings of Karl Marx, as opposed to the theory and practice of socialism and communism that both preceded and followed him. This discussion also relates to more immediate radical tactics, short-term radical approaches, so long as these are critically conceived and practiced within or integral to the long-term strategy. For example, there is a range of struggles around "access" taking place at present. These include access to the "given" educational opportunities by individuals and groups previously excluded; access to learning in nonconventional environments and access to alternative and usually more critical sources of knowledge. From the perspective of this author, all of these tactical struggles can have authentically radical potential if those involved in the challenge locate their approach within the broader strategy for revolutionary social transformation. In this article, I refer to that transformation as socialism, assuming this to be a process of preparation for a communist social formation; however, I use these terms in the sense that they were promulgated by Karl Marx not in terms of what we have either witnessed or experienced thus far in history.

We should not expect or even desire a methodological blueprint for radical or socialist practice. Working out an appropriate approach to any form of cultural action, i.e. education broadly conceived, for socialism requires a critical analysis of the specific context in which it is to be applied. However there is much that we can learn from the writings of Paulo Freire. At least this is my conclusion; therefore in this article I will rely on supporting my argument by utilizing extensive quotations from his writings so that the reader can be the judge of whether this conclusion is correct.

In Britain an unfortunate and, I think, damaging tendency has arisen regarding the work of Freire, especially when his ideas are implicitly or explicitly contrasted to those of the Italian Communist, Antonio Gramsci. Rather than learning from each of them, radical educators frequently have viewed their ideas as incompatible. Freire has come to be associated with process, or pedagogy, and Gramsci with knowledge, content and organization.[1]

In fact a wider debate about emphasising content rather than process, or vice versa, is rife throughout education in Britain. I would argue that both the wider debate and its expression within radical adult education (or any other site of radical practice) exemplify the tendency within bourgeois praxis to separate or dichotomize that which belongs together. In addition to the necessary dialectical unity between process and content, process contains a content of its own which can either complement or contradict the explicit content. Any content or body of extant knowledge is the result of methodological processes, which may work either dialectically or ideologically. (The distinction between these two processes should become clear as the discussion proceeds.) Because of this methodological processes must be considered critically alongside the content. Both Freire and Gramsci were acutely aware of the relation between process and content, and their strategies for educational and political work derive from a concern for grasping the dialectical unity between the two. Unfortunately space limitations prevent me from comparing the ideas of Freire and Gramsci in this article.[2]

As with any writing, the ideas of Freire presented in this article are a selection; however, my intention is that it is not an eclectic one. This consideration of Freire's contributions begins with some very brief and general comments on his background, i.e. the background in which he formed these ideas.

Paulo Freire is a Brazilian and is best known for his work in and influence upon mass literacy campaigns first in Brazil and then in Chile, and later in Guinea Bissau, Nicaragua and elsewhere. Even though Freire uses the broader terms, cultural action, and cultural revolution, he is usually associated with education. As a consequence it is easy to ignore that almost everything he has written also deals with the role of revolutionary leadership—the way in which socialist revolutionary leaders must work and learn with the people as well as their organizational role.

Even though I begin with some comments about his educational ideas, as far as possible I will attempt to avoid any separation between educational and political thought.

On a series of audio-tapes which Freire recorded while visiting Australia, he explains that his thinking about education began long before his doctoral studies or his work on mass literacy campaigns. It began when he was a young man who went to work with the rural and urban poor because of his Christian convictions. It was the poor conditions of existence and particularly the way they thought about these conditions that led him to the writings of Marx and other marxists (Freire, 1974a). A learning group with which I was involved in the early 1980s first listened to those tapes at the same time that we were seriously studying Freire's writings in order to formulate our own radical approach to adult education. This was about two years before I undertook an in-depth and comprehensive study of Marx's writings and therefore was before I understood either Marx's dialectical method of analysis or his negative concept of ideology. Therefore in our learning group's initial encounter with Freire I was unable to really fulfil my obligations and commitments as a radical educator because I did not understand how directly Freire's educational philosophy was based on Marx. In fact, Freire's writings assume of the reader a considerable grounding in Marx. This may be a fair assumption in Latin America but is clearly unfounded with reference to a North American or British readership; and this may go some way towards explaining why some of his ideas have been so readily incorporated by liberal/progressive educators.[3]

I will cite just a few examples of dialectical analysis, which could be read as interesting metaphors in the absence of an understanding of Marx's dialectical analysis. But first I must briefly describe the basis of that analysis. Careful study of Marx's writings renders it clear that he assumes that the principle of change in the social condition is dialectical contradictions; therefore he focuses his analysis on these types of contradictions. A dialectical contradiction is not the same as a logical contradiction but could lead to the latter in a given explanation. A dialectical contradiction is a unity or internal relation of two opposites that could not exist, as they presently do or have done historically, outside the way in which they are related. When such a relation is antagonistic, producing domination and subordination, and so on, the idea for the radical activist is to abolish or radically transform the relation, rather than to simply improve the position, within the relation, of the subordinate opposite (Marx and Engels, 1956: 49–54). Two examples of these contradictions in a capitalist society, which are directly related to this particular social form, are labor and capital and production and exchange or consumption; however there are many others at which radical educators must also direct their energies. For example, men and women, black people and white people, people with disability and those supposedly with none; these contradictions, relations of oppression, do not arise from capitalism but are shaped within the social relations of capitalism.

In discussing the oppressed, i.e. the subordinate opposite, Freire says: At this level, their perception of themselves as opposites of the oppressor does not yet signify involvement in a struggle to overcome the contradiction; the one pole aspires not to liberation but to identification with its opposite pole. (Freire, 1972: 22)

Even though the translator footnotes the word "contradiction" and explains that in this book it means "the dialectical conflict between opposing forces", it is not much help—unless one also knows that a dialectical contradiction is the unity of two opposites which could not exist as they are outside their relation to each other. One also misses the point that to liberate themselves the oppressed must engage in what Marx called "the negation of the negation" by negating their relation with the oppressor thereby negating themselves as a separate and oppressed class or group. Freire continues: In this situation the oppressed cannot see the "new [person]" as the [person] to be born from the revelation of the contradiction in the process of oppression giving way to liberation. For them the new [person] is themselves become oppressors. (Freire, 1972: 22–23)[4]

Drawing on Marx's dialectical theory of consciousness, i.e. the idea which conceives of consciousness as a dialectical unity between thought and action, praxis, Freire says: World and [people] do not exist apart from each other, they exist in constant interaction. Marx does not espouse such a dichotomy, nor does any other critical, realistic thinker. What Marx criticized and scientifically destroyed was not subjectivity, but subjectivism and psychologism. Just as objective reality exists not by chance, but as a product of human action, so it is not transformed by chance. If [humans] produce social reality (which in the "inversion of the praxis" turns back on them and conditions them), then transforming that reality is an historical task for [human beings]. (Freire, 1972: 27)

Of course, from this a reader can glean some idea about what Freire is implying. However, without Marx's detailed explanation of how a limited praxis, i.e. one which, even when aimed at resistance, simply reproduces the given social relations or dialectical contradictions, produces the inversion and of how revolutionary or critical praxis must both critique the resulting ideological explanations and transform the relations which constitute the social contradictions, I am not sure how someone can put Freire's ideas into practice with any sort of precision (Marx and Engels, 1976). For readers well-grounded in Marx, Freire's writings can be read in a much more analytical and strategical way, and his analytical rather than merely philosophical debt to Marx becomes clear. With such a grounding a much deeper meaning can be derived from the following where he is discussing a critical (dialectical) perception of reality developing amongst the oppressed.

This perception is necessary, but not a significant condition by itself for liberation; it must become the motivation force for liberating action. Neither does the discovery by the oppressed that they stand in dialectical relationships as antithesis to the oppressor who could not exist without them in itself constitute liberation. The oppressed can overcome the contradiction in which they are caught only when this perception enlists them in the struggle to free themselves (Freire, 1972: 26).

To free themselves means, in terms of long-term strategy, to free themselves from the relation of the dialectical contradiction rather than only to obtain political freedom in the traditional democratic sense. Again with Marx as a background, Freire could not be clearer; but without that background, readers will take from Freire what seems meaningful to them. Furthermore, I know from my own experience that if you abstract Freire's ideas from their Marxist theoretical context, you will miss the precision of his analysis and ignore the revolutionary intent of his work.

One of Freire's most important contributions to education or any form of cultural action for socialism and to marxism itself, stems from his understanding of Marx's theory of consciousness and his negative or critical concept of ideology in which ideology, or ideological, refers neither to a "system of beliefs" or "false consciousness" but to explanations, or actions and symbols based on such explanations, which are partial and fragmented and thereby distorted. Freire shares Marx's concern about how ideology, and what Freire also calls "a naive consciousness" (Freire, 1976)[5] can serve to sustain an oppressive social formation. His educational projects are based on developing a critical (dialectical) perception of reality amongst the participants (Freire, 1972: footnote 15 and 26–29). He expects socialist cultural workers and revolutionary leaders to have already developed this perception. Their role, however, is not to tell the people what to think but to enable them also to think critically (Freire, 1972: 99–101). His contribution (which I will discuss in detail in the next section) is an analysis of how to be with the people so that they can develop this way of thinking. Without it there will be no motivation for struggle and no authentic revolution. However, one of Freire's primary concerns is about how the ideology of the oppressors can continue to affect even those who have a critical perception of reality.

For Freire, as for Marx, ideology results from human beings' experiences within real relations or dialectical, social contradictions. Therefore according to Freire, when revolutionary leaders communicate with the people they must do so within relations which are the opposite of the oppressors' (Freire, 1972: 97). As mentioned above, ideology is not just a matter of ideas or explanations but entails ways of relating and behaving. In the following he warns revolutionary leaders that they may be reflecting to the people a less than revolutionary option: I believe that one of the most difficult problems confronting a revolutionary party in the preparation of militant cadres consists in rising above the canyon between the revolutionary option formulated verbally by the militants and the practice which is not always revolutionary. The petit bourgeois [liberal-democrat] ideology that permeated them in their class conditions interferes with what should be their revolutionary practice . . . It is in this sense that methodological errors are always an expression of an ideological vision . . . In so doing, all they do is reproduce this dichotomy typical of a class society—between teaching and learning . . . They refuse to learn with the people . . . Because of all this I am convinced that the effort to clarify the process of ideologizing must make up one of the introductory points in every seminar for preparing militants, simultaneously with the exercise of dialectical analysis of reality. (Freire, 1985: 163)

One of the most basic tenets of Freire's approach, then, is that cultural action for socialism is about developing a critical (dialectical) consciousness, a critical praxis, but this pertains equally to the leaders or educators as it does to the people even if the former have a "theoretical" or analytical head start (Freire, 1985: 156–163).

From what has been said thus far—and I will return to this in detail later—Freire understands revolution to be a process with an important and essential educational component (Freire, 1972: 43, 106). However, he also understands education to be a thoroughly political process, not just his approach to education but all education and every aspect of it (Freire, 1972: 52 and Freire, 1974a). To Freire every educational or cultural process can be seen as one which either domesticates people or as one which aims to liberate them, or rather to prepare them to collectively liberate themselves (Freire, 1985: 101–104). Hopefully it is clear that, for Freire, liberation is not aimed at individuals but, of course, will have a profound effect on them. Freire offers a very persuasive argument that educators' claims to neutrality are an impossibility. If educators are not encouraging people to question (to see their reality as a problem), to challenge and to change their reality, then they must be enabling them to accept it, adapt to it and to engage in its reproduction, unless, of course, their approach enables those with whom they work to see the latter as a tactic linked to the former. Therefore educators and every other cultural worker must make a political choice between domestication and liberation and in making that choice to be clear about whose interests they are serving (Freire, 1985 and 1974a).

Needless to say, those who have claimed that Freire's approach to education is non-prescriptive have, in certain ways, interpreted him incorrectly. At the level of prescription, which suggests what educators "ought" to do, he is unequivocal. This, in turn, links back to the essential prescription he shared with, and probably came to through his readings of, Marx. Both of them think that it is our human vocation to become more fully human (Freire, 1972: 20). In Marx's terms this would mean being at one with our "species being" or that which makes our species distinctive from others. According to this analysis of human ontology human beings are alienated from their human potential. Marx and Freire urge human beings to engage in a revolutionary process which would deliver human history into "human hands", i.e. making it the critical and creative product of all human beings. There is no doubt that this is prescriptive, but we should not forget that it is no more so than the laissez-faire "flip-side" prescription. The difference therefore is not one between prescription and non-prescription, but one between the ethical basis of the prescription. The idea of being more fully human is at the core of Freire's thought; therefore we should examine this idea in more detail.

Freire stresses that both humanization and dehumanization are real possibilities but only the former is the vocation of the human species. To exist humanly, or to engage in the process of humanization, we need not wait for a revolution. We can begin, even in the most limiting situations, to perceive those limits, our reality, critically and engage in the struggle to transform our societies (Freire, 1972: 72–73). For Freire, humanization is not some philosophical or Utopian demand but a real, historical possibility. It is the dialectical opposite of dehumanization, and to date it is constantly negated by dehumanization, or exploitation and domination; "Yet it is affirmed by that very negation . . . by the yearning of the oppressed for freedom and justice" (Freire, 1972: 20). He continues, stressing that dehumanization is a concrete historical fact rather than the natural destiny of humankind:

> Dehumanization, which marks not only those whose humanity has been stolen but also (though in a different way) those who have stolen it, is a distortion of the vocation of becoming

more fully human. This distortion occurs within history but it is not an historical vocation. Indeed to accept dehumanization as an historical vocation would lead to either cynicism or total despair. The struggle for humanization, for the emancipation of labor [from its relation with Capital] for the overcoming of alienation, for the affirmation of men as persons would be meaningless. This struggle is possible only because dehumanization, although a concrete historical fact, is not a given destiny but the result of an unjust order that engenders the violence in the oppressors, which in turn dehumanizes the oppressed.

(Freire, 1972: 20–21)

A critical perception of reality enables people to know what needs changing, but it has two other very essential functions. This critical, dialectical, perception together with an engagement in creating our conditions of existence, is what it means to be fully human, and it is the right of every person not some privileged few (Freire, 1972: 61). Furthermore it is this perception of reality that creates the will or the motivation in people to risk themselves in revolutionary struggle.

A deepened consciousness of their situation leads [people] to apprehend that situation as an historical reality susceptible of transformation. Resignation gives way to a drive for transformation and inquiry, over which [people] feel themselves in control. If [people], as historical beings, necessarily engaged with other [people] in a movement of inquiry, did not control that movement, it would be (and is) a violation of [their] humanity. Any situation in which some [people] prevent others from engaging in the process of inquiry is one of violence. The means used are not important; to alienate [people] from their own decision-making is to change them into objects. (Freire, 1972: 58)

Once again he is not just commenting on the oppressors but cautioning revolutionary leaders about their relations with the people. This passage also indicates that Freire thinks dehumanization is widespread. It is not just the poor who are alienated from decision-making and critical thinking but the vast majority of people living in the world regardless of their form of government. Related to this is Freire's distinction between "being in the world" and "being with the world" (Freire, 1985: 67–71).

According to Freire animals are "beings in the world"; they must respond and adapt to given conditions. People, too, can be "beings in the world" either when they lack a scientific understanding of the natural world or the necessary "scientific" (dialectical) understanding of their social formation. To be thoroughly, humanly "with the world" means that people would have developed a critical perception and collectively would have taken their environmental, social, political and economic destiny into their own hands. But even to begin that struggle is to become "beings with the world".

As mentioned earlier, Freire's most important contribution to marxist thought is his analysis of how socialist educators and political activists can work with people to enable them to think critically or dialectically about their reality. Repeatedly he emphasizes that such a perception cannot be given to or imposed on people (Freire, 1972: 97–101). This concern is firmly located in Freire's understanding of Marx's negative concept of ideology and his dialectical method of analysis. For Freire, grasping the dialectical content of reality is the necessary precondition for the beginnings of a human history created by all human beings (Freire 1972: 84–87). In a section where he discusses the program content of education for liberation—"the 'universe of themes' in dialectical contradiction"—he says:

In such a situation, myth creating irrationality [ideology] itself becomes a fundamental theme. Its opposing theme, the critical and dynamic view of the world, strives to unveil reality, unmask its mythicization and achieve the full realization of the human task: the permanent transformation of reality in favor of the liberation of [human beings].

(Freire, 1972: 74)

In a later section, he refers to a particular myth and in so doing encapsulates his approach to being with the people:

> Scientific [dialectical] and humanist revolutionary leaders . . . cannot believe in the myth of the ignorance of the people. They do not have the right to doubt for a single moment that it is only a myth, [an element of the oppressor's ideology] . . . Although they may legitimately recognize themselves as having, due to their revolutionary consciousness, a level of revolutionary knowledge different from the level of empirical knowledge held by the people, they cannot sloganize the people but must enter into dialogue with them, so that the people's empirical knowledge of reality, nourished by the leaders critical knowledge gradually becomes transformed into knowledge of the causes [dialectical contradictions] of reality.
>
> (Freire, 1972: 104)

In the next section I will be describing the principles and strategies which underpin this approach to working with people. However, before going on to those details, it is important to make two further points.

When Freire says we do not have the right to think that others are ignorant, he is not saying that we simply accept their perceptions of reality. These perceptions must be represented as a problem, because they may be limited by naive fatalism, permeated by the dominant class's ideology or locked into a limited awareness of a singular form of oppression (Freire, 1972: 80–83, 149–150). Freire's ideas have been enthusiastically embraced by a variety of reformist campaigns, and his concept of conscientization (the process of developing the critical/dialectical perception) is often equated with "consciousness raising". The following passages clearly challenge these reformist interpretations and will hopefully help to set the record straight for radicals who may have dismissed Freire more because of the practices which claim to be based on his ideas than because of what he actually says:

> . . . human beings do not get beyond the concrete situation, the conditions in which they find themselves, only by their consciousness or their intentions however good these may be . . . praxis is not blind action . . . It is action and reflection . . . In this sense, subjectivism—throwing itself into simple verbal denunciation of social injustice . . . while leaving intact the structure of society is just as negative as mistrusting a rigorous and permanent scientific [dialectical] analysis of objective reality.
>
> (Freire, 1985: 154–155)
>
> manipulated by the ruling classes' myths, the dominated classes reflect a consciousness which is not properly their own. Hence their reformist tendencies. Permeated by the ruling class ideology, their aspirations, to a large degree, do not correspond to their authentic being. These aspirations are superimposed by the most diversified means of manipulation.
>
> (Freire, 1985: 159)[6]

Freire's approach involves starting with "where people are" but moving with them to an increasingly critical consciousness. Such a consciousness would enable people to understand how their own experience of oppression, e.g. race, class, gender and so on, is linked to a total structure of oppression and to redefine their aspirations accordingly.

Freire's Approach

Clearly this approach is about working with people rather than working for them or on them, but we must consider now the transformations which are essential to establishing this relationship with others. In very general terms, Freire's approach involves challenging and transforming the relations, which pertain in traditional (bourgeois) cultural practices. The immediate goal of these transformations is the conscientization I referred to earlier. Freire uses the Latin American equivalent of this term to embrace in one word his advocacy of the need for a critical, dialectical perception of reality in unity with a critical, revolutionary practice (Freire, 1985: 82–87). The term conscientization expresses the inseparable unity between critically acting to transform relations and the critical transformation of consciousness. In other words, it is only within the experience of struggling to transform relations and the experience of the transformations that our critical consciousness can fully develop.

To initiate a Freirian approach, then, involves a detailed analysis of the relations which will need to be transformed. Although these may vary considerably in different social and historical contexts, two relations, in particular, seem to me relevant within any formal or non-formal educational setting and have important implications for many other areas of cultural work. For readers who are familiar with Freire's work, the relation between teachers and learners will be well known, but I must argue that it is frequently misunderstood.

The following discussion is based on a dialectical analysis of bourgeois education,[7] which draws heavily on Freire's ideas. Teachers and learners are a unity of opposites, or in other words a dialectical contradiction. Each group is what it is by virtue of its relation to the other. For Freire this is an antagonistic contradiction which must be overcome. The teacher possesses "already existing knowledge" which learners need. An antagonism results because learners, due to their dependency, are subordinate and teachers as a dialectical consequence are dominant. Therefore teachers and learners constitute different groups in which the processes of teaching and learning have become separated or dichotomized. Another consequence of this is that the "act of creating new knowledge" becomes totally separated from the "act of acquiring extant knowledge". All of these separations are antagonistic because they limit the learning and creative potential of both groups.

With Freire's approach, the idea is to conceive teaching and learning as two internally related processes within each person. This is why he uses the rather cumbersome terms, teacher–learners and learner-teachers, to express the necessary transformations. Teachers do not cease being teachers but cease being the exclusive or only teacher in the learning group. They will need to relinquish authoritarianism but not authority. He emphasizes that teacher-learners must have plans, projects and goals or an overall intent within which they work, including their own learning (Freire, 1972 and 1974a). Learner-teachers likewise do not cease being learners but join together with teachers in a mutual process, a unity, of teaching and learning. However, as simple and straightforward as this transformation may sound, it is extremely difficult. Teachers on their own cannot transform this relation. They can initiate the change by challenging learners to consider the limitations of existing relations, but it is only when the learners accept the challenge that the actual, the collective, struggle to transform the relations begins. It is the beginning of the struggle because to truly establish the unity between teaching and learning within each person, the transformation of yet another relation must be sought simultaneously.

It is impossible authentically to effect the transformation of the teacher-learner relation until both teachers and learners transform their relation to knowledge (Freire, both 1972: 53 and 1974a). In other words, being or relating differently is inextricably bound up with knowing differently. Given Marx's theory of consciousness (praxis), and Freire's understanding and use of it, this should not be surprising. I only want to emphasize that both transformations must be struggled for simultaneously. The task is all the more difficult in bourgeois societies because our relations to knowledge and our concepts of knowledge, our epistemologies, are constituted within and penetrated by bourgeois ideology. Both Marx and Freire stress that certain residues of the capitalist social formation will linger even after a socialist revolution. Bourgeois epistemology is one such residue, which, until it is challenged and transformed, will remain a barrier to the realization of socialism (Freire, 1972: 128). In this century it has proven itself to be a very real and pervasive barrier.

Like everything else, which, in fact, results from social relations, bourgeois knowledge is perceived as a "thing", a commodity. If we possess it, it affects who we are, our status and self-esteem, and if we do not possess it, there is an equal and opposite effect on who we are and how we think about ourselves. A transformed relation to knowledge involves constantly scrutinizing what we know, and constantly testing its adequacy as a tool for illuminating our real conditions and informing our action. Knowledge therefore cannot be conceived as a static possession but only as a mediation or tool between people and the world, which either helps or hinders a critical perception of reality. And this is also true for the knowledge, which may have resulted from grasping the dialectical movements of reality at a particular point in time. In fact it is because social reality moves and develops according to dialectical processes that knowledge cannot be perceived as static (Freire, 1972: 146–147; 1985: 87–90, 105–107).

In Freire's approach to education, knowledge—the expert's and our own—becomes an object to which we direct our critical thought. Since knowledge is used to deepen our understanding of the themes or issues which arise from our material conditions, it must be constantly tested, questioned or problematized. All sorts of knowledge—academic, radical critique, personal are central to Freire's approach but as something we use rather than simply acquire. Therefore, any knowledge is a means by which we begin learning rather than an end in itself. When knowledge enables us to unmask the dialectical contradictions of our reality it becomes the springboard for the creation of new knowledge or a deeper understanding of the world, which we will need for developing a revolutionary praxis. When, on the other hand, the critical scrutinizing of a form of knowledge reveals that it is concealing those contradictions, it can be used to inform us of ideological processes and results.

Some radical educators in Britain appear to have rejected Freire's ideas because they can see no space for a consideration of radical content. Nothing could be further from the case; but perhaps the role of content or knowledge in Freire's approach is only clear given an understanding of Marx's negative concept of ideology and the epistemological and ontological shifts required by Freire's approach.

In order to effect the transformation of teacher-learner relations and relations to knowledge, Freire proposed that learning must take place within a revolutionary form of communication, namely dialogue. He calls it "the seal of the transformed relations", but it is also the process which enables these transformations to take place:

> Only dialogue, which requires critical thinking, is also capable of generating critical thinking. Without dialogue there is no [real] communication, and without communication there can be no true education. Education which is able to resolve the contradiction between teacher and student takes place in a situation in which both address their act of cognition [understanding] to the object by which they are mediated.
>
> (Freire, 1972: 65)

With reference to the last point and perhaps more clearly elsewhere, he says:

> While in education for domestication one cannot speak of a knowledge object but only of knowledge which is complete, which the educator possesses and transfers to the educatee; in education for liberation there is no complete knowledge possessed by the educator, but a knowable object which mediates educator and educatees as subjects in the knowing process. Dialogue is established as the seal of the epistemological relationships between subjects in the knowing process.
>
> (Freire, 1974b: 20–21)

Dialogue is not achieved easily. It involves the struggle to transform the relations I have just discussed; therefore it is a form of critical praxis (Freire, 1972: 99; also see Allman and Wallis, 1990). It is a form of communication, which is appropriate for cultural action for socialism, or any arena of radical praxis (Freire, 1972: 98–99).

In dialogue, teachers and learners learn to relate differently to each other by relating differently to knowledge and vice versa. I can best explain dialogue and these different relations by contrasting it to two traditional forms of educational communication, lecture and discussion. On one of the tapes in the series mentioned earlier (Freire, 1974a), Freire tries to clarify his approach by contrasting it to what he calls "banking education". However, it becomes clear, in his description of the banking teacher, that what he is criticizing is not a method—the lecture—but the teacher's relation to knowledge which now affects how the method is used. The gist of what he says is that the teacher goes to her study or the library and researches the topic for the lecture. She prepares her notes and organizes the appropriate order of presentation, and in this process her "act of knowing" is completed. She has only now to transmit the results to the learners. Freire says he is convinced of just the opposite. For me to know, I need another subject of knowing . . . "Because of you [the other subject of knowing] I know that I can know more." I would argue that the same "banking" relations to knowledge pertain in most discussions as well as the vast majority of progressive pedagogy. For example, let's look at what takes place in a discussion.

People enter into discussions in order to articulate what they already know or think. If the discussion takes place in an educational context, the teacher will want to use the discussion method to be sure that the students have understood and can express or apply what they have learned prior to the discussion. The discussion method also helps people to learn the skill of arguing their interpretation or their knowledge against that which is expressed by others. Discussion is an ordered and managed communication of monologues. If everyone in the group shares a similar understanding, discussion can be an extremely self-confirming or reassuring experience. However, often there is a fair amount of conflict and therefore competition amongst the monologues. As a consequence, there must be a discussion leader who can guarantee equal time and space to each participant. This leader should also be able to manage the dynamics of the group so as to contain conflict and assure the harmony and cohesion of the group. In an educational context, the leader-teacher should also acknowledge the correct understanding when it is voiced or re-pose the question to yet another participant when the previous one has either got it all wrong or at least not quite right. In other words, there is some knowledge, which it is the objective to know and to correctly express and/or apply.

Dialogue, in contrast and complete opposition, involves the critical investigation of knowledge or thinking. Rather than focusing only on what we think, dialogue requires us to ask of each other and ourselves why we think what we do. In other words, it requires us to "problematize" knowledge (Freire, 1972: Ch 3). This means all sorts of knowledge, academic and personal knowledge as well as how we have come to a subjective knowledge or "feeling" about some issue. All of these types of knowledge are susceptible to ideological contamination; and therefore they must be critically scrutinized by the learning group.

> By stimulating "perception of the previous perception" and "knowledge of previous knowledge," [dialogue] stimulates the appearance of a new perception and the development of new knowledge ... potential [critical] consciousness supersedes real [limited] consciousness. (Freire, 1972: 87)

Since some of the knowledge under investigation will be central to the way which individual participants think about themselves and their world, trust is essential to dialogue. However, real feelings of trust amongst the members of a learning group will not pre-exist the struggle to achieve dialogue. Trust is created within that struggle (Freire, 1972: 137). What does accelerate the achievement of dialogue is at least some level of commitment, amongst participants, to develop a deeper and more critical understanding of their reality. In dialogue everyone helps each other, and is helped, to explore the historical and material origins of their thought.

Dialogue, therefore, is a collaborative form of communication and learning which, even though it involves challenge, creates trust rather than animosity. Most fundamentally it is a form of communication, which enables people to grasp the dialectical movements of their reality. The struggle to transform the antagonistic relations and to keep them transformed demands the constant unity of action and critical reflection. The unity of action and reflection in dialogue is a form of critical praxis just as it is in political action. We don't think, then act and turn off our critical reflection. Nor can we think critically without an active struggle to do so. Freire says: Let me emphasize that my defense of praxis implies no dichotomy by which this praxis could be divided into a prior stage of reflection and a subsequent stage of action. Action and reflection occur simultaneously ... Critical reflection is also action. (Freire, 1972: 99)

Pedagogy of the Oppressed contains the most fully elaborated explication of Freire's educational philosophy. However, what is often ignored is that this book is also about revolutionary strategy. Freire argues that revolution must entail two phases. One he calls "cultural action" and the other "cultural revolution".[8] Cultural action refers to any type of project which attempts to transform relations prior to the taking of power at the exact moment of political revolution. The aim of these projects is to enable people to develop a critical perception of their oppression and, as far as possible prior to the revolution, to prepare themselves for full active engagement in cultural revolution (Freire, 1972: 30–31, 103–107). Cultural revolution is a permanent process in which conscientized people engage in the continuous creation and recreation of their society. Instead of taking place in opposition to the state, it is supported by the revolutionary state or whatever political organization replaces the bourgeois state (Freire, 1985:Ch 7).

At several points in his writing Freire addresses the problem of revolutionary leaders or socialist educators who think there is no possibility of education for liberation within capitalist state institutions. He says that many of them believe in dialogue with the people but think that it will only be possible after power has been wrested from the bourgeoisie (Freire, 1972: 105). In answer to their doubt, he argues:

> One aspect of the reply is to be found in the distinction between systematic education which can only be changed by political power, and educational projects, which should be carried out with the oppressed in the process of organizing them. The pedagogy of the oppressed ... has two distinct stages. In the first, the oppressed unveil the world of oppression and, through praxis, commit themselves to its transformation. In the second stage, in which the reality of oppression has been transformed, this pedagogy ceases to belong to the oppressed and

becomes the pedagogy of all [people] in the process of permanent liberation. In both stages, it is always through action in depth that the culture of domination is culturally confronted. In the first stage, this confrontation occurs through the change in the way the oppressed perceive the world of oppression; in the second stage, through the expulsion of myths created and developed in the old order which, like spectres, haunt the new structure emerging from the revolutionary transformation.

(Freire, 1972: 30)

Again, speaking about revolutionary leaders, he says: When they deny the possibility that leaders can behave in a critically educational fashion before taking power, they deny the revolution's educational quality as cultural action preparing to become cultural revolution (Freire, 1972: 106). One of the reasons why cultural revolution must continue after the decisive revolutionary moment was stated above; that is, to rid the new society of all of the ideological residue—Marx called it "muck"—of the previous one (Marx and Engels, 1976: 60). Freire also stresses another reason. With science harnessed to meeting and enriching human needs, human beings will create more complex societies. Therefore they must be critically vigilant regarding what they create so that technology is not allowed to replace human choice as the determining factor in human history (Freire, 1985: 88–89).

Throughout his writings Freire expresses his concern that we must guard against one form of oppression replacing another. This is why he urges revolutionary leaders to enter into the same types of relations with the people that he has proposed for teachers and learners. Like the socialist educator, the political activist or any other cultural worker must begin with people's understanding of the world but then reframe this perception as a problem. Re-posed as a problem, reality becomes the object of their critical inquiry:

Cultural synthesis . . . does not mean that the objectives of revolutionary action should be limited by the aspirations expressed in the world view of the people. If this were to happen (in the guise of respect for that view), the revolutionary leaders would be passively bound to that vision. Neither invasion by the leader of the people's world view nor mere adaptation by the leaders to the (often naive) aspirations of the people is acceptable . . . Cultural synthesis serves the ends of organization; organization serves the ends of liberation . . . the oppressed, in order to become free, also need a theory of action . . . Nor can the people—as long as they are crushed and oppressed, internalizing the image of the oppressor—construct by themselves a theory of their liberating action. Only in the encounter of the people with the revolutionary leaders—in their praxis—can this theory be built.

(Freire, 1972: 149–150)

Freire clearly sees the need for leaders, but leaders who work and learn with people rather than for them. The leaders do bear the responsibility for co-ordination—and, at times, direction—as leaders who deny praxis to the oppressed thereby invalidate their own praxis. By imposing their word on others, they falsify that word and establish a contradiction [a logical one] between their methods and their objectives. If they are truly committed to liberation, their action and reflection cannot proceed without the action and reflection of others. Revolutionary praxis must stand opposed to the praxis of the dominant elites, for they are by nature antithetical (Freire, 1972: 97).

With Freire, this is not just a matter of principles but is an historical necessity. It is the only means by which we can make certain that one form of oppression is not simply replaced by another. His concern is related to his analysis of the "oppressor within" (Freire, 1972: 23ff).

The oppressor within is the psychological result of the social and material relations between the oppressors and oppressed. The oppressor's ideology of ways of thinking—motives—ways of behaving—actually penetrates the subjectivities of the oppressed. They have no model, other than the oppressor, of what they might aspire to be. This can be true for their leaders as well. Therefore Freire urges that the only way to counter this tendency is for socialist educators and revolutionaries—in every aspect of their "being"—to offer a model of the revolutionary option (Freire, 1972: 104–107). To do this and to sustain it means that everyone who joins the struggle for socialist revolution will have to understand the necessity for the continuous critical examination of the oppressor within themselves (Freire, 1972: 36–37). This is especially important during the stage of cultural action when structural change has not yet occurred.

During this stage we can only ever experience some aspects of the revolutionary option in an abbreviated form. But even that form should offer a clearer or more concrete idea of what we are seeking to become. It is crucial for prefigurative struggle to offer a "glimpse" of the socialist alternative. People need to experience and feel the difference rather than just hear or read about it, if their consciousness is to undergo an authentic change. Dialogue, as a form of education and political communication, is one example of what I mean by a "glimpse". It is an extremely important one, because it enables people to do far more than see the alternative. Dialogue enables us to experience the alternative or certain aspects of it for a period of time. The real defeat of the oppressor within, the elimination from our thought and desires of all the "muck of bourgeois society", is what the process of socialism, or what Freire calls "cultural revolution", aims to achieve.

I have tried to select the ideas of Paulo Freire which offer the most important contributions to radical educators. For those who, in the past, have either embraced him or dismissed him, as well as for radical educators who have yet to encounter Freire's ideas, I can only hope this discussion has provided a useful challenge.

People have asked me whether one could list Freire's contributions in a way which would present clearly his legacy to radical adult education. I think this would be misleading. Clearly there is a legacy but, to date, it is comprised of both positive and negative effects. As I have tried to indicate, here, the positive contributions can be culled if one engages in a rigorous analysis of Freire's ideas together with an equally rigorous, and continuously scrutinized, effort to apply them in the development of a radical educational approach. However, without this effort, the legacy is bound to be one with logically contradictory or negative outcomes. The results will be a continuation of what has happened thus far, only perhaps with even more negative consequences as Freire is received within the prevailing consciousness of the post-modern condition.[9] What I mean by this is that his ideas will be relativized, made the ripe pickings for an eclecticism devoid of any coherent, theoretical "guiding thread", and therefore amenable to being incorporated into educational practices that have no real radical intent. Worse still, radical educators with real radical intentions, as defined in this article, will remain divided and will be deprived of Freire's valuable contributions. Instead of this current nebulous legacy, we could be using Freire's philosophy to begin to create a coherent theory capable of developing a truly radical educational/political practice.

Notes

1. For example see Field, John (1987) "Power and knowledge" in Workers' Education. 1, pp 15–18.
2. It is important to consider, e.g. what Gramsci says about educational relationships on pages 349–350 of Gramsci, A. (1929–1935) Selections from the Prison Notebooks, Hoare, Q. and Smith, G.N. (editors and translators, Lawrence and Wishart, 1971).

3. A great deal of progressive adult education has been influenced by the psychologists of "personal freedom" such as Carl Rogers. Rogers himself has claimed affinity with Freire and there have been numerous articles in educational journals which attempt to conflate Freire and Rogers' ideas. Two learning colleagues (students), James Calvey and Janet Galpin, have written excellent Diploma dissertations which demolish these claims.

4. In addition see Freire's Politics of Education (1985), where he says: "Marx underlined, in The Holy Family, the conscious action of the proletariat in the abolition of themselves as a class by the abolition of the objective conditions that constitute that class." (p 162) Also, please note that when I quote Freire I alter his use of gender language by using whenever I can, without distorting the meaning, plural nouns and pronouns. These and altered verb tenses are indicated in brackets.

5. Writers' and Readers' Publishing Co-operative published their edition in 1976. Please note that due to the publication date readers often think this text post-dates Pedagogy of the Oppressed but in fact it was written in 1967. Here I am referring to p 44.

6. Also see pp 160–162 in Freire, 1985.

7. "Bourgeois education" is education which has developed within or been further developed within capitalist social relations. Bourgeoisie is the term used to designate the capitalist class.

8. Freire uses an anthropological definition of the term "culture". He is not just referring to "high" culture but also to every material object and every aspect of social consciousness that is produced by the social being of people living within a specific cultural variation of a social formation.

9. For a materialist, i.e. Marxist, analysis of the post-modern condition see Harvey, D. (1989), The Condition of Post-Modernity, Oxford: Blackwell. His description of the post-modern condition and his analysis of its causes have important implications for anyone trying to form a critical understanding of current trends in adult education, particularly in the UK and the rest of the so-called "developed" world.

References

Allman, P. and Wallis, J. (1990). "Praxis: implications for 'really' radical education", in Studies in Adult Education, 22, pp 14–30

Freire, P. (1972). Pedagogy of the Oppressed, Harmondsworth: Penguin

Freire, P. (1974a). Authority versus Authoritarianism, an audio-tape in the series "Thinking with Paulo Freire", Sydney, Australia: Australian Council of Churches

Freire, P. (1974b). "Education: domestication or liberation", in Lister, I. (ed). De-Schooling, Cambridge: Cambridge University Press

Freire, P. (1976). Education: The Practice of Freedom, Writers' and Readers' Publishing Cooperative

Freire, P. (1985). The Politics of Education, Macmillan

Marx, K. and Engels, F. (1956). The Holy Family, Lawrence and Wishart

Marx, K. and Engels, F. (1976) The German Ideology, Moscow: Progress

Suggested Readings for Future Study

Alverman, D. E., Moon, J. S., & Hagwood, M. C. (1999). *Popular culture in the classroom: Teaching and researching critical media literacy.* Newark: DE: International Reading Association.

Anyon, J. (1981). "Social class and school knowledge," *Curriculum Inquiry,* 11(1): 3–42.

Apple, M. and Buras, K. L. (2005). *The Subaltern Speaks: Curriculum, Power, and Education Struggles.* New York: Routledge.

Apple, M. W. (1993). *Official knowledge: Democratic education in a conservative age.* New York: Routledge.

Apple, M. and Christian-Smith, L., eds. (1991). *The politics of the textbook.* New York: Routledge.

Arriaza, G. (2003). "Schools, Social Capital and Children of Color." *Race, Ethnicity and Education* (6)1, 71–93.

Artiles, A. J. and Trent, S. C. (1994). "Overrepresentation of minority students in special education: A continuing debate." *The Journal of Special Education,* 27(4): 410–437.

Baker, Colin (2006). *Foundations of bilingual education and bilingualism.* Buffalo, NY: Multilingual Matters.

Baynton, D. (2001). *Disability and the justification of inequality in American history.* In P. Longmore & L. Umansky (eds.), *The new disability history: American perspectives* (pp. 33–57). New York: New York University Press.

Berliner, D.C. and Biddle, B.J. (1995). *The manufactured crisis: myths, fraud, and the attack on America's public schools.* Cambridge: Perseus Books.

Beyer, L. & Apple, M. (1998). *The curriculum: Problems, politics and possibilities.* New York: SUNY Press.

Bourdieu, P. and Passeron, J. C. (1977). *Reproduction in education, society, and culture.* Beverly Hills, CA: Sage.

Bowles, S. and Gintis, H. (1976). *Schooling in capitalist America.* New York: Basic Books.

Comer, J. P. (2004). *Leave no child behind.* New Haven: Yale University Press.

Cummins, J. (1983). "Bilingualism and special education: Program and pedagogical issues," *Learning Disabilities Quarterly,* 6: 373–386.

Dance, L. J. (2002). *Tough Fronts: The Impact of Street Culture on Schooling.* New York: Routledge.

D'Ambrosio, U. (1999). "Literacy, Matheracy, and Technocracy: A Trivium for Today," *Mathematical Thinking and Learning* (1)2: 131–153.

Davis, L. J. (1995). *Enforcing normalcy: Disability, deafness and the body.* London: Verso.

Davis, L. J. (1997). *The disability studies reader.* New York: Routledge.

Dewey, J. (1916). *Democracy and education: An introduction to the philosophy of education.* New York: Macmillan.

Espinoza-Herold, M. (2003). *Issues in Latino Education: Race, School, Culture and the Politics of Academic Success,* Boston: Pearson Education Group.

Erevelles, N. (2000). "Educating unruly bodies: Critical pedagogy, disability studies, and the politics of schooling," *Educational Theory,* 50(1): 25–47.

Fine, M. (1991). *Framing Dropouts: Notes On the Politics of an Urban Public High School.* Albany, NY: SUNY.

Flecha, Ramon. *Sharing Words—Theory and Practice of Dialogic Learning,* Lanham, MD: Rowman & Littlefield.

Foster, M. (1997). *Black teachers on teaching.* New York: New Press.

Gabel, S. (ed.) (2005). *Disability Studies in Education: Readings in theory and Method.* New York: Peter Lang.

Gleeson, B. (1999). *Geographies of Disability.* London and New York: Routledge.

Gutstein, E. (2005). *Reading and Writing The World With Mathematics: Toward a Pedagogy for Social Justice.* Oxford: RoutledgeFalmer.

Gutstein, E. (2003). "Teaching and Learning Mathematics for Social Justice in an Urban, Latino School," *Journal for Research in Mathematics Education,* 34(1), 37–73.

Irvine, J. J. (1990). *Black students and school failure: Policies, practices, and prescriptions.* New York: Praeger.

Kozol, J. (1991). *Savage inequalities: Children in America's schools.* New York: Crown.

MacLeod, J. (1995). *Ain't no makin' it: aspirations and attainment in a low-income neighborhood.* Boulder: Westview.

McLaren, P. (1989). *Life in schools: An introduction to critical pedagogy in the foundations of education.* New York: Longman.

Monahan, T. (2005). *Globalization, Technological Change and Public Education.* New York: Routledge.

Moschkovich, J. "A Situated and Sociocultural Perspective on Bilingual Mathematics Learners. *Mathematical Thinking and Learning* 4(2&3): 189–212.

Oakes, J. (1985). *Keeping Track: How Schools Structure Inequality.* New Haven: Yale University Press.

Olsen, L. (1997). *Made in America: Immigrant Students in Our Public Schools.* New York: The New Press.

Perry, T., Steele, C. and Hilliard, A. G. (2003). *Young, gifted and Black: Promoting high achievement among African-American students.* Boston: Beacon Press.

Skrtic, T. (ed.) (1995). *Disability and Democracy: Reconstructing [special] education for postmodernity.* New York: Teachers College Press.

Part Seven

*Critical Pedagogy and
Teacher Education*

Introduction to Part Seven

Schools are one of the primary social institutions at work in the reproduction of social inequalities, while simultaneously portraying a humanist vision of their redemptive and transformative power. In light of the impact of schools on students' lives and futures, critical pedagogy identifies teacher education as one of the key ideological state apparatuses implicated in the production and transmission of capitalist values and the hegemonic procurement of consent. Teacher education is also the space in which classroom educators are socialized and initiated into pedagogical attitudes and practices that support the power asymmetries of the larger society.

The struggle for social justice and school transformation, then, must engage the politics of teacher education as a primary site of contestation, in the forging of a school culture that functions in the interest of disenfranchised populations. As such, much of the work within teacher education entails the struggle over the meaning and practice of democracy. More specifically, this includes the role of teachers as ideological agents at the service of a corporatized world, or as transformative intellectuals committed to a liberatory ethos of schooling. The notion of teachers as intellectuals, with a focus on the art and science of teaching and its democratically inspired possibilities, has been at the forefront of all major proposals made by progressive educators in the last century.

In concert with this tradition, critical pedagogy proposes a new arrangement of power relations in teacher preparation, to facilitate the formation of teachers as cultural workers preoccupied with the formation of critical citizenship and civic engagement. In contrast to the guiding neoliberal vision of schools as engines for the global economy, critical pedagogy proposes an emancipatory formation of teachers—one that socializes teachers through a language of critique and possibility, by which they can begin to sidestep the transmission of hegemonic values. This speaks to a teacher education project grounded upon liberatory ideals and teacher preparation as an important form of "cultural politics," where issues of power, economics, history, culture, language, and pedagogy are all employed to both confront and transform historical oppressions associated with public schooling in America.

Summary of Articles

"Teacher Education and Democratic Schooling," by Henry Giroux, provides an important and comprehensive analysis of the failure of teacher education to engage in democratic practices. In this article, Giroux identifies the ideological rites and cultural assumptions that support teacher education as one of the most pernicious public institutions in the reproduction of social inequalities. In its place, Giroux proposes an emancipatory culture of teacher preparation, where teachers learn the craft of democracy, problematize asymmetrical structures of power, and embrace a commitment to the education of oppressed populations. Through such a culture, teachers engage with students as historical subjects and transformative agents of social change, as well as integrate the curriculum as a vehicle for critical dialogue. Giroux further proposes the integration of critical inquiry into questions of ideology, through which a concrete pedagogical praxis can be developed to facilitate the examination of different forms of subordinated knowledge within the official curriculum. Just as Dewey and Freire before him, Giroux affirms the incorporation of students' lives, experiences, cultures, and languages into their process of learning, in order to reaffirm their identities and create the conditions for their social and economic empowerment.

In "Fighting for Our Lives," Gloria Ladson-Billings addresses the failure of teacher education programs in the United States to prepare classroom educators to effectively work with African-American students. She brings clarity to our understanding of the historical collusion of traditional teacher education values and the dominant society, in its perpetuation of a deficit view of African-American students, enacted through attitudes and practices that strip Black students of their culture and language. By advocating for a neutral, color-blind, one-size-fits all pedagogy, teacher education, unwittingly, negates the humanity of students of color and reinscribes within schools the racism of US society. In its place, Ladson-Billings proposes a culturally responsive teacher education approach that takes into account the unique experiences of African-American students. She specifically suggests the need for radical transformation in the way teachers see themselves, where they do their fieldwork, and how they use specific pedagogies to teach school curriculum. Ladson-Billings rightly advocates for a culturally relevant teacher education, where teachers learn how to promote academic achievement, based on cultural competency and a language of critique. Lastly, Ladson-Billings insists that any teacher preparation program that seeks to effectively prepare teachers to work with African-American students, must reassess admission procedures, examine the curriculum, restructure field experiences, and recruit and retain African-American faculty in the program.

Similarly, Sonia Nieto argues in "Bringing Bilingual Education Out of the Basement and Other Imperatives for Teacher Education" that it is high time for teacher education to accept the fact that language minority students are a reality of classroom life across the United States. She argues that teacher preparation needs to be reconceptualized to prepare teachers to work with second language learners and their communities. Nieto proposes that all educators, not only bilingual teachers, should learn a second language, know the history of immigration, be familiar with language policies and practices, and develop a working knowledge of the language, culture and traditions of the communities in which they teach. In line with this proposal, teacher education should include general education courses that teach students basic knowledge of first and second language acquisition, as well as critical pedagogical practices to modify the curriculum for second language learners. She invites colleges and schools of education to make a concerted commitment to language minority education in both their mission and conceptual frameworks, and most importantly, to hire teacher educators who are fully competent in languages other than English.

Questions for Reflection and Dialogue

1. Identify the hidden discourse of teacher preparation programs, centered on account-ability schemes, testing, standardization, and teacher-proof curricula.

2. Why do most traditional teacher preparation programs advocate a vision of neutral, color-blind education?

3. According to Henry Giroux, what are the most important elements of a critical teacher preparation program that aims to prepare teachers as transformative intellectuals and cultural workers?

4. Why does Gloria Ladson-Billings believe that the teaching of African–American students should be a primary focus of teacher preparation?

5. What critical features does Ladson Billings advocate for a well-designed teacher education program that seeks to meet the needs of African-American students?

6. Explain what is meant by culturally relevant pedagogy? What does it mean to be a culturally competent teacher?

7. What does Sonia Nieto mean when she states that bilingual education should be taken out of the closet?

8. What does Nieto say about the opposition to bilingual education? Why do you believe there has been so much opposition to bilingual education? What is the relationship of this opposition to the assimilationist role of schools?

9. Have you heard that teachers recommend parents of English language learners to speak only English at home with their children? Do you think this is a biased and racist statement? Explain.

10. How does Nieto's article impact your understanding of teacher education and the potential role of critical pedagogy, in the preparation of future teachers?

22

Teacher Education and Democratic Schooling

Henry A. Giroux

As far back as 1890, a New England teacher named Horace Willard cogently argued that in contrast to members of other professions, teachers lived "lives of mechanical routine, and were subjected to a machine of supervision, organization, classification, grading, percentages, uniformity, promotions, tests, examination."[1] Nowhere, Willard decried, was there room in the school culture for "individuality, ideas, independence, originality, study, investigation."[2] Forty years later, Henry W. Holmes, dean of Harvard University's new Graduate School of Education, echoed these sentiments in his criticism of the National Survey of the Education of Teachers in 1930. According to Holmes, the survey failed to support teachers as independent critical thinkers. Instead, it endorsed a view of the teacher that George Counts termed a "routine worker under the expert direction of principals, supervisors, and superintendents."[3] Holmes was convinced that if teachers' work continued to be defined in such a narrow fashion, schools of education would eventually respond by limiting themselves to forms of training that virtually undermined the development of teachers as critically minded intellectuals.

At different times both of these noteworthy critics of American education recognized that any viable attempt at educational reform must address the issue of teacher education. Most important was their conviction that teachers should function professionally as intellectuals, and that teacher education should be inextricably linked to critically transforming the school setting and, by extension, the wider social setting.

In the early part of the twentieth century, a number of experimental teacher education programs managed to shift the terrain of struggle for democratic schooling from a largely rhetorical platform to the program site itself. One such program was organized around New College, an experimental teacher training venture affiliated with Teachers College at Columbia University between 1927 and 1953. Spokespersons from New College proclaimed "that a sound teacher education program must lie in a proper integration of rich scholarship, educational theory, and professional practice."[4] Furthermore, New College embarked on a training program based on the principle that "it is the peculiar privilege of the teacher to play a large part in the development of the social order of the next generation."[5] New College's first announcement claimed that if teachers were to escape from the usual "academic lockstep ... [they] required contact with life in its various phases and understanding of it—an understanding of the intellectual, moral, social, and economic life of the people."[6]

The idea that teacher education programs should center their academic and moral objectives on the education of teachers as critical intellectuals, while advancing democratic interests, has invariably influenced the debates on the various "crises" in education over the last fifty years.[7] Moreover, it has been precisely because of the presence of such an idea that a rationale eventually could be constructed which linked schooling to the imperatives of democracy and classroom pedagogy to the dynamics of citizenship. This is not to suggest, however, that either public education or teacher training programs were over-burdened by a concern for democracy and citizenship.[8] Nevertheless, the historical prece-dent for educating teachers as intellectuals and making schools into democratic sites for social transformation might begin to define the way in which public education and the education of teachers could be appropriately perceived today. I wish, in other words, to build on this precedent in order to argue for the education of teachers as transformative intellectuals. As I have pointed out previously, the term "transformative intellectual" refers to one who exercises forms of intellectual and pedagogical practice that attempt to insert teaching and learning directly into the political sphere by arguing that schooling represents both a struggle for meaning and a struggle over power relations. I am also referring to one whose intellectual practices are necessarily grounded in forms of moral and ethical dis-course exhibiting a preferential concern for the suffering and struggles of the disadvan-taged and oppressed. Here I extend the traditional view of the intellectual as someone who is able to analyze various interests and contradictions within society to someone capable of articulating emancipatory possibilities and working toward their realization. Teachers who assume the role of transformative intellectuals treat students as critical agents, question how knowledge is produced and distributed, utilize dialogue, and make knowledge mean-ingful, critical, and ultimately emancipatory.[9]

I further develop in this chapter a theme that has permeated this book; that is, within the current discourse on educational reform[10] there exists, with few exceptions,[11] an omin-ous silence regarding the role that both teacher education and public schooling should play in advancing democratic practices, critical citizenship, and the role of the teacher as intel-lectual. Given the legacy of democracy and social reform bequeathed to us by our edu-cational forebears, such as John Dewey and George Counts, not only does this silence suggest that some of the current reformers are suffering from political and historical amnesia; it also points to the ideological interests that underlie their proposals. Regrettably, such interests tell us less about the ills of schooling than they do about the nature of the real crisis facing this nation—a crisis which, in my view, not only augurs poorly for the future of American education, but underscores the need to reclaim a democratic tradition presently in retreat. Bluntly stated, much of the current literature on educational reform points to a crisis in American democracy itself.

The discourse of recent educational reform characteristically excludes certain pro-posals from consideration. For instance, missing from the various privileged discourses that have fashioned the recent reform movement, and absent from the practices of public school teachers whose participation in the current debate on education has been less than vigorous, are concerted attempts at democratizing schools and empowering students to become critical, active citizens. This reluctance of teachers has had a particu-larly deleterious effect, since the absence of proposals for rethinking the purpose of schools of education around democratic concerns has further strengthened the ideo-logical and political pressures that define teachers as technicians and structure teachers' work in a demeaning and overburdening manner. Kenneth Zeichner underscores this concern when he writes:

> It is hoped that future debate in teacher education will be more concerned with the question of which educational, moral and political commitments ought to guide our work in the field

rather than with the practice of merely dwelling on which procedures and organizational arrangements will most effectively help us realize tacit and often unexamined ends. Only after we have begun to resolve some of these necessarily prior questions related to ends should we concentrate on the resolution of more instrumental issues related to effectively accomplishing our goals.[12]

The current debate provides an opportunity to critically analyze the ideological and material conditions—both in and out of schools—that contribute to teachers' passivity and powerlessness. I also believe that recognition of the failure to link the purposes of public schooling to the imperatives of economic and social reform provides a starting point for examining the ideological shift in education that took place in the 1980s and for developing a new language of democracy, empowerment, and possibility in which teacher education programs and classroom practices can be defined. My central concern is to develop a view of teacher education that defines teachers as transformative intellectuals and schooling as part of an ongoing struggle for democracy. In developing my argument, I will focus on four considerations. First, I will analyze the dominant new conservative positions that have generated current educational reforms in terms of the implications these viewpoints hold for the reorganization of teacher education programs. Second, I will develop a rationale for organizing teacher education programs around a critical view of teachers' work and authority, one that I believe is consistent with the principles and practices of democracy. Third, I will present some programmatic suggestions for analyzing teacher education as a form of cultural politics. Finally, I will argue for a critical pedagogy that draws upon the many-sided conversations and voices that make up community life.

Education Reform and the Retreat from Democracy

Underlying the educational reforms proposed by the recent coalition of conservatives and liberals, conveniently labeled "the new conservatives," is a discourse that both edifies and mystifies their proposals. Capitalizing upon the waning confidence of the general public and of a growing number of teachers in the effectiveness of public schools, the new conservatives argue for educational reform by faulting schools for a series of crises that include everything from a growing trade deficit to the breakdown of family morality.[13] The new conservatives have seized the initiative by framing their arguments in a terse rhetoric that resonates with a growing public concern about downward mobility in hard economic times, that appeals to a resurgence of chauvinistic patriotism, and that reformulates educational goals along elitist lines. Such a discourse is dangerous not only because it misconstrues the responsibility schools have for wider economic and social problems—a position that has been convincingly refuted and need not be argued against here[14]—but also because it reflects an alarming ideological shift regarding the role schools should play in society. The effect of this shift, launched by the New Right's full-fledged attack on the educational and social reforms of the 1960s, has been to redefine the purpose of education so as to eliminate its citizenship function in favor of a narrowly defined labor market perspective. The essence and implications of this position have been well documented by Barbara Finkelstein.

> Contemporary reformers seem to be recalling public education from its traditional utopian mission—to nurture a critical and committed citizenry that would stimulate the processes of political and cultural transformation and refine and extend the workings of political

democracy. . . . Reformers seem to imagine public schools as economic rather than political instrumentalities. They forge no new visions of political and social possibilities. Instead, they call public schools to industrial and cultural service exclusively. . . . Reformers have disjoined their calls for educational reform from calls for a redistribution of power and authority, and the cultivation of cultural forms celebrating pluralism and diversity. As if they have had enough of political democracy, Americans, for the first time in a one hundred and fifty-year history, seem ready to do ideological surgery on their public schools—cutting them away from the fate of social justice and political democracy completely and grafting them onto elite corporate, industrial, military, and cultural interests.[15]

It is important to recognize that the new conservative attack on the reforms of the last decade has resulted in a shift away from defining schools as agencies of equity and justice. There is little concern with how public education could better serve the interests of diverse groups of students by enabling them to understand and gain some control over the socio-political forces that influence their destinies. Rather, through this new discourse, and its preoccupation with accountability schemes, testing, accreditation, and credentializing, educational reform has become synonymous with turning schools into testing centers. It now defines school life primarily by measuring its utility against its contribution to economic growth and cultural uniformity. Similarly, at the heart of the present ideo-logical shift is an attempt to reformulate the purpose of public education around a set of interests and social relations that define academic success almost exclusively in terms of the accumulation of capital and the logic of the marketplace. This represents a shift away from teacher control of the curriculum and toward a fundamentally technicist form of education that is more directly tied to economic modes of production. Moreover, the new conservatives provide a view of society in which authority derives from technical expertise and culture embodies an idealized tradition that glorifies hard work, industrial discipline, domesticated desire, and cheerful obedience. Edward Berman has deftly captured the political nature of this ideological shift.

> Architects of the current reform have, to their credit, dropped the rhetoric about the school as a vehicle for personal betterment. There is little pretense in today's reports of the resultant programs that individual improvement and social mobility are important concerns of a reconstituted school system. The former rhetoric about individual mobility has given way to exhortations to build educational structures that will allow individual students to make a greater contribution to the economic output of the corporate state. There are few rhetorical flourishes to obfuscate this overriding objective.[16]

The ideological shift that characterized the current reform period is also evident in the ways in which teacher preparation and classroom pedagogy are currently being defined. The rash of reform proposals for reorganizing schools points to a definition of teachers' work that seriously exacerbates conditions that are presently eroding the authority and intellectual integrity of teachers. In fact, the most compelling aspect of the influential reports, especially the widely publicized *A Nation at Risk: Action for Excellence*, and *A Nation Prepared: Teachers for the 21st Century*, is their studious refusal to address the ideological, social, and economic conditions underlying poor teacher and student per-formance.[17] For example, as Marilyn Frankenstein and Louis Kampf point out, public school teachers constantly confront conditions "such as the overwhelming emphasis on quantification (both in scoring children and keeping records), the growing lack of control over curriculum (separating conception from execution) and over other aspects of their work, the isolation from their peers, the condescending treatment by administrators, and the massive layoffs of veteran teachers."[18]

Instead of addressing these issues, many of the reforms taking place at the state level further consolidate administrative structures and prevent teachers from collectively and creatively shaping the conditions under which they work. For instance, at both the local and federal levels, the new educational discourse has influenced a number of policy recommendations, such as competency-based testing for teachers, a lockstep sequencing of materials, mastery learning techniques, systematized evaluation schemes, standardized curricula, and the implementation of mandated "basics."[19] The consequences are evident not only in the substantively narrow view of the purposes of education, but also in the definitions of teaching, learning, and literacy that are championed by the new management-oriented policymakers. In place of developing critical understanding, engaging student experience, and fostering active and critical citizenship, schools are redefined through a language and policies that emphasize standardization, competency, and narrowly defined performance skills.

Within this paradigm, the development of curricula is increasingly left to administrative experts or simply adopted from publishers, with few, if any, contributions from teachers who are expected to implement the new programs. In its most ideologically offensive form, this prepackaged curriculum is rationalized as teacher-proof and is designed to be applied to any classroom context regardless of the historical, cultural, and socioeconomic differences that characterize various schools and students.[20] What is important to note is that the deskilling of teachers appears to go hand in hand with the increasing adoption of management-type pedagogies.

> Viewing teachers as semiskilled, low-paid workers in the mass production of education, policymakers have sought to change education, to improve it, by "teacher-proofing" it. Over the past decade we have seen the proliferation of elaborate accountability schemes that go by acronyms like MBO (management by objectives), PBBS (performance-based budgeting systems), CBE (competency-based education), CBTE (competency-based teacher education), and MCT (minimum competency testing).[21]

The growing removal of curriculum development and analysis from the hands of teachers is related to the ways technocratic rationality is used to redefine teachers' work. This type of rationality increasingly takes place within a social division of labor in which thinking is removed from implementation and the model of the teacher becomes that of the technician or white-collar clerk. Likewise, learning is reduced to the memorization of narrowly defined facts and isolated pieces of information that can easily be measured and evaluated. The significance of the overall effects of this type of rationalization and bureaucratic control on teachers' work and morale has been forcefully articulated by Linda Darling-Hammond. She writes:

> In a Rand study of teachers' views of the effect of educational policies on their classroom practices, we learned from teachers that in response to policies that prescribe teaching practices and outcomes, they spend less time on untested subjects, such as science and social studies; they use less writing in their classrooms in order to gear assignments to the format of standardized tests; they resort to lectures rather than classroom discussions in order to cover the prescribed behavioral objectives without getting "off the track"; they are precluded from using teaching materials that are not on prescribed textbook lists, even when they think these materials are essential to meet the needs of some of their students; and they feel constrained from following up on expressed student interests that lie outside of the bounds of mandated curricula. . . . And 45 percent of the teachers in this study told us that the single thing that would make them leave teaching was the increased prescriptiveness of teaching content and methods—in short, the continuing deprofessionalization of teaching.[22]

As previously stated, the ideological interests that inform the new conservative proposals are based on a view of morality and politics that is legitimated through an appeal to national unity and tradition. Within this discourse, democracy loses its dynamic character and is reduced to a set of inherited principles and institutional arrangements that teach students how to adapt rather than to question the basic precepts of society. What is left in the new reform proposals is a view of authority constructed around a mandate to follow and implement predetermined rules, to transmit an unquestioned cultural tradition, and to sanctify industrial discipline. Couple these problems with large classes, excessive paperwork, fragmented work periods, and low salaries, and it comes as no surprise that teachers are increasingly leaving the field.[23]

In effect, the ideological shift at work here points to a restricted definition of schooling, one that almost completely strips public education of a democratic vision where citizenship and the politics of possibility are given serious consideration. When I argue that the recent conservative or "blue-ribbon" reform recommendations lack a politics of possibility and citizenship, 1 mean that primacy is given to education as economic investment, that is, to pedagogical practices designed to create a school–business partnership and make the American economic system more competitive in world markets. Of course, there is a less influential but equally anti-utopian and pedestrian conservative approach to school reform. In this view, critical learning and citizenship are reduced to an elitist, Platonic notion of pedagogy in which the complexity of the knowledge/power relation is held hostage by a claim to the virtues of a reductionist notion of cultural literacy. In this case, culture and knowledge are treated statically as either a warehouse of great books or a list of information that need only be transmitted to willing and grateful students. A politics of possibility and citizenship, by contrast, refers to a conception of schooling in which classrooms are seen as active sites of public intervention and social struggle. Moreover, this view maintains that possibilities exist for teachers and students to redefine the nature of critical learning and practice outside the imperatives of the corporate marketplace. The idea of a politics and project of possibility is grounded in Ernst Bloch's idea of "natural law" wherein "the standpoint of the victims of any society ought to always provide the starting point for the critique of that society."[24] Such a politics defines schools as sites around which struggles should be waged in the name of developing a more just, humane, and equitable social order both within and outside schools.

I have spent some time reemphasizing the new conservative discourse and the ideological shift it represents because in my view the current reforms, with few exceptions, pose a grave threat to both public schooling and the nature of democracy itself. The definition of teaching and learning provided by this discourse ignores, as I have pointed out, the imperative of viewing schools as sites of social transformation where students are educated to become informed, active, and critical citizens. The gravity of this ideological shift is hardly ameliorated by the fact that even public schooling's more liberal spokespersons have failed to develop a critical discourse that challenges the hegemony of dominant ideologies. For example, the highly publicized reports by John Goodlad, Theodore Sizer, Ernest Boyer, and others neither acknowledge nor utilize the radical tradition of educational scholarship.[25] Although the liberal position does take the concepts of "equality of opportunity" and "citizenship" seriously, we are, nevertheless, left with analyses of schooling that lack a sufficiently critical understanding of the ways in which power has been used to favor select groups of students over others. In addition, we are given only a cursory treatment of the political economy of schooling, with its scattered history of dishonorable linkages to corporate interests and ideology. Furthermore, we are provided with little understanding of how the hidden curriculum in schools works in a subtly discriminating way to discredit the dreams, experiences, and knowledges associated with students from specific class, racial, and gender groupings.[26]

In the absence of any competing critical agenda for reform, the new conservative discourse encourages institutions for teacher education to define schools primarily as training sites that provide students with the technical expertise required to find a place within the corporate hierarchy. Thomas Popkewitz and Allan Pitman have characterized the ideology underlying the current reform proposals, moreover, as betraying a fundamental elitism since it basically adopts a perspective of society that is undifferentiated by class, race, or gender. The logic endemic to these reports, the authors argue, demonstrates an attachment to possessive individualism and instrumental rationality. In other words: "Quantity is seen as quality. Procedural concerns are made objects of value and moral domains. The teacher is a facilitator . . . or a counselor. . . . Individualization is pacing through a common curriculum . . . Flexibility in instruction is to begin where the student is ready to begin. . . . There is no discussion of what is to be facilitated or the conceptions of curriculum to guide procedures."[27]

Furthermore, Popkewitz and Pitman see a distinctive shift from a concern with equity to a slavish regard for a restricted notion of excellence. That is, the concept of excellence that informs these new reports "ignores the social differentiations while providing political symbols to give credibility to education which only a few can appreciate."[28] What is rightly being stressed is that the concept of excellence fashioned in the reports is designed to benefit "those who have already access to positions of status and privilege through accidents of birth."[29]

Given the context in which teaching and learning are currently being defined, it becomes all the more necessary to insist on an alternative view of teacher education, one which, in refusing to passively serve the existing ideological and institutional arrangements of the public schools, is aimed at challenging and reforming them.

Teacher Education: Democracy and the Imperative of Social Reform

I want to return to the idea that the fundamental concerns of democracy and critical citizenship should be central to any discussion of the purpose of teacher education. In doing so, I will organize my discussion around an initial effort to develop a critical language with which to reconstruct the relationship between teacher education programs and the public schools, on the one hand, and public education and society, on the other.

If teacher education programs are to provide the basis for democratic struggle and renewal in our schools, they will have to redefine their current relationship to such institutions. As it presently stands, schools of education rarely encourage their students to take seriously the imperatives of social critique and social change as part of a wider emancipatory vision. If and when education students begin to grapple with these concerns at the classroom level, it is invariably years after graduation. My own experience in teacher education institutions—both as a student and as an instructor—has confirmed for me what is generally agreed to be commonplace in most schools and colleges of education throughout the United States: that these institutions continue to define themselves essentially as service institutions which are generally mandated to provide the requisite technical expertise to carry out whatever pedagogical functions are deemed necessary by the various school communities in which students undertake their practicum experiences.[30] In order to escape this political posture, teacher education programs need to reorient their focus to the critical transformation of public schools rather than to the simple reproduction of existing institutions and ideologies.[31]

One starting point would be to recognize the importance of educating students in the languages of critique and possibility; that is, providing teachers with the critical terminology and conceptual apparatus that will allow them not only to critically analyze the democratic and political shortcomings of schools, but also to develop the knowledge and skills that will advance the possibilities for generating curricula, classroom social practices, and organizational arrangements based on and cultivating a deep respect for a democratic and ethically based community. In effect, this means that the relationship of teacher education programs to public schooling would be self-consciously guided by political and moral considerations. Dewey expressed well the need for educators to make political and moral considerations a central aspect of their education and work when he distinguished between "education as a function of society" and "society as a function of education."[32] In simple terms, Dewey's distinction reminds us that education can function either to create passive, risk-free citizens or to create a politicized citizenry educated to fight for various forms of public life informed by a concern for justice, happiness, and equality. At issue here is whether schools of education are to serve and reproduce the existing society or to adopt the more critical role of challenging the social order so as to develop and advance its democratic imperatives. Also at issue is developing a rationale for defining teacher education programs in political terms that make explicit a particular view of the relationship between public schools and the social order, a view based on defending the imperatives of a democratic society.

Public Schools as Democratic Public Spheres

My second concern is directed to the broader question of how educators should view the purpose of public schooling. My position echoes Dewey's in that I believe public schools need to be defined as democratic public spheres. This means regarding schools as democratic sites dedicated to self- and social empowerment. Understood in these terms, schools can be public places where students learn the knowledge and skills necessary to create a critical democracy. Contrary to the view that schools are extensions of the workplace or frontline institutions in the corporate battle for international markets, schools viewed as democratic public spheres center their activities on critical inquiry and meaningful dialogue. In this case, students are given the opportunity to learn the discourse of public association and civic responsibility. Such a discourse seeks to recapture the idea of a critical democracy that commands respect for individual freedom and social justice. Moreover, viewing schools as democratic public spheres provides a rationale for defending them, along with progressive forms of pedagogy and teachers' work, as agencies of social reform. When defined in these terms, schools can be defended as institutions that provide the knowledge, skills, social relations, and vision necessary to educate a citizenry capable of building a critical democracy. That is, school practice can be rationalized in a political language that recovers and emphasizes the transformative role that schools can play in advancing the democratic possibilities inherent in the existing society.[33]

Rethinking the Nature of Teacher Education

I would like to bring the foregoing discussion to bear on the more practical mission of reconstructing teacher education programs around a new vision of democratic schooling and teaching for critical citizenship. Consequently, I will devote the remainder of my discussion to outlining, in detailed and programmatic terms, what I believe are some essential components and categories for a teacher education curriculum and a critical pedagogy in the schools. But before discussing this issue, I want to argue against some of the more recent calls for the abolition of schools of education. I maintain that many schools of education as they are currently organized need to be drastically reformed; the issue for me is reform, not abolition. The proposal to retain schools of education rests on a number of considerations. The nature of public schooling demands that prospective teachers be introduced to a notion of theory and practice that is forged outside the disciplinary boundaries that primarily characterize undergraduate liberal arts programs. In other words, the education of teachers cannot be reduced to forms of learning in which students are required merely to master the cognate disciplines. The nature of public schooling requires that teachers know more than the subject matter they will be teaching. They also need a fundamental understanding of issues specific to the economic, political, and cultural nature of schooling itself. That is, they need to learn an interdisciplinary language that focuses on the history, sociology, philosophy, political economy, and political science of schooling. Teachers need to be able to theorize in a language that includes but goes far beyond the limits of traditional disciplines; they need to understand the sociology of school cultures, the meaning of the hidden curriculum, a politics of knowledge and power, a philosophy of school/state relations, and a sociology of teaching. They also need to develop approaches to research, methods of inquiry, and theory that are directly tied to the problems and possibilities of schooling. It is also important to stress that if the education of teachers is left to liberal arts programs, the wedge between the university and schools will widen. Liberal arts programs take as their first concern a view of learning organized around the disciplines; they do not focus on public school problems; they contain no mechanisms for developing school/community relations; and they have no reason to reform the theory and practice relation so as to allow teachers to work as reflective researchers in collaboration with university teachers and students. These concerns can only be taught within a school of education, one that embraces the notion of educating teachers as transformative intellectuals around the demands of a critical pedagogy and a cultural politics. To abolish schools of education is to undermine the possibility of developing them as centers for democratic learning and as public spheres that can work organically with the communities in which they are located.

Of course, most teacher education programs have been, and continue to be, entirely removed from a vision and a set of practices dedicated to the fostering of critical democracy and social justice. A repeated criticism made by educators working within the radical tradition has been that, as it currently exists, teacher education rarely addresses either the moral implications of societal inequalities within our present form of industrial capitalism or the ways in which schools function to reproduce and legitimate these inequalities.[34]

When classroom life is discussed in teacher education programs, it is usually presented as a fundamentally one-dimensional set of rules and regulative practices, rather than as a cultural terrain where a variety of interests and practices collide in a constant and often chaotic struggle for dominance. Thus, prospective teachers frequently receive the impression that classroom culture is essentially free from ambiguity and contradiction. According to this view, schools are supposedly devoid of all vestiges of contestation, struggle, and cultural politics.[35] Furthermore, classroom reality is rarely presented as if it were socially constructed, historically determined, and reproduced through institutionalized relationships of class, gender, race, and power. Unfortunately, this dominant conception of schooling vastly contradicts what the student teacher often experiences during his or her practicum of fieldsite work, especially if the student is placed in a school largely populated by economically disadvantaged and disenfranchised students. Yet student teachers are nevertheless instructed to view schooling as a neutral terrain devoid of power and politics. It is against this transparent depiction of schooling that prospective teachers, more often than not, view their own ideologies and experiences through a dominant theoretical and cultural perspective that remains largely unquestioned. Most important, teachers in this situation have no grounds upon which to question the dominant cultural assumptions that shape and structure the ways in which they respond to and influence student behavior.

Consequently, many student teachers who find themselves teaching working-class or minority students lack a well-articulated framework for understanding the class, cultural, ideological, and gender dimensions that inform classroom life. As a result, cultural differences among students often are viewed uncritically as deficiencies rather than as strengths, and what passes for teaching is in actuality an assault on the specific histories, experiences, and knowledges that such students use both to define their own identities and to make sense of their larger world. I use the term "assault" not because such knowledge is openly attacked—but because it is devalued through a process that is at once subtle and debilitating. What happens is that within the dominant school culture, subordinate knowledge is generally ignored, marginalized, or treated in a disorganized fashion. Such knowledge is often treated as if it did not exist, or treated in ways that disconfirm it. Conversely, ideologies that do not aid subordinate groups in interpreting the reality they actually experience often pass for objective forms of knowledge. In this process prospective teachers lose an understanding of the relationship between culture and power as well as a sense of how to develop pedagogical possibilities for their students from the cultural differences that often characterize school and classroom life. In the next section, I discuss the elements that, in my view, should constitute a new model of teacher education, one that addresses the above issue more specifically.

Teacher Education as Cultural Politics

My concern here is with reconstituting the grounds upon which teacher education programs are built. This means implementing an alternative form of teacher education that conceptualizes schooling as taking place within a political and cultural arena where forms of student experience and subjectivity are actively produced and mediated. In other words, I wish to state once again the idea that schools do not merely teach academic subjects, but also, in part, produce student subjectivities or particular sets of experiences that are in themselves part of an ideological process. Conceptualizing schooling as the construction and transmission of subjectivities permits us to understand more clearly the idea that the curriculum is more than just an introduction of students to particular subject disciplines and teaching methodologies; it also serves as an introduction to a particular way of life.[36]

Here, I must forego a detailed specification of teaching practices and instead attempt to briefly sketch out particular areas of study crucial to the development of a reconceptualized teacher education curriculum. I assign the term "cultural politics" to my curriculum agenda because I believe that this term permits me to capture the significance of the sociocultural dimension of the schooling process. Furthermore, the term allows me to highlight the political consequences of interaction between teachers and students who come from dominant and subordinate cultures. A teacher education curriculum as a form of cultural politics assumes that the social, cultural, political, and economic dimensions are the primary categories for understanding contemporary schooling.[37] Within this context, school life is conceptualized not as a unitary, monolithic, and ironclad system of rules and regulations, but as a cultural terrain characterized by varying degrees of accommodation, contestation, and resistance. Furthermore, school life is understood as a plurality of conflicting languages and struggles, a place where classroom and street-corner cultures collide and where teachers, students, and school administrators often differ as to how school experiences and practices are to be defined and understood.

The imperative of this curriculum is to create conditions for student self-empowerment and self-constitution as an active political and moral subject. By "empowerment" I mean the process whereby students acquire the means to critically appropriate knowledge existing outside their immediate experience in order to broaden their understanding of themselves, the world, and the possibilities for transforming the taken-for-granted assumptions about the way we live. Stanley Aronowitz has described one aspect of empowerment as "the process of appreciating and loving oneself."[38] In this sense, empowerment is gained from knowledge and social relations that dignify one's own history, language, and cultural traditions. But empowerment means more than self-confirmation. It also refers to the process by which students are able to interrogate and selectively appropriate those aspects of the dominant culture that will provide them with the basis for defining and transforming, rather than merely serving, the wider social order.

The project of "doing" a teacher education curriculum based on cultural politics consists of linking critical social theory to a set of stipulated practices through which student teachers are able to dismantle and critically examine preferred educational and cultural traditions, many of which have fallen prey to an instrumental rationality that either limits or ignores democratic ideals and principles. One of my main concerns focuses on developing a language of critique and demystification that is capable of analyzing the latent interests and ideologies that work to socialize students in a manner compatible with the dominant culture. I am equally concerned, however, with creating alternative teaching practices capable of helping to empower students both inside and outside schools. Although it is impossible to provide a detailed outline of the courses of a curriculum for cultural politics, I want to comment on some important areas of analysis that are central to such a program. These include the critical study of power, language, history, and culture.

Power

A pivotal concern of a teacher education curriculum that subscribes to a cultural politics approach is to assist student teachers in understanding the relationship between power and knowledge. Within the dominant curriculum, knowledge is often removed from the issue of power and is generally treated in a technical manner; that is, it is seen in instrumental terms as something to be mastered. That such knowledge is always an ideological construction linked to particular interests and social relations generally receives little consideration in teacher education programs. An understanding of the knowledge/power relationship raises important issues regarding what kinds of knowledge educators can provide to empower students to understand and engage the world around them as well as to exercise the kind of courage needed to change the social order where necessary. Of considerable concern, then, is the need for student teachers to recognize that power relations correspond to forms of school knowledge that both distort the truth and produce it. That is, knowledge should be examined both for the way in which it might misrepresent or mediate social reality and for the way in which it actually reflects people's experiences and, as such, influences their lives. Understood in this way, knowledge not only reproduces reality by distorting or illuminating the social world, but also has the more concrete function of shaping the day-to-day lives of people through their felt, relatively unmediated world of commonsense assumptions. This suggests that a curriculum for democratic empowerment must examine the conditions of school knowledge in terms of how it is produced and what particular interests it might represent; in addition, it should scrutinize the effects of such knowledge at the level of everyday life. In short, prospective teachers need to understand that knowledge does more than distort; it also produces particular forms of life. Finally, knowledge contains hopes, desires, and needs that resonate positively with the subjective experience of a particular audience, and such knowledge needs to be analyzed to find the Utopian promises often implicit in its claims.[39]

Language

In traditional approaches to reading, writing, and second-language learning, language issues are primarily defined by technical and developmental concerns. Although such concerns are indeed important, what is often ignored in mainstream language courses in teacher education programs is how language is actively implicated in power relations that generally support the dominant culture. An alternative starting point to the study of language recognizes the significance of Antonio Gramsci's notion that every language contains elements of a conception of the world. It is through language that we come to consciousness and negotiate a sense of identity, since language does not merely reflect reality but plays an active role in constructing it. As language constructs meaning, it shapes our world, informs our identities, and provides the cultural codes for perceiving and classifying the world. This implies, of course, that within the available discourses of the school or the society, language plays a powerful role because it serves to "mark the boundaries of permissible discourse, discourage the clarification of social alternatives, and makes it difficult for the dispossessed to locate the source of their unease, let alone remedy it."[40] Through the study of language within the perspective of a cultural politics, prospective teachers can gain an understanding of how language functions to "position" people in the world, to shape the range of possible meanings surrounding an issue, and to actively construct reality rather than merely reflect it. As part of language studies, student teachers would become more knowledgeable about and sensitive to the omnipresence and power of language as constitutive of their own experiences and those of their potential students.[41] Student teachers would also benefit from an introductory understanding of European traditions of discourse theory and the textual strategies that characterize their methods of inquiry.[42] Furthermore, through an exposure to the semiotics of mass and popular cultures, students could at least learn the rudimentary methods of examining the various codes and meanings that are constitutive of both their own personal constructions of self and society and those of the students they work with during their practicum or on-site sessions.[43]

History

The study of history should play a more expansive role in teacher education programs.[44] A critical approach to history would attempt to provide student teachers with an understanding of how cultural traditions are formed; it would also be designed to bring to light the various ways in which curricula and discipline-based texts have been constructed and read throughout different historical periods. Furthermore, such an approach would be self-consciously critical of the problems surrounding the teaching of history as a school subject, since what is conventionally taught overwhelmingly reflects the perspectives and values of white, middle-class males. Too often excluded are the histories of women, minority groups, and indigenous peoples. This exclusion is not politically innocent when we consider how existing social arrangements are partly constitutive of and dependent on the subjugation and elimination of the histories and voices of those groups marginalized and disempowered by the dominant culture. In addition, the concept of history can also help illuminate what kinds of knowledge are deemed legitimate and promulgated through the school curriculum. Conventional emphasis on chronological history, "which traditionally saw its object as somehow unalterably 'there,' given, waiting only to be discovered,"[45] would be supplanted by a focus on how specific educational practices can be understood as historical constructions related to the economic, social, and political events of a particular time and place. It is primarily through this form of historical analysis that students can recover "subjugated knowledges."[46] My use of this term directs us to those aspects of history in which criticism and struggle have played a significant role in defining the nature and meaning of educational theory and practice. For example, students will have the opportunity to examine critically the historical contexts and interests at work in defining what forms of school knowledge become privileged over others, how specific forms of school authority are sustained, and how particular patterns of learning become institutionalized.

Within the format of a curriculum as a form of cultural politics, it is also necessary that the study of history be theoretically connected to both language and reading. In this context, language can be subsequently studied as "the bearer of history" and history can be analyzed as a social construction open to critical examination. The important linkage between reading and history can be made by emphasizing that "reading occurs within history and that the point of integration is always the reader."[47] In analyzing this relationship, teachers can focus on the cultural meanings that students use to understand a text. Such a focus will better equip student teachers to understand how the process of reading occurs within a particular student's cultural history and in the context of his or her own concerns and beliefs. This will also assist student teachers to become more critically aware of how students from subordinate cultures bring their own sets of experiences, as well as their own dreams, desires, and voices to the reading act. In other words, student teachers must develop a critical theory of learning that includes an analysis of how students produce rather than just receive knowledge. This entails understanding how students bring their own categories of meaning into play in the exchange between school knowledge and their own subjectivities and histories.

Culture

The concept of culture, varied though it may be, is essential to any teacher education curriculum aspiring to be critical. I am using the term "culture" here to signify the particular ways in which a social group lives out and makes sense of its "given" circumstances and conditions of life.[48] In addition to defining "culture" as a set of practices and ideologies from which different groups draw to make sense of the world, I want to refashion the ways in which cultural questions become the starting point for understanding the issue of who has power and how it is reproduced and manifested in the social relations that link schooling to the wider social order. The link between culture and power has been extensively analyzed in critical social theory over the past ten years. It is therefore possible to offer four insights from that literature that are particularly relevant for illuminating the political logic that underlies various cultural/power relations. First, the concept of culture has been intimately connected with the question of how *social relations are structured* within class, gender, race, and age formations that produce forms of oppression and dependency. Second, culture has been analyzed within the radical perspective not simply as a way of life, but as a *form of production* through which different groups in either their dominant or subordinate social relations define and realize their aspirations through asymmetrical relations of power. Third, culture has been viewed as a *field of struggle* in which the production, legitimation, and circulation of particular forms of knowledge and experience are central areas of conflict. Fourth, the production of culture has been analyzed primarily through analysis of language as the constitutive and expressive signifier of meaning. What is important here is that each of these insights raises fundamental questions about the ways in which inequalities are maintained and challenged in the sphere of culture.

The study of cultures—or, more specifically, what has come to be known as "cultural studies"—should become the touchstone of a teacher education curriculum. It can provide student teachers with the critical categories necessary for examining school and classroom relations as social and political practices inextricably related to the construction and maintenance of specific relations of power. Moreover, by recognizing that school life is often mediated through the clash of dominant and subordinate cultures, prospective teachers can gain some insight into the ways in which classroom experiences are necessarily intertwined with their students' home life and street-corner culture. This point is meant to be more than a rallying cry for relevance; rather, it asserts the need for prospective teachers to understand the systems of meaning that students employ in their encounters with forms of dominant school knowledge and social relations. It is important, therefore, that student teachers learn to analyze expressions of mass and popular culture, such as music videos, television, and film. In this way, a successful cultural studies approach would provide an important theoretical avenue for teachers to comprehend how ideologies become inscribed through representations of everyday life.

More specifically, a cultural studies program can be organized around a variety of core courses in which the issues of power, history, language, and culture can be approached in an interdisciplinary context. Cultural studies would provide a more interdisciplinary foundation in order to analyze the limits of the traditional disciplines in addressing educational problems as well as to reconstruct relationships among faculty and students. The potential a cultural studies program has for reshaping relationships among faculty as well as between faculty and students is enormous. Generally, schools of education are divided into a number of departments that have few programmatic links to each other. Programs are usually organized around areas such as educational psychology, educational administration, foundations of education, curriculum and instruction, and guidance and counseling and often function in an insular fashion with few or no opportunities for faculty or students from these, different programs to work together.

A cultural studies program would offer a number of mandatory courses to be taken by students in the various departments. Such courses would work in conjunction with disciplinary specialists in order to provide students with a language and a method of inquiry that allow them to understand both the limits and the strengths of the disciplinary matrix. In addition, the program would utilize faculty from the different departments to teach interdisciplinary courses and to engage in collaborative research. For example, courses offered could be developed around themes like language and power in educational administration, reading educational psychology as historical texts, analyzing diverse curricula languages as a form of cultural production, analyzing pedagogy as an ethical discourse, and so on. Such a program could also be used to engage faculty and students in shared research projects that could not ordinarily take place within mainstream disciplines and methods of inquiry.

A cultural studies program could also become a site for initiating new relations between public schools and the community at large. For example, productive relations could be developed between public school teachers and the faculty and students of the cultural studies program around some of the concrete problems facing public schools. This could be particularly productive around race, gender, ethnic, language, and class considerations as they present themselves in various aspects of the schooling process. Similarly, teachers and staff members could participate in study groups and seminars designed to further the groups' collective knowledge and possibilities for working together around common problems. A cultural studies program could also provide the basis for establishing organic links with surrounding communities. The histories, resources, public services, and voices of the community could be researched and brought together through the cultural studies program in order to develop curriculum projects, elements of a critical pedagogy, and policy initiatives. Such projects developed in relation with community groups could serve as an ongoing vehicle for mutual dialogue, learning, and collective action. Although these suggestions are general and schematic, they do provide a glimpse of the theoretical and practical possibilities that could be developed in rethinking the nature of a teacher education program in which cultural studies is viewed as one of its major programmatic concerns.

Toward a Critical Pedagogy for the Classroom

In the previous sections I highlighted the importance of viewing schools as social and political sites involved in the struggle for democracy. In addition, I reconsidered the relationship between authority and teachers' work and attempted to develop the theoretical rudiments of a program in which teacher education would be viewed as a form of cultural politics. In this final section, I shift the focus from questions of institutional purpose and teacher definition to the issues of critical pedagogy and student learning. In so doing, I state some of the fundamental theoretical elements that I believe can be used to construct a critical pedagogy in which the issue of student interests and motivation is linked to the dynamics of self- and social empowerment. I wish to underscore here that the public schools shape and reinforce the attitudes that prospective teachers bring to their clinical experiences. By focusing on some of the theoretical elements that constitute a critical pedagogy, I attempt to clarify the link between our notion of a teacher education curriculum as a form of cultural politics and the actual dynamics of classroom pedagogy. With this in mind, I will now sketch out the rudiments of a critical discourse that defines classroom pedagogy within the parameters of a political project centering on the primacy of student experience, the concept of voice, and the importance of transforming schools and communities into democratic public spheres.

The Primacy of Student Experience

The type of critical pedagogy I am proposing is fundamentally concerned with student experience insofar as it takes the problems and needs of the students themselves as its starting point. As a historical construction and lived practice that is produced and legitimated within particular social forms, student experience becomes an object of inquiry rather than an unproblematic given. As part of a pedagogy of possibility, student experience provides the basis for analyzing the social forms that reconstruct the subjective character of the stories, memories, and meanings that are in place when students come to schools. A critical pedagogy in this instance encourages a critique of dominant forms of knowledge and social practices that semantically and emotionally organize meanings and experiences that give students a sense of voice and identity; similarly, it attempts to provide students with the critical knowledge and skills necessary for them to examine their own particular lived experiences and cultural resources. As I have mentioned previously, this means assisting students to draw on their own voices and histories as a basis for engaging and interrogating the multiple and often contradictory experiences that provide them with a sense of identity, worth, and presence. In this form of pedagogy, knowledge is being made for these students inside their language and histories and not outside history. The historicity of knowledge and experience provides the basis for helping students to develop a respect for their own experiences so they can be legitimate and reclaim their own language and histories. The important pedagogical principle at work here is to validate students' experience in order to empower them and not merely to please them.

Student experience must be given preeminence in an emancipatory curriculum. But learning how to understand, affirm, and analyze such experience means not only understanding the cultural and social forms through which students learn how to define themselves, but also learning how to engage student experience in a way that neither unqualifiedly endorses nor delegitimates it. In part, this suggests that teachers learn how to create an affirmative and critical continuity between how students view the world and those forms of analyses that provide the basis for both analyzing and enriching such perspectives. To do so is to acknowledge that at the heart of any critical pedagogy is the necessity for teachers to work with the knowledges that students actually have. Although this may seem risky and in some cases dangerous, it provides the basis for validating the way in which students read the world as well as for giving them the intellectual content for putting knowledge and meaning into their own categories of meaning and cultural capital. This suggests that school knowledge as produced and modified through the voice of the teacher has to be made meaningful to students before it can be made critical. School knowledge never speaks for itself; rather, it is constantly filtered through the ideological and cultural experiences that students bring to the classroom. To ignore the ideological dimensions of student experience is to deny the ground on which students learn, speak, and imagine.

The important pedagogical implications for student teachers is that they should be educated to understand how student experience produced in the various domains and layers of everyday life gives rise to the often contradictory *and* different voices students employ to give meaning to their own existence in relation to both the communities in which they live and the wider society. What should be recognized is that in the multiple experience, meanings, and voices that students inhabit there are tensions and contradictory beliefs that need to be analyzed regarding the interests and values they celebrate and legitimate. It is crucial, therefore, that educators address the question of how aspects of the social world are experienced, mediated, and produced by students in often contradictory ways and how the forms of meaning that arise out of these contradictions collectively disable or enable the possibilities open to students within the existing society. Failure to do so not only will prevent teachers from tapping into the drives, emotions, and interests that give students their own unique voice, but also will make it equally difficult to provide the momentum for learning itself.

While the concept of student experience is being offered as central to a critical pedagogy, it should also be recognized as a central category of teacher education programs. This suggests that student practicums should be seen as sites where the question of how experience is produced, legitimated, and accomplished becomes an object of study for teachers and students alike. Unfortunately, most student practicums are viewed as either a rite of passage into the profession or merely a formal culminating experience in the teacher education program.

Student Voice and the Public Sphere

The concept of voice constitutes the focal point for a theory of teaching and learning that generates new forms of sociality as well as new and challenging ways of confronting and engaging everyday life. Voice, quite simply, refers to the various measures by which students and teachers actively participate in dialogue. It is related to the discursive means whereby teachers and students attempt to make themselves "heard" and to define themselves as active authors of their worlds. Displaying a voice means, to cite Mikhail Bakhtin, "retelling a story in one's own words."[49] More specifically, the term "voice" refers to the principles of dialogue as they are enunciated and enacted within particular social settings. The concept of voice represents the unique instances of self-expression through which students affirm their own class, cultural, racial, and gender identities. A student's voice is necessarily shaped by personal history and distinctive lived engagement with the surrounding culture. The category of voice, then, refers to the means at our disposal—the discourses available to use—to make ourselves understood and listened to, and to define ourselves as active participants in the world. However, as I have stressed previously, the dominant school culture generally represents and legitimates the voices of white males from the middle and upper classes to the exclusion of economically disadvantaged students, most especially females from minority backgrounds.[50] A critical pedagogy takes into account the various ways in which the voices that teachers use to communicate with students can either silence or legitimate them.

The concept of voice is crucial to the development of a critical classroom pedagogy because it provides an important basis for constructing and demonstrating the fundamental imperatives of a critical democracy. Such a pedagogy attempts to organize classroom relationships so that students can draw on and confirm those dimensions of their own histories and experiences that are deeply rooted in the surrounding community. In addition, by creating active links with the community, teachers can open up their classrooms to its diverse resources and traditions. This presupposes that teachers familiarize themselves with the culture, economy, and historical traditions that belong to the communities in which they teach. In other words, teachers must assume a pedagogical responsibility for attempting to understand the relationships and forces that influence their students outside the immediate context of the classroom. This responsibility requires teachers to develop their curricula and pedagogical practices around those community traditions, histories, and forms of knowledge that are often ignored within the dominant school culture. This can, of course, lead to a deeper understanding by both teachers and students of how both "local" and "official" knowledges get produced, sustained, and legitimated.

Teachers need to develop pedagogical practices that link student experiences with those aspects of community life that inform and sustain such experiences. For example, student teachers could compile oral histories of the communities in which they teach, which could then be used as a school and curricula resource—particularly in reading programs. In addition, they could work in and analyze how different community social agencies function so as to produce, distribute, and legitimate particular forms of knowledge and social relations. This would broaden their notions of pedagogical practices and help them understand the relevance of their own work for institutions other than schools. Similarly, prospective teachers could develop organic links with active community agencies such as business, religious organizations, and other public spheres in an attempt to develop a more meaningful connection between the school curriculum and the experiences that define and characterize the local community. The concept of voice can thus provide a basic organizing principle for the development of a relationship between knowledge and student experiences and, at the same time, create a forum for examining broader school and community issues. In other words, teachers must become aware of both the transformative strengths and structures of oppression of the community-at-large and develop this awareness into curriculum strategies designed to empower students toward creating a more liberating and humane society. In short, teachers should be attentive to what it means to construct forms of learning in their classrooms that enable students to affirm their voices within areas of community life, that is, within democratic public spheres needing constant criticism, safeguarding, and renewal.

Steve Tozer has written on this issue:

> The process of fitting students for community life, then, is an effort to prepare students both for the existing community and to bring them to understand and to appreciate the historical values and ideas which point to a more ideal community than the one that exists ... the teacher's duty is to recognize the historical ideals which make community life worth living, ideals upon which the larger society is founded: ideals of human dignity and equality, freedom, and mutual concern of one person for another. ... This is not to say that teachers should prepare students for some nonexistent utopia. Rather, teachers must develop an understanding of the community as it exists and an understanding of what kind of people will be required to make it better. They can try to develop for themselves an ideal of the community their students should strive for, and they should help their students with the knowledge, the values and the skills they will need if they are to be resilient enough to maintain high standards of belief and conduct in an imperfect society.[51]

It is an unfortunate truism that when communities are ignored by teachers, students often find themselves trapped in institutions that not only deny them a voice, but also deprive them of a relational or contextual understanding of how the knowledge they acquire in the classroom can be used to influence and transform the public sphere. Implicit in the concept of linking classroom experiences to the wider community is the idea that the school is best understood as a polity, as a locus of citizenship. Within this locus, students and teachers can engage in a process of deliberation and discussion aimed at advancing the public welfare in accordance with fundamental moral judgments and principles. To bring schools closer to the concept of polity, it is necessary to define them as public spaces that seek to recapture the idea of critical democracy and community. In effect, I want to define teachers as active community participants whose function is to establish public spaces where students can debate, appropriate, and learn the knowledge and skills necessary to live in a critical democracy.

By "public space" I mean, as Hannah Arendt did, a concrete set of learning conditions where people come together to speak, to engage in dialogue, to share their stories, and to struggle together within social relations that strengthen rather than weaken possibilities for active citizenship.[52] School and classroom practices should in some manner be organized around forms of learning that serve to prepare students for responsible roles as transformative intellectuals, as community members, and as critically active citizens outside schools.[53]

I began this chapter by arguing that teacher education should be seriously rethought along the lines of the critical democratic tradition, a tradition which, regrettably, has been all but excluded from the current debates on American schooling. I have argued that this tradition provides the basis for rethinking the relationship of schooling to the social order and for restructuring the education of prospective teachers so as to prepare them for the role of transformative intellectuals. Moreover, I have argued that teacher education programs must assume a central role in reforming public education and, in so doing, must assert the primacy of a democratic tradition in order to restructure school-community relations.

In my view, the search for a creative democracy undertaken at the beginning of the century by Dewey and others is presently in retreat, having been abandoned by liberals and radicals alike. This situation presents a dual challenge to critical educators: there is now an urgent need not only to resurrect the tradition of liberal democracy, but to develop a theoretical perspective that goes beyond it. In the current age of conservatism, public education must analyze its strengths and weaknesses against an ideal of critical democracy rather than the current corporate referent of the capitalist marketplace. Similarly, public education must fulfill the task of educating citizens to take risks, to struggle for institutional and social change, and to fight for democracy and against oppression both inside and outside schools. Pedagogical empowerment necessarily goes hand in hand with social and political transformation.

My position is indebted to Dewey but attempts to extend his democratic project. My position accentuates the idea that schools represent a very important site in the struggle for democracy. But it is different from Dewey's view because it perceives the self- and social empowerment of students as involving not just the politics of classroom culture, but also political and social struggle that occurs outside school sites. Such an approach acknowledges that critical pedagogy is but one intervention—albeit a crucial one—in the struggle to restructure the ideological and material conditions of everyday life. I am convinced that teacher education institutions and public schools can and should play an active and productive role in broadening the possibilities for the democratic promise of American schooling, politics, and society.

Notes

1. Arthur G. Powell, "University Schools of Education in the Twentieth Century," *Peabody Journal of Education*, 54(1976), 4.
2. Ibid., p. 4.
3. George Counts, quoted in Powell, "University Schools," p. 4.
4. As quoted in Lawrence A. Cremin, David A. Shannon, and Mary Evelyn Townsend, *A History of Teachers College, Columbia University* (New York: Columbia University Press, 1954), p. 222.
5. Ibid., p. 222.
6. As quoted by George Counts in Ibid., p. 222.
7. For an interesting discussion of this issue, see Ira Katznelson and Margaret Weir, *Schooling for All: Class, Race, and the Decline of the Democratic Ideal* (New York: Basic Books, 1985).
8. See especially the work of the revisionist historians of the 1960s. Among the representative works are Michael B. Katz, *The Irony of Early School Reform: Educational Innovation in Mid-Nineteenth Century Massachusetts* (Boston: Beacon Press, 1968); Colin Greer, *The Great School Legend* (New York: Basic Books, 1972); and Clarence J. Karier, Paul Violas, and Joel Spring, *Roots of Crisis: American Education in the Twentieth Century* (Chicago: Rand McNally, 1973).
9. See Stanley Aronowitz and Henry A. Giroux, *Education under Siege: The Conservative, Liberal, and Radical Debate over Schooling* (South Hadley, Mass.: Bergin and Garvey, 1985).
10. I am using the term "discourse" to mean "a domain of language use subject to rules of formation and transformation," as quoted in Catherine Belsey, *Critical Practice* (London: Methuen, 1980), p. 160. Discourses may also be described as "the complexes of signs and practices which organize social existence and social reproduction. In their structured, material persistence, discourses are what give differential substance to membership of a social group or class or formation, which mediate an internal sense of belonging, and outward sense of otherness," as quoted in Richard Terdiman, *Discourse-Counter-Discourse* (New York: Cornell University Press), p. 54.
11. Aronowitz and Giroux, *Education under Siege*; and Ann Bastian, Colin Greer, Norm Fruchter, Marilyn Gittel, and Kenneth Haskins, *Choosing Equality: The Case for Democratic Schooling* (New York: New World Foundation, 1985).
12. Zeichner, "Alternative Paradigms of Teacher Education," *Journal of Teacher Education*, 34(1983), 8.
13. Some of the more representative writing on this issue can be found in Diane Ravitch, *The Troubled Crusade. American Education 1945–1980* (New York: Basic Books, 1983); John H. Bunzel, ed, *Challenge to American Schools: The Case for Standards and Values* (New York: Oxford University Press, 1985); Diane Ravitch, *The Schools We Deserve: Reflections on the Educational Crises of Our Time* (New York: Basic Books, 1985); and Edward Wynne, "The Great Tradition in Education: Transmitting Moral Values," *Educational Leadership*, 43(1985), 7.
14. Some of the best analyses are Lawrence C. Stedman and Marshall S. Smith, "Recent Reform Proposals for American Education," *Contemporary Education Review*, 53(1983), 85–104; Walter Feinberg, "Fixing the Schools: The Ideological Turn," *Issues in Education*, 3(1985), 113–38; Edward H. Berman,"The Improbability of Meaningful Educational Reform," *Issues in Education*, 3(1985), 99–112; and Aronowitz and Giroux, *Education under Siege*.
15. Barbara Finkelstein, "Education and the Retreat from Democracy in the United States, 1979–1982," *Teachers College Record*, 86(1984), 280–81.
16. Berman, "Improbability," p. 103.
17. I am using the term "influential" to refer to those reports that have played a major role in shaping educational policy at both the national and local levels. These include The National Commission on Excellence in Education, *A Nation at Risk: The Imperative for Educational Reform* (Washington, D.C.: GPO, 1983); Task Force on Education for Economic Growth, Education Commission of the States, *Action for Excellence. A Comprehensive Plan to Improve Our Nation's Schools* (Denver: Education Commission of the States, 1983); The Twentieth Century Fund Task Force on Federal Elementary and Secondary Education Policy, *Making the Grade* (New York: The Twentieth Century Fund, 1983); Carnegie Corporation, *Education and Economic Progress: Toward a National Education Policy* (New York: Author, 1983); and Carnegie Forum on Education and the Economy, *A Nation Prepared: Teachers for the 21st Century* (Hyattsville, Md.: Author, 1986). Also considered are other recent reports on teacher education reform: The National Commission for Excellence in Teacher Education, *A Call for Change in Teacher Education* (Washington, D.C: American Association of Colleges in Teacher Education, 1985); C. Emily Feistritzer, *The Making of a Teacher* (Washington, D.C.: National Center for Education Information, 1984); "Tomorrow's Teachers: A Report of the Holmes Group" (East Lansing, Mich.: Holmes Group, 1986); and Francis A. Maher and Charles H. Rathbone, "Teacher Education and Feminist Theory: Some Implications for Practice," *American Journal of Education*, 101(1986), 214–35. For an analysis of many of these reports see Catherine Cornbleth, "Ritual and Rationality in Teacher Education Reform," *Educational Researcher*, 15:4 (1986), 5–14. The Holmes Report has been the subject of a number of articles; some of the most insightful are to be found in *Teachers College Record*, 88:3 (Spring 1987).

18. Marilyn Frankenstein and Louis Kampf, "Preface," in Sara Freedman, Jane Jackson, and Katherine Boles, "The Other End of the Corridor: The Effect of Teaching on Teachers," *Radical Teacher*, 23(1983), 2–23. It is worth noting that the Carnegie Forum's *A Nation Prepared* ends up defeating its strongest suggestions for reform by linking teacher empowerment to quantifying notions of excellence.

19. Stedman and Smith, "Recent Reform Proposals," pp. 85–104.

20. I am not automatically opposed to all forms of curricular software and technologies, such as interactive video disks and computers, as long as teachers become aware of the limited range of applications and contexts in which these technologies may be put to use. Certainly, I agree that some prepackaged curricula are more salient than others as instruments of learning. Too often, however, the use of such curricula ignores the contexts of the immediate classroom situation, the larger social milieu, and the historical juncture of the surrounding community. Furthermore, classroom materials designed to simplify the task of teaching and to make it more cost-efficient often separate planning or conception from execution. Many of the recent examples of predesigned commercial curricula are largely focused on competencies measured by standardized tests, precluding the possibility that teachers and students will be able to act as critical thinkers. See Michael W. Apple and Kenneth Teitelbaum, "Are Teachers Losing Control of Their Skills and Curriculum?" *Journal of Curriculum Studies*, 18 (1986), 177–84.

21. Linda Darling-Hammond, "Valuing Teachers: The Making of a Profession," *Teachers College Record*, 87(1985), p. 209.

22. Ibid.

23. For an excellent theoretical analysis of this issue, see Freedman, Jackson, and Boles, "The Other End of the Corridor." For a more traditional statistical treatment, see Darling-Hammond, *Beyond the Commission Reports: The Coming Crisis in Teaching*, R-3177-RC (Santa Monica, Calif,: Rand Corporation, July 1984); National Education Association, *Nationwide Teacher Opinion Poll*, 1983 (Washington, D.C.: Author, 1983); and American Federation of Teachers, *School as a Workplace: The Realities of Stress*, volume 1 (Washington, D.C.: Author, 1983).

24. Dennis J. Schmidt, "Translator's Introduction: In the Spirit of Bloch," in Ernst Bloch, *Natural Law and Human Dignity*, trans. Dennis J. Schmidt (Cambridge, Mass.: MIT Press, 1986), p. xviii.

25. John Goodlad, *A Place Called School: Prospects for the Future* (New York: McGraw-Hill, 1983); Theodore Sizer, *Horace's Compromise: The Dilemma of the American High School* (Boston: Houghton Mifflin, 1984); and Ernest Boyer, *High School: A Report on Secondary Education in America* (New York: Harper and Row, 1983).

26. For an overview and critical analysis of this literature, see Henry A. Giroux, "Theories of Reproduction and Resistance in the New Sociology of Education: A Critical Analysis," *Harvard Educational Review*, 53(1983), 257–93.

27. Popkewitz and Pitman, "The Idea of Progress and the Legitimation of State Agendas: American Proposals for School Reform," *Curriculum and Teaching*, 1 (1986), p. 21.

28. Ibid., p. 20.

29. Ibid, p. 22.

30. Zeichner, "Alternative Paradigms"; and Jesse Goodman, "Reflections on Teacher Education: A Case Study and Theoretical Analysis," *Interchange*, 15(1984), 7–26. The fact that many teacher education programs have defined themselves as synonymous with instructional preparation has often given them a debilitating practical slant, leading to a limited conception of teaching as exercises in classroom management and control. Isolated courses on classroom management have had a tragic effect on how teachers are able to critically interrogate the political implications of curricular decision making and policy development. This predicament can be traced to a history of the academic politics that grew out of the separation of colleges of education from the liberal arts tradition and the arts and sciences faculty; see Donald Warren, "Learning from Experience: History and Teacher Education," *Educational Researcher*, 14:10 (1985), 5–12.

31. For an excellent analysis of this issue, see National Coalition of Advocates for Students, *Barriers to Excellence: Our Children at Risk* (Boston: Author, 1985).

32. As quoted in Frank Lentricchia, *Criticism and Social Change* (Chicago: University of Chicago Press, 1985); see also John Dewey, *Democracy and Education* (New York: Free Press, 1916) and *The Public and Its Problems* (New York: Holt, 1927).

33. Dewey, "Creative Democracy—The Task Before Us," in *Classic American Philosophers*, ed. Max Fisch (New York: Appleton-Century-Crofts, 1951), pp. 389–94; and Richard J. Bernstein, "Dewey and Democracy: The Task Ahead of Us," in *Post-Analytic Philosophy*, ed. John Rajchman and Cornel West (New York: Columbia University Press, 1985), pp. 48–62.

34. Zeichner, "Alternative Paradigms"; Henry A. Giroux, *Ideology, Culture, and the Process of Schooling* (Philadelphia: Temple University Press, 1981); and John Sears, "Rethinking Teacher Education: Dare We Work Toward a New Social Order?" *Journal of Curriculum Theorizing*, 6(1985), 24–79.

35. Of course, this is not true for all teacher education programs, but it does represent the dominant tradition characterizing them; see Zeichner, "Alternative Paradigms."

36. See John Ellis, "Ideology and Subjectivity," in *Culture, Media, Language*, ed. Stuart Hall, Dorothy Hobson, Andrew Lowe, and Paul Willis (Hawthorne, Australia: Hutchinson, 1980), pp. 186–94; see also Julian Henriques, Wendy Hollway, Cathy Urwin Couze Venn, and Valerie Walkerdine, *Changing the Subject* (New York: Methuen, 1984).

37. Henry A. Giroux and Roger Simon, "Curriculum Study and Cultural Politics," *Journal of Education*, 166(1984), 226–238.

38. Stanley Aronowitz, "Schooling, Popular Culture, and Post-Industrial Society: Peter McLaren Interviews Aronowitz," *Orbit*, 17(1986), p. 18.

39. Foucault, "The Subject of Power," in *Beyond Structuralism and Hermeneutics*, ed. Hubert Dreyfus and Paul Rabinow (Chicago: University of Chicago Press, 1982), p. 221.

40. T.J. Jackson Lears, "The Concept of Cultural Hegemony: Problems and Possibilities," *American Historical Review*, 90(1985), pp. 569–70.

41. Gary Waller, "Writing, Reading, Language, History, Culture: The Structure and Principles of the English Curriculum at Carnegie-Mellon University," unpublished manuscript, Carnegie-Mellon University, 1985, p. 12.

42. I am primarily referring to the French school of discourse theory, as exemplified in the writings of Foucault; see his *The Archaeology of Knowledge*, trans. A.M. Sheridan Smith (London: Tavistock, 1972); see also the following works by Foucault: *Language, Counter-Memory, Practice. Selected Essays and Interviews*, trans. Donald F. Bouchard and Sherry Simon (Ithaca: Cornell University Press, 1979) and "Politics and the Study of Discourse," *Ideology and Consciousness*, 3(1978), pp. 7–26.

43. For an introduction to such issues, see Umberto Eco, *A Theory of Semiotics* (Bloomington: Indiana University Press, 1976); Roland Barthes, *Elements of Semiology*, trans. Annette Labers and Colin Smith (New York: Hill and Wang, 1964); Roland Barthes, *Mythologies* (New York: Hill and Wang, 1957).

44. Waller, "Writing, Reading, Language," p. 12.

45. Ibid., p. 14.

46. Foucault, "Two Lectures," in *Power/Knowledge*, ed. Colin Gordon (New York: Pantheon, 1980), pp. 78–108.

47. Waller, "Writing, Reading, Language," p. 14.

48. Giroux, *Ideology, Culture, and the Process of Schooling*.

49. As quoted in Harold Rosen, "The Importance of Story," *Language Arts*, 63 (1986), p. 234.

50. For a thorough analysis of this, see Arthur Brittan and Mary Maynard, *Sexism, Racism and Oppression* (New York: Blackwell, 1984).

51. Steve Tozer, "Dominant Ideology and the Teacher's Authority," *Contemporary Education*, 56(1985), 152–53.

52. Arendt, *The Human Condition* (Chicago: University of Chicago Press, 1958).

53. Attempts to link classroom instruction to community contexts are nowhere more important than during teachers' clinical experiences. On these occasions, prospective teachers should be assisted in making connections with progressive community organizations, especially those affiliated with local governmental council meetings, and in interviewing community leaders and workers in various community agencies linked to the school. This enhances the possibility that prospective teachers will make critically reflective links between classroom practices and the ethos and needs of the surrounding social and cultural milieu.

23

Fighting for Our Lives: Preparing Teachers to Teach African American Students

Gloria Ladson-Billings

During the 1970s, school desegregation in U.S. northern cities became a national focal point. In Boston, a contested court order had parents, teachers, administrators, students, school committee members, and community members struggling with school busing to achieve desegregation. One African American parent, caught on the documentary film footage of the award winning civil rights series, "Eyes on the Prize" (Hampton, 1986), exclaimed, "When we fight about education, we're fighting for our lives." This urgent perspective of "fighting for our lives" informs the discussion about preparing teachers to teach African American students effectively. This article addresses the dearth of literature about preparing teachers to teach African American students, the attempts by scholars to fill this void, and the need for ongoing research in this area.

The Silence of the Literature

With very few exceptions, the literature does not expressly address the preparation of teachers to teach African American learners effectively (Ladson-Billings, 1994b). Instead, references to the educational needs of African American students are folded into a discourse of deprivation. Searches of the literature base indicate that when one uses the descriptor, "Black education," one is directed to see, "culturally deprived" and "culturally disadvantaged." Thus, the educational research literature, when it considers African American learners at all, has constructed all African American children, regardless of economic or social circumstance, within the deficit paradigm (Bettleheim, 1965; Bloom, Davis, & Hess, 1965; Ornstein & Viaro, 1968).

The literature is reflective of a generalized perception that African American culture is not a useful rubric for addressing the needs of African American learners, and thus, that African American culture is delegitimized in the classroom. Rather than seeing African Americans as possessing a distinctive culture, African American learners often are treated as if they are corruptions of White culture, participating in an oppositional, counter-productive culture (Ogbu, 1987). Schools and teachers treat the language, prior knowledge, and values of African Americans as aberrant and often presume that the teacher's job is to rid African American students of any vestiges of their own culture.

I would argue that the educational literature is silent on the issue of teaching African American students because much of the educational research has relied on generic models of pedagogy (Shulman, 1987) that position themselves as "culture neutral" when they actually support the learning of mainstream students. The emphasis on a "one best system" (Tyack, 1974) emerges from the 19th-century Americanization model that was designed to merge all students, regardless of ethnic and cultural origins, into one ideal "American" model (Olneck, 1995). Of course, this Americanization process considered only those immigrant and cultural groups from Europe. Indigenous peoples and people of African descent were not thought educable and therefore not a part of the mainstream educational discourse.

For many years, the education of African American learners was left solely to the African American community via state-supported segregated schools (Anderson, 1988). And, although not consistent with professed national ideals of equity and justice, there is some evidence to suggest that some segregated schools did meet the educational needs of African American students (Anderson, 1988; Siddle Walker, 1996). Community access and involvement, trust between teachers and parents, and concern and caring for students were all hallmarks of these schools where the needs of African American students were paramount. Foster (1990) indicates that African American teachers in segregated schools felt more comfortable introducing and discussing issues of race and racism in their all-Black settings than in the integrated schools in which they subsequently taught. Furthermore, Foster suggests that effective teaching of African American students almost always involves some recognition and attention to the ways that race and racism construct and constrict peoples' lives.

With the increasing diversity of the school population, more literature has emerged that addresses the needs of non-White students from the standpoint of language and culture (Banks, 1997). However, some of this literature has compressed the experiences of all non-White groups into a singular category of "other" without recognizing the particularity of African American experience and culture. It is important for teachers (current and prospective) to understand the specific and unique qualities of the African American cultural experience.

The Uniqueness of the African American Cultural Experience

Two concepts I attempt to have my own teacher education students grapple with are the notions of "equivalent" and "analogous," because discussions of racism, discrimination, inequality, and injustice sometimes degenerate into a "hierarchy of oppression;" that is, discussants want to talk in terms of who has suffered most. However, when we understand the ways in which oppression has worked against many groups of people based on their race, culture, class, gender, disability, and sexual orientation, we must recognize that there may be analogous experiences that are not necessarily equivalent ones. Thus, the displacement and forced removal of indigenous groups throughout the Americas and the internment of Japanese Americans during World War II are both examples of oppression. However, they are not equivalent experiences. Our understanding of the commonalities of oppression cannot wash out the particularities and specifics of each experience.

The African American social and cultural experience, like those of each cultural group, is unique. African Americans are the only group forcibly brought to the Americas for the expressed purpose of labor exploitation through racial slavery (Franklin & Moss, 1988). As one of the earliest nonindigenous groups to appear in the Americas, African Americans have a history in this country that predates most European Americans.[1]

The creation of a racial hierarchy with White and Black as polar opposites has positioned all people in American society (King, 1994) and reified "whiteness" in ways that suggest that the closer one is able to align oneself to whiteness, the more socially and culturally acceptable one is perceived to be. Thus, when European Americans of various ethnic groups assert, "My people faced discrimination, and they made it. Why can't Blacks pull themselves up like we did?" they are ignoring the very different historical trajectories from which these cultural groups were launched and the very different symbol system that has been created to reinscribe blackness and whiteness as fundamentally opposite (Morrison, 1991).

The ideology of White supremacy (Allen, 1994) argued that African Americans were genetically inferior and not fully human. Thus, the expectation for educating them was (and continues to be) low. Early efforts at state-supported education for African Americans was directed at training for manual labor and domestic service (Anderson, 1988). Scholarly arguments to the contrary (DuBois, 1903/1953; Woodson, 1933) failed to make their way into the mainstream literature. Thus, separate and unequal education continued for many decades past the Civil War.

As a group, African Americans have been told systematically and consistently that they are inferior, that they are incapable of high academic achievement. Their performance in school has replicated this low expectation for success. In addition to being told that they cannot perform at high levels, African American students often are taught by teachers who would rather not teach them (Grant, 1989; Haberman, 1989).

By the time the landmark Brown v. Board of Education (1954) decision was rendered, many African Americans were arguing from a position of sameness (Tate, Ladson-Billings, & Grant, 1993). That is, they were asserting that African American and White children were alike and deserved the same educational opportunities. This rhetoric of "equality means sameness" tended to ignore the distinctive qualities of African American culture and suggested that if schools were to make schooling experiences identical for African Americans, we somehow could achieve identical results.

However, because African American learners do not begin at the same place as middle-class White students either economically or socially, and because what may be valued in African American culture (Boykin & Tom, 1985) differs from what may be valued in schools, applying the same "remedy" may actually increase the educational disparities. For example, in the case of gender differences, we know that female students do not perform as well as male students in mathematics. A variety of reasons have been posited to explain this differential. Some reasons are related to females' abilities in spatial relations. Others (Gilligan, 1993; Houston, 1994) examine the ways that male students dominate classroom discussion and teacher time. Still, others (Campbell, 1995; Willis, 1992) argue about the way mathematics is organized and presented. The way to improve female performance, however, is not merely to continue to give female students more of the same, but rather to reorganize mathematics education in some fundamental ways. For example, all-female mathematics classes, integration across math areas (algebra, geometry, trigonometry), and more obvious and specific connections of math to everyday lives, are being employed to improve the performance of female students (and students of color) in school mathematics. Uncovering optimal learning environments for female students may mean deciding on very different strategies for male versus female mathematics learners. The same thing may be true in developing effective strategies for African American learners. As we begin to learn more about successful teaching for African American learners (Hollins & Spencer, 1990; Ladson-Billings, 1994a), we are better able to address their needs through curricular and pedagogical strategies.

Strategies for Improving the Education of Teachers

Teacher preparation is culpable in the failure of teachers to teach African American students effectively. Most teachers report that their preservice preparation did little or nothing to prepare them for today's diverse classrooms (Ladson-Billings, 1994b). Reviews of the literature on multicultural teacher education (Grant & Secada, 1990; Ladson-Billings, 1995a, 1996; Zeichner, 1992) indicate that most preservice approaches rely on individual courses and diverse field experiences to satisfy legislative and professional association calls for meeting the needs of diverse students.

However, no single course or set of field experiences is capable of preparing preservice students to meet the needs of diverse learners. Rather, a more systemic, comprehensive approach is needed. Work that uses autobiography, restructured field experiences, situated pedagogies, and returning to the classrooms of experts can each provide new opportunities for improving teaching.

Autobiography

Jackson (1992) argues that autobiography provides an opportunity for the "critical examination and experience of difference" (p. 4). She further asserts that autobiography allows individuals to speak as subjects with their own voices, "representing themselves and their stories from their own perspectives" (p. 3). This use of one's own story is also employed by Gomez and Tabachnick (1992) as a way to get preservice teachers to reflect on their practicum experiences in diverse classrooms. Hollins (1990) refers to "resocializing preservice teachers in ways that help them view themselves within a culturally diverse society" (p. 202) through the construction of personal/cultural autobiographies. Similar to this, King and Ladson-Billings (1990) link critical education theory and multicultural teacher education to help prospective teachers "consciously re-experience their own subjectivity when they recognize similar or different outlooks and experiences" (p. 26), both in courses and field experiences.

Restructured Field Experiences

The practical aspects of learning to teach are overwhelmingly valued by teachers as the most important part of their preparation. Unfortunately, many of these field experiences occur in White middle-income communities that offer a different set of challenges and opportunities from those that teachers can expect to encounter in the urban classrooms populated by African American students. Thus, when new teachers enter urban settings, they experience a mismatch between what they expect based on their preservice preparation and what they find in urban schools.

Some teacher education programs require that part of the field experience occur in a "diverse" setting (Zeichner, 1993). However, sometimes these "diversity requirements" are seen by students as hurdles in the way of their "real" student teaching (i.e., in middle income, suburban schools). Spending limited time in urban classrooms often serves to reinforce students' stereotypes and racist attitudes toward African American students because they are not accompanied with requisite understanding about African American culture and cultural practices.

Other programs stress "immersion" experiences in diverse communities (Mahan, 1982; Noordhoff & Kleinfeld, 1991), placing students in community (as opposed to school) settings to help them understand the daily lives of the children in context. Moving away from the predictability of the classroom with its rules, routines, and rituals, prospective teachers may recognize that limited access to goods and services, poor health care facilities, uneven police and fire protection, and unsafe and dilapidated playgrounds, all work against students' willingness to participate in school tasks.

At the same time, community experiences also can help students to see the strengths that reside in a culture. Self-governing bodies such as churches, lodges, social clubs, and neighborhood associations serve as purveyors of culture. Students may learn that families use a variety of child-rearing practices that may or may not map neatly onto schooling practices. They may learn of the role of "other mothers" (Collins, 1991) who, although not blood relatives of particular children, serve in a maternal capacity. Learning to see students with strengths as opposed to seeing them solely as having needs may inform the pedagogical practices of novice teachers in positive ways.

Situated Pedagogies

The literature of educational anthropologists has addressed culturally specific pedagogies (e.g., see Au & Jordan, 1981; Cazden & Leggett, 1981; Mohatt & Erickson, 1981; Vogt, Jordan & Tharp, 1987). This work has described teachers' attempts to make the school and home experiences of diverse learners more congruent. The majority of this literature has dealt with smallscale, encapsulated communities where cultural practices are easily recognizable and not as intertwined with other cultures.

Critical scholars have posited theoretical, conceptual, and research possibilities for situated pedagogies that consider race, class, and gender (e.g., see Ellsworth, 1989; hooks, 1989; McLaren, 1989). By addressing the specifics of particular diverse communities, this literature avoids the platitudes and unsubstantiated generalities of generic pedagogical perspectives. This work asks teacher educators to think more carefully about the relationship of teacher preparation to the communities in which they are located and the school populations that their graduates are likely to serve.

Returning to the Classrooms of "Experts"

In my work on successful teachers for African American students (Ladson-Billings, 1995b), I began looking for common beliefs and practices among such teachers. What I discovered were three prepositional notions about how they conceived of their practice that form the basis of what I term culturally relevant pedagogy (Ladson-Billings, 1994a, 1995b). These propositions involve academic achievement, cultural competence, and sociopolitical critique.

Academic achievement. In the classrooms I observed, teaching and learning were exciting, symbiotic events. Although teachers established routines and rituals, the classrooms were never dull. Students were regularly reminded that they were expected to learn and that learning would be rigorous and challenging. Some of the teachers taught from what might be considered a constructivist (Fennema, Carpenter, Franke, & Carey, 1992) position (i.e., students' own knowledge forms the basis of inquiry either as part of the official curriculum or as it interacts with the official curriculum). Standards were high in these classrooms. Students were expected to work hard, and they welcomed this responsibility.

Cultural competence. In addition to promoting learning and academic achievement, culturally relevant teachers foster and support the development of cultural competence. Cultural competence refers to the ability to function effectively in one's culture of origin (Ladson-Billings, 1995b). For African American students, this means understanding those aspects of their culture that facilitate their ability to communicate and relate to other members of their cultural group (Gay & Baber, 1987). Because of the pervasive negative representations of Black culture (Merelman, 1995), students may unwittingly ally themselves with schooling that works to promote their disaffiliation and alienation from African American culture.

Cultural competence can be supported in the classroom by acknowledging the legitimacy of students' home language and using it as a bridge to American Edited English.[2] It also is supported through the use of curriculum content selections that reflect the full range of humanity extant in students' cultures.

Sociopolitical critique. Perhaps if teachers could get students to achieve academically and manifest cultural competence, they might be more than satisfied with their pedagogical efforts. However, culturally relevant teachers recognize that education and schooling do not occur in a vacuum. The individual traits of achievement and cultural competence must be supported by sociopolitical critique that helps students understand the ways that social structures and practices help reproduce inequities. This aspect of culturally relevant teaching links it closely with a critical pedagogy that argues for students and teachers alike to participate in a collective struggle (Boggs, 1974). Thus, students must be challenged to ask questions about the ways that whole groups of people are systematically excluded from social benefits.

Antiracist Teacher Education: A Promising Practice

Autobiography, restructured field experiences, situated pedagogies, and examining the classrooms of experts all provide glimpses of possibility for facilitating the pedagogy of teachers who teach African American students. However, each has the potential to fail to confront the major stumbling block in preparing teachers for success with African American students: racism.

Although many teacher education programs include some form of multicultural education (Grant & Secada, 1990; Ladson-Billings, 1995a), confronting issues of racism in a deliberately antiracist framework is less common (Cochran-Smith, 1995; Kailin, 1994). Discussions of race and racism are absent from educational discourse even when our conceptions of race are more embedded and fixed than ever before. Teacher educators who have attempted to bring issues of race and racism to the forefront of their preparation programs have been subjected to resistance and harsh criticism from students (Ahlquist, 1991; Tatum, 1994).

Lee (1985) states that the "aim of [anti-racist education] is the eradication of racism in all its various forms. Anti-racist education emerges from an understanding that racism exists in society and, therefore, the school, as an institution of society, is influenced by racism" (p. 8). Thus, teacher education that embraces an antiracist perspective recognizes that prospective teachers' and "teachers' sensibilities are shaped by the same forces that mold us in the society at large" (Kailin, 1994, p. 173). However, antiracist educators understand racism as learned behavior and, as such, it can be unlearned.

Kailin's (1994) approach to antiracist staff development for teachers addresses two perspectives on racism: individual and institutional. The individual aspect of her work requires teachers to know and understand themselves, a process also used by King and Ladson-Billings (1990). Kailin employed strategies for developing collective auto-biography, understanding teachers' social backgrounds, participating in multicultural and race awareness exercises, examining teacher expectations of student competency, and exploring the manifestation of individual racism in teacher–student interactions and in school culture. At the institutional level, Kailin's approach prompts teachers to examine the historical roots of institutional racism in the United States as well as the ways that texts and curricula and schools as institutions support racism.

To prepare teachers to be successful with African American students, teacher educators must help prospective teachers recognize the ways that race and racism structure the everyday experiences of all Americans. More specifically, teachers must understand how race and racism negatively impact African American students and their ability to success-fully negotiate schools and classrooms. Some of the recommendations for change in teacher education that may lead us to more positive outcomes include:

Reassessing admissions procedures. A good deal of our struggle in teacher education resides at the admission door. Haberman (1989) argues that we will not get better teachers until we admit better people into the profession. Current admission procedures continue to screen out potentially excellent teacher candidates who desire to teach in African American communities, while at the same time including many candidates who have no intention or desire to serve those communities.

Reexamining course work. Dissatisfaction with teacher education course work has been widely expressed by both those within and outside of the profession. One of the places where course work is particularly weak is in its lack of attention to the perspectives and concerns of African Americans. Many of the foundations and methods courses fail to mention African Americans except as "problems." Course work that addresses the legitim-acy of African American culture and problematizes Whiteness can begin to make preserv-ice course work more meaningful for those who teach African American students.

Restructuring field experiences. As previously mentioned, field experiences tend to leave a lasting impression on teachers. Restructuring these field experiences may help students to understand the complexities of communities and cultures. Rather than having prospect-ive teachers dread going into African American communities, field experiences may play a role in addressing the stereotypes and racist attitudes that they may hold.

Recruiting and retaining African American scholars. For too many prospective teachers, their only encounter with African Americans is as subordinates. Increasing the numbers of African American faculty can help to disrupt some of the preconceived notions that they may have about the competencies and abilities of African Americans. Certainly, African American faculty can serve as a resource and counterbalance to prevailing notions of African American communities, for both adults and children.

Ultimately, the work of education in a democracy is to provide opportunities for all citizens to participate fully in the formation of the nation and its ideals. These ideals can never be fully realized if significant portions of our society are excluded from high-quality education and the opportunity to play public roles in the society. African American stu-dents are suffering in our schools at an alarming rate. They continue to experience high drop-out, suspension, and expulsion rates. Although possessing a high school diploma is no guarantee of success in U.S. society, not having one spells certain economic and social failure. Thus, when we fight about education, we indeed are fighting for our lives.

Notes

1. The European American slave trade was legally ended in 1848. The bulk of European immigration occurred in the 1890s. Thus, most African Americans have historical roots in this country that predate those of most European Americans.
2. Rather than the term Standard English I use American Edited English to refer to the particular formal language used in the United States.

References

Ahlquist, R. (1991). Power and imposition: Power relations in a multicultural foundations class. The Journal of Negro Education, 60, 158–169.

Allen, T. (1994). The invention of the White race. London: Verso.

Anderson, J. (1988). The education of blacks in the South, 1860–1935. Chapel Hill: University of North Carolina Press.

Au, K., & Jordan, C. (1981). Teaching reading to Hawaiian children: Finding a culturally appropriate solution. In H. Trueba, J. Guthrie, & K. Au (Eds.), Culture and the bilingual classroom: Studies in classroom ethnography (pp. 139–152). Rowley, MA: Newbury House.

Banks, J. (1997). Teaching strategies for ethnic studies (6th ed.). Boston: Allyn & Bacon.

Bettleheim, B. (1965). Teaching the disadvantaged. National Education Association Journal, 54, 8–12.

Bloom, B., Davis, A., & Hess, R. (1965). Compensatory education for cultural deprivation. New York: Holt, Rinehart & Winston.

Boggs, G.L. (1974). Education: The great obsession. Harvard Educational Review (Monograph No. 2, pp. 61–81).

Boykin, A.W., & Tom, F. (1985). Black child socialization: A conceptual framework. In H. McAdoo & J. McAdoo (Eds.), Black children: Social, educational and parental environments (pp. 33–51). Beverly Hills, CA: Sage.

Brown v. Board of Education, 347 U.S. 483 (1954).

Campbell, P. (1995). Redefining the "girl problem in mathematics." In W. Secada, E. Fennema, & L.B. Adajian (Eds.), New directions for equity in mathematics education (pp. 225–241). Cambridge, UK: Cambridge University Press.

Cazden, C., & Leggett, E. (1981). Culturally responsive education: Recommendations for achieving Lau remedies II. In H. Trueba, J. Guthrie, & K. Au (Eds.), Culture and the bilingual classroom: Studies in classroom ethnography (pp. 69–86). Rowley, MA: Newbury House.

Cochran-Smith, M. (1995). Uncertain allies: Understanding the boundaries of race and teaching. Harvard Educational Review, 65, 541–570.

Collins, P.H. (1991). Black feminist thought. New York: Routledge.

DuBois, W.E.B. (1953). The souls of Black folks. New York: Fawcett. (Original work published 1903)

Ellsworth, E. (1989). Why doesn't this feel empowering? Working through repressive myths of critical pedagogy. Harvard Education Review, 59, 297–324.

Fennema, E., Carpenter, T., Franke, M., & Carey, D. (1992). Learning to use children's mathematics thinking: A case study. In C. Maher & R. Davis (Eds.), Relating schools to reality (pp. 93–118). Needham Heights, MA: Allyn & Bacon.

Foster, M. (1990). The politics of race: Through African American teachers' eyes. Journal of Education, 172, 123–141.

Franklin, J.H., & Moss, A.A. (1988). From slavery to freedom (6th ed.). New York: Knopf.

Gay, G., & Baber, W. (1987). Expressively Black: The cultural basis of ethnic identity. New York: Praeger.

Gilligan, C. (1993). Joining the resistance: Psychology, politics, girls, and women. In L. Weis & M. Fine (Eds.), Beyond silenced voices (pp. 143–168). Albany: State University of New York Press.

Gomez, M.L., & Tabachnick, B.R. (1992). Telling teaching stories. Teaching Education, 4, 129–138.

Grant, C.A. (1989). Urban teachers: Their new colleagues and curriculum. Phi Delta Kappan, 70, 764–770.

Grant, C.A., & Secada, W. (1990). Preparing teachers for diversity. In W.R. Houston, M. Haberman, & J. Sikula (Eds.), Handbook of research on teacher education (pp. 403–422). New York: Macmillan.

Haberman, M. (1989). More minority teachers. Phi Delta Kappan, 70, 771–776.

Hampton, H. (Executive Producer). (1986). Eyes on the Prize [PBS video series]. Blackside Production, Boston.

Hollins, E.R. (1990). Debunking the myth of a monolithic White American culture, or moving toward cultural inclusion. American Behavioral Scientist, 34, 201–209.

Hollins, E.R., & Spencer, K. (1990). Restructuring schools for cultural inclusion: Changing the schooling process for African American youngsters. Journal of Education, 172, 89–100.

hooks, b. (1989). Talking back: Thinking feminist, thinking Black. Boston: South End Press.

Houston, B. (1994). Should public education be gender free? In L. Stone (Ed.), The education feminism reader (pp. 122–134). New York: Routledge.

Jackson, S. (1992, April). Autobiography: Pivot points for the study and practice of multiculturalism in teacher education. Paper presented at the annual meeting of the American Educational Research Association, San Francisco.

Kailin, J. (1994). Anti-racist staff development. Teaching and Teacher Education, 10, 169–184.

King, J.E. (1994, January). Rethinking the Black/White duality of our time. Paper presented at the Visiting Minority Scholars lecture series, Wisconsin Center for Educational Research, Madison.

King, J.E., & Ladson-Billings, G. (1990). The teacher education challenge in elite university settings: Developing critical perspectives for teaching in a democratic and multicultural society. European Journal of Intercultural Studies, 1, 15–30.

Ladson-Billings, G. (1994a). The dreamkeepers: Successful teachers for African American children. San Francisco: Jossey Bass.

Ladson-Billings, G. (1994b). Who will teach our children? Preparing teachers to teach African American learners. In E. Hollins, J. King, & W. Hayman (Eds.), Teaching diverse learners: Formulating a knowledge base for teaching diverse populations (pp. 129–158). Albany: State University of New York Press.

Ladson-Billings, G. (1995a). Multicultural teacher education: Research, policy, and practices. In J.A. Banks & C.M. Banks (Eds.), Handbook of research on multicultural education (pp. 747–759). New York: Macmilian.

Ladson-Billings, G. (1995b). Toward a theory of culturally relevant pedagogy. American Educational Research Journal, 32, 465–491.

Ladson-Billings, G. (1996). "Your blues ain't like mine": Keeping issues of face and racism on the multicultural agenda. Theory Into Practice, 35(4), 248–255.

Lee, E. (1985). Letters to Marcia: A teacher's guide to anti-racist education. Toronto, Ontario: Cross-Cultural Communication Centre.

Mahan, J. (1982). Native Americans as teacher trainers: Anatomy and outcomes of a cultural immersion project. Journal of Educational Equity and Leadership, 2, 100–110.

McLaren, P. (1989). Life in schools: An introduction to critical pedagogy in the foundations of education. White Plains, NY: Longman.

Merelman, R. (1995). Representing Black culture. New York: Routledge.

Mohatt, E., & Erickson, E (1981). Cultural differences in teaching styles in an Odawa School: A sociolinguistic approach. In H. Trueba, J. Guthrie, & K. Au (Eds.), Culture and the bilingual school: Studies in classroom ethnography (pp. 105–119). Rowley, MA: Newbury House.

Morrison, T. (1991). Playing in the dark: Whiteness and the literary imagination. Cambridge, MA: Harvard University Press.

Noordhoff, K., & Kleinfeld, J. (1991, April). Preparing teachers for multicultural classrooms: A case study in rural Alaska. Paper presented at the annual meeting of the American Educational Research Association, Chicago.

Ogbu, J. (1987). Variability in minority school performance. A problem in search of an explanation. Anthropology and Education Quarterly, 18, 312–334.

Olneck, M. (1995). Immigrants and education. In J. Banks & C.M. Banks (Eds.), Handbook of research on multicultural education (pp. 310–327). New York: Macmillan.

Ornstein, A., & Viaro, P. (Eds.). (1968). How to teach disadvantaged youth. New York: David McKay.

Shulman, L. (1987). Knowledge and teaching: Foundations of the new reform. Harvard Educational Review, 57, 1–22.

Siddle Walker, E.V. (1996). Their highest potential: An African American community school in the segregated south. Chapel Hill: University of North Carolina Press.

Tate, W.E., Ladson-Billings, G., & Grant, C.A. (1993). The Brown decision revisited: Mathematizing social problems. Educational Policy, 7, 255–275.

Tatum, B.D. (1994). Teaching white students about racism: The search for white allies and the restoration of hope. Teachers College Record, 95, 462–476.

Tyack, D. (1974). The one best system: A history of American urban education. Cambridge, MA: Harvard University Press.

Vogt, L., Jordan, C., & Tharp, R. (1987). Explaining school failure, producing school success: Two cases. Anthropology and Education Quarterly, 18, 276–286.

Willis, S. (1992). The power of mathematics: For whom? In J. Kenway & S. Willis (Eds.), Hearts and minds: Self esteem and the schooling of girls (pp. 191–212). London: Falmer.

Woodson, C.G. (1933). The miseducation of the Negro. Washington, DC: Association Press.

Zeichner, K. (1992). Educating teachers for cultural diversity. East Lansing, MI: National Center for Research on Teacher Learning.

Zeichner, K. (1993). Traditions of practice in U.S. preservice teacher education programs. Teaching & Teacher Education, 9, 1–13.

24

Bringing Bilingual Education Out of the Basement and Other Imperatives for Teacher Education

Sonia Nieto

Introduction

Think about the bilingual program in your school or other schools that you know: Is it in the basement or next to the boiler room? Is it located in a closet or under the stairs? Is it in a temporary mobile unit? All of these are indications that the bilingual program (the same can often be said about the special education program) has a low position in the school and community. The "basement" is an apt metaphor for the place and status that bilingual education and other issues of concern for language minority students have in most schools.

In this chapter, I address the issue of teacher education, with a lens on language minority students. In my answer to the question, "What do teachers and prospective teachers need to know about language minority students and why?", I suggest that there has often been a widespread assumption that language minority students are the responsibility of specialists such as ESL and bilingual teachers, and perhaps after leaving the program, of special education teachers. But we can no longer delude ourselves that this is the case. Language minority children and young people are found, or soon will be found, in almost every classroom around the country. As a result, all teachers of all backgrounds who teach in all schools need to be adequately prepared to teach them. Hence, I suggest that teachers need to develop competence in specific subject matters and, even more significantly, in the attitudes and values they have concerning young people of language minority backgrounds.

Schools and colleges of education by and large have failed to adequately prepare future and practicing teachers to teach language-minority students. Those teacher education programs that offer specializations in bilingual education and/or ESL, and even more so those that combine these strands, are well equipped to prepare teachers to face the challenges of the growing language-minority student population in our nation. But programs without such strands are frequently guided by the assumption that the job of schools of education is to train teachers to work in "regular"—that is, monolingual English—classrooms. They give little consideration to the fact that *all* classrooms in the future will have students whose first language is not English, even if they do not currently serve such students.

The number and variety of language-minority students have escalated tremendously in the past several years. For example, according to a 1996 report (Macías & Kelly, 1996), there were 3,184,696 students classified as having limited proficiency in English, almost a 5 percent increase in just one year. The same report indicated that students of limited

English proficiency represent 7.3 percent of all public school students, and that far fewer than 50 percent of these students were enrolled in federal or state programs in bilingual education. As a result, over half of all students whose native language is other than English spend most or part of their day in monolingual English classrooms. This situation is reason enough to propose that all teachers, not only bilingual teachers, need to be prepared to work with language-minority students.

In this chapter, I suggest that, although schools and colleges of education need to teach specific skills and strategies for working with language-minority students, it is even more essential that teacher education programs help teachers to develop positive attitudes and beliefs toward these students. After all, questions of language are *pedagogical* as well as *ideological*. Ideologies reflect a deeply ingrained system of beliefs, and they generally include a political program for action. In terms of linguistic differences, ideologies reflect positive or negative values concerning specific languages and the people who speak them. In addition, ideologies either uphold or challenge established authority and existing policies. In the case of language diversity, ideologies can either engage human efforts behind pluralism and social equality, or they can support the status quo.

What is the responsibility of schools and colleges of education to prepare teachers to work with students who speak native languages other than English? What should *all* teachers know about language-minority students, and what kinds of skills do teachers need to be effective with these students? In the case of bilingual and ESL teachers, what distinct competencies do they need to develop? In what follows, I review the kinds of knowledge that schools and colleges of education need to develop in all their teacher candidates, whether these future teachers expect to work in bilingual settings or not. I will also mention a number of explicit areas of study that bilingual and ESL teachers need. But I will focus my attention on the values, beliefs, and attitudes that I believe should be at the core of teacher education programs. I propose three imperatives for teacher education programs as they prepare teachers for the new generation of Americans, many of whom are language-minority students. Specifically, I suggest that teacher education programs need to

1. take a stand on language diversity;
2. bring bilingual education out of the basement;
3. promote teaching as a lifelong journey of transformation.

What should Teachers Know?

Students who are speakers of languages other than English are found in classrooms in all communities throughout the United States, from the most urban to the most rural and from the ethnically diverse to the seemingly homogeneous (Macías & Kelly, 1996). Yet most teacher education programs continue to behave as if language-minority students were found only in ESL or bilingual classrooms. As a result, teachers who have taken traditional courses in pedagogy and curriculum or who have had typical practicum experiences in English monolingual settings will not be prepared to teach the growing number of language-minority students who will end up in their classrooms. Even when language-minority students are primarily in ESL or bilingual settings, presuming that these students are the sole responsibility of ESL and bilingual teachers strengthens the perception that these youngsters should be in separate classrooms, halls, and even schools rather than integrated with their peers whenever pedagogically possible.

Because language-minority students are often physically isolated from their English-speaking peers, this separation adds to their alienation. The same is true of bilingual teachers, who in most schools are both physically and emotionally separated from other teachers. Bilingual teachers report feeling estranged, dismissed, or simply ignored by their peers and supervisors (Montero-Sieburth & Pérez, 1987). Consequently, the relationships among bilingual and "mainstream" teachers, and among students in bilingual and English-monolingual classrooms, are regularly fraught with misunderstanding. The emotional and physical separation experienced by bilingual and nonbilingual teachers does not lend itself to developing collegial relationships or opportunities to work collaboratively.

What might allow collaborative relationships between bilingual and nonbilingual teachers? One way to promote opportunities for them to work together is to start off all teachers with common knowledge concerning language diversity. All teachers, not only bilingual and ESL teachers, need to develop the following kinds of knowledge:

- familiarity with first- and second-language acquisition
- awareness of the sociocultural and sociopolitical context of education for language-minority students
- awareness of the history of immigration in the United States, with particular attention to language policies and practices throughout that history
- knowledge of the history and experiences of specific groups of people, especially those who are residents of the city, town, and state where they will be teaching
- ability to adapt curriculum for students whose first language is other than English
- competence in pedagogical approaches suitable for culturally and linguistically heterogeneous classrooms
- experience with teachers of diverse backgrounds and the ability to develop collaborative relationships with colleagues that promote the learning of language-minority students
- ability to communicate effectively with parents of diverse language, culture, and social-class backgrounds

In addition to these skills, all teacher candidates, regardless of the setting in which they will be working, should be strongly encouraged to learn a second language, particularly a language spoken by a substantial number of students in the community in which they teach or intend to teach. No matter how empathic teachers may be of the ordeal that students go through to learn English, nothing can bring it home in quite the same way as going through the process themselves. Bill Dunn, a doctoral student of mine who "came out of the closet" as a Spanish speaker a number of years ago, wrote eloquently about this experience in a journal he kept (Nieto, 1999). Bill teaches in a town with a student body that is about 75 percent Puerto Rican, and after twenty years in the system, he realized that he understood a good deal of Spanish. He decided to learn Spanish more systematically through activities such as taking a Spanish class at a community center, sitting in on bilingual classes in his school, and watching Spanish-language television shows. Although Bill had been a wonderful teacher before learning Spanish, the experience of placing himself in the vulnerable position of learner taught him many things: a heightened respect for students who were learning English; a clearer understanding of why his Spanish-speaking students, even those who were fluent in English, made particular mistakes in grammar and spelling; and a renewed admiration for the bilingual teachers in his school. The skills and knowledge listed above are a common starting point for all teachers, but for those who are preparing to become bilingual and/or ESL teachers, the knowledge base needs to be expanded to include:

- fluency in at least one language in addition to English
- knowledge of the conceptual and theoretical basis for bilingual education
- knowledge of specific pedagogical strategies that promote language development
- ability to serve as cultural mediators between students and the school
- knowledge of various strategies for assessing students' language proficiency and academic progress

This list is not meant to be exhaustive, but rather to suggest that there are numerous specific strategies and approaches that teachers of language-minority backgrounds need to learn. But in spite of the importance of knowing particular strategies and approaches, I believe that the focus of teacher educators has to be elsewhere. Although bilingual education is about language and pedagogy, it is equally about power and ideology. That is, questions of *which* language to use, *when* and *how* to use it, and *why* it should be used are above all ideological questions. In the final analysis, native-language education brings up questions of whose language has legitimacy and power, and of how far our society is willing to allow differences to exist and even flourish. These questions go to the heart of what our schools are for, and what we value as a society. Consequently, I suggest that besides pedagogy and curriculum, schools and colleges of education need to help teachers develop critical perspectives about education. This means that the *values, beliefs,* and *attitudes* that underscore particular approaches also need to become the subject matter of their study and analysis.

The Ideological Underpinnings of Bilingual Education

As we have previously discussed, ideology is a systematic set of principles usually linked with political action that either upholds or challenges the status quo. A generation ago, Paulo Freire's (1970) assertion that education is always political was greeted with denial or skepticism in many quarters in our society. The claim that education is political—that is, that it is fundamentally concerned with issues of power and dominance—flies in the face of education as understood in the United States, where we have always asserted that education is universal, equal, and fair. But the ideological basis of education is exposed through such blatant practices as vastly differentiated funding for rich and poor school districts (Kozol, 1991), and the detrimental effects of ability tracking and other sorting practices on students of diverse socioeconomic, racial, ethnic, and linguistic backgrounds (Oakes, 1985; Spring, 1989). The political nature of education has also been evident in the case of bilingual education, which has been under attack since its very inception (Nieto, 1992). Scholars of bilingual education have always known that it is political, and some books on the subject discuss openly its political nature and include reference to it in their titles (Arias & Casanova, 1993; Crawford, 1992).

But what does it mean to say that bilingual education is political? For one thing, it means that every discussion of bilingual education is based on a philosophical orientation concerning language diversity in our society and on the official status that languages other than English are to be given. It also means that all educational decisions about bilingual education—when and how to use which language, the nature of the program, who should teach in such programs, and the educational expectations of students who speak languages other than English—reflect a particular worldview. Prospective teachers need to understand that the mere existence of bilingual education affronts one of the most cherished ideals of our public schools, that is, the assimilation of students of nondominant backgrounds into the cultural mainstream. And because bilingual education challenges the assimilationist agenda of our schools and society, I believe that the greatest fear among its opponents is that *bilingual education might in fact work*. If this were not the case, why so much opposition to it?

Prospective teachers need to know that bilingual education developed in the 1960s as a result of the civil rights era; that linguistic democracy has been as crucial a civil rights issue for language-minority communities as desegregation has been for African American communities; and that language is a central value and birthright that many families treasure and seek to maintain. Prospective teachers also need to understand that the families of language-minority students want their children to become fluent speakers of English because they know that this knowledge will provide their children with their greatest opportunity for academic and economic success. Many of these families insist, however, that their children also maintain and use their first language.

The curriculum, as well as the quality and quantity of materials, available to students in bilingual programs, and decisions about when to move students from bilingual to nonbilingual classes are all political, and not merely pedagogical, decisions. Language-minority students in the United States are overwhelmingly poor and powerless, and their dominated status is related in no small way to how they are perceived and to the nature of the education they receive. For instance, because bilingual education is ordinarily a program for economically disadvantaged and oppressed communities, city and state boards of education are often unenthusiastic about spending money on a program they perceive as too expensive and "wasteful." But in middle-class neighborhoods, the costs associated with teaching children a second language are rarely challenged.

Imperatives for Teacher Education

If indeed all teachers will at some time or another be faced with teaching students whose first language is other than English, what is the responsibility of teacher educators and teacher preparation programs? Let me suggest three imperatives for teacher education: first, teacher educators and teacher preparation programs need to take a stand concerning the education of language-minority students; second, they need to bring bilingual education out of the basement, both literally and figuratively; and third, they need to prepare future teachers to think of teaching as a lifelong journey of transformation. I will comment briefly on the first two, and more thoroughly on the third of these imperatives.

Take a Stand on Language Diversity

Schools and colleges of education need to decide what they stand for concerning education in general, as well as in the specific case of language diversity and language-minority students. They can begin this process by asking a number of key questions, the answers to which they may assume are shared, but which very often are not:

- *What is the purpose of education? What are schools for?*

Other than to prepare lofty mission statements that have little to do with their day-to-day practice, it is rare for faculties of education to get together to discuss the very purposes of education: Is the purpose of schools to fit students into society? Is it to prepare students for specific jobs? Or is it to prepare students to become productive and critical citizens of a democratic society? Must schools replicate societal inequities? Should they seek to prepare a few good managers and many compliant workers? Or is the role of schools to prepare students for the challenges of a pluralistic and rapidly changing society? Answers to these questions can determine the scope and quality of a teacher preparation program curriculum and the field experiences provided to students. If, for example, the faculty determines that the primary objective of education is to prepare students for our rapidly changing and pluralistic society, then attention to language diversity becomes a key component in their course offerings.

- *What do we do about language diversity?*

The issue of difference lies at the heart of the way that U.S. schools have defined their responsibility to educate young people. From the time that compulsory schooling in the United States began, the ideals of equality and fairness have struggled with the ideals of pluralism and diversity (Dewey, 1916; Spring, 1997; Weinberg, 1977). That is, the balance between *unum* and *pluribus* has always been contested. Many times, the zeal to assimilate and homogenize all students to one norm has won out; rarely has diversity been highlighted as a value in its own right.

In the case of language diversity, Luis Moll (1992) has pointed out the singular focus on the English language taken by many educators and society at large, suggesting that

> the obsession of speaking English reigns supreme—as if the children were somehow incapable of learning that language well, or as if the parents and teachers were unaware of the importance of English in U.S. society—and usually at the expense of other educational or academic matters. (pp. 20–21)

Historically, answers to the question of what to do about language diversity have ranged from grudging acceptance, to outlawing the use of languages other than English in instruction, to brutal policies, especially those directed at Mexican Americans and American Indians, that enforced the use of the English language at the exclusion of other languages (Crawford, 1992; Deyhle & Swisher, 1997; Donato, 1997). How schools of education answer these questions can help them either to focus on assimilation as a goal, or to think of ways to use language diversity as a resource.

Bring Bilingual Education Out of the Basement

The basement is a fitting metaphor for the status of bilingual education, both in elementary and secondary schools and in schools and colleges of education. Basements are dark, dank places where people store what they do not want to display in their homes. Bilingual programs are frequently found in basements next to the boiler room, in supply closets, or in trailers or hallways isolated from the rest of the school. Their very physical placement is a giveaway to their low status in schools and among the general public. But language-minority students will not disappear simply because they are hidden from sight. If it is true that the number of language-minority students will increase over the coming years, then all teachers need to learn how to best teach them. Further, all schools and colleges of education, no matter how remote they may be from the urban areas where most language-minority students live, have to prepare teachers who will specialize in teaching these students, because no geographic area will remain a monolingual enclave of English for long.

In schools and in teacher preparation programs, bilingual education needs to be moved out of the basement and onto the first floor. Figuratively speaking, at the university level, this means giving bilingual education and language diversity issues a place of prominence in the teacher education curriculum. Although there is a need to continue to offer specialized courses for bilingual and ESL teachers who will spend the bulk of their time with language-minority students, as a profession we can no longer afford to teach about bilingual education only to prospective bilingual teachers. Rather, all courses should be infused with content relating to language diversity, from those in secondary science methods to those in reading. Courses in educational foundations, history, and policy matters also should include reference to bilingual education. Pre-practicum and practicum placements, other field experiences, course assignments, and course readings also need to reflect support for language diversity. In addition, schools of education might rethink their requirements for admission, giving priority to those candidates who are fluent in at least one language other than English. In sum, language and language diversity issues would become part of the *normal experience* for all prospective teachers. In this way, it becomes clear that the responsibility for teaching language-minority students belongs to all teachers.

An approach that gives language diversity a high status in teacher preparation programs will invariably mean that teacher educators will face a good deal of resistance from some prospective teachers. It is by now a truism that most prospective teachers are White, middle-class, monolingual English-speaking women with little experience with people different from themselves, and that most of them believe—or at least hope—they will teach in largely White, middle-class communities (Aaronsohn, Carter, & Howell, 1995). Having to take courses that focus on students whom they may not want to teach, and that give weight to issues that they may want to dismiss, will certainly cause some tension. In fact, teaching courses that focus on diversity in any way usually results in conflict, and there is ample demonstration of this fact in the literature (Chávez Chávez & O'Donnell, 1998). But infusing the curriculum with content in language diversity may also result in expanding the vision and therefore enriching the perspectives of prospective teachers. In turn, their success and effectiveness with language-minority students may also be positively affected. As is the case with teachers, most teacher educators are also White, middle-class, monolingual English speakers, and many have had little experience or training in language diversity issues. This means that teacher educators must themselves rethink how their courses need to be changed to reflect language diversity, and they need to be given the support and time to do so. Likewise, if we are serious about giving language diversity a positive status in the general teacher education program, we must recognize that the current teacher education faculty needs to be diversified. Consequently, another implication of bringing bilingual education out of the basement is that schools of education will have to recruit a more diverse faculty with specific training and experience in bilingual education, second-language acquisition, and the education of language-minority students.

Recruiting a diverse faculty does not in and of itself guarantee that the result will be a faculty that is more diverse in ideological perspective. For example, not all Latinos/as are supporters of bilingual education, nor should they be recruited for this reason. However, recruiting a faculty that is diverse in training and expertise, as well as in background and experience, will probably ensure a broader diversity of perspectives than is currently the case.

Promote Teaching as a Lifelong Journey of Transformation

Teacher educators have the lofty but frightening responsibility to prepare future teachers and other educational leaders. In terms of diversity, I believe that our major responsibility is twofold: to help teachers and prospective teachers affirm the linguistic, cultural, and experiential diversity of their students while at the same time opening up new vistas, opportunities, and challenges that expand their worlds. But because teaching is above all a matter of forming caring and supportive relationships, the process of affirming the diversity of students begins as a journey of the teachers. A journey always presupposes that the traveler will change along the way, and teaching is no exception. However, if we expect teachers to begin their own journey of transformation, teacher educators must be willing to join them because until we take stock of ourselves, until we question and challenge our own biases and values, nothing will change for our students.

Affirming the diversity of students is not just an individual journey, however. It is equally a collective and institutional journey that happens outside individual class-rooms and college courses. How do teachers prepare for the journey, and what is the role of teacher educators? Let me suggest several central points to keep in mind as teachers and faculty begin this journey (these are discussed in much greater detail in Nieto, 1999).

Teachers Need to Face and Accept Their Own Identities
As we have mentioned, most teachers in the United States are White, monolingual, middle-class females who are teaching a student body that is increasingly diverse in native language, race, ethnicity, and social class. Due to their own limited experiences with people of diverse backgrounds, including language-minority backgrounds, many teachers perceive of language diversity as a problem rather than an asset. This is probably due to the fact that they have internalized the message that their culture is the norm against which to measure all others. As a result, they seldom question their White-skin or English-language privilege (McIntosh, 1988). Schools and colleges of education need to provide prospective teachers with opportunities to reflect on all of these issues before teaching children from diverse backgrounds.

Because of the assimilationist nature of U.S. schooling, most people of European American background have accepted the "melting pot" as a true reflection of our society's experience with cultural pluralism. The immigration of Europeans is generally presented as the model by which all other groups should be measured, as if it represented the reality of others whose history, race, culture, and historical context differ greatly. Many teachers of European American descent, who are drawn primarily from working-class backgrounds, are quick to accept the myths about diversity, merit, success, and assimilation that they have learned along the way. In a compelling essay written over a quarter of a century ago, Mildred Dickeman (1973) explained how such myths operate:

> All mythologies serve to interpret reality in ways useful to the perpetuation of a society. In this
> case an ideology arose which interpreted the existence of ethnic diversity in America in ways
> supportive of the sociopolitical establishment. Probably the schools played an important role
> in the creation of this ideology. Certainly they came to serve as the major institutions for its
> propagation. (p. 8)

The myths to which Dickeman alludes include the perception that people of nonmain-stream backgrounds must completely "melt" in order to be successful; that individual effort is superior to community and collective identity and action; and that all it takes is hard work and perseverance to make it, with no attention paid to the structural barriers and institutional biases that get in the way of equality. If they believe these myths, it becomes easy for teachers to compare African American, Latino, American Indian, and Asian and Asian American students with the portrait of successful European immigrants they have accepted as the norm, and to blame students who do not achieve academically. Generally, the blame is couched in terms of the inferior culture or race of the students, or on passivity or lack of concern on the part of their parents.

One consequence of accepting these deficit views is that because only students of backgrounds visibly different from the mainstream are thought to have a culture, culture itself is defined as a problem. But teachers also have cultural identities, even though they have learned to forget or deny them. As cultural beings, they come into teaching with particular worldviews, values, and beliefs, and these influence all of their interactions with their students. For the most part, however, teachers of European American backgrounds are unaware that they even possess a culture, or that their culture influences them in any substantive way save for holiday celebrations or ethnic festivals they may still attend. All teachers of all backgrounds need to recognize, understand, and accept their own diversity and delve into their own identities before they can learn about and from their students. Specifically in the case of teachers of European American backgrounds, Dickeman suggests that they begin to uncover and recover their own histories:

> Coming as we do from a range of ethnic and cultural identities, and by the mere fact of
> recruitment primarily from the lower and lower middle classes, we have available to us, how-
> ever forgotten, repressed or ignored, the experiences of self and family in the context of
> pressure for assimilation and upward mobility. . . . When teachers begin to recognize that their
> own ethnic heritages are valuable, that their own family histories are relevant to learning and
> teaching, the battle is half won. (p. 24)

Recovering their ethnic identities invariably leads European American teachers to a confrontation with their racial, linguistic, and social-class privilege (Howard, 1999; McIntosh, 1988), a painful but ultimately life-changing experience for many of them. For teacher preparation programs, this implies that opportunities and support need to be provided for teachers and prospective teachers to go through this process. These opportunities also need to be made available to teachers and future teachers from nondominant backgrounds. Although teacher educators often assume that prospective teachers of African American, Hispanic, and Asian American backgrounds are somehow automatically prepared to teach students of diverse backgrounds simply by virtue of their own backgrounds, this is not always true (Nieto, 2001). That is, having an identity that differs from the mainstream— for example, being Chicana—does not necessarily guarantee sensitivity or knowledge about Vietnamese students. Likewise, being Chicana does not even mean that a teacher will be more knowledgeable about her Chicano students. Although it is generally true that teachers of nondominant backgrounds bring substantial skills, knowledge, and passion to their jobs, this is not always the case. Teacher preparation programs need to understand this, and they need to provide *all* prospective teachers, not just those of European American background, with the skills and attitudes to teach students of all backgrounds.

Teachers Need to Become Learners and Identify With Their Students

Without denying the need to teach students the cultural capital that they need to help them negotiate society, teachers also need to make a commitment to become *students of their students*. This implies at least two kinds of processes. First, teachers need to learn *about* their students, a change from the one-way learning that usually takes place in classrooms. For this to happen, teachers must become researchers of their students. Second, teachers need to create spaces in which they can learn *with* their students, and in which students are encouraged to learn about themselves and one another.

If we think of teaching and learning as reciprocal processes, as proposed by Paulo Freire (1970), then teachers need to become actively engaged in learning through their inter- actions with students. Developing a stance as learners is especially consequential if we think about the wide gulf that currently exists in the United States between the language backgrounds and other experiences of teachers and their students. Given this situation, the conventional approach has been to instruct students in the ways of White, middle-class, English-speaking America and, in the process, to rid them of as many of their differences as possible.

Learning about one's students is not simply a technical strategy, or a process of picking up a few cultural tidbits. It is impossible for teachers to become culturally or linguistically responsive simply by taking a course where these concerns are reduced to strategies. This does not mean that teaching is always an intuitive undertaking, although it certainly has this quality at times. But even more pivotal are the attitudes of teachers when they are in the position of learners. That is, teachers need to be open to their language-minority students' knowledge in order to find what can help them learn, and then change their teaching accordingly.

Defining the teacher as a learner is a radical departure from the prevailing notion of the educator as repository of all knowledge, a view that is firmly entrenched in society. Ira Shor (Shor & Freire, 1987) critiqued this conventional portrait of teachers vis-à-vis their stu- dents: "The students are not a flotilla of boats trying to reach the teacher who is finished and waiting on the shore. The teacher is also one of the boats" (p. 50). Yet in spite of how terrifying it may be for teachers to act as all-knowing sages, the conception of *teacher as knower* is a more familiar and, hence, less threatening one than *teacher as learner*. Once teachers admit that they do not know everything, they make themselves as vulnerable as their students. But it is precisely this attitude of learner on the part of teachers that is needed, first, to convey to linguistically diverse students that nobody is above learning; and second, to let students know that they also are knowers, and that what they know can be an important source of learning for others as well. It follows from this perspective that there needs to be a move away from the deficit model to a recognition of the cultural and linguistic knowledge and resources that students bring to their education. Teachers need to build on this knowledge as the foundation of their students' academic learning.

Teachers Need to Become Multilingual and Multicultural

Teachers can talk on and on about the value of cultural diversity, and about how beneficial it is to know a second language, but if they themselves do not attempt to learn another language, or if they remain monocultural in outlook, their words may sound hollow to their students. Even if their curriculum is outwardly supportive of students' linguistic and cultural diversity, if teachers do not demonstrate through their actions and behaviors that they truly value diversity, students can often tell.

Teachers who can call on their own identities of linguistic and cultural diversity usually have an easier time of identifying with their students of diverse backgrounds. But absent such connections with diversity, what is the responsibility of teacher preparation programs? I suggest that we need to find ways to engage future teachers in a process of becoming multicultural and multilingual, and I have already recommended a number of ways in which we can do so. I would just add that schools of education need to make their prospective teachers an offer they cannot refuse; that is, they need to make it worth their while to become multilingual and multicultural by having incentives that help future teachers view diversity as an asset. These incentives can include credit for learning another language; refusing to accept course work that does not reflect attention to diversity; and support for academic work that is tied to community service.

Becoming multilingual and multicultural is often an exhilarating experience, but it can also be uncomfortable and challenging because the process decenters students from their world. It necessarily means that students have to learn to step out of their comfortable perspectives and try to understand those of others. In the process, however, they usually gain far more than they give up: a broader view of reality, a more complex understanding of their students' lives, and a way to approach their students so that they can learn successfully.

Teachers Need to Learn to Confront Racism and Other Biases in Schools

If teachers simply follow the decreed curriculum as handed down from the central office, and if they go along with standard practices such as rigid ability tracking or high-stakes testing that result in unjust outcomes, they are unlikely ever to question the fairness of these practices. But when they begin to engage in a personal transformation through such actions as described above—that is, when they become learners with, of, and for their students and forge a deep identification with them; when they build on students' talents and strengths; and when they welcome and include the perspectives and experiences of their students and families in the classroom—then they cannot avoid locking horns with some very unpleasant realities inherent in the schooling process, realities such as racism, sexism, heterosexism, classism, and other biases. For instance, teachers begin to discover the biased but unstated ideologies behind some of the practices that they had previously overlooked. As a result, teachers have no alternative but to begin to question the inequitable nature of such practices. They become, in a word, critical educators. In this respect, helping prospective teachers become critical is a fundamental role of teacher education programs, and it means challenging not only the policies and practices of schools but also those of the very teacher education programs they are in. A critical stance challenges the structure of schools at the elementary and secondary school levels so that teachers begin to question, among other school realities, the following:

- seemingly natural and neutral practices such as asking parents to speak English at home with their children (in fact, teachers who are supportive of language diversity begin to ask their students' parents to do just the opposite: to speak their native language at home, and to promote literacy in all forms in their native language whenever possible);
- the lack of high-level courses in students' native languages (critical teachers begin

to ask, for example, whether schools have parallel and equal courses in science, math, social studies, and other subject areas in students' native languages);

- counseling services that automatically relegate students of some language backgrounds to nonacademic choices (critical teachers become aware of both subtle and overt messages that students are incapable of doing high-level academic work because they are not yet proficient in English, as if English proficiency were the primary barometer of intelligence).

At the teacher education level, a critical stance means that faculty and prospective teachers begin to question the following:

- the isolation of bilingual education as a separate strand in the teacher education program, and the separation between bilingual education and ESL (as if this separation made sense in the real world where students are struggling to become bilingual and where bilingualism is, in all other settings except for school, a highly valued skill);
- screening practices that make it impossible for a more diverse student body to become teachers (these include an overemphasis on grades with little attention paid to skills they might already have in language ability and cultural awareness; during interviews, a rigid conception of how the "ideal teacher" behaves, without acknowledging how cultural and social-class differences might influence their responses; a bias against prospective teachers who have an accent; and so on);
- how faculty are recruited and hired, and how these practices might militate against the possibility of retaining a faculty that is diverse in language and culture (for example, by failing to include competencies in culture and language in the job descriptions for nonbilingual positions, even though such competencies could be highly effective in those positions).

Facing and challenging racism and other biases is both an inspiring and a frightening prospect. It means upsetting business as usual, and this can be difficult even for committed and critical teachers. It is especially difficult for young teachers, who recognize that they have little power or influence among more seasoned school staffs. As a result, they often either lose hope or become solitary missionaries, and neither of these postures can accomplish any appreciable changes.

Help Future Teachers Learn to Develop a Community of Critical Friends

What I suggest instead is that we teach future teachers to become *critical colleagues,* that is, teachers who are capable of developing respectful but critical relationships with their peers. Working in isolation, no teacher can single-handedly effect the changes that are needed in an entire school, at least not in the long term. In fact, isolation builds walls, allowing teachers to focus on only their own students. In this way, it becomes far too easy to designate language-minority students as the responsibility of only the bilingual and ESL teachers. But developing a community of critical friends opens up teachers' classrooms—and their perspectives—so that they can acknowledge that the concerns of language-minority students are everyone's concerns, not just of one or two teachers in the school building.

Time and again, teachers in my classes have spoken about the need to develop a cadre of peers to help them and their school go through the process of transformation. But what is needed is not simply peers who support one another—essential as this may be—but also peers who debate, critique, and challenge one another to go beyond their current ideas and practices. This is especially useful in terms of bilingual education, a hotly contested issue seldom discussed in an in-depth way among teachers. Developing a community of critical friends is one way of facing difficult issues, and it is one more step in the journey of transformation.

Prospective teachers also need to build bridges to their students' families and to other members of the communities in which they work. Rather than viewing families and other community members as adversaries, prospective teachers need to develop skills in interacting effectively with them. Yet how many teachers have learned about these issues in their teacher education programs? Even in bilingual programs, where both parent involvement and communication with families are seen as central, there are few examples of actual exposure to these ideas. At the very least, teacher preparation programs need to provide courses, seminars, and practicum experiences so that prospective teachers learn to work with families.

In the end, teachers who work collaboratively with their peers and families in a spirit of solidarity will be better able to change schools to become more equitable and caring places for students of linguistically and culturally diverse backgrounds. Even personal transformation is best accomplished as a *collective* journey that leads to change in more than just one classroom. This means that prospective teachers need to learn to communicate and work with colleagues of varying perspectives; they need to learn to support and affirm one another, but also to question and confront one another to envision other possibilities.

That bilingual education works is a given. Rather than continue to endlessly debate its effectiveness, what are needed are strategies to improve it. What has *not* worked, on the other hand, are the approaches used by schools of education to prepare future teachers for the great diversity—linguistic, cultural, and socioeconomic, among others—that new teachers will face. These programs have a long way to go in preparing prospective teachers to respect and affirm the languages and identities of all the students who will inevitably be present in their classrooms in the coming years.

The three imperatives and numerous suggestions I have made in this chapter are only a beginning stage in the kinds of changes that are needed to help schools and universities shift from a focus on assimilation as their goal to an agenda of respect and affirmation for all students of all backgrounds. If teacher education faculties take these imperatives to heart, it means that they are willing to undergo a profound transformation in outlook, ideology, and curriculum. It also means that programs in general and faculty members in particular will welcome change, even though it may be a difficult prospect for many of us. But in the process of transformation, schools and colleges of education can become more hopeful places, because in the long run, we will be preparing better teachers for all students, including our bilingual and language-minority students. And the promise of social justice and equal educational opportunity for all students, an elusive dream in many places, will be closer to becoming a reality.

References

Aaronsohn, E., Carter, C.J., & Howell, M. (1995). Preparing monocultural teachers for a multicultural world: Attitudes toward inner-city schools. *Equity and Excellence in Education, 28*, 5–9.

Arias, M.B., & Casanova, U. (Eds.). (1993). *Bilingual education: Politics, practice, research.* Chicago: University of Chicago Press.

Chávez Chávez, R., & O'Donnell, J. (Eds.). (1998). *Speaking the unpleasant: The politics of non-engagement in the multicultural education terrain.* Albany: State University of New York Press.

Crawford, J. (1992). *Hold your tongue: Bilingualism and the politics of "English Only."* Reading, MA: Addison-Wesley.

Dewey, J. (1916). *Democracy and education.* New York: Free Press.

Deyhle, D., & Swisher, K. (1997). Research in American Indian and Alaska Native education: From assimilation to self-determination. In M.W. Apple (Ed.), *Review of research in education* (vol. 22, pp. 113–194). Washington, DC: American Educational Research Association.

Dickeman, M. (1973). Teaching cultural pluralism. In J.A. Banks (Ed.), *Teaching ethnic studies: Concepts and strategies* (pp. 4–25). Washington, DC: National Council for the Social Studies.

Donato, R. (1997). *The other struggle for equal schools: Mexican Americans during the civil rights era.* Albany: State University of New York Press.

Freire, P. (1970). *Pedagogy of the oppressed.* New York: Seabury Press.

Howard, G. (1999). *We can't teach what we don't know: White teachers, multiracial schools.* New York: Teachers College Press.

Kozol, J. (1991). *Savage inequalities; Children in America's schools.* New York: Crown.

Macías, R.F., & Kelly, C. (1996). *Summary report of the survey of the states' limited English proficient students and available educational programs and services 1994–1995.* Washington, DC: United States Department of Education, Office of Grants and Contracts Services, George Washington University.

McIntosh, P. (1988). *White privilege and male privilege: A personal account of coming to see correspondences through work in women's studies* (Working Paper No. 189). Wellesley, MA: Wellesley College Center for Research on Women.

Moll, L.D. (1992). Bilingual classroom studies and community analysis: Some recent trends. *Educational Researcher, 21*(2), 20–24.

Montero-Sieburth, M., & Pérez, M. (1987). *Echar pa'lante,* moving onward: The dilemmas and strategies of a bilingual education. *Anthropology and Education Quarterly, 18,* 180–189.

Nieto, S. (1992). We speak in many tongues: Language diversity and multicultural education. In C. Díaz (Ed.), *Multicultural education for the 21st century* (pp. 112–136). Washington, DC: National Education Association.

Nieto, S. (1999). *The light in their eyes: Creating multicultural learning communities.* New York: Teachers College Press.

Nieto, S. (2001). Conflict and tension; growth and change: The politics of teaching multicultural education courses. In D. Macedo (Ed.), *Tongue-tying multiculturalism.* Boulder, CO: Rowman & Littlefield.

Oakes, J. (1985). *Keeping track: How schools structure inequality.* New Haven, CT: Yale University Press.

Shor, I., & Freire, P. (1987). *A pedagogy for liberation: Dialogues on transforming education.* New York: Bergin & Garvey.

Spring, J. (1989). *The sorting machine revisited: National education policy since 1945.* New York: Longman.

Spring, J. (1997). *Deculturalization and the struggle for equality: A brief history of the education of dominated cultures in the United States* (2nd ed.). New York: McGraw-Hill.

Weinberg, M. (1977). *A chance to learn: A history of race and education in the U.S.* Cambridge, Eng.: Cambridge University Press.

Suggested Readings for Future Study

Beyer, L. E. and Zeichner, K. (1987). "Teacher education in cultural context: Beyond reproduction," in T. S. Popkewitz (ed.), *Critical Studies in Teacher Education*. Philadelphia: The Falmer Press.

Beyer, L. E. (1989). "Reconceptualizing teacher preparation: Institutions and ideologies," *Journal of Teacher Education*, 40: 22–26.

Carr, W. and Kennis, S. (1986). *Becoming Critical: Education Knowledge and Action Research*. New York: Routledge.

Claus, J. (1999). "You Can't Avoid the Politics: Lessons for Teacher Education from a Case Study of Teacher-Initiated Tracking Reform," *Journal of Teacher Education*, Vol. 50, No 1.

Cochran-Smith, M. & Lytle, S. L. (eds.) (1993). *Inside/outside: Teacher research and knowledge*. New York: Teachers College.

Cochran-Smith, M. (2005). "Studying teacher education. What we know and need to know," *Journal of Teacher Education*, 56: 301–306.

Cochran-Smith, M. (2001). "Sticks, stones, and ideology: the discourse of reform in teacher education," *Educational Researcher*, 30(8): 3–15.

Darling-Hammond, L. (2006). "Constructing 21st-century teacher education," *Journal of Teacher Education*, 57(3): 300–314.

Denzin, N. K. (2003). *Performance Ethnography: Critical Pedagogy and the Politics of Culture*. London: Sage.

Ellsworth, E. (1997). *Teaching positions: Difference, pedagogy and the power of address*. New York: Teachers College Press.

Finn, P. J. and Finn, M. E. (2007). *Teacher Education with an Attitude: Preparing Teachers to Educate Working-Class Students in their Collective Self-Interest*. New York: SUNY Press.

Freire, P. (2005). *Teachers as Cultural Workers*. Boulder, CO: Westview.

Harman, R. (2007). "Critical Teacher Education in Urban Contexts: Discursive Dance of a Middle School Teacher," *Language and Education*, 21(1): 31–45.

hooks, b. (1994). *Teaching to transgress. Education as the practice of freedom*. New York: Routledge.

Keesing-Styles, L. (2003). "The Relationship between Critical Pedagogy and Assessment in Teacher Education," *Radical Pedagogy*. Retrieved on January 16, 2008. (http://radicalpedagogy.icaap.org/content/issue5_1/03_keesing-styles.html)

Kincheloe, J., Bursztyn, A., and Steinberg, S. R. (2004). *Teaching Teachers: Building a Quality School of Urban Education*. New York: Peter Lang.

Kincheloe, J., Slattery, P., and Steinberg, S. R. (2000). *Contextualizing Teaching: Introduction to Education and Educational Foundations*. New York: Longman.

Kincheloe, J. (1993). *Toward a critical politics of teacher thinking: Mapping the Posmodern*. Westport, Connecticut: Bergin and Garvey.

Kincheloe, J. (2003). *Teachers as researchers: Qualitative inquiry as a path to empowerment*. New York: RoutledgeFalmer.

King, J. E. (2005). *Black Education: A Transformative Research and Action Agenda for the New Century*. New York: Lawrence Erlbaum.

Lipman, P. (2003). *High Stakes Education: Inequality, Globalization, and Urban School Reform*. Oxford: RoutledgeFalmer.

Morrell, E. and Collatos, A.M. (2002). Toward a critical teacher education: High school student sociologists as teacher educators. *Social Justice*, 29(4): 60–71.

Poetter, T. (2004). *Critical perspectives on the curriculum of teacher education*. Lanham, MD: University Press of America.

Popkewitz, T. S. (2007). *Cosmopolitanism and the Age of School Reform*. New York: Routledge.

Popkewitz, T. S. (1987). *Critical studies in teacher education: Its folklore, theory and practice*. New York: Falmer Press.

Torres, M. N. and Mercado, M. D. (2007). *The need for critical media literacy in teacher education core curricula.* In D. Macedo and S. Steinberg (eds.), *Media literacy: A reader*, pp. 538–558. New York: Peter Lang.

Zeichner, K. M. (1999). The new scholarship in teacher education. *Educational Researcher*, 28(9): 4–15.

Zeichner, K. M. (1996). "Teachers as reflective practitioners and the democratization of school reform," in K. M. Zeichner, S. Melnik, and M. L. Gomez (eds.), *Current of reforms in preservice teacher education*. New York: College Press.

Part Eight

Issues Beyond the Classroom

Introduction to Part Eight

In this first decade of the twenty-first century, our minds are bombarded daily with fear inspiring images of brutality and turmoil, while thin promises of normalcy dangle alongside the plunder and greed of a fierce globalized economy. This spectacle has been capriciously reproduced and publicly enacted through the most powerful hegemonic force of our time—a mass media muzzled and controlled by the corporate elite. In the midst of increasing job insecurity, the privatization of public welfare resources, and the ever-widening gap between the rich and poor, the US population has been forced to contend with the deleterious impact of two major national tragedies and the mendacity of the Bush administration's foreign policy.

In the first five years alone, the nation underwent three historically defining moments. September 11, 2001 (9/11) signaled the first suicide terrorist attack on the US mainland. On March 20, 2003 war was declared on Iraq, as an orchestrated retaliation tied to the "War on Terrorism." And, in late August 2005, New Orleans experienced massive destruction at the hands of Hurricane Katrina—not only one of the most intense, but the costliest hurricane on record in the country's history. There are those who would deem these three disasters (one political, one military, and one "natural") as direct or indirect consequences of internationalized neoliberal policies—namely, poverty, racism, ecological devastation, and the massive ideological corruption of the corporatized media.

These historical tragedies—along with military torture in Abu Ghraib and Guantanamo; the Patriot Act and its intensification of public surveillance; the Halliburton, Enron and Blackwater scandals; numerous national crises tied to unemployment, child poverty, health care, education, immigration, housing, and youth incarceration; and the culture industry's promotion of unchecked consumerism—have all deeply influenced our view of the world, whether we are conscious of this or not. In the wake of these conditions, critical educators are left to contend with the crushing blow of media distortions and misrepresentations on our critical faculties. In the hope of dislodging adherence to uncritical acceptance reinforced by the power of the airwaves, there is the need to cultivate pedagogical conditions beyond the classroom, where alternative readings of the world can emerge through community praxis. This summons the pedagogical power of people's lives and community traditions in the formation of an organic critical literacy—a literacy that can counter the impact, for example, of blind patriotism or mindless accumulation which obscure critical readings of the world.

To gain a better understanding of the impact of economic and political conditions on prevailing social views, it is useful to also examine the manner in which the current ecological crisis is unquestionably linked to the destructive structural conditions savagely proliferated around the globe. This is so, whether examining relationships between profit-generated pollution and devastating changes in weather patterns, or the justification of prisoner abuse and the infringement of civil rights, or the use of mass-scale technology in the fabrication of hegemonic consent and the repression of political dissent. Moreover, in all these instances, the break with our synergetic existence with nature and all organic life potentially leaves us estranged and disaffected. Inherent, here, is a need to counter the potential narcissistic indifference to the suffering of "the Other," by laying the groundwork for establishing the community solidarity and universal kinship, in and out of schools, necessary to forging a larger struggle for social justice, human rights, and democratic life.

This emancipatory feature of solidarity and kinship within communities is an often-overlooked legacy of Freire's work to critical pedagogy—a feature that grounded much of his early approach to the development of literacy. Much of the impetus, in fact, for his groundbreaking treatise *Pedagogy of the Oppressed*, was actually not his work in the formal classroom, but rather his pedagogical relationships within poor rural communities of Brazil, where illiterate men and women lived and labored. It should then come as no surprise that critical pedagogy is conceived as a living and organic pedagogy, one that by definition extends beyond the classroom walls. This is particularly important in keeping with a dialectical understanding of knowledge as dialectically tied to the larger social order and shaped by historical events, changing economic conditions, technological advances, and shifting political landscapes.

With this in mind, an emancipatory pedagogy, rooted in a praxis of reflection, dialogue, and action, can be enacted wherever subordinate populations struggle to affirm, challenge, resist, and transform the dehumanizing conditions of their existence. Anchored in a solid commitment to a vision of social justice and human rights, many critical educators, cultural workers, and community activists integrate critical pedagogy in alternative sites, such as adult education, community organizing, youth cultural arts programs, health care initiatives, worker education, and independent media programming. Within these community spaces, an array of untold possibilities can emerge as children, youth, and adults create opportunities together to grapple with meaningful issues and identify solutions that make sense in their world. Such efforts assist us to unveil the deep hegemonic impact of public institutions, the mainstream media, public surveillance, and unbridled consumerism, so that we might counter the forces of domination and exploitation and meet the challenge of creating an ecologically harmonious and life-affirming future.

Summary of Articles

In "Patriotism, Pedagogy, and Freedom: On the Educational Meanings of September 11," Michael Apple utilizes his own response to 9/11 to problematize the "phenomenological" experiences of teachers and school district officials to the tragedy. At the core of his discussion is the question: How do we make meaning of these horrific acts and how do we create spaces within our classroom to try to interpret this tragic event? In particular, Apple attempts to complicate the patriotic discourses and pedagogical practices which resulted from individual and collective contradictory emotions and disparate political readings of the tragedy. He grounds his discussion in the contentious arena of the Madison, Wisconsin School Board's response to 9/11, to illustrate how the politics of patriotism functioned to narrow the possibilities of critical dialogue about US politics and economic power. Apple contends that hegemonic alliances, grounded in patriotism, only succeed when conservatives coalesce patriotic fervor with the fears and worries of those suffering from the negative impact of the political economy. He calls for critical educators to embrace a more complicated political understanding of such concepts as democracy and freedom, if we are to counter the hegemonic projects that seek to redefine democracy as patriotic fervor, and freedom as the free market.

The corporate monopoly control of the media and the impact of its unproblematic commonsense constructions of social class are central concerns for Pepi Leistyna and Loretta Alper in their article "Critical Media Literacy for the Twenty-First Century." Particularly at issue is the manner in which entertainment television is implicated in the perpetuation of an economically stratified society, through its hegemonic portrayals of life in America. They show how television programming, in complicity with the political economy, perpetuates class hierarchical notions that reinforce the myth of meritocracy and the false promises of upward mobility stirred by the "American dream." Leistyna and Alper provide an incisive critique that points to the manner in which class roles are reinscribed, while the larger structures of class, gendered, and racialized inequalities are camouflaged. The consequence, they argue, is that working-class men and women are left to contend with false readings of their lives as deficient and unworthy of more, despite the fact that the advancement of capitalism and its internationalization would not have been possible without the intelligence, skills, and productivity of working people. Leistyna and Alper conclude with a discussion of the possibilities of critical media literacy, insisting that any movement to raise consciousness and democratize economic, social and technological relations must reflect the interest and lived histories of the working class.

Richard Kahn, in "Towards Ecopedagogy: Weaving a Broad-based Pedagogy of Liberation for Animals, Nature, and the Oppressed People of the Earth," provides an important critique to critical pedagogy, speaking of the urgent need to integrate matters of ecological significance to the struggle for emancipatory life. Kahn details the ravages of a globalized technocapitalism on the planet's ecosystem and exposes the increasing threat of extinction upon us, as well as the need for educators to become critically conscious of our inextricable interconnection with all living beings. He carefully provides the beginnings of a theoretical and historical foundation for a planetary ecopedagogy movement. In contrast to traditional environmental education "for sustainable development," Kahn calls for a radical ecopedagogy, anchored in both educational and ethical ecoliteracies, which challenges our old assumptions and can assist us to build broad-based solidarities for liberation.

William Westerman begins his discussion of "Folk Schools, Popular Education, and a Pedagogy of Community Action" with the notion that what makes pedagogy revolutionary is not simply the content, but rather an engaged communication process. Drawing on the influences of the Danish Folk Schools, the work of the Highlander School in Tennessee, and the literacy campaigns of Paulo Freire in Brazil, Westerman maintains that a teachers understanding of the "folk culture" or popular culture must be central to critical emancipatory practices of schooling and community activism. In concert, he asserts that an emancipatory pedagogy must be tied to the histories and realities of everyday people. He equally affirms the significance of integrating an analysis of class and social reality to liberatory pedagogical efforts in schools and communities. Westerman reinforces Freire's respect and faith in the people, stressing that answers to their own problems must be found in the realities of their daily existence.

Questions for Reflection and Dialogue

1. Explain what Michael Apple means when he says that hegemonic alliances can only succeed when they connect with elements of "good sense" of the people. What are the implications here for those who struggle for change in schools?

2. What does Apple mean when he says democracy and freedom "act as sliding signifiers?" Why is this an important concept for classroom teachers to understand?

3. Do you remember September 11, 2001? Where were you? What were your experiences in the classroom as a student or a teacher? Was the issue discussed? What were the main sentiments you remember? How do you connect Apple's experience and ideas about 9/11 to your own experience?

4. Define "social class" and discuss the three separate ways in which it is experienced.

5. What are the television representations of social class that Leistyna and Alper discuss? How are each of these linked to stereotypical beliefs about class and how do they function to preserve false readings of working-class men and women?

6. Identify examples of current television entertainment and provide an analysis of how these programs perpetuate or disrupt stereotypes of working-class people.

7. What is "critical media literacy?" In what ways can critical media literacy support the development of political consciousness and the forging of a truly democratic process?

8. According to Richard Kahn, what are the features of a radical ecopedagogy? In what ways is a radical ecopedagogy different from traditional notions of environmental education?

9. What is Kahn's critique of critical pedagogy? In what ways does the article challenge your own practices and old assumptions of the earth, life, and liberation?

10. What are the commonalities and differences in the revolutionary educational projects that William Westerman examines in his discussion?

11. In what ways can the integration of popular culture enhance the pedagogical possibilities within schools and communities?

25

Patriotism, Pedagogy, and Freedom: On the Educational Meanings of September 11

Michael W. Apple

Amid the volumes of material that have been published on the September 11 attacks—some of it uncritically patriotic and some of it more thoughtful and nuanced in its search for answers to why there may be such hatred toward the United States—little attention has been paid to the effects of this tragedy on education.[1] I do not think that the terrifying acts of September 11th (9/11) can be understood in isolation from the international and national contexts out of which they arose (see, e.g., Chomsky, 2002). Yet I also believe that we must pay close attention to the very personal ways in which 9/11 was experienced phenomenologically by teachers such as myself and the little-known effects it has had on pedagogy and the political urge to have schools participate in a complicated set of patriotic discourses and practices that swept over the United States in the wake of the disaster.[1]

Given this focus, parts of my analysis in this article will need to be personal. I do this not because I think that I have any better purchase on reality than the reader but because all of us may be better able to understand the lived effects of 9/11 by exploring what it meant to identifiable social actors and educators like myself. Thus, I explore in this essay the tension I felt as an educator who wanted to create both space within my university classroom for students to express their anger and outrage and also to raise some fundamental questions about why there are people in many parts of the world who have such extremely negative feelings toward the United States and the global capitalism our economy fosters that they would go to any extreme to call attention to their cause. I start at the personal level, but my aim is to participate in a collective project in which people from many different social locations and positions tell the stories of what 9/11 meant, and continues to mean, for their lives and educational practices. I then discuss the impact of 9/11 on the politics of the school board in Madison, Wisconsin, where I live. Here we see that the politics of patriotism made it much more difficult for schools at all levels to engage in social criticism or meaningful dialogue about U.S. policies and economic power. As we shall also see, 9/11 had powerful and worrisome effects that are often hidden in our rush to use schools for patriotic purposes.

Like many people, I am certain, I sat and watched the TV coverage of September 11th for hours—interviews and screaming people running away or running toward, but always running or seeking cover. A contradictory welter of emotions and political understandings and interpretations constantly surged within me. Then, by that night and throughout the days and nights that followed, the ruling pundits took charge of the public expression of what were the legitimate interpretations of the disaster. Given this media spin, I realized that the important question for educators at all levels of the educational system was how do we make meaning of these horrific acts and how do we create spaces within our classrooms to try to interpret this tragic event. I tried to come to grips with this in the context of my observation that, speaking very generally, the American public has little patience with the complexities of international relations and even less knowledge of the United States's complicity in supporting and arming dictatorial regimes, nor does it have a developed and nuanced understanding of U.S. domination of the world economy, of the negative effects of globalization, of the environmental effects of its wasteful energy policies and practices, and so much more, despite the nearly heroic efforts of critics of U.S. international policy such as Noam Chomsky (see, e.g., Chomsky, 1999). This speaks to the reality of the selective tradition in official knowledge and in the world beyond our borders that the news portrays (Apple, 2000). Even when there have been gains in the school curriculum—environmental awareness provides a useful example—these have been either adopted in their safest forms (see Fraser, 1989) or they fail to internationalize their discussions. Recycling bottles and cans is "good"; connections between profligate consumption of a disproportionate share of the world's resources and our daily behavior are nearly invisible in schools or the mainstream media. In this regard, it is helpful to know that the majority of nonbusiness vehicles purchased in the United States are now pick-up trucks, mini-vans, and sport utility vehicles—a guarantee that energy conservation will be a discourse unmoored in the daily practices of the U.S. consumer and an even further guarantee that the relationship between U.S. economic and military strategies and the defense of markets and, say, oil resources will be generally interpreted as a fight to protect the "American Way of Life" at all costs.

I mention all this because it is important to place what happened in the wake of 9/11 in a context of the "American" psyche and of dominant American self-understandings of the role the United States plays in the world.[2] In the domestic events surrounding 9/11, we had now become the world's oppressed. The (always relatively weak) recognition of the realities of the Palestinians or the poor in what we arrogantly call the third world was now evacuated. Almost immediately, there were a multitude of instances throughout the nation of people who looked Arabic being threatened and harassed on the street, in schools, and in their places of business. Less well known, but in my mind of great importance because they show the complexities of people's ethical commitments in the face-to-face relations of daily life, were the repeated instances of solidarity including university and community demonstrations of support for Islamic students, friends, and community members. Yet these moments of solidarity, though significant, could not totally make up for such things as Islamic, Punjabi, Sikh, and other students in high schools and at universities being threatened with retaliation and, in the case of some Punjabi secondary school students, being threatened with rape as an act of revenge for 9/11. This documents the connections between some elements of national identity and forms of masculinity, a relationship that cries out for serious analysis (Weaver-Hightower, 2002).

At the universities, some teachers ignored the horror, perhaps for much the same reason that I, as a young teacher in 1963, had dealt with the Kennedy assassination by simply resorting to normality as a defense against paralysis and continuing to give a spelling test as though nothing had happened. In other university classes, days were spent in discussions of the events. Sadness, disbelief, and shock were registered. But just as often, anger and a resurgent patriotism came to the fore. Any critical analysis of the events and of their roots in the hopelessness, denial of dignity, and despair of oppressed peoples—as I and a number of my colleagues put forward in our classes and seminars—had to be done extremely cautiously, not only because of the emotionally and politically charged environment even at a progressive university like my own but also because many of us were not totally immune from some of the same feelings of anger and horror. Even for progressive educators, the events of 9/11 worked off of the contradictory elements of good and bad sense we too carry within us and threatened to pull us in directions that, in other times, would have seemed to be simplistic and even jingoistic. But at least for me, and the vast majority of my colleagues and graduate students, the elements of good sense won out.

Given these elements of good sense, it was clear that pedagogical work needed to be done. But this wasn't a simple issue because a constant question, and tension, was always on my mind. How could one condemn the murderous events, give one's students an historical and political framework that puts these events in their larger critical context, and provide a serious forum where disagreement and debate could fruitfully go on so that a politics of marginalization didn't occur in the classes—and at the same time not be seen as somehow justifying the attacks. Although I had very strong feelings about the need to use this as a time to show the effects of U.S. global economic, political, and cultural policies, I also had strong "teacherly" dispositions that this was also not the time to engage in a pedagogy of imposition. One could not come across as saying to students or the public, "Your understandings are simply wrong; your feelings of threat and anger are selfish; any voicing of these emotions and understandings won't be acceptable." This would be among the most counterproductive pedagogies imaginable. Not only would it confirm the already just-near-the-surface perceptions among many people that somehow the left is unpatriotic, but such a pedagogy also could push people into rightist positions, in much the same way as I had argued in my own work about why people "became right" (Apple, 1996). This required a very strategic sense of how to speak and act, both in my teaching and in my appearances on national media.

Take my teaching as a major example. I wanted my students to fully appreciate the fact that the U.S.-led embargo of Iraq caused the death of thousands upon thousands of children each year that it was in place. I wanted them to understand how U.S. policies in the Middle East and in Afghanistan helped create truly murderous consequences. However, unless their feelings and understandings were voiced and taken seriously, the result could be exactly the opposite of what any decent teacher wants. Instead of a more complex understanding of the lives of people who are among the most oppressed in the world—often as a result of Western and Northern economic and political policies (Greider, 1997)—students could be led to reject any critical contextual understanding largely because the pedagogical politics seemed arrogant. In my experiences, both as an activist and a scholar, this has happened more often than some theorists of "critical pedagogy" would like to admit.[3] None of us is a perfect teacher, and I am certain that I made more than a few wrong moves in my attempts to structure the discussions in my classes so that they were open and critical at the same time. But, I was impressed with the willingness of the vast majority of students to reexamine their anger, to put themselves in the place of the oppressed, to take their more critical and nuanced understandings and put them into action. Indeed, one striking effect was that some students in my classes formed a coalition to engage in concrete actions in their own schools and communities, as well as in the university, to interrupt the growing anti-Islamic and jingoistic dynamics that were present even in progressive areas, such as Madison and the University of Wisconsin.

This politics of interruption became even more important because these complicated pedagogical issues and the contradictory emotions and politics that were produced in the aftermath of 9/11 were felt well beyond the walls of the university classroom. At times, they also had the effect of radically transforming the politics of governance of schooling at a local level in communities throughout the United States. One example from Madison can serve as a powerful reminder of the hidden effects of the circulation of discourses of patriotism and "threat" as they move from the media into our daily lives.

Patriotism, the Flag, and the Control of Schools

On an October evening that hinted at the coming of cooler weather, more than 1,200 persons packed the auditorium where the Madison Board of Education had called a special public hearing. Flags were everywhere—in hands, on lapels, pasted on jackets. The old and trite phrase that "you could cut the tension with a knife" seemed oddly appropriate here. The tension was somehow physical; it could literally be felt, almost like an electrical current that coursed through your body. And for some people present at the hearing, the figures behind the front table deserved exactly that. They needed to be electrically shocked.

In August 2001, well before the 9/11 disasters, the seeds of this conflict had been planted in what were seemingly innocuous ways. Smuggled into the Wisconsin state budget was a bit of mischief by conservative legislators seeking to gain some arguing points for the next election. There was a section in the budget authorization bill that required that students in all public (state funded) schools publicly recite The Pledge of Allegiance or that schools play or sing "The Star Spangled Banner," a national anthem that is a strikingly militaristic song with the added benefit of being nearly impossible for most people—and certainly most children—to sing. Even though the legislation allowed for nonparticipation, given the long and inglorious history of legislation of this kind in the United States, there was a clear implication that such lack of participation was frowned upon. This was something of a time bomb just waiting to explode. And it did.

In the midst of the growing patriotic fervor following 9/11, the Madison, Wisconsin, School Board voted in early October to follow the law in the most minimalist way possible by mandating that administrators play only instrumental versions of the anthem. For some board members, the law seemed to be the wrong way to teach patriotism. Rote memorization was not the best approach if one actually wanted to provide the conditions for the growth of thoughtful citizenship. For others, the law was clearly a political ploy by conservative legislators to try to gain more support among right-wing voters in an upcoming election that was felt to be a close call. And for other board members, there were a number of principles at stake. The state should not intervene into the content of local school board decisions of this type. Further, not only had the new law not been subject to close public scrutiny and serious debate, but it also threatened the cherished (at least in theory) constitutional right of freedom of dissent. For all of these reasons, a majority of people on the school board voted not to have the reciting of the Pledge or the singing of the anthem in the Madison Public Schools.

The School Board did actually comply with the law by having the music—if not the lyrics—of the anthem played over the loudspeaker. This would eliminate the more warlike words that accompanied the music. Some members of the board felt that in a time of tragedy in which so many innocent lives had been lost, the last thing that students and schools needed were lyrics that to some glorified militarism. The solution was a compromise: play an instrumental version of the anthem.[4]

Within hours, the furor over their decision reached boiling point. The media made it their major story. Prominent headlines in a local conservative newspaper stated such things as "School Board Bans Pledge of Allegiance." This negative coverage occurred even though the board had actually complied with the formal letter of the law and had indeed held public hearings prior to their actions, where many people had objected to the law and to the saying of the Pledge and the singing of the anthem. Conservative politicians and spokespersons, colonizing the space of fear and horror over the destruction of the World Trade Center, quickly mobilized. This could not be tolerated. It was not only unpatriotic, but it was disrespectful, both to the women and men who died in the disaster and to our military overseas. To those being mobilized, it also was a signal that the board was out of touch with "real" Americans—one more instance of elite control of schools that ignored the wishes of the "silent majority" of "freedom loving" and patriotic Americans.

At the meeting of the school board approximately 50% of the speakers from the audience supported the board's original decision to require neither the Pledge nor the singing of the anthem, a fact that was deeply buried in the news accounts that consistently highlighted the conservative mobilization against the board. This is in part because the voices of those supporting the board's vote were often drowned out by those who opposed it. A cacophony of hisses, boos, chants, and phrases reminiscent of earlier periods of "red-baiting" greeted each speaker who spoke out in favor of the board's actions. Meanwhile, those who spoke out against the board were greeted with applause and loud cheers. (It almost sounded like an Olympic event in which the chant "USA, USA" could be heard.)

Throughout it all, the board members tried to remain civil and not respond to what were at times quite personal attacks on their patriotism. In many ways, the hours upon hours of meeting time and the intense conflicts and debates that ensued could be interpreted as an example of democracy in action. In part such an interpretation is undoubtedly correct. Yet the harshness of the language, the theater of patriotic symbols, the echoes of war fever, all of this also added up to a politics of intimidation at times as well. Having said this, however, there was also a sense of genuine expression of pain and hurt, a recognition that "ordinary Americans" had been killed and that schools had to recognize the deaths as having occurred among "people like ourselves."

The populist notes being struck here are crucial because hegemonic alliances can only succeed when they connect with the elements of "good sense" of the people (Apple, 1996, 2001). Popular worries over one's children and the schools they attend in a time of radical corporate downsizing and capital flight, worries about social stability and cultural traditions that are constantly being subverted by the commodifying processes and logics of capital, and so much more, all of this allows conservative groups to suture these concerns into their own antipublic agenda. Thus, rampant and fearful conservatism and patriotism are not the only dynamics at work in this situation, even though the overt issue was about the Pledge and the anthem. None of this could have happened without the growing fear of one's children's future and over the nature of an unstable paid labor market, and especially without the decades-long ideological project in which the right had engaged to make so many people believe that big government was the source of the social, cultural, and economic problems we faced (Apple, 1996, 2001; Katz, 2001).

Yet there were more conjunctural reasons for this response as well. It is always wise to remember that although the State of Wisconsin was the home of much of the most progressive legislation and of significant parts of the democratic socialist tradition in the United States, it also was the home of Senator Joseph McCarthy—yes, the figure for whom McCarthyism is named. Thus, behind the populist and social democratic impulses that have had such a long history here, there lies another kind of populism. This one is what, following Stuart Hall (1980), I have called authoritarian populism, a retrogressive assemblage of values that embodies visions of "the people" that has been just as apt to be nationalistic, anti-immigrant, anticosmopolitan, anticommunist, promilitary, and very conservative in terms of religious values (Apple, 2001). In times of crisis, these tendencies can come to the fore. And they did, with a vengeance.

Of course, we cannot understand any of this unless we understand the long history of the struggles over the very meaning of freedom and citizenship in the United States (Foner, 1998). For all of the protagonists in the school board controversy what was at stake was freedom. For some, it was the danger of international terrorism destroying our free way of life. Nothing must interfere with the defense of American freedom, and schools were on the front lines in this defense. Thus, an uncritical and unquestioning pedagogy of patriotism was what the schools needed to foster at this time of national crisis. For others, such freedom was in essence meaningless if it meant that citizens couldn't act on their freedoms, especially in times of such crises. Silencing dissent and imposing forms of compulsory patriotism were the very antithesis of freedom. A hidden curriculum of compulsory patriotism would, in essence, do exactly this.

This documents an important point. Concepts such as freedom are sliding signifiers. They have no fixed meaning but are part of a contested terrain in which different visions of democracy exist on a social field of power in which there are unequal resources to influence the publicly accepted definitions of key words. In the words of one of the wisest historians of such concepts:

> The very universality of the language of freedom camouflages a host of divergent connotations and applications. It is pointless to attempt to identify a single "real" meaning against which others are to be judged. Rather than freedom as a fixed category or predetermined concept, . . . it [is] an "essentially contested concept," one that by its very nature is the subject of disagreement. Use of such a concept automatically presupposes an ongoing dialogue with other, competing meanings.
>
> (Foner, 1998, p. xiv)

The realization of how concepts such as democracy and freedom both act as sliding signifiers with no fixed meaning and can be mobilized by varying groups with varying agendas returns us to a point I made earlier—the ideological project in which the economic and cultural right have engaged. We need to understand that the widely successful effects of what Roger Dale and I have called conservative modernization have been exactly that—widely successful (Apple, 2001; Dale, 1989/1990). We are witnessing—living through is a better phrase—a social/pedagogic project to change our common sense, to radically transform our assumptions about the role of "liberal elites," of government and the economy, about what are "appropriate" values, the role of religion in public affairs, gender and sexuality, "race," and a host of other crucial areas. Democracy has been transformed from a political concept to an economic one. Collective senses of freedom that were once much more widespread (although we need to be careful of not romanticizing this) have been largely replaced by individualistic notions of democracy as simply consumer choice. Although this has had major effects on the power of labor unions and on other kinds of important collective social movements, it also has created other hidden needs and desires besides those of the rational economic actor who makes calculated individual decisions in a market (Apple, 2000, 2001; Kintz, 1997). I think these needs and desires have also played a profound role in the mobilization of the seemingly rightist sentiment I have been describing.

Underneath the creation of the unattached individualism of the market is an almost unconscious desire for community. However, community formation can take many forms, both progressive and retrogressive. At the time of 9/11, both came to the fore. The school board's decision threatened the "imagined community" of the nation at the same time as the nation actually seemed to be under physical threat (Anderson, 1991). It also provided a stimulus for the formation of a "real" community, an organization to "win back" the space of schooling for patriotism. The defense of freedom is sutured into the project of defending the nation, which is sutured into a local project of forming a (rightist) counterhegemonic community to contest the antipatriotic and ideologically motivated decisions by urban liberal elites. Thus, the need to "be with others," itself a hidden effect of the asocial relations of advanced capitalism, has elements of good and bad sense within it. Under specific historical circumstances these elements of good sense can be mobilized in support of a vision of democracy that is inherently undemocratic in its actual effects on those people in a community who wish to uphold a vision of freedom that not only legitimates dissidence but provides space for its expression.[5]

In saying this, do not read me as being totally opposed to ideas of nation or of the building of imagined communities. In my mind, however, social criticism is the ultimate act of patriotism. As I say in *Official Knowledge* (Apple, 2000), rigorous criticism of a nation's policies demonstrates a commitment to the nation itself. It says that one demands action on the principles that are supposedly part of the founding narratives of a nation and that are employed in the legitimization of its construction of particular kinds of polities. It signifies that "I/we live here" and that this is indeed our country and our flag as well. No national narrative that excludes the rich history of dissent as a constitutive part of the nation can ever be considered legitimate. Thus, in claiming that the board had acted in an unpatriotic manner, the flag-waving crowd and the partly still inchoate movement that stood behind it in my mind was itself engaged in a truly unpatriotic act, one which showed that the national narrative of freedom and justice was subject to constant renegotiation and struggle over its very meaning.[6] The 9/11 tragedy provided the conditions for such struggles at a local level, not only in the classrooms at universities such as my own but also in the ordinary ways we govern our schools.

In Madison, even with the forces arrayed against it, the threat to call a special election to oust all of the board members who voted against the mandatory Pledge and singing stalled. In fact, the recall campaign failed by a wide margin. The conservative organizers were not able to get anywhere near the number of votes needed to force a new election. This is a crucial element in any appraisal of the lasting effects of 9/11. In the face of resurgent patriotism and anger, in the face of calls for an enhanced national security state and for schools to be part of the first line of defense, at the local level in many communities wiser heads, ones with a more substantive vision of democracy, prevailed. Yet this is not the end of this particular story. The pressure from the right did have an effect. The board reversed its policy, leaving it up to each individual school to decide if and how they would enforce the mandated patriotism. This decision defused the controversy in a way that has a long history in the United States. Local decisions will prevail, but there is no guarantee that the decisions at each local school will uphold a vision of thick democracy that welcomes dissent as itself a form of patriotic commitment.

Still, the issues surrounding thick democracy at a local level do not end with the question of whether dissent is welcome or not. To document why we must go further, I need to point to other crucial dynamics that were at work and that were the unforeseen results of this controversy. When the recall campaign failed, conservatives rededicated themselves to winning the next school board election. Two of the seats of people who had been among the majority of members who had originally taken the controversial decision were to be contested. Here, too, the conservatives failed and both seats were taken by progressives.

This again seems as if our story had a relatively happy ending. Yet simply leaving the story there would miss one of the most important hidden effects of the 9/11-Pledge connection. Instead, what I shall now describe shows something very different—that often the effects of seeming victories against rightist mobilization must themselves be understood as complicated and as occurring along multiple dynamics of power.

Because of the tensions, controversies, and personal attacks that developed out of the board's deliberations, one of the members who had voted for the board's minimalist response resigned right before the closing date for registering as a candidate for the next election. That member, an African American who had been on the board for a number of years, was "worn out" by the controversy. In essence, although it is trite to say so, it became the straw that broke the camel's back. It had taken so much energy and time to fight the battles over funding cuts, over the development of programs that were aimed specifically at Madison's growing population of children of color, over all those things that make being one of the few minority members of a school board so fulfilling and frustrating, that the emotional labor and time commitments involved in the compulsory patriotism conflict and in its aftermath created an almost unbearable situation for him. Even though a progressive write-in candidate did win the seat that had been vacated, a cogent voice, one representing communities of color in the community, had been lost.

This points to a crucial set of unintended results. The legislation smuggled into the budget bill had echoes of dynamics that were very different from those overtly involved in the conflict over the Pledge, but these echoes still were profound in their effects. In the context of 9/11, this seemingly inconsequential piece of legislation not only created the seeds of very real conflicts and conservative mobilizations but also, through a long chain of events, it led to the loss of a hard-won gain. An articulate, African American elected board member who had fought for social justice in the district could take it no more. In the conjunctural and unpredictable events both of and after the horror of 9/11, a bit of "mischief" in which Republican legislators sought to protect their right flank, rebounds back on the realities of differential power at the local level. Obviously, race was not necessarily on the minds of the legislators who placed that piece of legislation into the budget bill.[7] However, the effects to which it led ultimately were, profoundly, racial at the level of local governance.

I want to stress the importance of these effects. In any real situation there are multiple relations of power. Any serious understanding of the actual results of 9/11 on education needs to widen its gaze beyond what we usually look for. As I have shown, in the aftermath of 9/11 the politicization of local school governance occurred in ways that were quite powerful. Yet without an understanding of "other" kinds of politics, in this case race, we would miss one of the most important results of the struggle over the meaning of freedom in this site. September 11 has had even broader effects than we recognize.

Conclusion

In the account I have given in the second half of this article, it is unclear then who really won or lost here. But one thing is clear: No analysis of the effects of 9/11 on schools can go on without an understanding of the ways in which the global is dynamically linked to the local. Such an analysis must more fully understand the larger ideological work and history of the neoliberal and neoconservative project and its effects on the discourses that circulate and become common sense in our society. And no analysis can afford to ignore the contradictory needs and contradictory outcomes that this project has created at multiple levels and along multiple axes of power.

Thus, I argue that educators—whether teaching a university class or participating in local school board decision making—must first recognize our own contradictory responses to the events of 9/11. We must also understand that these responses, although partly understandable in the context of tragic events, may create dynamics that have long-lasting consequences. And many of these consequences may themselves undercut the very democracy that we believe we are upholding and defending. This more complicated political understanding may well be a first step in finding appropriate and socially critical pedagogic strategies to work within our classes and communities to interrupt the larger hegemonic projects—including the redefinition of democracy as patriotic fervor—that we will continue to face in the future.

Notes

1. I would like to thank James A. Beane for his comments and for his help on the material used in this essay. Amy Stuart Wells also provided important and insightful suggestions on the content of this article. A different version of this paper will appear in the Australian journal *Discourse*.

2. Even though I used this word before in my text, I have put the word "American" in quotation marks for a social purpose in this sentence because it speaks to the reality I wish to comment on at this point in my discussion. All of North, Central, and South America are equally part of the Americas. However, the United States (and much of the world) takes for granted that the term refers to the United States. The very language we use is a marker of imperial pasts and presents. See Said (1978) for one of the early but still very cogent analyses of this.

3. This is one of the reasons that, even though parts of the points may have been based on only a limited reading of parts of the critical pedagogical traditions, I have some sympathy with a number of the arguments made in Luke and Gore (1992)—and not a lot of sympathy for the defensive over-reactions to it on the part of a number of writers on critical pedagogy. Political/educational projects, if they are to be both democratic and effective, are always collective. This requires a welcoming of serious and engaged criticism.

4. This too led to some interesting and partly counterhegemonic responses. At one school, a famous Jimi Hendrix rendition of "The Star Spangled Banner" was played over the loudspeaker system. This version—dissonant and raucous—was part of the antiwar tradition of music during the Vietnam-era protests. This raised even more anger on the part of the "patriots" who were already so incensed about the board's vote.

5. Of course, the conservative groups that mobilized against the Board's initial decision would claim that they were exercising dissent, that their members were also engaged in democratic action. This is true as far as it goes. However, if one's dissent supports repression and inequality, and if one's dissent labels other people's actions in favor of their own constitutional rights as unpatriotic, then this is certainly not based on a vision of "thick" democracy. I would hold that its self-understanding is less than satisfactory.

6. In this regard, it is important to know that the Pledge of Allegiance itself has always been contested. Its words are the following:

   I pledge allegiance to the flag of the United States of America, and to the republic for which it stands, one Nation, under God, with liberty and justice for all.

   Yet the phrase "under God" was added during the midst of the McCarthy period in the early 1950s as part of the battle against "God-less communists." Even the phrase "to the flag of the United States of America" is a late addition. The Pledge was originally written by a well-known socialist and at first only contained the words "I pledge allegiance to the flag." In the 1920s, a conservative women's group, the Daughters of the American Republic, successfully lobbied to have the words "of the United States of America" added as part of an anti-immigrant campaign. They were deeply fearful that immigrants might be pledging to another nation's flag and, hence, might actually be using the pledge to express seditious thoughts.

7. As I have argued in *Educating the "Right" Way* (Apple, 2001), however, race and the politics of "whiteness" have played a significant role in the historical development of neoliberal, neoconservative, and authoritarian populist anger at the state and in the development of their proposals for school reform.

References

Anderson, B. (1991). *Imagined communities*. New York: Verso.

Apple, M.W. (1996). *Cultural politics and education*. New York: Teachers College Press.

Apple, M.W. (2000). *Official knowledge* (2nd ed.). New York: Routledge.

Apple, M.W. (2001). *Educating the "right" way: Markets, standards, god, and inequality*. New York: Routledge.

Chomsky, N. (1999). *Profit over people*. New York: Seven Stories Press.

Chomsky, N. (2002). *9–11*. New York: Seven Stories Press.

Dale, R. (1989/1990). The Thatcherite project in education. *Critical Social Policy, 9*, 4–19.

Foner, E. (1998). *The story of American freedom*. New York: Norton.

Fraser, N. (1989). *Unruly practices*. Minneapolis: University of Minnesota Press.

Greider, W. (1997). *One world, ready or not*. New York: Simon & Schuster.

Hail, S. (1980). Popular democratic vs authoritarian populism. In A. Hunt (Ed.), *Marxism and democracy*. London: Lawrence and Wishart.

Katz, M.B. (2001). *The price of citizenship*. New York: Metropolitan Books.

Kintz, L. (1997). *Between Jesus and the market*. Durham, NC: Duke University Press.

Luke, C., & Gore, J. (1992). *Feminisms and critical pedagogy*. New York: Routledge.

Said, E. (1978). *Orientalism*. New York: Pantheon.

Weaver-Hightower, M. (2002). The gender of terror and heroes? *Teachers College Record*.

26

Critical Media Literacy for the Twenty-First Century: Taking Our Entertainment Seriously

Pepi Leistyna and Loretta Alper

While capitalism consists of a structural reality built on political and economic processes, institutions, and relationships, its proponents also rely on the formative power of culture to shape the kinds of meaning, desire, subjectivity, and thus identity that can work to ensure the maintenance of its logic and practice. Corporate bodies take very seriously the fact that culture shapes our sense of political agency and mediates the relations between everyday struggles and structures of power.[1] In fact, in this age of postmodern technologies that can saturate society with media messages, elite private interests have worked diligently to monopolize the means of production and distribution of information and ideas so as to be able to more effectively circulate, legitimate, and reproduce a vision of the world that suits their needs; a world where profit trumps people at every turn.

While there is a plethora of ways in which agencies of knowledge production like schools, houses of faith, and the media are strategically used to engineer history and shape public consciousness, one of the pedagogical forces that needs to be watched more closely is entertainment television. Though media executives and producers insist that television is meant to entertain and not to educate, TV shows have undeniably played a pivotal role in shaping our perceptions of the world (Allen & Hill, 2004; Bourdieu, 1996; Carey, 1995; Durham & Kellner, 2001; Hall, 1997; Parenti, 1992). However, because we generally see television as just entertainment, we readily disregard its impact on our thinking. It is precisely because we believe television is merely entertainment, that we need to take its power and influence seriously.[2]

Television in the United States is largely controlled by five massive transnational corporations: Time Warner (which among its many assets, owns and operates CNN, Turner Classic Movies, HBO, Court TV, TNT, TBS, and the Cartoon Network), Disney (owns ABC, ESPN, the Disney Channel, the History Channel, A&E, Biography, Military History, Lifetime, E, the Style Network, and Soapnet), News Corporation (owns Fox, National Geographic Channel, Direct TV, FX, and STAR), General Electric (owns NBC, Telemundo, Bravo, MSNBC, CNBC, Sci Fi, Paxon, the USA Network, and Sundance—which is a joint venture with CBS), and Viacom (owns CBS, MTV, Showtime, Comedy Central, BET, TV Land, VH1, CMT, Nick at Nite, Spike TV, and Nickelodeon). As the Federal Communications Commission continues to pass legislation that allows these conglomerates to further monopolize the use of public airwaves (McChesney, 2004)—while it buries research that clearly shows how such forces are breaking the law by neglecting to serve the needs of the general populace—such private interests have been effective in using this medium to disseminate messages that serve their ideological and economic imperatives. This chapter provides an example of this common practice as it examines how the working class in the United States has been framed by corporate media in ways that reinforce classist, racist, and sexist stereotypes that serve to justify the inequities inherent in capitalism's class structure.[3]

Class Matters

Because the subject of class is so taboo in the United States, we lack a conceptual framework for understanding television's portrayal of the working class. Having a basic definition of class will not only give us insight into why people occupy their class positions, it will also enable us to make sense of TV's representations and their broader social implications.

Social class—an essential component of capitalist social relations—is experienced in three separate but interconnected ways. Economic class pertains to one's income and how much wealth/or capital a person has accumulated. Political class is the amount of power that a person has to influence the workplace and the larger social order; this includes social capital—those interpersonal connections that make it easier to effect change. Cultural class has more to do with taste, education, and lifestyle, or what is also referred to as cultural capital. While the economic, political, and cultural are always in flux, so is the definition of class.

Since the early colonial years, the United States has largely been built on the interests of the elite business classes, which, needless to say, have benefited greatly from a longstanding denial of the structural realities of a class system. Intended to perpetuate faith in the "American dream"—which ironically implies a class hierarchy as it romanticizes movement from the bottom to the top of the economic ladder—this disavowal is buttressed by an ideology that reinforces the myth of meritocracy where hard work and persistence are perceived as the essential ingredients for success; with no mention of any of the critical factors that inhibit upward mobility such as labor, wage, and tax laws that favor the wealthy, a public school system that is largely funded through property taxes, or gender discrimination and racism—just to name a few. Far beyond the limits of individual virtue, class divisions and conflicts in the United States are inherent to an economic system that not only unjustly discriminates against different groups of people, but also subdivides power along the lines of owners and professional, managerial, and working classes.

In what is now a post-industrial society in the United States—one that relies on service industries, knowledge production, and information technologies rather than industrial manufacturing to generate capital—the average wage is 29% less than it was during the days of industry. Class mobility in this country is more restricted than ever before, unless of course the direction is downward. Within these economic shifts, the middle class is imploding into the working class, which in turn is imploding into the working poor who are literally relegated to life on the streets.[4]

Census data show that the gap between the rich and the poor in this country is the widest it has been since the government started collecting information in 1947. In fact, with the exception of Russia and Mexico, the United States has the most unequal distribution of wealth and income in the industrialized world. Nevertheless, in this post-Katrina economic climate—where federal malfeasance unwittingly exposed the raw poverty that exists in this country—the current administration and both Republican-run houses, just before Christmas, pushed through $50 billion in spending cuts to such social programs as food stamps and Medicaid.[5]

Since 2000, unemployment in the United States has hovered between 5% and 6%, and millions of jobs have been lost during this period.[6] These job losses are neither merely layoffs caused by hard economic times nor are they a direct result of 9/11 as conservatives would have us believe. With capital flight and global out-sourcing, both blue-collar and white-collar jobs have been and continue to be exported by U.S. corporations to nations that pay below a living wage and that ensure that workers have no protection under labor unions and laws that regulate corporate interests and power. By cheap labor, we are often talking between 13.5 and 36 cents an hour; we're also talking about a total disregard for child-labor laws and environmental protections (National Labor Committee for Worker and Human Rights, 2003). Moreover, as the Federal Reserve has noted, these jobs will not be returning, even if there is a major upswing in the U.S. economy.

The current administration has bragged about creating new jobs for Americans, but it fails to inform the public that these are overwhelmingly part-time, adjunct, minimum-wage positions that provide no pension, union protection, or healthcare benefits. Part-time, temp, or subcontracted jobs currently make up 30% of the workforce, and this number is rapidly increasing.

As the federal minimum wage is currently $5.15 an hour—a wage that is sustained by powerful corporate lobbyists—full-time workers in the United States make about $10,712 a year. Keep in mind that the federal poverty level for an individual is $9,214. This makes it impossible to afford adequate housing throughout the country. "In fact, in the median state a minimum-wage worker would have to work 87 hours each week to afford a two-bedroom apartment at 30% of his or her income, which is the federal definition of affordable housing" (National Coalition for the Homeless, 1999, p. 3). It is no wonder that one out of every five homeless people is employed. It is important to note that contrary to popular myth, the majority of minimum-wage workers are not teenagers: 71.4% are over the age of 20. Nonetheless, in March 2005, the Republican majority-Senate voted once again against an increase in the minimum wage.

The average income in the United States is shrinking and workers are earning less, adjusting for inflation, than they did a quarter century ago. Real wages are falling at their fastest rate in 14 years. Meanwhile, median CEO pay at the 100 largest companies in Fortune's survey rose 14 percent last year to $13.2 million. Still, average CEO pay in *Business Week's* survey was $7.4 million. It would take 241 years for an average worker paid $30,722 to make that amount (Sklar, 2003, p. 4).

The ratio of average CEO pay in the United States to the average blue-collar pay in the same corporation is 470 to 1.

As far as political influence is concerned, in the United States "some 80% of all political contributions now come from less than 1% of the population" (Collins, Hartman, & Sklar, 1999, p. 5). It should thus come as no surprise that most of the public policy debate in this country remains in the confines of the Wall Street and Fortune 500 agenda. The richest 1% of Americans control about 40% of the nation's wealth; the top 5% have more than 60%. While the nation's median household income is $44,389—down 3.8% from 1999—the average income for the top 0.1% of the population is $3 million.

According to *Forbes Magazine* (2006), for the fourth consecutive year, the rich got richer: The collective net worth of the nation's wealthiest has climbed to $1.25 trillion. For the first time, everyone on the list is a billionaire.

Even the current tax system in this country is structured to perpetuate the class hierarchy. "People making $60,000 paid a larger share of their 2001 income in federal income, Social Security and Medicare taxes than a family making $25 million, the latest Internal Revenue Service data show" (Ivins, 2005, p. 1).

The nation's wealthiest 10% own almost 90% of all stocks and mutual funds (Dollars & Sense & United for a Fair Economy, 2004). While one in two Americans does not own stocks, the ubiquitous numbers from Wall Street imply that the market will help those in need and the country as a whole. Meanwhile, the poor and the rich are depicted as living on the polar edges of society's economic spectrum, which is predominantly occupied by a grand middle class—a romanticized category that works to obfuscate the realities of class conflict.[8] According to the mythology, the rich, the poor, and the working and middle classes are not dialectically intertwined given that one's class position is a product of individual efforts rather than structural forces.[9]

The working class is in fact the majority of the population in this country. As Michael Zweig notes:

> It turns out that in the United States about 62% of the labor force are working-class people. That is, people who go to work, they do their jobs, they go home, they go to another job, but they don't have a lot of control or authority over their work. These are people who are blue collar, white collar, and pink collar. That's the working-class majority. Those are most people in this country.
>
> (interview in *Class Dismissed: How TV Frames the Working Class*, 2005)

However, regardless of the aforementioned conditions that the working-class majority endures on a regular basis, corporate-managed media have constructed their own tales about the lives of everyday people. It is very important to look at the stories they tell and to ask the critical question: Whose interests are served by such representations?

Class Identity in the Age of Television

While the working class is largely missing from the public discourse, it has always had a place in the world of entertainment television. In fact in the early days, working-class and immigrant families were a regular part of the TV repertoire on shows like I *Remember Mama* (1949–1957), *The Goldbergs* (1949–1955), and *Life with Luigi* (1952–1953), which featured Norwegian, Jewish, and Italian families.[10]

As TV evolved as a commercially sponsored medium, advertisers began to play an increasingly important role in creating programs. Their impact went far beyond on-screen sponsorship to having a hand in the actual production, including scriptwriting and hiring of talent (Barnouw, 1978). Due to their power and influence, advertisers were able to redefine the meaning of the American Dream, from the search for a better life to the pursuit of a consumer lifestyle.

Different from radio, where many of the earlier shows got their start, on television one can really see what the assimilation process is supposed to look like according to the advertising-driven media. It is the acquisition of consumer goods, becoming less ethnic, and looking more like aspirational middle-class American families (Lipsitz, 2002). As Bambi Haggins points out:

> In the late 40s and the early 1950s there is a very specific instruction on consumerism that takes place within narratives . . . that if we have these products then we can move into this different

place on this socio-economic hierarchy. *The Goldbergs* is an excellent example of the ethnicom that starts out in urban America then moves to the suburbs. And in that movement you get a very specific idea of the things you need to have in order to gain access to the suburban American dream. Even in a show like *Amos and Andy* [1950–1953], which is problematic for a lot of reasons, you have Sapphire wanting to buy a new dining room table because that table is going to afford her access to a higher social and intellectual strata.

(interview in *Class Dismissed*, 2005)

Working together, producers and advertisers understood that associating products with middle- and upper-class lifestyles would increase both ratings and sales. The stark contrast between the gritty image of working-class life and the shiny sanitized world of consumer advertising proved to be irreconcilable (Barnouw, 1978). As television became more con-solidated in the late 1950s and the early 1960s, working-class and immigrant families would gradually disappear. On the contrary, programs that could provide a pristine setting for product placement and articulate the needs of a healthy, successful middle-class family living the American dream would take center stage—shows such as: *I Married Joan* (1952–1955), *The Adventures of Ozzy and Harriet* (1952–1966), *Make Room for Daddy* (1953–1965), *Father Knows Best* (1954–1960), *Leave it to Beaver* (1957–1963), *Dennis the Menace* (1959–1963), and *The Dick Van Dyke Show* (1961–1969).

In part, the reason that the working class seems to disappear from public discourse and from the world of entertainment television is because there was a real economic boom going on at the time. Within this post-WW II economic climate, many workers, especially white workers, did achieve a better standard of living. This was due to organizing and collective bargaining, as well as to government programs that provided a real safety net. However, there is also an ideological reason for the disappearance of class from the public eye. The country was moving into the cold war—the McCarthy era—and it is ironic that unions, the very organizations that enabled workers to achieve a better standard of living, are seen as a real threat now. Any effort to further democratize industry, technology, and economic and social relations gets branded as communist and has to be crushed. As Zweig explains:

> So what we had was this presentation of living standards as the measure of class because the old notion of class as power was being wiped out, was being crushed. That was the left . . . "Oh you're a communist. Let's not talk about class that way. What we really want to talk about is that you're doing better than you ever have before. Workers in this country are all middle class now . . ." And even union leaders talk about how they made their members middle class. Well they didn't make their members middle class. They made their working-class members have a better standard of living. That's a very different thing.

(interview in *Class Dismissed*, 2005)

Television would continue to play a central role in touting the great openness and comforts of the middle class.

From the Margins to the Middle

In the 1950s as the white working class was disappearing into the classless middle, African Americans and other racially subordinated groups continued to endure the horrors of white supremacy coupled with the exploitative logic of capital.[11] Disregarding these harsh realities, TV's fantasy land only allowed people of color to be visible as happy servants or entertainers on programs like *Beulah* (1950–1953) and *The Nat "King" Cole Show* (1956–1957) (Riggs, 1991; Gray, 1995).[12]

In order to gain broader access to television, blacks and other marginalized groups would have to learn to play by TV's rules—namely to have faith in the American Dream.[13] While this logic has served television's commercial imperatives, it has also reduced struggles for economic justice and social equality to a simple matter of inclusion.

In the post-civil rights era, the arrival of African Americans onto primetime television with shows like *Sanford and Son* (1972–1977), *Fat Albert and the Cosby Kids* (1972–1980), *Good Times* (1974–1979), *Grady* (1975–1976), *What's Happening?* (1976–1979), and *That's My Momma* (1974–1975), suggests that there is no need for the redistribution of wealth and power because on TV there is plenty of room for everyone. As Marlin Riggs (1991) notes in his documentary film *Color Adjustment*, in large part these sitcoms cast ghetto life in a happy light where opportunity was simply a question of initiative. He also reveals how *Good Times* showed real potential to take on some of the harsh realities of class exploitation and racism—potential that was quickly extinguished because of the transparent political content of some of the earlier episodes. Furthermore, in the spirit of the American Dream and meritocracy, by the last episode—as with so many of these programs[14]—the family escapes the ghetto and moves into the middle class.

The other storyline running through black sitcoms during this period dealt with this idea of "moving on up." However, these shows did not address economic hardship at all. The best known example is *The Jeffersons* (1975–1985) with the self-made man, George Jefferson. George's hard work and entrepreneurial spirit ensure the success of his dry cleaning business and consequently allow his family to "move on up" to the East Side. As Robin Kelly argues:

> He proves that black people are successful, so therefore the Civil Rights Movement is over. He proves that there is no need for affirmative action because he is a self-made man. He proves that there is no need for welfare because these people can make it on their own.
>
> (interview in *Class Dismissed*, 2005)

This message is clear in the following scene with the Jeffersons' neighbors:

> *Mrs. Willis:* Your family started at zero and look at what you've got now: a son going to college, a lovely wife, a successful business, and a beautiful apartment.
> *Louise (George's wife):* And you did it all by yourself.
> When Mr. Willis (Tom, the white husband) tries to shake George's hand in acknowledgment and celebration of his success, George pushes it away as if to say I do not need your help, or anybody else's for that matter.[15]

The Cosby Show (1984–1992) was also controversial in this respect. While the sitcom provided an important non-stereotypical image of a black family that countered the overwhelmingly pejorative representations that preceded it, the show nonetheless disregarded the harsh realities faced by poor and working-class people of color (Dyson, 1993; Jhally & Lewis, 1992; Riggs, 1991). As Herman Gray argues: "It *[The Cosby Show]* continues to do the general work of affirming the openness of a kind of middle-class society and an arrival of racial difference into that . . ." (interview in *Class Dismissed*, 2005). It is important to note that, while still very popular, the show went off the air the same year as the L.A. uprisings.

This same ideology of openness and arrival is embedded in more recent shows that feature African Americans such as *Martin* (1992–1997), *The Hughleys* (1998–2002),[16] *The Bernie Mac Show* (2001–present), *My Wife and Kids* (2001–2005), *All of Us* (2003–present), and *That's So Raven* (2003–present). While these shows depict the everyday lives of people, they are scripted outside of the reality that 30.4% of black workers and 39.8% of Latino/a workers earn low wages (Economic Policy Institute, 2004/2005). The median income of racially subordinated families is $25,700, as compared with white families—$45,200 (Dollars & Sense & United for a Fair Economy, 2004). The unemployment rate for African Americans and Latino/as over the years has remained more than double that of whites. While about 10% of white children live in poverty in the United States, over 30% of African American and Latino/a kids experience economic hardship. Representations that capture these realities are at best few and far between.

There have been some black working-class characters on situation comedies; for example, the *Fresh Prince of Bel Air* (1990–1996). This character played by actor Will Smith is having some trouble in the ghetto and so he is shipped off to live with his rich relatives in Bel Air—leaving his single mom behind in the hood. In this post-Cosby world, there is no need for government programs to provide social services and economic support because there are wealthy black families that can rescue troubled youths and offer them all of the necessities for social advancement.[17]

There are other shows like *Eastside Westside* (1963), *Frank's Place* (1987–1988), and *Roc* (1991–1994) that have taken up some of the complexities of race and class politics. However, either because of the controversial nature of the material or the fact that networks have done such a poor job of promoting these shows and building audiences for them, they do not last long.

With the exception of a few prominent roles (featuring middle- and upper-middle-class characters) on shows like *ER* (1994–present), *Law & Order: Special Victims Unit* (1999–present), and *Grey's Anatomy* (2005–present), Asian Americans are still largely excluded from prime time or relegated to bit parts (Hamamoto, 1994). In addition, while the growing importance of the Latino demographic has resulted in a small increase in representations, e.g., *The Brothers Garcia* (2000–2004), *Resurrection Blvd.* (2000–2002), and *American Family* (2002–2004), most Latinos are still confined to cable and Spanish-language networks and are overwhelmingly middle class (Davila, 2001; Negrón-Muntaner, 2004; Rodriguez, 1997).[18] The only show to feature a working-class Latino character since *Chico and the Man* (1974–1978) is *The George Lopez Show* (2002–present).[19] However, different from the characters of the ghetto sitcom era who are trying to move out of the working class, George Lopez has already left it behind and moved up to the comfortable familiarity of the middle-class family sitcom.

The George Lopez Show is a perfect example of how the American dream is supposed to work. A former assembly line worker, George is promoted to manager of the factory. Suddenly he has no problems. He lives in a beautiful space. His family has no problems other than what typical American middle-class families supposedly go through. In fact, the only thing that marks him as working class is his mom and his buddies back at the factory who refer to him as "Mr. Clipboard."[20] It is pretty comical that the producers chose to use *Low Rider* as the theme song for the show. While this is a song about urban Latino culture, there is a total disconnect between the song and who this middle-class character is—there is nothing low rider about George Lopez. In fact, if anything, the show eclipses the reality that the overwhelming majority of Latino/as in the United States suffer the abuses of immigration discrimination, labor exploitation, unemployment, and racism.[21]

Women Have Class

While they have never been excluded like other underrepresented groups, television largely ignores the economic realities faced by many women in this country (Bettie, 2003;

Douglas, 1995; Press, 1991). Across the board, women earn less than men regardless of education, and they often work a double shift as part of the paid labor force and as unpaid caretakers of the home and family. On average, women make 77 cents to a man's dollar. The median income for men in the United States is $40,800; for women, it is $31,200. The leading occupations for women are all lower-middle and working-class jobs. In addition, the majority of jobs at the bottom of the economic scale are held by women, especially women of color. In 2003, "33.9% of Black women and 45.8% of Latinas earned low wages" (Economic Policy Institute, 2004/2005, p. 130). Not only does television disregard these realities, it rarely even depicts work as an economic necessity. This is evident in older shows that feature female characters such as *Bewitched* (1964–1972) and *The Brady Bunch* (1969–1974) (where even Alice, the family maid, is happy and carefree),[22] and in more recent programs like *Friends* (1994–2004) and *Sex & the City* (1998–2004).

In the last three decades, the number of households headed by single moms has remained fairly constant, at around 9%. With an average income of only $24,000, single moms experience poverty at a rate that is substantially higher (28%) than the national average (13%) (U.S. Census Bureau, 2003). Single moms, in shows like *Julia* (1968–1971), *The Partridge Family* (1970–1974), *One Day at a Time* (1975–1984), *Murphy Brown* (1988–1998), *Ally McBeal* (1997–2002), *Judging Amy* (1999–2005), *The Parkers* (1999–2004), *The Gilmore Girls* (2000–present), and *Reba* (2001–present) do not reflect the reality of single mothers' lives.[23]

We have only seen a handful of working-class female characters on entertainment television. Most women, even single moms, have been middle-class characters in career jobs where money is not paramount. The few shows that have portrayed women struggling economically don't deal directly with class issues.[24] These are women who are simply down on their luck (e.g., *Alice* (1976–1985)) either because they have lost their husbands or they have made a really bad choice for a husband. A perfect example of this is *Grace under Fire* (1993–1998). She is divorced with two kids. She is a recovering alcoholic. Her ex-husband Jimmy, also an alcoholic, offers the family very little support. While she deals with serious issues, what this show is really about is one woman's determination to not make the same mistakes that she has made in the past. In other words, her obstacles are self-imposed and so it is her responsibility to transcend them. As she tells her children in one episode:

> I really want you to get a fair shake out of life and that's not gonna happen if you take the easy way out. It's a bad habit to get into, because then you will get into some relationship that you don't want, or some job, and the next thing you know you'll be doing the hootchie-coo on top of a Formica table wearin' a bunch of blue eye shadow in front of a bunch of tractor salesmen that don't even tip real good . . .

Really the only show to put gender and class together is *Roseanne* (1988–1997).[25] It aired in the late 1980s at a time when network ratings were down, and ABC was willing to take a chance on it. It is important to note that the decision to air the show was not made in order to democratize the air waves by finally including the realities and struggles of a working-class family. With ratings down, the corporate media were simply desperate for new and attractive ideas. In addition, as Rhoda Zuk (1998) reveals, the production company responsible for putting the program together was able to hire non-union workers for all aspects of the show:

> Such activity gives the lie to an apparently well-meaning production designed to communicate the affective life of a large group materially disadvantaged by the overriding of workers' organization. (p. 3)

Roseanne also appears in the midst of a feminist backlash where the ideology is essentially that women have won equal rights, they have arrived, and they do not need feminism anymore. However, what was really going on at the time was an attack against all working women, who were being blamed for the disruption in the family for going to work.

Regardless of the pressures to tone down the program and her public political persona, Roseanne insisted that her sitcom be a feminist show about a working-class family. As Andrea Press notes:

> *Roseanne* is a show that addresses issues that are basic to feminism: the division of labor in the family, the need for good childcare for women who work, the need for working-class women to work . . . on *Roseanne* you saw an image of a working-class woman who felt she was a great mother. She worked around some of the challenges she faced not having a lot of extra money, not having a lot of extra time, and not really being able to purchase a lot of advantages for her children.
>
> (interview in *Class Dismissed*, 2005)

Barbara Ehrenreich adds: "Now and then it would actually follow Roseanne into her workplace, her confrontations with her bosses; that is a rare event on TV—might give people ideas I guess so they do not show it too often" (interview in *Class Dismissed*, 2005).

Roseanne was also revolutionary in that it did not use the father figure to reinforce the stereotype that working-class men are all a bunch of buffoons (Freed, 2002).[26]

Class Clowns

In order to reinforce its middle-class ideology, television must account for the members of the working class who have not made it. TV reproduces the deeply ingrained belief that workers' inadequacies are to blame for their lack of advancement. In reality, most Americans do not change their class position, and the boundaries of social class are now more restrictive than ever. As Stanley Aronowitz argues:

> For a very long time, I believe ending in the early 1980's or the late 1970's, it was possible for a quarter of the working class to move beyond its class origins to professional and managerial categories. And that developed into both mythology as well as an ideology. The mythology was that everybody in America can gain social mobility. The ideology was that it's a personal question.
>
> (interview in *Class Dismissed*, 2005)

Television representations either perpetuate the idea that the cream always rises to the top, or they reinforce stereotypes about workers' failure to succeed due to their inferior qualities such as bad taste, lack of intelligence, reactionary politics, poor work ethic, and dysfunctional family values (Aronowitz, 1992; Butsch, 2002).[27]

One of the flaws that is supposedly characteristic of the working class that is widely circulated in popular culture, and TV plays an important role in that circulation, pertains to taste, lifestyle, and leisure. A stereotypical image that we get is a bunch of slobs sitting around on some cheesy couch drinking beer, preferably brown bottle or can beer, and staring endlessly at the tube. Given their love of junk culture, we do not get the sense that they are deserving of the finer things in life—they would not appreciate them anyway. This stereotype is exemplified in an episode of *Yes Dear* (2000–present):

Wife: I'm just trying to give your family a little culture [they don't like her gazpacho soup]. Bet if I shoved it in a Hot Pocket and smothered it in Velveeta the four of you would be out back wrestlin' over it.

On entertainment television, we do not get the idea that working-class characters are economically deprived; rather, their low tolerance and limited access to the "virtues of high culture" are attributed to personal taste and choice.

When working-class characters do try to move out of this space and hob-knob with the middle and upper classes, it is made really laughable because they are so awkward in this new environment—they do not have the cultural capital to navigate it. TV plays off of this, in particular sitcoms (e.g., older shows like *Laverne & Shirley* (1976–1983) and more recent programs such as *The Nanny* (1993–1999)). This ridicule is evident in the following scene in *The King of Queens* (1998–present):

> *Well-to-do neighbor:* It's really nice of you to have us over. *Neighbor's husband:* Yeah thanks, this is for you. Scotch, hope you like it. *Doug's wife:* Like it? He loves it! Big scotch guy right here. *Doug (a delivery service driver):* Scotch is great. Love the drink. Love the tape.[28]

One way for the working class to fit into this upper-class world is to get a personal make-over. There are a slew of reality shows that are dedicated to this process.[29] In the opening credits of *I Want to Be a Hilton* (2005), a "poorly dressed" young woman is standing in front of her trailer-like home and says into the camera, "I want to trade in my blue-collar life." This statement is followed by all the contestants on the show proclaiming, "I want to be a Hilton," that is, a member of the wealthy hotel family, as they prepare themselves for the etiquette classes and challenges that the multi-millionaire matriarch will put them through in order to win this status.

Joe Millionaire (2003–2004) is another prime example of this make-over process where members of the working class are equipped with the necessary social skills and etiquette to pass as money.

There are a number of other shows that are about physical transformation and class advancement. The idea that bodily perfection leads to upward mobility is reinforced on shows like *The Swan* (2004) and *Extreme Makeover* (2003–2005), where people even go under the knife in order to change the way they look. This myth is also perpetuated by the slew of talk shows like *Oprah* (1986–present) that dedicate enormous amounts of airtime transforming guests with the help of hair, make-up, and style experts. And not only that, now you can makeover your house on shows like *Trading Spaces* (2000–present) and *Design on a Dime* (2003–2006), as well as your junk box car—on *Pimp My Ride* (2004–present). Then there's *Queer Eye for the Straight Guy* (2003–present) that goes for the whole package—the body and the house.[30]

This ideological thread has been woven into Web TV as well. The new program, *Brawny Academy.com* (2006) is an attempt to clean up sloppy men.[31]

None of these things actually changes a person's class position or the economic conditions that have created their situation in the first place. If you want a real class makeover, you are going to have to radically change the economic system. Now that would make for a really interesting reality show![32]

Another debilitating characteristic of this group of people according to the stereotype is that working-class men lack intelligence. It is obvious they were not good students. They often fumble the language and a lot of basic stuff just goes right over their heads. The classic character of the lovable but laughable buffoon that is still very much with us today is played by Jackie Gleason in *The Honeymooners* (1955–1956) in the character of Ralph Cramden (Aronowitz, 1992; Butsch, 2002). This show was preceded by *Life of Riley* (1945–1950) where Gleason played the bumbling father.[33]

In *The Honeymooners*, Gleason is a city bus driver who hates his job. He is loud and blustery and always coming up with ridiculous money-making schemes; and the real joke is that we know that he is not that smart. He has this sidekick, Ed Norton, who is this dimwitted, but lovable, happy-go-lucky sewer worker. While eating, Ed tells Ralph, "Man: I'm telling you if pizzas were manhole covers, the sewer would be a paradise!"

These class clowns get reproduced in the 1960s with *The Flintstones* (1960–1966). Even though it is set back in the Stone Age, Fred is the direct descendant of Ralph Cramden, and Barney is definitely the son of Ed Norton. And what follows is a whole parade of dumb working-class guys whose stupidity is the brunt of the joke (e.g., *Gittigan's Island* (1964–1967), *Welcome Back Kotter* (1975–1979), *Taxi* (1978–1983), *Working Stiffs* (1979), *Cheers* (1982–1993), *Momma's Family* (1983–1990—which was taken from a skit on *The Carol Burnett Show* (1967–1978)), *Married with Children* (1987–1997), *The Simpsons* (1989–present), *Dinosaurs* (1991–1994), *The Drew Carey Show* (1995–2004), *King of the Hill* (1997–present), *The King of Queens* (1998–present), *My Name Is Earl* (2005–present), and *Lucky Louie* (2006–present)).[34]

The Honeymooners is also an important prototype for a particular gender dynamic. Because these husbands are so lacking in common sense, and the wives are obviously smarter, it is the women who end up ruling the roost (Butsch, 2002; Riggs, 1991). As Ralph's wife Alice demands:

Now you listen to me Ralph. You are not going bowling!
Ralph: I gotta go Alice, I promised the guys!
Alice: The guys? What about me Ralph? What about your job? What about our future?

What we end up with is a reversal of traditional gender roles where these caricatures of men are essentially incapable of taking their place at the head of the household. Take, for example, this scene in the more recent show *Rodney* (2004–present):

Rodney: I just gambled away my paycheck, that's all.
Rodney's wife Trina: You lost that too? Rodney, we don't have money to gamble!
Rodney: I know, that's why I was trying to get it back.
Trina: Rodney, we agreed that you were going to use that paycheck to pay off our property taxes.
Rodney: Trina, I have a problem.
Trina: You don't have a problem! I do, I'm married to an idiot!

It is not just the wives. In a typical working-class household, even the kids are smarter than the dad. This is really evident in shows like *The Simpsons* (1989–present), in the father–son relationship in *Married with Children* (1987–1997), and in *Still Standing* (2002–present).

The working class is being blamed for not being educated enough to compete in a global economy, and yet we have one of the most educated workforces in the world regardless of the fact that our public education system is highly class based. It is also ironic that given this claim of lack of education, corporations are moving to "Third-World" countries, where there is enormous illiteracy in order to find "cheap" labor.

On corporate-run TV, there is a recurring representation that the working class has no interest in education as they wallow in anti-intellectualism. They have no interest in reading, unless it is the sports page, the comics, or a tabloid of some sort. Aronowitz asks:

> Why do we get this image of the anti-intellectual and the stupid worker even though workers historically were the reasons we have public education because their organizations among others were people who fought for the public education system . . . and that working-class kids now go to community colleges and four-year colleges in record numbers . . .
>
> (interview in *Class Dismissed*, 2005)

There is a reason for these stereotypes: They distract us from the structural realities, especially the unequal distribution of resources in public education, that inhibit people's lives. However, what is worse is they disregard the fact that the overwhelming majority of working-class parents really do care about their kids' education.

The working class is also represented as being uninterested in politics, which is ridiculous if you think about working-class history and the struggle for basic rights and a living wage. This supposed apathy is embodied in a classic scene on *Cheers* (1982–1993) where Norm and Cliff bump into Senator John Kerry in front of the bar. Kerry is talking to a gentleman in a trench coat. The man (a typical character that one would find in the wealthy Back Bay area of Boston) walks off after Kerry gives him the thumbs up as a sign that the two men had understood and agreed with one another:

Norm (excited): Oooh, Oooh, look at that. Look what we got here.
Cliff: What?
Norm: Look!
Cliff: Oooh, it's the film critic . . . Channel 11.
Norm: It's the anchorman . . . Channel 8. (Both are excited.)
Norm: You wanna get an autograph?
Cliff: Yeah, yeah!
Norm (to Kerry): Excuse me . . .
Kerry: Hi Guys, how ya doing, how are you?
Cliff (nervous): We're really big fans of yours (he fumbles the language a bit), can we have . . . can we get your autograph?
Kerry: Yeah, sure . . . Ah, here, let me get something to write on. (Cliff and Norm both search for a pen in their pockets—of course only as a gesture as they both know that they don't have a writing utensil on them; a sign of their lack of professionalism.)
Cliff: You know, I love that . . . that report you did on that train wreck. Ya know, they oughta get you at 60 *minutes* as an anchor.
Norm: Pulitzer Prize.
Kerry: No, I'm John Kerry, Senator Kerry from Massachusetts.
Norm: Oh, our senator, I'm sorry man, so sorry.
Both: Sorry to bother you pal (they both walk away and head down the bar entrance stairs; Kerry puts his hands in the air as if to say, what was that all about).
Cliff (on the way down the stairs): Hey wait, hold on. Maybe he knows Senator Gopher from *The Love Boat*.
Norm (both men running back up the stairs to catch up with Kerry): Hey, yo!

When we do get characters that are interested in politics, they are almost always staunch conservatives, bigots, and closed-minded. The archetypal figure here is Archie Bunker from *All in the Family* (1971–1979). As Ehrenreich states:

> So, while we laughed, it also made me very uncomfortable because Archie Bunker was a stand in for so many blue-collar guys. But the upper-middle class and the upper classes have always liked to believe they are the enlightened ones and it's the working class that is full of these bozos.
>
> (interview in *Class Dismissed*, 2005)

Perhaps the most blatant representational crime against the working class by the corporate media is this image of this lazy incompetent worker who is complacent and not interested in improving his or her lot in life. In *Still Standing* (2002–present), Bill, a toilet salesman, is talking with his wife's sister's date:

Date: Actually, I'm a psychologist. If I wanted to be a psychiatrist, I'd have to go through medical school and residency and all that.

Bill: Yeah, I know how you feel, buddy. I was going to take the management course at work, but it was like three Saturdays.

These characters have no leadership skills, and they are in constant need of supervision. As we see on *King of the Hill* (1997–present), when Hank is showing a wealthy investor around town and the two come across a construction site where the workers are on break:

Potential customer: Something's wrong.

Hank: Yeah it's the dam unions. Come on boys, finish up them Little Debbies and get back to work!

In this era of globalization with enormous job loss, outsourcing and off-shoring, corporations need a scapegoat for their avarice activity and the scapegoat is the working class whose members are not working hard enough, and yet, since 1975, productivity is way up (163%). Furthermore, they are supposedly asking for too much money, and yet wages are stagnant (115%), and profits are through the roof (758%).

When it comes to family values, in the late 1980s and early 1990s there is a dramatic shift away from the omnipresent image of the happy homogeneous nuclear family. This era that is often referred to as "Loser TV" gave birth to shows like *Married with Children*, *The Simpsons*, *Jerry Springer* (1991–present), and *Beavis and Butthead* (1993–1997). These shows appear at the tail end of eight years of Ronald Reagan, when the country was going through some serious economic turmoil. However, instead of looking at downsizing, lay-offs, unemployment, and corporate greed, these working-class couples are seen as the poster child of bad parenting, and hence the source of all of society's ills. They certainly lack the wisdom, discipline, and morality of the middle-class parents of other shows.[35]

These families give rise to a couple of different kinds of children; either they are smart and talented, which reinforces the myth of meritocracy—these kids are going to make it out regardless of the circumstances; or they are deviant in a number of ways—the Bart Simpson type.[36]

The two biggest troublemakers are definitely Beavis and Butthead. These guys celebrate stupidity, and they live for sex and violence. The show plays on a generation of youths raised on a media saturated society of junk culture, commodity, and alienation where the parents are driven out of the home and into the labor force and where the TV becomes the babysitter and the role model (Kellner, 1997). As Doug Kellner notes, there surely is an element of working-class revenge for these two guys who come from broken homes in a disintegrating community where school and work in the fast-food industry are meaningless, and where they are downwardly mobile with a bleak future, if any. Shows like *The Simpsons* and *Beavis and Butthead* do offer a critique of our corporate-driven society. These characters know that something is wrong. However, the problem is that their actions are just individualized acts of rebellion—their response is to trash stuff. As a consequence, such behavior ends up being self-destructive rather than transformative.

No Class

Outside of the comic frame, there is a different and more threatening image of the working class on crime shows. Because this genre does not use class as a lens to view criminal behavior, deviance is most often framed in racial or cultural terms. As Kelly notes:

> Something happens in the 70s and 80s where all these cop shows really put a lot of emphasis on working in ghetto communities. They are the most dangerous places to work. And it coincides again, with this image that the black poor, or black criminal behavior, is a result of a lack of guidance, the lack of strong father figures, a matriarchy that explains criminal violence because these mothers are not able to control their youth; and in a criminal culture, it also reinforces, I think, white, and black fears in some ways, that youth, particularly young males in inner-city communities, are dangerous. They are all suspect. They deserve to go to jail.
> (interview in *Class Dismissed*, 2005)[37]

The more recent incarnation of such shows, e.g., *Cops* (1989–present), *Homicide: Life on the Street* (1993–1999), *NYPD Blue* (1993–2005), *Oz* (1997–2003), *The Shield* (2002–present), and *Dog the Bounty Hunter* (2004–present) continue to do important ideological work. They justify the growing prison population with a record 2.1 million people behind bars—over 70% of whom are non-white. African American males make up the largest number of those entering prisons each year in the United States. Racially subordinated women are also being incarcerated in epidemic proportions. As Loic Wacquant (2002) states, "The astounding upsurge in Black incarceration in the past three decades results from the obsolescence of the ghetto as a device for caste control and the correlative need for a substitute apparatus for keeping (unskilled) African Americans in a subordinate and confined position—physically, socially, and symbolically" (p. 23).

Addressing the links between the racialization and criminalization of people and television's role in this pedagogical process, Herman Gray notes:

> Even the attempts to mediate it by having black authority figures like black lieutenants and black judges [on TV shows] doesn't necessarily change the logic by which these two forms of meaning come together; that is to say, blackness and criminality.
> (interview in *Class Dismissed*, 2005)[38]

Of course, these images are scripted outside of any analysis of racism and the poverty caused by capitalism.

Thirty-seven million people in this country live in poverty, a number that is up 1.1 million from 2003. According to the U.S. Department of Agriculture, there are 25.5 million people who rely on food stamps to avoid hunger—a number that is up 2 million from 2004. In other words, 6.8 million families live in poverty, and 17% of the nation's children, or about 12 million kids, are compelled to endure inhumane economic conditions. An Urban Institute study has revealed that about 3.5 million people are homeless in the U.S. [a number projected to increase 5% each year], and 1.3 million (or 39%) of them are children (National Coalition for the Homeless, 2002).

The largest group of poor people in the United States is white. However, we have a very limited understanding of who they are because their images historically have been so few and far between. Because whiteness is associated with a dominant culture, poor and working-class whites are usually portrayed as cultural outcasts or a subculture. While TV mocks their condition, it gladly uses their image to entertain us.

The rural working class is nearly invisible in mainstream culture. What we find on television are these twisted comedic images, which, like the ghetto sitcoms, really pastoralize poverty. The earlier images were of hillbilly characters popularized on shows like *Ma & Pa Kettle* (1954) and *The Real McCoys* (1951–1963). These are followed by the "idiot sitcom era," with country bumpkin shows like *The Beverly Hillbillies* (1962–1971), *Andy Griffith* (1961–1968), *Gorner Pyle* (1964–1970), *Green Acres* (1965–1971), and *Petticoat Junction* (1963–1970), which featured characters who were simple-minded, non-threatening, and really easy to laugh at. These shows would be followed by *Hee-Haw* (1969–1993), *The Dukes of Hazard* (1979–1985), *Newhart* (1982–1990), *Enos* (1980–1981), and *The Dukes* (1983–1984).[39]

The person who has resurrected the hillbilly and given it new life as "redneck pride" is Jeff Foxworthy. From comedy tours to films to a cable show, *Blue Collar TV* (2004–present), being a redneck seems like a lifestyle which includes NASCAR and country music. More specifically, Foxworthy has taken what in reality is an economic position and made it look like a lifestyle choice.

> *Foxworthy on comedy tour:* Sophisticated people invest their money in stock portfolios. Rednecks invest our money in commemorative plates. Yeah, that's the legends of NASCAR series right there . . .

Co-opting redneck pride is also a way that the Republican party has tried to brand itself as a friend of working people and to develop its political clout in the so-called red states.

> *George W. Bush (describing NASCAR while at the race):* This is more than an event, it's a way of life for a lot of people.
> *Female organizer for the Republican party at NASCAR:* This is the first time that we have done this. We recognize that this is a happy hunting ground for new Republican voters.

The hypocrisy and deceit here are difficult to swallow—not that the Democrats have done much for the working class lately, but the Republican agenda has always been a war against the working class, working poor, and unemployed.

As the effects of the economic downturn become more visible, so is this more threatening image of the white poor who are being popularized as white trash. All these types, the hillbilly, the redneck, and white trash are racially coded terms to describe a genetic subset of white people—lowlifes. So Jerry Springer, who introduces his show with a television in the trashcan, is where all the qualities associated with white trash are on display: a lack of desire to work, sexual perversion, incest, and so on. In a similar spirit, *Geraldo* (1987–1998—hosted by Geraldo Rivera), created a perverse spectacle that was described by *Newsweek* as "trash TV." It is interesting because this is a multiracial world—it is a sort of equal opportunity spectacle. The common link that brings them all together is social class. As Lisa Henderson argues:

> I think that it's important to recognize that all those so-called practices, airing dirty laundry, fighting, cheating, are things that middle-class people do too, but when they do them, they are screwed up; when working-class people do them, especially on television, well, that's just the way they are, they're trash.
>
> (interview in *Class Dismissed*, 2005)

While presented with a touch of seriousness and professionalism, there is a similar entertainment strategy used on talk shows such as *Sally Jesse Raphael* (1985–2002), *Montel Williams* (1991–present), *Jenny Jones* (1991–2003), *Ricki Lake* (1993–2004), and *The Maury Povich Show* (1998–present). They often have programs about working-class children who are out of control. A popular response is to send these deviant youths to military boot camp or prison and televise the spectacle.

Courtroom series also play a role in reproducing the image of working-class cheats and buffoons, e.g., *Judge Judy* (1996–present) and *Judge Joe Brown* (1998–present).

Class Action: Media Literacy for the Twenty-First Century

While television has long used the image of the working class to entertain us, current labor conditions are no laughing matter. Today's workers face a declining standard of living and the loss of job security. They also risk falling victim to corporate greed and malfeasance such as the recent atrocities of Enron, Tyco, Wal-Mart, Worldcom, or any of the other over 20,000 acts of corporate lawbreaking that are documented annually. The working class is also experiencing a concerted effort to dismantle the democratizing force of organized labor. While workers in unions earn 30% more than non-union people doing the same job and get far more guaranteed benefits such as a pension and healthcare, the Republican assault on organized labor has been devastating. By 2002, only 13.2% of wage and salary workers were union members—a number that is getting smaller every year (Bureau of Labor Statistics, 2003). Regardless of the federal law (Section 7 of the National Labor Relations Act) that states that

> Employees shall have the right to self organization, to form, join or assist labor organizations, to bargain collectively through representatives of their own choosing and to engage in other concerted activities for the purpose of collective bargaining or other mutual aid or protection . . .

the harsh reality is that those who try to organize often face serious repercussions. Human Rights Watch has recorded that ten to twenty thousand people a year are fired or punished for trying to unionize. Low-wage earners in particular face an atmosphere of intimidation and as a result many, desperate for work, steer clear of union activity.

Regardless of the neoliberal promise of prosperity for all, it is more than obvious that the structural dimensions of social class within this economic logic remain profoundly in place. In fact, economic conditions for millions of people in the United States and for billions of people worldwide are worsening as a direct result of privatization, deregulation, and restructuring; as well as by the ways in which elite private powers have been successful in using the State to protect corporate interests and dismantle many of the rights and protections achieved locally and internationally by grassroots activists, organized labor, and social democracies.

Corporate media's narrow, unrealistic images conceal the extent of this assault on

America's workforce, so we can no longer afford to ignore TV's framing of the working class or see it as just entertainment.[40]

The media reform movement has already begun to educate the general population about the political economy of the mass media—that is, ownership and regulation of this industry—and challenge the FCC and Congress to democratize the airwaves and new technologies and to diversify representations that reflect both the new realities of work and the changing face of the working class in the United States.

A key component of any activist effort should be to encourage the widespread development of critical media literacy, that is, the ability to read the values and beliefs embedded in the knowledge that is circulated throughout society so as to be able to defend ourselves from propaganda and participate in its eradication.

A critical model of media literacy is primarily concerned with the kinds of theories and practices that encourage people to develop an understanding of the interconnecting relationships among ideology, power, meaning, and identity that constitute *culture*. Literacy of this sort entails understanding culture as a pedagogical force in which the multiplicity of aural and visual signifying systems that people are inundated with every day, through language, TV, advertising, radio, print journalism, music, film, and so on, are ideological and formative, rather than merely vehicles for expression or reflections of reality. They are the conduits through which values and beliefs that work to shape how people see, interpret, and act as socialized and political beings are promoted.

Critical media literacy encourages us to not only think about culture politically, but also to think about politics culturally. Political consciousness and action do not take place in a vacuum. As argued in the introduction of this chapter, oppression not only consists of a structural reality built on political and economic processes and relationships, it also relies on symbolic systems to shape the kinds of meaning, identity, desire, and subjectivity that can work to ensure the maintenance of what Antonio Gramsci referred to throughout his work as the hegemony of "common sense."

The ability to demystify social reality requires both theory and action. *Theory* in this sense is how people interpret, critique, and draw generalizations about *why* the social world spins the economic, cultural, political, and institutional webs that it does. From this working definition, theory is the ability to make sense of all levels of the everyday—that is, the *why* and *how* of what has been happening in people's lives, and not simply a focus on *what* is occurring and how to effectively respond. As an integral part of any political project, theorizing also presents a constant challenge to imagine and materialize alternative political spaces and identities and more just and equitable economic, social, and cultural relations. It makes possible consciousness raising, coalition building, resistance, activism, and structural change.

In such undemocratic times, it is not surprising that critical media literacy is often discouraged. As people, especially students, are distracted or lured away from critically reading historical and existing social formations, in particular those that maintain abuses of power, they often become the newest wave of exploited labor power and reproducers, whether they are conscious of it or not, of oppressive social practices.

On the contrary, critical media literacy is rooted in a democratic project that emphasizes new theories and languages of critique, resistance, and possibility capable of engaging the oppressive social practices that maintain the de facto social code in the United States. These new theories and languages provide the necessary analytic stepping stones for realizing a truly democratic process through which we can better identify the sociopolitical realities that shape our lives and where necessary, transform our practices.

As argued throughout this chapter, any such movement to raise consciousness and democratize economic, social, and technological relations has to reflect the diverse interests and experiences of the working class. In this battle for economic justice and racial and social equality, TV, regardless of its sordid past, can play an important role.

Notes

1. Anti-colonial activists have long recognized how material conditions, politics, and culture are interlaced and how subordination, resistance, and opposition take place in both the physical and symbolic realm.

2. It is also important to look at how the news media and Hollywood frame the working class. For information about how labor is depicted in the news media, see Puette, William (1992). *Through Jaundiced Eyes: How the Media View Organised Labor*, Ithaca, NY: Cornell University Press; Buckingham, David (2000). *The Making of Citizens: Young People, News and Politics*. New York: Routledge; and Martin, Christopher (2004). *Framed: Labor and the Corporate Media*. Ithaca, NY: Cornell University Press. For an analysis of Hollywood films and their depiction of the working class, see Booker, Keith (1999). *Film and the American Left: A Research Guide*. Westport, CT: Greenwood Press; Buhle, Paul & Wagner, Dave (2002). *Radical Hollywood*. New York: The New Press; Ross, Steven (1998). *Working-Class Hollywood*. Princeton, NJ: Princeton University Press; and Horne, Gerald (2001). *Class Struggles in Hollywood: 1930–1950*. Austin: University of Texas Press.

3. This process is far more complicated than simply a bunch of media moguls and corporate heads sitting around making these decisions together—which needless to say, does happen. Someone like Rupert Murdoch is very clear about his political agenda, and that agenda is evident in the representations circulated by FOX. The same goes for the rest of the so-called liberal media, which in reality are also in favor of monopolizing the airwaves and circulating corporate logic (Herman & Chomsky, 2002). This is no conspiracy. These people are simply protecting their own best interests. At the same time, while major decisions are made by bigger power brokers, writers and producers do not really need big brother around to monitor their work. In most cases, they have been properly educated so as to know what is appropriate and what is not. At the same time, writers and producers may not be conscious of the fact that they are reproducing oppressive ideologies. They too are the product of representation, and their sense of humor, for example, is constructed within accepted discourses and circulated through society's institutions—they have already been called into that ideological space and thus know what will make people laugh or cry. In the end, whether they are conscious of it or not, they play a central role in reproducing discriminatory images and social practices.

4. It is important to note that the use of class stratification here is referring to standard of living and not to class as a category of power.

5. 45.8 million Americans lack health insurance, which includes 9.2 million kids. "Overall, nearly 1 in 5 full-time workers today goes without health insurance; among part-time workers, it is 4 to 1" (Krim & Witte, 2004, p. A01). As compared with 2001, there were 5 million fewer jobs providing health insurance in 2004. These statistics are particularly interesting given that "the average compensation for the top health care executives at the top 10 managed healthcare companies, not including unexercised stock options, is $11.7 million per year" (Jackson, 2001, p. 3).

6. It is important to note that the Census also bypasses the long-term unemployed and the homeless.

7. Of course Republicans are working to do away with the capital gains tax so as to reap the full benefits of their stock portfolios and other investments.

8. The super rich are made virtually invisible—other than showing off their lavish lifestyles on entertainment television or their wealth and power in the Forbes report. As Michael Parenti (2000) points out, 1% of the population goes undocumented in income distribution reports because U.S. Census Bureau surveys are not distributed to the wealthiest of Americans such as Bill Gates who is worth $53 billion, or Warren Buffett who has accumulated a cool $46 billion.

9. The best way to attain upward mobility is the old fashioned way—to inherit it. Republicans are working diligently to do away with inheritance taxes, or what they strategically refer to as "death taxes." Countering this strategic use of language, many people trying to keep the laws in place refer to this tax as the "Paris Hilton tax."

10. While it wasn't a regularly scheduled program, *Many* (1953), the story of the everyday life of a butcher living in an urban environment provided an interesting image of the working class.

11. While racism can't simply be conflated with the economic base of capitalism, we certainly need to look at the ways in which it is used to exploit diverse groups within capitalist social relations. It is also crucial to look at the ways in which historically racism, and sexism for that matter, has served an important role in keeping at bay working-class unity and maintaining a system of labor exploitation.

12. A classic example of this is the character "Rochester" on *The Jack Benny Program* (1951–1965). It is important to note that *The Nat "King" Cole Show* ran up against racist sponsors, which ultimately led to its premature death.

13. This can be seen in shows like *Julia* (1968–1971) and *I Spy* (1965–1968) which featured a young Bill Cosby.

14. Fred and Lionel get out of the ghetto and move to Arizona, and in 1977 a spin off of *Sanford and Son* is released—*The Sanford Arms*. The storyline is about turning the old rooming house into a successful hotel. Archie Bunker also makes it out of his working-class neighborhood and opens a bar. The featured characters on *What's Happening* either escape the ghetto or enter the middle-class therein.

15. Kelly adds: "Another example of 'moving on up' suggests that what black youths need are white people to come in and step in with superior parenting skills and resources to basically bring them out of the ghetto. *Diff'rent Strokes* [1976–1986] is a classic example." He also uses the show *The White Shadow* (1978–1981) to illustrate this point.

16. As in the typical format, the family moves from the inner city to the suburbs.

17. *704 Hawser Street* (1994) is a show with African American, working-class characters. They live in Archie Bunker's old house in Queens, NY. While the two parents are portrayed as "typical working-class, blue collar liberals," their son is very conservative and fancies a Jewish girl from the neighborhood. While this may be Norman Lear's attempt to make up for pigeon-holing the working class through the earlier depiction of Archie Bunker as a working-class yahoo, the show only lasted for six episodes. In 1996, Bill Cosby initiated and co-produced the show *Cosby*. The short-lived sitcom was based on a retired old man who loses his job and searches for another. Most of the episodes are preoccupied with this character driving his wife crazy. What is interesting is that the show was based on the English program *One Foot in the Grave* (1990–2001), which entertained some serious political criticism. On the contrary, Cosby lightened the humor and thus the content of his version. *The PJs* (1999–2001), an animated show created by actor Eddie Murphy, offered insight into life in a housing project and the chief superintendent, but is was more about comical adventures than any explicit critique of the formation of such projects. *The Tracy Morgan Show* (2003) is built around the life of an African American family in a tiny Brooklyn apartment, and while Tracy struggles working as an auto mechanic, the show, in its short life, was preoccupied with trying to fulfill his dream of expanding his business. *Everybody Hates Chris* (2005–present) is set in Brooklyn, New York during the early 1980s. Chris is sent to a primarily white middle school, and so while it has the potential to reveal some of the realities of that world, it is more about coming of age.

18. Latino/a characters have appeared on shows like *Norm* (1999–2001), *Walker, Texas Ranger* (1993–2001), (1999–2001), *Gideon's Crossing* (2000–2001), *Third Watch* (1999–2005), *Nash Bridges* (1996–2001), *That 70s Show* (1998–2006); and Latino/a characters have appeared in secondary roles on such shows as *ER* (1994–present) *Jag* (1995–2001), *Felicity* (1998–2002), and *Family Law* (1999–2002).

19. The show *CHIPS* (1977–1983) did feature Erik Estrada as officer Frank "Ponch" Poncherello.

20. In this racialized space, his father is missing and is assumed to have abandoned the family.

21. There are no programs that take up the conditions of persons with disabilities. Disability is also a class issue in that two-thirds of people with disabilities are unemployed. The material conditions of the elderly are also neglected by the corporate media. When they are included it is in drug commercials, retirement success stories on advertisements, or on shows where money is not an issue, such as *The Golden Girls* (1985–1992).

22. All of the maids/housekeepers/butlers/servants on TV are depicted as complacent, without serious worries, and often empowered to question the boss; e.g., *Beulah, Hazel* (1961–1966), Mr. French on *A Family Affair* (1966–1971), Florence on the *The Jeffersons*, Bentley, Florida on *Maude*, Geoffrey on *The Fresh Prince of Bel Air*, Paul Hogan on *Joe Millionaire*. There are no scenes of them scrubbing toilets and taking abuse.

23. While beyond the scope of this chapter, it is important to take up the stereotype of working-class women as trashy and slutty, especially "fake blonds." It would then be interesting to analyze *The Anna Nicole Smith Show* (2002–2003), as we have the movement of a woman from Texas, where she was abandoned by her father and raised by her mother and aunt, to exotic dancer, to billionaire, to see what she brings to that new class status. The opposite is also true in *The Simple Life* (2002–2003) with Paris Hilton, which mocks everyone.

24. The cartoon *As Told by Ginger* (2000–2004) offered an interesting perspective of a working-class girl living with her single mom. Ginger's mom is a nurse who is on strike and works for her own cleaning business. While the show is by no means radical, it does move a bit beyond the typical TV content.

25. The show *Maude* (1972–1978) did provide a good deal of feminist critique, but it was coming from an upper-middle-class white woman, who had a housekeeper.

26. While *Roseanne* was a breath of fresh air, the show was more about working-class moms getting the recognition that they deserve than what would need to change in order to democratize wealth and power in this country. When I asked Ehrenreich about this critique of the show, she responded with a giggle, "These are capitalist media, they're supported by sponsors . . . You're gonna have to make those shows if that's what you want."

27. Advertising also relies on these stereotypes. The strategy is to use humor to create fear by showing the audience what they should avoid.

28. It is interesting how these shows often assume class integration in neighborhoods, and unlike the rather bleak household settings depicted in some of the earlier shows, today's working-class families usually live in very comfortable homes that are equipped with all the modern amenities associated with the good life.

29. The reality show *Survivor* (2000–present) drew a great deal of attention because of Susan Hawk, a Midwestern truck driver whose accent and etiquette epitomized the stereotype of the tacky abrasive working-class character.

30. Since the early 1990s, television has cautiously opened the door to a few gay and lesbian characters, e.g., *The Real World* (1992–present), *Ellen* (1994–1998), and her newest talk show (2003), *ER* (1994–present), *Spin City* (1996–2002), *The View* (1997–present), *Will & Grace* (1998–2006), *Queer as Folk* (2000–2005), *Survivor* (2000–present), *Six Feet Under* (2001–2005), *The Amazing Race* (2001–present), *The L-Word* (2004–present), and in many soap operas. Queer visibility on prime time as with other marginalized groups is due in part to changing social conditions and also with the networks' need to spice up existing repertoires with small variations, but at the exclusion of working-class, gender variant, and other non-conforming individuals.

31. Reality shows like *Wife Swap* (2004–present) also play this role.

32. While reality shows such as *American Chopper* (2003–present), *Dirty Jobs* (2003–present), *Deadliest Catch* (2005–present), and *Miami Ink* (2005–present) don't provide any substantive critique of society, they do offer an interesting view into the lives of a diversity of working-class people.

33. An interesting show that needs further attention when it comes to these representations is *The Three Stooges* (1930–2006).

34. Comedy shows like *Saturday Night Live* (1975–present), *In Living Color* (1990–1994), and *Mad TV* (1995) all have characters and skits that mock the working class. While they also poke fun at the rich, the impact is surely not the same.

35. One of the most fascinating examples of shows that romanticize the virtues of family even in the worst of conditions is *The Waltons* (1972–1981). Taking place during the Depression, the family survives the hard times because of the caring and dedication of the entire family. In the mythology, this is what pulled the country out of trouble, not F.D.R.'s socialist response in the form of the New Deal, or the economic revitalization caused by the war.

36. While the shows *Nanny 911* (2004–present) and *The Super Nanny* (2005–present) help fix families from most diverse backgrounds, the majority of the troubled families screaming for help are working class.

37. The crime shows of the 1970s and 1980s include: *Streets of San Francisco* (1972–1977), *The Rookies* (1972–1976), *Kojak* (1973–1978), *Police Woman* (1974–1978), *Starsky & Hutch* (1975–1979), *Baretta* (1975–1978), *S.W.A.T.* (1975–1976), *Hunter* (1984–1991), *Hill Street Blues* (1981–1987), *Miami Vice* (1984–1991), and *21 Jump Street* (1987–1991).

38. *Law and Order* (1990–present) occasionally provides some interesting political commentary about race, class, and gender discrimination, as do the shows *Cold Case* (2003–present) and *CSI* (2000–present), *CSI Miami*, 2002–present).

39. For a long time now, cartoons such as *Deputy Dog* (1959–1972) have often played off of this country-bumpkin stereotype.

40. While this chapter and research are not about audience reception, that is, how people interpret these messages, we would argue that workers themselves often internalize this stigma. They may see themselves as working men and women, working families, but they reject the label working class. As a result they do not have a sense of class solidarity or class-consciousness.

References

Allan, Robert & Hill, Annette (Eds.) (2004). *The Television Studies Reader*. New York: Routledge.

Aronowitz, Stanley (1992). "Working-Class Culture in the Electronic Age." In: *The Politics of Identity: Class, Culture, Social Movements*. New York: Routledge.

Barnouw, Erik (1978). *The Sponsor: Notes on a Modern Potentate*. New York: Oxford University Press.

Bettie, Julie (2003). *Women without Class: Girls, Race, and Identity*. Berkeley: University of California Press.

Bourdieu, Pierre (1996). *On Television*. New York: The New Press.

Butsch, Richard (2002). "Ralph, Fred, Archie and Homer: Why Television Keeps Recreating the White Male Working-Class Buffoon." In *Gender, Race and Class in Media*. (Eds.) Gail Dines and Jean Humez. Thousand Oaks, CA: Sage.

Carey, Alex (1995). *Taking the Risk out of Democracy: Corporate Propaganda Versus Freedom and Liberty*. Chicago: University of Illinois Press.

Class Dismissed: How TV Frames the Working Class (2005). A project by Pepi Leistyna, narrated by Ed Asner, co-written and produced with Loretta Alper, executive producer Sut Jhally, directed by Loretta Alper. Northampton, MA: Media Education Foundation. (All of the interview references are from this source.)

Collins, Chuck, Hartman, Chris & Sklar, Holly (1999). "Divided Decade: Economic Disparity at the Century's Turn." United for a Fair Economy. Available at: www.ufenet.org/press/archive/1999/ Divided_Decade/divided_decade. html

Davila, Arlene (2001). *Latinos Inc.: The Marketing and Making of a People*. Berkeley, CA: University of California Press.

Dollars & Sense and United for a Fair Economy (Eds.) (2004). *The Wealth Inequality Reader*. Cambridge, MA: Economic Affairs Bureau.

Douglas, Susan (1995). *Where the Girls Are: Growing Up Female with the Mass Media*. New York: Three Rivers Press.

Durham, Meenakshi Gigi & Kellner, Douglas (2001). *Media and Cultural Studies: Key Works*. Maiden, MA: Blackwell.

Dyson, Michael Eric (1993). *Reflecting Black: African-American Cultural Criticism*. Minneapolis: University of Minnesota Press.

Economic Policy Institute (2004/2005). *The State of Working America*. Ithaca, NY: ILR Press.

Forbes (2006). "The 400 Richest Americans." Available at: http://www.forbes.com/lists/

Freed, Rosanna (2002). "The Gripes of Wrath: Roseanne's Bitter Comedy of Class." *Television Quarterly*. Available at: www.emmyonline.org/tvq/articles/30–2-l5.asp

Gray, Herman (1995). *Watching Race: Television and the Struggle for "Blackness."* Minneapolis: University of Minnesota Press.

Hall, Stuart (Ed.) (1997). *Representation: Cultural Representations and Signifying Practices*. London: Sage.

Hamamoto, Darrell (1994). *Monitored Peril: Asian Americans and the Politics of TV Representation*. Minneapolis: University of Minnesota Press.

Herman, Edward & Chomsky, Noam (2002). *Manufacturing Consent: The Political Economy of the Mass Media*. New York: Pantheon.

Ivins, Molly (2005). "April 15th: You're Getting Screwed." AlterNet. Available at: http://www.alternet.org/ story/21760

Jackson, Derrick (2001). "Who's Better Off This Labor Day? Numbers Tell." Available at: www.raisethefloor.org/ press_bostonglobe.html.

Jhally, Sut & Lewis, Justin (1992). *Enlightened Racism: The Cosby Show, Audiences, and the Myth of the American Dream*. Boulder, CO: Westview.

Kellner, Douglas (1997). "Beavis and Butt-Head: No Future for Postmodern Youth." In: *Kinder-Culture: The Corporate Construction of Childhood*. (Eds.) Steinberg, Shirley & Joe Kincheloe. Boulder, CO: Westview.

Krim, J. & Witte, G. (2004, December 31). "Average Wage Earners Fall Behind: New Job Market Makes More Demands but Fewer Promises." Washington Post, p. A01.

Lipsitz, George (2002). "The Meaning of Memory: Family, Class and Ethnicity in Early Network Television." In: *Gender, Race and Class in Media* (Eds.) Gail Dines & Jean Humez. Thousand Oaks, CA: Sage.

McChesney, Robert (2004). *The Problem of the Media: U.S. Communication Politics in the Twenty-First Century*. New York: Monthly Review Press.

Meiksins Wood, Ellen (1995) *Democracy against Capitalism: Renewing Historical Materialism*. Cambridge: Cambridge University Press.

National Coalition for the Homeless (1999). Available at: www.nationalhomeless.org/jobs.html

National Coalition for the Homeless (2002). Available at: www.nationalhomeless.org/who.html

National Labor Committee for Worker and Human Rights (2003). Available at: www.nlcnet.org

Negrón-Muntaner, Frances (2004). *Boricua Pop: Puerto Ricans and the Latinization of American Culture*. New York: New York University Press.

Parenti, Michael (1992). *Make-Believe Media: The Politics of Entertainment*. Belmont, CA: Wadsworth.

Parenti, Michael (2000). "The Super Rich Are out of Sight." Available at: www.michaelparenti.org/ Superrich.html

Press, Andrea (1991). *Women Watching Television: Gender, Class, and Generation in the American Television Experience*. Philadelphia: University of Pennsylvania Press.

Riggs, Marlon (1991). *Color Adjustment*. San Francisco: California Newsreel.

Rodriguez, Carla (Ed.) (1997). *Latin Looks: Images of Latinas and Latinos in the US. Media*. Boulder, CO: Westview.

Sklar, Holly (2003). "CEO Pay Still Outrageous." Available at: www.raisethefloor.org/press_ceo_oped.html

U.S. Census Bureau (2003, September 15). "Poverty in the United States: 2003." Report.

Wacquant, Loic (2002). "Deadly Symbiosis: Rethinking Race and Imprisonment in Twenty-First-Century America." *Boston Review: A Political and Literary Forum*. 27(2) (April/May): 23–31.

Zuk, Rhoda (1998). "Entertaining Feminism: *Roseanne* and Roseanne Arnold." *Studies in Popular Culture*. Available at: http://pcasacas.Org/SPC/spcissues/21.l/kuk.htm

27

Towards Ecopedagogy: Weaving a Broad-based Pedagogy of Liberation for Animals, Nature, and the Oppressed People of the Earth

Richard Kahn

> It is urgent that we assume the duty of fighting for the fundamental ethical principles, like respect for the life of human beings, the life of other animals, the life of birds, the life of rivers and forests. I do not believe in love between men and women, between human beings, if we are not able to love the world. Ecology takes on fundamental importance at the end of the century. It has to be present in any radical, critical or liberationist educational practice. For this reason, it seems to me a lamentable contradiction to engage in progressive, revolutionary discourse and have a practice which negates life. A practice which pollutes the sea, the water, the fields, devastates the forests, destroys the trees, threatens the birds and animals, does violence to the mountains, the cities, to our cultural and historical memories.
>
> Paulo Freire[1]

The Edge of the Abyss: The Dance of Global Capital and Ecological Catastrophe

As we begin the 21st century on Earth, the living inhabitants of the planet stand positioned at the foot a great wave of social crisis and global ecological catastrophe. They are already nearly drowned in an ocean of Post-WWII social transformations, in economies of capital, and in the cultural revolution that has resulted from rapid advances in military science and technology—that which is frequently referred to under the moniker of "globalization."[2] Thus, our moment is new—never before have the collected mass beings of the planet Earth been so thoroughly threatened with extinction as they are now and never before have so many of us raised this problem consciously and desperately together in the hopes of transforming society towards a better, more peaceable kingdom as a result. And yet, the present does not arise in a vacuum, but rather out of the concreteness of history itself. We move, then, in a sea of possibilities and swirling energies. Amidst these energies arises the great wave; and it is crashing and we who are threatened with annihilation and asked to threaten others with the same are its driftwood. Will we then be smashed to splinters upon the polluted beach of no tomorrow? Will we surf the awesome tube of this grave peril and move laterally across it into newly imagined freedoms? Or will we head outward into deeper waters still, floating upon unfathomable depths, along with dangers and possibilities even as of yet unforeseen?

To think and live historically is to be ecological, to move in a bed of context. The anthropologist Gregory Bateson pointed out that the code for understanding the basic ecological unit of survival is "organism plus environment." This relationship—to think ecologically is to think about the relationships between things—declares that a threat to either the organism or its environment is a movement towards the ecology of death: the life process requires *both* and any process that so binds the one or the other so as to threaten "both" is in some sense courting death and moving away from the love of life.[3] Ecologies, then, come in good and bad varieties. There is the sustainable ecology of a cultural commons dwelling in a relationship with a biodiverse habitat and there is the unsustainable ecology proffered by virtual networks of global investment into corporate industries bent on maximizing profit over people and places. To quote Bateson again, "There is an ecology of bad ideas, just as there is an ecology of weeds."[4] Transnational technocapitalism, as we know it today, has arisen historically as a conscious threat to both organisms and their environment, turning both into little more than "natural resources" for its own assault on a greater rate of surplus value production. It plays the one against the other to their mutual demise and while technocapitalist heroes, such as Bill Gates, imagine a new "friction-free" capitalist world in which services and money are exchanged much like oxygen and carbon-dioxide used to be (and now we have carbon trading credits!), the fact of the matter is that capitalism as we know it rests by definition upon friction. It is predicated first and foremost by competition and growth, a predatory survival of the fittest approach to life in which "fittest" means most mighty and therefore able to grow further and out-compete rivals. There is no ecology of symbiosis in the dominant system today, no ecology of mutuality and compassion; and again, this lack exists not by accident but rather as the result of concrete historical forces at work in our world—many of which have coalesced into a global technocapitalist spectacle during only these last few decades.

In his book, *The Enemy of Nature*, the ecosocialist and activist Joel Kovel begins by documenting the terrible legacy of natural resource degradation that spans the approximately forty years that have now elapsed since the first Earth Day and the release of the Club of Rome's benchmark economic treatise *The Limits to Growth* (1969). Echoing the findings of eminent environmental and ecological groups such as The Union of Concerned Scientists and personages such as the species conservationist Peter Raven, the picture that emerges from Kovel's work is that of an institutionalized, transnational, phase-changing neoliberalism that acts as a cancer upon the Earth, a form of "endless growth" political economy that is literally over-producing and consuming the planet towards death.[5] Wholly without precedent, the human population has nearly doubled during this time period, increasing by nearly 3 billion people. Similarly, markets have continued to worship the gods of efficiency and quantity and refused to conserve. The use and extraction of "fossil fuel" resources like oil, coal, and natural gas—the non-renewable energy stockpiles— followed and exceeded the trends set by the population curve despite many years of warnings about the consequences inherent in their over-use and extraction, and this has led to a corresponding increase in the carbon emissions known to be responsible for global warming.[6]

Likewise, living beings and organic habitats are being culled and destroyed in the name of human production and consumption at staggering rates. Tree consumption for paper products has doubled over the last forty years, resulting in about half of the planet's forests disappearing, while throughout the oceans, global fishing also has doubled resulting in a recent report finding that approximately 90% of the major fish species in the world's oceans have disappeared.[7] Forty-mile-long drift nets are routinely used to trawl the ocean bottoms, causing incalculable damage to the ocean ecosystem. Giant biomass nets, with mesh so fine that not even baby fish can escape them, have become the industry standard in commercial fishing and as a result there is expected to be no extant commercial fishery left active in the world by 2048.[8] Further, such nets are commonly drowning and killing about 1000 whales, dolphins, and porpoises daily—some of the very highly sentient species already near extinction from centuries of commercial hunting—and there has even been a startling move towards the re-introduction of commercial whaling by the International Whaling Commission due to pressure from countries such as Norway, Iceland and Japan.[9] As with forests and oceans, since the end of the 1960's, half of the planet's wetlands have either been filled or drained for development, and nearly half of the Earth's soils have been agriculturally degraded so as not to support life.[10] Finally, as giant corporate agribusinesses have consumed the family farm and as fast food has exploded from being a cultural novelty to a totalizing cultural staple, vast, unimaginable slaughterhouses—brutal production-lines in which thousands of animals are murdered for meat harvesting every hour—have also become the business standard. In his book, *Dominion*, Matthew Scully estimates that nothing less than 103 million pigs, 38 million cows and calves, 250 million turkeys, and 8 billion chickens are slaughtered annually in America alone.[11] When we add to these the numbers of animals that are hunted each year for sport or pelt, those that are killed by global transportation systems and those that are cruelly vivisected and killed in scientific experimentation practices, the numbers magnify by many tens of millions more. All told, then, running alongside the contemporary growth of the world's environmental move-ment is the red stain of trillions of dead animals—a symbol of the radical amplification of global capitalism that has occurred in our lifetimes.

Almost all of these trends are escalating and most are accelerating. Even during what recently amounted to an economic downturn for many, transnational markets and devel-opment continue to flow and evolve, and the globalization of technocapital is fueling yet another vast reconstruction of the myriad planetary political, economic, and socio-cultural forces into a futuristic network society.[12] Over the last four decades, then, human-ity has unfolded like a shock wave across the face of the Earth, one which has led to an exponential increase of transnational marketplaces and startling achievements in science and technology, but one which has also had devastating effects upon planetary ecosystems both individually and as a whole. Most telling has been the parallel tendency over this time period toward mass extinction for the great diversity of species deemed non-human, including vast numbers of mammals, birds, reptiles, amphibians and insects. Comparing the numbers involved in this catastrophe with the handful of other great extinctions existing within the prehistoric record has led the esteemed paleoanthropologist Richard Leakey to coin this age as the time of "the Sixth Extinction," a great vanishing of creatures over the last thirty-odd years such as the planet has not seen during its previous sixty-five million.[13] Mirroring these findings, the United Nations Environment Programme's *GEO-3* report of 2002 found that a vision of continued economic growth and global development akin to that which is now underway is consonant only with planetary extinction and specifically they conclude that: either great changes are made in our global lifestyle now or irrevocable social and ecological upheavals will grip the world by 2032.

Lest we make the mistake of thinking that our present globalization crisis proceeds along the simple lines of human flourishing and natural resource wasting, then it cannot be stated strongly enough that even as world gross economic product has nearly tripled since 1970, these gains have been pocketed by a relatively few advanced capitalist nations (and then a smaller class within them still) at the expense of the planet's poor.[14] Recently, the United Nations Development Programme issued its *Human Development Report 1999* which found that the top twenty percent of the people living in advanced capitalist nations have eighty-six percent of the world gross domestic product, control eighty-two percent of the world export markets, initiate sixty-eight percent of all foreign direct investment, and possess seventy-four percent of the communication wires. Meanwhile, the bottom twenty percent of the people hailing from the poorest nations represent only about one percent of each category respectively. The divide between rich and poor has been gravely exacerbated, with the gap between the two nearly doubling itself from an outrageous factor of 44:1 in 1973 to about 72:1 as of the year 2000. Much of this is directly related to a series of loans begun by the World Bank and the World Trade Organization in the 1990's, which ultimately increased Third World debt by a factor of eight compared with pre-globalization figures.[15]

So, as approximately 1.2 billion people live on less than $1 per day and nearly 3 billion live on less than $2 per day, the roaring heights of global technocapitalism have been unfortunate indeed for nearly half of the human population.[16] Globalization has been especially torturous upon poor women and children, who are denied basic human rights en masse and who, in the attempt to combat their situations of mass starvation and homelessness, enter by the millions each year into the relations of slave-labor and the horrors of the global sex trade. Even more tragically, millions of additional poor (many of whom are women and children) have been violently pressed into the circumstance of outright slavery! Thus, when this is properly related to the neo-colonialist conditions fostered upon the Third World by the explosion of transnational capitalist development, we can rightly assert that these very same cultural, economic and politically hegemonic practices constitute a form of global "family terrorism" meant to oppress those who already suffer the most.[17] As these Third World families almost invariably disclose themselves along racial and ethnic lines when compared with their over-developed Caucasian counterparts, it should be noted that such family terrorism constitutes the oppression of planetary difference generally.

New advances in capitalist lifestyle and practice are then directly responsible for grave exacerbations of widespread poverty and suffering, species genocide, and environmental destruction. It is axiomatic for this essay, then, that the exploitation of species, of the environment, and of the poor by the rich, have a single underlying cause (and those fighting in the name of these, a single enemy)—the globalization of technocapitalism.[18] Those interested in animal liberation and its correlates must find and develop solidarity with those working towards the conservation and preservation of nature; and each of these groups must also expand their reach—both theoretically and practically—to include the fight for social justice. Clearly, the project before us is immense; we face nothing less than the unprecedented transformation and domination of the planet. Hence, one might wonder about the efficacy of our successfully seeing through an international revolution that is capable of unifying many different social movements together under the banner of immediate socio-ecological crisis.[19]

It will not happen without education, but to speak of education—as has the U.N.[20]—as a key process by which we might fend off the worst aspects of today's globalization, and realize more of the utopia in which non-human animals, oppressed human peoples, and the planet are not wholly exterminated but rather ecumenically brought into a new ecological society generally, may be misreading what present educational practices can in fact accomplish. For instance, examining the evolution of the burgeoning movement for environmental education over the last forty years, we can trace both its positive and negative pedagogical effects—the ways in which it has contributed to progressive causes and fostered forms of ecoliteracy, on the one hand, and the manner in which it became co-opted by establishment powers, functioned technocratically, and has remained altogether marginal in schools of education, on the other. Sensing the limitations of environmental education theorized merely as experiential forms of "outdoor education" (e.g., "No Child

Left Inside"), the United Nations began in 2005 the Decade of Education for Sustainable Development with the hope that a new field of sustainable development education (ESD) that engages with social, cultural, and environmental themes will become better theorized, evaluated and ultimately instituted around the world in both academic and non-academic domains.

Tomorrow's sustainable society—one that sustains all life, and not just its most powerful elements—if reliant upon education, will require a pedagogical revolution equal to its present socio-economic counterpart. The field of critical pedagogy has arguably been the leading source of revolutionary pedagogical ideas and practices to date, but as the philosopher of education Ilan Gur-Ze'ev has noted, "Until today, Critical Pedagogy almost completely disregarded not just the cosmopolitic aspects of ecological ethics in terms of threats to present and future life conditions of all humanity. It disregarded the fundamental philosophical and existential challenges of subject–object relations, in which 'nature' is not conceived as a standing reserve either for mere human consumption or as a potential source of dangers, threats, and risks."[21] What is required, I argue, is therefore a dialectical blending of critical pedagogy and environmental education that will allow each to overcome their previous theoretical limitations towards the realization of a more inclusive, critical and transformative ecopedagogy—a goal that appears to have represented Freire's own final position on the matter, it should be noted.

In what follows, I will thus attempt to provide the beginnings of a theoretical and historical foundation for a planetary ecopedagogy movement by first providing a summary critique of environmental education trends to demonstrate why ecopedagogy cannot and must not be reduced or simply tethered to existing environmental education curricula and standards, even when they are conceived as education for sustainable development. In closing, I will then go on to call for an expansion of environmental literacy towards ecoliteracy and survey the forms of ecological literacy that I believe are presently relevant for the development of ecopedagogy generally.

Environmental Education's Big Bang and Fizzled Finale

Just as there is now a socio-ecological crisis of serious proportions, there is also a crisis in environmental education over what must be done about it. Over the last half-century, the modern environmental movement has helped to foster widespread social and cultural transformation. In part, it has developed ideas and practices of environmental preservation and conservation, struggled to understand and reduce the amount of pollution and toxic risks associated with industrialized civilization, produced new modes of counterculture and morality, outlined the need for appropriate technologies, and led to powerful legislative environmental reforms as well as a wide range of alternative institutional initiatives. As a form of nonformal, popular education it has stirred many people to become self-aware of the role they play in environmental destruction and to become more socially active in ways that can help to create a more ecological and sustainable world.

In terms of formal educational programs, federal and state legislatures have mandated that environmental education be included as part of the public education system's curricular concerns with passage of legislation such as the National Environmental Education Act of 1990. Correlatively, over the last 35 years the North American Association for Environmental Education—the world's flagship environmental education organization—has grown from being a fledgling professional society to its current state as the coordinator, in over 55 countries worldwide, of thousands of environmental organizations towards the certification and legitimation of environmental education as a professional research field. These educational programs have apparently made their case, as a comprehensive set of studies were completed in 2005 which found that:

- 95% of all American adults support having environmental education programs in schools;
- 85% of all American adults believe that governmental agencies should support environmental education programs; and that
- 80% believe that corporations should train their employees in how to solve environmental problems.[22]

In many ways, then, the foundation for comprehensive and powerful forms of environmental literacy and ecoliteracy has never been more at hand throughout society.

However, despite environmental education's significant pedagogical accomplishments, there have also been numerous setbacks and a tremendous amount of work remains to be done. For example, the same studies that revealed Americans' overwhelming support for environmental education programs reported a variety of findings that demonstrate that most Americans continue to have an almost shameful misunderstanding of the most basic environmental ideas. Thus, it was found that an estimated:

- 45 million Americans think the ocean is a fresh source of water;
- 125 million Americans think that aerosol spray cans still contain stratospheric ozone-depleting chlorofluorocarbons (CFCs) despite the fact that they were banned from use in 1978;
- 123 million Americans believe that disposable diapers represent the leading landfill problem when they in fact only represent 1% of all landfill material; and
- 130 million Americans currently believe that hydropower is the country's leading energy source when, as a renewable form of energy, it contributes only 10% of the nation's total energy supply.[23]

More troubling still, there has been a burgeoning rise in social and ecological disasters that are resulting from a mixture of unsustainable economic exploitation and environmentally unsound cultural practices. These are ecological issues that require a much deeper and more complex form of ecoliteracy than is presently possessed by the population at large if there still remains significant confusion as to whether or not the ocean is salty. In this context, while it may be unfair to lay the blame for social and ecological calamity squarely on environmental education for its inability to generate effective mass pedagogy, it must still be noted that the field of environmental education has been altogether unable to provide either solutions or stop-gaps for the ecological disasters that have continued to mount due to the mushrooming of transnational corporate globalization over the last few decades.

In fact, during this same time period, environmental education has tended to become isolated as a relatively marginal academic discipline.[24] It is rarely integrated across the curriculum in either teacher-training, educational leadership or educational research programs of study and is instead generally confined to M.A.-level environmental education certification programs. Further, these degree programs themselves are often lacking rigorous theoretical and politicized coursework, usually focusing instead on promoting the sort of outdoor educational experiences that can advance outdated, overly-essentialized and dichotomous views about nature and wilderness.[25] As Steven Best and Anthony Nocella have theorized, such views as these are of a kind typical of the first two waves of (predominantly white, male, and middle-class) U.S. environmentalism, and have proven insufficient and even harmful towards promoting multiperspectival ecological politics and environmental justice strategies that seek to uncover collective environmental action across differences of race, class, gender, species and other categories of social difference.[26] Hence, so-called "outdoor" environmental education programs stand in need of radical reconstruction. Lastly, a form of relatively depoliticized environmental literacy has become rooted as the field standard since William Stapp (1969), who is considered the "founder" of the environmental education movement, first stressed that the goals of environmental education were: knowledge of the natural environment, interdisciplinary exploration, and an inquiry-based, student-centered curricular framework that could be used for overcoming intractable conflict and ideology in society.[27]

A poster-child example for this form of environmental literacy is the School of Environmental Studies, known as the "Zoo School," in Apple Valley, Minnesota. Here high school-aged juniors and seniors attend school on the zoo grounds, treating the institution and a nearby park as an experiential learning lab where they conduct independent studies and weave environmental themes into their curricular work and projects. A 2003 pamphlet by Michele Archie, though funded and promoted by the United States Environmental Protection Agency, entitled *Advancing Education Through Environmental Literacy*, lauds the school as one which is "using the environment to boost academic performance, increase student motivation, and enhance environmental literacy." But the literacy aspects of this education, which accord with the aims put forth previously by Stapp and now by the North American Association for Environmental Education, lack the deep critical, social and ethical focus that contemporary environmentalism demands.[28]

For instance, the heads of the Zoo School do not have the students pose problems into the history and nature of zoos—a highly problematical social and environmental institution—or become active in the fight against the zoo's own sordid history and policies. As regards the latter project, for example, it would be a worthwhile educational venture to have students become involved in banning dolphins from the zoo (hardly a species native to Minnesota) and to have them returned to either a sanctuary or non-domesticated oceanic habitat. Instead, as of 2006, one can pay $125 to swim with the zoo's dolphins, a practice generally condemned by marine ecologists and environmentalists/animal rightists alike as both inhumane and beyond the bounds of good environmental stewardship. Alternatively, Zoo School students could be collectively organized to learn to name and oppose the corporate marketing and ideology presently taking place within the zoo. As an example, instead of developing their environmental literacy (as is currently done) through explorative experiences of the zoo's Wells Fargo Family Farm, a place according to the zoo that can foster experiences for children "to explain and also to learn about how food gets from farms to tables" (http://www.mnzoo.com/animals/family_farm/index.asp), students could gain literacy in how to organize collectively in opposition to such practices and in how to demand answers from responsible parties as to why high-ranking executives of a leading corporate agribusiness like Cargill presently sit on the zoo's Board of Directors. Additionally, students could learn to read the exhibit against the grain in order to politically problematize why the zoo doesn't create exhibits explaining the ins and outs of truly ecological diets like veganism, but conversely appears to naturalize and support (at least tacitly) as sustainable and conservationist the standard American heavily meat-based diet and the factory farming and slaughterhouse industry which supports it.

However, the Zoo School is promoted within leading environmental education circles as a leader because it is, in the words of the Environmental Education & Training Partnership, "Meeting Standards Naturally."[29] That is, it is motivating students in a new way to go to school and meet or even surpass national curricular and testing standards of a kind consistent with the outcome-orientation of the No Child Left Behind Act. As with other schools that have adopted environmental education as the central focus of their programs, the Zoo School apparently shines—not because it is producing ecological mindsets and sustainable living practices capable of transforming society in radically necessary ways, but because its students' reading and math scores have improved, and they have performed better in science and social studies, developed the ability to transfer their knowledge from familiar to unfamiliar contexts, learned to "do science" and not just learn about it, and showed a decline in the sort of overall behavior classified as a discipline problem.[30] Obviously, regardless of whatever good pedagogy is taking place at the Zoo School, this laudatory praise of its environmental literacy program by environmental educators is little more than the present-day technocratic standardization movement in education masquerading as a noteworthy "green" improvement. Put bluntly: this is environmental literacy as a greenwash.[31]

Worse still, however, is that here environmental literacy has not only been co-opted by corporate state forces and morphed into a progressively-styled, touchy-feely method for achieving higher scores on standardized tests like the ACT and SAT, but in an Orwellian turn typical of the Bush-era it has come to stand in actuality for a real illiteracy about the nature of ecological catastrophe, its causes, and possible solutions. As I have insisted, our current course for social and environmental disaster (though highly complex and not easily boiled down to a few simple causes or solutions) must be traced to the evolution of an anthropocentric worldview grounded in what the sociologist Patricia Hill Collins has referred to as a "matrix of domination," a global technocapitalist infrastructure that relies upon market-based and functionalist versions of literacy to instantiate and augment its socioeconomic, cultural and environmental control. Conversely, the type of environmental literacy standards now showcased at places like the Zoo School as Michele Archie's "Hallmarks of Quality" are those that fail to develop the type of radical and partisan subjectivity in students which might be capable of deconstructing their socially and environmentally deleterious hyper-individualism or their obviously socialized identities that tend towards state-sanctioned norms of competition, hedonism, consumption, marketization and a form of quasi-fascistic patriotism that they unflinchingly belong to "the greatest nation on earth."

It is clear, then, that despite the effects and growth of environmental education over the last few decades, it is a field that is ripe for a reconstruction of its literacy agenda. Again, while something like the modern environmental movement (conceived broadly) should be commended for the role it has played in helping to articulate many of the dangers and pitfalls that contemporary life now affords, it is also clear that environmental education has thus far inadequately surmised the larger structural challenges now at hand and has thus tended to intervene in a manner far too facile to demand or necessitate a rupture of the status-quo. What has thereby resulted is a sort of crisis of environmental education generally and, as a result, recently the field has been widely critiqued by a number of theorists and educators who have sought to expose its theoretical and practical limitations.

From Environmental Education to Education for Sustainable Development

It was during 1992, at the first Earth Summit in Rio de Janeiro, Brazil, that an attempt to make a systematic statement about the interrelationship between humanity and the Earth was conceived of and demanded—a document that would formulate the environmental concerns of education once and for all in both ethical and ecological (as opposed to merely technocratic and instrumentalist) terms. This document, now known as the Earth Charter (http://www.earthcharter.org), failed to emerge from Rio, however. Instead, Chapter 36 of the *1992 Earth Summit Report* went on to address the issue in the following manner:

> Education is critical for promoting sustainable development and improving the capacity of the people to address environment and development issues. . . . It is critical for achieving environmental and ethical awareness, values and attitudes, skills and behavior consistent with sustainable development and for effective public participation in decision-making.[32]

In 1994, the founding director of the United Nations Environment Programme and organizer of the Rio Earth Summit, Maurice Strong, along with Mikhail Gorbachev, renewed interest in the Earth Charter and received a pledge of support from the Dutch government. This led to a provisional draft of the document being attempted in 1997, with the completion, ratification, and launching of the Earth Charter Initiative at the Peace Palace in The Hague occurring on June 29, 2000. The initiative's goal was to build a "sound ethical foundation for the emerging global society and to help build a sustainable world based on respect for nature, universal human rights, economic justice, and a culture of peace."[33] While hardly a perfect document or initiative, the Earth Charter's announced mission was still nothing short of revolutionary, as it attempted a bold educational reformulation of how humans should perceive their cultural relationship to nature, thereby casting environmental and socio-economic/political problems together in one light and demanding long-term, integrated responses to the growing planetary social and ecological problems.[34]

It was hoped that at the 2002 Earth Summit meetings in Johannesburg, South Africa (i.e., the World Summit for Sustainable Development) the United Nations would adopt and endorse the Earth Charter. However, the summit proved disappointing in many respects, and while Kofi Annan optimistically closed the summit by announcing that $235 million worth of public–private partnerships had been achieved because of the conference and that this put sustainable development strategies firmly on the map, social and environmental activists found the World Summit for Sustainable Development to be a sham for mostly the same reason. Thus, the W$$D (as its critics called it, due to its apparent pro-business agenda and bad taste in staging an Olympics-style, posh event on the outskirts of the Soweto shantytowns' appalling poverty) articulated a central divide between large-scale corporate and governmental technocrats and the more grassroots-based theorists, activists, and educators proper. As a result of the considerable pressure exerted by the U.S. delegates (and the additional political and economic interests of the other large states and non-governmental organizations), the 2002 summit ultimately refused to consider ratification of the holistic, pointedly socialist in spirit, and non-anthropocentric Earth Charter educational framework.[35] Instead, the Decade of Education for Sustainable Development was announced by the U.N. in 2005 and education for sustainable development was promoted as the new crucial educational field to be integrated across the disciplines and at all levels of schooling.

A leading international critic of environmental education has been Edgar González-Gaudiano, who rightly charges that all-too-often the theories, policies, and discursive themes of environmental education have represented voices of the advanced capitalized nations of the global North, as the perspectives of the global South were ignored.[36] For González-Gaudiano this means that the issue of environmental justice, which highlights the cultural racism inherent in mainstream sustainable (and unsustainable) development strategies, is problematically overlooked by most educational programs currently dealing with environmental issues.[37] In opposition, he has developed an intersectional ecological concept of "human security" that could displace commonplace ideas of national security in favor of a problem-posing pedagogy that seeks knowledge of how the environmental factors that contribute to disease, famine, unemployment, crime, social conflict, political repression and other forms of sexual, ethnic or religious violence can be examined as complex social and economic problems deserving of everyone's attention. In this context, towards a consideration of education for sustainable development, González-Gaudiano has remarked that like environmental education before it, education for sustainable development might be a "floating signifier" or "interstitial tactic" capable of providing diverse groups opportunities to produce alliances as part of the construction of a new educational discourse. However, he also finds it troubling that non-environmental educators "either appear to be uninformed or have shown no interest in the inception of a Decade that concerns their work."[38]

For his part, lead editor of the *Canadian Journal of Environmental Education*, Bob Jickling, is additionally worried by the apparently instrumentalist and deterministic nature of education for sustainable development thus far. In his opinion, it is extremely troubling that education for sustainable development's tendency as a field to date is to treat education as merely a method for delivering and propagating experts' ideas about sustainable development, rather than as a participatory and metacognitive engagement with students over what (if anything) sustainable development even means.[39] Indeed, if this is all that is to be expected of and from education for sustainable development, then it may be concluded that it basically amounts to the latest incarnation of what Ivan Illich cynically referred to as the prison of the "global classroom."[40] Yet it should be pointed out that despite his serious reservations, Jickling notes that there may be many educators already doing good work under this moniker as well.

Like Jickling and González-Gaudiano, I believe that critical ecopedagogues should make strategic use of the opportunities afforded by the Decade of Education for Sustainable Development but must refrain from becoming boosters for it who fail to advance rigorous critiques of its underlying political economy. To my mind, it is clear that this economy is mainly the political and economic global Third Way of so-called liberal centrists like Tony Blair and Bill Clinton, whom the *New York Times* has referred to as the "Impresario of Philanthropy" because of his Clinton Global Initiative and his work on behalf of disaster relief related to the recent Asian tsunami and Hurricane Katrina. The rhetoric of this approach now champions *sustainable development* as a win-win-win for people, business, and the environment, in which the following policy goals are upheld: (1) development "meets the needs of the present without compromising the ability of future generations to meet their own needs" and (2) development improves "the quality of human life while living within the carrying capacity of supporting ecosystems."[41] In its tendency to deploy progressive slogans, Clintonian Third Way politics claims that it wants to put a human face to globalization and that it supports inclusive educational, medical, and civic development throughout the global South in a manner much akin to that demanded by leaders in Latin

America and Africa. But if this Third Way political vision really intends to deliver greater equity, security, and quality of life to the previously disenfranchised, it is especially note-worthy that it also mandates that "existing property and market power divisions [be left] firmly off the agenda."[42]

A 2000 speech by Clinton to the University of Warwick exemplifies this claim and so reveals why astute globalization critics such as Perry Anderson have characterized Third-wayism as merely "the best ideological shell of neo-liberalism today."[43] In his speech, Clinton rhetorically plugs building the necessary "consensus" to allow for the opening of previously closed markets and rule-based trade, such as that sponsored by the Inter-national Monetary Fund, in the name of a global humanitarianism, which can overcome disasters such as global warming, disease, hunger, and terrorism:

> I disagree with the anti-globalization protestors who suggest that poor countries should some-how be saved from development by keeping their doors closed to trade. I think that is a recipe for continuing their poverty, not erasing it. More open markets would give the world's poorest nations more chances to grow and prosper.
>
> Now, I know that many people don't believe that. And I know that inequality, as I said, in the last few years has increased in many nations. But the answer is not to abandon the path of expanded trade, but, instead, to do whatever is necessary to build a new consensus on trade.[44]

The neoliberal market mechanism remains largely the same, then, in both Third Way welfarism and the aggressive corporatism favored by the current Bush administration. The only difference between them may be the nature of the trade rules and goals issued by the governing consensus. In this, the Clinton Global Initiative is a poster child for the ideology of most U.S. centrist liberals who believe that administrations can learn to legislate tem-perance by creating more and more opportunities for intemperate economic investment in alternative, socially responsible markets. The sustainable development vision thereby maintained is of a highly integrated world society, centered and predicated on economic trade, presided over by beneficent leaders who act in the best interests of the people (while they turn an honest profit to boot). However, in this respect we might wonder in a more stringent manner than did the ecologist Garrett Hardin, "*Quis custodies ipsos custodes?*—Who shall watch the watchers themselves?"[45]

Sustainable development has thus increasingly become a buzzword uttered across all political lines; one is as likely to hear it in a British Petroleum commercial as on the Pacifica radio network. As noted, it is now trumpeted also by the United Nations over and against environmental education, thereby challenging every nation to begin transforming its educational policies such that a global framework for ecological and social sustainability can be built in relatively short order. But just what kind of sustainable development is education for sustainable development supposed to stand for though? Is it consonant with alter-globalization views, or is it rather synonymous with neoliberalism in either its Bush or Clinton variants? It charges institutions (especially educational institutions) with altering their norms and behavior in the name of environmental and cultural conservation, but can a top-down movement for organizational change really address the fundamental failures of present institutional *technique*? The ecosocialist and founder of the German Green Party, Rudolf Bahro, noted that most institutional environmental protection "is in reality an indulgence to protect the exterministic structure," which removes concern and responsibility from people so that "the processes of learning are slowed down."[46] Does education for sustainable development amount to something radically different from this? Due to the inherent ideological biases currently associated with the term "sustainable development," education for sustainable development demands careful attention and analysis by critical ecopedagogues over the next decade.

From Environmental Literacy to Ecoliteracies

Jim Cummins and Dennis Sayers effectively delineate three broad categorical types of literacy: the functional, the cultural and the critical.[47] Functional literacy, in their view, constitutes the basics of reading, writing, arithmetic and vocational skills that allow people to negotiate life in an industrialized society. Cultural literacies highlight larger anthropological levels of meaning—that people live in shared communities which have particular traditions of meaning and knowledge expectations, as well as specific forms of agreed upon social interaction depending upon the community. Lastly, critical literacy illuminates the unequal workings of power in societies, allows people to understand the sociocultural workings of domination and oppression and acts as an ethical spur that demands the transformation of society in favor of greater justice and equality.

Cummins and Sayers's framework can be utilized to delineate complementary forms of environmental literacies as well. As we have seen, functional environmental literacies, as proposed by field founders such as William Stapp or governmental agencies such as the Environmental Protection Agency's Environmental Education Division, involve goals of learning to understand basic scientific ecology, geology and biology to the degree that they are relevant to social life, on the one hand, and how society can affect basic ecological systems for better or worse, on the other. At another level, it should also be realized that so-called environmental literacies can have a cultural aspect (i.e., different cultures have different ways of relating to and understanding nature). Here mainstream definitions of environmental literacy must be found to be generally lacking, as neither is there any explicit demand for a multicultural ecological outlook and practice, nor is there any clear recognition that literacy requirements for responsible citizenship are themselves particular forms of culturally specific requirements that should not be offered as universal goods for all to learn. Further, to speak of cultural environmental literacies is to enact a crucial move from an environmental to an ecological order of knowledge. For once an understanding has been reached that culture and nature are in dialectical relationship, even as ideas about nature are themselves related across any given culture or interactionally across multiple cultures, to speak simply of "environmental literacy" is inaccurate and insufficient. For the literacy itself no longer relates primarily to an (or the) environment, but rather it aims to delineate potential knowledge about an ecology of relations between particular cultures and the way in which those cultures inhabit their bioregions and habitats. Thus, to realize a primary cultural-aspect of environmental literacy is immediately to recognize the necessary move from an environmental literacy to a cultural ecoliteracy.

But there are various forms of ecoliteracy and while the development of cultural ecoliteracies is absolutely essential if a goal of sustainability is ever to be realized throughout the planet, I seek to argue that we must also realize forms of a higher-order critical ecoliteracy. A critical ecoliteracy involves the ability to articulate the myriad ways in which cultures and societies unfold and develop ideological political systems and social structures that tend either towards ecological sustainability and biodiversity or unsustainability and extinction. In addition, critical ecoliteracy means being able to recognize one's own critical ecoliteracy as a form of ethical epiphany that individuates the state of planetary ecology as a whole at any given time, and which contains within itself a range of transformative energies, life forces, and liberatory potentials capable of affecting the future. Moreover, in the particular example of Western society, a critical ecoliteracy would mean (amongst other things) understanding: the historical roles that waves of colonialism and imperialism have had both socially and environmentally, the ways in which industrial capitalism (including modern science and technology) has worked ecologically and anti-ecologically on the planet both locally and globally, the manner in which an ideological image of "humanity" has served to functionally oppress all that has been deemed Other than human by interested parties, and the historical wrong through which ruling class culture and politics terrorizes planetary life whilst marginalizing, intimidating, confronting, jailing and sometimes even murdering socio-ecological freedom fighters. As literacies involve practical dimensions too, a Western critical literacy would doubtless involve (at a minimum) taking action on these issues at both an individual and collective level, engaging with ecological and sustainable countercultures, rescuing animals and habitats whenever possible, and working for revolutionary counter-hegemonic social change generally in favor of abolishing civic hierarchies based on race, class, gender and other categories of identified social difference.

While frameworks for environmental education and education for sustainable development still represent the two leading programs for potentially addressing ecological concerns within education, then, a variety of smaller cultural and critical ecoliteracy projects have arisen that deserve attention in conjunction with the rise of a movement for ecopedagogy. While critiques can (and should) be advanced that engage with all these versions of ecoliteracy, it should be concluded that, taken altogether in conjunction with developments in critical pedagogy, they represent a mosaic of leading-edge, progressive theories of socio-ecological education and literacy.

A founding figure of the ecoliteracy movement is undoubtedly Frijtof Capra, the Chair of the Center for Ecoliteracy (http://www.ecoliteracy.org). In his recent work, Capra draws upon the systems-oriented nature of biological systems and ecological thinking in calling for an education for sustainability that favors the ability to synthesize instead of analyze experience and which seeks to describe life as complex systems of relationships that work in an ever-evolving, holistic and qualitative perspective.[48] Some transformative educators like Brian Swimme of the California Institute of Integral Studies are experimenting with Capra's notion of ecoliteracy by combining it with other pedagogical models, such as Alfred North Whitehead's rhythm of ideas and process-orientation, Loren Eiseley's literary naturalism and Pierre Teilhard de Chardin's notion of an evolving spirit of mind and grace. On the other hand, in the United Kingdom, Capra's work is also being importantly applied alongside the critique of capitalism by Stephen Sterling.[49] Still, a potential to depoliticize humanity's current ecological crisis through a failure to articulate a broad-based, inclusive vision of critical ecoliteracy are problems that Capra's movement must continue to seek to address.

In this respect, a promising bridge has begun to be made by Edmund O'Sullivan between Capra's systems-oriented pedagogy and the transformative, social justice orientation of critical pedagogy.[50] O'Sullivan, and those associated with him at the University of Toronto's Transformative Learning Centre (http://www.oise.utoronto.ca/tlcentre), have begun to imaginatively combine visions of transformative education with a biocentric approach that is also critical of contemporary geo-political practices and which attempts to foster a literacy for positive pedagogical experiences of the art, beauty and spirit of the planet as we might know it. O'Sullivan himself promotes the Earth Charter as a meaningful example of how radical social positions can be articulated within global institutional frameworks. Further, drawing upon the eco-theologian Thomas Berry's notion of the important role of cosmology in education, O'Sullivan has called for "a new story" that will value the arrival of the "Ecozoic age" in which visions of the Earth and of planetary equity can take the place in our cultural stories of now pervasive notions of oppressive domination and repressive violence.

Another founding figure of the ecoliteracy movement is David Orr. In his work, Orr wonders why environmental education has proven inadequate to quell ecological crisis.[51] In part, his answer is that built into the emerging environmental discourse of the last three decades has been a sort of equivocation of terms—as is the case, he argues, with the talk surrounding sustainability. On the one hand, says Orr, many (chiefly politicians and CEOs) have called for a "sustainable society" that is really a code for a form of "techno-logical sustainability." Technological sustainability views the human predicament as a rationally-solvable, anthropocentric, scientifically-directed state of affairs, one that will solve its problems through the proper top-down management of an endless-growth economy. On the other hand, many others (chiefly environmentalists) have talked about a "sustainable society" in terms of "ecological sustainability"—a view that questions human rationality and motives, emphasizes the importance of natural systems and their equilibrium for life, and which sides with a critical view of the dominant social practices that appear to breed disequilibrium.

Orr's notion of ecological literacy ultimately attempts to arbitrate the problems inherent in these disputes over environmental education (and now education for sustainable development) by resolving them within a postmodern "both/and" logical approach which integrates and incorporates insights from all of the various models previously enumerated. While critical of the potential complicity of environmental education curricula and policies with truly unsustainable lifestyle practices, Orr nonetheless feels that they too have something to contribute in the attempt to avert a further manifestation of an ecological crisis situation. While likewise drawing upon Capra's notion of holistic systems, from critical pedagogy's conceptions of literacies into power and of critical dialogue, and from ideas about an Earth-centered cosmology akin to O'Sullivan's, Orr's ecoliteracy also calls for a functional balancing of personal experiences of the natural world with scientific perspectives on ecological systems. However, in surpassing a functional environmental literacy approach, Orr describes functional literacy as being but the beginning of a fuller emerging literacy into the full range of human ontic and existential life. As students move beyond the mere observation and understanding of natural and social systems, always with an eye towards ecological harmony and balance, Orr contends that students inherently come to recognize an additional ethical responsibility (as did figures like Henry David Thoreau, John Muir, and Aldo Leopold) to model such balance within their own life practices and relationships with people, other species and the planet. Thus, while Orr recognizes a responsibility to act on behalf of the world (potentially radically when it is being fiercely degraded), he also realizes that part of becoming ecologically literate is the adoption of a perspective for behavior that values complexity, process, and the sort of temperance that is bred only by being actively involved in a lifelong practice of critical understanding and spiritual wonder. Ultimately, Orr's ecoliteracy therefore asks of us that we each remain open to listening to a manifold of different knowledge systems, that we act collaboratively with a diversity of others (in a non-anthropocentric fashion), that we remain rigorous and critical in our ethical stance towards life, and that we constantly integrate our own life experiences towards the general end of helping our home planet Earth to sustain the rich and beautiful tapestry of life which it both supports and provides.

Another key new ecoliteracy movement is that which is developing under the moniker of humane education. Humane education has a long pedigree associated primarily with the movement for non-human animal welfare and as such humane curricula presently focus on ecoliteracy campaigns to help homeless pets, combat animal cruelty in society, promote humane-certified foodstuffs in school cafeterias, raise awareness about the fur trade, and generate greater familiarity with wild animals amongst school-aged children. The move to envision and create a more radicalized, holistic and inclusive form of ecoliteracy for humane education is probably best charted by movement theorist David Selby.[52] Selby's work documents with great nuance the exciting myriad of historical vectors that are presently coalescing around the movement for humane education and attempts to argue that humane education can embody the integration of seven literacy areas: development education, environmental education, human rights education, peace education, gender equity education, and race equity education. Yet, Selby has also noted with disappointment that humane education, especially of a variety that he is calling for, is essentially below the horizon line of academic disciplines. Indeed, this lack of university support has made funding for humane education programs difficult and the lack of these programs has prevented humane education's further integration into schools and other local educational institutions.

Lastly, no survey of contemporary ecoliteracy frameworks would be complete without mention of the movement for ecojustice education chiefly theorized by C.A. Bowers.[53] Bowers and his associates, which include educators and theorists such as Rebecca Martusewicz,[54] have also developed a Center for EcoJustice Education (http://www.centerforecojusticeeducation.org) that seeks to promote ecojustice aims at the grassroots level, within the academy and for policy initiatives. Besides serving as a central hub for ecojustice educators, it publishes an online journal and houses a dictionary wherein key socio-ecological concepts are defined from an ecojustice perspective.

Though Bowers has spent voluminous pages in excoriating the theorists of critical pedagogy[55] for promoting a version of literacy that focuses on developing "critical" capacities—which Bowers believes are ideologically linked to a post-Enlightenment culture of autonomous selves that co-construct the modern domination of nature proper—Bowers's own version of ecoliteracy radically integrates cultural and critical capacities as it draws upon influences such as the Frankfurt School of critical theory, Jacques Ellul, Gregory Bateson and Ivan Illich in an attempt to reveal how a culture predicated on liberal Western individualism has produced ecological crisis through the pervasive homogenization, monetization and privatization of existence. In Bowers's view, the extension of Western liberal ideology through cultural means results in the alienation of community, the loss of forms of inter-generational wisdom that teach sustainability and commonality, and the imperialist/colonialist translation of cultural diversity into a global cosmopolitanism. Against this, Bowers calls for literacy into the way in which indigenous (and other) cultures that have long-standing traditions of sustainability in their cultural practices understand and relate to the world. In this, ecojustice literacy works alongside the ecological literacy aims of indigenous educators themselves.[56] Additionally, in an age now characterized by the rampant globalization of cultures, Bowers feels ecojustice literacy must further knowledge of how sustainable cultures are presently resisting their assimilation by re-defining themselves around vernacular social practices that strengthen community and commons-based approaches to living well. Finally, Bowers's ecojustice version of ecoliteracy calls for students to question deeply the latest fetish for technological infusions of computers and other digital paraphernalia into culture and education and he seeks to mount a larger collective cynicism about the current role naïve constructivist-oriented pedagogies are playing in and around schools.

Though the potential significance of (at least some of) the ecojustice critique made of critical pedagogy distinguishes ecojustice theory from other ecoliteracy approaches, it is in many respects also its greatest downfall. Far too much energy has been spent in promoting and demolishing critical pedagogy as a straw man for all that is presently wrong with mainstream education vis-à-vis its relationship to ecoliteracy. While critical pedagogy is undoubtedly a leading movement amongst progressive educators, to imagine that the field of education proper is somehow working in concert with the demands of the educational left is a kind of propaganda that is better left to rightist organizations like the Heritage Foundation. However, especially because the progressives are marginalized in professional education circles and because critical pedagogy currently does have the ear of many leftist educators, it would be more productive in my opinion for ecojustice educators to find ways to bridge differences between the two camps, undertake the furtherance of critical but respectful dialogue between the two movements, and so work towards forging a more united front in education for the social and ecological betterment of all.

Concluding Remarks

Space prevents me from engaging with the real history of ecopedagogy as a movement born primarily in a Latin American context during the 1990s within Freirean circles, including important personages like Moacir Gadotti, Francisco Gutierrez and Cruz Prado, as well as Leonardo Boff. Much of their work remains untranslated into English and while it is stimulating revolutionary developments in education internationally, such work has yet to become rooted in Northern or Western educational contexts on the whole. But just as in relation to his own work, when Paulo Freire said "the progressive educator must always be moving out on his or her own, continually reinventing me and reinventing what it means to be democratic in his or her own specific cultural and historical context,"[57] so too now is there the challenge to develop forms of ecopedagogy relevant to the advanced capitalist nations, their cultures, and their histories. One way in which I am attempting to do this is to forge a creative affiliation of scholars, teachers, leaders of non-governmental organizations, activists and other citizens called Ecopedagogy Association International (http://ecopedagogy.org) to provide forums for productive dialogues on what ecopedagogy is, what it is not, and what it needs to be.

As I have argued, one thing we can say is that ecopedagogy cannot be reduced to environmental education. While environmental education appears to be growing professionally as a field in many ways and should continue to become ever-more central to educational and political discourse over the next decade(s) under the banner of sustainability, or more aptly education for sustainable development, the immediate institutional trend for even broad-based forms of environmental education is a depressing move away from the types of radical ecoliteracies I believe are now demanded by the imminent threats posed to life by the mounting social and ecological crises. This is an ominous indicator on the educational field's horizon line (and on society's as well)—one that speaks to a deep fracture that exists between the majority of the people in and around institutions of education that favor a rational planning and "wise use" economic approach and the revolutionary minority that are bent on realizing an ethical "revaluation of all values" that will ultimately be capable of meeting the present challenge set before us by the growing global catastrophes.

Now, simply, we must strive to challenge our old assumptions as educators—even as critical educators—and to build our solidarities and organize a common language and ways of being together more than ever before. This plan for action as I can name it is for a radical ecopedagogy—a term delineating both educational and ethical literacies. Undoubtedly, in the age of standardized everything, educational institutions stand in need of reconstruction and re-dreaming to be set a-right. Yet, education remains a primary institution towards affecting social and ecological change for the better, and so it deserves to be fought for, transformed by the needs of the day, and so wizened by lessons of the past. Though however limited in power, the ecopedagogues are placing their feet inside the doors of school buildings everywhere even now and calling for the demonstration of the emancipatory feelings inside each and every one of us: let's storm the entrance and let love live! It is one thing to do in these desperate times. I believe it is worth the chance—it could mean the difference between today's rage and tomorrow's hope. What will you do?

Notes

1. Paulo Freire, *Pedagogy of Indignation* (Boulder, CO: Paradigm Publishers, 2004).
2. On "globalization," as the growth of Western technocapitalism since World War II, and its contemporary meanings, see Steven Best and Douglas Kellner, *The Postmodern Adventure: Science, Technology and Cultural Studies at the Third Millennium* (New York, Guilford Press, 2001), pp. 205–53. On resistance movements to globalization, see Richard Kahn and Douglas Kellner, "Resisting Globalization" in George Ritzer (ed.), *The Blackwell Companion to Globalization* (Maiden, MA: Blackwell Publishers, 2007).
3. On the ecological consequences of states of biophilia and necrophilia, see Erich Fromm, *The Heart of Man* (New York: Harper & Row, 1964). I have expanded on this idea elsewhere in Richard Kahn, "The Educative Potential of Ecological Militancy in an Age of Big Oil: Towards a Marcusean Ecopedagogy" in Douglas Kellner, Tyson Lewis, and Clayton Pierce (eds.), *Marcuse's Challenge to Education* (Lanham, MD: Rowman & Littlefield, forthcoming).
4. Gregory Bateson, *Steps to an Ecology of Mind* (Chicago: University of Chicago Press, 1972), p. 492.
5. Joel Kovel, *The Enemy of Nature* (New York, Zed Books, 2002), pp. 38–39. For the Union of Concerned Scientists, see "World Scientists' Warning to Humanity" in Paul R. Ehrlich and Anne H. Ehrlich, *Betrayal of Science and Reason: How Anti-Environmental Rhetoric Threatens Our Future* (Washington, D.C.: Island Press, 1996), pp. 242–50. For Raven, see "What We Have Lost, What We Are Losing," in Michael J. Novacek (ed.), *The Biodiversity Crisis: Losing What Counts* (New York: New Press, 2001), pp. 58–62.
6. Al Gore, *An Inconvenient Truth* (New York, NY: Rodale Books, 2006). It should be noted that despite the media spectacle tethering vehicular gas mileage to global warming as a primary cause of global climate change, the global livestock industry contributes far and away more global warming emissions than all forms of transportation combined and should be considered a grave ecological harm. For instance, see the U.N.'s Food and Agriculture Organization's 2006 report *Livestock's Long Shadow*. Gore has himself been the subject of recent critique by animal rights organizations like PETA and some environmental groups such as Sea Shepherd Conservation Society for leaving livestock and dietary practices out of his agenda to combat global climate change.
7. Rick Weiss, "Key Ocean Fish Species Ravaged, Study Finds," *Washington Post* (May 15, 2003).
8. Boris Worm, et al., "Impacts of Biodiversity Loss on Ocean Ecosystem Services," *Science*, Vol. 314, No. 5800, (2006), pp. 787–90.
9. Joseph B. Verrengia, "Scientists Raise Alarm Over Sea-Mammal Deaths," *The Associated Press* (June 16, 2003).
10. The statistics in this paragraph, unless otherwise noted, are listed in Joel Kovel, *The Enemy of Nature*, pp. 3–5.
11. Matthew Scully, *Dominion: The Power of Man, the Suffering of Animals, and the Call to Mercy* (New York: St. Martin's Press, 2002), pp. 284–85.
12. Douglas Kellner, "Theorizing Globalization," *Sociological Theory*, Vol. 20, No. 3, (2002), pp. 285–305.
13. Richard Leakey and Roger Lewin. *The Sixth Extinction* (New York: Doubleday, 1995).
14. Joel Kovel, *The Enemy of Nature*, p. 4.
15. Joel Kovel, *The Enemy of Nature*, p. 4.
16. World Bank, *World Development Report 1998* at http://www.worldbank.org.
17. For a thorough discussion relating globalization to the oppression of poor women and children, see Rhonda Hammer, *Antifeminism and Family Terrorism: A Critical Feminist Perspective* (Lanham, MD: Rowman & Littlefield, 2002), pp. 187–94.

18. This oft-quoted memo from when Lawrence Summers, President of Harvard and former Treasury Secretary for Bill Clinton, worked for the World Bank serves as the penultimate articulation of how oppression of the environment and poor are linked together by technocapitalist elites:

> Just between you and me, shouldn't the World Bank be encouraging more migration of the dirty industries to the LDCs [less developed countries]? . . . I think the economic logic behind dumping a load of toxic waste in the lowest wage country is impeccable and we should face up to that . . .
>
> I've always thought that under-populated countries in Africa are vastly under-polluted; their air quality is probably vastly inefficiently low [sic] compared to Los Angeles or Mexico City.—in John Bellamy Foster, *Ecology Against Capitalism* (New York: Monthly Review Press, 2002), p. 60.

19. In this light, see Tom Athanasiou, *Divided Planet: The Ecology of Rich and Poor* (Athens: University of Georgia Press, 1998).

20. "Even the most casual reading of the earth's vital signs immediately reveals a planet under stress. In almost all the natural domains, the earth is under stress—it is a planet that is in need of intensive care. Can the United States and the American people, pioneer sustainable patterns of consumption and lifestyle, (and) can you educate for that? This is a challenge that we would like to put out to you."—Noel J. Brown, United Nations Environment Programme, *National Forum on Education about the Environment* (October 1994).

21. Ilan Gur-Ze'ev, (ed.), *Critical Theory and Critical Pedagogy Today: Toward a New Critical Language in Education* (Haifa: Haifa University, 2005), p. 23.

22. Kevin Coyle, *Environmental Literacy in America. What 10 Years of NEETF/Roper Research and Related Studies Say About Environmental Literacy in the U.S.* (Washington, D.C.: The National Environmental Education & Training Foundation, 2005).

23. Kevin Coyle, *Environmental Literacy in America.*

24. Indeed, in 2001, it was revealed at the International Standing Conference for the History of Education at the University of Birmingham, UK, that aside from one purely Australian effort, as of yet there has been no rigorous attempt to reconstruct the history of environmental education proper—it is literally a discourse without a chronicle.

25. Though it must be noted that even fields like outdoor education are contested terrains in which norms and boundaries can be pushed to advance progressive agendas. For instance, see Connie Russell, et al., "Queering Outdoor Education," in *Pathways: The Ontario Journal of Outdoor Education*, Vol. 15, No. 1, (2003), pp. 16–19.

26. Steven Best and Anthony Nocella, II, "A Fire in the Belly of the Beast: The Emergence of Revolutionary Environmentalism," in Best and Nocella, II (eds.), *Igniting a Revolution: Voices in Defense of the Earth* (Oakland, AK Press, 2006).

27. William Stapp, "The Concept of Environmental Education," in *Journal of Environmental Education*, Vol. 1, No. 3, (1969), pp. 31–36.

28. In its 2000 report, *Excellence in Environmental Education: Guidelines for Learning (K-12)*, the North American Association of Environmental Education lists four essential aspects to environmental literacy: 1) Developing inquiry, investigative, and analysis skills, 2) Acquiring knowledge of environmental processes and human systems, 3) Developing skills for understanding and addressing environmental issues, and 4) Practicing personal and civic responsibility for environmental decisions. While the third and fourth aspects respectively gesture to the possibility of a politicized version of environmental education, the lack of a specific demand for critical social thought on the part of students or for the understanding of the role of power in society, coupled with the field's traditionally "bi-partisan" approach to conflict resolution, means that the potential in this literacy agenda to foment positive ecological change through educative means is significantly undermined.

29. Michele Archie, *Advancing Education Through Environmental Literacy*, Alexandria, VA: Association for Supervision and Curriculum Development.

30. Joanne Lozar Glenn, *Environment-based Education: Creating High Performance Schools and Students* (Washington, D.C.: National Environmental Education and Training Foundation, 2000).

31. Wikipedia (http://en.wikipedia.org/wiki/Greenwash) defines "greenwash" thus: Greenwash (a portmanteau of green and whitewash) is a pejorative term that environmentalists and other critics use to describe the activity of giving a positive public image to putatively environmentally unsound practices.

32. United Nations Conference on Environment and Development, "Promoting Education, Public Awareness and Training," in *Agenda 21* (Geneva: UN, 1992), pp. 221–27.

33. See http://www.earthcharter.org/innerpg.cfm?id_page=95.

34. See David Gruenewald, "A Foucauldian Analysis of Environmental Education: Toward the Socioecological Challenge of the Earth Charter," in *Curriculum Inquiry*, Vol. 34, No. 1, (2004), pp. 71–107.

35. Moacir Gadotti, "Paulo Freire and the Culture of Justice and Peace: The Perspective of Washington vs. The Perspective of Angicos," in Carlos Torres and Pedro Noguera (eds.), *Paulo Freire and the Possible Dream* (Denmark: Sense Publishers, forthcoming).

36. See Edgar González-Gaudiano, "Education for Sustainable Development: Configuration and Meaning," in *Policy Futures in Education*, Vol. 3, No. 3 (2005), pp. 243–50.

37. Peter McLaren and Edgar González-Gaudiano, "Education and Globalization, An Environmental Perspective— An Interview with Edgar González-Gaudiano," in *International Journal of Educational Reform*, Vol. 4, No. 1 (1995), pp. 72–78.

38. Edgar González-Gaudiano, "Education for Sustainable Development: Configuration and Meaning," p. 244.

39. Bob Jickling, "Sustainable Development in a Globalizing World: A Few Cautions," in *Policy Futures in Education*, Vol. 3, No. 3 (2005), pp. 251–59.

40. Ivan Illich and Etienne Verne, *Imprisoned in the Global Classroom* (London: Writers & Readers, 1981).

41. See respectively Gro Harlem Brundtland, *Our common future: Report of the World Commission on Environment and Development* (Oxford: Oxford University Press, 1987) and David Munro and Martin W. Holdgate (eds.), *Caring for the earth. A strategy for sustainable living* (Gland, Switzerland: The World Conservation Union, United Nations Environment Programme, and World Wildlife Fund, 1991).

42. Doug Porter and David Craig, "The third way and the third world: Poverty reduction and social inclusion in the rise of 'inclusive' liberalism," in *Review of International Political Economy*, Vol. 11, No. 2 (2004), pp. 387–423.

43. Perry Anderson, "Renewals," in *New Left Review*, Vol. 11, No. 1 (2000), p. 11.

44. William J. Clinton, "Remarks by the president to the community of the University of Warwick." (December 14, 2000).

45. Garrett Hardin, "The tragedy of the commons," *Science*, Vol. 162 (1968), pp. 1243–48.

46. Rudolf Bahro, *Avoiding social and ecological disaster: The politics of world transformation* (Bath, U.K.: Gateway Books, 1994).

47. Jim Cummins and Dennis Sayers, *Brave New School: Challenging Cultural Illiteracy through Global Learning Networks* (New York: St. Martin's Press, 1999).

48. See Frijtof Capra, *The Hidden Connections: Integrating the Biological, Cognitive, and Social Dimensions of Life into a Science of Sustainability* (New York, NY: Doubleday, 2002) and his "Ecoliteracy: A Systems Approach to Education," in Zenobia Barlow (ed.), *Ecoliteracy: Mapping the Terrain* (Berkeley, CA: Learning in the Real World, 2000), pp. 27–35.

49. Stephen Sterling, *Sustainable Education: Re-visioning Learning and Change* (Bristol, Vermont: Green Books, 2001).

50. Edmund O'Sullivan, *Transformative Learning: Educational Vision for the 21ˢᵗ Century* (London: Zed Books, 1999). See also, Edmund O'Sullivan and Marilyn Taylor, *Learning Toward an Ecological Consciousness: Selected Transformative Practices* (New York, NY: Palgrave, 2004).

51. See David Orr, *The Nature of Design: Ecology, Culture and Human Intention* (Oxford: Oxford University Press, 2002), *Earth in Mind: On Education, Environment, and the Human Prospect* (Washington, DC: Island Press, 1994) and *Ecological Literacy: Education and the Transition to a Postmodern World* (Albany, NY: SUNY Press, 1992).

52. David Selby, "Humane Education: Widening the Circle of Compassion and Justice," in Tara Goldstein and David Selby (eds.), *Weaving Connections: Educating for Peace, Social and Environmental Justice* (Toronto, CA: Sumach Press, 2000) and his *Earthkind: A teacher's handbook on humane education* (Stoke-on-Trent: Trentham, 1995). Another more inclusive vision of human education is Zoe Weil, *The Power and the Promise of Humane Education* (British Columbia, Canada: New Society Publishers, 2004).

53. For instance, C.A. Bowers, *Transforming Environmental Education: Making the Renewal of the Cultural and Environmental Commons the Focus of Educational Reform* (EcoJustice Press, 2006). Online at: https://scholarsbank.uoregon.edu/dspace/bitstream/1794/3070/6/transEE-rev.pdf; also his *Educating for Eco-Justice and Community* (Athens: University of Georgia Press, 2001) *and Education, Cultural Myths, and the Ecological Crisis: Toward Deep Changes* (New York: SUNY Press, 1993).

54. See Rebecca Martusewicz, *Seeking Passage* (New York, NY: Teachers College Press, 2001) and Rebecca Martusewicz and Jeff Edmundson, "Social Foundations as Pedagogies of Responsbility and Eco-Ethical Commitment," in Dan Butin (ed.), *Teaching Social Foundations of Education: Contexts, Theories, and Issues* (Mahwah, N.J.: Lawrence Erlbaum, 2005).

55. Besides those already mentioned, see for example C.A. Bowers, "Can Critical Pedagogy Be Greened?" in *Educational Studies*, Vol. 34 (2003), pp. 11–21.

56. For example, see the work of Gregory Cajete (ed.), *A People's Ecology: Explorations in Sustainable Living: Health, Environment, Agriculture, Native Traditions* (Santa Fe, NM: Clear Light Publishers, 1999).

57. Paulo Freire, et al., *Mentoring the Mentor* (New York, NY: Peter Lang, 1997), p. 308.

28

Folk Schools, Popular Education, and a Pedagogy of Community Action

William Westerman

What can make pedagogy revolutionary is not just the content, but the process, and the question of who is the teacher and who is the student. There are the dualities—reading/writing, listening/speaking, answering/questioning, accepting/investigating—but in much formal schooling, equal emphasis is not given to both halves of an engaged communicative process. Conceivably, though not always, teaching and studying can exist in a dialogic relationship that in itself is a revolutionary reformulation of the standard classroom technique. Beyond that, occasionally the educational process can lead to further action and to social change. This chapter concerns itself with the act of study as a proto- and prerevolutionary act, an act of questioning and an act of challenging the existing social order. More accurately, this essay addresses historical examples when the act of study was a force advancing a revolutionary process. In fact, the kind of pedagogy I discuss is one in which the student's actions and questions, and the authority of daily life, are given a primacy that they do not have in static educational models.

In particular, this chapter focuses on two strands of revolutionary pedagogy—one that originated in the folk schools of Denmark and took root in the mountains of Tennessee, influencing the Civil Rights movement as well as generations of labor organizing in the United States and one that originated in the slums of Brazil, took a detour through Portuguese West Africa, and took hold in revolutionary and religious communities in Central America and parts of South America before moving on to the wider developing world. These two strands, the northern thread spun by Danish nationalists and Myles Horton and the southern spun by Paulo Freire and Amilcar Cabral, intertwined briefly before the deaths of Horton and Freire in the 1990s. What ties the two together are themes of freedom, empowerment, and emancipation, on the one hand, and techniques of developing literacy, orality, and knowledge of the community, on the other. It turns out that an understanding and an appreciation of folk culture is central to both. In the conclusion, I attempt to braid these threads with a third strand, that of folklife studies, to examine the qualities inherent in a discipline that studies popular culture which make it so suitable for an activist pedagogy.[1] It will be my contention that there is something about these three pedagogical disciplines that in combination make for an education that is truly revolutionary: critical literacy, orality (not in the sense of rote recitation but in the sense of mastering oral skills and being able to wield the spoken word), and knowledge, including self-consciousness, of one's folk culture.

The Danish Folk Schools and their Influence

One of the manifestations of Romantic nationalism in Europe was the collection and study of folklore materials, in such nascent nations as Finland, Italy, and Germany. Following the philosophical influence of Herder, proto-folklorists roamed the countryside, collecting songs and tales *(Märchen)*, from peasants, in the process elevating and romanticizing the peasant class within their own society while asserting the nationhood of their own people. But all was not just a matter of nationalism. Another feature of this elevation concerned the education of the peasantry as part of the process of civilizing them and preparing them for political participation in the rising nation. As the influence of monarchies waxed and waned in the decades following the French Revolution, and as national boundaries were being drawn and redrawn, it was also important that the peasants were kept clear about their national and linguistic allegiances. Political and intellectual elites in smaller European countries were concerned about losing national identities and wanted to bolster claims of national autonomy. In the wake of the Napoleonic Wars, devastated nations looked to assert national cultures once more. Some middle-class intellectuals harbored democratic impulses, too, and after the revolutions of 1848 looked to the peasant class as future citizens in post-feudal constitutional societies with bicameral parliaments, at least one chamber of which was to be popularly elected.

In the Scandinavian countries and in Denmark in particular, the task of educating the peasant was part of the work of establishing cultural and linguistic identity. In 1830, Henrik Wegeland, a Norwegian poet, wrote a theoretical essay called "Encouragement to Country Folks to See to Their Own Education" (Paulston 1974, p. x). Similar ideas were developing in Denmark, which had lost land to Germany and which was faced with the spreading influence and increasing use of the German language by its southern elites (Begtrup et al. 1926, pp. 94–95; Coe 2000; Rørdam 1980, p. 40). A Lutheran minister who also happened to be a student of Norse mythology, N.F.S. Grundtvig (1783–1872), developed the idea in 1834 that one remedy was a form of popular education not just for elites but for the peasants as well, those who "have to feed themselves and the officials too" (Adams 1975, p. 20; Manniche 1939, p. 84). In that way, while not challenging the idea of monarchism with democracy, at least the rural folk could participate in the strengthening of a Danish nation. Grundtvig established the first of these "Folk Schools" ten years later, in 1844 (Manniche 1939, p. 87; Paulston 1974, p. x). His school failed, but a second, more successful school was founded by Christian Kold (1816–70) seven years later with one-tenth the initial start-up money (Begtrup 1926, pp. 95–99). Together these schools spawned a movement that over the course of the next 80 years educated some 300,000 Danish citizens (Adams 1975, p. 20). By the mid-1920s, as many as 30 percent of the rural population of Denmark had attended a folk school (Hart 1926, p. 41).

Directed at farmers, peasants, and rural artisans, the Folk High Schools ultimately offered a curriculum consisting of Danish language, history, and social conditions, Norse mythology and literature, agricultural studies, music, and physical education, in combination with (literal) "field work," time spent developing better manual agricultural and domestic skills. More hours were spent studying history and social conditions than any other subject. There were no books; everything was oral, including poetry and song (Adams 1975, p. 20; Hart 1926). Grundtvig believed that "Academic life tends peculiarly to lead bookish men into false paths unless it is continuously corrected by an education that comes not out of books, but out of the life and the work of the people" (Hart 1926, p. 106). His work was furthered by his disciples Kold and Ludvig Schrøder, who "believed in 'the poetry of human activity, the romance of daily work' " (Manniche 1939, p. 95). All believed strongly that education had to have application in everyday life. Wrote Grundtvig, "Dead are letters even if they be written with the fingers of angels, and dead is all knowledge which does not find response in the life of the reader" (Manniche 1939, p. 83).

Grundtvig's belief was shared by many Romantics in nineteenth-century Europe. Leo Tolstoy wrote in 1862 "the home conditions ... the field labor, the village games, and so forth ... are the chief foundation of all education ... Every instruction ought to be only an answer to the questions put by life" (Tolstoy 1862, pp. 14–15). But folk schools maintained an explicitly activist agenda as well: "Facts enlarge life when they are *in* life. And the task of education, as of civilization, is that of finding some way of getting the facts we know used in the reordering of the world," wrote one American disciple (Hart 1926, p. 85).

Grundtvig's overarching operational theory in his "school for life" involved three factors involved in this definition of folk school education as an approach that, in the words of one modern interpreter:

> (a) arises from life, i.e. it is rooted in the life of the individual and the people. It speaks into the life situation of the young and it is inspired by the people's myths and history ... (b) is living. That is to say ... not based on the book, but on the living, spoken word, above all conversation ... (c) aims at life. The education has the task of shedding light both on human life as such and on the individual's life.
>
> (Bugge 2001, pp. 65–66)

Above all, unlike much state-run education, folk schools were "not examination schools. Their aim is not to enable the student to pass a particular exam" (Bugge 2001, p. 67).

Language, culture, and music held special roles in Grundtvig's thought and, later on, in the schools. Grundtvig had traveled to England three times between 1829 and 1831, to study Anglo-Saxon texts, including Beowulf, which he copied to bring back to Denmark (Begtrup et al. 1926, pp. 84–85). He also translated works from Latin into Danish, because of the importance of "a living voice speaking the mother tongue" (Begtrup et al. 1926, p. 83). As for music, a later American visitor wrote, "It is a delightful experience to hear the students sing hymns, ballads, folk songs, and patriotic songs. All of them sing and most of them sing well" (Knight 1927, p. 81). Eventually, a high school song book became part of the folk school curriculum, and went into at least 16 editions by 1974; the largest included over 800 songs (Rørdam 1980, p. 110).

The folk school movement lay behind many political and economic changes in Denmark during the late nineteenth century, including the development of agricultural cooperatives, land reform, and the rise of participatory democracy through Left parties and politics in general, including successively larger electoral victories by Leftist parties in 1872, 1884, and 1901 (Knight 1927; Rørdam 1980). Not all the schools were politically radical (Whisnant 1983, pp. 130–136), but they had an impact on the economic structure of Denmark, at least. One American visitor, education professor Edgar Wallace Knight of the University of North Carolina wrote admiringly that:

> Since 1864 [Denmark] has restored herself, has developed an effective system of general education and of adult and agricultural education, perfected an agricultural system that is unexcelled anywhere, created cooperative agencies which are the marvel of Europe and America, removed illiteracy among the people, converted tenants into owners of homes, organized the farmers and enabled them to protect their interests, and brought to the masses of the Danish people a high level of intelligence and culture and material prosperity. Education has transformed rural

Denmark. The right kind of education properly directed can transform any rural community in the United States.

(Knight 1927, p. 10)[2]

The Danish Folk Schools showed remarkable longevity, and were still expanding into the twentieth century. In 1921, an International People's College opened in Elsinore, attracting the attention of people far beyond Scandinavia (Manniche 1939, p. 21). American writer Joseph Hart, in a glowing profile of the folk schools published in New York entitled *Light from the North*, captured the essence of the folk school philosophy in this description:

> [The Danes] do not create the minds that develop in those schools. They do not control those minds. They do not tie old forms of culture to those minds in order to make sure that they will be cultured later on. They provide the proper soils for growth; they take young people at just the right season of their lives; they cultivate them intelligently; they surround them with the climates of cultural growth; they trust the processes of development; they provide that "silence and long time" which John Keats held to be foster-mother of culture; and, for the most part, they reap the expected harvest in due time. They are culturers of minds; they work with nature; and they get the rewards that intelligence deserves.

(Hart 1926, pp. 78–79)

The education, as Hart saw it, was in the cultivation process, not, metaphorically speaking, in the crop or the seeds themselves. Later on, there would be specific folk high schools devoted to Danish handicrafts (founded in Kerteminde in 1952), language (founded in Kalø in 1952), and art (founded in Holbæk in 1965) (Rørdam 1980, pp. 183–185).

Several American educators in particular were impressed enough by the idea to travel to Denmark and use the folk schools as a model in their own work. Olive Dame Campbell authored a 1928 book on the topic (Campbell 1928) and then went on to found the John C. Campbell Folk School in the Appalachians (named after her husband), with which folklorists might be familiar, since it has been discussed more critically by David Whisnant in his book *All that is Native and Fine* (1983). In her study, Olive Dame Campbell had noted that Grundtvig "emphasized the importance of an experience in the common life and labor of the everyday man" (1928, p. 58) and she included the study of social and economic conditions in her curriculum, though she avoided some of the more politically radical elements of the Danish schools' analysis (Whisnant 1983, p. 136).[3]

The Highlander School

The influence of Danish Folk Schools in the United States was spread even more widely through the efforts of Myles Horton (1905–90), who spent a year in Denmark in 1931, following the onset of the worldwide Great Depression. Born in mountainous Savannah, Tennessee in 1905, Horton came from a poor rural background. Though his grandfather had been illiterate, his parents stressed education, and after college, he had ended up studying at Union Theological Seminary under Reinhold Niebuhr, "to try to find out," in his words, "how to get love and social justice together" (Horton 1990, pp. 32–35). He followed this with a year of studying sociology at the University of Chicago, and while in Chicago Horton met Jane Addams and participated in programs at Hull House (Horton 1990, pp. 47–48). He first became introduced to the folk schools after attending a community folk dance session at Reverend Aage Møller's Danish Lutheran church in

Chicago. Møller and another pastor, Enok Mortensen, told Horton about the Folk School movement and suggested he visit Denmark (Glen 1996, p. 16; Horton 1990, p. 50).

Horton would also likely have been aware not only of John C. and Olive Dame Campbell's work with folk schools, but with more political interpretations being published in the United States as well. Knight's study, cited above, concluded with this declaration:

> Too many of the farm workers in the United States are in the toils of the vicious system of tenancy, owning not an inch of the soil they live on nor a single shingle in the roofs under which they sleep. The Danes have been able through education and cooperation to reduce social injustice and to increase the wellbeing of all the people.
>
> (Knight 1927, p. 236)

Such sentiments would have been very attractive for Horton, who was trying to figure out at that time how to put his ideals into practice. Indeed, at the Danish Folk Schools, Horton was drawn by the sense of community, by the belief that school was a social experience, and by the appeal of placing home life in its larger context. Students, he wrote, "could learn not only what to do at home but have a chance to study social forces at work" (Horton 1989, p. 30). The radical potential of "these democratic schools" and their Danish founders also impressed Horton, who later wrote admiringly of Grundtvig's "creative powers . . . and . . . emotional energy . . . which enabled him to strike out, almost single handed, against the economic and spiritual poverty that enslaved the people" (Horton 1944, pp. 23–24).[4]

He returned to the United States in 1932, interested in education in a local community setting, like the folk schools, rather than mass educational reform where results were harder to gauge. Being tied to a community was paramount (Horton 1938, pp. 280, 295; 1990, p. 56). Enlisting Niebuhr's help in the fundraising and organizational effort, he planned to open "The Southern Mountains School" in North Carolina, "for the training of labor leaders in the southern industrial areas" (Horton 1990, p. 61). Thus, unlike the Danish Folk Schools that had not been overtly concerned with the political process, Horton introduced into his concept of folk school the express purpose of effecting political change in the region. This signaled a switch in the development of folk schools, in the words of one historian, after which they came "to secure generally liberating rather than adjustive outcomes" (Paulston 1974, p. ix). But Horton's view was also holistic; he wrote shortly after founding Highlander that "Schools must combine the economic, social, intellectual, esthetic, and moral elements of our culture, just as ordinary people combine them in ordinary life" (Horton 1938, p. 267).

Horton intended his school to be the first of many such schools in the region with this social agenda. "The Southern Mountains School"—a name initially chosen strictly for fundraising purposes—Horton and his associates renamed the Highlander, choosing a term, interestingly enough, that had been coined and made popular by John C. Campbell (Campbell 1921; Horton 1990, p. 63). The Monteagle, Tennessee location was selected for the very practical reason that Dr. Lillian Johnson, a former college president and student of John Dewey, donated her land to the project (although threatening to withdraw support because at first she found the enterprise too radical) (Horton 1990, pp. 63–65). The first two classes offered there were in psychology and cultural geography, a discipline close to, if not overlapping, folklife studies. Niebuhr, Joseph Hart, and Norman Thomas were among the school's charter advisory board members (Horton 1989, p. 46).

Over the next three decades in particular, Highlander sharpened its mission. The first students and trainees concentrated on labor organizing, including building unions and planning rallies. Highlander even became an official training center for the Congress of

Industrial Organizations (CIO) in the South, for example (Horton 1990, p. 87). Yet, it was in the education and training of activists for integration wherein Highlander came to national prominence, as the cradle of the Civil Rights movement. Rosa Parks, John Lewis, and Martin Luther King, Jr. were among the most prominent of hundreds of Civil Rights activists who received training at Highlander, one of the few integrated institutions in the entire South.

Three aspects of the curricular philosophy at Highlander were particularly important and novel within the American context. The first was the idea of experiential education that Horton clearly adapted from Grundtvig (and Tolstoy and Jean Jacques Rousseau). People learn by experience in real-life settings:

> If we are to think seriously about liberating people to cope with their own lives, we must refuse to limit the educational process to what can go on only in schools. The bars must come down; the doors must fly open; nonacademic life—*real* life—must be encompassed by education. Multiple approaches must be invented, each one considered educative in its own right.
>
> (Horton 1973, p. 331)

However, Horton expanded the concept of experiential education from the Danes' emphasis on agricultural fieldwork and artisanship to include the experience of democracy, cooperative economics, and participation in labor strikes within the learning environment (Horton 1990, pp. 68–69). The Highlander Folk Cooperative, a cannery, opened in 1934, while participation in strikes, including having the students join picket lines at major actions in the region, was also one of the earliest features of the school (Horton 1989, p. 54).

Horton also went further than the Danish Folk Schools in the belief that the people, including students, held the answers to their own problems based on the experiences of their lives. Horton later described this change in his point of view:

> [W]e saw problems that we thought we had the answers to, rather than seeing the problems and the answers that the people had themselves. That was our basic mistake. Once you understand that, you don't have to have answers, and you can open up new ways of doing things.
>
> (Horton 1990, p. 68)

The method was in the ability, as he wrote, "to learn how people learn, and respect what they already know" (Horton 1990, p. 69).

Horton's cultivation of leadership was also one of Highlander's greatest strengths and innovations. He did not articulate this much in his published work, but occasionally revealed the philosophy behind his method:

> It is, of course, impossible to bring together more than a small percentage of the people, but this is all that is necessary. Leaders are aroused people, who, like the aroused atom, start a chain reaction which is self-propagating. It is the multiplication of leadership that gives power to the people and enables them to make reality of dreams . . .

And then, with a nod to folklore:[5]

> The key that will release the people's power will not be found in the hands of a Paul Bunyan or a John Henry, but in the hands of the Johnny Appleseeds.
>
> (Horton 1947, p. 82)

The incorporation of cultural activities into the curriculum, the third significant and novel element of Highlander pedagogy, was part and parcel of the educational as well as political process. Horton got the idea of community singing from Grundtvig and the Danes and dancing from his time in Chicago (Horton 1973, p. 329; 1983, p. 29). In personal notes written around 1931, he suggested "School and community life should be built around get-togethers such as singing, dancing, discussions, dinners, etc." (Horton 1989, p. 30). As he noted on the use of crafts in elementary education, "Handicraft and artwork should be presented in such a way that beautiful things would not be thought of as unattainable luxury, but as necessary parts of life," and that knowledge "of local trees, flowers, herbs, and wild life" was an important part of this curriculum, too (Horton 1938, p. 287).

Horton's first wife, Zilphia Johnson Horton (1910–56) has only recently been recognized as a major figure in the pedagogy of Highlander, and has not yet been fully recognized for her significance in American cultural work and folklore (Carter 1994; Glen 1996; Horton 1989). She came to the school in 1935 and introduced singing into the school curriculum (Horton 1990, p. 75) as well as the off-campus work of labor organizing and striking (Carter 1994, p. 8). Myles credited her with adding a new dimension to the school: "I learned a tremendous lot from Zilphia, my wife, who brought in a whole new cultural background, drama and dance and music, oral history, storytelling—all kinds of things that I'd grown up knowing but just hadn't thought of as being related to learning" (Horton and Freire 1990, p. 41). She collected folk and labor songs, transformed and wrote new lyrics for others, composed new ones, and encouraged the students to do the same (Glen 1996, pp. 46–47, 66; Horton 1989, p. 120), One book of her collected songs had an introduction by John L. Lewis, president of the United Mine Workers (Adams 1975, pp. 72, 225). Students would go out to picket lines and collect songs from one strike, and often, later on, transmit those songs to strikers on other picket lines, thus acting as agents of transmission in the labor folk tradition. Zilphia Horton later said in an interview, "The people can be made aware that many of the songs about their everyday lives—songs about their work, hopes, their joys and sorrows—are songs of merit" (Adams 1975, p. 76). Singing was also popular on the school grounds, and the BBC even broadcast a concert from Highlander in 1937 (Glen 1996, p. 47). It was at Highlander that "We Shall Overcome" was adapted by Zilphia Horton in 1946 to become the anthem of an embryonic political movement; she adapted the words, slowed down the tempo, and provided accordion accompaniment (Carter 1994, p. 15). Other songs of Civil Rights—"We Shall Not Be Moved," "This Little Light of Mine," and "Keep Your Eyes on the Prize"—were first associated with the movement there during her time, whether in their original or rewritten forms (Glen 1996, pp. 176–177).[6]

The cultural component of the Highlander experience continued with the arrival of folklorist, collector, and singer Guy Carawan in the 1950s, and later his wife Candie Carawan (they eventually became the directors after Myles Horton's death), and frequent visits from Pete Seeger. But participation, not performance, was the key. The Civil Rights activist, SNCC chairman and later Congressman, John Lewis wrote, "Besides the workshops and the speakers and the discussions, we did a lot of singing at Highlander. It didn't matter whether you could carry a tune or not, everyone sang. Even me, and I *cannot* sing" (Lewis 1998, p. 90). Social folk dance was equally a part of community building, as it came to be in Denmark too, and square dances were a regular feature of life at Highlander. Labor dramas were developed or written by staff and students for tours of the South, perhaps as many as a hundred in all (Adams 1975, p. 72), and largely under Zilphia Horton's direction, as she had studied drama and advocated it as a technique for social change (Carter 1994, p. 10). The school also encouraged worker-students to set down their first person narratives of life in the labor movement, and many of these were published in the school newspaper or in mimeographed anthologies (Horton 1989, p. 121). Myles Horton would later sum up, "Ballads, hymns, folk songs, songs of protest: all these have done much to arouse people to awareness and to the sense of community" (1973, p. 330). In many of these areas, Zilphia provided the initial spark.

Both the Danish Folk Schools and the Highlander School took as their starting point the education of rural adults, educating them beyond basic skills and encompassing critical thinking and participatory democracy. If a radical message was implicit in the work of some of the Danes, Myles and Zilphia Horton made that a more explicit and important part of their work. In that sense, the work of Highlander always strove to be revolutionary, reaching its epitome in the Civil Rights movement of the 1950s and 1960s. At the same time, to the south, Latin American revolutionary educational movements were also developing, and they too would become part of larger social revolutions.

Paulo Freire, Literacy, and Popular Education

A contemporary of Horton, Paulo Freire (1921–97), embarked on a similar path and concerned himself with adult education and literacy throughout Latin America. He did not learn from the Danish Folk Schools directly, but participated in political movements of the poor in his native Brazil. Even more than Horton, Freire developed a specific pedagogical methodology that was to have an impact on a political plane that reached higher than protest into the very workings of revolutionary government. Freire's work began in Brazil, but as a result of political circumstances, his temporary exile, and his travels later as an acknowledged innovator, his ideas were put into practice in Chile, Central America, particularly Nicaragua, and three formerly Portuguese colonies in Africa as they reached independence, as well as in poor neighborhoods and literacy campaigns throughout the Americas. As with Horton, Freire's work began with seemingly basic skills but placed them within a context of culture and the recognition of prevalent socioeconomic conditions.

Freire's now well-known method involves a radical reformulation of the teacher-student relationship. In formal educational models, the teacher traditionally holds all the knowledge, and deposits information into students, who function as mere receptacles. Freire introduced a more critical model of the educational relationship, which recognizes the role of the student's life experience in making sense of the surrounding social reality. The student's understanding and critique of social reality not only become part of the educational dialogue between student and teacher (since all learning, according to Freire, is based in a dialogic relationship) but also become the concrete bases for the teaching of literacy skills. The student's life becomes part of the curriculum. The student learns to read not meaningless phrases with no social context, but phrases with a bearing on everyday life experience. Thus, the student is learning to read the world in addition to the word, to use Freire's phrase from his seminal work, *Pedagogy of the Oppressed* (Freire 1970). In other words, what sets Freire's method apart is that the student becomes an active participant in the educational process, through questions, dialogue, and the introduction of life experience; the teacher does not have all the answers, and the contents of the reading primers are no longer irrelevant phonetic phrases, but sentences that reflect on the everyday life reality of the student.

Freire pioneered these methods in Brazil (and later Chile) in the late 1950s and early 1960s. Because of his literacy campaigns and outspokenness against the government, he was jailed and eventually exiled by the Brazilian dictatorship. But Brazil was hardly the only country involved in adult literacy campaigns or in the analysis of social conditions during the 1960s, 1970s, and 1980s. Because of its sheer size, it was harder to have a nationwide influence there. In fact, the first great national literacy campaign in Latin America began in Cuba on April 15, 1961, ironically the very day of the Bay of Pigs invasion (Kozol 1978, p. 354).[7] As with Freire's method, which begins with the analysis of a drawing by the students, the Cuban lessons began with the social analysis and discussion of a photograph (Kozol 1978, p. 353). In both cases, the teaching of literacy begins with the social realities of the students.

In a study of the folk school movement in Bangladesh, the Danish scholar of folk schools, K.E. Bugge discusses Freire's work as the natural outgrowth of Grundtvig's method played out in the economic context of developing countries. He finds extraordinary similarity in Grundtvig's and Freire's outlook. Both were concerned with empowerment, emancipation from oppression (be it cultural or economic), equity,[8] and most of all, freedom (Bugge 2001, pp. 69–73). Methodologically both were similar as well, emphasizing education drawing on life experience, and the importance of both literacy and oral expression. As Bugge notes, both Grundtvig and Freire believed "that backward social groups have lost the urge and ability to express themselves orally" (Bugge 2001, p. 74).

The most widespread and successful application of Freire's approach took place in Nicaragua beginning in early 1980, where a revolutionary government sought to use literacy to extend a political revolution into a social one. In fact, during a visit to Nicaragua three months after the Sandinista revolution that toppled Anastasio Somoza, Freire reportedly "stressed the importance of providing opportunities for learners to practice their creativity" (Cardenal and Miller 1981, p. 17).[9] As in Cuba, a literacy campaign was one of the first initiatives of the Sandinista revolutionary government.[10] In the 1980 "Crusade," illiteracy was lowered from approximately 50 to 13 percent nationwide and it has been estimated that "more than one-fifth of the population participated directly in the campaign" (Berryman 1984, p. 237; Chacón and Pozas 1980; Miller 1985, p. 200).

As in Cuba, the reading primer was developed around thematic chapters that reflected the lives of peasants and fishing communities, rather than readings with no social context. The first reader included such topics as a biography of Sandino, the "struggle for national liberation," "exploitation by foreign and national elites," the "rights and responsibilities of the new citizenry," land reform, health care, and women's rights (Arnove 1986, p. 22). Words introduced in the first reader included *revolución* (revolution), *liberación* (liberation), *genocidio* (genocide), and *masas populares* (popular masses) (Arnove 1986, p. 22). The official guidelines indicated that a central goal was "to actively engage students in the observation, interpretation, and analysis of their life circumstances" (Arnove 1986, p. 50), and specifically promote a basic understanding of "the national development plan, and the emerging political and economic structures" of the postrevolutionary society (Cardenal and Miller 1981, p. 6). One science textbook included the following statement on pedagogy: "We can only say we have learned something when we are capable of applying [knowledge] to transform little by little our reality" (Arnove 1986, p. 50). In other words, this pedagogical style was a three-part process, involving "discovering reality, interpreting it, and transforming it," while "the learner . . . also teaches and the teacher . . . also learns" (Suarez quoted in Miller 1985, p. 94).

Moreover, the *brigadistas* who were deployed in what was also known as "the cultural insurrection" to teach literacy, also became involved in manual labor, farming, craft production, and other efforts to integrate theater, dance, oral poetry, and festivals in the countryside into the literacy campaign (Cardenal and Miller 1981, pp. 8, 21; Chacón and Pozas 1980; Whisnant 1995, pp. 239–240).[11] Some 450 students were enlisted in "cultural brigades" that did not participate in literacy teaching but who were deployed to study culture and collect oral histories and other folk cultural knowledge (Miller 1985, p. 67). Fernando Cardenal, the Minister of Education, wrote in December of 1979 that there were plans to include as part of the literacy campaign the collection of national songs, refrains, folktales, and legends (Cardenal 1981, p. 35).

Most ambitiously, perhaps, Cardenal announced a plan to record two thousand oral histories of the insurrection to be deposited in a future "museum of oral history of the struggle for our freedom" (Cardenal 1981, p. 36). Within five months of the commencement of the campaign, some 7,000 oral history interviews had been conducted (Equipo DEI 1981, p. 144), though it is not clear whether all were recorded on audiotape. One Ministry commission later wrote, at the second congress reviewing the progress of the campaign in September 1980, that projects to develop a cultural atlas, collect information on folk medicines, and to incorporate art "as an instrument to deepen the mechanism of learning" would be included (Equipo DEI 1981, pp. 226, 229). The commission also announced plans to develop a National Museum of Literacy, with exhibits on literacy, including many essays and poems written by newly literate peasants, as well as collections of "our popular [folk] songs and our legends" (Equipo DEI 1981, p. 238). Eventually an Institute of the History of Nicaragua was founded under the Sandinistas in 1987, and all the materials from the Literacy Crusade and the oral history project, including cassette tapes, are archived there, at what is now the combined Institute of the History of Nicaragua and Central America, located at the Universidad Centroamericana in Managua.

The Nicaraguan case was clearly revolutionary, not only politically, but also in the sense that educational work and cultural work were literally brother disciplines. The literacy campaign was in many ways the centerpiece of the Sandinista government's initial work and arguably its most successful project, as it had been in other countries where Freire had been involved (see, e.g., Freire 1981). Not only was it the most successful application of Freire's method in terms of scope and short-term results, but also its qualitative impact went far beyond literacy and accomplished more than the reform of an educational system. While the idea of the literacy campaign was top-down (as it was with the Danes and Olive Dame Campbell), Freire's method is, to the fullest extent possible, dialogic and bottom-up, in his words, revolutionary rather than reformist (Cardenal and Miller 1981, p. 17). In Nicaragua this approach was put fully into practice during an intensive half-year period. What may be surprising is how integrally the understanding of popular culture was interwoven in that pedagogical process.

Freire's method was also applied in the teaching of adult literacy in El Salvador, during its attempted revolution in the 1980s. In contrast to Nicaragua, the Salvadoran campaign did not have the backing of a government newly in power, and education took place in villages, guerrilla camps, and "liberated zones" (Hammond 1998), carried but by the guerrillas as well as by nonviolent political activists in the so-called popular movements. Among the first syllables taught to Salvadoran peasants were "*cam-pe-si-no*" (the Spanish word for "peasant"). This was very much based precisely on the model not only from Freire but also from the war of independence in Guinea-Bissau and Cape Verde advanced by Amilcar Cabral (1924–73), whom Freire had influenced personally, and who in turn influenced Freire's later work as well.[12]

At the same time that literacy campaigns were underway in Nicaragua, El Salvador, and elsewhere, another movement, Liberation Theology, with similar aims and methods was becoming widespread throughout Latin America. The emergence and ideals of this move-ment showed the influence of Freire's approach beyond literacy and into the realm of religion. A radical reformulation of church teaching, favoring interpretation from the perspective of the poor and oppressed, Liberation Theology developed as an outgrowth of Vatican II by theologians, clergy, and laity concerned about social conditions in Latin America, including Brazil, Peru, and Central America. The method for disseminating this approach came in the form of so-called Christian Base Communities, discussion groups among urban and rural poor in which doctrine was discussed and debated in the context of the social conditions of people's lives, not as dogma. The structure of these Communities was similar to the structure of the literacy classes, with a high value placed on critique, questioning, life knowledge, and the reassignment of intellectual authority. Literacy, religious practice, and culture were part of a holistic social transformation, employing similar methods even though on a surface level they might appear to be distinct.

Typically, Base Community leaders would begin by reading passages from the Bible and prompting discussion, placing authority for interpretation in the hands of the parish-ioners, rather than in defending their own unquestionable authority.[13] Base Community work could also involve the exchange of knowledge between the community members and the leaders. It could really be said that the Base Community experience was an even less formal kind of popular education than literacy campaigns or folk schools, largely because its social structure was so radically different. According to one Salvadoran former Base Community lay worker I interviewed in 1985, "70% of the whole [popular political] movement in El Salvador" had come from a background "in a base community, religious base community." He described his experiences as a leader:

> There is this ambience, this feeling, I mean, the situation in, when you come into the area, when we were coming into the neighborhood, into the shantytowns, like we feel that, you know, there was the place in which we will have to be. Because when we were coming in: "Hello, how are you?" and everyone [came] to hug us, you know, and to say, "How you been?" and "Listen, I have this mango here . . . Do you want the half? I'll take the other half, I haven't eaten," you know, and there is all, all the situation of sharing *everything*. Everything.
>
> Yeah, it's a community of sharing, of giving. Rather than you know receiving, just receiving. . . .
>
> We sat in different groups . . . Usually in each group there were at least ten people, and we were five, seven people going at the time. We were talking about 70 to 100 people many times, sitting you know, underneath a tree, to the shade of the tree, on roads, on the, you know, on the land, on the grass . . .
>
> It wasn't a lecture. It never was a lecture. Because in order to [make] people really realize, and to make—not just realize but to make them understand and that from this understanding could [one] take a step, it had to be a discussion, it had to be a, you know—like, I learned a lot from them, a lot. Even, you know, the way that plants have to be grown, and what type of help have to be used to cure different things. I mean that type of things. . . .
>
> It's very incredible. I mean, the first time that I went over there, you know, I was study—in my . . . senior high school and thought, I thought, you know, I'm going to, to *teach* them. And it was the opposite. I went to learn. Not to learn about the herbs, and stuff, but to learn how they were managing to live with those conditions. From the first time that I went over there, that was it. That made it. Everyone changed from that first time . . .
>
> [We were] between 18 years, 30, I think 30 years. Young people, I think . . . We were really young, most of us. And the people that we were talking to were old, young, and children . . . Many times there were the whole family in one group.
>
> (Rolando Interview, May 29, 1985)[14]

This Base Community model illustrates, in a way, Freire's more secular notion of education as joint process:

> Every thematic investigation which deepens historical awareness is thus really educational,
> while all authentic education investigates thinking. The more educators and the people investi-
> gate the people's thinking, and are thus jointly educated, the more they continue to investigate.
> Education and thematic investigation, in the problem-posing concept of education, are simply
> different moments of the same process.
>
> (Freire 1970, p. 101)

The Base Communities, particularly in Central America, were applying this approach in religious terms, and anticipating an outgrowth into social action.

While literacy campaigns involved reading primers and even photographs as a basis for the social analysis that leads to an enriched literacy, Base Communities used Biblical texts, particularly the Gospel, as the starting point for a discussion of social inequity and injustice. While the movement certainly produced its share of written theology, it is also noteworthy for some of the well-documented examples of community life and religious interpretation, particularly Ernesto Cardenal's four volumes of base community transcripts, *The Gospel in Solentiname* (Cardenal 1982).

This approach, which became known also as the popular church ("popular" meaning "people's" but also being the closest equivalent in Spanish of the English word "folk" [see Paredes 1969]), was part of the larger scope of people's movements, including popular literacy and adult educational campaigns, popular organizing and labor movements, guer-rilla armies, and popular music, such as *Nueva Canción* (the "New Song" movement originating in Chile and spreading beyond the Andes throughout Latin America), with an overt political message. Such movements began in the countryside with peasant popula-tions, but also included the urban poor. There was an open acknowledgment within these movements that the cultural, the political, and the pedagogical were closely connected, and that culture was not something that belonged only to an elite few.

It is important to recognize that popular culture was part of these growing movements from the earliest days of Freire's work in the early 1960s, and that, as was the case at Highlander, music and art were integral to this kind of work. As Freire wrote in an autobiographical essay:

> It is no accident that the words culture and popular were so frequently present in the move-
> ment's vocabulary. Popular Culture Movement. Cultural centers. Cultural circles. Cultural
> squares. Popular theater. Popular education. Popular medicine. Popular poetry. Popular music.
> Popular festivals. Popular mobilization. Popular organization. Popular art. Popular literature.
>   One of the stated objectives of the movement was the preservation of popular culture
> traditions: the people's festivals, their stories, their mythic figures, and their religiousness. In
> all this we found not only the resigned expression of the oppressed but also their possible
> methods of resistance . . . none of th[is] ever escaped the movement's notice.
>
> (Freire 1996, p. 117)

More specifically, he wrote upon a visit to Port-au-Prince that he saw the local popular painting as a crucial expressive form:

> It was as if the Haitian popular classes, forbidden to be, forbidden to read, to write, spoke or
> made their discourse of protest, of denunciation and proclamation, through art, the sole
> manner of discourse they were permitted.
>
> (Freire 1994, p. 161)

Again there was the same pattern of education of the poor, political transformation, and folk or popular culture that existed in the work of Highlander and the Civil Rights Movement.

The joining of popular culture into what developed as bottom-up models of social change are what made these movements unique. In Latin America, two interrelated social movements—the literacy approach of Paulo Freire and the Base Community movement of Liberation Theology—emerged between 1957 and 1985 to confront military power and economic injustice. In North America, the Civil Rights Movement in the 1950s and 1960s was based on a strategy of grassroots organizing that later led to collaborative research for social action (e.g., the work of Appalshop, and the later work of Highlander on issues such as the rights of miners and environmental issues [Carawan and Carawan 1993]). Both cases (as well as the ideas of Grundtvig and Cabral, for that matter) linked common features: a triad of adult education/politics/popular culture; an educational strategy that incorporated life and field experience; methodologies that placed authority and analysis in the hands of the poor, particularly the rural poor; a sense that teaching as solidarity is ultimately an act of love and risk; and an ideal that the resulting transformation of social reality is the apex of the educational process. These models have differed from many other radical movements in two striking ways; they all questioned traditional hierarchical, top-down structures of education and political movements (even while there was a tension between that ideal and the realities of such issues as leadership and curriculum development), and they all depended upon a thorough understanding of the forms, customs, agricultural practices, land use, language, music, dance, and beliefs—in short, the folklife—of the communities in which they were situated.

The intellectual leaders of these movements were able to transmit (as well as develop) their ideas through small group gatherings, religious meetings, and other open discussions, as well as in educational institutions and informal settings, training a generation (or two) of cultural and community activists that shaped work for social justice in the Americas thereafter. They did so not by teaching abstract theory, but by teaching that theory could be synthesized from the lived experiences of oppressed people. And they did so, ideally, by teaching through a process that respected the idea of dialogue and promoted it as an egalitarian tool in the learning process. Still, for them, theory and practice were and are inseparable. Not just in the typical sense, that a theory is necessary in advance of a successful practice, but that, in Freire's words, "without practice there's no knowledge" (Horton and Freire 1990, p. 98), so the two are in a constant dialectic, and the synthesis is what Freire refers to as "praxis."

In the vein that runs from the Danish Folk Schools through the popular literacy campaigns in Central America there remains the ideal that the observation and analysis of social reality are at the core of pedagogy, whether teaching literacy, science, or ethics. Suffice it to say that for those pedagogues involved in this kind of work, there was, and is, a preference for observing social reality from the perspective of the poor, marginalized, and oppressed, a perspective usually ignored and overlooked in typical state curricula. Furthermore, reality as any of us live it is constructed by social forces, as Peter Berger and Thomas Luckmann famously point out (1966). Horton, Freire, and their students would be quick to point out that that reality has a validity (particularly when planning the transformation of the world into a more equitable habitat). It may not be the reality in an absolute sense, but it is a social perspective, no less real for not being absolute, which has been left out of state-sponsored schoolbooks for too long.

Perhaps it will be no surprise then that toward the end of their lives, Freire and Horton collaborated on a book, *We Make the Road by Walking* (1990), consisting entirely of extended dialogues between the two. The dialogic approach was not just representative of Freire's mode of teaching, it also was a practical consideration given Horton's frailty at the time, and indeed, Horton died within two weeks of his last meeting with Freire to review the manuscript. The book is more significant for showing the confluence of the two educators' ideas, rather than one's influence on the other, although we know that Horton knew of Freire's work at least as early as 1972 (Horton 1973). Both agree on the dialogic and dialectic nature of true education, where the teachers learn from the students, and that "believing in the people, but not in a naive way," as Freire says, is "necessary" (Horton and Freire 1990, p. 247). This leads to a bottom-up effect on the community organizer:

> [T]here is an interpretive and necessary moment in which the leaders who are trying to mobilize and organize have to know better what they are doing ... They will change their language, their speech, the contents of their speech to the extent that in mobilizing the people they are learning from the people. And then the more they learn from the people the more they can mobilize.
>
> (Horton and Freire 1990, pp. 121–122)

Likewise, theory and knowledge are dialectical, and forever changing based on new information and historical circumstances. In Freire's words:

> I cannot fight for a freer society if at the same time I don't respect the knowledge of the people ... Knowledge is changed to the extent that reality also moves and changes. Then theory also does the same. . . .
>
> (Horton and Freire 1990, p. 101)

Freire's motivation is shaping social reality. Nowhere do we see more clearly than in this book that Horton, who also was raised within the culture in which he would later work, matches Freire in motive and technique.

One of the central points Horton makes in this dialogue, which speaks for the approach of both men, is that his school, his method, were not about reform:

> I think the poor and the people who can't read and write have a sense that without structural changes nothing is worth really getting excited about. They know much more clearly than intellectuals do that reforms don't reform. They don't change anything ... Now if you could come to them with a radical idea ... where they see something significant, they'd become citizens of the world ...
>
> So to embolden people to act, the challenge has got to be a radical challenge. It can't be a little simplistic reform that reformers think will help them. It's got to be something that they know out of experience could possibly bring about a change. And we sell people like that short by assuming that they can take a little baby step and isn't this wonderful ... But that kind of analysis doesn't fit the national situation in any way here in this country. So it leaves us working with the remnants, leaves us working with the little pockets of hope and adventurism wherever we can find it.
>
> (Horton and Freire 1990, pp. 93–94)

This is the crux of the issue for Horton, who wrote relatively little. Later on he leaves no doubt about the revolutionary nature of his concept of pedagogical process:

> We concluded that reform within the [educational] system *reinforced* the system, or was co-opted by the system. Reformers didn't change the system, they made it more palatable and justified it, made it more humane, more intelligent. We didn't want to make that contribution to the schooling system.
>
> (Horton and Freire 1990, p. 200)[15]

Therein lies the difference between what Olive Dame Campbell and Myles Horton took from the Danish Folk School system, and why Freire's technique of literacy training was such an important part of revolutions from Nicaragua to Guinea-Bissau and the community organizing that laid the groundwork for future revolutions. It was not just a question of making the system more functional or palatable, it was an opportunity to remake the entire system.

A Synthesis of Approaches

Comparing the educational philosophy behind the Danish Folk Schools and Highlander, on the one hand, and the popular literacy movements of Paulo Freire and in Central America and Guinea-Bissau and Cape Verde, on the other, makes some obvious similarities stand out. The participants were largely from peasant and rural classes. Educational praxis was experiential. Authority for knowledge and understanding of social reality rested in large part with the students; even when they didn't have certain skills, which could be taught, they had the insight and life experience. Music, dance, and artisanship were essential parts of the curriculum. And synonymous words were used to describe the overall education: folk/*Volk* in the Germanic-speaking countries, and *popular* in the Romance-speaking ones.

On a more subtle, and perhaps fundamental, level is the recognition in all these examples of the importance of language as an essential tool in the process of emancipation. Literacy, being able to read and write in your language, is without doubt a basic skill. But if that skill is not connected to using one's native language, or to thinking critically about social reality, then it is incompletely developed. In societies that are not completely oral, reading and writing are forms of thinking (Freire 1985, pp. 13–14). Beyond literacy, being able to speak, and to have control over one's words and one's own language, is part of an emancipatory education. Henry Giroux writes "The political nature of language is revealed in its use to structure and shape the communicative process" (Giroux 1981, p. 138). I would add that its *ability* to structure and shape the local culture renders language even more "political." In other words, whether asserting one's Danishness under a Germanic sphere of influence, asserting one's civil and human rights, or asserting one's liberation from colonialist socioeconomic structures, one has to be able to form and speak one's own words. Freire calls this "naming the world." It is a question of not being rendered silent and powerless, but being able to speak, speak out, or even sing out, to assert one's cultural, civil, and economic rights. Ownership of one's own language is a vital, and political, step. Freire concludes, "The fact is that language is inevitably one of the major preoccupations of a society which, liberating itself from colonialism and refusing to be drawn into neocolonialism, searches for its own re-creation. In the struggle to re-create a society, the reconquest by the people of their own word becomes a fundamental factor" (Freire 1978, p. 176).

The concept of orality was central to the work of Grundtvig and his followers, Horton, and Freire. While this clearly involves being able to formulate and give voice to one's own thoughts and sentiments (and those of the community, cultural, or class group affiliation), it also involves a mastery of the oral tradition. But mastery of the oral tradition is seldom a passive recitation of the words of others. Those who master the oral traditions know how to shape and reshape, form, create and re-create the words and ideas they have inherited and give them new meaning in new performance. Contrary to the orthodox academic belief that literacy by and large supersedes orality, the folk and popular school models presuppose that orality and literacy exist alongside one another as parallel and mutually necessary skills.[16] Freire is never more clear on this point than when he concludes one article: "The five-year program will eliminate illiteracy in São Tomé and Príncipe. The people will speak their word" (Freire 1981, p 30).

In order to speak or sing from a position of empowerment, knowing one's traditions is practically a prerequisite—not merely to have an awareness of where one stands in society, in terms of class, historical background, ethnicity, and so on, but to have an appreciation for and indeed an ownership of one's own culture, customs, holidays, sacred beliefs, means of cultivation and sustenance. This goes beyond self-knowledge to mean instead a knowledge of where and how one relates culturally to the world, an understanding of the folk traditions, lifeways, work and occupational culture,[17] beliefs, ethics, and aesthetics (Freire 1998, p. 38), music, and physical movement that place us within a local culture and a larger nation-state.

If the basics in primary education for children are the accepted "reading, writing, and 'rithmetic," it would not be farfetched to say that under the adult pedagogies of folk and popular schools, the basics for adult education are reading, speaking, and folklife. This would indeed be a radical transformation of educational priorities, of course, away from mastery of mere skills, and toward a critical knowledge of how to employ linguistic and ethnographic techniques in the service of self-understanding and socioeconomic liberation.

Folklife and Democratic Participation

Since my academic training is as a folklorist, I would like to conclude my argument by looking through the lens my home discipline provides me. Folklife studies—which I refer to as a broader category than Folklore as a discipline—originated in the study of peasant tales, customs, and beliefs, and emphasizes craft and music as being as deeply laden with purpose and meaning as more materialist aspects of social life. Where the study of antiquities, later called "folklore," focused on oral and verbal genres in the eighteenth and nineteenth centuries, the larger rubric, folklife, included ways of living, surviving, and other customs of the peasant class. Folk literature was collected to assert independent national identities, and the study of folklore has been linked to Romantic nationalism. Folklife was documented also to establish a differential identity, but since food and housing were also studied, then issues of class moved to the fore. In general, folklife (known as ethnology in much of the world) became more widely practiced in subjugated nations, poor or isolated regions within nations, and nations bordering the major powers: Ireland, Wales, Scotland, Denmark, Sweden, Hungary, the Pennsylvania German and Appalachian regions of the United States, and southern Italy.

The significance of this context is twofold. First, in all of these places education outside of universities, not just collection, became an important feature of ethnological work; folk schools and open-air and indoor museums have democratically made knowledge available again to "the folk." Second, folklife added a second dimension beyond romantic nationalism—which could and has become its own instrument of exclusion and persecution (see Abrahams 1993)—that of democratization, the other side of Romanticism. In this regard, it is no accident that Freire frequently mentions beauty, aesthetics, and of course freedom, that Horton cites Percy Bysshe Shelley as a major influence (Horton 1990, pp. 29–31; Horton and Freire 1990, pp. 34–35), that American visitors to Denmark invoked John Keats, or that revolutionary songs or songs extolling human dignity became part of the curriculum in Denmark, Nicaragua, and elsewhere.

This emphasis on experiential education finds modern practical incarnation in the form of participant observation, the basic technique of ethnographic investigation. That we learn by doing fieldwork is true whether it is labor in the field or field research, and in fact, the Nicaraguan literacy workers were expected to keep field diaries, which themselves became pedagogical tools (Miller 1985). Participation in life rather than reliance on book knowledge is the source of knowledge in folklife as a discipline. Another important shared principle is that the authority rests with the people in the community, whether they are studying or being studied, organizing or being organized. Or to use Freire's terms, people are subjects in their own history, rather than objects of someone else's research (Freire 1985, p, 199). This is the hallmark of traditional folklife research, particularly in areas such as Ireland, Wales, and Scandinavia where we see the purest form of this intellectual paradigm.[18] It is this very acknowledgment of where authority lies that distinguishes folklife work in more modernized milieux, and I would argue what sets the folklife as a discipline apart from other approaches. This is what I maintain is most epistemologically revolutionary about the folklife method, whether it is taking place in folk schools or folklife departments. In a given social reality, the authority rests with those who experience, and often struggle against, that reality, rather than with those who study it from afar.

Lost, perhaps, is the idea Horton, Freire, and their followers made explicit—that the analysis of class and social reality are features not just of some revolutionary or social change movements, but of everyday educational settings as well. Such a pedagogy depends only partly on content, the lived experience of the oppressed. Content is important, but it is trumped by method. How do we, or any students of culture, observe, listen, analyze, and come to know? How can we do fieldwork except by dialogue? I would go even further to say that in the study and analysis of the reality of everyday life, which we best access through field research—by its very nature involving dialogue as well as reciprocity—there is potential for radical community transformation. We share a method that values trust and authority in people rather than in books, recognizes the importance of cultural expression, sends people out into the field, looks at society from the bottom up, and analyzes the bonds of community while reinforcing them. All of these techniques were shared by the "teachers" in the folk schools, popular literacy campaigns, and base communities, while ostensibly teaching language and literacy. If we as students go as far as our predecessors did in the observation and analysis of social reality, what about that third step, the transformation of reality, the practice that would in turn sharpen and extend our theory?

The challenge of studying Grundtvig, Horton, and Freire is that they implicitly and explicitly tell us that knowledge applied is the highest theoretical calling (while we who have been trained in universities have been conditioned to believe that such an ideal or outcome—i.e., that high theory would develop better from praxis rather than from disinterested research—is counterintuitive). Such humanistic values as listening and observing in the field, engaging in analysis through dialogue and discussion, and then developing an applied methodology that encourages us to utilize our research in solving social problems, may be the last pedagogical hope for constructive revolutions that are not based on ideals of hate and devastation.

Notes

The author would like to extend special thanks to Dorothy Noyes and Margaret Mills for their continuous encouragement to contribute to this conference and volume, to Tom Ewing for insightful and helpful editorial suggestions, and to

Margaret Randall, Gioconda Belli, David Azzolina, Nancy Gadbow, and Carlos Fernando Chamorro for research assistance and answering last-minute questions.

1. These elements in part constitute the hidden political history of folklore studies in America.

2. This reverential tone would be echoed, some 55–60 years later, in reports back from U.S. delegations visiting postrevolutionary Nicaragua. The historical parallel, however, was disrupted by the fact that the Reagan administration was far more threatened by Nicaragua and actively pursued its overthrow. Denmark, especially in comparison to the much larger Soviet Union, presented no such threat in the 1920s.

3. Whisnant makes the point that, to some extent, the folk school movement was so diverse that people tended to emphasize those aspects of its curriculum and ideology they were most sympathetic to.

4. This appears in an article for a general readership published in *Mountain Life and Work*, the magazine of the Southern Mountain Workers.

5. Or *fakelore*.

6. The Zilphia Horton collection in the Tennessee State Historical Archives contains over 1,300 song texts, including historical information, biographical notes on the composers, and the changes made at different points in the folk process. There are also 85 songs on tape, and 11 songbooks published at Highlander while she was there (Tennessee State Library and Archives 1967). The range of the songs varies from popular songs and composed standards ("As Time Goes By," "Anchors Aweigh," "The Star-Spangled Banner," "Old Folks at Home," and "On Wisconsin" are all in the collection) to a range of folk and labor songs, some widely-known and some topical. There are songs on race and injustice, such as "Black Man in Prison," "Ballad of the Blue Bell Jail," and "Scottsboro Boys Shall Not Die"; songs on politics, "The Guy that I Send to Congress," "There'll Always be a Congress," "Doing the Reactionary," "The Youth Act Must be Passed this Year," and "There is Mean Things Happening in this Land"; and songs on labor, such as "Bread and Roses," of course, as well as the less well-known "Workers' Marseillaise," "Ten Little Sweatshops," "Ten Little Textile Workers," "Song of the Danville Strikers and Their Children," "Battle Hymn of the Farmers' Union," "Ballad of the Southern Summer School," "Everett, November Fifth," "Fifty Thousand Lumberjacks," "Give Me that Textile Workers Union," "I'm Too Old to Be a Scab," "March of the Toilers," "Oh, Tortured and Broken," "Siamese Out of Work Song," "Song of Local 102 (ILGWU)," "Song of the Munitions Workers," "Southern Tenant Farmers' Union Song" "The Steel Workers' Battle Hymn" "There Are Crowds That Make You Grumpy," "The Twenty-Third Shirt Factory Psalm," "Victory Song of the Dressmakers" "Victim of Priorities" "Waitresses' Song," "We Have Fed You all for a Thousand Years," "You'll Wish You Were One of Us," "You'll Wish You'd Listened to Us," and many other irresistible titles. Her collection also includes letters from Ben Botkin, Alan Lomax, Woody Guthrie, Tom Glazer and, as expected, Pete Seeger, and from representatives of such notable unions as the IWW, the ILGWU, the CIO, and the UAW (Tennessee State Library 1967).

7. In an odd historical quirk, the Nicaraguan literacy campaign began on March 24, 1980 (Chacón and Pozas 1980), the very day Archbishop Oscar Romero was assassinated in neighboring El Salvador. While coincidental, literacy and the forces of counterrevolution are linked in some cosmic or in this case metaphoric sense.

8. "Equity" as opposed to "equality," which connotes "sameness." Grundtvig even specifically chose—and coined (Begtrup et al. 1926, p. 82)—the Danish word *ligelighed* in contradistinction to *lighed*, which means "equality," for that reason. In one of his songs he wrote of "equal dignity in castle and cottage" (Bugge 2001, p. 73).

9. Horton first went to Nicaragua in 1980 (Horton 1990, pp. 202ff.) and Highlander sponsored a conference in Managua on North/South education in 1983 (Glen 1996, p. 275).

10. In Nicaragua, there had been two previous literacy campaigns with strikingly different political objectives. In the 1960s, under the Somoza dictatorship, one political party had launched a literacy campaign following Freire's techniques in the late 1960s (Berryman 1984, p. 59). A decade later, the Somoza government launched a literacy campaign as a tactic to infiltrate the popular oppositional movement and identify Sandinista sympathizers (Cardenal and Miller 1981, p. 4).

11. Whisnant does not address the literacy campaign as much as one would hope in his intensive study of the politics of culture in Nicaragua, *Rascally Signs in Sacred Places* (1995), perhaps because the literacy campaign was run from the Ministry of Education rather than the Ministry of Culture (as the two ministries were headed by brothers, Fernando and Ernesto Cardenal respectively, one could hardly imagine the programs could have been much closer). It would make an interesting point of comparison, since in his earlier work Whisnant faults Olive Dame Campbell's cultural and educational work in Appalachia for its avoidance of radical political ideology and social change (1983, pp. 135–136). Some of the Danish folk schools Campbell encountered were politically and explicitly radical, while she was more of a reformer than a revolutionary. Whisnant writes about what Campbell omitted from the Danes, but his own underemphasis of the literacy campaign in Nicaragua and, more surprisingly perhaps, his lack of mention of Horton and Highlander—they appear just in one endnote in *All that is Native and Fine* (1983, p. 299)—are curious.

12. See, notably, Freire (1978), but also Freire and Macedo (1987). Freire said, tantalizingly, "One of my dreams, which went unfulfilled, was to conduct a thorough analysis of Amilcar Cabral's work . . . In this book I would have

drawn a clear distinction between 'revolutionary pedagogue' and 'pedagogue of the revolution.' We have some revolutionary pedagogues; but we don't have many pedagogues of the revolution. Amilcar is one of them" (Freire and Macedo 1987, p. 103). Cabral's—and Freire's—work was important not only in Guinea-Bissau and Cape Verde, which shared a revolutionary movement but are now distinct nations, but also the much smaller island nation of São Tomé and Príncipe, further to the south but also colonized by Portugal, where the basic reading primers were called the *Popular Culture Notebooks* (Freire 1981, p. 28). As a point of comparison, as of the year 2000, these three countries together had a population of under two million; compared with Nicaragua, which had nearly five million, Denmark, which had about half a million more than that, El Salvador, which had over six million, and Cuba, which now has over eleven million people. This is a little deceptive for use in this paper, because Denmark's population growth was much slower in the twentieth century. A more useful comparison has to do with area, since transportation and diffusion of educational resources were probably more equivalent in nineteenth-century Denmark and twentieth-century Nicaragua. One realizes how all the more extraordinary the Nicaraguan literacy campaign was by observing that Nicaragua has three times the land mass of Denmark and around one-tenth the number of passenger vehicles. (For more information on the transportation difficulties, see Cardenal and Miller [1981, pp. 12–13].)

13. The bibliography on Liberation Theology is vast, but one of the best overviews of the movement in practice is Berryman (1984).

14. Ellipses between paragraphs represent questions posed, which have been edited out for reasons of space, or in one case an answer to a question not relevant here.

15. These are hard words to hear and take to heart during tough economic times. See also Coe (2000, p. 40) for similar concerns in a discussion of the Scandinavian folk schools.

16. The importance of orality in revolutionary situations was also demonstrated in the small contemporaneous 1979–83 revolution in Grenada, in which oral poetry, calypso, and the role of Creole all played a large part, even though the nation already had a very high rate of literacy (Searle 1983, pp. 92ff.).

17. Freire was more explicitly coming from the intellectual tradition of Antonio Gramsci, for whom self-knowledge in terms of class and history is critical: "The starting point of critical elaboration is the consciousness of what one really is, and is 'knowing thyself' as a product of the historical process to date which has deposited in you an infinity of traces, without leaving an inventory" (Gramsci 1971, p. 324). Although Gramsci was certainly interested in the question of rural intellectuals, he observed that the transition to industrialization, in eliminating skilled trades, also wiped out a layer of specialized knowledge that skilled laborers would have cultivated through the study of their trades. In schools run by the working class, intellectual studies and manual labors would be combined in the curriculum (Gramsci 1985, pp. 42–43), as indeed they were in the folk high schools in Denmark and at Highlander. Freire, citing Gramsci, also sees a false dichotomy between "muscular-nervous effort" and "intellectual-cerebral elaboration" (Freire 1985, pp. 71, 94 n. 13; Gramsci 1971, p. 9).

18. Nowhere more explicitly, for example, as in one of my favorite folklife book titles: *Ask the Fellows Who Cut the Hay* (Evans 1956). Or, for that matter, in the case of Brazil, in the revelations unearthed by the folklorist-protagonist in Jorge Amado's novel, *Tent of Miracles* (Amado 1971).

References

Abrahams, Roger D. 1993. "Phantoms of Romantic Nationalism in Folkloristics." *Journal of American Folklore* vol. 106, pp. 3–37.

Adams, Frank with Myles Horton. 1975. *Unearthing Seeds of Fire: The Idea of Highlander.* Winston-Salem: John F. Blair.

Amado, Jorge. 1971. *Tent of Miracles.* Translated by Barbara Shelby. New York: Avon Books. [Orig. published 1970.]

Arnove, Robert F. 1986, *Education and Revolution in Nicaragua.* Westport, Conn.: Praeger.

Begtrup, Holger, Hans Lund, and Peter Manniche. 1926. *The Folk High Schools of Denmark and the Development of a Farming Community.* London: Oxford University Press.

Berger, Peter L. and Thomas Luckmann. 1966. *The Social Construction of Reality.* Garden City, N.Y.: Doubleday & Company.

Berryman, Phillip. 1984. *The Religious Roots of Rebellion.* Maryknoll, N.Y.: Orbis Books.

Bugge, K.E., 2001. *Folk High Schools in Bangladesh.* Translated by David Stoner. Odense: Odense University Press.

Campbell, John C. 1921. *The Southern Highlander and His Homeland.* New York: Russell Sage Foundation.

Campbell, Olive Dame. 1928. *The Danish Folk School.* New York: Macmillan Company.

Carawan, Guy and Candie Carawan. 1993. "Sowing on the Mountain: Nurturing Cultural Roots and Creativity for Community Change." In *Fighting Back in Appalachia: Traditions of Resistance and Change.* Stephen L. Fisher, ed. Philadelphia: Temple University Press, pp. 245–261.

Cardenal, Ernesto. 1982. *The Gospel in Solentiname.* Translated by Donald D. Walsh. Maryknoll, N.Y.: Orbis Books. [Orig. published 1975.]

Cardenal, Fernando. 1981, "Objetivos de la Cruzada Nacional de Alfabetización." In *Nicaragua: Triunfa en la Alfabetización: Documentos y Testimonios de la Cruzada Nacional de Alfabetización*. San José, Costa Rica: DEI and Ministry of Education. [Orig. published 1979.] pp. 27–45.

—— and Valerie Miller. 1981. "Nicaragua 1980: The Battle of the ABCs." *Harvard Educational Review* vol. 51, pp. 1–26.

Carter, Vicki K. 1994. "The Singing Heart of Highlander Folk School." *New Horizons in Adult Education* vol. 8, no. 2 (Spring), pp. 4–24.

Chacón, Alicia and Victor S. Pozas, eds., 1980, *Cruzada Nacional de Alfabetización: Nicaragua Libre 1980*. Managua: Ministry of Education.

Coe, Cati. 2000. "The Education of the Folk: Peasant Schools and Folklore Scholarship." *Journal of American Folklore* vol. 113, pp. 20–43.

Equipo DEI (Departamento Ecuménico de Investigaciones). 1981. *Nicaragua: Triunfa en la Alfabetización: Documentos y Testimonios de la Cruzada Nacional de Alfabetización*. San José, Costa Rica: DEI and Ministry of Education.

Evans, George Ewart. 1956. *Ask the Fellows Who Cut the Hay*. London: Faber and Faber.

Freire, Paulo. 1970. *Pedagogy of the Oppressed*. Repr. translated by Myra Bergman Ramos. New York: Seabury Press. [Orig. published 1968.]

—— . 1978. *Pedagogy in Process: The Letters to Guinea-Bissau*. Translated by Carman St. John Hunter. New York: Seabury Press.

—— . 1981. "The People Speak Their Word: Learning to Read and Write in São Tomé and Principe." Translated by Loretta Porto Slover. *Harvard Educational Review* vol. 51, pp. 27–30.

—— 1985. *The Politics of Education*. Translated by Donaldo Macedo. South Hadley, Mass.: Bergin & Garvey Publishers, Inc.

—— . 1994. *Pedagogy of Hope*. Translated by Robert R. Barr. New York: Continuum.

—— . 1996. *Letters to Cristina: Reflections on My Life and Work*. Translated by Donaldo Macedo, Quilda Macedo, and Alexandre Oliveira. New York: Routledge.

—— . 1998. *Pedagogy of freedom: Ethics, Democracy, and Civic Courage*. Translated by Patrick Clarke. Lanham, Md.: Rowman & Littlefield Publishers, Inc.

—— and Donaldo Macedo. 1987. *Literacy: Reading the Word and the World*. South Hadley, Mass.: Bergin & Garvey Publishers, Inc.

Giroux, Henry A. 1981. *Ideology, Culture, and the Process of Schooling*. Philadelphia: Temple University Press.

Glen, John M. 1996. *Highlander: No Ordinary School*. 2nd ed. Knoxville: University of Tennessee Press.

Gramsci, Antonio. 1971. *Selections from the Prison Notebooks*. Edited and translated by Quintin Hoare and Geoffrey Nowell Smith. New York: International Publishers.

—— . 1985. *Selections from the Cultural Writings*. David Forgacs and Geoffrey Nowell-Smith ed. Translated by William Boelhower. Cambridge: Harvard University Press. [Orig. published 1920.]

Hammond, John L. 1998. *Fighting to Learn: Popular Education and Guerrilla War in El Salvador*. New Brunswick, N.J.: Rutgers University Press.

Hart, Joseph K. 1926. *Light from the North: The Danish Folk High Schools—Their Meanings for America*. New York: Henry Holt & Co.

Horton, Aimee Isgrig. 1989. *The Highlander Folk School: A History of Its Major Programs*. Brooklyn: Carlson.

Horton, Myles. 1938. "The Community Folk School." In *The Community School*. Samuel Everett, ed. New York: D. Appleton-Century Company, pp. 265–297.

—— . 1944. "Grundtvig and Danish Folk Schools." *Mountain Life and Work* vol. 20, no. 1, pp. 23–25.

—— . 1947. "Farm-Labor Unity." *Prophetic Religion* vol. 8, pp. 79–82, 93.

—— . 1973. "Decision-Making Processes." In *Educational Reconstruction: Promise and Challenge*. Nobuo Shimahara, ed. Columbus: Charles E. Merrill Publishing Co., pp. 323–341.

—— . 1983. "Influences on Highlander Research and Education Center, New Market, Tennessee, USA." In *Grundtvig's Ideas in North America*. Copenhagen: The Danish Institute, pp. 17–31

—— . 1990. *The Long Haul*. With Judith Kohl and Herbert Kohl. New York: Anchor Books, Doubleday.

—— and Paulo Freire. 1990. *We Make the Road by Walking: Conversations on Education and Social Change*. Brenda Bell, John Gaventa, and John Peters, eds. Philadelphia: Temple University Press.

Knight, Edgar Wallace. 1927. *Among the Danes*. Chapel Hill: University of North Carolina Press.

Kozol, Jonathan. 1978. "A New Look at the Literacy Campaign in Cuba." *Harvard Educational Review* vol. 48, pp. 341–377.

Lewis, John, with Michael D'Orso. 1998. *Walking with the Wind*. New York: Simon & Schuster.

Manniche, Peter. 1939. *Denmark, A Social Laboratory*. Oxford: Oxford University Press.

Miller, Valerie. 1985. *Between Struggle and Hope: The Nicaraguan Literacy Crusade*. Boulder, Colo.: Westview Press.

Paredes, Américo. 1969. "Concepts About Folklore in Latin America and the United States." *Journal of the Folklore Institute* vol. 6, pp. 20–38.

Paulston, Rolland G. 1974. *Folk Schools in Social Change: A Partisan Guide to the International Literature*. Pittsburgh: University of Pittsburgh.

Rolando (pseudonym). 1985. Interviewed by author, in English, Philadelphia. May 29.

Rørdam, Thomas. 1980. *The Danish Folk High Schools*. Revised 2nd ed. Translated by Alison Borch-Johansen. Copenhagen: The Danish Institute.

Searle, Chris. 1983. *Grenada: The Struggle Against Destabilization*. London: Writers and Readers Publishing Cooperative Society Ltd.

Tennessee State Library and Archives, Manuscript Division. 1967. *Zilphia Horton, 1910–1956. Folk Music Collection, 1935–1956*. Nashville: Tennessee State Archives, Registers no. 6.

Tolstoy, Leo. 1862 [1967 reprint]. "On Popular Education." In *Tolstoy on Education*. Leo Wiener, Trans. Chicago: University of Chicago Press.

Whisnant, David. 1983. *All That is Native and Fine*. Chapel Hill: University of North Carolina Press.

—— . 1995. *Rascally Signs in Sacred Places: The Politics of Culture in Nicaragua*. Chapel Hill: University of North Carolina Press.

Suggested Readings for Future Study

Allman, P. (2001). *Revolutionary Social Transformation: Democratic hopes, politic possibilities and critical education.* Westport, CT: Bergin & Garvey.

Anyon, J. (2005). *Radical Possibilities: Public Policy, Urban Education, and A New Social Movement.* New York: Routledge.

Ayers, W. (2004). *Teaching the Personal and the Political: Essays on Hope and Justice.* New York: Teachers College Press.

Bagdikian, B. (2004). *The New Media Monopoly.* Boston: Beacon.

Boal, A. (1998). *Legislative Theatre: Using Performance to Make Politics.* New York: Routledge.

Boykoff, J. (2006). *The Suppression of Dissent.* New York: Routledge.

Buckingham, D. (2003). *Media Education: Literacy, learning and contemporary culture.* Malden: MA: Blackwell.

Buckingham, D. (2003). "Media education and the End of the Critical Consumer," *Harvard Educational Review*, 73(3): 309–328.

Butsch, R. (2007). *Media and public spheres* (pp. 122–135). New York: Palgrave Macmillan.

Canaan, J. E. (2002). "Theorizing Pedagogic Practices in the Contexts of Marketization and of September 11, 2001, and Its Aftermath," *Anthropology & Education Quarterly*, 33(3): 368–382.

Carlson, D. and Apple, M. W. (1998). *Power, Knowledge, and Pedagogy: The meaning of democratic education in unsettling time.* Boulder, CO; and Oxford: Westview Press.

Carty, V. and Onyett, J. (2006). "Protest, cyberactivism and new social movements: The reemergence of the peace movement post 9/11," *Social Movement Studies*, 5(3): 229–249.

Casella, R. (2006). *Selling Us the Fortress.* New York: Routledge.

Cole, M. (2006). *Education, Equality and Human Rights.* New York: Routledge.

Conway, J. (2006). *Praxis and politics: Knowledge production in social movements.* New York: Routledge.

Coyer, K. (2005). "If it Leads it Bleeds: The participatory newsmaking of the Independent Media Centre," in W. de Jong et al. (eds.), *Global activism, global media* (pp. 165–178). Ann Arbor: MI: Pluto.

Davidson H. S. (1995). *Schooling in a "Total Institution": Critical Perspectives on Prison Education.* Westport, CT: Bergin & Garvey.

de Jong, W., Shaw, M., and Stammers, N. (eds.) (2005). *Global activism, global media.* Ann Arbor, MI: Pluto.

Dolby, N. and Rizvi, F. (2007). *Youth Moves: Identities and Education in Global Perspective.* New York: Routledge.

Dolby, N. (2003). "Popular Culture and Democratic Practice," *Harvard Educational Review*, 73(3): 258–284.

Downing, J. (2001). *Radical Media: Rebellious communication and social movements.* Thousand Oaks: CA: Sage.

Fields, B. A. and Feinberg, W. (2001). *Education and Democratic Theory: Finding a Place for Community Participation in Public School Reform.* New York: SUNY Press.

Feinberg, W. (2006). *For Goodness Sake. Religious Schools and Education for Democratic Citizenry.* New York: Routledge.

Fischman, G., et al. (eds.) (2005). *Critical Theories, Radical Pedagogies, and Global Conflicts.* Lanham, MD: Rowman and Littlefield Publishers.

Forester, J. (1985). *Critical theory and public life.* Cambridge, MA: MIT Press.

Frechette, J. D. (2002). *Developing Media Literacy in Cyberspace: Pedagogy and Critical learning for the twenty-first century classroom.* Westport: CT: Greenwood.

Freire, P. (2004). "Television Literacy," in *Pedagogy of Indignation* (pp. 87–95). Boulder, CO: Paradigm.

Freire, P. (1998). *Pedagogy of freedom: Ethics, democracy, and civic courage.* Lanham, MD: Rowman and Littlefield.

Freire, P. (1996). *Pedagogy of hope.* New York: Continuum.

Freire, P. (1973). *Education for critical consciousness.* New York: Continuum.

Freire, P. (1985). *The politics of education.* MA: Bergin & Garvey.

Garrido, M. and Halavais, A. (2003). "Mapping networks of support for the zapatista movement: Applying social-networks analysis to study contemporary social movements." In M. McCaughey and M. Ayers (eds.), *Cyberactivism: Online activism in theory and practice* (pp. 165–184). New York: Routledge.

Gilmore, R. (2007) *Golden Gulag: Prisons, Surplus, Crisis, and Opposition in Globalizing California*. University of California Press.

Ginwright, S., Cammarrota, J., and Noguera, P. (2006). *Beyond Resistance! Youth Activism and Community Change*. New York: Routledge.

Giroux, H. (2007). *The University in Chains: Confronting the Military-Industrial-Academic Complex*. Boulder, CO: Paradigm Publishers.

Giroux, H. (2006). *America on the Edge: Henry Giroux on Politics, Culture, and Education*. New York: Palgrave Macmillan.

Giroux, H. (2006). "Breaking into the Movies: Film as Cultural Politics." In *America on the Edge: Henry Giroux on Politics, Culture, and Education* (pp. 1117–128). New York: Palgrave Macmillan.

Giroux, H. (2005) *Against the New Authoritarianism: Politics After Abu Ghraib*. Winnipeg, MB: Arbeiter Ring Publishing.

Giroux, H. (2001). *The Mouse that Roared: Disney and the End of Innocence*. Lanham, MD: Rowman and Littlefield.

Giroux, H. (1997). *Pedagogy and the politics of hope: Theory, culture and schooling*. Boulder, CO: Westview.

Giroux, H. (1994). *Disturbing pleasures: Learning popular culture*. New York: Routledge.

Giroux, H. (1989). *Popular Culture: Schooling and everyday life*. Westport, CT: Bergin & Garvey.

Giroux, H. (1988). *Schooling and the struggle for public life: Critical pedagogy in the modern age*. Minneapolis: University of Minnesota Press.

Giroux, H. (1988). *Teachers as intellectuals: Toward a critical pedagogy of learning*. South Hadley, MA: Bergin & Garvey.

Gitlin, A. (1994). *Power and Method: Political Activism and Educational Research*. New York: Routledge.

Goodman, S. (2003). *Teaching youth media: A critical guide to literacy, video production, and social change*. New York: Teachers College.

Greene, D. (2007). "Gatekeepers: The Role of Adult Education Practitioners and Programs in Social Control," *Journal of Critical Education Policy Studies*, vol. 5 no. 2 (November).

Greene, M. (2000). *Releasing the imagination: Essays on education, the arts and social change*. New York: Jossey-Bass.

Halleck, D. (2002). *Hand-held visions: The impossible possibilities of community media*. New York: Fordham University.

Herman, E. and Chomsky, N. (2002). *Manufacturing consent: The political economy of the mass media* (2nd ed.). New York: Pantheon.

Holst, J. (2002). *Social Movements, Civil Society, and Radical Adult Education*. Westport, Conn: Bergin & Garvey.

Holtz, H. and Associates (1988). *Education and the American dream: Conservatives, liberals and radicals debate the future of education*. MA: Bergin & Garvey.

hooks, b. (1994). *Outlaw Culture: Resisting Representations*. New York: Routledge.

Horton, M. (2003). "What is Liberating Education?" In Jacobs, D. (ed.) *The Myles Horton Reader* (pp. 184–189). Knoxville, TN: University of Tennessee.

Kellner, D. (2005). *Media spectacle and the crisis of democracy: Terrorism, war, and election battles*. Boulder, CO: Paradigm.

Kellner, D. (2001). *Media and Cultural Studies: Keyworks* (pp. 1–38). Malden, MA: Blackwell.

Kid, D. (2003). Indymedia.org: A new communications commons. Cyberactivism: Online activism in theory and practice (pp. 47–69). New York: Routledge.

Kincheloe, J.L. and S. R. Steinberg (2004). *The Miseducation of the West: How Schools and the Media Distort Our Understanding of the Islamic World*. Westport, CT: Praeger Publishers.

Kincheloe, J. (1998). *How Do We Tell the Workers?: The Socioeconomic Foundations of Work*. Westview.

Kincheloe, J. and Steinberg, J., eds. (1995). *Thirteen Questions: Reframing education's conversation*. New York: Peter Lang Publishers.

Kohl, H. (1998). *The discipline of hope: Learning from a lifetime of teaching*. New York: The New Press.

Lankshear, C. and Knobel, M. (2006). *New literacies: Everyday practices & classroom learning*. Maidenhead, England: Open University.

Lankshear, C. and Knobel, M. (2005). "Paulo Freire and Digital Youth in Marginal Spaces." In *Critical Theories, Radical Pedagogies, and Global Conflicts* (pp. 293–306). Lanham, MD: Rowman and Littlefield.

Ledwith, M. (2005). *Community Development: A Critical Approach*. Cambridge, UK: The Polity Press.

Ledwith, M. (2001). "Community work as critical pedagogy: re-envisioning Freire and Gramsci," *Community Development Journal*, 36: 171–182.

Leistyna, P. and Alper, L. (2007). "Critical media literacy for the twenty-first century." In D. Macedo and S. Steinberg (eds.), *Media literacy: A reader* (pp. 54–78). New York: Peter Lang.

Macedo, D. and Steinberg, S. (eds.) (2007). *Media literacy: A reader*. New York: Peter Lang.

Marino, D. (1997). *Wild Garden: Art, Education, and the Culture of Resistance*. Toronto: Between the Lines Production.

McChesney, R. (2000). *Rich media, poor democracy: Communication politics in dubious times*. New York: New York Press.

McChesney, R. (2004). *The problem of the media: U.S. communication politics in the twenty-first century*. New York: Monthly Review.

McCullagh, C. (2002). *Media power*. New York: Palgrave.

McDonnell, L., Timpane, P.M., and Benjamin, R., eds. (2000). *Rediscovering the democratic purposes of education*. Kansas: University Press of Kansas.

McLaren, P. (2001). *Revolutionary Social Transformation: Democratic Hopes, Political Possibilities and Critical Education*. Greenwood Publishing.

McLaren, P. (2000), *Che Guevara, Paulo Freire, and the Pedagogy of Revolution*. Lanham, Boulder, New York, Oxford: Rowman & Littlefield Publishers, Inc.

McLaren, P. (1995). *Critical Pedagogy and Predatory Culture*. New York: Routledge.

McLaren, P. (1997). *Revolutionary Multiculturalism: Pedagogies of Dissent for the New Millennium*. Boulder: Westview.

McLaren, P. and Lankshear, C. (1994). *Politics of liberation: Paths from Freire*. New York: Routledge.

Meiners, E. R. (2007). *Right to be Hostile: Schools, Prisons, and the Making of Public Enemies*. New York: Routledge.

Merideth E. (1994). "Critical Pedagogy and Its Application to Health Education: A Critical Appraisal of the Casa en Casa Model," in *Health Education & Behavior*, 21(3): 355–367.

Morrell, E. (2002). "Toward a critical pedagogy of popular culture: Literacy development among urban youth," *Journal of Adolescent & Adult Literacy*, 46(1): 72–77.

Oaks, J., Rogers, J., and Lipton, M. (2006). *Learning Power: Organizing for Education and Justice*. New York: Teachers College Press.

O'Cadiz, M., Wong, P., & Torres, C. (1998). *Education and democracy: Paulo Freire, social movements and educational reform in Sao Paulo*. Boulder, CO: Westview.

Oldenski, T. (1997). *Liberation Theology and Critical Pedagogy in Today's Catholic Schools: Social Justice in Action*. New York: Routledge.

PuettCross, T. (2005). "On Transforming the World: Critical Pedagogy for Interfaith Education," in *Currents*, Vol. 55, No. 2 (Summer).

Purpel, D. (1989). *The Moral and Spiritual Crisis in Education: A curriculum for justice and compassion in education*. South Hadley, MA: Bergin & Garvey.

Saltman K. J. (2007). *Schooling and the Politics of Disaster*. New York: Routledge.

Shor, I. and Freire, P. (1987). *A pedagogy for liberation: Dialogues on transforming education*. South Hadley, MA: Bergin & Garvey.

Steinberg, S. R. (1997). *Kinderculture: The Corporate Construction of Childhood*. Boulder, CO: Westview.

Steiner, S. (1999). *Freireian Pedagogy, Praxis, and Possibilities: Projects for the New Millennium*. Oxford: Routledge-Falmer.

Tierney, W. (1993). *Building communities of difference: Higher education in the twenty-first century*. Westport, CT: Bergin & Garvey.

Tisdell, E. and Thompson, M. (2007) *Popular culture and entertainment media in adult education*. San Francisco: Jossey-Bass.

Trend, D. (2003). "Merchants of death: Media violence and American empire," *Harvard Educational Review*, 73(3): 285–307.

Epilogue

Teaching as an Act of Love: Reflections on Paulo Freire and His Contributions to Our Lives and Our Work

Antonia Darder

> As individuals or as peoples, by fighting for the restoration of [our] humanity [we] will be attempting the restoration of true generosity. And this fight, because of the purpose given it, will actually constitute an act of love. (p. 29)
>
> Paulo Freire, *Pedagogy of the Oppressed* (1970)

For days, I have reflected on the writings of Paulo Freire; and with every turn of ideas, I've been brought back to the notion of love and its manifestation in our work and our lives. Here, let me say quickly that I am neither speaking of a liberal, romanticized, or merely feel-good notion of love that so often is mistakenly attributed to this term nor the longsuffering and self-effacing variety associated with traditional religious formation. Nothing could be further from the truth. If there was anything that Freire consistently sought to defend, it was the freshness, spontaneity, and presence embodied in what he called an "armed loved—the fighting love of those convinced of the right and the duty to fight, to denounce, and to announce" (Freire, 1998, p. 42). A love that could be lively, forceful, and inspiring, while at the same time, critical, challenging, and insistent. As such, Freire's brand of love stood in direct opposition to the insipid "generosity" of teachers or administrators who would blindly adhere to a system of schooling that fundamentally transgresses every principle of cultural and economic democracy.

Rather, I want to speak to the experience of love as I came to understand it through my work and friendship with Freire. I want to write about a political and radicalized form of love that is never about absolute consensus, or unconditional acceptance, or unceasing words of sweetness, or endless streams of hugs and kisses. Instead, it is a love that I experienced as unconstricted, rooted in a committed willingness to struggle persistently with purpose in our life and to intimately connect that purpose with what he called our "true vocation"—to be human.

A Commitment to Our Humanity

> A humanizing education is the path through which men and women can become conscious about their presence in the world. The way they act and think when they develop all of their capacities, taking into consideration their needs, but also the needs and aspirations of others.
>
> (Freire & Betto, 1985, pp. 14–15)

For Freire, a liberatory education could never be conceived without a profound commitment to our humanity. Once again, I must point out that his notion of humanity was not merely some simplistic or psychologized notion of "having positive self-esteem," but rather a deeply reflective interpretation of the dialectical relationship between our cultural existence as individuals and our political and economic existence as social beings. From Freire's perspective, if we were to solve the educational difficulties of students from oppressed communities, then educators had to look beyond the personal. We had to look for answers within the historical realm of economic, social, and political forms, so that we might better understand those forces that give rise to our humanity as it currently exists. In so many ways, his work pointed to how economic inequality and social injustice dehumanize us, distorting our capacity to love ourselves, each other, and the world. In the tradition of Antonio Gramsci before him, Freire exposed how even well-meaning teachers, through their lack of critical moral leadership, actually participate in disabling the heart, minds, and bodies of their students—an act that disconnects these students from the personal and social motivation required to transform their world and themselves.

There is no question that Freire's greatest contribution to the world was his capacity to be a loving human being. His regard for children, his concern for teachers, his work among the poor, his willingness to share openly his moments of grief, disappointment, frustration, and new love, all stand out in my mind as examples of his courage and unrelenting pursuit of a coherent and honest life. I recall our meeting in 1987, six months after the death of his first wife, Elza. Freire was in deep grief. During one of his presentations, he literally had to stop so that he could weep the tears that he had been trying to hold back all morning. For a moment, all of us present were enveloped by his grief and probably experienced one of the greatest pedagogical lessons of our life. I don't believe anyone left the conference hall that day as they had arrived. Through the courageous vulnerability of his humanity—with all its complexities and contradictions—Freire illuminated our understanding of not only what it means to be a critical educator, but what it means to live a critical life.

In the following year, I experienced another aspect of Freire's living praxis. To everyone's surprise, Freire remarried a few months later. Many were stunned by the news and it was interesting to listen to and observe the responses of his followers in the States. Some of the same radical educators who had embraced him in his grief now questioned his personal decision to remarry so quickly after the death of Elza. Much to my surprise, the news of his marriage and his public gestures of affection and celebration of his new wife, Nita, were met with a strange sort of suspicion and fear. Despite these reverberations, Freire spoke freely of his new love and the sensations that now stirred in him. He shared his struggle with loneliness and grief and challenged us to *live and love* in the present—as much personally as politically.

Fear and Revolutionary Dreams

> The more you recognize your fear as a consequence of your attempt to practice your dream, the more you learn how to put into practice your dream! I never had interviews with the great revolutionaries of this century about their fears! But all of them felt fear, to the extent that all of them were very faithful to their dreams.
>
> (Shor & Freire, 1987, p. 57)

Challenging the conditioned fears with which our dreams of freedom are controlled and the "false consciousness" that diminishes our social agency are common themes in Freire's work. In *Pedagogy of the Oppressed* (1970), he wrote of the *fear of freedom* that afflicts us, a fear predicated on prescriptive relationships between those who rule and those who are expected to follow. As critical educators, he urged us to question carefully our ideological beliefs and pedagogical intentions and to take note of our own adherence to the status quo. He wanted us to recognize that every *prescribed behavior* represents the imposition of one human being upon another—an imposition that moves our consciousness away from what we experience in the flesh to an abstracted reality and false understanding of our ourselves and our world. If we were to embrace a pedagogy of liberation, we had to prepare ourselves to replace this conditioned fear of freedom with sufficient autonomy and responsibility to struggle for an educational praxis and a way of life that could support democratic forms of economic and cultural existence.

Freire often addressed the notion of fear in his speeches and in his writings. In his eyes, fear and revolutionary dreams were unquestionably linked. The more that we were willing to struggle for an emancipatory dream, the more apt we were to know intimately the experience of fear, how to control and educate our fear, and finally, how to transform that fear into courage. Moreover, we could come to recognize our fear as a signal that we are engaged in critical opposition to the status quo and in transformative work toward the manifestation of our revolutionary dreams.

In many ways, Freire attempted to show us through his own life that facing our fears and contending with our suffering are inevitable and necessary human dimensions of our quest to make and remake history, of our quest to make a new world from our dreams. Often, he likened our movement toward greater humanity as a form of *childbirth, and a painful one*. This *labor of love* constitutes a critical process in our struggle to break the *oppressor-oppressed* contradiction and the conflicting beliefs that incarcerate our humanity. Freire's description of this duality is both forthright and sobering.

> The oppressed suffer from the duality which has established itself in their innermost being. They discover that without freedom they cannot exist authentically. Yet, although they desire authentic existence, they fear it. They are at one and the same time themselves and the oppressor whose consciousness they have internalized. The conflict lies in the choice between wholly themselves or being divided; between ejecting the oppressor within or not ejecting him; between human solidarity or alienation; between following prescriptions or having choices; between being spectators or actors, between acting or having the illusion of acting through the action of the oppressors; between speaking out or being silent, castrated in their power to create and re-create, in their power to transform the world.
>
> (Freire, 1970, p. 33)

Freire firmly believed that if we were to embrace a pedagogy of freedom, we had to break out of this duality. We had to come to see how the domesticating power of the dominant ideology causes teachers to become ambiguous and indecisive, even in the face of blatant injustice. Critical educators had to struggle together against a variety of punitive and threatening methods used by many administrators to instill a fear of freedom. Because if this domesticating role were not rejected, even progressive teachers could fall prey to *fatalism*—a condition that negates passion and destroys the capacity to dream—making them each day more politically vulnerable and less able to face the challenges before them.

Fatalism is a notion that Freire, until the end, refused to accept. At every turn, he emphatically rejected the idea that nothing could be done about the educational consequences of economic inequalities and social injustice. If the economic and political power of the ruling class denied subordinate populations the space to survive, it was not because "it should be that way" (Freire, 1997, p. 41). Instead, the asymmetrical relations of power that perpetuate fatalism among those with little power had to be challenged. This required teachers to problematize the conditions of schooling with their colleagues, students, and parents, and through a critical praxis of reflection, dialogue, and action, become capable of *announcing justice*. But such an announcement required a total *denouncement of fatalism*, which would unleash our power to push against the limits, create new spaces, and begin redefining our vision of education and society.

Capitalism as the Root of Domination

> Brutalizing the work force by subjecting them to routine procedures is part of the nature of the capitalist mode of production. And what is taking place in the reproduction of knowledge in the schools is in large part a reproduction of that mechanism.
>
> (Freire & Faundez, 1989, p. 42)

The question of power is ever present in Freire's work, as is his intimacy with the struggle for democracy. At this juncture, it is vitally important that we turn to Freire's ideological beginnings—a dimension of his work that often has been negated or simply ignored by many liberals and progressives who embraced his pedagogical ideas. A quick scan of the writings cited in *Pedagogy of the Oppressed* clearly illustrates that Freire's work was unabashedly grounded in Marxist-Socialist thought. Without question, when Freire spoke of the *ruling class* or the *oppressors*, he was referring to historical class distinctions and class conflict within the structure of capitalist society—capitalism was the root of domination. As such, his theoretical analysis was fundamentally rooted in notions of class formation, particularly with respect to how the national political economy relegated the greater majority of its workers to an exploited and marginalized class. However, for Freire, the struggle against economic domination could not be waged effectively without a humanizing praxis that could both engage the complex phenomenon of class struggle and effectively foster the conditions for critical social agency among the masses.

Although heavily criticized on the left for his failure to provide a more systematic theoretical argument against capitalism, Freire's work never retreated from a critique of capitalism and a recognition of capitalist logic as the primary totalizing force in the world. This is to say that he firmly believed that the phenomenon of cultural invasion worldwide was fundamentally driven by the profit motives of capitalists. During my early years as a critical educator, I, like so many, failed to adequately comprehend and incorporate this essential dimension of Freire's work. For critical educators of color in the United States, we saw racism as the major culprit of our oppression and insisted that Freire engage this issue more substantively. Although he openly acknowledged the existence of racism, he was reticent to abandon the notion of class struggle and often warned us against losing sight of the manner in "which the class factor is hidden within both sexual and racial discrimination" (Freire, 1997, p. 86). Our dialogues with him on this issue often were lively and intense because in many ways, Freire questioned the limits of cultural nationalism and our blind faith in a politics of identity. At several different conferences, where educators of color called for separate dialogues with him, he told us that he could not understand why we insisted on dividing ourselves. With true angst, Freire explained to us: "I cannot perceive in my mind how Blacks in America can be liberated without Chicanos being liberated, or how Chicanos can be liberated without Native Americans being liberated, or Native Americans liberated without Whites being liberated" (Freire, 1987). He insisted that the struggle against oppression was a human struggle in which we had to build solidarity across our differences, if we were to change a world engulfed by capitalism. "The lack of unity among the reconcilable 'different' helps the hegemony of the antagonistic 'different'. The most important fight is against the main enemy" (Freire, 1997, p. 85). As might be expected, many of us walked away frustrated. Only recently have I come to understand the political limits of our parochial discourse.

The world economy has changed profoundly since the release of *Pedagogy of the Oppressed*, yet Freire's message remains more relevant than ever. As capital, labor, and knowledge increasingly are conceived of in global terms, the influential role of capital is expanded exponentially, and the globalization of national and local economies is changing the underlying basis of the nation-state (Carnoy, 1997), these structural changes are reflected in the theories and practices of public schooling. As a consequence, "there is now a radical separation in the curriculum between the programs that do the most concrete training for jobs and the programs that do the most critical reflection. Such job separation reduces the capacity of workers to challenge the system" (Shor & Freire, 1987, p. 47).

Moreover, as Ladislau Dowbor (1997) eloquently argues in his preface to *Pedagogy of the Heart*, we must remove the blinders and see capitalism as the generator of scarcity. We cannot afford to ignore the growing gap between the rich and the poor caused by an increasing economic polarization that belies neoliberal theories of the trickle-down effect. And despite an abundance of technological devices flooding the market place, clean rivers, clean air, clean drinking water, chemical-free food, free time, and the space for adult and children to socialize freely has diminished. "Capitalism requires that free-of-charge happiness be substituted for what can be bought and sold" (p. 26). Yet, seldom do we find with the resounding praises paid to technology a discussion of how technological revolutions have exposed the wretchedness of capitalism—millions of people dying from starvation alongside unprecedented wealth. And even more disconcerting is the deleterious impact of globalized capitalism upon the social and environmental interests of humanity—interests that seem to receive little concern next to the profit motives of transnational corporations.

Challenging Our Limitations

> In order to achieve humanization, which presupposes the elimination of dehumanizing oppression, it is absolutely necessary to surmount the limit-situations in which men [and women] are reduced to things.
>
> (Freire, 1970, p. 93)

Although Freire's historical, regional, and class experiences were different from many of ours, his political purpose was clear and consistent. To achieve a liberatory practice, we had to challenge those conditions that limit our social agency and our capacity to intervene and transform our world. In light of this, Freire's frequent response to questions about issues that perpetuate educational injustice was to challenge us to consider the nature of the limits we were confronting and how we might transcend these limitations in order to discover that beyond these situations, and in contradiction to them, lie *untested feasibilities* for personal, institutional, and socioeconomic restructuring. For example, in thinking back to how many educators of color responded to Freire's insistence that we create alliances to struggle against capitalism, many of us could not break loose from our deep-rooted (and objectified) distrust of "Whites," nor could we move beyond our self-righteous justification of our sectarianism. These represented two of the limit situations that prevented us from establishing the kind of democratic solidarity or *unity within diversity* that potentially could generate profound shifts in the political and economic systems that intensify racism. Freire knew this and yet listened attentively to our concerns and frustrations within the context of our dialogues, always with respect and a deep faith in the power of our political commitment and perseverance.

Freire deeply believed that the rebuilding of solidarity among educators was a vital and necessary radical objective because solidarity moved against the grain of "capitalism's intrinsic perversity, its anti-solidarity nature" (Freire, 1998, p. 88). Throughout his writings, Freire warned us repeatedly against sectarianism. "Sectarianism in any quarter is an obstacle to the emancipation of [human] kind" (Freire, 1970, p. 22). "While fighting for my dream, I must not become passionately closed within myself" (Freire, 1998, p. 88). In many instances, he linked our ability to create solidarity with our capacity for *tolerance.*

At a critical scholars' conference in Boston during the summer of 1991, I came face to face with Freire's notion of tolerance. The meetings had been quite intense, particularly with respect to the concerns of feminist scholars within the field. Rather than exemplifying dialogue, I felt the exchanges began to take on a rather virulent tone. In my frustration, I stood up and fired away at one of the presenters. Freire seemed upset with my response. The following day during my presentation, I again proceeded to critique passionately the lack of substantive commitment to the principles of dialogue and solidarity among the group, focusing my critique on issues of cultural and class differences among many of us. Freire's response to my comments that afternoon remain with me to this day. He was particularly concerned with what he judged as my lack of tolerance and beseeched me to behave with greater tolerance in the future, if I was to continue this work effectively. With great political fervor, I rejected Freire's position making the case that what we needed was to be more *intolerant*—of oppression and social injustice! For years, I licked my wounds over being *scolded* in public by Freire. But eight years later, I must confess that I recognize great wisdom in Freire's advice. Despite my undeniable political commitment, I was lacking tolerance as "revolutionary virtue—the wisdom of being able to live with what is different, so as to be able to fight the common enemy" (Freire & Faundez, 1989, p. 18).

Let us stop for a moment and recognize that just as we all face limit situations in our world and within ourselves, Freire, too, faced such issues in his private and public life. In 1964, after launching the most successful national literacy campaign Brazil had ever known, he was imprisoned and exiled by the right-wing military dictatorship that had overthrown the democratically elected government of Joao Goulart. Freire remained in exile for almost 16 years. But despite the pain and hardships he and his family experienced, Freire's work as an educator and cultural worker continued unabated. In reminiscences of those years, I recall most the sense that Freire clearly understood domination and exploitation as a worldwide phenomenon. As such, he recognized that within the political struggle for a socialist democracy, a myriad of legitimate political projects existed that, regardless of location, were unequivocally linked by their purpose and commitment to economic and cultural democracy. On a more personal level, he spoke of enduring the pain and suffering of exile, while at the same time not reducing his life to grieving alone. "I do not live only in the past. Rather, I exist in the present, where I prepare myself for the possible" (Freire, 1998, p. 67). Hence, Freire's experience of exile was as much a time of facing a multitude of fears, sorrows, and doubts within unfamiliar contexts as it was a time for remaking himself anew and restoring the dreams that had been shattered.

As Freire's work became more prominent within the United States, he also grappled with a variety of issues that both challenged and concerned him. For almost three decades, feminists across the country fiercely critiqued the sexism of his language. In some arenas, Marxist scholars criticized him brutally for his failure to provide a systematic analysis of class, capitalism, and schooling. To the dismay of many scholars, educators, and organizers of color, Freire seemed at times unwilling (or unable) to engage, with greater depth and specificity, the perverse nature of racism and its particular historical formations within the United States. Neither could he easily accept, from a historical materialist perspective, the legitimacy of the Chicano movement and its emphasis on a mythological homeland, Atzlan. Along the same lines, Freire also questioned the uncompromising resistance or refusal of many radical educators of color to assume the national identity of "American"—an act that he believed fundamentally weakened our position and limited our material struggle for social and economic justice. Beyond these issues, he also harbored serious concerns over what he perceived as the splintered nature of the critical pedagogy movement in the United States. Yet, most of these issues were seldom engaged substantively in public, but rather were the fodder of private dialogues and solitary reflections.

Given this history, it is a real tribute to Freire, that in *Pedagogy of the Heart* (or *Under the Shade of the Mango Tree*—its original title), written shortly before his death, Freire demonstrated signs of change and deepening in his thinking about many of these issues. For example, the language in the book finally reflected an inclusiveness of women when making general references, which had been missing in his earlier writings. He spoke to the issue of capitalism more boldly than ever before and considered the nature of globalization and its meaning for radical educators. He also addressed issues of diversity and racism, acknowledging openly that, "[w]e cannot reduce all prejudice to a classist explanation, but we may not overlook it in understanding the different kinds of discrimination" (p. 86). And more forcefully than ever, he spoke to the necessity of moving beyond our reconcilable differences so that we might forge an effective attack against the wiles of advanced capitalism in the world.

The Capacity to Always Begin Anew

> This capacity to always begin anew, to make, to reconstruct, and to not spoil, to refuse to bureaucratize the mind, to understand and to live as a process—live to become—is something that always accompanied me throughout life. This is an indispensable quality of a good teacher.
> (Freire, 1993, p. 98)

The examples above are shared not to diminish, in any way, Freire's contribution or the memory of his work, but rather to remember him within his totality as a human being, with many of the conflicts and contradictions that confront us all, and yet with an expansive ability for sustained reflection, inquiry, and dialogue. But most important, he had an incredible capacity to reconstruct and *begin always anew*. For Freire, there was no question that he, others, and the world were always in a state of becoming, of transforming, and reinventing ourselves as part of our human historical process. This belief served as the foundation for his unrelenting search for freedom and his unwavering hope in the future. In the tradition of Marx, he believed that we both make and are made by our world. And as such, all human beings are the makers of history. In Freire's view, knowledge could not be divorced from historical continuity. Like us, "history is a process of being limited and conditioned by the knowledge that we produce. Nothing that we engender, live, think, and make explicit takes place outside of time and history" (Freire, 1998, p. 32). And more important, educators had to recognize that "it was when the majorities are denied their right to participate in history as subjects that they become dominated and alienated" (Freire, 1970, p. 125).

In light of this, Freire was convinced that this historical process needed to take place within schools and communities, anchored in relationships of solidarity. Freire urged critical educators to build communities of solidarity as a form of *networking*, to help us in problematizing the debilitating conditions of globalized economic inequality and in confronting the devastating impact of neoliberal economic and social policies on the world's population. Freire believed that teachers, students, parents, and others could reproduce skills and knowledge through networks formed around schools and adult education, youth organizations, and religious organizations that have a common democratic interest to enhance individual and collective life. More important, through *praxis*—the authentic union of action and reflection—these education networks could enter into the re-making of a new culture of capital, both as sites for the integration of disassociated workers and for the development of critical consciousness (or *conscientizacao*), ultimately shaping the future of local and national politics, and hence, altering the nature of the global economy. Freire's notion of establishing critical networks is a particularly compelling thought considering the current political struggles in California for the protection of immigrant rights, affirmative action, and bilingual education.

In many ways, the idea of critical networks is linked directly with the struggle for democracy and an expanded notion of citizenship. Freire urged us to strive for *intimacy with democracy*, living actively with democratic principles and deepening them so that they could come to have real meaning in our everyday life. Inherent in this relationship with democracy was a form of citizenship that could not be obtained by chance. It represented a construction that was always in a state of becoming and required that we fight to obtain it. Further, it demanded *commitment, political clarity, coherence, and decision* on our part. Moreover, Freire insisted that:

> No one constructs a serious democracy, which implies radically changing the societal structures, reorienting the politics of production and development, reinventing power, doing justice to everyone, and abolishing the unjust and immoral gains of the all-powerful, without previously and simultaneously working for these democratic preferences and these ethical demands.
>
> (Freire, 1989, p. 67)

Freire also repeatedly associated the work of educators with an unwavering *faith in the oppressed*, who, too, were always in a state of becoming anew. "Never has there been a deeper need for progressive men and women—serious, radical, engaged in the struggle for transforming society, to give testimony of their respect for the people" (Freire, 1997, p. 84). Freire consistently identified this respect for and commitment to marginalized people as an integral ingredient to the cultivation of dialogue in the classroom. "Dialogue requires an intense faith in [others], faith in their power to make and remake, to create and re-create, faith in [their] vocation to be more fully human (which is not the privilege of an elite but the birthright of all)" (Freire, 1970, p. 79). Moreover, he insisted that true dialogue could not exist in the absence of love and humility. But for Freire, dialogue also implied a critical posture as well as a preoccupation with the meanings that students used to mediate their world. He believed it was impossible to teach without educators knowing what took place in their students' world. "They need to know the universe of their dreams, the language with which they skillfully defend themselves from the aggressiveness of their world, what they know independently of the school, and how they know it" (Freire, 1998, p. 73). Through such knowledge, teachers could support students in reflecting on their lives and making individual and collective decisions for transforming their world. As such, dialogue, through reflection and action, could never be reduced to blind action, deprived of intention and purpose.

Indispensable Qualities of Progressive Teachers

> It is impossible to teach without the courage to try a thousand times before giving up. In short, it is impossible to teach without a forged, invented, and well-thought-out capacity to love.
>
> (Freire, 1998, p. 3)

In *Teachers as Cultural Workers*, Freire (1998) wrote *Letters to Those Who Dare to Teach*. Again, he brings us back to an ethics of love and challenges us to reconsider our practice in new ways and to rethink our pedagogical commitment. Freire argued that the task of a teacher, who is always learning, must be both joyful and rigorous. He firmly believed that teaching for liberation required seriousness and discipline as well as scientific, physical, and emotional preparation. Freire stressed often that teaching was a task that required a love for the very act of teaching. For only through such love could the political project of teaching possibly become transformative and liberating. For Freire, it could never be enough to teach only with critical reason. He fervently argued that we must dare to do all things with feeling, dreams, wishes, fear, doubts, and passion.

> We must dare so as never to dichotomize cognition and emotion. We must dare so that we can continue to teach for a long time under conditions that we know well: low salaries, lack of respect, and the ever-present risk of becoming prey to cynicism. We must dare to learn how to dare in order to say no to the bureaucratization of the mind to which we are exposed every day. We must dare so that we can continue to do so even when it is so much more materially advantageous to stop daring.
>
> (Freire, 1998, p. 3)

To be a progressive teacher who dares to teach requires, in Freire's eyes, a set of very particular and indispensable qualities. He believed these qualities could protect radical teachers from falling into the trappings of *avant-gardism*, by helping them become more conscious of their language, their use of authority in the classroom, and their teaching strategies. Through striving to develop these qualities, teachers could also come to understand that they cannot liberate anyone, but rather that they were in a strategic position to invite their students to liberate themselves, as they learned to read their world and transform their present realities.

Unlike the traditional pedagogical emphasis on specific teaching methodologies, particular classroom curricula, and the use of standardized texts and materials, Freire's *indispensable qualities* focus on those human values that expand a teacher's critical and emotional capacity to enter into effective learning-teaching relationships with their students. Freire begins with a *humility* grounded in courage, self-confidence, self-respect, and respect for others. In many ways, he believed that humility is the quality that allows us to listen beyond our differences, and as such represents a cornerstone in developing our intimacy with democracy. Freire associated humility with the *dialectical* ability to live an *insecure security*, which means a human existence that did not require absolute answers or solutions to a problem but rather that, even in the certainty of the moment, could remain open to new ways, new ideas, and new dreams. This anti-authoritarian position also works to prevent teachers from squelching expressions of resistance in their students—resistance that, in fact, is not only meaningful, but necessary to their process of empowerment. Inherent in this quality of humility also is the ability of teachers to build their capacity to express a *lovingness* rooted in their commitment to consistently reflect on their practice and to consider the consequences of their thoughts, words, and actions within the classroom and beyond.

In keeping with his consistent emphasis on the necessity of confronting our fears, Freire identified *courage* as another indispensable quality of educators. Courage here implies a virtue that is born and nourished by our consistent willingness to challenge and overcome our fears in the interest of democratic action—an action that holds both personal and social conseqeunces. Freire believed that as teachers become clearer about their choices and political dreams, courage sustains our struggle to confront those myths, fueled by the dominant ideology, that fragment and distort our practice. Key to this process is our critical ability to both accept and control our fear.

> When we are faced with concrete fears, such as that of losing our jobs or of not being promoted, we feel the need to set certain limits to our fear. Before anything else, we begin to recognize that fear is a manifestation of our being alive. I do not hide my fears. But I must not allow my fears to immobilize me. Instead, I must control them, for it is in the very exercise of this control that my necessary courage is shared.
>
> (Freire, 1998, p. 41)

Tolerance is another of the indispensable qualities on Freire's list. Without this virtue, he contends, no authentic democratic experience can be actualized in the classroom or our own lives. But it is important to note that tolerance "does not mean acquiescing to the intolerable; it does not mean covering up disrespect; it does not mean coddling the aggressor or disguising aggression" (Freire, 1998, p. 43). Freire adamantly stressed that tolerance is neither about *playing the game*, nor a civilized gesture of hypocrisy, nor a coexistence with the unbearable. Instead, the critical expression of tolerance is founded on the basic human principles of respect, discipline, dignity, and ethical responsibility.

Finally, Freire assigned *decisiveness, security*, the *tension between patience and impatience*, and the *joy of living* to the set of indispensable qualities. He wholeheartedly believed that the ability to make decisions, despite the possibility of rupture, is an essential strength of our work as progressive educators. He argued that teachers who lack this quality often resort to irresponsible practices of permissiveness in their teaching, a condition that is as damaging to students as the abuse of teacher authority. Further, a lack of confidence was often linked to indecision, although security (or confidence), on the other hand, stems from a sense of competence, political clarity, and ethical integrity.

The ability of teachers to practice their pedagogy within the *dialectical tension* of *patience and impatience* represented for Freire a significant leap in an educator's development. This virtue allows teachers to both feel the urgency of the difficult conditions they are facing within schools and at the same time respond with thoughtful and reflective tactics and strategies, rather than *blind activism*. Key to understanding this concept is recognizing the problematics of those who espouse an ethic of *absolute patience* on one hand, and those who manifest an *uncontainable impatience* on the other. Both can impair our ability to participate pedagogically in effective ways.

At no time is the ability to cultivate a *dialectical* understanding of the world more necessary than when we as educators are asked to live within the tension of two seemingly contradictory concepts of responses. This is to say, living an *impatient patience* or *insecure security* is predicated on our willingness and ability to grapple with the complexity and ambiguity of the present, despite a heightened level of tension we may experience. And, as such, to respond in *coherence* with our democratic dream, rather than to seek prescribed formulas or quick-fix recipes to alleviate the tension, potentially is a creative and liberating force in our lives. This dialectical competence also implies a *verbal parsimony*, which helps us to rarely lose control over our words or exceed the limits of considered, yet energetic, discourse—a quality that Freire consistently demonstrated over the years during his participation in difficult dialogues.

Freire placed great significance on our ability to live joyfully despite the multitude of external forces that constantly challenge our humanity. The indispensable quality of *teaching with a joy of living* personifies most the ultimate purpose in both Freire's work and life. In retrospect, I am filled with wonderful memories of Freire—the beauty of his language, the twinkle in his eyes, his thoughtful and respectful manner, the movement of his hands when he spoke, his lively enthusiasm when contemplating new ideas, and his candid expressions of love and gratitude. In his words and his deed, Freire persistently invited teachers to fully embrace life, rather than to surrender our existence to the stifling forces of economic and social injustice.

> By completely giving myself to life rather than to death—without meaning either to deny death or to mythicize life—I can free myself to surrender to the joy of living, without having to hide the reasons for sadness in life, which prepares me to stimulate and champion joy in the school.
>
> (Freire, 1998, p. 45)

Although Freire does not explicitly speak of activism in his *Letters to Those Who Dare to Teach* (1998), his theoretical work was never disassociated from his activism. Moreover, he argued tirelessly for the inseparability of political consciousness and political action in our teaching and in our lives. Hence, teachers as intellectuals, cultural workers, and community activists must "aspire to become an association of truly serious and coherent people, those who work to shorten more and more the distance between what they say and what they do" (Freire, 1997, p. 83). The transformation of schools can only take place when teachers, working in solidarity, take ownership and struggle to radically change the political and economic structures of power that defile our revolutionary dreams.

> Thus I can see no alternative for educators to unity within the diversity of their interests in defending their rights. Such rights include the right to freedom in teaching, the right to speak, the right to better conditions for pedagogical work, the right to paid sabbaticals for continuing education, the right to be coherent, the right to criticize the authorities without fear of retaliation . . . and to not have to lie to survive.
>
> (Freire, 1998, p. 46)

References

Carnoy, M. (1997), Foreword to *Pedagogy of the heart* by P. Freire. New York: Continuum.

Dowbor, L. (1997). Preface to *Pedagogy of the heart* by P. Freire. New York: Continuum.

Freire, P. (1970). *Pedagogy of the oppressed.* New York: Seabury.

Freire, P. (July, 1987). People of Color Caucus Dialogue. Critical Pedagogy Conference, University of California, Irvine, CA.

Freire, P. (1993). *Pedagogy of the city*. New York: Continuum.

Freire, P. (1997). *Pedagogy of the heart*. New York: Continuum.

Freire, P. (1998). *Teachers as cultural workers: Letters to those who dare to teach*. Boulder, CO: Westview.

Freire, P., & Betto, F. (1985). *Essa escola chamada vida*. São Paulo: Atica.

Freire, P., & Faundez, A. (1989). *Learning to question: A pedagogy of liberation*. New York: Continuum.

Macedo, D., & Araujo Freire, A. (1998). Foreword to *Teachers as cultural workers: Letters to those who dare to teach* by P. Freire. Boulder, CO: Westview.

McLaren, P. (1997). "Paulo Freire's legacy of hope and struggle," *Theory, Culture & Society*. 14(4), 147–153.

Shor, I., & Freire, P. (1987). *A pedagogy for liberation*. MA: Bergin and Garvey.

About the Editors

Antonia Darder is a Professor of Educational Policy Studies and Latina/Latino Studies at the University of Illinois, Urbana-Champaign. She is the author of *Reinventing Paulo Freire: A Pedagogy of Love.*

Marta P. Baltodano is an Associate Professor of Education at Loyola Marymount University in Los Angeles.

Rodolfo D. Torres is Associate Professor of Urban and Regional Planning at the University of California, Irvine. He is the co-editor of *Latino Social Movement* (Routledge).

Permissions

Apple, Michael, "Patriotism, Pedagogy, and Freedom: On the Educational Meanings of September 11," *Teachers College Record*, vol. 104, no. 8, 2002, pp. 1760–1772.

Leistyna, Pepi and Loretta Alper, "Critical Media Literacy for the Twenty-first Century" from *Media Literacy: A Reader* edited by Donaldo Macedo and Shirley Steinberg, pp. 54–78. © 2006 by Peter Lang. Reprinted with permission of the publisher.

Kahn, Richard, "Towards Ecopedagogy: Weaving a Broad-based Pedagogy of Liberation for Animals, Nature, and the Oppressed People of the Earth". First appeared in *Journal of Critical Animal Studies*, Vol. 1, No. 1 (2003). Reprinted with permission of author. For more information on how education can help to avert planetary ecological crisis, please visit: http://www.richardkahn.org

Westerman, William, "Folk Schools, Popular Education, and a Pedagogy of Community Action" in *Revolution and Pedagogy* edited by E. Thomas Ewing, 2005, Palgrave Macmillan. Reproduced with permission of Palgrave Macmillan.

Darder, Antonia, "Teaching as an Act of Love: Reflections on Paulo Freire and His Contributions to Our Lives and Our Work," from *An Occasional Paper Series for Entering the 21st Century*, California Association of Bilingual Education. © 1998 Antonia Darder.

Index

Please note that references to Notes will have the letter 'n' following the note